DATE DUE

DEMCO 128-5046

SOMETHING ABOUT THE AUTHOR®

Something about
the Author *was named
an "Outstanding
Reference Source,"
the highest honor given
by the American
Library Association
Reference and User
Services Association.*

ISSN 0276-816X

something ABOUT THE AUThOR®

**Facts and Pictures about Authors
and Illustrators of Books for Young People**

**EDITED BY
ALAN HEDBLAD**

VOLUME 108

GALE GROUP

*Detroit
San Francisco
London
Boston
Woodbridge, CT*

STAFF

Editor: Alan Hedblad
Associate Editor: Melissa Hill
Autobiography Features Coordinator: Motoko Fujishiro Huthwaite

Contributing Editors: Sara L. Constantakis, Catherine Goldstein, Maria Job, Arlene M. Johnson
Editorial Assistant: Erin E. White

Editorial Technical Specialist: Karen Uchic

Managing Editor: Joyce Nakamura
Publisher: Hal May

Research Manager: Victoria B. Cariappa
Project Coordinator: Corrine A. Boland
Research Specialists: Barbara McNeil, Cheryl L. Warnock
Research Associates: Tamara C. Nott, Wendy K. Festerling, Tracie A. Richardson, Robert Whaley
Research Assistants: Phyllis J. Blackman, Tim Lehnerer, Patricia L. Love

Permissions Manager: Maria L. Franklin
Permissions Associates: Sarah Chesney, Edna Hedblad, Michele Lonoconus

Production Director: Mary Beth Trimper
Production Assistant: Deborah Milliken

Graphic Artist: Gary Leach
Image Database Supervisor: Randy Bassett
Imaging Specialists: Robert Duncan, Michael Logusz
Imaging Coordinator: Pamela A. Reed

Library of Congress Catalog Card Number 72-27107

ISBN 0-7876-3217-1
ISSN 0276-816X

Printed in the United States of America

10 9 8 7 6 5 4 3 2 1

Contents

Authors in Forthcoming Volumes

Below are some of the authors and illustrators that will be featured in upcoming volumes of *SATA*. These include new entries on the swiftly rising stars of the field, as well as completely revised and updated entries (indicated with *) on some of the most notable and best-loved creators of books for children.

*Ariane Dewey: Author and illustrator Dewey is noted for her use of bright, primary colors and simple lines, and for her stories that tweak history or myth with a dose of humor.

Edward Field: An accomplished poet with several volumes of verse to his credit, Field based *Magic Words,* his latest collection of poetry for children, on native Eskimo songs and stories gathered by Danish explorer Knud Rasmussen.

Robert Roger Ingpen: Ingpen's impressive body of work spans two decades and earned the Australian author and illustrator the Andersen Medal in 1986. Among his best-known books are the self-illustrated *The Idle Bear, The Age of Acorns,* and *The Dreamkeeper.*

*Nancy Jewell: Picture-book author Jewell has collaborated with such esteemed illustrators as Leonard Weisgard and Elizabeth Sayles. Her most recent works include *Christmas Lullaby* and *Silly Times with Two Silly Trolls,* the second volume in the adventures of her rambunctious protagonists, Nip and Tuck.

Jess Mowry: With works such as *Way Past Cool* and *Babylon Boyz* that reflect his experiences growing up in Oakland, California's inner city, Mowry has risen above his tumultuous childhood to become an accomplished author and role model for the street kids with whom he works and writes about.

*Walter Dean Myers: The winner of five Coretta Scott King Awards, as well as numerous other honors, Myers is regarded as one of the best contemporary American writers for children and young adults, and is credited with helping to redefine the image of blacks in juvenile literature.

*Gillian Paton Walsh: English author Paton Walsh is perhaps best known as the writer of realistic and historical fiction for older primary graders and young adults. Acknowledged for her range and versatility, she has contributed to a diverse number of other genres, including science fiction, picture books, original folktales, mysteries, and short stories.

J. K. Rowling: Rowling's highly publicized, best-selling debut book, *Harry Potter and the Sorcerer's Stone,* is the first of seven books featuring the boy wizard. Other titles in the wildly popular series include *Harry Potter and the Chamber of Secrets* and *Harry Potter and the Prisoner of Azkaban.*

*Ruth Sanderson: In addition to bringing to life the works of a host of popular picture-book authors such as William Sleator, Jane Yolen, and Clyde Robert Bulla, Sanderson has recently illustrated her own texts, including *The Twelve Dancing Princesses* and *Papa Gatto: An Italian Fairy Tale,* with her rich, detailed paintings.

Art Spiegelman: Spiegelman made a name for himself on the underground comics scene before publishing the two-volume *Maus: A Survivor's Tale,* which marked a zenith in his artistic career. Both autobiographical and historical commentary, the *Maus* books are based on the experiences of Spiegelman's father, a Holocaust survivor.

Diana Wieler: Considered one of Canada's finest writers for young adults, Wieler has garnered a host of prestigious awards for her work. Respected for both the style and content of her fiction, Wieler writes openly, respectfully, and insightfully about themes and issues relevant to contemporary teens.

Introduction

Something about the Author (*SATA*) is an ongoing reference series that examines the lives and works of authors and illustrators of books for children. *SATA* includes not only well-known writers and artists but also less prominent individuals whose works are just coming to be recognized. This series is often the only readily available information source on emerging authors and illustrators. You'll find *SATA* informative and entertaining, whether you are a student, a librarian, an English teacher, a parent, or simply an adult who enjoys children's literature.

What's Inside SATA

SATA provides detailed information about authors and illustrators who span the full time range of children's literature, from early figures like John Newbery and L. Frank Baum to contemporary figures like Judy Blume and Richard Peck. Authors in the series represent primarily English-speaking countries, particularly the United States, Canada, and the United Kingdom. Also included, however, are authors from around the world whose works are available in English translation. The writings represented in *SATA* include those created intentionally for children and young adults as well as those written for a general audience and known to interest younger readers. These writings cover the entire spectrum of children's literature, including picture books, humor, folk and fairy tales, animal stories, mystery and adventure, science fiction and fantasy, historical fiction, poetry and nonsense verse, drama, biography, and nonfiction.

Obituaries are also included in *SATA* and are intended not only as death notices but also as concise overviews of people's lives and work. Additionally, each edition features newly revised and updated entries for a selection of *SATA* listees who remain of interest to today's readers and who have been active enough to require extensive revisions of their earlier biographies.

New Autobiography Feature

Beginning with Volume 103, *Something about the Author* will feature three or more specially commissioned autobiographical essays in each volume. These unique essays, averaging about ten thousand words in length and illustrated with an abundance of personal photos, present an entertaining and informative first-person perspective on the lives and careers of prominent authors and illustrators profiled in *SATA*.

Two Convenient Indexes

In response to suggestions from librarians, *SATA* indexes no longer appear in every volume but are included in alternate (odd-numbered) volumes of the series, beginning with Volume 57.

SATA continues to include two indexes that cumulate with each alternate volume: the Illustrations Index, arranged by the name of the illustrator, gives the number of the volume and page where the illustrator's work appears in the current volume as well as all preceding volumes in the series; the Author Index gives the number of the volume in which a person's biographical sketch, autobiographical essay, or obituary appears in the current volume as well as all preceding volumes in the series.

These indexes also include references to authors and illustrators who appear in Gale's *Yesterday's Authors of Books for Children, Children's Literature Review,* and *Something about the Author Autobiography Series.*

Easy-to-Use Entry Format

Whether you're already familiar with the *SATA* series or just getting acquainted, you will want to be aware of the kind of information that an entry provides. In every *SATA* entry the editors attempt to give as complete a picture of the person's life and work as possible. A typical entry in *SATA* includes the following clearly labeled information sections:

- *PERSONAL:* date and place of birth and death, parents' names and occupations, name of spouse, date of marriage, names of children, educational institutions attended, degrees received, religious and political affiliations, hobbies and other interests.

- *ADDRESSES:* complete home, office, electronic mail, and agent addresses, whenever available.

- *CAREER:* name of employer, position, and dates for each career post; art exhibitions; military service; memberships and offices held in professional and civic organizations.

- *AWARDS, HONORS:* literary and professional awards received.

- *WRITINGS:* title-by-title chronological bibliography of books written and/or illustrated, listed by genre when known; lists of other notable publications, such as plays, screenplays, and periodical contributions.

- *ADAPTATIONS:* a list of films, television programs, plays, CD-ROMs, recordings, and other media presentations that have been adapted from the author's work.

- *WORK IN PROGRESS:* description of projects in progress.

- *SIDELIGHTS:* a biographical portrait of the author or illustrator's development, either directly from the biographee—and often written specifically for the *SATA* entry—or gathered from diaries, letters, interviews, or other published sources.

- *FOR MORE INFORMATION SEE:* references for further reading.

- *EXTENSIVE ILLUSTRATIONS:* photographs, movie stills, book illustrations, and other interesting visual materials supplement the text.

How a SATA Entry Is Compiled

A *SATA* entry progresses through a series of steps. If the biographee is living, the *SATA* editors try to secure information directly from him or her through a questionnaire. From the information that the biographee supplies, the editors prepare an entry, filling in any essential missing details with research and/or telephone interviews. If possible, the author or illustrator is sent a copy of the entry to check for accuracy and completeness.

If the biographee is deceased or cannot be reached by questionnaire, the *SATA* editors examine a wide variety of published sources to gather information for an entry. Biographical and bibliographic sources are consulted, as are book reviews, feature articles, published interviews, and material sometimes obtained from the biographee's family, publishers, agent, or other associates.

Entries that have not been verified by the biographees or their representatives are marked with an asterisk (*).

Contact the Editor

We encourage our readers to examine the entire *SATA* series. Please write and tell us if we can make *SATA* even more helpful to you. Give your comments and suggestions to the editor:

BY MAIL: Editor, *Something about the Author,* The Gale Group, 27500 Drake Rd., Farmington Hills, MI 48331-3535.

BY TELEPHONE: (800) 877-GALE

BY FAX: (248) 699-8054

Acknowledgments

Grateful acknowledgment is made to the following publishers, authors, and artists whose works appear in this volume.

ADDY, SHARON HART. Addy, Sharon Hart, photograph. Reproduced by permission of the author.

ANDERSON, KIRSTY. Anderson, Kirsty, photograph. Reproduced by permission of the author.

AVI. Cover of *S. O. R. Losers,* by Avi. Avon Camelot Books, 1986. Reproduced by permission of Avon Books, Inc. / Cover of *The True Confessions of Charlotte Doyle,* by Avi. Avon Flare Books, 1992. Reproduced by permission of Avon Books, Inc. / Cover of *Beyond the Western Sea, Book 1: The Escape from Home,* by Avi. Avon Camelot Books, 1997. Reproduced by permission of Avon Books, Inc. / Catalanotto, Peter, illustrator. From a jacket of *Nothing But the Truth: A Documentary Novel,* by Avi Wortis. Orchard Books, 1991. Jacket illustration © 1991 by Peter Catalanotto. Reproduced by permission of Orchard Books, New York. / Wortis, Avi, photograph by Jim Shea. AP/Wide World Photos. Reproduced by permission.

BAIUL, OKSANA. Half title page of *Oksana: My Own Story,* by Oksana Baiul, as told to Heather Alexander. Random House, 1997. Cover photograph by SportsChrome USA. Reproduced by permission. / Baiul, Oksana, photograph by Betty Marshall/Shooting Star. Reproduced by permission.

BLOOM, LLOYD. Bloom, Lloyd, illustrator. From an illustration in *Arthur, For the Very First Time,* by Patricia MacLachlan. HarperTrophy, 1980. Illustrations copyright © 1980 by Lloyd Bloom. Reproduced by permission of HarperCollins Publishers.

BREWER, JAMES D. Brewer, James D., photograph. Reproduced by permission of the author.

BYARS, BETSY. Byars, Betsy Cromer, one year old, photograph. Reproduced by permission. / Byars, Betsy Cromer with her father, Guy Cromer, in the galley of the *Nan-a-Bet,* summer, 1942, photograph. Reproduced by permission. / Byars, Betsy, about 4, and sister, Nancy, about 6, posing with their mother, photograph. Reproduced by permission. / Byars, Betsy with Ed Byars, June 23, 1950, photograph. Reproduced by permission. / Byars, Betsy, with husband, Ed, and daughters Laurie and Betsy Ann, 1956, photograph. Reproduced by permission. / Byars, Betsy with husband, Ed, Clemson, South Carolina, photograph. Reproduced by permission./ Byars, Betsy with sister, Nancy, photograph. Reproduced by permission. / Byars, Betsy, standing with college roommates Barbara Ann Jobes and Fronie Mims, Graduation Day, June, 1950, photograph. Reproduced by permission. / Byars, Betsy, receiving Newbery Medal, awards ceremony, June, 1971, photograph. Reproduced by permission. / Byars, Betsy with husband, Ed, Morgantown, West Virginia, 1974, photograph. Reproduced by permission. / Byars, Betsy with family, on daughter's wedding day, December 17, 1977, photograph. Reproduced by permission. / Byars, Betsy, with husband, Ed, Newcastle, Virginia, September, 1984, photograph. Reproduced by permission. / Byars, Betsy, photograph. Reproduced by permission. / Byars, Betsy, photograph. Reproduced by permission. / Rugheimer, Grandfather, photograph. Reproduced by permission. / Cromer, Guy and Nan Rugheimer, c. 1924, photograph. Reproduced by permission.

CHAMBERS, AIDAN. Jacket of *Dance on My Grave,* by Aidan Chambers. Harper & Row, 1982. Jacket © 1982 by Harper & Row, Publishers, Inc. Reproduced by permission of HarperCollins Publishers. / Chambers, Aidan, photograph by Lydia van der Meer. Reproduced by permission of the author.

COLEMAN, MICHAEL. Ward, John R., photographer. From a cover of *Internet Detectives,* by Michael Coleman. Bantam Skylark Books, 1997. Reproduced by permission of Bantam Books, a division of Random House, Inc. / Coleman, Michael, photograph. Reproduced by permission of the author.

COOK, GLEN. Jainschigg, Nicholas, illustrator. From a cover of *She Is the Darkness,* by Glen Cook. Tom Doherty Associates Books, 1997. Copyright © 1997 by Glen Cook. Reproduced by permission. / Cook, Glen, photograph. © 1998 Olan Mills. Reproduced by permission of the author.

COPE, JANE. Cope, Jane, illustrator. From an illustration in *The Cherry Blossom Tree,* by Jan Godfrey. Augsburg, 1996. © 1996 Jane Cope. Reproduced by permission of Augsburg Fortress. / Cope, Jane, photograph. Reproduced by permission of the author.

COX, CLINTON. Cover of *Come All You Brave Soldiers: Blacks In The Revolutionary War,* by Clinton Cox. Scholastic Press, 1999. Reproduced by permission. / Cox, Clinton, photograph. Reproduced by permission of the author.

DALTON, SHEILA. Beeson, Bob, illustrator. From a cover of *Bubblemania,* by Sheila Dalton. Orca Book Publishers, 1992. Illustrations © 1992 by Bob Beeson. Reproduced by permission. / Dalton, Sheila, photograph by Gordon Wyatt. Reproduced by permission.

DEDMAN, STEPHEN. Dedman, Stephen, photograph by Amanda Godecke. Reproduced by permission of the author.

DePAOLA, TOMIE. dePaola, Tomie, illustrator. From an illustration in his *Nana Upstairs & Nana Downstairs.* G. P. Putnam's Sons, 1998. Text copyright © 1973 by Tomie dePaola. Illustrations copyright © 1998, 1973 by Tomie dePaola. Reproduced by permission of G. P. Putnam's Sons, a division of Penguin Putnam Inc. / dePaola. Tomie, illustrator. From an illustration in his *Watch Out for the Chicken Feet in Your Soup.* Aladdin Paperbacks, 1974. Copyright © 1974 by Tomie dePaola. Reproduced by permission of Aladdin Paperbacks, an imprint of Simon & Schuster Macmillan. / dePaola, Tomie, illustrator. From an illustration in his *Strega Nona.* Aladdin Paperbacks, 1975. Copyright © 1975 by Tomie dePaola. Reproduced by permission of Aladdin Paperbacks, an imprint of Simon & Schuster Macmillan. / dePaola, Tomie, illustrator. From a cover of *The Legend of the Bluebonnet: An Old Tale of Texas,* retold by Tomie dePaola. G. P. Putnam's Sons, 1983. Jacket art © 1983 by Tomie dePaola. Reproduced by permission of G. P. Putnam's Sons, a division of Penguin Putnam Inc. / dePaola, Tomie, photograph by Suki Coughlin. © Suki Coughlin. Reproduced by permission of the author.

DEWAN, TED. Dewan, Ted, illustrator. From an illustration in *The Sorcerer's Apprentice,* by Ted Dewan. Doubleday Books for Young Readers, 1998. Copyright © 1997 by Ted Dewan. Reproduced by permission of Transworld Publishers Ltd, a division of the Random House Group Ltd. In North America by Random House Children's Books, a division of Random House, Inc.

FITCH, SHEREE. Bobak, Molly Lamb, illustrator. From a cover of *Toes in My Nose and Other Poems,* by Sheree Fitch. Boyds Mills Press, 1987. Illustrations copyright © 1987 by Molly Lamb Bobak. Reproduced by permission. / Labrosse, Darcia, illustrator. From an illustration in *If You Could Wear My Sneakers!,* by Sheree Fitch. Doubleday Canada Limited, 1997. Poetry © 1997, 1998 Sheree Fitch. Illustrations © 1997 Darcia Labrosse. Reproduced by permission. / Fitch, Sheree, photograph by Paul Darrah. Reproduced by permission of the author.

FRENCH, JACKIE. Guthridge, Bettina, illustrator. From a cover of *Annie's Pouch,* by Jackie French. Angus & Robertson, 1995. Cover and internal illustrations copyright © Bettina Guthridge 1995. Reproduced by permission of Angus & Robertson, an imprint of HarperCollins Australia.

GHIGNA, CHARLES. Gorton, Julia, illustrator. From a cover of *Riddle Rhymes,* by Charles Ghigna. Hyperion Books for Children, 1995. Jacket illustration © 1995 by Julia Gorton. Reproduced by permission. / Ghigna, Charles, photograph. Reproduced by permission of the author.

GOLDSMITH, HOWARD. Kent, Jack, illustrator. From a cover of *The Twiddle Twins' Haunted House,* by Howard Goldsmith. Mondo, 1997. Cover illustration © 1985 by Jack Kent. All rights reserved. Reproduced by permission of Mondo Publishing, One Plaza Road, Greenvale, NY 11548

GRIECO-TISO, PINA. Grieco-Tiso, Pina, photograph. Reproduced by permission of the author.

HAMBLY, BARBARA. Cover of *Star Trek: Crossroad,* by Barbara Hambly. Pocket Books, 1994. Copyright © 1994 by Paramount Pictures. All rights reserved. Reproduced by permission. / Struzan, Drew, illustrator. From a cover of *Star Wars: Children of the Jedi,* by Barbara Hambly. Bantam Books, 1995. Cover art copyright © 1995 Lucasfilm Ltd. & TM. All rights reserved. Reproduced by permission of Lucasfilm Ltd. / Seder, Jason, illustrator. From a cover of *A Free Man of Color,* by Barbara Hambly. Bantam Books, 1997. Cover art © 1998 by Jason Seder. Reproduced by permission of Bantam Books, a division of Random House, Inc. / Hambly, Barbara, photograph by Jay Kay Klein. © Jay Kay Klein. Reproduced by permission.

HASHMI, KERRI. Hashmi, Kerri, photograph. Reproduced by permission of the author.

HENKES, KEVIN. Henkes, Kevin, illustrator. From an illustration in his *Owen.* Greenwillow Books, 1993. Copyright © 1993 by Kevin Henkes. Reproduced by permission of Greenwillow Books, a division of William Morrow and Company, Inc. / Cover of *A Weekend With Wendell,* by Kevin Henkes. Mulberry Paperback Books, 1995. Reproduced by permission of Mulberry Paperback Books, a division of William Morrow and Company, Inc. / Henkes, Kevin, illustrator. From an illustration in his *Lilly's Purple Plastic Purse.* Greenwillow Books, 1996. Copyright © 1996 by Kevin Henkes. Reproduced by permission of Greenwillow Books, a division of William Morrow and Company, Inc. / Henkes, Kevin, photograph by Tom Beckley. Reproduced by permission of the author.

Jon Krakauer. Doubleday, 1990. Cover photography © Ned Gillette & Adventure Photo & Film. Reproduced by permission of Doubleday, a division of Random House, Inc. / Cover of *Into the Wild,* by Jon Krakauer. Anchor Books, 1997. Reproduced by permission of Doubleday, a division of Random House, Inc.

LAIRD, CHRISTA. Duffy, Daniel Mark, illustrator. From a cover of *Shadow of the Wall,* by Christa Laird. Beech Tree Books, 1997. Cover illustration © 1997 by Daniel Mark Duffy. Reproduced by permission of Beech Tree Books, a division of William Morrow and Company, Inc. In the UK by permission of Random House UK Limited. / Duffy, Daniel Mark, illustrator. From a cover of *But Can the Phoenix Sing?,* by Christa Laird. Beech Tree Books, 1998. Cover illustration © 1998 by Daniel Mark Duffy. Reproduced by permission of Beech Tree Books, a division of William Morrow and Company, Inc. In the UK by permission of Random House UK Limited.

LENT, JOHN. Lent, John, photograph by Jude Clarke. Reproduced by permission.

MARGOLIS, JEFFREY A. Berndt, Eric R., photographer. From a cover of *Teen Crime Wave: A Growing Problem,* by Jeffrey A. Margolis. Enslow Publishers, Inc., 1997. Copyright © 1997 by Jeffrey A. Margolis. Reproduced by permission.

MASSIE, ELIZABETH. Norcia, Ernie, illustrator. From a cover of *Patsy's Discovery,* by Elizabeth Massie. Pocket Books, 1997. Reproduced by permission of Pocket Books, an imprint of Simon & Schuster Macmillan.

McGRATH, BARBARA B. McGrath, Barbara B., photograph. Reproduced by permission.

MEYERS, SUSAN. Tang, Susan, illustrator. From a cover of *Meg and the Secret Scrapbook,* by Susan Meyers. Troll Associates, 1995. Cover illustration © 1995 by Susan Tang. Reproduced by permission of Troll Communications, LLC.

MORRISON, LILLIAN. Cook, Joel, illustrator. From a cover of *Whistling the Morning In,* by Lillian Morrison. Wordsong, 1992. Jacket design and illustrations © 1992 by Joel Cook. Reproduced by permission. / Dunaway, Nancy, illustrator. From a cover of *I Scream, You Scream,* by Lillian Morrison. August House Little Folk, 1997. Jacket illustration © 1997 by Nancy Dunaway. Reproduced by permission. / Morrison, Lillian, photograph by Eyre de Lanux. Reproduced by permission.

MOSS, THYLIAS. Pinkney, Jerry, illustrator. From an illustration in *I Want to Be,* by Thylias Moss. Dial Books for Young Readers, 1993. Text copyright © 1993 by Thylias Moss. Pictures copyright © 1993 by Jerry Pinkney. Reproduced by permission of Dial Books for Young Readers, a division of Penguin Putnam Inc. / Moss, Thylias, photograph by D. C. Goings. University of Michigan Photo Services. Reproduced by permission of the author.

MURRAY, KIRSTY. Murray, Kirsty, photograph by B. MacNamara. Reproduced by permission.

PARKS, GORDON. Parks, Gordon, photograph. Corbis-Bettmann. Reproduced by permission.

PECK, ROBERT NEWTON. Peck, Robert Newton, all photographs reproduced by permission of the author.

PETERSON, JEAN SUNDE. Coates, David, photographer. From a cover of *Talk with Teens about Self and Stress: 50 Guided Discussions for School and Counseling Groups,* by Jean Sunde Peterson. Edited by Pamela Espeland. Free Spirit Publishing Inc., 1993. Copyright © 1993 by Jean Sunde Peterson. Reproduced by permission. / Peterson, Jean Sunde, photograph. Reproduced by permission.

PETTIT, JAYNE. Pettit, Jayne, photograph by Bin Pettit. Reproduced by permission of the author.

PORTER, JANICE LEE. Porter, Janice Lee, photograph. Reproduced by permission of the author.

ROCK, MAXINE. Verstraete, Randy, illustrator. From a cover of *Totally Fun Things to Do with Your Dog,* by Maxine Rock. John Wiley & Sons, Inc., 1998. Reproduced by permission. / Rock, Maxine, photograph. Reproduced by permission.

SALISBURY, GRAHAM. Cover of *Blue Skin of the Sea,* by Graham Salisbury. Delacorte Press, 1994. Reproduced by permission of Delacorte Press, a division of Random House, Inc. / Lieder, Rick, illustrator. From a jacket of *Shark Bait,* by Graham Salisbury. Delacorte Press, 1997. Jacket illustration © 1997 by Rick Lieder. All rights reserved. Reproduced by permission of Delacorte Press, a division of Random House, Inc. / Salisbury, Graham, photograph. Reproduced by permission of Graham Salisbury.

SAYLES, ELIZABETH. Sayles, Elizabeth, illustrator. From a cover of *Not in the House, Newton!,* by Judith Heide Gilliland. Clarion, 1995. Jacket illustrations copyright © 1995 by Elizabeth Sayles. Reproduced by permission of Houghton Mifflin Company. / Sayles, Elizabeth, illustrator. From a cover of *Millions of Snowflakes,* by Mary McKenna Siddals. Clarion, 1995. Jacket illustrations copyright © 1998 by Elizabeth Sayles. Reproduced by permission of Houghton Mifflin Company. / Sayles, Elizabeth, with daughter, Jessica Dow, photograph by Anne Pollack. Reproduced by permission.

STILES, MARTHA BENNETT. Thomas, Larry, illustrator. From a cover of *James the Vine Puller: A Brazilian Folktale,* retold by Martha Bennett Stiles. Carolrhoda Books, 1992. Text and illustrations copyright © mcmlxxiv by Carolrhoda Books, Inc. Reproduced by permission. / Stiles, Martha Bennett, photograph by Susan Lippman. Reproduced by permission.

STOTTER, MIKE. Stotter, Mike, photograph. Reproduced by permission of the author.

STRUG, KERRI. Tieleman, Al, photographer. From a cover of *Landing on My Feet: A Diary of Dreams,* by Kerri Strug with John P. Lopez. Andrews McMeel Publishing, 1997. Reproduced by permission of *Sports Illustrated.* / Strug, Kerri, photograph by Dave Joiner. Archive Photos, Inc. Reproduced by permission.

SWAN, SUSAN. Swan, Susan, photograph. Reproduced by permission of the author.

SWEENEY, JOYCE. Cover of *The Tiger Orchard,* by Joyce Sweeney. Laurel-Leaf Books, 1993. © 1993 by Joyce Sweeney. Reproduced by permission of Dell Publishing, a division of Random House, Inc. / Cover of *Piano Man,* by Joyce Sweeney. Laurel Leaf Books, 1994. Reproduced by permission of Random House Children's Books, a division of Random House, Inc. / Ducak, Danilo, illustrator. From a cover of *Free Fall,* by Joyce Sweeney. Laurel-Leaf Books, 1997. Cover illustration © 1996 by Danilo Ducak. Reproduced by permission of Random House Children's Books, a division of Random House, Inc. / Cover of *Shadow,* by Joyce Sweeney. Laurel-Leaf Books, 1996. Reproduced by permission of Random House Children's Books, a division of Random House, Inc. / Meltzer, Ericka, illustrator. From a cover of *The Spirit Window,* by Joyce Sweeney. Delacorte Press, 1998. Jacket illustration © 1998 by Ericka Meltzer. Reproduced by permission of Delacorte Press, a division of Random House, Inc. / Sweeney, Joyce, photograph by Jay Sweeney. © Joyce Sweeney. Reproduced by permission of Sterling Lord Literistic, Inc.

TRUESDELL, SUE. Truesdell, Sue, illustrator. From an illustration in *Santa's Short Suit Shrunk: And Other Christmas Tongue Twisters,* by Nola Buck. HarperTrophy, 1997. Text © 1997 by Nola Buck. Illustrations © 1997 by Susan G. Truesdell. Reproduced by permission of HarperCollins Publishers. / Truesdell, Sue, illustrator. From a cover of *Ghost Trap: A Wild Willie Mystery,* by Barbara M. Joosse. Clarion Books, 1998. Jacket illustration © 1998 by Sue Truesdell. Reproduced by permission of Houghton Mifflin Company.

VOJTECH, ANNA. Vojtech, Anna, illustrator. From an illustration in *The First Strawberries: A Cherokee Story,* retold by Joseph Bruchac. Dial Books for Young Readers, 1993. Pictures copyright © 1993 by Anna Vojtech. Reproduced by permission of Dial Books for Young Readers, a division of Penguin Putnam Inc. / Vojtech, Anna, illustrator. From an illustration in *Marushka and the Month Brothers,* a folktale retold by Anna Vojtech and Philemon Sturges. North-South Books, 1996. Illustrations © 1996 by Anna Vojtech. Used with permission of North-South Books, Inc., New York.

WARNER, SUNNY. Warner, Sunny, photograph. Reproduced by permission.

WILBUR, RICHARD. Diaz, David, illustrator. From an illustration in *The Disappearing Alphabet,* by Richard Wilbur. Harcourt Brace & Company, 1997. Illustrations © 1998 by David Diaz. Reproduced by permission of Harcourt, Inc. / Wilbur, Richard, photograph by Constance Stuart Larrabee. Reproduced by permission of the author.

YOUNGER, BARBARA. Younger, Barbara, photograph. Reproduced by permission of the author.

ZARIN, CYNTHIA. Zarin, Cynthia, photograph by Joseph Goddu. Photo © 1997 by Joseph Goddu. Reproduced by permission of Sterling Lord Literistic, Inc.

SOMETHING ABOUT THE AUTHOR

ADDY, Sharon Hart 1943-

Personal

Born February 3, 1943, in Oak Creek, WI; daughter of Earl (a bricklayer and janitor) and Gertrude (a caterer; maiden name, Ueberfluss) Hart; married Gordon Addy (a hydraulic repairman), August 9, 1969; children: Mari Jo Burri, Jill. *Education:* University of Wisconsin, Whitewater, B.E., 1964. *Religion:* Catholic. *Hobbies and other interests:* Gardening.

Addresses

Home and office—4098 E. Studio Lane, Oak Creek, WI 53154.

Career

Freelance writer, speaker and teacher. Fifth-grade teacher in Stone Bank, WI, 1964-66, Commerce City, CO, 1966, and Oak Creek, WI, 1967-70; substitute teacher in Oak Creek, WI, 1983-87; Community Newspapers, Inc., Milwaukee, WI, staff and features writer, 1985-90. Institute of Children's Literature, West Redding, CT, instructor, 1995—. *Member:* Society of Children's Book Writers and Illustrators.

Writings

We Didn't Mean To ("Life and Living from a Child's Point of View" series), illustrated by Jay Blair, Raintree, 1981.

A Visit with Great-Grandma, illustrated by Lydia Halverson, Albert Whitman, 1989.

Kidding Around Milwaukee: What to Do, Where to Go, and How to Have Fun in Milwaukee, John Muir, 1997.

Right Here on This Spot, illustrated by John Clapp, Houghton Mifflin, 1999.

Contributor of short story "The Breakwater" to *Wisconsin Seasons: Classic Tales of Life Outdoors,* Cabin

Sharon Hart Addy

Bookshelf, 1998. Contributor of short stories, poems, and articles to children's magazines, including *Highlights for Children, The Friend,* and *The Pennywhistle Press.*

Work in Progress

Research on blacksmithing in the late 1800s and on Milwaukee's German community in the early 1900s.

Sidelights

Sharon Hart Addy told *SATA:* "One of my strongest memories from second grade is walking home from school thinking about becoming a writer. I wanted to write stories as wonderful as the ones I read.

"When I reached ninth grade, I discovered I could handle words pretty well. That year my English teacher accused me of plagiarism over my description of a leaf rustling down the street. Three years later, the same teacher sent an article I wrote for the school paper to the local newspaper. They published it with my byline.

"Unfortunately, by this point my dream of becoming a writer was supplanted by the practical decision to become an elementary school teacher. In college I kept my vision of writing to myself. Real writers certainly didn't spend as much time as I did on a single paragraph!

"After graduation from college, I taught fifth grade for several years, then married and left teaching to raise my family. I started writing while my girls watched *Sesame Street,* and I've been at it ever since. I write anything I get a good idea for—stories, articles, poetry, riddles, books.

"I wrote *We Didn't Mean To* after I learned that a series of books about problems children encounter could use a book on vandalism. *A Visit with Great-Grandma* grew out of an article I did as a feature writer for the local newspaper. My editor asked for a story about people who immigrated to America. The great-grandmas I interviewed didn't speak English very well, but they both enjoyed visiting with their great-grandchildren. I wondered how they communicated. As I played 'What if?' the story came together.

"A call from an editor looking for a Milwaukee-based writer led to *Kidding Around Milwaukee,* a guide to the Milwaukee area for kids. Exploring my own childhood for ideas led me to write "The Breakwater," a story in the adult outdoor anthology *Wisconsin Seasons.*

"*Right Here on This Spot* grew from an idea for a magazine article. A children's magazine planned an issue on the Great Lakes. Since I live near Lake Michigan and find archaeology interesting, I contacted the Great Lakes Archaeological Research Center and set up an interview with the Center's archaeologist. The day we met he didn't have time to talk, so he handed me a report on one of his digs. The magazine rejected the article, but I never forgot what I read in the report. He excavated a spot just a few miles from my house and found evidence that humans hunted at the edge of Ice Age glaciers. I got to thinking about all the people who lived on the land we occupy today. The result was *Right Here on This Spot.*

"The stack of folders beside my computer contains notes for a novel, ideas for picture books, and several unfinished stories. When one project stalls, I set it aside to let my subconscious mind work on it and pick up another one. Now I know: Writers do take a long time to perfect their work. They even do a lot of research to write fiction."

For More Information See

PERIODICALS

Booklist, April 15, 1989, p. 1460.
School Library Journal, March, 1982, p. 142; June, 1989, p. 81.

*   *   *

ALAGOA, Ebiegberi Joe 1933-

Personal

Born March 14, 1933, in Okpoma, Rivers State, Nigeria; son of Joseph Ayibatonye (a chieftain) and Jane Furombogha (Obasi) Alagoa; married Mercy Gboribusuote Nyananyo, September 26, 1961; children: David Ayibatonye. *Education:* University College, Ibadan, Nigeria, B.A. (with honors); University of Wisconsin, Ph.D. (history), 1966.

Addresses

Office—School of Humanities, University of Port Harcourt, Port Harcourt, Rivers State, Nigeria, PMB 5234.

Career

National Archives Nigeria, Kaduna, Nigeria, archivist, 1959-62; University of Lagos, Lagos, Nigeria, lecturer in African history, 1965-67, Centre of Cultural Studies, director, 1972-77; Institute of African Studies, University of Ibadan, senior research fellow, 1967-72; School of Humanities, University of Port Harcourt, Port Harcourt, Rivers State, Nigeria, dean, beginning 1977. Rivers State Council of Arts and Culture, chair, 1973-75. *Member:* American Anthropology Association, Historical Society of Nigeria.

Writings

FOR YOUNG PEOPLE

Jaja of Opobo: The Slave Who Became a King (nonfiction), Longman (London), 1970.
King Boy of Brass (nonfiction), Heinemann Educational (London), 1975.

(Editor, with T. N. Tamuno) *Eminent Nigerians of the Rivers State,* Heinemann Educational, 1980.

OTHER

(Compiler) *Special List of Records Related to Historical, Anthropological, and Social Studies among Provincial Administration Record Groups at National Archives, Kaduna,* National Archives (Kaduna, Nigeria), 1962.

The Small Brave City-State: A History of Nembe-Brass in Niger Delta, University of Wisconsin Press (Madison), 1964.

Kien abibi onde fa pugu. Nembe numerals, Nembe Cultural Association, Lagos (Lagos, Nigeria), 1967.

(With Adadonye Fombo) *A Chronicle of Grand Bonny,* Ibadan University Press (Ibadan, Nigeria), 1972.

A History of the Niger Delta: An Historical Interpretation of Ijo Oral Tradition, Ibadan University Press, 1972.

War Canoe Drums and Topical Songs from Nembe, Rivers State, Rivers State Council for Arts and Culture (Nigeria), 1974.

(Editor) *More Days, More Wisdom: Nembe Proverbs,* University of Harcourt Press (Harcourt, Nigeria), 1983.

(Editor) *Oral Tradition and Oral History in Africa and the Diaspora: Theory and Practice,* Centre for Black and African Arts and Civilization (Lagos, Nigeria), 1990.

Sidelights

Nigerian historian and educator Ebiegberi Joe Alagoa has written numerous works about his homeland, the Rivers State region of Nigeria. Many of these works deal with history and folklore as incorporated into the oral tradition of Africa. In *The Small Brave City-State: A History of Nembe-Brass in Niger Delta,* Alagoa chronicles the history of the Nembe people who have lived near the Brass River estuary of the Niger Delta since the fifteenth century. Drawing on oral sources preserved in the national archives, as well as other published sources, Alagoa describes the social and political organizations, commerce, and politics of the Nembe Brass. He also describes the Akassa War between the Nembe and the British colonial trading-company.

Many commentators have praised Alagoa's contribution to the recorded history of Nigeria. Judging Alagoa to be "well equipped to fuse the oral traditions of the Nembe people with the more standard sources," Robert O. Collins, writing in the *American Historical Review,* called *The Small Brave City-State* "first a most useful contribution to the local history of the delta region and second a scholarly addition to the history of Nigeria as a whole." Collins added, "the chapter on the Akassa War is particularly useful to the African historian." A critic for *Choice* called the work "well written," praising Alagoa's "excellent analysis" of the region's institutions. "Alagoa has written a historical study rather than an ethnography, thus omitting many cultural features which would interest anthropologists," noted Donald C. Simmons in a review for *American Anthropologist.* "However, anyone interested in the area can glean much background ethnological information from this interesting, well-documented study, whose minor faults are due not to the author but to the paucity of data available for reconstructing Nembe history."

For young readers, Alagoa has contributed to London publisher Heinemann's "African Historical Biographies" series. The goal of this series is to present African history from a native point of view, rather than from the colonial perspective so frequently employed. Thus, *King Boy of Brass* tells the story of a nineteenth-century boy-king of the Niger Delta, who is at first a disappointment to his father but redeems himself as an astute trader and a fine ambassador for his country in dealings with Europe. Abiola Odejide, writing in *Reading Teacher,* contended that Alagoa's book turned the reader into a "detached observer, an auditor rather than a vicarious participant of a past experience." "The authors in all the Heinemann series are strongly aware of the historical perspective, leading to an overwhelming factual tone and the relegation of literary quality to the background," stated Odejide. On the other hand, the critic offered a more favorable estimation of another of Alagoa's works for young people, *Jaja of Opobo: The Slave Who Became a King.* Young readers are more likely to become absorbed in this book, maintained Odejide, because the author offers a fictionalized glimpse of the early life of Jaja, describing him as "a troublesome boy who exhibits great fighting spirit in his experience as a slave sold many times over."

Works Cited

Collins, Robert O., review of *The Small Brave City-State: A History of Nembe-Brass in Niger Delta, American Historical Review,* April, 1965, pp. 880-81.

Odejide, Abiola, review of *King Boy of Brass* and *Jaja of Opobo: The Slave Who Became a King, Reading Teacher,* March, 1987, pp. 642-43.

Simmons, Donald C., review of *The Small Brave City-State: A History of Nembe-Brass in Niger Delta, American Anthropologist,* June, 1965, pp. 793-94.

Review of *The Small Brave City-State: A History of Nembe-Brass in Niger Delta, Choice,* February, 1965, p. 584.*

*　　*　　*

ANDERSON, Kirsty 1978-

Personal

Born February 28, 1978, in Melbourne, Australia; daughter of William K. (a historian) and Esther Margaret (a scientist) Anderson. *Education:* University of Melbourne, B.A. *Politics:* Labor. *Religion:* Christian.

Addresses

Home—17 Sunbury Cresent, Surrey Hills, Victoria, Australia. *Electronic mail*—Gilland@eisa.net.au.

Kirsty Anderson

Career

Writer. Also works as creative dance assistant; volunteer adult literacy tutor; volunteer with UNICEF and Guide Dogs for the Blind. *Member:* Fellowship of Australian Writers, Amnesty International.

Awards, Honors

John Morrison Short Story Award, Fellowship of Australian Writers; Mavis Thorpe Clarke Award.

Writings

Kingdoms of the Seventh Pool, Holy Angels Publishing (North Fitzroy, Australia), 1998.
Lumis Wars, Holy Angels Publishing, in press.

Work in Progress

Catabasis, a young adult fantasy journey to the underworld; *Grey Children of the Rooftop,* a young adult fantasy.*

ANDERSON, Lisa G. 1963-

Personal

Born June 28, 1963, in Detroit, MI; daughter of Leonard (a steel broker) and Barbara (Moquin) Sytek; married Charles H. Anderson Jr. (a computer program analyst), June 28, 1986. *Education:* Macomb Community College, A.A.S., 1989; Northwood University, BBA, 1995.

Addresses

Home—47886 Addario, Shelby Township, MI 48316. *E-mail*—andersoc062886@webtv.com.

Career

United States Army Tank Automotive Command, clerk typist, 1982-84, procurement clerk, 1984-89, procurement assistant, 1989, contract specialist, 1990-95. Currently retired from U.S.A. Tank Automotive Command, 1995—. Also a Christian songwriter; active in Children's Ministry of Zion Christian Church, Troy, MI; public speaker for Macomb Literacy Partners Inc., a program of the Macomb County Library, MI. *Member:* Macomb Literacy Partners Inc., Macomb County Library.

Writings

Proud to Be Me: Peewee Platypus, Ridge Enterprises, 1990.

Author of numerous articles and poems.

Work in Progress

No Problem Is Too Big for You, in press; a series of books for preschoolers in conjunction with community literacy project called "Read to Me."

Sidelights

Public speaker and poet Lisa G. Anderson is the author of a number of inspirational poems and speeches aimed at celebrating human diversity. Anderson, who was born with cerebral palsy and diagnosed with multiple sclerosis in 1993, is determined to turn the slights and taunts that plagued her own childhood into a positive force for change. Her 1990 book, *Proud to Be Me: Peewee Platypus,* tells the story of Peewee, who is embarrassed by his species' configuration of broad muzzle and webbed feet when he begins to explore the world. The other animals laugh at him, but then he meets Professor Peacock, who explains that all creatures are unique and therefore beautiful. The professor introduces Peewee to other unusual animals, such as a giraffe and a flamingo. By the close of the story, Peewee has come to love and respect himself and to appreciate the diversity of nature.

Anderson, a Michigan resident who worked for several years for the U.S. Army as a procurement specialist, has taken the *Peewee* story to elementary schools and community groups. She receives letters from educators, counselors, and children with disabilities telling her about the positive impact *Peewee Platypus* has had on them. An accomplished public speaker and author of numerous poems, Anderson is involved in writing a series of books for young readers designed to work in conjunction with the community literacy program "Read to Me." Anderson's title character, Peewee, has become the "spokesplatypus" for the "Read to Me" program, which helps prepare children ages one through five for school.

Anderson told *SATA:* "Everyone has the wonderfully unique ability to contribute to our world, no matter how small. I believe little is much when God's in it. I always encourage people to savor each and every moment. We have to celebrate life."

*   *   *

AVI 1937-
(Avi Wortis)

Personal

Full name is Avi Wortis; given name is pronounced "Ah-vee"; born December 23, 1937, in New York, NY; son of Joseph (a psychiatrist) and Helen (a social worker; maiden name Zunser) Wortis; married Joan Gabriner (a weaver), November 1, 1963 (divorced); married Coppelia Kahn (a professor of English); married Linda C. Wright (a businesswoman); children: Shaun Wortis, Kevin Wortis; stepchildren: Gabriel Kahn (second marriage), Hayden, Catherine, Robert, Jack Spina. *Education:* Attended Antioch University; University of Wisconsin-Madison, B.A., 1959, M.A., 1962; Columbia University, M.S.L.S., 1964.

Addresses

Home—Denver, CO. *Agent*—Gail Hochman, Brandt & Brandt, 1501 Broadway, New York, NY 10036.

Career

Writer, 1960—. New York Public Library, New York City, librarian in Performing Arts Research Center, 1962-70; Lambeth Public Library, London, England, exchange program librarian, 1968; Trenton State College, Trenton, NJ, assistant professor and humanities librarian, 1970-86. Has also taught a variety of college courses pertaining to children's literature for Simmons College, UCLA extension, Wesleyan University, and Illinois Wesleyan. Visiting writer in schools across the United States and in Canada and Denmark, conducting workshops and seminars with children, parents and educators. *Member:* Authors Guild.

Awards, Honors

Best Book list, British Book Council, 1973, for *Snail Tale: The Adventures of a Rather Small Snail;* Grants from New Jersey State Council on the Arts, 1974, 1976,

Avi

and 1978; runner-up for Edgar Allan Poe Award, Mystery Writers of America, 1975, for *No More Magic,* 1979, for *Emily Upham's Revenge,* and 1984, for *Shadrach's Crossing;* Christopher Book Award, 1981, for *Encounter at Easton;* Children's Choice Award, International Reading Association, 1980, for *Man from the Sky,* and 1988, for *Romeo & Juliet—Together (& Alive) at Last;* Best Books, *School Library Journal,* 1980, for *Night Journeys;* Scott O'Dell Award for historical fiction, *Bulletin of the Center for Children's Books,* and Best Books for Young Adults, American Library Association (ALA), both 1984, both for *The Fighting Ground;* Best Books for Young Adults, ALA, 1986, Best Books, *School Library Journal,* 1987, Best Books of the Eighties, *Booklist,* 1988, Virginia Young Readers' Award, 1990, all for *Wolf Rider: A Tale of Terror;* Best Books, Library of Congress, 1989, for *Something Upstairs,* and 1990, for *The Man Who Was Poe;* Golden Kite Award, Society of Children's Book Writers and Illustrators, Best Books, *School Library Journal,* Editor's Choice, *Booklist,* and Books for the Teen Age, New York Public Library, all 1990, and Newbery Honor Book, ALA, Notable Book, ALA, *Boston Globe-Horn Book* Award, and Judy Lopez Memorial Award, all 1991, all for *The True Confessions of Charlotte Doyle;* Rhode Island Award, 1991, Volunteer State Award, 1991-92, Sunshine State Young Readers Award, 1992, all for *Something Upstairs: A Tale of Ghosts;* Notable Trade Book in the Field of Social Studies, National Council for the Social Studies and Children's Book Council (NCSS-CBC), Editor's Choice, *Booklist,* and Best Books, *Horn Book, School Library Journal,* and *Publishers Weekly,* all 1991,

Newbery Honor Book, ALA, Honor Book, *Boston Globe-Horn Book,* Books for the Teen Age, New York Public Library, Blue Ribbon Book, *Bulletin of the Center for Children's Books,* Best Books, Library of Congress and Bank Street Teachers' College, all 1992, and Best YA's from the last twenty-five years, Young Adult Library Services Association (YALSA-ALA), 1994, all for *Nothing but the Truth;* One Hundred Titles for Reading and Sharing, New York Public Library, Editor's Choice, *Booklist,* and Best Books, *School Library Journal,* all 1992, Pick of the Lists, American Booksellers Association (ABA), and Notable Book, ALA, both 1993, all for *"Who Was That Masked Man, Anyway?";* Books for the Teen Age, New York Public Library, and Best Books for Young Adults, ALA, both 1993, both for *Blue Heron;* Books for the Teen Age, New York Public Library, 1994, for *City of Light/City of Dark;* Children's Books of the Year, Bank Street, and Pick of the Lists, ABA, both 1994, both for *The Bird, the Frog, and the Light;* Children's Books of the Year, Bank Street, Pick of the Lists, ABA, and Editor's Choice, *Booklist,* all 1994, and Notable Book, ALA, 1995, all for *The Barn;* Best Books, *School Library Journal, Booklist,* and New York Public Library, all 1995, and *Boston Globe/Horn Book* Award and Notable Book, ALA, 1996, all for *Poppy;* Notable Children's Book in the Language Arts, National Council of Teachers of English, 1997, for *When I Was Your Age;* Blue Ribbon Book, *Bulletin of the Center for Children's Books,* Notable Trade Book in the Field of Social Studies, NCSS-CBC, and Best Books for Young Adults, ALA, all 1997, all for *Beyond the Western Sea;* Top 10 Fantasy Novels for Youth, *Booklist,* 1999, for *Perloo the Bold.*

Writings

Things That Sometimes Happen, illustrated by Jodi Robbin, Doubleday, 1970.
Snail Tale: The Adventures of a Rather Small Snail, illustrated by Tom Kindron, Pantheon, 1972.
No More Magic, Pantheon, 1975.
Captain Grey, illustrated by Charles Mikolaycak, Pantheon, 1977.
Emily Upham's Revenge; or, How Deadwood Dick Saved the Banker's Niece: A Massachusetts Adventure, illustrated by Paul O. Zelinsky, Pantheon, 1978.
Night Journeys, Pantheon, 1979.
Encounter at Easton (sequel to *Night Journeys*), Pantheon, 1980.
Man from the Sky, illustrated by David Weisner, Knopf, 1980.
History of Helpless Harry: To Which Is Added a Variety of Amusing and Entertaining Adventures, illustrated by Paul O. Zelinsky, Pantheon, 1980.
A Place Called Ugly, Pantheon, 1981.
Who Stole the Wizard of Oz?, illustrated by Derek James, Knopf, 1981.
Sometimes I Think I Hear My Name, Pantheon, 1982.
Shadrach's Crossing, Pantheon, 1983, reprinted as *Smuggler's Island,* Morrow, 1994.
S.O.R. Losers, Bradbury, 1984.
Devil's Race, Lippincott, 1984.
The Fighting Ground, Lippincott, 1984.

Bright Shadow, Bradbury, 1985.
Wolf Rider: A Tale of Terror, Bradbury, 1986.
Romeo & Juliet—Together (& Alive) at Last (sequel to *S.O.R. Losers*), Orchard, 1987, Avon, 1988.
Something Upstairs: A Tale of Ghosts, Orchard Books, 1988.
The Man Who Was Poe, Orchard Books, 1989.
The True Confessions of Charlotte Doyle, Orchard Books, 1990.
Windcatcher, Bradbury, 1991.
Nothing but the Truth, Orchard Books, 1991.
Blue Heron, Bradbury, 1992.
"Who Was That Masked Man, Anyway?", Orchard Books, 1992.
Punch With Judy, illustrated by Emily Lisker, Bradbury, 1993.
City of Light/City of Dark: A Comic Book Novel, Orchard Books, 1993.
The Bird, the Frog, and the Light: A Fable, illustrated by Matthew Henry, Orchard, 1994.
The Barn, Orchard, 1994.
Tom, Babette, & Simon: Three Tales of Transformation, illustrated by Alexi Natchev, Macmillan, 1995.
Poppy, illustrated by Brian Floca, Orchard, 1995.
Beyond the Western Sea, Book One: The Escape from Home, Orchard, 1996.
Beyond the Western Sea, Book Two: Lord Kirkle's Money, Orchard, 1996.
What Do Fish Have to Do with Anything?: And Other Stories, illustrated by Tracy Mitchell, Candlewick, 1997.
Finding Providence: The Story of Roger Williams, illustrated by James Watling, HarperCollins, 1997.
Poppy and Rye, illustrated by Brian Floca, Avon, 1998.
Perloo the Bold, illustrated by Marcie Reed, Scholastic, 1998.
Abigail Takes the Wheel, illustrated by Don Bolognese, HarperCollins, 1999.
Ragweed, illustrated by Brian Floca, Avon, 1999.
Midnight Magic, Scholastic, 1999.

Also author of numerous plays. Contributor to books, including *Performing Arts Resources, 1974,* edited by Ted Perry, Drama Book Publishers, 1975. Contributor to periodicals, including *New York Public Library Bulletin, Top of the News, Children's Literature in Education, Horn Book, ALAN Review, Journal of Youth Services in Libraries, Voice of Youth Advocates,* and *Writer.* Book reviewer for *Library Journal, School Library Journal,* and *Previews,* 1965-73.

Translations of Avi's books have been published in Germany, Austria, Denmark, Norway, Spain, Italy, and Japan.

A recording of *The Fighting Ground* was produced by Listening Library, *The Man Who was Poe* by Audio Bookshelf; many others of Avi's books have been recorded on audio cassette, including: *The Barn, Beyond the Western Sea, Blue Heron, Bright Shadow, Man from the Sky, Night Journeys, Perloo the Bold, Poppy, Poppy and Rye, Punch With Judy, Romeo & Juliet—Together (& Alive) at Last, Something Upstairs, Smuggler's*

Island, The True Confessions of Charlotte Doyle, What Do Fish Have to Do with Anything?, "Who Was That Masked Man, Anyway?," and *Wolf Rider.*

Adaptations

Emily Upham's Revenge, Shadrach's Crossing, Something Upstairs, The Fighting Ground, The True Confessions of Charlotte Doyle, Nothing but the Truth, and *Read to Me* were produced on the radio programs "Read to Me," Maine Public Radio, and "Books Aloud," WWON-Rhode Island; *True Confessions of Charlotte Doyle, City of Light/City of Dark, Sometimes I Think I Hear My Name, Something Upstairs,* and *Night Journeys* have all been optioned for film; *Something Upstairs* was adapted as a play performed by Louisville (KY) Children's Theater, 1997; *Nothing but the Truth* was adapted for the stage by Ronn Smith and has been performed in numerous schools.

Work in Progress

Ereth's Birthday, for Avon; *The Good Dog,* for DK Ink; *Prarie School,* for HarperCollins.

Sidelights

An inventive and prolific writer, Avi is well-known to critics, teachers, parents, and especially to young readers for his inviting, readable novels. Even reluctant readers are swept away by Avi's fast-paced, adventurous, and imaginative plots. Because he uses a variety of genres, such as mystery, adventure, historical, coming-of-age, and fantasy, to tell his stories, Avi broadens his audience with each new work. In a statement for *Twentieth-Century Children's Writers,* the talented author summarized his goals as a young adult novelist: "I try to write about complex issues—young people in an adult world—full of irony and contradiction, in a narrative style that relies heavily on suspense with a texture rich in emotion and imagery. I take a great deal of satisfaction in using popular forms—the adventure, the mystery, the thriller—so as to hold my reader with the sheer pleasure of a good story. At the same time I try to resolve my books with an ambiguity that compels engagement. In short, I want my readers to feel, to think, sometimes to laugh. But most of all I want them to enjoy a good read."

Born in Manhattan in 1937 and raised in Brooklyn, Avi is from a long line of artists. His great-grandparents, a grandmother, an aunt, and his parents were writers, while two uncles were painters and another a composer. Many members of his close and extended family are active in the arts, including Avi's twin sister, who is also a writer. Avi's family was quite politically active in ways considered radical; they actively worked against racism, and for the rights of women and laborers, addressing concerns emanating from the Great Depression of the 1930s. The author once explained in an interview with *Something about the Author (SATA)* that his extended family comprised "a very strong art community and what this meant for me as a child was

that there was always a kind of uproarious sense of debate. It was all a very affectionate sharing of ideas—arguing, but not arguing in anger, arguing about ideas."

Growing up, Avi was an avid reader. He experienced difficulties in writing, however, which eventually caused him to flunk out of one school. It was later discovered that he has a dysfunction known as dysgraphia, an impairment that causes him to reverse letters or misspell words. "One of my aunts said I could spell a four letter word wrong five ways," he told *SATA.* "In a school environment, I was perceived as being sloppy and erratic, and not paying attention." Avi, however, kept writing and credits his family's emphasis on books for his perseverance. When papers came back to him covered in his teachers' red ink, he simply saved them, corrections and all.

Just after junior high, despite his writing difficulties, Avi became fixed on becoming a writer. A tutor, hired by his parents to improve his spelling and writing skills, fed his interest in writing, as did his own avid reading habits. Avi claims he learned more from reading—everything from comic books and science magazines to histories, plays, and novels—than he learned in school. In a *Booklist* interview with Hazel Rochman, Avi said, "I love to write. No, let's start first, I love to read. No, start even before, I love stories. My strength as a writer is my strength as a reader."

When he reached college age, Avi enrolled in playwriting classes at Antioch University. "That's where I really started to write seriously," he told *SATA.* One of the plays Avi wrote in college won a contest and was published in a magazine. There were many other plays—"a trunkful of plays," said the author, "but I would say ninety-nine percent of them weren't very good."

After receiving his master's degree, Avi worked at a variety of jobs. Capitalizing on his experience as a playwright, he took a job in the theater collection of the New York Public library. This career move led to his interest in becoming a librarian. He enrolled in Columbia University's library science program and eventually became a librarian—a career that lasted twenty-five years. While a librarian, he continued to write. It wasn't until his two sons were born that he considered writing for a younger audience. Avi enjoyed telling his boys stories, and they enjoyed listening and participating in the storytelling process. Eventually Avi wrote some of his stories down, illustrated them, then submitted them to several publishers. In 1970, Doubleday accepted the text for one of his stories, *Things That Sometimes Happen.* Explaining his abbreviated pen name, Avi told *SATA* that his agent called asking what name to put on the book cover, and without much thought Avi responded, "'just put Avi down' and that was the decision. Just like that."

Things That Sometimes Happen, a collection of "Very Short Stories for Very Young Readers," was designed with Avi's young sons in mind. For several years he continued to write children's books geared to his sons' advancing reading levels, but he told *SATA:* "At a certain point they kept growing and I didn't. I hit a fallow period, and then I wrote *No More Magic.* Suddenly I felt 'This is right! I'm writing novels and I love it.' From then on I was committed to writing novels."

Avi has penned novels for many different genres. Because several of his early works, including *Captain Grey, Night Journeys,* and *Encounter at Easton,* are set in colonial America, he quickly earned a reputation as an historical novelist. Avi's 1984 novel *The Fighting Ground,* winner of the Scott O'Dell Award for historical fiction for children, presents one event-filled day in the life of Jonathan, a thirteen-year-old boy caught up in the Revolutionary War. The novel begins as Jonathan slips away from his family's New Jersey farm one morning in order to take part in a skirmish with the Hessians (German mercenary soldiers hired by the English). Jonathan sets out full of unquestioned hatred for the Hessians, the British, and the Americans who were loyal to the British—the Tories. He hopes for a chance to take part in the glory of battle. "O Lord, he said to himself, make it be a battle. With armies, big ones, and cannons and flags and drums and dress parades! Oh, he could, *would* fight. Good as his older brother. Maybe good as his pa. Better, maybe. O Lord, he said to himself, make it something *grand!"*

Avi portrays no grandeur in the war. Jonathan can barely carry his six-foot long musket, and has a worse time trying to understand the talk among the men with whom he marches. The small voluntary group's leader is a crude man who lies to the men and is said to be "overfond of killing." After a bloody and confusing skirmish, Jonathan is captured by three Hessians and briefly comes to understand them as individual human beings. Later, when he is called upon to be the brave soldier he had yearned to be, Jonathan's harrowing experience reveals the delusion behind his wish. The close of the novel brings the reader and Jonathan an understanding of what war means in human terms. *The Fighting Ground* was widely praised by critics, many of whom expressed sentiments similar to these from Zena Sutherland of *Bulletin of the Center for Children's Books,* who asserted: "[The novel] makes the war personal and immediate: not history or event, but experience; near and within oneself, and horrible."

More interested in telling a good story and providing a means of imagining and understanding the past than in teaching a specific historical fact, Avi's style is well-suited to the historical fiction genre. "The historical novel is a curious construction," he once told *SATA.* "It represents history but it's not truly accurate. It's a style." He elaborated in an interview with Jim Roginski in *Behind the Covers:* "Somewhere along the line, I can't explain where, I developed an understanding of history not as fact but as story. That you could look at a field and, with only a slight shift of your imagination, suddenly watch the battle that took place there . . . . You have to have a willingness to look beyond *things . . . .* Take the Battle of Bunker Hill during the Revolution.

The leader of the American troops was Dr. Warren, who was killed during the battle. His body had been so dismembered and disemboweled, the only way he could be identified was by the nature of his teeth. And it was Paul Revere who did it. When you tell the story of war that way, a much stronger statement about how ghastly war really is, is made."

Taking readers back in time to pre-Civil War America, Avi combined elements of historical novel, ghost story, and science fiction, to create *Something Upstairs: A Tale of Ghosts.* When the book's main character discovers the ghost of a murdered slave in the historic house his family recently moved into in Providence, Rhode Island, he travels back in time to the days of slave trading. There, the young man uncovers information about the murder and, perhaps more importantly, about the manner in which American history is collectively remembered. Although Avi was praised for his historical representation in this work, the author told *SATA* that "the irony is that in those Providence books there is nothing historical at all; it's a kind of fantasy of my neighborhood." Like his narrator in *Something Upstairs,* Avi moved from Los Angeles to Providence; in fact, he moved into the historic house featured in this novel.

The Man Who Was Poe, Avi's fictionalized portrait of nineteenth-century writer Edgar Allan Poe, intertwines fiction and history on several levels. Historically, Poe went through a period of severe depression and poverty, aggravated by alcoholism during the two years preceding his death in 1849. Avi, whose novel focuses on this period, said he became fascinated with Poe because he was so extraordinary and yet such "a horrible man." In the novel, a young boy, Edmund, has recently immigrated to Providence from England with his aunt and twin sister in order to look for his missing mother. When both aunt and sister disappear, the penniless boy must elicit help from a stranger—who happens to be Edgar Allen Poe. Poe, noticing similarities between Edmund's story and his own life, detects material for his writing and agrees to help the boy. Between maddening bouts of drunkenness, Poe ingeniously finds a trail of clues to the family's disappearance. Edmund, who has been taught to defer to adults, alternates between awe of the great man's perceptive powers and despair at his madness.

Vividly reflecting the macabre tone of Poe's fiction, Avi portrays the old port city of Providence as a bleak and chaotic world in which compassion and moral order seem to have given way to violence and greed. The character Poe, with his morbid imagination, makes an apt detective in this realm until it becomes clear that he wants the "story" of Edmund's family to end tragically. Edmund's plight is a harsh one, relying on Poe as the only adult who can help him, while at the same time attempting to ensure that Poe's vision does not become a reality. Roger Sutton of the *Bulletin of the Center for Children's Books,* called the novel "a complex, atmospheric thriller." "Avi recreates the gloom of 1840s Baltimore [*sic*] with a storyteller's ease," remarked Sutton, "blending drama, history, and mystery without a hint of pastiche or calculation. And, as in the best mystery stories, readers will be left in the end with both the comfort of puzzles solved and the unease of mysteries remaining."

In another unique twist on the convention of historical novels, *The True Confessions of Charlotte Doyle* presents the unlikely story of a very proper thirteen-year-old girl who, as the sole passenger and only female on a transatlantic ship in 1832, becomes involved in a mutiny at sea. Holding her family's aristocratic views on social class and demeanor, Charlotte begins her voyage trusting only Captain Jaggery, whose fine manners and authoritative command remind her of her father. She is thus shocked to find that Jaggery is a viciously brutal shipmaster. This discovery, along with her growing fondness for members of the ship's crew, gradually leads Charlotte to question—and discard—the values of her privileged background. As she exchanges her finishing school wardrobe for a common sailor's garb and joins the crew in its work, she reveals the strength of her character, initially masked by her restrictive upbringing.

In the adventures that follow, including a mysterious murder, a storm, and a mutiny, Charlotte's reeducation and emancipation provide a new version of the conventionally male story of rugged individualism at sea. The multi-award-winning novel has received accolades from critics for its suspense, its evocation of life at sea, and particularly for the rich and believable narrative of its protagonist as she undergoes a tremendous change in outlook. The impact of Charlotte's liberation from social bonds and gender restrictions in *The True Confessions of Charlotte Doyle* has a powerful emotional effect on many of its readers. Avi told *SATA* that "many people, mostly girls, and even adults," have told him of "bursting into tears" at the book's ending—tears of relief that Charlotte finds the freedom to realize herself as she chooses. In her *Five Owls* review of *The True Confessions of Charlotte Doyle*, Cathryn M. Mercier wrote that Charlotte's "struggle will fully engage readers, who will find themselves cheering the improbable but deeply satisfying conclusion." Avi addressed Ms. Mercier's contention of an "improbable conclusion" in his *Boston Globe-Horn Book* Award acceptance speech, in which he commented: "I am deeply grateful for the award you have given me today. But I hope you will understand me when I tell you that if the 'improbable' life I wrote lives in someone's heart as a life *possible,* then I have already been given the greatest gift a writer can receive: a reader who takes my story and endows it with life by the grace of their own desire."

Other historical novels by Avi are *The Barn*, published in 1994, and the two-volume *Beyond the Western Sea*, published in 1996. Set in 1850's Oregon, *The Barn* features an intelligent nine-year-old boy named Ben who must return home from boarding school to care for his widowed, invalid father. Ben decides that he wants to fulfill his father's dream of building a barn on their farm. His brother and sister reluctantly agree to help, and after three long months, they finish the barn. That evening, though, their father dies in his sleep, never seeing the barn. While his brother and sister eventually move on,

A thirteen-year-old girl, the sole passenger and only female on a transatlantic ship in 1832, becomes involved in a mutiny at sea in Avi's unique twist on the conventional historical novel.

Ben stays on the farm with the memory of his father linked to the barn. Deeply affected by the novel, *Booklist*'s Hazel Rochman raved, "This small, beautiful historical novel has a timeless simplicity. It's the best thing he's done."

With *Beyond the Western Sea: The Escape from Home,* the first book in his Victorian-modeled series, Avi created an exciting cliffhanger with plenty of adventure and a cast of colorful characters. "While you actually do have to turn the pages for yourself here," wrote Roger Sutton of *Bulletin of the Center for Children's Books,* "the task soon feels like it's out of your hands as Avi's tense, twisting storytelling takes over." The story begins in 1850s Ireland during the potato famine, with Maura and Patrick O'Connell and their mother being forced out of their home by their relentless landlord, Lord Kirkle. Like many others during this infamous period, the O'Connells plan to sail to America to join their father. Mother, however, decides to stay behind, leaving the children on their own. Who should the children meet in Liverpool while en route but Sir Laurence Kirkle—the eleven-year-old son of Lord Kirkle. Laurence, they learn, is running away from his father. By book's end, Laurence is a stowaway facing big trouble. Mary M. Burns of *Horn Book* maintained: "The ending leaves one of the main characters 'in dire straits,' as the old-fashioned melodramas used to say, insuring that readers will be eagerly awaiting the promised sequel." As evidence of those eagerly awaiting readers, *Voice of Youth Advocates* contributor Kathleen Beck offered, "no sooner had *Escape from Home* been published than [a young library patron] was breathlessly requesting this sequel."

With the second installment, *Beyond the Western Sea, Book Two: Lord Kirkle's Money,* Avi transforms the first book into what Burns called a "blockbuster epic ... totaling 675 pages." While readers of book two find that Laurence is safe, they also learn about the harsh realities and discrimination that the Irish-born characters face in America. Patrick and Maura discover that their father is dead, and each character learns to survive independently. Concluding her positive review of the "Beyond the Western Sea" series, *Horn Book*'s Burns declared, "an adventure in grand style, the story benefits from its historical foundation and skillful plotting."

Avi, although an enthusiastic reader of history, is by no means tied to the historical novel and delights in finding new ways to structure his stories. He told *SATA:* "People constantly ask, 'How come you keep changing styles?' I think that's a misquestion. Put it this way, 'What makes you so fascinated with technique?' You know that there are a lot of ways to tell a story. To me that's just fun." With his extensive background in theater, it is no surprise that many of Avi's novels have roots in drama.

In 1984, Avi published *S.O.R. Losers,* a funny contemporary novel about a group of unathletic boys forced by their school (which is based on Avi's high school in New York City) to form a soccer team. Opposing the time-honored school ethic that triumph in sports is the American way, the boys form their own opinions about winning at something that means little to them. In a team meeting, they take stock of who they are and why it's so important to everyone *else* that they should win their games. The narrator, who is the team's captain, sums it up: "Every one of us is good at something. Right? Maybe more than one thing. The point is *other* things ... . But I don't like sports. I'm not good at it. I don't enjoy it. So I say, so what? I mean if Saltz here writes a stinko poem—and he does all the time—do they yell at him? When was the last time Mr. Tillman came around and said, 'Saltz, I *believe* in your being a poet!'"

Avi makes a clear statement with his humor in *S.O.R. Losers.* He once told *SATA* that he sees an irony in the American attitude toward education. "On the one hand, our culture likes to give a lot of lip service to support for kids, but on the other hand, I don't think the culture as a whole likes kids. And kids are caught in this contradiction. I ask teachers at conferences 'How many of you

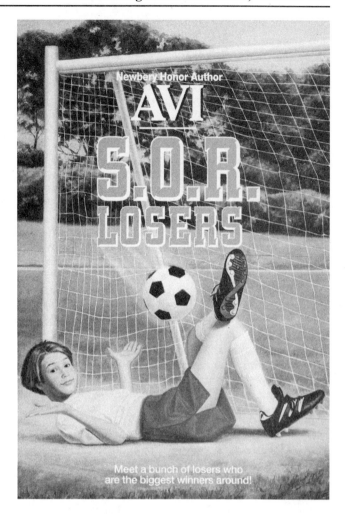

Avi's funny contemporary novel features a group of unathletic boys forced by their school to form a soccer team and pressured to win despite their disinterest.

have athletic trophies displayed in your schools?' You know how many raise their hands. And I ask, 'How many of you have trophy displays for the best reader or writer?' Nobody raises their hands. And I say 'What is it therefore that stands as the essential achievement in your school?' With test scores falling, we need to make kids better readers, but instead we're interested in a minority of kids, mostly males, whose primary focus is sports."

With its narrator's deadpan reporting of the fiascos of a consistently losing sports team, *S.O.R. Losers* does more than make a point—it's funny. *Horn Book* contributor Mary M. Burns, who called the novel "one of the funniest and most original sports sagas on record," particularly praised Avi's skill with comedic form. "Short, pithy chapters highlighting key events maintain the pace necessary for successful comedy. As in a Charlie Chaplin movie, emphasis is on individual episode—each distinct, yet organically related to an overall idea." Avi has written several other comic novels, including his sequel to *S.O.R. Losers, Romeo & Juliet—Together (& Alive) at Last,* and two well-received spoofs on nineteenth-century melodrama, *Emily Upham's Revenge* and *History of Helpless Harry.*

Avi is also the author of several acclaimed contemporary coming-of-age novels, including *A Place Called Ugly* and *Sometimes I Think I Hear My Name.* His 1992 Newbery honor book, *Nothing but the Truth,* is the story of Philip Malloy and his battle with an English teacher, Miss Narwin. Kept off the track team with bad grades in English, Philip repeatedly breaks school rules by humming the national anthem along with the public address system in Miss Narwin's home room. Eventually, the principal suspends Philip from school. Because the school happens to be in the midst of elections, various self-interested members of the community exploit this story of a boy being suspended for his patriotism. Much to everyone's surprise, the incident in homeroom snowballs into a national media event that, in its frenzied patriotic rhetoric, thoroughly overshadows the true story about a good teacher's inability to reach a student, a young man's alienation, a community's disinterest in its children's needs, and a school system's hypocrisy.

Nothing but the Truth is a book without a narrator, relating its story through school memos, diary entries, letters, dialogues, newspaper articles, and radio talk show scripts. Presented without narrative bias, the story takes into account the differing points of view surrounding the incident, allowing the reader to root out the real problems leading to the incident. Avi explained to *SATA* that he got the idea for the structure of this novel from a form of theater that arose in the 1930s called "Living Newspapers"—dramatizations of issues and problems confronting American society presented through a "hodge podge" of document readings and dialogues.

Displaying Avi's obvious sympathy for the "outsider" position of adolescence is *Nothing but the Truth*'s main character, Philip Malloy. In all the national attention Philip receives as a patriotic hero, no one asks him what he feels or thinks, and no one seems to notice that he changes from a fairly happy and enthusiastic youth to a depressed and alienated adolescent. Philip's interest in *The Outsiders,* S. E. Hinton's novel about rival gangs of teenagers (written when Hinton was only seventeen years old), reveals that Philip would like to read about a world that looks like his own, with people experiencing problems like his. The Shakespeare plays assigned in school do not reach him. Avi explained to *SATA:* "It's not an accident that in the last decades the book most read by young people is *The Outsiders.* I wish Stephen King's novels were taught in the schools, so that kids could respond to them and talk about them." Avi does not hesitate to set complexities and harsh truths before his readers because, he noted, these truths are already well-known to children. "I think writers like myself say to kids like this, 'We affirm your sense of reality.' We help frame it and give it recognition."

In his 1997 work *What Do Fish Have to Do with Anything?: And Other Stories,* Avi offers seven stories in which young adult protagonists realize the power they hold over their lives, as well as the lives of others. For example, in "What's Inside," a thirteen-year-old boy is able to convince his older cousin not to commit suicide. "Whether facing a domineering mother, divorced par-

ents, or a reputation as the bad guy, the protagonists take positive steps forward," wrote *School Library Journal* contributor Carol A. Edwards. It is each individual's choice of good over bad, "the halo over the pitchfork, that makes these stories inspiring," added Edwards. *Booklist* reviewer Michael Cart praised the "authentic emotional insights that provide the surprises and right-on rites of passage."

Avi has also successfully penned fantasy fiction. *Poppy,* which received a *Boston Globe-Horn Book* Award in 1996, is an example of Avi's highly regarded fantasy writing. In this story two deer mice, Ragweed and Poppy, are about to marry when the self-proclaimed king of Dimwood Forest—an owl named Mr. Ocax—eats Ragwood, supposedly as punishment for neglecting to seek his permission to marry. Although Mr. Ocax eats Ragwood, Poppy escapes. Soon, the other mice go to Mr. Ocax for permission to move to New House, where there is more food. He refuses their request, using Poppy's disobedience as an excuse, but Poppy suspects that Mr. Ocax has another motive for keeping the mice

In Avi's novel, related through memos, diary entries, newspaper articles, and other written documents, an adolescent suspended from school finds himself at the center of a media event originated by vote-hungry local politicians. (Cover illustration by Peter Catalanotto.)

nearby and sets out to find it so she can save her family. Ann A. Flowers of *Horn Book* called *Poppy* "a tribute to the inquiring mind and the stout heart." *Bulletin of the Center for Children's Books* critic Roger Sutton wrote: "Sprightly but un-cute dialogue, suspenseful chapter endings, and swift shifts of perspective between Ocax and Poppy will make chapter-a-day readalouds cause for anticipation." Avi followed *Poppy* with the sequels *Poppy and Rye* and *Ragweed.*

Although writing on a full-time basis, Avi maintains regular interaction with children by traveling around the country, talking in schools about his work. "I think it's very important for me to keep these kids in front of my eyes. They're wonderfully interesting and they hold me to the reality of who they are." Avi once told *SATA* that children are passionate and honest readers who will either "swallow a book whole" if they like it, or drop it "like a hot potato" if they don't. In an article in *School Library Journal,* he provides a telling anecdote about his approach to children: "Being dysgraphic, with the standard history of frustration and anguish, I always ask to speak to the learning-disabled kids. They come in slowly, waiting for yet another pep talk, more instructions. Eyes cast down, they won't even look at me. Their anger glows. I don't say a thing. I lay out pages of my copy-edited manuscripts, which are covered with red marks. 'Look here,' I say, 'see that spelling mistake. There, another spelling mistake. Looks like I forgot to put a capital letter there. Oops! Letter reversal.' Their eyes lift. They are listening. And I am among friends."

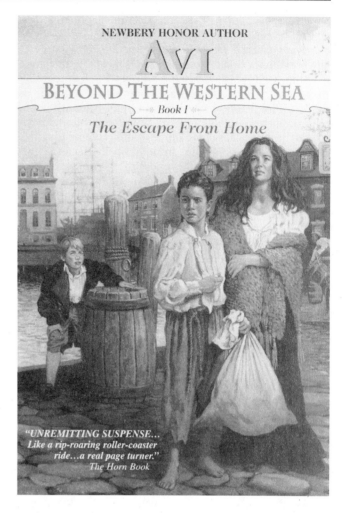

In the first book of his "Beyond the Western Sea" series, Avi presents an exciting cliffhanger with plenty of adventure and a cast of colorful characters.

Works Cited

Avi, "All That Glitters," *Horn Book,* September-October, 1987, pp. 569-76.

Avi, *Boston Globe-Horn Book* Award acceptance speech, *Horn Book,* January-February, 1992, pp. 24-27.

Avi, *The Fighting Ground,* Lippincott, 1984.

Avi (with Betty Miles), "School Visits: The Author's Viewpoint," *School Library Journal,* January, 1987, p. 21.

Avi, *S.O.R. Losers,* Bradbury, 1984.

Avi, autobiographical statement in *Twentieth-Century Children's Writers,* St. Martin's, 1989, pp. 45-46.

Beck, Kathleen, review of *Beyond the Western Sea, Book Two: Lord Kirkle's Money, Voice of Youth Advocates,* December, 1996, p. 267.

Burns, Mary M., review of *Beyond the Western Sea, Book One: The Escape from Home, Horn Book,* July-August, 1996, p. 461.

Burns, Mary M., review of *Beyond the Western Sea, Book Two: Lord Kirkle's Money, Horn Book,* November-December, 1996, p. 731.

Burns, Mary M., review of *S.O.R. Losers, Horn Book,* January-February, 1985, p. 49.

Cart, Michael, review of *Poppy, Booklist,* November 15, 1997, p. 557.

Cart, Michael, review of *What Do Fish Have to Do with Anything?: And Other Stories, Booklist,* November 15, 1997, p. 560.

Edwards, Carol A., review of *What Do Fish Have to Do with Anything?: And Other Stories, School Library Journal,* December, 1997, p. 120.

Review of *The Fighting Ground, Bulletin of the Center for Children's Books,* June, 1984, p. 180.

Flowers, Ann A., review of *Poppy, Horn Book,* January-February, 1996, p. 70.

Mercier, Cathryn M., review of *The True Confessions of Charlotte Doyle, Five Owls,* January-February, 1991, pp. 56-57.

Rochman, Hazel, "A Conversation with Avi," *Booklist,* January 15, 1992, p. 930.

Rochman, Hazel, "Focus: How to Build a Barn," *Booklist,* September 1, 1994, p. 40.

Roginski, Jim, *Behind the Covers: Interviews with Authors and Illustrators of Books for Children and Young Adults,* Libraries Unlimited, 1985, pp. 33-41.

Sutherland, Zena, review of *The Fighting Ground, Bulletin of the Center for Children's Books,* June, 1984, p. 180.

Sutton, Roger, review of *Beyond the Western Sea, Book One: The Escape from Home, Bulletin of the Center for Children's Books,* February, 1996, p. 183.

Sutton, Roger, review of *The Man Who Was Poe, Bulletin of the Center for Children's Books,* October, 1989, p. 27.

Sutton, Roger, review of *Poppy, Bulletin of the Center for Children's Books,* January, 1996, p. 154.

For More Information See

BOOKS

Bloom, Susan P. and Cathryn M. Mercier, *Presenting Avi,* Twayne, 1997.

Markham, Lois, *Avi,* Learning Works (Santa Barbara, CA), 1996.

PERIODICALS

Booklist, March 15, 1993, p. 1312; April 15, 1994, p. 1538; February 1, 1996, p. 930; February 1, 1997, p. 949; May 15, 1998, p. 1625; April 1, 1999, p. 1424.

Bulletin of the Center for Children's Books, October, 1992, p. 35; December, 1994, p. 120; March, 1997, p. 240.

Horn Book, January-February, 1989, p. 65; January-February, 1995, p. 57; January-February, 1997, pp. 40-43; March-April, 1999, p. 206.

Kirkus Reviews, October 1, 1993, p. 1268; September 15, 1995, p. 1346.

Publishers Weekly, September 14, 1990, p. 128; September 6, 1991, p. 105; September 5, 1994, p. 112; June 15, 1998, p. 60; May 10, 1999, p. 68.

School Library Journal, April, 1994, p. 95; November, 1998, p. 116; May, 1999, p. 85.

Voice of Youth Advocates, April, 1992, p. 21; June, 1996, p. 92.

B

BAIUL, Oksana 1977-

Personal

Born November 16, 1977, in Dnepropetrovsk, Ukraine, of the former Union of Soviet Socialist Republics (USSR); immigrated to the United States, 1994, naturalized citizen; daughter of Sergei (estranged from his wife and daughter from 1979 on) and Marina (a French teacher) Baiul, who died in 1991.

Oksana Baiul

Addresses

Home—Newark, DE. *Agent*—Shelly Schultz, William Morris Agency, 1325 Avenue of the Americas, New York, NY 10019.

Career

Ice skater, 1991 to present. Recipient of second-place award in the women's figure skating European Championships, 1993; first-place award in the women's World Figure Skating Championships, 1993; and won the Gold Medal for women's figure skating at the 1994 Olympic Games in Lillehammer, Norway. Baiul now skates professionally. She has co-authored two books about her life and skating.

Writings

Oksana: My Own Story, as told to Heather Alexander, Random House (New York), 1997.
Secrets of Skating, compiled by Christopher Sweet, with original photography by Simon Bruty, foreword by Dorothy Hamill, Universe Publishers (New York), 1997.

Sidelights

Oksana Baiul began to receive national attention as a figure skater in 1991, when she placed twelfth in the Soviet Championships. By 1993 she was receiving international attention as the second-place winner in the European Championships in Helsinki, and later that year, as winner of the World Championships in Prague. The following year, Baiul became a household name throughout the world, winning the Gold Medal for women's figure skating at the 1994 Olympic Games at the age of sixteen.

Baiul overcame great odds to make it to the top of her sport; her story is told in her skating autobiography, *Oksana: My Own Story.* But she also paid a great price as a result of her instant notoriety and sudden riches, a story her book leaves out, but which has been followed by all those interested in skating and sports news in general.

Oksana: My Own Story traces Baiul's origins to Dnepropetrovsk, the Soviet missile factory town in the Ukraine where she was born in 1977. Baiul was raised by her mother and maternal grandparents from the age of two, when her father Sergei deserted the family. It was her grandfather who got her started in skating by buying Oksana her first pair of skates when she was four. He foresaw a future in dance for her, and viewed the skating rink as a "training ground" for a career in the ballet. But Baiul took to the ice instantly, and there she remained under the training of Stanislav Korytek, called "one of the finest Ukrainian coaches" by Ami Walsh in *Newsmakers 1995*. Bauil's mother Marina managed to cover the costs of her daughter's training from her salary as a French teacher. But Marina Baiul's life was cut short in 1991, at the age of thirty-six, when she died of ovarian cancer. Having already lost her grandparents, and only having glimpsed her father at her mother's funeral, Baiul was effectively orphaned by her mother's death.

Fortunately for her and for the future of women's skating, Baiul's coach Korytek, who defected to Canada within a few weeks of Marina Baiul's death, begged Galina Zmievskaya, another excellent skating coach, to help Baiul. Zmievskaya's protege and later son-in-law Victor Petrenko encouraged her to coach Baiul, having sensed the young skater's potential. Within a short time Baiul was living with Zmievskaya in her small Odessa apartment, sharing her youngest daughter's bedroom.

Within two years Baiul began to win medals in major competitions, including a win at the World Championships in 1993. But the pressure of these events was hardly comparable to the upcoming Winter Olympic Games. If the pressure of the games themselves was not enough, women's figure skating was in the spotlight more than usual that year because of the intensive coverage of the Tonya Harding-Nancy Kerrigan scandal. The scandal began in January, 1994, when a man (who was later discovered to have been hired by figure skater Harding's boyfriend) attacked Kerrigan as she trained in Detroit's Cobo Arena. Although Kerrigan's knee was injured in the attack, she was able to skate at the Olympic Games, as was Harding, who had not been disqualified by her boyfriend's actions. Baiul had her own injuries to contend with going into the final competition; she ran into another skater while training on the night before the finals and suffered a bad cut to her shin and bruises on her back. But despite the overwhelming attention being focused on women's skating, and despite her own painful injuries, Baiul skated a nearly flawless program and managed to beat the heavily favored Kerrigan by a narrow margin. In so doing, Baiul arrested the attention of one of the largest television viewing audiences ever, and secured herself place in the figure-skating pantheon.

Baiul's book ends at this climactic point. Reviews of *Oksana: My Own Story* were generally positive, although some reviewers waxed more enthusiastic than

Baiul's autobiography traces her success as an Olympic skater, as well as personal tragedies and triumphs. (Cover photo by SportsChrome.)

others. Writing for *School Library Journal*, Janice C. Hayes admired the book's high-quality photographs and heavy, snow-flake embossed paper, as well as its "charming and heartwarming story." Conversely, Deborah Stevenson, writing for the *Bulletin of the Center for Children's Books*, called the book "a hardcover souvenir brochure" that does not bring readers "any real closeness to the glamorous world" they are eager to read about. *Booklist* reviewer Chris Sherman felt the book would appeal to preteen skating fans, noting that, while the book doesn't reveal much new information, it does provide "interesting reading."

Works Cited

Hayes, Janice C., review of *Oksana: My Own Story, School Library Journal,* May, 1997, p. 142.

Sherman, Chris, review of *Oksana: My Own Story, Booklist,* May 1, 1997, pp. 1489-91.

Stevenson, Deborah, review of *Oksana: My Own Story, Bulletin of the Center for Children's Books,* May, 1997, pp. 312-13.

Walsh, Ami, *Newsmakers 1995,* Gale, 1995.

For More Information See

PERIODICALS

People Weekly, June 23, 1997, pp. 71-75.
Time, January 26, 1998, pp. 64-67.

*   *   *

BASTYRA, Judy

Addresses

Home—13 Elms Avenue, Muswell Hill, London N10
2JN, England.

Career

Editor and writer; restaurant consultant. Has appeared on
radio and television broadcasts. Has worked as an editor
for Benn Brothers Ltd., 1965-67; Haymarket Press,
1968-69; Thomson Publications, 1969-70; Ambassador
Publications, 1970-71; Peter Dunbar Associates, 1972-
78; and Marshall Cavendish, 1973-79. Media and
resource consultant for Marie Stopes International (an
international charity).

Writings

Caribbean Cooking, Windward, 1987.
(With Julia Canning) *A Gourmet's Book of Fruit,* Salaman-
    der, 1989.
(With Judy Hindley) *Make, Bake, Grow and Sew,* Collins,
    1989.
Busy Little Cook, illustrated by Nicola Smee, Conran
    Octopus, 1990.
(With Sandra Alexander) *Love Bites,* Robson Books, 1993.
Get, Set ... Go Vegetables, photographs by Michael
    Michaels, Franklin Watts, 1994.
Get, Set ... Go Fruit, photographs by Michael Michaels,
    Franklin Watts, 1994.
Get, Set ... Go Bread, photographs by Michael Michaels,
    Franklin Watts, 1995.
Get, Set ... Go Cheese, photographs by Michael Michaels,
    Franklin Watts, 1995.
Hanukkah Fun, Kingfisher, 1996.
Fun Food, Collins, 1996.
Look and Make: I Can Cook, Franklin Watts, 1996.
Homeless, Evans, 1996.
Cooking with Dad, Bloomsbury, 1996.
Kids' Guide to Making Money and Keeping It!, Blooms-
    bury, 1997.
Cookie Fun, Kingfisher, 1997.
Pizza Fun, Kingfisher, 1997.
Parties for Kids, Kingfisher, 1998.
Making the Most of Being a Student, Kogan Page, 1998.

Contributor to books, including *The Encyclopaedia of
Herbs, Spices and Flavourings,* Dorling Kindersley,
1992; *Cook's Companion,* Webster, 1991; *Sainsbury's
Book of Food,* Webster, 1989; and *Have You Started
Yet?,* Piccolo, 1980. Contributor to magazines, including
*BBC Good Food, Busy Needles, Company, Confident
Cooking, Covent Garden Courier, Doctor's Answer,*
*Essentials, Family Circle, Food & Entertainment, Food
Illustrated, Homes and Gardens, Inspirations, Look &
Learn, Nice N'Easy, Stitch by Stitch, Taste, The Big
Issue, Woman, Woman & Home, Woman's Own.* Con-
tributor to newspapers, including *London Daily News,
Today, Daily Star, Jewish Chronicle, Hampstead &
Highgate Express, Times (London).**

*   *   *

BLACKLIN, Malcolm
See CHAMBERS, Aidan

*   *   *

BLEDSOE, Glen L(eonard) 1951-

Personal

Born April 10, 1951, in Gary, IN; son of John William
(a steel worker) and Loretta Radcliffe (a child care
provider; maiden name, Dix) Bledsoe; married Karen
Elizabeth Lytle (a teacher and writer), June 28, 1992;
children: Gabriel Scott, James Wesley Solonika (stepson). *Education:* Indiana University—Bloomington,
B.A., 1983; attended School of the Art Institute of
Chicago, 1980; Willamette University, M.A.T., 1991.
Hobbies and other interests: Guitar, shin-shin toitsu
aikido.

Addresses

Home—Salem, OR. *Electronic mail*—GlnBledsoe@
aol.com and http://members.aol.com/SublimeArt/Stu-
dios.

Career

U.S. Steel Co., chemical technician, 1972-78; Rubino's
Music Center, Portage, IN, luthier and seller of musical
instruments, 1976-80; Keizer Elementary School, Keizer, OR, teacher, 1991—, team leader, 1995—, web page
designer and webmaster of http://keizer.salkeiz.
k12.or.us, 1995—. Lansing Art Gallery, Lansing, MI,
interim director, 1981; also works as artist in residence.
Willamette University, cochairperson of Education Con-
sortium, 1996—. *Member:* Society of Children's Book
Writers and Illustrators.

Writings

FOR CHILDREN; WITH KAREN BLEDSOE

Classic Ghost Stories II, Lowell House (Los Angeles, CA),
    1998.
Classic Sea Stories, Lowell House, 1999.
Creepy Classics III, Lowell House, 1999.
Classic Mysteries II, Lowell House, in press.
Classic Adventure Stories, Lowell House, in press.

OTHER

Contributor of articles to the periodicals *HyperCard* and
Computing Teacher; contributor of art to *Oregon Focus.*

Contributor of illustrations to the compact disc accompanying *Real World Bryce II* by Susan Kitchens.

Sidelights

Glen L. Bledsoe once commented: "My wife and I have our separate writing projects, but when we work together we have a unique approach. I usually write the first few chapters to a novel, then, using a y-cord, we both plug into my Macintosh computer. From there we take turns as inspiration moves us. We leap-frog through entire chapters very quickly that way. Later we swap chapters for editing and rewriting. The result is a flowing, seamless product. We have completed five novels, and have as many to finish."*

*   *   *

BLEDSOE, Karen E(lizabeth) 1962-

Personal

Born April 15, 1962, in Salem, OR; daughter of Don James (an accountant and Christmas tree farmer) and Harriet Elizabeth (a medical technologist and Christmas tree farmer; maiden name, Hiday) Lytle; married Glen Leonard Bledsoe (a teacher and writer), June 28, 1992; children: Gabriel Scott (stepson), James Wesley Solonika. *Education:* Willamette University, B.S., 1985, M.A.T., 1991; Oregon State University, M.S., 1988. *Hobbies and other interests:* Gardening, shin-shin toitsu aikido.

Addresses

Home—Salem, OR. *Office*—Division of Natural Science and Mathematics, Western Oregon University, Monmouth, OR 97361. *E-mail*—KestrelB@aol.com. *Agent*—Elisabet McHugh.

Career

Temporary and substitute teacher at public schools in Salem, OR, 1991-95; Western Oregon University, Monmouth, instructor in biology, 1995—. Oregon Academy of Science, science education co-chairperson and web page designer, 1996—; Oregon Collaborative for Excellence in the Preparation of Teachers, faculty fellow, 1997—; Oregon Public Education Network, team coach for Master WEBster web page design contest, 1998-99. U.S. Forest Service, seasonal biological technician, 1985; City of Salem, seasonal recreational leader and environmental educator, 1989-94. *Member:* Society of Children's Book Writers and Illustrators, National Biology Teachers Association, Oregon Science Teachers Association, Phi Delta Kappa.

Writings

FOR YOUNG PEOPLE; WITH GLEN L. BLEDSOE

Classic Ghost Stories II, Lowell House (Los Angeles, CA), 1998.
Classic Sea Stories, Lowell House, 1999.
Creepy Classics III, Lowell House, 1999.
Classic Mysteries II, Lowell House, in press.
Classic Adventure Stories, Lowell House, in press.

OTHER

(With Candyce Norvall) *365 Nature Crafts,* Publications International, 1997.
Best Friends, Publications International, 1997.
School Memories Album, Publications International, 1998.
Millennium Album, Publications International, 1998.

Sidelights

Karen E. Bledsoe comments: "Writing and teaching are natural careers for me. I've always liked telling what I know to a captive audience.

"Words have been my toys since I first taught myself to read at the age of three. I spent many hours manufacturing little books, hand-illustrated and bound with a stapler. Inventions were a favorite theme, followed closely by mysteries, code books, and adventure stories. When I wasn't writing, I was gobbling up books as fast as I could get my hands on them. Books were my best friends during my school years when we moved every year—sometimes twice a year. I was a wallflower and had difficulty making friends.

"In junior high and high school, when the family was more settled and I finally had friends again, I turned to more challenging themes in both my reading and writing: high fantasy, supernatural adventure, lengthy sagas. I churned out the usual dreary, self-pitying poetry characteristic of angst-ridden teen writers, wrote for the school yearbook, and got a fair start on a lengthy fantasy novel that I may yet finish. My best subjects were English and science, and I chose the life sciences as my college path.

"College and a disastrous marriage occupied the next eight years of my life. Though I had little energy to spare for it, I still dabbled at writing. With a sister-in-law, I completed my first novel, a cliche-ridden romantic spoof that will never see the light of print (nor was it meant to) but which taught me much about what it takes to finish a book. Earning my bachelor's degree and a master of arts in botany during this period taught me plenty about perseverance in adverse circumstances.

"Finding that teaching was more to my liking than scientific research, I enrolled in the master of arts in teaching program at Willamette University, where I earned my teaching certificate and met my current husband. The two events marked a new era in my life. In the mutually supportive environment we've nurtured in our home, we have both blossomed creatively. We always have projects going: novels in progress, web pages going up, art work, music, gardening, while the television slowly gathers dust. When we write, it is often literally together, with two keyboards plugged in series into the back of a Macintosh. Our publishing successes have been modest so far, but we intend to persevere until we can retire from teaching and earn our living as writers."*

*   *   *

BLOOM, Lloyd 1947-

Personal

Born January 10, 1947, in New York, NY. *Education:* Received undergraduate degree from Hunter College, 1972; Indiana University, M.F.A., 1975; studied at the Art Students League of New York City and the New York Studio School prior to and during college education.

Addresses

Home—Brooklyn, NY.

Career

Illustrator.

Awards, Honors

Fulbright Scholarship in painting, 1976; Friends of American Writers Juvenile Book Merit Award, 1980, for *Grey Cloud;* Golden Kite Award, and American Library Association (ALA) Notable Book, both 1980, both for *Arthur, for the Very First Time;* Irma Simonton Black Award, 1983, for *No One Is Going to Nashville;* Illustration Honor, *Boston Globe-Horn Book,* 1985, for *Like Jake & Me;* Award for Illustration, Jewish Book Council, 1987, for *Poems for Jewish Holidays. Yonder* was exhibited at the Biennale Illustrations Bratislava, International Board on Books for Young People, 1989.

Illustrator

Virginia F. Voight, *Bobcat,* Dodd, Mead, 1978.
Robert Burch, *Wilkin's Ghost,* Viking Penguin, 1978.
(Compiled by Phyllis R. Fenner) *A Dog's Life: Stories of Champions, Hunters, and Faithful Friends,* William Morrow, 1978.
Barbara Steiner, *Biography of a Bengal Tiger,* Putnam, 1979.
Uriel Ofek, *Smoke Over Golan: A Novel of the 1973 Yom Kippur War in Israel,* HarperCollins Children's Books, 1979, Jewish Publication Society, 1987.
Charlotte Towner Graeber, *Grey Cloud,* Four Winds, 1979, Simon & Schuster Children's, 1984.
Lillie D. Chaffin, *We Be Warm Till Springtime Comes,* Macmillan, 1980.
Patricia MacLachlan, *Arthur, for the Very First Time,* Harper & Row, 1980.
Francine Jacobs, *Fire Snake: The Railroad That Changed East Africa,* William Morrow, 1980.
Ethel J. Phelps, *The Maid of the North: Feminist Folk Tales from Around the World,* Henry Holt, 1981.
Jill Paton Walsh, *The Green Book,* Farrar, Straus & Giroux, 1982.

Mavis Jukes, *No One Is Going to Nashville,* Alfred A. Knopf, 1983.
Eric Suben, reteller, *The Elves and the Shoemaker,* Golden Books, 1983.
Sue Alexander, *Nadia the Willful,* Pantheon Books, 1983.
Mavis Jukes, *Like Jake & Me,* Alfred A. Knopf, 1984.
Robert Burleigh, *A Man Named Thoreau,* Atheneum, 1985.
Stan Steiner, *The Ranchers: A Book of Generations,* University of Oklahoma Press, 1985.
(Selected by Myra Cohn Livingston) *Poems for Jewish Holidays,* Holiday House, 1986.
(Selected and retold by Howard Schwartz) *Miriam's Tambourine: Jewish Folktales from Around the World,* Seth Press, 1986.
Gershon Winkler, *The Secret of Sambatyon,* Judaica, 1987.
Tony Johnston, *Yonder,* Dial, 1988.
Terry W. Treseder, *Hear O Israel: A Story of the Warsaw Ghetto,* Atheneum, 1990.
Dennis Haseley, *Ghost Catcher,* HarperCollins Children's, 1991.
Gloria Houston, *But No Candy,* Philomel, 1992.
Lenny Hort, reteller, *The Goatherd and the Shepherdess: A Tale from Ancient Greece,* Dial, 1995.
David A. Adler, *One Yellow Daffodil: A Hanukkah Story,* Gulliver (San Diego), 1995.
Anne Isaacs, *Treehouse Tales,* Dutton, 1997.
Barbara Santucci, *Anna's Corn,* W. B. Eerdmans (Grand Rapids, MI), 1997.
Margaret Willey, *Thanksgiving with Me,* Laura Geringer, 1998.
Helen Recorvits, *Goodbye, Walter Malinski,* Farrar, Straus & Giroux, 1999.
Libba Moore Gray, *When Uncle Took the Fiddle,* Orchard, 1999.

Sidelights

Lloyd Bloom is the illustrator of dozens of books for young readers that have won critical acclaim and industry citations for the depth and richness of their images. His first effort, published three years after Bloom earned an M.F.A. degree from Indiana University, was Virginia F. Voight's *Bobcat.* Bloom worked on other animal-centered books, such as *A Dog's Life: Stories of Champions, Hunters, and Faithful Friends* and Barbara Steiner's *Biography of a Bengal Tiger,* before completing pictures for 1979's *Smoke Over Golan: A Novel of the 1973 Yom Kippur War in Israel,* written by Uriel Ofek. Ofek's story was the first of several Jewish-themed works illustrated by Bloom, including the award-winning *Poems for Jewish Holidays, Miriam's Tambourine: Jewish Folktales from Around the World,* Terry W. Treseder's *Hear O Israel: A Story of the Warsaw Ghetto,* and David A. Adler's *One Yellow Daffodil: A Hanukkah Story.* Treseder's tale recounts one young boy's terrible experiences during the Holocaust in Poland. For Adler's 1995 story for primary graders, *One Yellow Daffodil,* Bloom depicts an aging survivor of Auschwitz who has buried many of his bad memories along with his observance of the traditional Jewish holidays. One December day two young customers invite florist Morris Kaplan to their home for Hanukkah, and the warmth of the family celebration helps the solitary Kaplan reconnect with others and his own Jewish childhood. The yellow daffodil of the title is what the Holocaust survivor once saw blooming in the mud of the concentration camp, a sight that provided him with hope in a seemingly hopeless situation. Kaplan brings his vintage menorah to his hosts the following day. "Bloom's rich acrylic paintings lend an appropriately thoughtful tone to the pensive text," maintained Kay Weisman of *Booklist.*

For Jill Paton Walsh's 1982 science fiction story *The Green Book,* Bloom depicted a fantastical utopian world that is called Shine by its settlers, who are refugees from earth. An essay on Bloom by *Children's Books and Their Creators* contributor Sally Holmes Holtze praised the illustrator for his "stylized landscape" of a planet where all vegetation is translucent and shimmering, a new world populated by human figures "exhibiting the sinewy grace typical of Bloom's style, and ... arranged in groups on a page in a way that frames the action with their bodies, composition lending strength to the novel's fable quality."

Bloom also won praise for his illustrations for Lenny Hort's *The Goatherd and the Shepherdess.* The 1995 picture book, a retelling of a love story from third-century Greece, features a pastoral setting and danger on the high seas. The story tells of the fateful romance between Daphnis, Chloe, and Dorcon, one of whom sacrifices a life for love. Lauralyn Persson, reviewing *The Goatherd and the Shepherdess* for *School Library Journal,* noted that Bloom's acrylic-tinted human figures "have a look of substance that recalls some of Picasso's neoclassical paintings." Persson commended his landscapes as "a place where creatures exist together in harmony." Other titles that Bloom has illustrated have also called upon his powers of imagination to re-create past worlds, among them *A Man Named Thoreau,* by Robert Burleigh, and Stan Steiner's *The Ranchers: A Book of Generations.* For Anne Isaacs's *Treehouse Tales,* Bloom created black and white pencil illustrations that depict three children of a Pennsylvania farm family of the 1880s. The Barrett children's beloved tree house is featured in two of the three tales; in the third, tomboy Emily proves she can ride a horse as well as her brothers can. The drawings, noted a *Publishers Weekly* critic, "mix a sweet nostalgia with mild folkloric humor."

Bloom's illustrations for Margaret Willey's 1998 picture book *Thanksgiving with Me* capture the warmth of family traditions and each household's own unique history. In this work, a young girl anticipates the arrival of her six uncles for a holiday dinner, while her mother recounts stories in verse about each of them. "As Mother describes her brothers, they come to life through her words as well as through the stylized pictures that brim with vitality and good cheer," asserted *Booklist* commentator Ilene Cooper. *Riverbank Review* critic Nora Wise-Halladay also cheered Bloom's renditions of the uncles, which "emphasize movement and gentle power; there is a sinewy grace to these big men. Even the landscape, strong and fluid, seems to carry the uncles to the mother and daughter's outstretched arms." Noting a

Lloyd Bloom's evocative illustrations reflect ten-year-old Arthur's wonder as he first experiences country life on his aunt and uncle's farm. (From Arthur, for the Very First Time, *written by Patricia MacLachlan.)*

pleasant but exceptional occurrence, Wise-Halladay wrote that in *Thanksgiving with Me,* "a perfectly wonderful text is matched by an inspiring set of illustrations."

Bloom re-created the hardships of the Great Depression in his pictures for Helen Recorvits's *Goodbye, Walter Malinski,* a story for middle graders published in 1999. The title character in this work is the adored older brother of Wanda, a ten-year-old whose father has been laid off from his job. Wanda's father plans to send 15-year-old Walter away for work, but the boy dies in a winter drowning accident with Wanda nearby. "Bloom's softly shaded black-and-white line illustrations, sometimes brooding, sometimes helpful," asserted a *Publishers Weekly* commentator, "punctuate each chapter and contribute to the emotional impact of the tale."

Works Cited

Cooper, Ilene, review of *Thanksgiving with Me, Booklist,* September 1, 1998, p. 135.

Review of *Goodbye, Walter Malinski, Publishers Weekly,* March 1, 1999, p. 69.

Holtze, Sally Holmes, essay on Bloom in *Children's Books and Their Creators,* Houghton Mifflin, 1995, pp. 64-65.

Persson, Lauralyn, review of *The Goatherd and the Shepherdess, School Library Journal,* March, 1995, p. 181.

Review of *Treehouse Tales, Publishers Weekly,* May 26, 1997, p. 86.

Weisman, Kay, review of *One Yellow Daffodil: A Hanukkah Story, Booklist,* November 1, 1995, p. 476.

Wise-Halladay, Nora, review of *Thanksgiving with Me, Riverbank Review,* Fall, 1998, pp. 28-29.

For More Information See

PERIODICALS

Booklist, February 1, 1995, p. 1010.

Horn Book, September-October, 1997, p. 572.

Publishers Weekly, January 9, 1995, p. 63; September 18, 1995, p. 92.

School Library Journal, October, 1995, p. 34; July, 1997, p. 69; September, 1998, p. 185.

*   *   *

BREWER, James D. 1951-

Personal

Born November 19, 1951, in Tiptonville, TN; son of Nellie V. Brewer; married Jan Caylor (a registered nurse), August 6, 1972; children: Bethany and Shannon. *Education:* Union University, B.S., 1972; Southern Baptist Theological Seminary, M.Div., 1975; University of South Carolina, M.A., 1989. *Politics:* Independent. *Religion:* Christian. *Hobbies and other interests:* martial arts, travel, music.

Addresses

E-mail—jbrewer@ne.infi.net.

Career

U.S. Army, various assignments in the Armored Cavalry, 1977-1995, retiring as major; *Armor* magazine, editor-in-chief; business writing and editorial consulting; college instructor and author. *Member:* Mystery Writers of America, Retired Officers Association.

Writings

"MASEY BALDRIDGE/LUKE WILLIAMSON MYSTERY" SERIES

No Bottom, Walker & Company, 1994.
No Virtue, Walker & Company, 1995.
No Justice, Walker & Company, 1996.
No Remorse, Walker & Company, 1997.

No Escape, Walker & Company, 1998.

OTHER

The Danger From Strangers: Confronting the Threat of Assault (self-help), Insight Books, 1994.
The Raiders of 1862 (historical novel), Praeger, 1997.

Work in Progress

Desoto's Cross, a mystery, and *Cashiered: The Thomas Worthington Story.*

Sidelights

While an officer in the U.S. Army, James D. Brewer began a second career as a freelance journalist. Writing non-fiction magazine articles led to his first book, a self-help title on protecting oneself entitled *The Danger From Strangers: Confronting the Threat of Assault.* Shortly thereafter, he found his "voice" as a fiction writer, drawing upon his heritage as the son of a third-generation Mississippi River family and his interest in historical legends, particularly those centering on the Reconstruction period. Brewer's work includes a series of mysteries in which two men forge an unlikely alliance to bring justice to the post-Civil War South.

Brewer told *SATA:* "I enjoy researching and writing about people and events often overlooked by general historians." Reflecting about his work as a mystery writer, he added: "When I write fiction, I seek, first and foremost, to tell a good story. If the reader happens to learn some history from the work, then that is an added value."

Brewer tackles the subject of personal defense in his first full-length book, *The Danger from Strangers: Confronting the Threat of Assault.* He profiles the types of people most likely to encounter assault, and explains steps to take to avoid becoming a victim. All aspects of attack are addressed, including tips on how to react if an attack is inevitable. In addition to exploring the issue of if and when to fight back, Brewer outlines the legal ramifications of being a Good Samaritan if one is confronted by a crime in progress or by a victim of one. Denise Perry Donavin, writing in *Booklist,* called *The Danger from Strangers* an "essential guide," and a *Book News* reviewer enthused: "By reading and practicing the conflict avoidance exercises brilliantly articulated in this book, everyone will gain confidence and recover some of the quality of life that the rampant fear of crime has stolen away."

Turning to fiction, Brewer penned *No Bottom,* the first in a series of five historical mysteries. *No Bottom* is set against a backdrop of the Mississippi River during Reconstruction. Hostility festers among Southerners defeated by a particularly ruthless Union Army unit, known as the Mississippi Marine Brigade. During the 1872 season, sons of the South take revenge by sinking steamboats piloted by former members of the unit. The main characters in *No Bottom* are an ex-Union gunboat pilot and an ex-Confederate soldier who now find

James D. Brewer

themselves on the same side trying to protect steamboat interests.

Luke Williamson, the gunboat-pilot-turned-riverboat-captain, and Masey Baldridge, the wounded Rebel turned insurance-claim investigator, meet after one of Williamson's steamers carrying passengers and cargo sinks outside Natchez. Together, the men uncover a plot to take control of river commerce by sinking certain boats, even as Williamson is planning his last trip of the season in his only other boat, the *Paragon*. A *Kirkus Reviews* critic applauded the book's "brawny riverboat intrigue," and a reviewer for *Publishers Weekly* commented that the author "fashions the uneasy alliance and the tensions of the post-Civil War South into a fine historical novel with a fully satisfying conclusion."

The precipitating event in the series' second title, *No Virtue,* begins near Memphis, where Cassie Pierce, a regular passenger on Williamson's paddle wheeler, is found dead. Police come immediately and arrest Williamson's trusted first mate, a black man, as the murderer. Williamson quickly sends for Masey Baldridge to find the real killer. Referring to Williamson and Baldridge as an "appealingly offbeat detective team," a critic in *Kirkus Reviews* added, they "have a

high old time bringing the culprits to book in this lively Reconstruction tale." Williamson and Baldridge believe the murder plot involves a rare gold coin thought to be part of the lost Confederate treasury. The mystery surrounding a purported cache of coins leads Baldridge to interview the former President of the Confederacy, Jefferson Davis, who confirms the coins exist and that they are missing. An action-packed search ensues. In her comments for *School Library Journal,* Linda Vretos asserted: "This is an intriguing story with well-developed characters." "An elusive suspect, a perspicacious prostitute, and conspiracy enliven this stand-alone sequel," said Rex E. Klett in *Library Journal.*

The third book in Brewer's mystery series, *No Justice,* introduces Salina Tyner, an aspiring sleuth who joins Baldridge in his search for Gatling guns missing from the army. Unlike previous stories, Baldridge is hired by another detective, Allan Pinkerton, to help—not to solve the crime, but to guide him through river country in search of thieves. The plot thickens when it becomes clear that the stolen guns are part of a plan to assassinate President Grant, who is scheduled to be on the maiden voyage of Williamson's new boat. Baldridge strikes out on his own to find the suspected robbers, leaving Tyner to fend for herself. Like the first two books in the series,

No Justice takes place along the Mississippi River in the years following the Civil War. Anita Short, in a review for *School Library Journal,* noted the unique perspective Brewer gives readers about former enemies who become friends after the war. She continued, "The sense of place is vivid, and the historical background is very much a part of the story." A *Kirkus Reviews* critic declared *No Virtue* "the liveliest and most inventive of [Brewer's] adventures to date," and *Booklist* reviewer George Needham maintained: "The structure of the novel, its sense of humor, and a well-drawn cast of characters combine to create some satisfying suspense."

An astute businessman as well as a riverboat captain, Luke Williamson expands his business interests to include a detective agency in *No Remorse.* Along with partners Masey Baldridge, a high-living detective who is fond of horses and liquor, and Salina Tyner, a former prostitute, he opens Big River Detective Agency. With some misgivings, the trio take on the murder case of Williamson's arch business rival, Hudson Van Geer, when Van Geer's widow asks them to help prove her son, Stuart, is innocent.

The three sleuths quickly find themselves embroiled in a family torn apart by deception and greed. To clear Stuart Van Geer, who refuses to help himself, the Big River team must delve into the Van Geers' family secrets. In *Voice of Youth Advocates,* critic Joanna Morrison stated: "*No Remorse* has strongly delineated, engaging characters and an intriguing sense of place . . . ." Wes Lukowsky expressed a like opinion in *Booklist,* maintaining: "This Baldridge-Williamson novel offers an exciting, often humorous caper set against a richly detailed Reconstruction background."

Brewer continues his successful series with a fifth book, *No Escape,* which returns to Memphis during the yellow fever epidemic of 1873. In this novel, a distraught mayor turns to Big River Detective Agency to track down a murderer roaming the streets of Memphis. Baldridge, Williamson, and Tyner pool their knowledge and wiles to find the killer, appropriately called Yellow Jack, amid a frightened citizenry already coping with the deadly, and rapidly spreading, disease.

Works Cited

Review of *The Danger From Strangers: Confronting the Threat of Assault, Book News,* September 4, 1994.

Donavin, Denise Perry, review of *The Danger From Strangers: Confronting the Threat of Assault, Booklist,* March 1, 1994, p. 1166.

Klett, Rex E., review of *No Virtue, Library Journal,* July, 1995, p. 126.

Lukowsky, Wes, review of *No Remorse, Booklist,* August, 1997, p. 1882.

Morrison, Joanna, review of *No Remorse, Voice of Youth Advocates,* April, 1998, p. 44.

Needham, George, review of *No Justice, Booklist,* June 1, 1996, p. 1678.

Review of *No Bottom, Kirkus Reviews,* January 1, 1994, p. 19.

Review of *No Bottom, Publishers Weekly,* January 31, 1994, p. 79.

Review of *No Justice, Kirkus Reviews,* May 1, 1996, pp. 641-42.

Review of *No Virtue, Kirkus Reviews,* June 15, 1995, p. 814.

Short, Anita, review of *No Justice, School Library Journal,* December, 1996, p. 150.

Vretos, Linda, review of *No Virtue, School Library Journal,* December, 1995, p. 142.

For More Information See

PERIODICALS

Booklist, March 1, 1994, p. 1166; April 15, 1998, p. 1378.

Kirkus Reviews, January 1, 1994, p. 19; June 15, 1995, p. 814; May 1, 1996, p. 641.

Library Journal, March 1, 1994, p. 123; March 15, 1997, p. 72; June 23, 1997, p. 139; July, 1998, p. 141.

Publishers Weekly, February 14, 1994, p. 74; May 8, 1995, p. 290.

School Library Journal, November, 1994, p. 140.

Autobiography Feature

Betsy Byars

1928

In 1968 my husband Ed and I went to our first soaring championship in Marfa, Texas. He was going to compete. I was going to be the crew chief. As crew chief, I was to help put the glider together, fill the wings with water, tow him to the start line, run his wing, then hook up the trailer and follow him around the course and pick him up if he landed away from the airport. The last thing I did before I left home was to buy a spiral notebook because I planned, in my spare time, to start a book.

The closer we got to Marfa, the worse I felt. A crew chief likes to see nice, mowed fields where her pilot can land, short fences, wide gates, and friendly farmers. What I saw was rocky, craggy, cactus-covered land, fences that went on for miles, and no farmers whatsoever.

I said, "Ed, where on earth do you land out here?"

He said, "On the road."

It then turned out that another of my duties was to stop truck traffic while he landed.

That night, unable to sleep in the Paisano Hotel, I wrote the first sentence in my spiral notebook. "The land is hard in southwest Texas."

Every day of the two week contest, I did something wrong, and I am not talking about minor errors. Once I didn't hook the trailer up properly and it fell off the car on a curve. Once I whipped into a gas station, pulled around the pumps, filled the gas tank, and then found out that my thirty-foot trailer was going to knock over the gas tank when I pulled out.

I tried to back up, but that made it worse. I tried to pull forward so that I could back up the other way, and that made it even worse. I ended up locked around those gas tanks so tightly it would take a miracle to get me out.

A miracle happened. Some men came out of a bar across the street, saw the crowd at the gas station and came over to help. They picked up the back of the trailer and moved it over about one inch. I then drove forward one inch. They then picked up the back of the trailer and moved it two inches. That is how I got out of the gas station, literally inch by inch. When I finally drove away, the entire crowd cheered.

My husband had been waiting for me all this time behind a mesa in the broiling sun. He said, "Where have you been?"

I described in detail the incident at the gas station and the angels of mercy who had come from the bar to help me.

He said, "Betsy, why didn't you just unhook the trailer from the car, guide it into the street, drive the car out and hook up again?"

I said, truthfully, that it would never have occurred to me in a million years. And if he hadn't told me, the next time it happened, I would have gone straight to the nearest bar to round up some drunks.

Well, what with one thing and another, when I got home, I still had only one sentence in my spiral notebook. But it was no longer just a sentence. It was the first sentence of my next book, *The Winged Colt of Casa Mia,* set in Marfa, Texas.

Some of the happiest moments in my writing career come when I have the first sentence in a book. I may not know what the plot will be, I may not know all my characters, but I can somehow get a feeling from that first sentence whether it's going to be a book or a few stray paragraphs.

One sentence. All I needed now were about 3,500 more sentences to go with it.

I had no intention of becoming a writer when I was growing up, but I had one thing in common with every other writer I've ever met. I loved books. My earliest memory is of a book.

I am sitting beside my father on the sofa, and he is reading *The Three Bears* to me. Only my father is not reading it correctly. Instead of "Somebody's been eating my porridge," he has the baby bear say, "Somebody's been eating my corn flakes."

This infuriates me. I am hitting my father, trying by brute force to make him read correctly.

It works. He does indeed read it right for a few lines. Then, as soon as I relax, and lose myself in the story, the mama bear says, "Somebody's been sleeping on my Beauty Rest mattress."

More fury. More hits. A great first memory for an author. Already I had respect for the written word.

My father was a hardworking, stern man with, surprisingly, a good sense of humor. He came from the agricultural part of South Carolina and went to the Citadel, a college on the coast.

While he was a cadet there, he met my mother. My mother was very pretty and lively, and I imagine he fell in

Betsy Byars

love with her instantly. My mother loved acting and music and appeared in amateur shows. She had taken lessons in college in speech and dramatics.

Her interest in speech continued after her marriage and when I was about five, she arranged for me to take a series of preschool lessons in what was then called Expression.

I enjoyed my Expression lessons a lot. I cannot recall any of the poems I memorized, but there was a comic one that allowed me to roll my eyes and make a lot of faces. My mother suffered through my comic recitation for a while, but plainly it was not what she had in mind for me. I had not inherited her dramatic charm, and I soon was diplomatically shifted to piano lessons.

I really had two lives as a child. In one, we lived in the city of Charlotte on 915 Magnolia Avenue, and I did city things. In the other, we lived in the country, close to the cotton mill where my father worked. My father had majored in civil engineering in college, but because times were hard and jobs scarce, he had gone to work in the office of a cotton mill. The community was named after the mill—Hoskins.

At Hoskins we had goats and rabbits, and because I loved animals, I thought life was wonderful. Only later did I realize how hard this move must have been for my pretty mother, how she must have hated the train tracks which ran

through our front yard, that her closest touch with culture was the rental library in the back of the drugstore.

We were there about three years and one of the highlights was a birthday party my mother gallantly staged for my sister Nancy.

At Hoskins, no one went to a store and bought a birthday present. Everyone just looked around their house until they found something that did not look too bad, and they wrapped it up and came to the party.

My sister got the oddest assortment of gifts that I had ever seen, and I, who loved odd things, was green with envy. One of the things she got was a pair of celluloid cuffs which office workers put on their arms to keep the sleeves of their blouses clean. I loved those celluloid cuffs. My sister could get me to do anything by letting me borrow the celluloid cuffs.

But the most memorable gift was a very tiny one, wrapped in a scrap of notebook paper. I must have been an unimaginative child, because I kept saying, "Open the little present. Open the little present."

My sister opened it at last and there was a dime.

That gift-wrapped dime stuck in my mind for years. And later, when I was writing *After the Goat Man*, I decided to pass it on in the school gift exchange to Harold V. Coleman. I hope someday to find a place in one of my books for the celluloid cuffs.

Betsy Byars and husband Ed at an informal soaring meet in 1984.

Nancy and I each had one party while we lived at the mill, but my sister got the best presents. I got things like a pair of pink socks that were too little and a china dog with the features washed off.

When I was in fourth grade, we moved back to 915 Magnolia Avenue, which was to be my home until I graduated from college.

Last year, I saw the house for the first time in thirty-five years. There was a For Sale sign out front. I made Ed stop the car and I went up and looked in the window, thinking the house was empty. I looked directly into the face of the woman who was looking out to see who I was. She very kindly invited me in, and I walked through the memory-filled rooms. No other house will ever hold so much of my life.

I was not particularly close to my grandparents, and I cannot remember any of them showing much interest in me. That suited me fine. That left me free to do what I wanted at their houses without getting caught.

I was, however, definitely interested in my Grandaddy Rugheimer's things. He was a dapper man, a tailor, of German descent. He collected rare coins, rare stamps, rare books, and rare tropical fish, all of which we were not allowed to touch. He also had a woodworking shop where he made incredibly beautiful things. We were allowed in there and the floor was always covered with beautiful curls

of wood, and we attached them to our heads and pretended we were Shirley Temple.

His rare stamps, books, and coins were kept in a large closet under the stairs. I went in one time to look at some of the books.

The one I remember was a large, gilt-edged book of Bible stories. I only saw the illustrations once, but they are etched into my mind as firmly as they were into the heavy cream paper. They were dark, detailed reflections of the terrible reality of biblical times.

The Jews Descending into the Fiery Furnace, Gabriel Wrestling with the Angel of Death—I can remember those pictures to this day. But the worst was Noah's Ark.

Noah's Ark was no happy scene with the animals clomping into the ark, two by two. The ark was already afloat, in the distance. In the front of the picture was the last mountain top where the remaining desperate people and animals struggled for survival.

I spent a lot of time looking at that picture, worrying about this mother and baby, that little lamb. I'm sure I asked my mother about it later, concealing where I had come across such a picture, but I never got a satisfactory answer.

As a writer, I have a good way of shedding these old childhood concerns—I pass them on to the characters in my books. So it is Harold V. Coleman, in *After the Goat Man*,

"My parents, Guy Cromer and Nan Rugheimer, during their courtship, 1924."

who gets my Noah's ark concern when he is cast as an extra hippopotamus in a Bible school production, and I can at last put my own concern aside.

My Grandaddy Cromer had a country store which was across the street from his house. I was over there one day at the candy counter, making my daily selection, when he said he was closing the store to go pay his respects to Mr. Joe. Did I want to come along? I did.

We drove out into the country and up to a farmhouse. We got out and went to the door. "We came to pay our respects to Mr. Joe," my grandfather said.

We went inside. Mr. Joe was in a hammered-together board coffin in the living room. We walked over and my grandfather picked me up so I could see over the side. My knee hit the coffin, jarring it, and Mr. Joe's mouth popped open.

It took me a long time to get rid of that concern, but I finally managed it in *The Pinballs*. It felt a lot better when Mr. Mason's knee hit the coffin instead of mine.

When I was in junior high, my father surprised us all by buying a boat. My father had never shown any interest in becoming a seafaring man, and my mother was convinced we would all go down in the Atlantic Ocean. In 1942 we came close.

This was before the age of really good weather forecasting, and so, on a beautiful Saturday, with not a cloud in the sky, we set out on the *Nan-a-Bet* (named for Nancy and me). We planned to pull into coves and behind islands along the South Carolina coast, anchor and spend the nights. My mother wisely remained on shore.

About five the next morning, we awoke and noticed that the boat was beginning to pitch a little. By six it was pitching a lot, and my father made the decision to head back to Charleston before things got really rough.

Things got really rough before we were anywhere near Charleston. My father was frantic. The waves were

enormous, and he was not a skilled seaman. This might even have been our maiden weekend voyage.

Nancy and I, however, thought it was wonderful. We sat in the cabin, laughing and composing our obituaries.

Finally, in midafternoon, we got a lucky break. We were slammed into shore by an enormous wave. My father tied up the boat and went looking for a phone. Nancy and I stayed with the *Nan-a-Bet*. This was fortunate because almost immediately some cute boys came to see if we needed any help.

All day my mother had been even more desperate than my father—pacing the floor, wringing her hands, crying. Her worst fear had been realized. Her husband and children were at the bottom of the Atlantic. Possibly she even chided herself for not drowning with us. As soon as she got my father's call, she drove to the site, rushed through the weeds and threw her arms around us.

This embarrassed us enormously in front of the cute boys. It was the only bad part of the whole day.

"Oh, Mother!" we said.

In all of my school years—from grade one through high school—not one single teacher ever said to me, "Perhaps you should consider becoming a writer." Anyway, I didn't want to be a writer. Writing seemed boring. You sat in a room all day by yourself and typed. If I was going to be a writer at all, I was going to be a foreign correspondent like Claudette Colbert in *Arise My Love*. I would wear smashing hats, wisecrack with the guys, and have a byline known round the world. My father wanted me to be a mathematician.

I hit high school in 1943, and the important thing—the only important thing—was to look exactly like everybody else. We wore dirty saddle shoes, angora socks, pleated

Betsy at one.

skirts, enormous sweaters (sometimes buttoned up the back) and pearls. If we were fortunate enough to be going with a high school athlete, we wore his sweater. We all had long hair with curved combs in the back so we could continuously comb our hair. We had mirrors taped inside our notebooks so we could check and make absolutely sure we looked exactly like everybody else.

We used lots of makeup, I particularly because my father had given me a twenty-five dollar war bond for not wearing makeup in junior high, and I had to make up for lost time.

We were constantly on the lookout for better beauty products than the dime stores had to offer. My best friend and I discovered one day, when we were shelling walnuts, that the outside rind was leaving a gorgeous stain on our hands. Without a thought we immediately started staining our legs.

We were enormously pleased with the result and promised not to tell any of our other friends how we'd done it, so they couldn't have gorgeous legs too. We went in the house to wash our hands, which were now stained up to the wrist in the same lovely color. We learned at the sink that the lovely color was permanent. Well, not permanent—it did wear off in a week or so, but the impact of the brown legs was definitely lessened by the brown hands.

I spent a good part of my school day arranging to accidentally bump into some boy or other. I would rush out of science, tear up three flights of stairs, say a casual "Hi" to a boy as he came out of English, and then tear back down three flights of stairs, rush into home ec and get marked tardy. I was tardy a lot.

The only actual course I can remember was in math, and certainly not because I excelled. Here's what I remember. When the teacher wrote Pi on the blackboard and we saw the numbers 31416 for the first time, someone said, "That's Cro's phone number!" My nickname was Cro, and I felt like a celebrity. I've had many phone numbers over the years, but that's the only one I remember.

My other memory of the class was fame of the other kind. I was caught cheating.

We were having a test on some formulas, and it just seemed simpler to copy the formulas down on the desk rather than go to all the trouble of memorizing them.

The teacher saw the formulas and called in everyone who sat in that particular seat throughout her daily classes. There were five of us. She then asked us to write the formulas from memory. The other four could. I couldn't.

We were having an assembly program on honesty that Friday, and part of my punishment (the other part was a 0 on the test) was to listen to the lecture seated on the front row beside the math teacher. I didn't mind the 0 at all, but the memory of sitting on the front row by the math teacher still makes me shudder.

We were never allowed to tell my father any bad news until after he had had his supper. This was my mother's ruling, and I can remember a lot of painful suppers, trying to eat, already filled with the knowledge that I had an item of bad news to break after the meal.

This particular bit of bad news was bad indeed, and I had come home from college for the weekend to break it in person. I was a sophomore, and the bad news was that I

Betsy about four in tam, sister Nancy about six with watch, and their mother.

was not going to be able to be a mathematician. I was flunking calculus.

When I had gone away to college, I had not put up any real struggle against majoring in math. The only thing I really loved to do was read, but I knew I couldn't get a job doing that. Besides, my sister whose actions I had been copying successfully for nineteen years was a math major, and I, like her, had always been very quick with those problems that start out, "If one farmer can plow ten fields in one-and-a-half days, how many . . . "

Until I hit calculus and came upon sine and cosine and tangent and cotangent and secant and cosecant, I thought there was nothing in the world I could not master if I put my mind to it. This—no matter how hard I tried, and I tried hard—I could not get.

It was a desperate semester for me. My father was paying hard-earned money for me to go to college and he expected me to do well. I had discovered early in life that things were easier all around if I lived up to my father's expectations. Even in high school when I was flitting through the halls, chasing boys, I made sure I never got a grade lower than B.

Grandaddy Rugheimer, "dapper even when hiking in the North Carolina mountains."

Now calculus. My father had been disappointed at my midterm calculus grade which had been, to my relief a C-. And here's the pathetic, desperate price I had paid for my C-.

Dr. Bowen would pass out the tests. I would wait a moment and then go up to his desk. I would say, "Dr. Bowen, would you please start me out on problem one? I've drawn an absolute blank. I know if you do the first line for me, I can finish."

I was the only girl in any of his classes and sort of a novelty. He would, in his enthusiasm for his own problem, work the whole thing.

I would go back to my seat, and I could actually feel the scorn and resentment of the other students as I passed their desks. I couldn't help it. I had to keep up my C-average.

I would try to do the next problem on my own. When I had a couple of meaningless rows of numbers and letters, I would go back to his desk and say, "Is this right? It just doesn't look the way yours did on the board last week."

He'd say, "Now, Miss Cromer, you know that's not right. Look at this."

And he'd work the second problem. The only calculus problems I ever got right were the ones he worked for me.

It was the thought of more and more desperate years like this, more and more scorn from my classmates, that sent me into the living room where my father sat in his chair by the radio, smoking a Camel cigarette.

Somehow I broke the bad news. I could not be a mathematician. Even worse, I was switching to English. There was not the terrible explosion that I had feared. To be honest, there usually wasn't.

On my final calculus exam, when Dr. Bowen was working one last problem for me, he asked if I was planning to continue with my math.

"No," I said, "I've decided not to be a mathematician." "Good," he said.

Nineteen forty-nine and fifty were great years. I was a senior at Queens College, just months away from getting out in the adult world where nobody could tell me what to do or what time I had to be in, and I had just met the man I wanted to marry. The sole cloud on the horizon of my life was that he might not ask me.

Ed was tall, good looking, witty, a wonderful dancer. He had a yellow Mercury convertible. Since he was left-handed, he had switched his gearshift over to the left side of the steering wheel, leaving his right arm free to be put around whatever lucky girl was beside him on the front seat. He had already graduated from college and was a man of the world, teaching Engineering at Clemson College. And, as if that weren't enough, he had a Stinson 1931 antique airplane. I was madly in love.

College regulations were very strict at that time at Queens College. We could only date on weekends, and even then we had to sign out and say exactly where we were going and with whom, etc.

One regulation which I obviously had to break was the one that you couldn't fly in an airplane without written permission from your parents. How could I tell a man of the world that I couldn't hop into his Stinson because I didn't have my mother's permission on file in the dean's office?

I remember one of our illegal flights well. We were on our way to Clemson for a football weekend, and we were lost a good bit of the time. The plane had very little in the way of navigational equipment, and the visibility was not good, but we finally got there by reading the names of the towns, which at that time were required to be painted on the top of the most prominent building. I thought it was great. A very cool, relaxed "Oh, that's Gaffney; we'll go this way" kind of navigation.

He proposed in the spring—or sort of proposed. I was sitting in the yellow Mercury convertible on the main street of Rock Hill, the town where his parents lived and he had grown up. He went in a store to speak to a friend. He came back and he said, "If you were going to get engaged, what kind of ring would you want?"

I said, "Oh, I don't know, maybe a diamond one."

He said, "Like this?" He reached into his pocket, took out a box, and, by a miracle, there it was, the most beautiful sight of my life.

I said, "Yes."

We were married two months later, on June 24. This was exactly three weeks after my college graduation.

It is no longer fashionable to admit this, but I was very happy to be getting married instead of looking for a job. I had no work ambition. I had always wanted marriage and a family. This was fortunate because my speciality as an English major had been Old English. I could rattle off words like bitraisshe, aungellyke, and fronceles and say the Prologue to *The Canterbury Tales* by heart, but there was not a big demand in the working world for a person who knew what a clow-gelofre was.

We were married on the hottest day of the year. As we were leaving on our honeymoon, some of the groomsmen rushed out and locked a cowbell and chain around Ed's neck. This was to make up for the fact that they had not been able to find the Mercury convertible and put dead fish in the hub caps.

When we finally got out of the city, there was the problem of the cowbell. Ed had said, "I think I may be able to slip the chain over my head," but of course he couldn't.

We finally found a garage that was open—it was late Saturday afternoon by this time—and in he went. I waited outside. In the garage, he laid his head on the work bench, a steady-handed mechanic sawed the chain in half, and our married life began.

For the next five years I was a young faculty wife at Clemson and married life agreed with me. Two of our daughters were born during those years—Laurie in October of 1951 and Betsy Ann in February of 1953. I was extremely happy.

My only writing consisted of letters and shopping lists.

In 1955 Ed decided to go to graduate school at the University of Illinois. If he was going to remain in teaching—which he intended to do—he would have to have his Ph.D. degree.

We rented our house, stored our furniture, loaned our dogs to Ed's mother, packed everything else in a red trailer and took off. It was a little like going West and I was excited about it.

When we pulled up two days later in front of the barracks where we would be living for the next two-and-a-half years, my excitement faded a little. When we went inside and I saw the barracks furniture, it faded even more.

Well, I told myself, I can fix the place up with posters, and pillows, and bright curtains. That took about a week. Now, I thought, I'm as settled as I'm ever going to be. I'm going to start making friends.

As it turned out, every other wife in the barracks complex either worked or was going to school. The last thing any of them wanted was to come to my house to chat. I got lonelier and lonelier. Ed went to work early in the morning and came home late. The kids, after an initial period of being picked on daily, had gotten over being the new kids and were part of the gang. I alone was at loose ends. The highlight of my day was the arrival of the grocery truck after lunch.

Now up until this point in my life, while I had never done any creative writing, I had always thought that I could write if I wanted to. I thought it couldn't be as hard as people say it is. I thought probably the reason professional writers claim it's so hard is because they don't want any more competition.

I got a typewriter so old I had to press the keys down an inch to make a letter. The *i* stuck, all the circular letters were filled in, the *t*'s were noticeably higher than the other letters. I was undaunted.

Years later, when I was writing *The 18th Emergency*, one of the letters started sticking on my electric typewriter,

Betsy and her father in the **Nan-a-Bet** *in 1942.*

"Sister mathematicians": Betsy (left) a senior in high school, Nancy, math major in college.

and this was so intolerable to me—I was in the middle of a chapter—that I rushed downtown in my shorts and bought a new Smith Corona.

When my husband came home and saw the old Smith Corona discarded on the floor, he asked what had happened. I explained about the stuck key, and he said, "You've got two other typewriters up in the attic. Why didn't you just get one of those down and use it?"

"I forgot," I said.

Anyway, back at the barracks apartment, I set the old typewriter by my place at the table, and that's where it stayed for two years. I would push it aside when I ate and pull it back when I got through. I wrote constantly.

My target was mainly the magazines. I would look through national magazines, see what they were publishing, write something similar and send it off. Sometimes this very amateurish approach worked.

My first sale was a short article to the *Saturday Evening Post* and I got seventy-five dollars for it. I was elated. I had known all along there was nothing to writing! Seven months passed before I sold a second article.

I was learning what most other writers have learned before me—that writing is a profession in which there is an apprenticeship period, oftentimes a very long one. In that, writing is like baseball or piano playing. You have got to practice if you want to be successful.

In my last year at Illinois—by this time our third daughter, Nan, had been born—I had become aware that I needed some help. I was selling short articles with some regularity, but I had done a mystery novel I couldn't sell and some children's books, and although I was not in despair, I certainly thought I might be able to shorten this endless apprenticeship period if I got some help.

I signed up for a writing course at the university.

I went to class on the first night with the greatest sense of hope and anticipation—not only because I was going to

get some valuable professional help, but also because I was going to be in the midst of people who were writing too—living, breathing writers.

I sat there, internally vibrating with excitement. The professor got up. He started the class with this sentence: "All the people in this town who are going to be professional writers are home right now, writing."

So much for my writing class.

We moved back to Clemson, back into our home, and I set up my typewriter in our bedroom on a card table. By this time writing had become an important part of my life. I had not been able to stop in Illinois, no matter how badly things went, because I needed writing to fill my life. Now I didn't need it in that way anymore, but I still couldn't stop. Now the reason was because I loved what I was doing.

I know of writers whose creative drive begins to fade in the face of seemingly endless rejection slips. Starting a new writing project does require enormous energy, and it gets harder and harder to sustain this creative energy when you are being continuously turned down.

In Illinois—out of necessity—I developed a kind of tough, I'll-show-them attitude that I have maintained to this day. Sort of—All right, you don't like that one, wait till you see this one. All right, you turned that down and you'll be sorry. I am now going to do the best book in the entire world.

And the truth was that each time I believed it really was going to be the best book in the world. It never occurred to me that complete and total success was not just one manuscript away.

The thing that was most difficult for me to understand during these years was why I could not get a children's book published. I had started writing them mainly because they looked so easy, but now I was really working on them. It seemed to me that my manuscripts were a hundred times better than any children's books I saw, and yet I couldn't get them published. Probably, I thought, publishers of children's books only publish books of friends and relatives.

I kept writing, and in my spare time I had a fourth child, a son, Guy, born in April of 1958.

In 1962, seven years after I rolled my first sheet of paper into that ancient typewriter, my first children's book was published. It had been turned down by nine publishers, so it was not exactly the book the world was waiting for, but I was absolutely wild with excitement.

I can remember the exact moment I first held the book in my hands. We were living in Morgantown, West Virginia, then. My husband had taken a job at West Virginia University.

I went to the mailbox. It was snowing. I only had on a sweater. I was shivering. I was always in a great hurry to get the mail.

I opened the box, pulled out the mail, and there was the package.

I knew it was my book. I ripped off the paper there at the end of the driveway and was cold no more. It was a moment of absolute magic.

All the work that I had done on the book—and I had worked hard—faded from memory. All the disappoint-

Graduation day, 1950, with roommates Barbara Ann Jobe and Fronie Mims.

ments, all the frustrations—and there had been lots of both of those too—were gone.

It was as if I had gotten an idea for a book that morning, come to the mailbox, and—presto—here it was. It was completely, absolutely, unforgettably—magic. I was an author at last.

In the same mail with the book came an ad from a clipping service. It said, "We know what they're saying about your book. Don't you want to know too?" I couldn't send my money off fast enough.

As it turned out, I didn't really want to know. The reviews were not good. One publication said that only libraries with unlimited budgets should even consider buying *Clementine*, thereby eliminating every single library in the nation.

So while I was at last an author, according to all the reviews, I still had a long way to go.

I finally sold a manuscript called *The Dancing Camel* to Viking and it didn't do well either. I did a book with Harper and Row—*The Groober*—same thing.

I was not discouraged. I'd show them yet.

About this time I signed up for a course in children's literature at West Virginia University, and this was one of the turning points in my career. For the first time I saw the realistic children's novel. There had not been any of those

when I was growing up. It was a Nancy Drew-Bobbsey Twins literary world, and I had been unaware there was any other.

What I had been writing up until this point were children's books about a troupe of pigs who went West to give shows, or an orangutan who enrolled in an all-girls academy—things like that. I had never even considered anything realistic.

Even now I did not jump in the sea of realism all at once. I don't think I could have. I waded in. I wrote a sort of semirealistic book called *Rama, the Gypsy Cat*. This was a book about a pioneer cat, and the character Rama was based on our own cat J. T. This, incidentally, was the only good we ever got out of that particular cat.

The book was published by Viking and, while praise wasn't heaped on it, it was praised. I felt I might be on the right track at last.

I followed *Rama* with a second pioneer novel—*Trouble River*. I had not yet learned to construct an intricate plot and so this, like *Rama,* was a journey book, one of the easiest kinds of books to write. You start your characters out at point A, take them to point B, and let them have some adventures along the way. Hopefully, you will think of the adventures as you progress.

By now I was getting the help I needed from what was to be a series of gifted editors. Annis Duff was the first. Whatever she told me to do, I did. If she said, "Cut," I cut.

If she said, "Add a character," I added. If she said, "This scene needs more work," I worked. If she said, "I'm not sure this will be a publishable book," as she said on the first reading of *Trouble River,* I wept.

And it was mainly through her patient help and keen insight that it turned out to be a publishable book after all.

As a writer, I have always been aware of the enormity of the gap between the brain and a sheet of paper. You write something that you think is hilarious; on paper it isn't funny at all. You write something sad; it's not. You write a story and you know exactly what the finished story should be; and it turns out to be something else.

The first book that turned out the way I had envisioned it was *The Midnight Fox.* (*Trouble River* had been written earlier but it was published after *The Midnight Fox.* As I recall it, we were still trying to make *Trouble River* publishable.)

I look on *The Midnight Fox* as another turning point of my career. It gave me a confidence I had not had before. I knew now that I was going to be able to do some of the things I wanted to do, some of the things I had not had the courage and skill to try. For this reason, and others, it remains my favorite of my books. I was now ready to start *The Summer of the Swans.*

My kids were all in grade school or junior high now, and I wrote during school hours. I never answered the phone while I was writing, so my kids had a secret ring for emergencies. They would dial our number, let the phone ring twice, hang up, and then dial again. Anytime I heard two rings, silence, and more rings, I answered the phone.

One morning the secret ring came. I answered the phone immediately and my daughter said in a broken, tearful voice, "Mom, the principal wants to see you." I said, "What for?" She said, "Just come!"

The day before the wedding, June 23, 1950.

I turned off my typewriter and went to school. In the principal's office my daughter was sitting on one side of the desk, her best friend on the other. Tears were rolling down every face but the principal's. Between the girls, resting on the principal's blotter, was an enormous drill.

My daughter and her friend had always been in the same room up until this year, and so they had decided it would be a good idea to drill a hole in the wall that separated their rooms so they could pass notes to each other. They had sneaked in during recess, taken the drill from Nan's book satchel, and were in the middle of drilling when the teacher came back for her sweater.

At the time, things like this were interruptions in my writing, but later they became my writing. The drill scene was to appear, years later, in *The Cybil War.*

In 1968, I participated in a volunteer program sponsored by West Virginia University. Anybody who was interested—truck drivers, housewives, miners—signed up to help kids who were having learning difficulties in school. I got a third-grade girl and a first-grade boy.

This was a stunning experience for me. Up until this time I had never been around kids who were having real problems in learning. I had not been aware of how much they suffered, not only because they had learning difficulties, but—more importantly—because of the way other kids treated them.

Charlie, the character in *The Summer of the Swans,* was neither of the kids I tutored, but I would never have written the book if I had not known them.

I did a lot of research on the character of Charlie in the Medical Library of W.V.U. I found three case histories of kids who had had brain damage because of high-fevered illnesses when they were babies, and that's where Charlie

came from. All the details of his life were from those three case histories. I made nothing up.

I worked hard on the book and I was proud of it. It was published in April of 1970 to a sort of resounding thud. It didn't sell well, it didn't get great reviews; in some papers it didn't get reviewed at all.

I went through a very discouraging period. Maybe, I thought, I am just not going to make it as a first-rate writer. Maybe I never will be good enough. Maybe I should consider doing something else. That fall I enrolled at West Virginia University to get my master's degree in special education.

I had now published seven books, but I had never had one of those long editorial lunches at a swanky New York restaurant that you read about. I had never been in a publisher's office. I had never even met an editor. My contacts with my editors had consisted of long letters and brief phone calls. I did not know a single other writer. Despite having published seven books, I was as green as grass.

I was leaving for class one morning in January when the phone rang. I answered it, and a woman's voice said, "This is Sara Fenwick and I'm Chairman of the Newbery-Caldecott Committee." My heart rose. "We've been in Los Angeles for the past week going over possible Newbery-Caldecott winners." My heart sank. I realized what she wanted now. She wanted to ask me some questions about writing *The Summer of the Swans,* and I would not be able to answer the questions intelligently and she would go back to the committee and say, "The woman is an idiot."

"And," she continued, "I am so pleased to tell you that your book *The Summer of the Swans* has won the Newbery Medal."

I was stunned. I went blank. I couldn't say a word. She said, "Mrs. Byars, are you there?"

I managed to say, "Yes."

She said, "Mrs. Byars, have you ever heard of the Newbery Medal?"

I said, "Yes."

Obviously, it was not one of my shining hours. At the end of the conversation, she said, "We're having a champagne reception on Thursday and we wish you could be with us."

I uttered my first complete sentence of the conversation. "I wish I could too."

It was midafternoon before my editor called. She said, "What time are you leaving for Los Angeles?"

I said I wasn't planning to go.

She said, "Of course you're going. Get your reservations and call me back."

I got the reservations, rushed downtown and bought two Newbery Award-type outfits. The next morning at seven o'clock I was on my way to Los Angeles. I was a nervous wreck.

When I got out there, it turned out that I had to be hidden for a day-and-a-half to keep people from suspecting I was the new winner. Actually I could have passed freely among all the librarians, not once falling under suspicion. In fact one of the things someone said after the announcement was, "It's so refreshing to have someone win that nobody ever heard of."

The announcement of the Newbery Award literally changed my life overnight. Up until this time I had had a few letters from kids. Now we had to get a bigger mailbox. I got tapes, questionnaires, invitations to speak, invitations to visit schools, requests for interviews. For the first time in my life, I started feeling like an author.

I got my medal in Dallas in June. I was extremely nervous about giving my speech. Just before we went to the awards dinner, Don Freeman, the wonderful author/illustrator, came up to me. He said, "I want to give you my calming stone so you won't be nervous." He gave me a small black stone, very smooth, and showed me how to hold it in the palm of my hand and rub my fingers against it.

I gave my Newbery speech with that calming stone in my hand, and it really worked. I don't save a lot of things, but I do still have both my Newbery medal and my calming stone.

When I was in second grade, at Hoskins mill school, there were two boys who terrorized the school—the Fletcher brothers, the absolute bullies of the world. Everyone was afraid of them—the teachers, even the principal. I can't remember anything they actually did, but what they were capable of gave me nightmares.

One of the Fletcher brothers was in my second grade. He was eleven years old. The other was thirteen. He was in my sister's room. Both of them were marking time until they became fourteen and would go to work in the mill. They relieved the boredom of this waiting by creating moments of stark, unrelieved terror at recess and after school.

The Fletcher boys stayed in my mind long after I had forgotten the names of my good friends at the mill, and I decided to do a book about a school bully. I really wanted to call the bully Fletcher, but I thought, well, those brothers are still out there somewhere. I settled on the name Marv Hammerman. I thought that had a good hard ring to it.

I wrote the book, it was published, and one day a few months later the phone rang. A voice said, "Is this Betsy Byars?" I said, "Yes, who is this?" The voice said, "Marv Hammerman." I almost dropped the phone. It turned out he was a sixth-grade teacher who had unwittingly started reading *The 18th Emergency* to his class. He was nice about it. He said his class was delighted to find out there were two terrible Marv Hammermans instead of one.

When I was writing this book, my sympathies were all with Mouse Fawley who was Hammerman's victim. I wanted all the readers to feel sorry for him too. Poor Mouse. Horrible Hammerman. Halfway through the book, it occurred to me what agony it must have been for the Fletcher brothers, both built more like men than boys, to sit in those tiny desks in Hoskins school, and I decided that at the end of the book, I'd pull a switch and let the reader see, just for a moment, what it would be like to be the bully.

It was something that I had not thought of until I was actually into the book, and it's not unusual for insights to come that way. My one regret about that book is that I didn't think to dedicate it to the Fletcher brothers until it was too late.

If we had not moved to West Virginia, I would never have been able to write *The Summer of the Swans, After the Goat Man, The House of Wings,* or *Good-Bye, Chicken*

The Byars family in Urbana, Illinois, 1956: "the barracks where I had two choices—write or lose my mind. I wrote."

Little, because the ideas for those four books came directly from our daily newspaper.

First, there was a story in the paper about an elderly man who was lost in the mountains around Morgantown. Hundreds of volunteers joined in the search for him. It turned out the old man had gotten bored with the picnic, walked home and gone to bed, but that didn't make the search any less dramatic to me. The story possibilities were great. That was the seed of *The Summer of the Swans.*

Another story—highway I-79 was coming through the area and dozens of people who had been living back in the hills all their lives were being forced to give up their land and move. There was a picture story of one of them—he was known locally as the Goat Man because he kept goats. I had only to look at the picture of him beside his cabin to know that this was wrong and that I wanted to do the book.

Then there was a story in the paper about a huge flying creature which had swooped down at a local farmer as he came from the barn. A follow-up story about a huge flying creature that had crashed into someone's TV antenna. One more story—the huge flying creature had scared some kids riding bikes on a country road. And by now the huge flying creature was known as the Morgantown monster.

The Morgantown monster turned out to be a sandhill crane, lost and injured in migration. Most readers lost interest in the story then, but mine was just beginning. *The House of Wings* was underway.

Finally, a tragic story. A man who had been drinking in a local bar tried to cross the frozen Monongahela river on a dare and went through the thin ice—the opening scene in *Good-Bye, Chicken Little.*

If not for living in West Virginia, I also would not have written *The TV Kid,* or, at any rate, it would have been a different book. The lake house that Lennie broke into was our lake house. Every spring, Ed and I went under the house on our backs in the crawl space to solder the pipes which had burst over the winter. Both of us worried about being bitten by a snake the whole time we were under there. After I published the book, I worried about it even more. Now if I got bitten, it wouldn't even be new material for me to write about.

I started on two master's degrees at West Virginia University, and although I didn't finish either one, my studies were invaluable. Particularly those in library science, because I learned exactly how and where to find what I want in the library.

For example, when I got interested in the news stories about the sandhill crane, I went to the library. What I was looking for was not books on the sandhill crane in the wild, where they make their nests, etc. I wanted to know what it would be like to have a sandhill crane living in the house with you.

I found fascinating stories. I found a story from Florida about two sandhill cranes who would come to a lady's house during fly season. She would let them in and they would eat all the flies off the screens.

· I found stacks of old *Audubon* magazines and my interest enlarged as I read. The stories I liked the most were written by men who weren't professional writers, but just men who had a way with injured birds. I was very moved by these stories.

They all started the same way, with the men remembering the exact date someone brought them the injured robin or crow. They remembered what had been wrong, what they had done, and they remembered in detail how the bird had acted in its long convalescence.

I read about a crow who liked to fly over to the dresser, walk past the mirror and admire himself. An owl who caught moths in the bathroom. A canary who would only sit on the frame of an ancestor's portrait.

The end of these stories was the same too. The men remembered the exact day they freed the bird. "It was a windy day, April 3," they would write. "He had a drink at the sink and he flew over and ate a Wheatie out of my bowl and then he flew to the windowsill. I opened the window and after five minutes he flew to the apple tree. Then he circled the orchard and was gone." And they always added, "I keep watching for him. I would be able to pick him out from a flock of a hundred birds."

By this time, I wanted to do the book about the injured crane, but I also wanted it to be about one of these gentle, patient men who love birds so much they set them free.

Ed and I were on one of our many gliding trips, and I rushed into a grocery store to get something to make him a sandwich before he took off. Making sandwiches is, unfortunately, another of my jobs as crew chief.

I came face to face with two elderly twins. They were probably eighty-five years old; they were dressed exactly alike—their hair was alike, their shoes and their purses. I had never seen anything like it. I followed them around the store for a half an hour. When I got back to the airport, Ed said as usual, "Where have you been?"

I said, "I have just been following the two most interesting people I have ever seen in my life, and as soon as I can, I'm going to put them in a book."

Now I have always been a wonderful eavesdropper and frequently hear bits of conversation that I put word for

The awards ceremony when Byars received her Newbery Medal, June, 1971.

word in my books. But this was the first time I had ever wanted to put living, breathing people into one.

My opportunity came in *The Pinballs*. I wanted one of the foster kids, Thomas J, to have an odd family and what odder family could I give him than eighty-five-year-old twins who were still dressing alike? I then proceeded to figure out for myself what their lives must have been like, what would account for the fact that they were still living together at age eighty-five. When I got through, I felt I was so close to the truth that if the elderly twins ever read *The Pinballs* they would sue me.

A few years later I was back in the same town, and I asked a local person about the twins, if they had always lived together, etc. "Oh no, they got married, moved away, had families, and then when their husbands died, they came home and started dressing alike again." I wish my Benson twins, Thomas and Jefferson, who had been named for their father's favorite president, had been as fortunate.

The Night Swimmers started out to be a mystery. I love mysteries and had always wanted to write one. I thought this was my opportunity.

The three characters, two brothers and a sister, were sneaking out at night to swim in other people's pools. While they were swimming, I planned, they would see something mysterious happening in one of the houses. They would not be able to tell anyone what they had seen because they weren't supposed to be there, and the mystery would develop.

Unfortunately, I could never think of anything mysterious for them to see. The kids were all but getting waterlogged, they had been in the swimming pool in the first chapter for so long. I was worried.

I was writing this book while I was packing to leave West Virginia. Ed and I and our four children had lived in the same house for twenty years and now Ed was changing jobs and we were going back to South Carolina. It was a hard time for me. I was having to throw memories away daily.

Like, one day I came across a small jewelry box tied with ribbon. It rattled. "What's this?" I untied the ribbon. The box contained baby teeth—all the little baby teeth I had taken out from under pillows in my role as tooth fairy. I burst into tears. I said, "Ed, I don't even know which teeth belong to which child." He said, "Betsy, throw those things out." I did, but it wasn't easy.

And one day I found a diary one of my daughters had kept in fifth grade. I would not have read it if I had come across it while she was keeping it, but now she was grown, had a daughter of her own, and I needed a good laugh. I opened it.

The whole diary was about how much she hated her sister. On every page was another reason for hating her more. The word *hate* had been written with such force that the letters were still pressed down into the page after all these years.

It made me remember that when my sister and I were growing up, my mother would come into the room which we shared and draw a chalk line down the center of the room to keep us from crossing over and killing each other.

That diary and that memory changed *The Night Swimmers* from a mystery to a book about brothers and sisters who get to the point where they hate each other. They made me realize that not only can brothers and sisters hate each other, but it may be the strongest hate they will ever feel in their lives. Certainly it was the only time in my own life that someone had to draw a chalk line to keep me from murder.

No professional writer that I know ever thinks—Oh, that's good enough. I'm tired of revising. I'll just send it on in. Who cares?

Even if I have rewritten a book seventeen times, if I feel it's not right, I'll write it again.

I had only done seven or eight drafts of *The Cybil War* when I sent it in. At that point, the book was written in the first person. Simon told the story himself.

I sent the manuscript to Viking, it was accepted, I got a contract. I did two or three more drafts. I sat down to read it once more before I sent it in for the last time.

Before I finished the second chapter, on what was supposed to be a quick, last-minute read, I found myself reading slower and slower, and with less and less pleasure. I could not shake the uneasy feeling that it had been a mistake to let Simon tell the story. I should have told it. What I need to do, I thought, is put this book in the third person.

Now, taking a book that is in the first person and changing it to third person is not simply a matter of changing all the *I*'s to *he*'s. Whole paragraphs have to be thrown out, even whole chapters. The things Simon tells, and the way he tells them, were not at all the way I, as narrator, would tell them. And I already had an advance for this book! I had already spent it!

I never hesitated. I was at my typewriter within minutes writing a new chapter one. When I was finally finished, the only thing about the book that remained the same was its title, my all-time favorite—*The Cybil War*.

In the twenty years that I lived in West Virginia, I wrote in a corner of our bedroom. I had a huge L-shaped desk in front of a big window where I could look out over the beautiful West Virginia hills. Sometimes, even when I wasn't writing, I'd sit there.

One of the things that bothered me most about moving was that I wouldn't have that corner and that desk and that view, and I didn't think I would be able to write without them. Also we were moving into a small, modern town house, and there wasn't any corner for my big desk. I didn't tell anybody, but I was absolutely certain I had written my last book.

Two weeks later, in my new town house, I wrote the opening chapter of *The Animal, the Vegetable, and John D. Jones,* the first of my South Carolina books. I was back where I had started, once again on the kitchen table.

I moved to a small desk upstairs with a beautiful view overlooking the lake and a new typewriter that could remember what I'd written and erase it. I started *The 2000-Pound Goldfish* on it. This book was a particular pleasure to write, not just because of the typewriter, but because I loved horror movies so much as a child that everyone said they would ruin my brain.

Then I got a word processor and wrote *The Glory Girl*, my second South Carolina book. Then *The Computer Nut,* my first collaboration—with my son Guy. Then *Cracker Jackson.* I'm now finishing *The Not-Just-Anybody Family.*

I used to think, when I first started writing, that writers were like wells, and sooner or later we'd use up what had happened to us and our children and our friends and our dogs and cats, and there wouldn't be anything left. We'd go dry and have to quit.

Betsy and Ed in his J-3 Cub, 1974.

Daughter Betsy's wedding day: sisters Nan (left) and Laurie flank the bride; her parents and brother Guy are seated, December 17, 1977.

I imagine we would if it weren't for that elusive quality—creativity. I can't define it, but I have found from experience that the more you use it, the better it works.

On April Fools' Day, 1983, I took my first flying lesson. I had been flying with Ed for thirty-five years, but I had never tried it myself. My thought was that flying, like writing, couldn't possibly be as hard as everyone said it was.

Like writing, it turned out to be harder. Months after I had learned how to take off and fly around and navigate, I still couldn't land. The ground was never exactly where I thought it was going to be. I made over a hundred landings before I did a good solid one, and then I made twenty before I did another.

On December 19, 1984, I got my pilot's license, and I am as proud of that as of anything in my writing career.

Uncle C. C. in *Good-Bye, Chicken Little* says, "There's two parts to a man's life. Forget all the junk you've heard about youth, teenage, middle age, old age. There's two parts to a man's life—up and down. Your life goes up like a fly ball and then, like it or not, it starts down. The people who are lucky have a long, long up and a quick down."

At age ninety-seven Uncle C. C. still felt he was on the way up. I, at age fifty-six, feel I am too.

Postscript (Spring of 1999)

A lot has changed in my life in the last fifteen years. I have eight grandchildren instead of two. My four children are all married. Two of my daughters—Laurie Myers and Betsy Duffey have started writing books of their own.

The biggest change of all is that my husband and I now live on an air strip in South Carolina. The lower floor of our house is a hangar so we can just taxi out and take-off, almost from our front yard.

But the basic things, particularly about my writing, haven't changed at all.

Here's the way I still rate the elements of a story in importance:

Characters
Plot
Setting
Good Scraps

(And most of the other things—like theme and mood—I don't think about.)

The plot of a book usually comes first. It's a seed, one idea, and what I'm looking for in this idea is something with possibilities—like kids swimming at night in someone's pool, like a character lost in the woods, like kids in a foster home.

But even though the plot comes first, it is not the most important thing. The characters are the key to the story. They unlock the plot. They make it happen.

One of the most important things, to me, is the character's name. Once I was writing one of the Blossom books, and I needed a name for a minor character, and the name "Bingo" popped into mind. But I liked the name too well to waste it, so I named the character something else and continued writing. But Bingo started taking over my mind. I knew how he got the name—that when he came into the world, the doctor said, "Bingo," that later he would say to his mom, "He wasn't naming me, Mom, he said that every time a baby was born," that later he would write in his journal, "Who knows what kind of person I would have become if the doctor had said, 'Richard.'" So I put aside the Blossoms and began *The Burning Questions of Bingo Brown.*

I sometimes change a name a dozen times, and my computer makes it easy. I use the command "Find and Replace" a lot. There was a character in *McMummy* and I couldn't get her personality because her name wasn't right. She was a would-be beauty contestant, and I'd tried Angeline, Ernestine, Hazelline, and then one day I was driving home, stopped at a red light and saw a sign that said Valvoline. I couldn't get home fast enough to ask my computer to find and replace.

The setting varies in importance. Sometimes it's very important, as in the book I'm working on now—*The Domino Effect,* and I spend a lot of time making the setting real to the reader. At other times the setting is not important at all, and so I use a generic setting, as in *The Pinballs.*

Plenty of good scraps are as important in making a book as in the making of a quilt.

I often think of my books as scrapbooks of my life, because I put in them all the neat things that I see and read and hear. I sometimes wonder what people who don't write do with all their good stuff.

Here are some of the neat things I have put in my books: A blacksnake on my front porch. Ninety-year-old twins who were still dressing alike. A man who could smell snakes. A cat named Five-thirty.

Here's how that happened. I was in the middle of writing a book about a dog called Tornado. There was a cat in the story and I didn't have a good name for her. We were visiting friends and their cat appeared and she said, "Oh, there's Five-thirty." I said, "Your cat is named Five-thirty?" She said, "Yes, she always shows up at that time." I said, "If you let me borrow that name, I'll dedicate my new book to you and your family." She said, "Deal." An extra hippopotamus. An owl in the bathroom. Puce tennis shoes. A gift-wrapped dime. A woman who ate road kill.

I'll tell you about that one, too. It came—as a lot of my scraps do—from the local newspaper. A woman who lived in the North Carolina woods lived alone. She ate what she could find in the forest and on the road. She gave recipes for how she cooked run-over squirrel and possum. At the time I read it, I thought, Well, that is too weird even for me, and I didn't save the article. Later, when I was writing *The Blossoms Meet the Vulture Lady,* I realized it wasn't too weird and the woman in the newspaper article became Mad Mary. Unfortunately I couldn't remember the recipes so had to leave them out. A boy who did imitations of whales. Garbage Dog. A cherry twig toothbrush. A dog with a turtle in his mouth.

I'll tell you about that one. When my daughter was about six, she had a small turtle, the kind you used to be able to buy in Woolworth's for fifty cents.

She cleaned the bowl and put the bowl and the turtle on the porch to get some sun. She went out an hour later and the turtle was gone.

This was a real mystery. The turtle could not have crawled out of the bowl, and every member of the family swore they hadn't hidden it for a joke.

Then we noticed that Rudy, a red dog from down the street, was sitting at the edge of the steps. Rudy looked worried, and we noticed that his mouth wasn't closed all the way. My daughter went over, forced Rudy's mouth open, and out popped the turtle, good as new

What had happened, we figured, was that Rudy had come along, seen the nice bowl of water, bent down to drink and ended up with a turtle in his mouth.

That was such a good scrap that I used it twice—once in *The 18th Emergency* and again in *Tornado.*

Here's the best thing about being a writer.

I am my own boss.

I work when I want to. If I don't feel like writing, I can go swimming or flying or snorkeling in Mexico. I can go on vacation when I want, and if I decide to take a month off, or a summer off, I can do that, too.

I am the boss not only of my life, but of the book I'm writing. I can pick what I want to write about, and if it doesn't work out, I can pick something else. I can make the things happen that I want to happen. If characters die (as both Pap and Mud did in an early version of *A Blossom Promise*), I can bring them back to life. I get a second chance and a third and a fourth. If it doesn't happen the way I want, I can do it over again and again until it does.

Here's the worst thing about me being a writer.

I am a terrible boss. I have been that way all my life. When I was little, my mother would say, "Where are you going?"

"Out."

"Not until you've done your homework."

"Mom, everyone's waiting on me."

"Not until you've done your homework."

"Mommmmmm . . ."

Byars today.

Early in my life I developed a lifelong love of two things: dogs and books. I cannot remember a time in my life when I didn't have the joy and comfort they could bring me.

Some lifelong loves came later. When I was a girl, my father took me to the airport on Saturdays to eat popcorn and watch the planes take off and land. I developed a love of flying, but I didn't have my first airplane ride until I was in college. During the summer before my senior year I fell madly in love with Ed Byars. Ed was a college professor, a man of the world with a yellow Mercury convertible and a 1931 Stinson airplane. He became my third lifelong love.

So while many things in my life change from year to year, my lifelong loves remain—books, dogs, flying, my husband . . . and, oh, yes, popcorn.

Writings

FOR CHILDREN

Clementine, illustrated by Charles Wilton, Houghton Mifflin, 1962.

Betsy and Ed in front of their home and hangar, Clemson, South Carolina, 1990s.

The Dancing Camel, illustrated by Harold Berson, Viking, 1965.

Rama, the Gypsy Cat, illustrated by Peggy Bacon, Viking, 1966.

The Groober (self-illustrated), Harper & Row, 1967.

The Midnight Fox, illustrated by Ann Grifalconi, Viking, 1968.

Trouble River, illustrated by Rocco Negri, Viking, 1969 .

The Summer of the Swans, illustrated by Ted CoConis, Viking, 1970.

Go and Hush the Baby, illustrated by Emily A. McCully, Viking, 1971.

The House of Wings, illustrated by Daniel Schwartz, Viking, 1973.

The Winged Colt of Casa Mia, illustrated by Richard Cuffari, Viking, 1973.

The 18th Emergency, illustrated by Robert Grossman, Viking, 1973.

After the Goat Man, illustrated by Ronald Himler, Viking, 1974.

The Lace Snail (self-illustrated), Viking, 1975.

The TV Kid, illustrated by Cuffari, Viking, 1976.

The Pinballs, Harper & Row, 1977.

The Cartoonist, illustrated by Cuffari, Viking, 1978.

Good-bye, Chicken Little, Harper & Row, 1979

The Night Swimmers, illustrated by Troy Howell, Delacorte, 1980.

The Cybil War, illustrated by Gail Owens, Viking, 1981.

The Animal, the Vegetable and John D. Jones, illustrated by Ruth Sanderson, Delacorte, 1982.

The 2000-Pound Goldfish, Harper & Row, 1982.

The Glory Girl, Viking, 1983.

(With Guy Byars) *The Computer Nut,* Viking, 1984.

Cracker Jackson, Viking, 1985.

The Golly Sisters Go West, illustrated by Sue Truesdell, Harper & Row, 1985.

The Not-Just-Anybody Family, illustrated by Jacqueline Rogers, Delacorte, 1986.

The Blossoms Meet the Vulture Lady, illustrated by Rogers, Delacorte, 1986.

The Blossoms and the Green Phantom, illustrated by Rogers, Delacorte, 1987.

A Blossom Promise, illustrated by Rogers, Delacorte, 1987.

The Burning Questions of Bingo Brown, illustrated by Cathy Bobak, Viking, 1988.

Beans on the Roof, illustrated by Melodye Rosales, Delacorte, 1988.

Bingo Brown and the Language of Love, illustrated by Bobak, Viking, 1989.

Hooray for the Golly Sisters!, illustrated by Truesdell, HarperCollins, 1990.

Bingo Brown, Gypsy Lover, Viking, 1990.

The Seven Treasure Hunts, illustrated by Jennifer Barrett, HarperCollins, 1991.

Wanted ... Mud Blossom, illustrated by Rogers, Delacorte, 1991.

The Moon and I (autobiography), Silver Burdett Press, 1992.

Bingo Brown's Guide to Romance, Viking, 1992.

Coast to Coast, Delacorte, 1992.

McMummy, Viking, 1993.

The Golly Sisters Ride Again, illustrated by Truesdell, HarperCollins, 1994.

The Dark Stairs: A Herculeah Jones Mystery, Viking, 1994.

Tarot Says Beware, Viking, 1995.

My Brother Ant, illustrated by Marc Simont, Viking, 1996.

Tornado, HarperCollins, 1996.

The Joy Boys, illustrated by Frank Remkiewicz, Delacorte, 1996.

A Bean Birthday, Macmillan, 1996.

Dead Letter: A Herculeah Jones Mystery, Viking, 1996.

Ant Plays Bear, illustrated by Simont, Viking, 1997.

Death's Door, Viking, 1997.

Disappearing Acts, Viking, 1998.

Me Tarzan, HarperCollins, 2000.

(With Betsy Duffey and Laurie Myers) *My Hero,* Holt, 2000.

Byars's writings have been translated into nine languages. Her manuscripts are housed at Clemson University, South Carolina.

C

CHAMBERS, Aidan 1934-
(Malcolm Blacklin)

Personal

Born December 27, 1934, in Chester-le-Street, County Durham, England; son of George Kenneth Blacklin (a funeral director) and Margaret (Hancock) Chambers; married Nancy Harris Lockwood (a former editor of *Children's Book News*), March 30, 1968. *Education:* Attended Borough Road College, London, 1955-57.

Aidan Chambers

Addresses

Home and office—Lockwood, Station Rd., South Woodchester, Stroud, Gloucestershire GL5 5EQ, England.

Career

English and drama teacher at various schools in England, 1957-68; full-time writer and editor, 1968—. Macmillan, London, general editor, "Topliners," "Club 75," "M Books," and "Rockets" series, 1967-85; *Signal: Approaches to Children's Books,* South Woodchester, Gloucestershire, publisher, 1969—; Thimble Press, proprietor and publisher, 1969—; Turton & Chambers, cofounder and editorial publisher, 1989—. Further Professional Studies Department, University of Bristol, tutor, 1970-82; Westminster College, Oxford, visiting lecturer, 1982-92; May Hill Arbuthnot Lecturer, University of Kansas at Little Rock, 1986. Writer and presenter of radio programs, including (with wife, Nancy Chambers) *Bookbox,* Radio Bristol, 1973-75; *Children and Books,* BBC Radio, 1976; *Ghosts,* Thames-TV, 1980; and *Long, Short, and Tall Stories,* BBC-TV, 1980—. Has produced children's plays for stage. *Military service:* Royal Navy, 1953-55. *Member:* Society of Authors.

Awards, Honors

Children's Literature Association Award, 1978, for article "The Reader in the Book"; Best Books, *School Library Journal,* 1979, for *Breaktime;* (with Nancy Chambers) Eleanor Farjeon Award, 1982; Best Books for Young Adults, American Library Association, 1983, for *Dance on My Grave;* Silver Pencil Award (Netherlands), 1983, 1985, and 1986.

Writings

FOR CHILDREN; FICTION

Cycle Smash, Heinemann, 1967.
Marle, Heinemann, 1968.
Don't Forget Charlie and the Vase, illustrated by Clyde Pearson, Macmillan, 1971.

Mac and Lugs, illustrated by Barbara Swiderska, Macmillan, 1971.

Ghosts Two (short stories), Macmillan, 1972.

Snake River, illustrated by Peter Morgan, Almqvist och Wiksell, 1975, Macmillan, 1977.

Fox Tricks (short stories), illustrated by Robin and Jocelyn Wild, Heinemann, 1980.

Seal Secret (novel), Bodley Head, 1980, Harper (New York), 1981.

The Present Takers (novel), Bodley Head, 1983, Harper, 1984.

Also author of *Ghost Carnival,* 1977. Contributor to *Winter Tales for Children 4,* Macmillan.

YOUNG ADULT NOVELS

Breaktime, Bodley Head, 1978, Harper, 1979.

Dance on My Grave, Bodley Head, 1982, Harper, 1983.

Now I Know, Bodley Head, 1987, published as *NIK: Now I Know,* Harper, 1987.

The Toll Bridge, Bodley Head, 1992, Harper, 1995.

Postcards from No Man's Land, Bodley Head, 1999.

PLAYS

Everyman's Everybody, produced in London, 1957.

Johnny Salter (produced in Stroud, Gloucestershire, 1965), Heinemann, 1966.

The Car (produced in Stroud, 1966), Heinemann, 1967.

The Chicken Run (produced in Stroud, 1967), Heinemann, 1968.

The Dream Cage: A Comic Drama in Nine Dreams (produced in Stroud, 1981), Heinemann, 1982.

Only Once: A Play for Young Actors, produced in Stroud, 1998.

EDITOR

(With Nancy Chambers) *Ghosts,* Macmillan, 1969.

I Want to Get Out: Stories and Poems by Young Writers, Macmillan, 1971.

(With Nancy Chambers) *Hi-Ran-Ho: A Picture Book of Verse,* illustrated by Barbara Swiderska, Longman, 1971.

(With Nancy Chambers) *World Minus Zero: A SF Anthology,* Macmillan, 1971.

(With Nancy Chambers) *In Time to Come: A SF Anthology,* Macmillan, 1973.

The Tenth [Eleventh] Ghost Book, Barrie & Jenkins, 2 volumes, 1975-76; published in one volume as *The Bumper Book of Ghost Stories,* Pan, 1976.

Fighters in the Sky, Macmillan, 1976.

Funny Folk: A Body of Comic Tales, illustrated by Trevor Stubley, Heinemann, 1976.

Men at War, Macmillan, 1977.

Escapers, Macmillan, 1978.

War at Sea, Macmillan, 1978.

(Under pseudonym Malcolm Blacklin) *Ghosts Four,* Macmillan, 1978.

Animal Fair, illustrated by Anthony Colbert, Heinemann, 1979.

Aidan Chambers' Book of Ghosts and Hauntings, illustrated by Antony Maitland, Viking, 1980.

Ghosts That Haunt You, illustrated by Gareth Floyd, Viking, 1980.

In Chambers's novel, a young man faces prosecution after living up to a promise made to his friend.

Loving You, Loving Me, Viking, 1980.

Ghost after Ghost, illustrated by Bert Kitchen, Viking, 1982.

Plays for Young People to Read and Perform, Thimble Press, 1982.

(With Jill Bennett) *Poetry for Children: A Signal Bookguide,* Thimble Press, 1984.

Out of Time: Stories of the Future, Bodley Head, 1984, Harper, 1985.

Shades of Dark: Ghost Stories, P. Hardy, 1984, Harper, 1986.

A Sporting Chance: Stories of Winning and Losing, Bodley Head, 1985.

(And contributor) *A Haunt of Ghosts,* Harper, 1987.

A Quiver of Ghosts, Bodley Head, 1987.

Love All, Bodley Head, 1988.

On the Edge, Macmillan, 1990.

FOR ADULTS

The Reluctant Reader, Pergamon Press, 1969.

Introducing Books to Children, Heinemann, 1973, revised edition, Horn Book, 1983.

Axes for Frozen Seas (lecture), Woodfield and Stanley, 1981.

Booktalk: Occasional Writing on Literature and Children, Harper, 1985.
The Reading Environment: How Adults Help Children Enjoy Books, Thimble Press, 1990, Stenhouse, 1996.
Tell Me: Children, Reading and Talk, Thimble Press, 1993, Stenhouse, 1996.

Contributor to periodicals, including *Books and Book-men, Books for Your Children, Children's Book News, Teachers' World,* and *Times Educational Supplement.* Author of columns "Young Reading," *Times Educational Supplement,* 1970-72, and "Letter from England," *Horn Book,* 1972-84.

OTHER

Haunted Houses, illustrated by John Cameron Jarvies, Pan, 1971.
More Haunted Houses, illustrated by Chris Bradbury, Pan, 1973.
Book of Ghosts and Hauntings, Viking, 1973.
Great British Ghosts, illustrated by Barry Wilkinson, Pan, 1974.
Great Ghosts of the World, illustrated by Peter Edwards, Pan, 1974.
Book of Flyers and Flying, illustrated by Trevor Stubley, Viking, 1976.
Ghost Carnival: Stories of Ghosts in Their Haunts, illustrated by Peter Wingham, Heinemann, 1977.
Book of Cops and Robbers, illustrated by Allan Manham, Viking, 1977.

Adaptations

The Toll Bridge was adapted for the stage and produced in Antwerp, Belgium, in 1998.

Sidelights

An accomplished novelist, dramatist, critic, and the author and editor of a variety of forms of fiction and nonfiction, Aidan Chambers is widely known as an outspoken advocate of children's literature. Many of Chambers's writings highlight a recurring theme: that children should be encouraged to read at an early age and allowed to develop their skills and reading preferences at an independent pace. "I can remember the day—evening rather—when I first learned to read," Chambers wrote in an essay for *Sixth Book of Junior Authors and Illustrators.* "That evening in winter I sat staring at a page of print, and suddenly I started to hear the words in my head, making sense. And the sense they were making was a story, with people talking in it, about an adventure on an island. Hearing those printed words suddenly making sense in my head is one of the most vivid and valued moments in my life." Chambers firmly believes that children respond best to subjects that are of interest to them. To this end, he has compiled anthologies about a variety of subjects, including ghosts, crime, and aviation. Chambers's fiction, primarily directed to young adults, is noted for its honest depiction of adolescent emotions and its sympathetic treatment of nontraditional young-adult themes like homosexuality. "Whether editing anthologies or writing or reviewing

children's books, Aidan Chambers takes his work seriously," asserted Christine Heppermann in *Children's Books and Their Creators.* "He believes children, like adults, deserve good books written just for them."

Born in 1934 in Chester-le-Street, a small town in the northeast part of England, Chambers came from a working-class family: his father was a skilled woodcraftsman and his mother cared for their home. His childhood home was dominated by a large, black, iron fireplace where all the food was cooked and the water heated; only a few books could be found, including a dictionary, a volume of *Aesop's Fables,* and a do-it-yourself medical book. Chambers did not read for pleasure, nor did he excel in primary school. "Throughout my ninth year I was beaten twice every Friday for not being able to do well enough in mental arithmetic tests," he recalled in the *Sixth Book of Junior Authors and Illustrators.* "School in Chester-le-Street was not a place you learned anything except how to avoid bullies."

Because he lived close to coal mines, Chambers got a firsthand look at the harsh realities of mining life. He described for *Something about the Author Autobiography Series (SAAS)* both the fascination and terror he associated with the pitmen: "Out of view at the head of the valley to my left was a coke factory, a huge, concrete affair from which oozed red-hot cinders in great vertical slabs like pus from a wound.... As I lay in the dark trying to get to sleep, for I never liked going to bed while my parents were still up, I could see through my back bedroom window the bobbing flashlights of pitmen as they walked to or from the mine along a path that skirted the top of the wood. I imagined they were night spirits invading my territory, and I was glad to be safe at home."

Chambers loved going to the movies. The cinematic image he remembers most vividly is the moment Judy Garland as Dorothy opened the black-and-white cottage door onto the dazzling colors of Oz in *The Wizard of Oz.* "'Going to the pictures' was the entertainment I looked forward to the most all through my childhood and youth," Chambers recalled in his autobiographical essay for *SAAS.* "I loved the snug hiddenness of the dark cinema, the smell, the smoke-filled beam of light shining onto the screen ... the utterly absorbed attention of an audience captured by a film.... I'm sure the way I write stories, perhaps even the way I read them, owes more to those hundreds of hours spent watching movies than to anything else."

After the war, Chambers's father took a job in the industrial town of Darlington. While Chambers was not happy about leaving his hometown, the move brought about one happy change—Darlington's school system was a good one, with attentive teachers and a challenging curriculum. Chambers was especially impressed by Jim Osborn, the head of the English department. With some prodding, Osborn convinced Chambers to join the debate and drama clubs. Chambers discovered that he loved public speaking and theatre. It was also about this time that Chambers realized that he wanted to become a fiction writer. He recalled for *SAAS:* "I wanted to write fiction. This impulse planted itself when I was fifteen, the night I finished D. H. Lawrence's *Sons and Lovers.* . . . Paul Morel's life seemed so like my own—the first time I experienced such a recognition—that I wished I could have written it."

Chambers did not have a lot of time to devote to his writing for the next few years. After he left school, he served two years of compulsory service in the armed forces. Upon his release from the service, Chambers entered college, where he produced some plays and wrote his own. Partially due to his background in literature and drama, Chambers got a job upon graduation, teaching English at a boys' school. "I arrived in Southend with just enough money to see me through to my first pay cheque, a suitcase of spare clothing, board and lodging arranged in a house near the school, and an exhilarating sense of an end and a beginning: an end to a constricted adolescence, to being a son supported by parents, . . . a student required to pass exams, and the beginning of an independent life," Chambers noted in his autobiographical essay.

Chambers enjoyed both his teaching position and living in Southend. He made a great many friends and rekindled his interest in religion, attending Anglo-Catholic services on a regular basis. Over time, he was drawn to the idea of joining a monastery. After looking into various religious orders, Chambers joined two brothers who were organizing a new type of order set up specifically to work with young people in the community. This led Chambers to a position at a local secondary school where the students were far from great readers. Responsible for their literary and drama instruction, Chambers spent several years in search of novels and plays appropriate for these students before finally deciding to write some of his own. The novels and plays were so successful that they were soon published.

Chambers lived as a monk for the next seven years. Although he enjoyed many aspects of the monastic life, he still felt unfulfilled. Both his writing and work outside the monastery often brought him into conflict with the other brothers of his order. After a great deal of thought, Chambers eventually decided to devote himself full time to teaching and to writing fiction. He served as the general editor for a young-adult series at Macmillan, and also continued to write plays, novels, and reviews. After marrying Nancy Lockwood in 1968, Chambers quit teaching to focus entirely on his writing. In 1969, he and his wife founded Thimble Press in order to publish *Signal* magazine, a periodical devoted to increasing the critical appreciation of children's literature.

As *Signal*'s circulation increased, Chambers's fiction writing took on a new voice. He told *SAAS:* "It happened like this. Having settled in, . . . my plan was to write another book of the kind I'd written before. But when I sat down to start, I realized that the prospect so bored me that I couldn't face it . . . . For days I sat and worried . . . . Finally, desperation took charge . . . . I grabbed a new notebook, a brand new pencil (I usually typed

everything I wrote), sat myself in an easy chair (I usually sat at a desk), and told myself to write the first thing that came into my head and to go on until I told myself to stop."

The result was the novel *Breaktime.* Told in a mixture of narrative modes, through narration, letters, stream-of-consciousness, and a diary, *Breaktime* follows seventeen-year-old Ditto on an eye-opening school holiday. While working on the novel, Chambers was concerned that both the story's strong sexual emphasis and free-form narrative structure would hurt its chances for publication. Despite the author's initial misgivings, *Breaktime* was published and met with a generally favorable critical response. "With humor and wit, with ingenuity and candor, the author has offered one piece of one kind of truth in a spirit of technical and emotional investigation," remarked Margery Fisher in *Growing Point.* Richard Yates of the *New York Times Book Review* found Ditto to be "an appealing young man," so appealing that the nature of his quest for adventure is one that "any number of readers can take to heart." A reviewer for *Horn Book* was equally laudatory, noting that Chambers "was interested in casting a teenage novel in a twentieth-century literary mode, and he has succeeded remarkably well . . . . In more ways than one . . . this book is strong meat—for its intellectualism as well as for its realism."

Chambers followed this first success with several more well-received novels for young adults. Similar to *Breaktime* in style, *Dance on My Grave* opens with a newspaper story describing the arrest of Hal Robinson for dancing on the fresh grave of his lover, Barry. Hal's account of the events leading up to this crime is revealed through notes taken during sessions with his social worker, as well as through letters, footnotes, and lists. After flipping over a boat on the Thames River in London, Hal is rescued by the older Barry, and the pair are brought together as friends and eventually as lovers. Consumed by his first, passionate love, Hal is both angry and jealous when he discovers that Barry has casually been with a girl. A fight ensues and Barry leaves on his motorbike; he is killed in an accident a short time later. A fast and hard-living young man, Barry had made Hal promise to dance on his grave after his death, and Hal does so, revealing to the world his long-hidden sexual orientation.

"*Dance on My Grave* is inventive, witty, stimulating," maintained Neil Philip in the *Times Educational Supplement,* adding that Barry and Hal's relationship "is related with a cool matter-of-fact humour which is most refreshing." Mary K. Chelton similarly asserted in *Voice of Youth Advocates:* "To have male feelings so well depicted is a rare treat, and to have the protagonist be a young gay male who survives a lost love with insight and joy, is rarer still . . . . Everything about this book is superb." Margery Fisher of *Growing Point* claimed that *Dance on My Grave* is "a book that makes its point through raucous good humor and implied feeling, through the sharp observation of a boy and his blundering apprehensions of the way others observe him. If teenage novels are to justify their existence, it will be by this kind of honest, particularized, personal writing."

Using framing devices similar to those employed in his previous young-adult novels, Chambers began his 1987 novel *Now I Know* with three separate narratives, taking place at three different times. As the three strands mesh together, they form the story of Nik, a seventeen-year-old agnostic who is persuaded by a history teacher to do the background research for a youth group that is creating an amateur film about the second coming of Christ. During the course of this work, Nik meets and falls in love with Julie, a Christian feminist who eventually loses her sight when she is injured by a terrorist bomb. After witnessing this attack, Nik decides to conclude his research through an experiment in the local junkyard; he engineers a "practice version" of the crucifixion.

"With its time shifts, word play, and discussions on such vexing theological problems as free will, suffering and affliction, doubt and belief, the novel is compelling but demanding. Yet it offers enormous rewards to thinking, mature young adults," asserted *Horn Book* reviewer Ethel L. Heins. Patty Campbell concluded in her *Wilson Library Bulletin* review of the U.S. version of the book, *NIK: Now I Know,* "Chambers in this many-layered novel has given us a work of stunning impact, a book in the tradition of C. S. Lewis and George MacDonald that lights the search but begs no easy answers."

The theme of self-discovery through conflict is continued in Chambers's novel *The Toll Bridge.* Borrowing from the Greek myth of Janus, the two-faced keeper of the gate to Hades, the novel introduces Piers, who symbolically has two faces as well. To escape the pressures of his parents, girlfriend, and school, Piers takes a job as the gatekeeper of a private toll bridge, living in isolation in the gate house. The one friend Piers *does* make is Tess, the estate manager's daughter, and the triangle is complete when a handsome, mysterious young man named Adam shows up one night. Unable to rid himself of his guest, Piers (renamed Jan when the three friends give each other new names) finds himself oddly drawn to Adam, as does Tess, though they know nothing of his past.

The Toll Bridge "is a rites of passage novel about identity and growth through friendship but it's also much more than that," maintained Melanie Guile in *Magpies.* "Moreover," continued Guile, "*The Toll Bridge*'s multifaceted form, together with its patterns of imagery (bridge, water, fire), enact crucial concerns in the novel: the fragmentation of personality that is an inevitable part of adolescence, and the struggle towards integration." A *Publishers Weekly* reviewer asserted: "Provocative in the best sense, this novel suggests even more than its intricate plot spells out, leaving readers with much for pleasurable contemplation."

Chambers's latest offering for young adults, *Postcards from No Man's Land,* contains the intricate, multi-layered plot elements characteristic of his previous novels. Jacob Todd travels to Amsterdam to represent his grandmother at a ceremony commemorating a battle in which his grandfather fought. While there, he visits the home of a Dutch family who sheltered his grandfather before his death. Jacob's adventures are interspersed with the story of Amsterdam native Geertrui Wesseling and her part in the war. Tony Bradman, writing in the London *Daily Telegraph,* called *Postcards from No Man's Land* "a terrific novel, chock-full of well-rounded characters and good writing." Dubbing the novel "provocative," *Magpies* reviewer Anne Briggs asserted that "Jacob's tentative but enthusiastic exploration of the world ... hit[s] just the right note for thoughtful adolescents teetering on the edge of adulthood."

Looking at Chambers's young-adult novels as a whole, *Twentieth-Century Young Adult Writers* essayist Robert Protherough observed that their "originality and driving power ... is undeniable.... Everything that Chambers has written can be seen as demonstrating the power of language and of active reading where 'the reader plays the text.'" "Chambers's work has forwarded children's literature in many respects," stated Heppermann in *Children's Books and Their Creators.* Focusing on Chambers's young-adult novels in particular, Heppermann added that these "works of fiction ... reflect his commitment to writing about situations and emotions familiar to his audience while simultaneously challenging and expanding their horizons with the unfamiliar." In order to convey these situations and emotions, Chambers employs a range of narrative techniques that many consider difficult for young readers. "His novels provide a challenge," continued Heppermann, "as he often experiments with narrative technique, attempting to convey ideas or sensations as authentically as possible." S. David Gill similarly pointed out in *ALAN Review:* "Admittedly, the stylized writing found in these novels may intimidate readers who like their novels 'once and fast,' but Chambers is worth the work: his writing rewards rereading." Gill added: "Rarely does a writer possess the skill to integrate so many elements into a cohesive narrative. Underlying this skill, however, are universal stories about adolescents struggling to deal with their worlds."

In his *SAAS* essay, Chambers admitted that his novels are actually a sequential body of work. He wrote: "This is how I think of it: I'm writing a portrait of a boy whose character is slowly emerging—is being created—as the books appear. *Breaktime* is largely to do with physical sensation—the life of the senses. *Dance on My Grave* is largely to do with the emotions—kinds of love, and our personal obsessions. *Now I Know* is largely about what people often call spiritual experience and about thought, and how they clash and blend and compliment each other."

According to Chambers, all of his novels are primarily concerned with how language defines individuals, language being the "god who makes us." Chambers takes a long time to write his fiction; sometimes it takes him years to fine-tune a novel or short story. Above all, Chambers views writing as a craft that demands great attention to detail. He continually struggles to find the right word or voice for his characters. "I have always found it a struggle to author books that matter to me," he wrote in his essay for *SAAS*. Chambers added: "I know that my life is privileged and rewarding beyond measure, and I'm thankful for that, but I do not think of myself as successful and won't until I have written a book that satisfies me by matching in its objectified, printed form the rich density of the imagined original. In this respect, nothing has changed since I was fifteen. I am also just as unsure of myself and as sure of failure, as unhappy with crowds of people; still prefer being at home to being anywhere else; still find in reading both the best of pleasures and the best means of keeping some kind of grip on life."

Works Cited

Bradman, Tony, "Stories of War, and the Pity of War," *The Daily Telegraph* (London), February 13, 1999.

Review of *Breaktime, Horn Book,* June, 1979, p. 307.

Briggs, Anne, review of *Postcards from No Man's Land, Magpies,* May, 1999, pp. 37-38.

Campbell, Patty, "The Young Adult Perplex," *Wilson Library Bulletin,* May, 1988, pp. 78-79.

Chambers, Aidan, essay in *Sixth Book of Junior Authors and Illustrators,* edited by Sally Holmes Holtze, Wilson, 1989, pp. 53-54.

Chambers, essay in *Something about the Author Autobiography Series,* Volume 12, Gale, 1991, pp. 37-55.

Chelton, Mary K., review of *Dance on My Grave, Voice of Youth Advocates,* October, 1983, p. 198.

Fisher, Margery, review of *Breaktime, Horn Book,* November, 1978, pp. 3418-19.

Fisher, review of *Dance on My Grave, Growing Point,* July, 1982, p. 3928.

Gill, S. David, "Aidan Chambers: Monk, Writer, Critic," *ALAN Review,* fall, 1997, pp. 11-12.

Guile, Melanie, review of *The Toll Bridge, Magpies,* May, 1993, p. 33.

Heins, Ethel L., review of *NIK: Now I Know, Horn Book,* January-February, 1989, pp. 76-77.

Heppermann, Christine, essay on Chambers in *Children's Books and Their Creators,* edited by Anita Silvey, Houghton, 1995, pp. 127-28.

Philip, Neil, "Adolescent Friction," *Times Educational Supplement,* September 10, 1982, p. 33.

Protherough, Robert, essay on Chambers in *Twentieth-Century Young Adult Writers,* St. James Press, 1994, pp. 111-13.

Review of *The Toll Bridge, Publishers Weekly,* June 19, 1995, p. 62.

Yates, Richard, "You Can and Can't Go Home Again," *New York Times Book Review,* April 29, 1979, p. 30.

For More Information See

PERIODICALS

American Book Review, November-December, 1997, pp. 1, 5.

Books for Keeps, November, 1992, p. 27.

Bulletin of the Center for Children's Books, September, 1995, p. 9.

School Library Journal, July, 1995, p. 92.

*   *   *

COLEMAN, Michael 1946-
(Fiona Kelly)

Personal

Born May 12, 1946, in London, England; son of John Francis (an engineer) and Grace Doris (Durney) Coleman; married Theresa Mary Murphy (a receptionist), October 10, 1968; children: Jennifer, Stephen, Catherine, Matthew. *Education:* City University, London, B.S., 1968.

Addresses

Home—29 West Downs Close, Fareham PO16 7HW, United Kingdom. *Agent*—Laurence Pollinger Ltd., 18 Maddox St., London W1R 0EU, United Kingdom. *Electronic mail*—michael.coleman@wordjuggling. freeserve.co.uk

Michael Coleman

Career

Marconi Co., Chelmford, Essex, England, computer programmer, 1968-69; Portsmouth University, Portsmouth, England, lecturer, 1969-88; IBM U.K. Laboratories, Winchester, England, quality assurer and consultant, 1988-93; author, 1988—. *Member:* Society of Authors.

Awards, Honors

Shortlist, Sheffield Children's Book Award, 1995, for *Hank the Clank,* 1997, for *Ridiculous!,* and 1998, for *Madame Retsmah Predicts;* shortlist, Best Children's Book, Writers' Guild, 1996, shortlist, Lancashire Children's Book Award and British Library Association Carnegie Medal, both 1997, both for *Weirdo's War;* shortlist, Norfolk Children's Book Award, 1998, for *Tag.*

Writings

PICTURE BOOKS

The Mum Who Was Made of Money, illustrated by Bhasia Bogdanowicz, Magi (London, England), 1993.
Hank the Clank, illustrated by Chris Mould, Oxford University Press (Oxford, England), 1994, Gareth Stevens (Milwaukee, WI), 1996.
Hank Clanks Again, illustrated by Mould, Oxford University Press, 1995.
Hank Clanks Back, illustrated by Mould, Oxford University Press, 1996.
Lazy Ozzie, illustrated by Gwyneth Williamson, Magi, 1994, Little Tiger (Wauwatosa, WI), 1996.
Ridiculous!, illustrated by Williamson, Magi, 1996, Little Tiger, 1996.
One, Two, Three, Oops!, illustrated by Williamson, Magi, 1998, Little Tiger, 1998.
George and Sylvia: A Love Story, Magi, 1999.

FICTION; FOR CHILDREN AND YOUNG ADULTS

Triv in Pursuit, Bodley Head (London, England), 1992, reprinted 1999.
Double Trouble, Learning Development Aids (Wisbech, England), 1992.
Tutankhamun Is a Bit of a Mummy's Boy ... And 50 Other Unpublished School Reports, Red Fox (London), 1992.
Gizmo Lewis, Fairly Secret Agent, Bodley Head, 1993, reprinted, 1999.
Fizzy Hits the Headlines, illustrated by Philippe Dupasquier, Orchard, 1993.
Fizzy Steals the Show, illustrated by Dupasquier, Orchard, 1994.
Redville Rockets, Orchard, 1994.
Shoot, Dad!, Scholastic (London, England), 1994.
Grounds for Suspicion/Race Against Time, Learning Development Aids, 1994.
Lexy Boyd and the Spadewell Sparklers, Bodley Head, 1994.
Fizzy TV Star, illustrated by Philippe Dupasquier, Orchard, 1995.
The Magic Sponge, illustrated by Nick Ward, Macdonald Young (Hove, England), 1996.

Weirdo's War, Orchard (London), 1996, Orchard (New York), 1998.
Fizzy in the Spotlight, illustrated by Philippe Dupasquier, Orchard, 1997.
Madame Retsmah Predicts, Scholastic, 1998.
Tag, Orchard, 1998.

FICTION; "MYSTERY KIDS" SERIES; ALL WRITTEN UNDER PSEUDONYM FIONA KELLY

Treasure Hunt (Mystery Kids 3), Hodder, 1995.
Funny Money (Mystery Kids 6), Hodder, 1995.
Wrong Number (Mystery Kids 9), Hodder, 1996.

THE "INTERNET DETECTIVES" SERIES

Net Bandits, Macmillan, 1996.
Escape Key, Macmillan, 1996.
Speed Surf, Macmillan, 1996.
Cyber Feud, Macmillan, 1996.
System Crash, Macmillan, 1996.
Web Trap, Macmillan, 1996.
(With Allan Frewin Jones) *Virus Attack,* Macmillan, 1997.
(With Jones) *Access Denied,* Macmillan, 1997.

THE "ANGELS F.C." SERIES; ALL ILLUSTRATED BY NICK ABADZIS

Touchline Terror, Orchard, 1997.
Dirty Defending, Orchard, 1997.
Handball Horror!, Orchard, 1997.
Gruesome Goalkeeping!, Orchard, 1997.
Goal Greedy!, Orchard, 1998.
Midfield Madness, Orchard, 1998.
Frightful Fouls!, Orchard, 1998.
Dazzling Dribbling!, Orchard, 1999.
Fearsome Free-Kicks!, Orchard, 1999.
Awful Attacking!, Orchard, 1999.

NONFICTION; "THE KNOWLEDGE" SERIES

Flaming Olympics, illustrated by Aiden Potts, Scholastic, 1996, 2nd edition, 2000.
Foul Football, illustrated by Harry Venning, Scholastic, 1997.
Wicked World Cup, illustrated by Venning, Scholastic, 1998.
Crashing Computers, Scholastic, 1999.

"TOP TEN" SERIES

Top Ten Bible Stories, illustrated by Michael Tickner, Scholastic, 1998.
Top Ten Fairy Stories, illustrated by Michael Tickner, Scholastic, 1999.

OTHER

Lexy Boyd and the Spadewell Sparklers was included in the anthology *Completely Wild Stories,* Red Fox, 1998; the books in the "Internet Detective" Series have been published in twenty-one languages; others of Coleman's books have been published in Czech, Norwegian, Italian, Spanish, Danish, and French.

Sidelights

Michael Coleman is the British author of dozens of books for young people, ranging from detective fiction to sports stories to nonfiction and picture books. A computer programmer and academic for over twenty years, Coleman began his second career while still working as a consultant for computer giant IBM in Winchester, England. As Coleman told *SATA*, "My writing career began with an embarrassment! I sent the first two chapters of a novel (*Triv in Pursuit*—about a school where the teachers are disappearing) to Red Fox. They rang me asking to see the remainder ... which I hadn't yet written! Needless to say, I did so and that was my first published book for children."

Aimed at middle graders, *Triv in Pursuit* follows the exploits of James "Triv" Trevellyan, an indifferent student at St. Ethelred's School. One Monday, all of the teachers begin disappearing, leaving only clever notes or odd clues behind. The note left by the music teacher, for instance, reads "I won't be coming Bach." With his friend Madeleine, Triv discovers that the local grocer, who works on the side as a hypnotist, is kidnapping the teaching staff for use in a conspiracy involving tea bags. Coleman interjects numerous jokes and comical moments leading up to Triv's cleverly plotted rescue, including pointed barbs directed at the school's headmaster, a zealous disciplinarian of the first order. Michael Kirby, reviewing *Triv in Pursuit* for *School Librarian,* maintained that the book is "written with great verve and humour," and dubbed it "a rollicking good read."

Lazy Ozzie is one of several picture books by Coleman written for younger readers. Set in a well-stocked barn, *Lazy Ozzie* centers on a young owl who is uninterested in learning how to fly, preferring instead to sit and appear wise. Ozzie's frustrated mother leaves him on a rafter one day, and tells him to be on the ground by the time she comes back; the already "wise" Ozzie simply hops down from animal to animal until he reaches his goal, but his mother has witnessed his ruse. "Coleman delivers the story in a comically rapid style, a crazy routine that ends in Ozzie's comeuppance," noted a *Kirkus Reviews* critic, who added that young audiences "will love and soon be able to predict the phases of Ozzie's descent."

Coleman has also written three well-received picture books for slightly older readers that center on a cemetery ghost. In the first title, *Hank the Clank,* Hank is in desperate want of a pal from the human world, but he frightens away any potential mates. With three of his spirit-world friends, he decides to haunt an elderly lady in earnest, but the woman remains comically unperturbed. Like many of Coleman's works aimed at primary graders, *Hank the Clank* and its sequels, *Hank Clanks Again* and *Hank Clanks Back,* are rife with puns and word-play. "Murky cartoon-style illustrations, a spiky handwritten text, and groaningly awful word play and jokes should ensure that Hank and his friends will not be short of companions of 7 and upwards," asserted *School Librarian* contributor Jill Bennett.

The "Fizzy" books are another of Coleman's series. Designed for early elementary readers and illustrated by

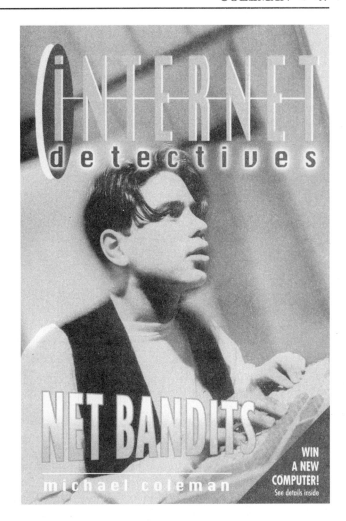

In Coleman's cyber-mystery, several young people try to locate the source of a frantic on-line message for help. (Cover photo by John R. Ward.)

Philippe Dupasquier, titles like *Fizzy Hits the Headlines* and *Fizzy in the Spotlight* feature the indomitable heroine Fiona "Fizzy" Izzard, whose love of adventure sometimes lands her in hot water. The author has also penned several soccer-themed books for boys that follow the exploits of the Angels Football Club, as well as a series of computer-dominated whodunit fiction called the "Internet Detectives." In the debut of the latter series, 1996's *Net Bandits,* young readers are introduced to Tamsyn and Josh, two computer-savvy classmates whose sleuthing skills are set in motion when they receive an e-mail message that they decode as a cry for help. Much of the action is related through e-mail messages reproduced on the page of the book. As a result of their work, the duo meet Rob, who is confined to a wheelchair, but is nevertheless able to join their escapade. Denia Hester of *Booklist* called *Net Bandits* "a tightly plotted story"; reviewing the second book in the series, *Escape Key,* Hester added that familiarity with computers was not a requirement for grasping the plot. "There's enough real chases and narrow escapes to keep everyone happy," Hester declared.

Coleman has also received praise for *Weirdo's War,* which was short-listed for a Carnegie Medal. The story relates the plight of Daniel, an intelligent loner teased by his classmates, who have nicknamed him "Weirdo." Daniel's father forces him to participate in a school field trip that is designed as an outdoor adventure experience. Daniel lands on the team with the meanest of the class bullies, and the story actually opens as the group is trapped in a limestone pit after a cave-in. Daniel's woes are recounted in flashback as he employs his powers of rational thinking and knowledge of science to extricate his team. "The first-person narrative achieves a depth of characterization unusual for a thriller," noted Mary M. Burns of *Horn Book,* who added: "In fact, [*Weirdo's War*] is much more than a thriller … it is a coming-of-age story of sorts and a tribute to the spirit of individuality. It's also a great read!"

Coleman continued to *SATA,* "I've written more than forty books [since my first], covering age ranges three to fourteen. They all set out, first and foremost, to entertain. Youngsters are a demanding audience and, unlike adults, do not see the point in soldiering on with a book they're not enjoying. So, whether it be humor or adventure, fact or fiction, I try to write something that they will enjoy reading.

"This is not to say that I don't think it's important to challenge the reader, I do. My science fiction books *Weirdo's War* and *Tag* both focus on characters who are faced with difficult personal and moral decisions. Even my picture books—like *Lazy Ozzie,* about an owl who tries to trick his mother—don't escape from this!

"If I had to advise a would-be writer, I'd say concentrate above all on developing unforgettable characters. Do this, and everything else follows. Be patient also; writing a book is like learning to juggle—it takes practice and mistakes, before everything falls into place. Oh, yes … and don't take yourself too seriously. Leave it to others!"

Works Cited

Bennett, Jill, review of *Hank the Clank, School Librarian,* February, 1995, p. 17.

Burns, Mary M., review of *Weirdo's War, Horn Book,* September-October, 1998, p. 605.

Hester, Denia, review of *Net Bandits* and *Escape Key, Booklist,* March 1, 1998, p. 1134.

Kirby, Michael, review of *Triv in Pursuit, School Librarian,* August, 1992, p. 17, p. 100.

Review of *Lazy Ozzie, Kirkus Reviews,* March 1, 1996, p. 371.

For More Information See

PERIODICALS

Booklist, January 1, 1999, p. 886.

Books for Keeps, September, 1993, p. 11; January, 1996, p. 10; September, 1996, p. 13.

Junior Bookshelf, October, 1992, p. 205.

Publishers Weekly, October 13, 1997, p. 75.

School Librarian, February, 1997, p. 46; November, 1997, p. 201.

*   *   *

COOK, Glen (Charles) 1944-
(Greg Stevens)

Personal

Born July 9, 1944, in New York, NY; son of Charles Albert (a civil servant) and Louella Mabel (Handy) Cook; married Carol Ann Fritz, June 14, 1971; children: three sons. *Education:* Attended University of Missouri, 1962-65. *Hobbies and other interests:* Stamp collecting.

Addresses

Home—4106 Flora Place, St. Louis, MO 63110. *Agent*—Russell Galen, Scovil-Chichak-Galen Literary Agency, 381 Park Ave. South, Suite 1112, New York, NY 10016.

Career

General Motors Corp., St. Louis, MO, auto assembler at Fisher Body Plant, 1965-67, Chevrolet Army Plant, munitions inspector, 1967-70, material controller, 1970-74, worker in grinding, plastic, and rework, 1974-76, material-control supervisor, 1976-78, truck assembler, 1977-88, auto assembler, 1989-91, worked in auto-electrical and electronics-systems repair, 1991-97. Also

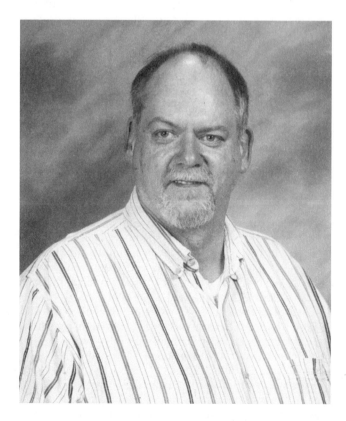

Glen Cook

worked as cook, restaurant manager, janitor, baker's helper, waiter, busboy, fruit packer, clerk, and forklift driver. *Military service:* Served eight years in U.S. Navy and Navy Reserve.

Writings

SCIENCE-FICTION AND FANTASY NOVELS

The Heirs of Babylon, Signet, 1972.
The Swordbearer, Timescape (New York City), 1982.
Passage at Arms, Warner Books, 1985.
A Matter of Time, Ace, 1985.
The Tower of Fear, Tor, 1989.
Sung in Blood, NESFA Press (Cambridge, MA), 1990.

Also author of *The Dragon Never Sleeps,* 1988.

FANTASY NOVELS; "DREAD EMPIRE" SERIES

Shadow of All Night Falling, Berkley, 1979.
October's Baby, Berkley, 1980.
All Darkness Met, Berkley, 1980.
The Fire in His Hands, Pocket, 1984.
With Mercy Toward None, Baen, 1985.
Reap the East Wind, Tor, 1987.
All Ill Fate Marshalling, Tor, 1988.

SCIENCE-FICTION NOVELS; "STARFISHERS" TRILOGY

Shadowline, Warner, 1982.
Starfishers, Warner, 1982.
Stars' End, Warner, 1982.

FANTASY NOVELS; "BLACK COMPANY" SERIES

The Black Company, Tor, 1984.
Shadows Linger, Tor, 1984.
The White Rose, Tor, 1985.
Annals of the Black Company (omnibus; includes *The Black Company, Shadows Linger,* and *The White Rose*) Doubleday, 1986.
Shadow Games, Tor, 1989.
The Silver Spike, Tor, 1989.
Dreams of Steel, Tor, 1990.
Bleak Seasons (first volume of "Glittering Stone" series), Tor, 1996.
She Is the Darkness (second volume of "Glittering Stone" series), Tor, 1997.
Water Sleeps (third volume of "Glittering Stone" series), Tor, 1999.

FANTASY NOVELS; "DARKWAR" TRILOGY

Doomstalker, Warner, 1985.
Warlock, Warner, 1985.
Ceremony, Warner, 1986.

FANTASY/MYSTERY NOVELS; "GARRETT FILES" SERIES

Sweet Silver Blues, New American Library, 1987.
Bitter Gold Hearts, New American Library, 1988.
Cold Copper Tears, New American Library, 1988.
Old Tin Sorrows, New American Library, 1989.
Dread Brass Shadows, Roc (New York City), 1990.
Red Iron Nights, Roc, 1991.
Deadly Quicksilver Lies, Roc, 1993.
Petty Pewter Gods, Roc, 1996.
Faded Steel Heat, New American Library, 1999.

OTHER

(Under pseudonym Greg Stevens) *The Swap Academy,* Publisher's Export Corp. (San Diego), 1970.

Work represented in anthologies, including *Clarion,* edited by Robin Scott Wilson, New American Library, 1971. Contributor to periodicals.

Work in Progress

Soldiers Live, the fourth volume in the "Glittering Stone" series; two novels in the "Garrett Files" series.

Sidelights

Glen Cook has worked a variety of jobs while doubling as an author of fantasy fiction. *St. James Guide to Fantasy Writers* essayist Gary Westfahl called Cook "the working man's fantasy writer" and observed that he "usually focuses his attention on the common people in his fantasy worlds, rather than the upper class." The 1989 novel *The Tower of Fear,* which marked Cook's debut in the hardcover market, was hailed by *Booklist* contributor Roland Green as "a thoroughly impressive effort" containing "grim but meticulous world-building," believable characters, and a "fascinating" plot full of political twists and turns.

Born in 1944, Cook briefly attended the University of Missouri before joining the working world. He got a job on the General Motors assembly line when he was twenty-one and stayed with the large auto-manufacturer in order to support his wife and growing family. Although he found time to indulge in his hobby, writing—Cook published his first book, *The Swap Academy,* pseudonymously in 1970—it wasn't until the early 1980s that he began turning out fantasies at a rapid rate.

Cook's first multi-volume saga is comprised of the novels collectively known as the "Dread Empire" books. This series began with the publication of *Shadow of All Night Falling* in 1979 and has grown to include seven volumes. Set in an imaginary world containing warring regions with parallels to Europe, the Far East, and the Middle East, Cook's "Dread Empire" books were followed by both the "Starfishers" and the "Darkwar" trilogies. The latter features the unusual heroine Marika, a psychic canine creature who is captured and put into the service of a tribe of militaristic witches. A *Booklist* critic commented of *Doomstalker,* the first novel in the "Darkwar" series: "its detailed characters and kinetic action are captivating."

In his fantasy novels, Cook's heroes are everyday people, rather than the wealthy nobles, beautiful princesses, and dashing knights that are typical of the genre. His popular "Black Company" books follow a group of merciless mercenaries who fight for good or evil, depending on which side pays the most. The soldiers are haunted by questions of the group's own origins, and their self-doubt tends to humanize them, making readers see that these soldiers fight out of necessity rather than by a moral choice of evil over good. The company's adventures are narrated by Croaker, a physician/soldier who heals his fellow company-members' battle wounds and who, while seemingly as cruel as the band he cares for, expresses an inner concern over the company's actions through his narration.

The first novel in the series, *The Black Company,* finds the group finishing up a job in the city of Beryl and taking up their next assignment—with a creature known only as Soulcatcher—only to realize that they are now in the employ of an evil force. Weaving ancient magic with down-and-dirty battle scenes, Cook's novel inspired *West Coast Review of Books* contributor Neil K. Citrin to comment: "Unless you're prepared to read for several hours, save this book for the weekend. It will grab you like a moray eel until the last page." Subsequent volumes in the "Black Company" series find evil growing in power, as the Dominator, the most evil of all creatures, prepares to walk once more among the living and turn the Earth into a world of chaos. Ultimately the evil sorceress who now controls the mercenary band, fearful that her petty tyranny will be overthrown, joins with the Black Company on the side of good in an effort to vanquish the Dominator. Reviewing *The White Rose* in *Voice of Youth Advocates,* Pam Spencer declared: "[Cook's] battle scenes are filled with guile and magic and make one want to leap on a flying carpet and unleash an arrow or two."

Cook began the "Black Company" series in 1984 intending it as a trilogy; readers enjoyed the fantastic setting and characters so much that the story has been carried through into nine novels since its debut. Cook has even made a side trip from his "Black Company" saga with the "Glittering Stone" series. In the first part, *Bleak Seasons,* the Black Company accepts a new leader as they work to fight the Shadowmasters, whose armies of demons are currently trapping the Company in the city of Dejagore, while at the same time, rival mercenary-bands within the city's walls wish to rid themselves of competition. While noting that a satisfactory reading of *Bleak Seasons* required fans to be familiar with the premise of the "Black Company" series, *Voice of Youth Advocates* contributor William J. White commented that "while seem[ing] somewhat experimental, playing with point of view shifts and non-linear narrative sequences, [*Bleak Seasons*] is among the best of the Black Company stories." Volume two, *She Is the Darkness* once again takes up the tale of the Company as the group moves closer toward discovery of its mystical origins when it reaches the city of Khatovar. It becomes a race against time, once the Company's demonic enemies begin to kill off members as a way of preventing those origins from being revealed. Bill White, in *Voice of Youth Advocates,* praised the novel's "complex and sophisticated story," and noted that the author "describes the villainy of the Company's antagonists with extraordinary power." Roland Green of *Booklist* called *She Is the Darkness* "wrenchingly realistic in both the details of war and the emotions of the characters."

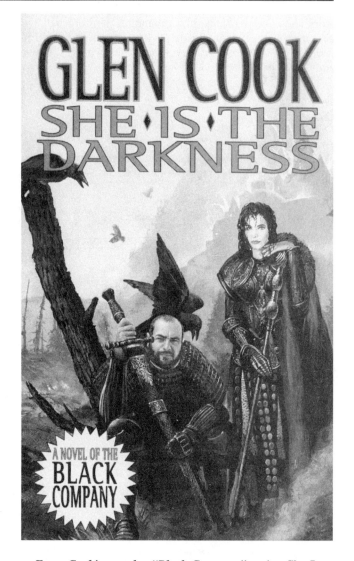

From Cook's popular "Black Company" series, **She Is the Darkness** *explores the uneasy alliance of two groups locked in a battle for dominance. (Cover illustration by Nicholas Jainschigg.)*

Cook changed course slightly in his "Garrett Files" series, which features a hard-boiled private eye as its pivotal character. While Garrett's sleuthing techniques may be familiar to readers, his cases are more unusual—the mysteries he solves involve elves, magicians, trolls, witches, and evil demons. In the 1996 novel *Petty Pewter Gods,* for instance, Garrett must find a key that has been hidden by the Earth's more powerful, dominant gods as a way to play a sort of "musical chairs" with less-powerful deities. The one who finds the key to the temple first gets to stay; the rest of the gods will be vanquished. And in *Cold Copper Tears,* a beautiful blonde woman seduces the hapless P.I. into taking on her case, which results in him taking on both the mob and a cult of fanatics during his search for relics lost by his client. Praising Cook's melding of the mystery and fantasy genres, *Kliatt* contributor Karen S. Ellis commented on the book's "colorful" language, "creative euphemisms," and "earthy humor." Several critics have also compared Cook's "Garrett" mysteries to those of writers like Raymond Chandler and Dashiell Hammett, due to the wry sense of humor Cook conveys in telling his tales. Other books in the "Garrett Files" series include *Bitter Gold Hearts, Red Iron Nights,* and *Sweet Silver Blues.*

Works Cited

Citrin, Neil K., review of *The Black Company, West Coast Review of Books,* July-August, 1984, p. 43.

Review of *Doomstalker, Booklist,* September 1, 1985, p. 31.

Ellis, Karen S., review of *Cold Copper Tears, Kliatt,* January, 1989, pp. 19-20.

Green, Roland, review of *She Is the Darkness, Booklist,* September 15, 1997, p. 216.

Green, review of *The Tower of Fear, Booklist,* September 15, 1989, p. 148.

Spencer, Pam, review of *The White Rose, Voice of Youth Advocates,* February, 1986, p. 393.

Westfahl, Gary, essay in *St. James Guide to Fantasy Writers,* St. James Press, 1996.

White, Bill, review of *She Is the Darkness, Voice of Youth Advocates,* April, 1998, p. 53.

White, William J., review of *Bleak Seasons, Voice of Youth Advocates,* April, 1997, p. 40.

For More Information See

BOOKS

St. James Guide to Science Fiction Writers, St. James Press, 1996, pp. 205-06.

PERIODICALS

Fantasy Review, December, 1984, p. 23; August, 1985, p. 17.

Kirkus Reviews, September 1, 1989, p. 1287; February 1, 1996, p. 181; July 15, 1997, p. 1074.

Kliatt, September, 1984, p. 25; March, 1996, p. 14.

Library Journal, September 15, 1989, p. 138.

Locus, April, 1994, pp. 33, 48.

Publishers Weekly, September 23, 1988, p. 68; March 4, 1996 p. 59; September 22, 1997, p. 74.

Science Fiction Chronicle, May, 1996, p. 57.

Voice of Youth Advocates, October, 1984, p. 205; April, 1996, p. 36.

*   *   *

COPE, Jane U(rsula) 1949-

Personal

Born April 4, 1949, in Portsmouth, England; daughter of Arthur (a naval architect) and Jeanette (Begarnie) Cope; married Ian Jay (a teacher); children: Tom. *Education:* University of Sussex, B.A. (with honors). *Politics:* "Generally left." *Religion:* "Nothing that can be labeled."

Jane U. Cope

Addresses

Home—7 Parkfield Way, Topsham, Exeter, Devon EX3 0DP, England. *Agent*—Linda Rogers, P.O. Box 330, London SE24 9WB, England.

Career

Freelance illustrator, 1979—. Held editorial positions with Egon Ronay and publisher G. Harrap, both London, England.

Awards, Honors

Book Award from *Times Educational Supplement,* 1990, for illustrating *Mathematical Eye.*

Writings

(With Anne Cope, and illustrator) *Leatherwork,* photographs by John Warren, Pan Books (London, England), 1979.

(With A. Cope, and illustrator) *Picture Framing,* photographs by Warren, Pan Books, 1981.

ILLUSTRATOR

Sheila Lane and Marion Kemp, adapters, *The Princess Who Wanted the Moon and Other Stories,* Ward Lock Educational (London), 1982.

Adrian Sington, *Test Your Memory,* Puffin, 1983.

Barbara Gilgallon and Sue Samuels, *The Calendar Quiz Book,* Puffin, 1984.

Adam Hart-Davis, *Scientific Eye,* Bell & Hyman, 1985.

Sheila K. McCullagh, *The Purse Full of Gold,* Collins Educational (London), 1985.

Helen Hollick, *Come and Tell Me,* Parkwest (New York City), 1986.

Frances Lindsay, *The Half-Price Bear,* Hodder & Stoughton (London), 1986.

Bernard Ashley, *Calling for Sam,* Orchard, 1987.

Ashley, *Taller Than Before,* Orchard, 1987.

Frances Lindsay, *Bim, the Very Special Bear,* Hodder & Stoughton, 1987.

Jacqueline Wilson, *Glubbslyme,* Oxford University Press (Oxford, England), 1987.

Paul Temple, *Creepy Crawlies,* Puffin, 1988.

Redmond O'Hanlon, *In Trouble Again,* Hamish Hamilton, 1988.

Bernard Ashley, *Down-and-Out,* Orchard, 1988.

Ashley, *The Royal Visit,* Orchard, 1988.

Ashley, *All I Ever Ask,* Orchard, 1989.

Ashley, *Sally Cinderella,* Orchard, 1989.

Adam Hart-Davis, *Mathematical Eye,* Unwin Hyman, 1989.

Frances Lindsay, *Runaway Bim,* Hodder & Stoughton, 1989.

Ginny Lapage, reteller, *The Basket-Maker's Donkey,* Collins Educational, 1990.

Peter Rowan, *Well, Well, Well,* Puffin (London), 1990.

Lesley Young, *Moorfield Finds a Friend,* Hodder & Stoughton, 1990.

Chris Meade, *Eureka! Finding Out Is Fun,* Puffin, 1991.

Jan Dyson, *Our Day Out,* Collins Educational, 1992.

Lesley Young, *Moorfield and the Forest Thief,* Hodder & Stoughton, 1992.

Janice M. Godfrey, *Who Made the Morning?,* Tamarind (London), 1993.

Eleanor Allen, *The Day Matt Sold Great-Grandma,* A. and C. Black (London), 1994.

Kathleen Crawford, *Have You Seen the Wind?,* Tamarind, 1994, published as *Have You Seen Wind?,* Chariot Victor, 1995.

Jan Mark, *Harriet's Turn,* Longman (Harlow, England), 1994.

Philip Wooderson, *Spooked,* A. and C. Black, 1994.

Karen King, *Where's God?,* Chariot Victor, 1995.

Julie Smart, *Investigating Design,* National Trust (London), 1995.

Susan P. Gates, *Waiting for Goldie,* Oxford University Press, 1996.

Clive Gifford, *The Case of the Toxic Trousers,* Hodder & Stoughton, 1996.

Anthony Wilson, *Space, The Science Museum Book of Amazing Facts,* Hodder Children's, 1996.

Janice M. Godfrey, *The Cherry Blossom Tree: A Grandfather Talks about Life and Death,* Augsburg (Minneapolis, MN), 1996.

Adele Geras, editor, *A Treasury of Jewish Stories,* Kingfisher (New York City), 1996.

Karen King, *Where's the Baby King?,* Standard Publishing (Cincinnati, OH), 1996.

Chris Oxlade, *Constructions,* Hodder & Stoughton, 1997.

John Farndon, *Astronomy, Activators,* Hodder's Children's, 1998.

Alan MacDonald, *The Goalie from Nowhere,* Tree Tops, Oxford University Press, 1998.

Malachy Doyle, *Trapped,* Tree Tops, Oxford University Press, 1999.

Sidelights

Jane U. Cope told *SATA:* "I think it's probably important to mention that I have no formal qualification in art or illustration. I graduated with a good degree in English

Grandfather shares his belief in God and an afterlife while discussing death with five-year-old Harriet in The Cherry Blossom Tree, *written by Jan Godfrey and illustrated by Cope.*

and worked for several years on the editing side of publishing. I left a full-time publishing job in order to travel and sail. When I returned, I started editing as a freelancer for various publishers. I wrote two books (one on picture framing and one on leatherwork), and while writing for another craft publication, I was asked to turn my drawings into finished art work. That's how I started.

"In the beginning, I split my time between freelance editing and a bit of illustration until I found myself an agent in London, in fact my current agent. The skills that I have were practiced and developed through doing the job, rather than training for it! It's not necessarily a route I'd advise anyone to follow; in fact, I regret not having spent time at art college.

"Illustrating is a lonely job, and you have to be self-motivated. One of the most rewarding spinoffs has been talking about my work in local primary schools, and of course my son and several of his friends have been models for various characters I've illustrated. (As our family name is Jay, I always try to include a jay [the bird] somewhere in each book.) We also have a growing collection of stuffed birds and animals, which are great reference material.

"I've never been single-minded enough to make a big career out of drawing. Family and friends are more important—and music, traveling, sailing, caving, cooking, sports—these all take their share of time too.

"I enjoy cartoon illustration. I still find it unbelievable that people pay me for drawing the sorts of silly things I love to draw! But that's only a part of the work I get, and much of the 'straighter' stuff requires a lot of effort and application. There are hundreds of dazzlingly talented illustrators around, and I'm not sure if that's inspirational or downright disheartening! My all-time favorite illustrator has to be Quentin Blake.

"Just recently I've been working on some ideas of my own, and ideally, that's what I want to do—write and illustrate my own stories."

*   *   *

COURTNEY, Dayle
See GOLDSMITH, Howard

*   *   *

COX, Clinton 1934-

Personal

Born June 10, 1934, in Sumter, SC; son of Lafayette Clinton (a Baptist minister) and Magdalene Elizabeth (a librarian; maiden name, Jackson) Cox; married Anita Beatrice Irwin (a telecommunications employee), April 28, 1965. *Education:* Goddard College, B.A., 1970; Columbia University, M.S., 1971. *Politics:* Independent. *Religion:* "Retired Baptist."

Clinton Cox

Addresses

Home—Schenectady, NY. *Electronic mail*—Clintx33@aol.com.

Career

Schenectady Union-Star, Schenectady, NY, reporter, 1968-69; Community News Service, New York City, reporter, 1972-73, city editor, 1974; *New York Daily News,* New York City, staff writer for Sunday magazine, 1974-78, political reporter, 1978-79; freelance magazine writer, 1980-90; *The City Sun,* Brooklyn, NY, columnist, 1990-93; author, 1990—. Advisory board member, Lorraine Hansberry/Robert Nemiroff Archival, Educational, and Cultural Fund. *Member:* Authors Guild.

Awards, Honors

Notable Children's Trade Book in the Field of Social Studies, National Council for the Social Studies and Children's Book Council (NCSS-CBC), for *Undying Glory, The Forgotten Heroes, Mark Twain, Fiery Vision,* and *Come All You Brave Soldiers;* Books for the Teen Age, New York Public Library, 1991, for *Undying Glory,* and 1993, for *Forgotten Heroes;* Books in the Middle: Outstanding Titles of 1995, *Voice of Youth Advocates,* for *Mark Twain.*

Writings

Undying Glory: The Story of the Massachusetts 54th Regiment, Scholastic, 1991.

The Forgotten Heroes: The Story of the Buffalo Soldiers, Scholastic, 1993.

Mark Twain: America's Humorist, Dreamer, Prophet, Scholastic, 1995.

Fiery Vision: The Life and Death of John Brown, Scholastic, 1997.

Come All You Brave Soldiers: Blacks in the Revolutionary War, Scholastic, 1999.

African American Healers, John Wiley, 1999.

African American Teachers, John Wiley, in press.

Work in Progress

Researching the history of black soldiers in the Civil War.

Sidelights

Clinton Cox's nonfiction studies for young adults present a view of American history that was once buried under longstanding prejudices. The longtime journalist, a native of South Carolina who has become a highly regarded writer on multicultural issues in New York City, began his career as an author of books for young people in 1991 with the publication of *Undying Glory: The Story of the Massachusetts 54th Regiment.*

Undying Glory reveals the origins and distinguished service record of the first African-American unit officially recruited in the North to serve in the Civil War. Formed in 1863 by New England abolitionists of both races, the 54th Regiment—whose story was also the basis for the motion-picture film *Glory*—was instrumental in changing attitudes about African-Americans and their patriotism. In *Undying Glory,* Cox explains how many Northerners, while opposed to slavery, had been initially uncomfortable with the notion of African-Americans serving in combat under the American flag. Furthermore, if any member of the 54th Regiment—one of whom was the son of abolitionist Frederick Douglass—had been captured by the Confederate Army of the secessionist Southern states, the prisoner of war would have been treated brutally as a slave who had mutinied. Cox chronicles the soldiers' exploits in battle, and explains how institutionalized racism thwarted and later dismissed their loyalty and valorous record. The men served under a white commander, and were compensated less than their white counterparts. Cox's extensive research, evident in the detailed bibliography, includes an account of the group's 1887 reunion. A *Kirkus Reviews* commentator called *Undying Glory* "a distinguished presentation of the historical record," and commended Cox's retelling of the battle scenes for their "compelling immediacy." Beverly Robertson, writing in *Voice of Youth Advocates,* praised Cox's "refreshingly frank style," and called his debut work "a fine contribution to the history of the Civil War, as well as to the history of racial injustices" in the United States.

Cox returned to the same military topic for his 1993 book *The Forgotten Heroes: The Story of the Buffalo Soldiers,* in which he chronicles the achievements and hardships of the 9th and 10th Cavalry units in the U.S.

Indian Wars in the 1870s and '80s. The Native Americans whom the African-American forces had been sent to fight gave them the tag "Buffalo soldiers," a term of respect for their bravery. As Cox explains, the African-American units had attracted volunteers looking for steady work and pay during a period of economic turmoil in the South, but were assigned menial tasks or dangerous assignments, for which they were provided substandard horses and equipment. Sent to protect white settlers in the West from Native American attacks, the black soldiers were sometimes assailed by the settlers themselves. *Forgotten Heroes* illustrates the ultimate irony of their assignment as an oppressed minority sent to quash Native American independence. Cox concludes his account with the actions of the 9th and 10th Cavalry at the decisive Battle of Wounded Knee in 1890. Lyn Miller-Lachmann, writing in *School Library Journal,* called the book "a thoroughly researched, well-written account," with "writing [that] reflects sensitivity toward the Indians." A *Kirkus Reviews* assessment found Cox's narrative "rich in carefully reconstructed episodes and acts of heroism."

For his next book, *Mark Twain: America's Humorist, Dreamer, Prophet,* Cox attempted to depict another side of the life of the acclaimed American writer. Twain, born Samuel Clemens into a slave-owning family in 1835, was the author of a number of popular books and one of the most famous figures of his era. As Cox explains in his biography, however, Twain was also the author of the controversial novel *Huckleberry Finn,* over which debate still rages about its characterization of African Americans. But Cox highlights how Twain's attitudes toward blacks progressed to the point where he used his eminence to speak forcefully against racism and the evils of slavery; he later endowed scholarships for African-American college students. Cox's work, though discussing Twain's writings in relation to his attitudes on African Americans, follows a chronological structure and steers clear of overt literary analysis. Deborah Stevenson of the *Bulletin of the Center for Children's Books* called *Mark Twain* "a timely, thoughtful, and readable approach" to the celebrated writer.

Cox wrote another biography for young adults, *Fiery Vision: The Life and Death of John Brown,* that chronicles the exploits of the leader of the most infamous anti-slavery revolt in the history of the antebellum South, in which radical abolitionists led by activist Brown seized the U.S. Arsenal at Harper's Ferry, Virginia. Cox's *Come All You Brave Soldiers: Blacks in the Revolutionary War* explores a rich source of forgotten subject matter in an account of the 5,000 blacks who fought for American independence against fierce Iroquois neighbors as well as British redcoats. Cox reveals their participation in and contributions to every major battle of the war, though the idea of blacks serving in the armed forces at that time was controversial: the text includes less-than-flattering portrayals of the attitudes of Presidents George Washington and Thomas Jefferson on the matter. Some of the black Revolutionary soldiers had enlisted outright, while others were slaves who were sent throughout the

Cox explores a forgotten subject in his account of the five-thousand blacks who fought for American independence against fierce Iroquois neighbors and British redcoats.

colonies to fight, but as Cox explains, the South feared slave revolts if blacks were exposed to military discipline. During and after the war, African Americans were treated shamefully despite their valor. Again, Cox's scholarship and lucid prose won praise from reviewers. In a *School Library Journal* review, Elaine Fort Weischedel compared *Come All You Brave Soldiers* to a few other books on the same topic, and found Cox's book a "superior treatment of an important subject." A *Kirkus Reviews* commentator maintained: "In addition to paying tribute to some overlooked figures, this book also demonstrates why one historical account is never enough to establish the facts, and the surprises to be found in good research."

Cox told *SATA:* "Growing up as an African American child who loved to read and was curious about American history, I was always puzzled by the absence of African Americans from the history books. I heard stories from my father, a chaplain for an all-black army unit, and other black veterans about their experiences in World War II, and yet I could not find those experiences in books or in the movies.

"As I grew older, I became determined to do all I could to see that other generations of youngsters would be able to find those experiences in books. Young people are hungry for the truth about themselves and the society they live in. There is a special hunger among those children who have been confined to the margins of society, whether they are African Americans, Native Americas, Latinos or poor whites.

"Every book I do is about a historical subject that has rarely, if ever, been told from the point of view of African Americans, even though they helped create that history. I have received many letters from both young people and adults thanking me for telling them about aspects of American history they had never heard of before. I hope to keep writing about these largely untold parts of our history, and bringing the truth to more readers."

Works Cited

Review of *Come All You Brave Soldiers, Kirkus Reviews,* December 1, 1998.

Review of *Forgotten Heroes, Kirkus Reviews,* December 1, 1993, p. 1521.

Miller-Lachmann, Lyn, review of *Forgotten Heroes, School Library Journal,* December, 1993, p. 142.

Robertson, Beverly, review of *Undying Glory, Voice of Youth Advocates,* December, 1991, p. 334.

Stevenson, Deborah, review of *Mark Twain, Bulletin of the Center for Children's Books,* September, 1995, p. 11.

Review of *Undying Glory, Kirkus Reviews,* October 1, 1991, p. 1285.

Weischedel, Elaine Fort, review of *Come All You Brave Soldiers, School Library Journal,* February, 1999, p. 115.

For More Information See

PERIODICALS

Booklist, February 15, 1999, p. 106.

Bulletin of the Center for Children's Books, January, 1992, pp. 121-22.

Voice of Youth Advocates, December, 1995, p. 322; April, 1999.

Wilson Library Bulletin, March, 1992.

D

DALTON, Sheila

Personal

Born in Middlesex, England; daughter of Christopher William (a contract administrator) and Vola Molly (a government office manager) Dalton; married Gordon Wyatt, 1982; children: Adam Dalton-Wyatt. *Education:* B.A. (Honors English), M.L.S. *Politics:* Liberal/Socialist. *Religion:* Agnostic. *Hobbies and other interests:* Insight meditation, herbalism, psychoanalysis, and psychology.

Sheila Dalton

Addresses

Home—Newmarket, Ontario, Canada. *Agent*—Carolyn Swayze. *E-mail*—sagespirit@hotmail.com.

Career

Freelance editor and reference librarian, 1982—. Previous positions include craftsperson, bartender and art gallery assistant. *Member:* The Writers' Union of Canada, League of Canadian Poets, Canadian Poetry Association, Canadian Society of Children's Authors, Illustrators, and Performers (CANSCAIP), Canadian Alliance in Solidarity with the Native Peoples.

Awards, Honors

"Our Choice" Award, Canadian Children's Book Centre, 1996, for *Doggerel;* "Our Choice" Award, Canadian Children's Book Centre, and shortlist for the Arthur Ellis Award, Juvenile Mystery category, Crime Writers of Canada, 1999, for *Trial by Fire;* Short Fiction Prize, Cross-Canadian Writers' Quarterly, 1984, for "Dreams of Freedom, Dreams of Need"; Runner-up, Kalamalka New Writers Society Award for book-length poetry manuscript, for *Blowing Holes through the Everyday.*

Writings

FOR CHILDREN

Bubblemania, illustrated by Bob Beeson, Orca Book Publishers (Victoria, British Columbia, Canada), 1992.

Doggerel, illustrated by Kim LaFave, Doubleday (Toronto, Ontario), 1996.

Catalogue, illustrated by Kim LaFave, Doubleday, 1998.

Trial by Fire (young adult), Napoleon Publications (Toronto), 1998.

Pig Tale, Doubleday, in press.

Contributor of titles *Leopards, Orangutans,* and *Gazelles* to the "Nature's Children" series, and *Japan* to the "Children of Other Lands" series, both published by Grolier. Also contributed entries to the "Discovery" series of science topics published by Houghton Mifflin Canada.

FOR ADULTS

Blowing Holes through the Everyday (poetry), HMS Press (London, Ontario), 1993.
Tales of the Ex Fire-Eater: A Novel, Aurora Editions (Winnipeg, Alberta), 1994.

Work in Progress

A novel for adults entitled *The Girl in the Box.*

Sidelights

Many of Canadian author and poet Sheila Dalton's works have been aimed at a juvenile audience. The author of the picture books *Bubblemania, Doggerel,* and *Catalogue,* Dalton is also the author of the adult novel *Tales of the Ex Fire-Eater,* and a poetry collection for adults entitled *Blowing Holes through the Everyday.*

Dalton's *Bubblemania,* with illustrations by Bob Beeson, is a counting book that relates the tale of David, a young boy who blows a big bubble that eventually traps his friends, relatives, and much of his town. To save his loved ones, David takes it upon himself to pop his wondrous creation. *Bubblemania* met with genial reviews. Rhea Tregebov in *Books in Canada* thought that the book's illustrations were somewhat "hectic," but praised Dalton's work as "energetic." Tregebov also noted that the story is suitable for all age groups, from "toddlers ... learning to count," to preschoolers learning to read and "early readers." Catherine McInerney in *Canadian Materials* hailed *Bubblemania's* "imaginative text," while Janet McNaughton in *Quill and Quire* concluded: "*Bubblemania* is not only a good counting book, it's the best one I've seen in a while."

In 1996, Dalton's *Doggerel* became available to child audiences. The book features illustrations of many different breeds and types of dogs done by Kim LaFave, with Dalton's light-hearted rhyming verses accompanying the pictures. This effort, too, met with rave reviews. Steve Pitt in the *Canadian Book Review Annual* announced that the author's "rhyme and rhythm standards [are] consistently high" in *Doggerel* while remaining "delightfully silly."

In the same vein, *Catalogue* showcases cats of all shapes, sizes, and attitudes. Commenting about *Catalogue* on Amazon.com, Dalton said, "I wrote *Catalogue* because I love cats, and I'd already written a kid's book about dogs, so I had to be fair!" Dalton went on to say that the book is a rhyming list of cats, "the snide, the cross-eyed, the clean and the lean, the furry and purry—even the brash, succotash.... I also wrote the book because I know kids like cats, and also want to learn to read, but in a fun way—and *Catalogue* has lots of words they can guess, and harder ones they can learn about in context, and a real bouncy rhythm I hope they enjoy."

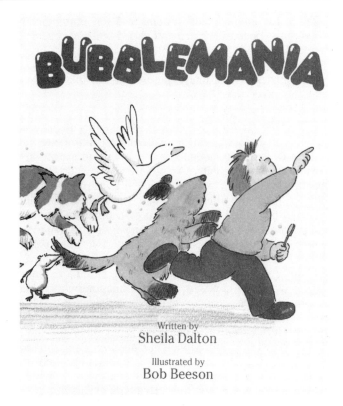

David blows a bubble so big that he must choose between the bubble and his family and neighbors in Dalton's whimsical counting book. (Illustrated by Bob Beeson.)

Dalton's young adult novel, *Trial by Fire,* is the story of a seventeen-year-old half-Cree boy named Nathan who tries to escape his past as well as his present. Nathan attempts to cope with people's prejudice while never having known his Native American father. When he meets Sally, Nathan thinks he has found someone who believes in him, but when Sally's house is set on fire, Nathan is considered a suspect. The boy then finds himself caught up in a tale of mystery and murder. Writing on Amazon.com, Dalton said: "I wrote this book because my husband is half-Cree, and he told me lots of stories about the Native American side of his family—how his grandmother starved to death on a reservation; how his father was adopted by white people in Saskatchewan; and how prejudice dogged his father's life. It was hard to listen to some of the stories, but fascinating, too. It made me think once again about prejudice and how hard it is to grow up feeling 'different.' It made me want to write a book that would be exciting and interesting, as well as thought provoking."

Blowing Holes Through the Everyday, Dalton's poetry collection for adults, discusses topics such as medical tests, being a tourist, and why some women sexually tease men. Bert Almon in *Canadian Book Review Annual* notes that Dalton includes a preface to this work in which she puts forth her theory that poetry offers the reader a connection to life's enigmas. Almon felt that the volume "assume[s] the mystery" more than it provides the reader an experience of it, but he did concede that

"Dalton has talent." Mark Young in *Scene* commented: "[Dalton's] poetry is as rich and varied . . . as any recent works I've read. She is capable of many poetic voices, yet is still able to imprint them with her own voice, which makes extraordinary these poems of the ordinary and the 'everyday.'"

Tales of the Ex Fire-Eater is no literary metaphor. The heroine of the book, whose real name is Antoinette but who is called Fido, actually is attempting to escape her past as a circus fire-eater. Antoinette is only fourteen but has lived with the circus all of her life, at first with her mother, then solo after her mother's disappearance. Her bisexual boyfriend, in training to be a tightrope walker, talks her into leaving with him and living in Toronto, where he abandons her for another boy. Eventually, Antoinette returns to the circus. Writing about the novel on Amazon.com, Dalton stated: "It's based on many experiences, and none—it is a very 'imaginary tale', but it came about because of real people and events . . . . It's my first novel, and one I'm very glad was published because it represents a younger me I may otherwise have lost touch with." Janet Money in *Canadian Book Review Annual* hailed the novel as "a fascinating web of characters and symbols" and predicted that it "would probably make a good film." Eva Tihanyi in *Books in Canada* praised *Tales of the Ex Fire-Eater* as well, citing "the remarkable consciousness of Antoinette herself" as superseding even the "wealth of colourful secondary characters."

Dalton once commented: "People sometimes ask me if I prefer writing for children or for adults. And I answer that I like both, for very different reasons. They seem to come from different parts of the psyche. Writing for diverse age groups keeps me in touch with different stages of life. Certainly, writing for children helps me create young characters in my books for adults, and vice-versa."

Works Cited

Almon, Bert, review of *Blowing Holes through the Everyday, Canadian Book Review Annual,* 1994, pp. 204-05.

Dalton, Sheila, commenting on *Catalogue,* Amazon.com, http://www.amazon.com (April 6, 1999).

Dalton, Sheila, commenting on *Tales of the Ex Fire-Eater,* Amazon.com, http://www.amazon.com (April 6, 1999).

Dalton, Sheila, commenting on *Trial by Fire,* Amazon.com, http://www.amazon.com (April 23, 1999).

McInerney, Catherine, review of *Bubblemania, Canadian Materials,* September, 1992, p. 207.

McNaughton, Janet, review of *Bubblemania, Quill and Quire,* May, 1992, p. 32.

Money, Janet, review of *Tales of the Ex Fire-Eater, Canadian Book Review Annual,* 1995, pp. 165-66.

Pitt, Steve, review of *Doggerel, Canadian Book Review Annual,* 1996, pp. 496-97.

Tihanyi, Eva, review of *Tales of the Ex Fire-Eater, Books in Canada,* October, 1995, p. 51.

Tregebov, Rhea, review of *Bubblemania, Books in Canada,* summer, 1992, p. 36.

Young, Mark, review of *Blowing Holes through the Everyday, Scene,* May-June, 1994, p. 8.

For More Information See

PERIODICALS

Quill and Quire, April, 1996, p. 38.

* * *

DEDMAN, Stephen 1959-

Personal

Born June 27, 1959, in Adelaide, South Australia; son of Kenneth John (an aircraft-engine fitter) and Janice Rae (a teacher; maiden name, McQueen) Dedman; married Elaine Kemp, August 28, 1993. *Education:* Curtin University, B.A. (English), and graduate diploma (writing). *Politics:* "Green." *Religion:* Agnostic. *Hobbies and other interests:* Travel, attending science-fiction conventions.

Addresses

Office—P.O. Box 276, Bayswater, Western Australia 6933. *Agent*—Richard Curtis, 171 East 7th St., New York, NY 10021. *E-mail*—dedmans@perth.dialix.oz.au.

Stephen Dedman

Career

Writer; actor, 1983-90; bookseller, 1985—; editorial assistant, 1987-94. *Eidolon* magazine, associate editor; Perth Writer's Festival, member of advisory committee, 1997-2001. *Member:* Science Fiction and Fantasy Writers of America; Horror Writers Association.

Writings

The Art of Arrow Cutting (novel), Tor (New York City), 1997.
Bone Hunters: On the Trail of Dinosaurs: An Extraordinary Story, Omnibus (Norwood, South Australia), 1998.
The Lady of Situations (short-fiction collection), Ticonderoga (Nedlands, Western Australia), 1999.

Also contributor of fiction to periodicals.

Work in Progress

Shadows Bite, a sequel to *The Art of Arrow Cutting; The Real Dracula,* young-adult nonfiction.

Sidelights

After twenty years of writing science-fiction and horror stories, Australian author Stephen Dedman had his first novel, *The Art of Arrow Cutting,* published by Tor Books. *The Art of Arrow Cutting* features protagonist Michelangelo Magistrale—known to his friends as Mage. Mage meets an alluring woman named Amanda Sharmon, who gives him the keys to her apartment after meeting him at a Greyhound bus station. While staying there, however, he is nearly killed by someone who claims to be looking for Amanda. Convinced he must warn Amanda of the danger, Mage embarks on an odyssey that covers much of the North-American continent. Along the way, he and the reader meet up with several interesting characters, including an actor and Japanese-demon expert, as well as a former professional basketball player-turned defense attorney. Mage also discovers that Amanda's key is the source of a magical power, known as "the focus," which he now possesses. Susan Hamburger, writing in *Library Journal,* applauded Dedman for the way he mixes "Japanese magic, organized crime, mystery, and memorable characters" in the novel. A critic for *Publishers Weekly* predicted that the book "should appeal to readers who enjoy urban fantasies of the sort made popular by Charles de Lint, Megan Lindholm and Emma Bull," while *Voice of Youth Advocates* contributor Laura Lent declared: "The power—the focus—draw one and all into its web of intrigue."

Dedman told *SATA:* "I began writing for fun when I was eight years old, because I loved stories, especially science-fiction and horror stories, and I lived half a mile from the nearest library and even further from any bookshop. I've always preferred to write the sort of story that I'd like to read, books that I'd buy if I saw them on the shelf, and while some of my work is suitable for children, much of my fiction isn't. While children and teenagers and adults all appreciate a good story and strong characters, they don't live in the same universe, and they don't have the same fears. Most adults have forgotten how it feels to live surrounded by mysteries and magic and giants, so they need the sort of stories I usually write much more than children do. When I do write for children, I prefer to tell true stories.

"*Bone Hunters* is the sort of book I would have loved to read when I was ten years old, but it's more than that; it's an attempt to show scientists, working in a field that fascinates most children, as human beings—fulfilling childhood dreams, having fun, occasionally playing jokes, but also working hard.

"My own working habits are straightforward; I set out to write a thousand words a day, minimum, and finish and submit one piece per month, usually a short story, even when I'm writing a novel or another book as well. I had many jobs before becoming a full-time writer, a few of them interesting, and my advice to anyone who wants to write is simple: write whenever you can. Write short stories—they're a good way to learn your craft—and set yourself deadlines to finish and submit them. Find yourself a good first reader who's not scared to criticise your work (I married mine). Read widely, but don't just write about what you read. See the world."

Works Cited

Review of *The Art of Arrow Cutting, Publishers Weekly,* May 19, 1997, p. 71.
Hamburger, Susan, review of *The Art of Arrow Cutting,* Library Journal, June 15, 1997, p. 101.
Lent, Laura, review of *The Art of Arrow Cutting, Voice of Youth Advocates,* December, 1997, pp. 323-24.

For More Information See

PERIODICALS

Kirkus Reviews, April 15, 1997, p. 596.
Voice of Youth Advocates, April, 1998, p. 12.

*   *   *

dePAOLA, Thomas Anthony 1934-
(Tomie dePaola)

Personal

Some sources cite surname as de Paola; name pronounced "Tommy de-*pow*la"; born September 15, 1934, in Meriden, CT; son of Joseph N. (a union official) and Florence (Downey) dePaola; married briefly in the late 1950s (marriage dissolved). *Education:* Pratt Institute, B.F.A., 1956; California College of Arts and Crafts, M.F.A., 1969; Lone Mountain College, doctoral equivalency, 1970. *Religion:* Roman Catholic.

Thomas Anthony dePaola

Addresses

Home—New London, NH. *Office*—c/o The Putnam & Grosset Book Group, 200 Madison Ave., New York, NY 10016.

Career

Author and illustrator of books for children. Professional artist and designer, and teacher of art, 1956—. Creative director of Whitebird Books, his imprint at publisher G. P. Putnam's Sons. Newton College of the Sacred Heart, Newton, MA, instructor, 1962-63, assistant professor of art, 1963-66; San Francisco College for Women (now Lone Mountain College), San Francisco, CA, assistant professor of art, 1967-70; Chamberlayne Junior College, Boston, MA, instructor in art, 1972-73; Colby-Sawyer College, New London, NH, associate professor, designer, and technical director in speech and theater department, writer and designer of sets and costumes for Children's Theatre Project, 1973-76; New England College, Henniker, NH, associate professor of art, 1976-78, artist-in-residence, 1978-79. Painter and muralist, with many of his works done for Catholic churches and monasteries in New England. Designer of greeting cards, posters, magazine and catalog covers, record album covers, and theater and nightclub sets. DePaola has also conducted workshops on children's literature, has made many school visits, and has been a guest artist on several episodes of the television program *Barney. Exhibitions:* Exhibitor in one-man shows in Arizona, Louisiana, Massachusetts, Minnesota, Nevada, New Jersey, New Hampshire, New York, and Vermont. Exhibitor at group shows in galleries, museums, libraries, and other venues in California, Colorado, Connecticut, Florida, Maine, Massachusetts, New Hampshire, New York, Ohio, Texas, Vermont, and Virginia as well as in Italy and Japan. Works are also included in many private collections. *Member:* Society of Children's Book Writers (member of board of directors), Authors Guild, National Advisory Council of the Children's Theater Company of Minneapolis, MN, Ballet of the Dolls Dance Company (member of board of directors), Minneapolis, MN.

Awards, Honors

Boston Art Directors' Club awards for typography and illustration, 1968; Child Study Association children's book of the year citations, 1968, for *Poetry for Chuckles and Grins,* 1971, for *John Fisher's Magic Book,* 1974, for *David's Window* and *Charlie Needs a Cloak,* and 1975, for *Strega Nona* and *Good Morning to You, Valentine,* 1986, for *Strega Nona's Magic Lessons, Tattie's River Journey, Tomie dePaola's Mother Goose,* and *The Quilt Story,* 1987, for *Teeny Tiny* and *Tomie dePaola's Favorite Nursery Tales;* Franklin Typographers Silver Award for poster design, 1969; three books included in American Institute of Graphic Arts exhibit of outstanding children's books: *The Journey of the Kiss,* 1970, *Who Needs Holes?,* 1973, and *Helga's Dowry,* 1979; two books included on *School Library Journal's* list of best picture books: *Andy, That's My Name,* 1973, and *Charlie Needs a Cloak,* 1974; Friends of American Writers Award as best illustrator of a children's book, 1973, for *Authorized Autumn Charts of the Upper Red Canoe River Country;* two books chosen as Children's Book Showcase titles: *Authorized Autumn Charts of the Upper Red Canoe River Country,* 1973, and *Charlie Needs a Cloak,* 1975; Brooklyn Art Books for Children Award, Brooklyn Museum and Brooklyn Public Library, 1975, for *Charlie Needs a Cloak,* and 1977, 1978, and 1979, for *Strega Nona,* which was also named a Caldecott Honor Book, 1976, and received the Nakamore Prize (Japan), 1978; *The Quicksand Book* and *Simple Pictures Are Best* were both chosen one of *School Library Journal's* Best Books for Spring, 1977; Chicago Book Clinic Award, 1979, for *The Christmas Pageant;* Children's Choice by the International Reading Association and the Children's Book Council, 1978, for *Helga's Dowry,* 1979, for *The Popcorn Book, Pancakes for Breakfast, The Clown of God, Four Scary Stories, Jamie's Tiger,* and *Bill and Pete,* 1980, for *Big Anthony and the Magic Ring* and *Oliver Button Is a Sissy,* 1982, for *The Comic Adventures of Old Mother Hubbard and Her Dog,* 1983, for *Strega Nona's Magic Lessons,* 1984, for *The Carsick Zebra and Other Animal Riddles,* 1985, for *The Mysterious Giant of Barletta;* Garden State Children's Book Award for Younger Nonfiction, New Jersey Library Association, 1980, for *The Quicksand Book;* Golden Kite Award for Illustration, Society of Children's Book Writers, 1982, for *Giorgio's Village,* and 1983, for *Marianna May and Nursey; Boston Globe-Horn Book* Award Honor Book for Illustration, 1982, and Critici in Erba commendation from Bologna Biennale, 1983, both for *The Friendly Beasts; Sing, Pierrot, Sing* was chosen one of *School*

Library Journal's Best Books, 1983; *Mary Had a Little Lamb* was chosen as a Notable Book by the Association of Library Service to Children (American Library Association), 1984; *The Clown of God* was selected a Notable Children's Film, 1984; *Sing, Pierrot, Sing* was selected a Notable Children's Trade Book in the Field of Social Studies by the National Council of Social Studies and the Children's Book Council, 1984, and *The Mysterious Giant of Barletta*, 1985; Award from the Bookbuilders West Book Show, 1985, for *Miracle on 34th Street; Redbook* Children's Picturebook Award Honorable Mention, 1986, for *Tomie dePaola's Favorite Nursery Tales; Horn Book* Honor List citation, 1986, for *Tomie dePaola's Mother Goose;* Golden Kite Honor Book for Illustration, 1987, for *What the Mailman Brought; The Art Lesson* was named one of the *New York Times* best picture books of the year, 1989. Several of dePaola's works were named Junior Literary Guild selections: *Charlie Needs a Cloak*, 1973; *Watch Out for the Chicken Feet in Your Soup*, 1974; *This Is the Ambulance Leaving the Zoo*, 1975; *Simple Pictures Are Best*, 1977; *Bill and Pete* and *The Popcorn Book*, both 1978; *Flicks*, 1979; *The Giants Go Camping*, 1979; *The Comic Adventures of Old Mother Hubbard and Her Dog*, 1981; *What the Mailman Saw*, 1987. DePaola has also received awards for his body of work: the Kerlan Award, University of Minnesota, 1981, for "singular attainment in children's literature"; the Regina Medal, Catholic Library Association, 1983, for "continued distinguished contribution to children's literature"; the David McCord Children's Literature Citation, 1986; the Smithson Medal, 1990; the Helen Keating Ott Award, 1993; the University of Southern Mississippi Medallion, 1995; and the Keene State College Children's Literature Festival Award, 1998. In 1990, dePaola was the American nominee in illustration for the Hans Christian Andersen Award, International Board on Books for Young People (IBBY).

Writings

FOR CHILDREN; UNDER NAME TOMIE dePAOLA

Criss-Cross, Applesauce, illustrated by B. A. King and his children, Addison House, 1979.
(Reteller) *The Legend of the Persian Carpet*, illustrated by Claire Ewart, Putnam, 1993.

AUTHOR AND ILLUSTRATOR; AUTOBIOGRAPHICAL AND SEMIAUTOBIOGRAPHICAL WORKS; PICTURE BOOKS, EXCEPT AS NOTED

Nana Upstairs and Nana Downstairs, Putnam, 1973, republished with full-color illustrations, Putnam, 1998.
Watch Out for the Chicken Feet in Your Soup, Prentice-Hall, 1974.
Oliver Button Is a Sissy, Harcourt, 1979.
Now One Foot, Now the Other, Putnam, 1981.
The Art Lesson, Putnam, 1989.
Tom, Putnam, 1993.
The Baby Sister, Putnam, 1996.
26 Fairmount Avenue: A Chapter Book (story), Putnam, 1999.

"STREGA NONA" SERIES; PICTURE BOOKS

Strega Nona: An Old Tale, Prentice-Hall, 1975, published as *The Magic Pasta Pot*, Hutchinson (London), 1979, and as *Strega Nona Classic Board Book*, Simon & Schuster, 1997.
Big Anthony and the Magic Ring, Harcourt, 1979.
Strega Nona's Magic Lessons, Harcourt, 1982.
Merry Christmas, Strega Nona, Harcourt, 1986.
Strega Nona Meets Her Match, Putnam, 1993.
Strega Nona: Her Story, Putnam, 1996.
Big Anthony: His Story, Putnam, 1998.

"BILL AND PETE" SERIES; PICTURE BOOKS

Bill and Pete, Putnam, 1978.
Bill and Pete Go Down the Nile, Putnam, 1987.
Bill and Pete to the Rescue, Putnam, 1998.

"KITTEN KIDS" SERIES; BOARD BOOKS

Pajamas for Kit, Simon & Schuster, 1986.
Katie and Kit at the Beach, Simon & Schuster, 1986.
Katie's Good Idea, Simon & Schuster, 1986.
Katie, Kit and Cousin Tom, Simon & Schuster, 1986.
Tomie dePaola's Kitten Kids and the Big Camp-Out, D & R Animation, 1988.
Tomie dePaola's Kitten Kids and the Haunted House, D & R Animation, 1988.
Tomie dePaola's Kitten Kids and the Missing Dinosaur, D & R Animation, 1988.
Tomie dePaola's Kitten Kids and the Treasure Hunt, D & R Animation, 1988.

OTHER BOOKS FOR CHILDREN; PICTURE BOOKS, CONCEPT BOOKS, RETELLINGS, ADAPTATIONS, AND COMPILATIONS

The Wonderful Dragon of Timlin, Bobbs-Merrill, 1966.
Fight the Night, Lippincott, 1968.
Joe and the Snow, Hawthorn, 1968.
Parker Pig, Esquire, Hawthorn, 1969.
The Journey of the Kiss, Hawthorn, 1970.
The Monsters' Ball, Hawthorn, 1970.
(Reteller) *The Wind and the Sun*, Ginn, 1972, reissued by Silver Press, 1995.
Andy, That's My Name, Prentice-Hall, 1973.
Charlie Needs a Cloak, Prentice-Hall, 1973.
The Unicorn and the Moon, Ginn, 1973, reissued by Silver Press, 1995.
The Cloud Book: Word and Pictures, Holiday House, 1975.
Michael Bird-Boy, Prentice-Hall, 1975.
Things to Make and Do for Valentine's Day, Watts, 1976.
When Everyone Was Fast Asleep, Holiday House, 1976.
Four Stories for Four Seasons, Prentice-Hall, 1977.
Helga's Dowry: A Troll Love Story, Harcourt, 1977.
The Quicksand Book, Holiday House, 1977.
The Christmas Pageant, Winston, 1978, published as *The Christmas Pageant Cutout Book*, 1980.
(Reteller) *The Clown of God: An Old Story*, Harcourt, 1978.
Pancakes for Breakfast, Harcourt, 1978.
The Popcorn Book, Holiday House, 1978.
Flicks, Harcourt, 1979.
The Kids' Cat Book, Holiday House, 1979.
Songs of the Fog Maiden, Holiday House, 1979.
The Family Christmas Tree Book, Holiday House, 1980.

The Knight and the Dragon, Putnam, 1980.

The Lady of Guadalupe, Holiday House, 1980.

(Reteller) *The Legend of the Old Befana: An Italian Christmas Story,* Harcourt, 1980.

(Reteller) *The Prince of the Dolomites: An Old Italian Tale,* Harcourt, 1980.

The Comic Adventures of Old Mother Hubbard and Her Dog, Harcourt, 1981.

(Reteller) *Fin M'Coul, the Giant of Knockmany Hill,* Holiday House, 1981.

The Friendly Beasts: An Old English Christmas Carol, Putnam, 1981.

The Hunter and the Animals: A Wordless Picture Book, Holiday House, 1981.

Francis, the Poor Man of Assisi, Holiday House, 1982.

Giorgio's Village: A Pop-up Book, Putnam, 1982.

(Reteller) *The Legend of the Bluebonnet: An Old Tale of Texas,* Putnam, 1983.

Marianna May and Nursey, Holiday House, 1983.

(Reteller) *Noah and the Ark,* Winston, 1983.

Sing, Pierrot, Sing: A Picture Book in Mime, Harcourt, 1983.

(Reteller) *The Story of the Three Wise Kings,* Putnam, 1983.

(Reteller) *David and Goliath,* Winston, 1984.

(Reteller) *Esther Saves Her People,* Winston, 1984.

The First Christmas: A Festive Pop-Up Book, Putnam, 1984.

(Reteller) *The Mysterious Giant of Barletta: An Italian Folktale,* Harcourt, 1984.

Tomie dePaola's Country Farm, Putnam, 1984.

Tomie dePaola's Mother Goose Story Streamers, Putnam, 1984.

Tomie dePaola's Mother Goose (also see below), Putnam, 1985.

(With others) *Once Upon a Time: Celebrating the Magic of Children's Books in Honor of the Twentieth Anniversary of Reading Is Fundamental,* Putnam, 1986.

(Reteller) *Queen Esther,* Winston, 1986, revised edition, Harper, 1987.

Tomie dePaola's Favorite Nursery Tales, Putnam, 1986.

An Early American Christmas, Holiday House, 1987.

(Adapter) *The Miracles of Jesus,* Holiday House, 1987.

(Adapter) *The Parables of Jesus,* Holiday House, 1987.

Tomie dePaola's Book of Christmas Carols, Putnam, 1987.

Tomie dePaola's Diddle, Diddle, Dumpling and Other Poems and Stories from Mother Goose (selections from *Tomie dePaola's Mother Goose*), Methuen (London), 1987.

Tomie dePaola's Three Little Kittens and Other Poems and Songs from Mother Goose (selections from *Tomie dePaola's Mother Goose*), Methuen, 1987.

Baby's First Christmas, Putnam, 1988.

Hey Diddle Diddle: And Other Mother Goose Rhymes (selections from *Tomie dePaola's Mother Goose*), Putnam, 1988.

Tomie dePaola's Book of Poems, Putnam, 1988.

(With others) *The G.O.S.H. ABC Book,* Aurum Books for Children (England), 1988.

The Legend of the Indian Paintbrush, Putnam, 1988.

Bob and Bobby, Puffin (London), 1988.

Haircuts for the Woolseys, Putnam, 1989.

My First Chanukah, Putnam, 1989.

Tony's Bread: An Italian Folktale, Putnam, 1989.

Too Many Hopkins, Putnam, 1989.

Little Grunt and the Big Egg: A Prehistoric Fairy Tale, Holiday House, 1990.

(Reteller) *Tomie dePaola's Book of Bible Stories,* Putnam/Zondervan, 1990.

My First Easter, Putnam, 1991.

My First Passover, Putnam, 1991.

My First Halloween, Putnam, 1991.

Bonjour, Mr. Satie, Putnam, 1991.

(With others) *To Ride a Butterfly,* Bantam, 1991.

Jamie O'Rourke and the Big Potato: An Irish Folktale, Putnam, 1992.

Patrick: Patron Saint of Ireland, Holiday House, 1992.

My First Thanksgiving, Putnam, 1992.

Jingle, the Christmas Clown, Putnam, 1992.

(With others) *The Big Book for Our Planet,* Dutton, 1993.

Christopher: The Holy Giant, Holiday House, 1994.

The Legend of the Poinsettia, Putnam, 1994.

Kit and Kat, Grosset & Dunlap, 1994.

Tomie dePaola's Book of the Old Testament (selections from *Tomie dePaola's Book of Bible Stories*), Putnam, 1995.

Country Angel, Country Christmas, Putnam, 1995.

Mary: The Mother of Jesus, Holiday House, 1995.

The Bubble Factory, Grosset & Dunlap, 1996.

Get Dressed, Santa!, Grosset & Dunlap, 1996.

Days of the Blackbird: A Tale of Northern Italy, Putnam, 1997.

Tomie's Little Mother Goose Board Book, Putnam, 1997.

Tomie dePaola's Make Your Own Christmas Cards, Price Stern Sloan, 1998.

Las Posadas, Putnam, 1999.

ILLUSTRATOR; UNDER NAME TOMIE dePAOLA

Lisa Miller (pseudonym of Bernice Kohn Hunt) *Sound,* Coward, 1965.

Pura Belpre, *The Tiger and the Rabbit and Other Tales,* Lippincott, 1965.

Lisa Miller, *Wheels,* Coward, 1965.

Jeanne B. Hardendorff, editor, *Tricky Peik and Other Picture Tales,* Lippincott, 1967.

Joan M. Lexau, *Finders Keepers, Losers Weepers,* Lippincott, 1967.

Melvin L. Alexenberg, *Sound Science,* Prentice-Hall, 1968.

James A. Eichner, *The Cabinet of the President of the United States,* Watts, 1968.

Leland B. Jacobs, compiler, *Poetry for Chuckles and Grins,* Garrard, 1968.

M. L. Alexenberg, *Light and Sight,* Prentice-Hall, 1969.

Robert Bly, *The Morning Glory,* Kayak, 1969.

Sam and Beryl Epstein, *Take This Hammer,* Hawthorn, 1969.

Mary C. Jane, *The Rocking-Chair Ghost,* Lippincott, 1969.

Nina Schneider, *Hercules, the Gentle Giant,* Hawthorn, 1969.

Eleanor Boylan, *How to Be a Puppeteer,* McCall, 1970.

Duncan Emrich, editor, *The Folklore of Love and Courtship,* American Heritage Press, 1970.

Duncan Emrich, editor, *The Folklore of Weddings and Marriage,* American Heritage Press, 1970.

Sam and Beryl Epstein, *Who Needs Holes?,* Hawthorn, 1970.

Joey is embarrassed by his old-fashioned Italian grandmother until his friend thoroughly enjoys visiting her. (*From* Watch Out for the Chicken Feet in Your Soup, *written and illustrated by dePaola.*)

Barbara Rinkoff, *Rutherford T. Finds 21B,* Putnam, 1970.

Philip Balestrino, *Hot as an Ice Cube,* Crowell, 1971.

Sam and Beryl Epstein, *Pick It Up,* Holiday House, 1971.

John Fisher, *John Fisher's Magic Book,* Prentice-Hall, 1971.

William Wise, *Monsters of the Middle Ages,* Putnam, 1971.

Peter Zachary Cohen, *Authorized Autumn Charts of the Upper Red Canoe River Country,* Atheneum, 1972, revised edition, Silver Press, 1995.

Sibyl Hancock, *Mario's Mystery Machine,* Putnam, 1972.

Jean Rosenbaum and Lutie McAuliff, *What Is Fear? An Introduction to Feelings,* Prentice-Hall, 1972.

Rubie Saunders, *The Franklin Watts Concise Guide to Babysitting,* Watts, 1972, published as *Baby-Sitting: For Fun and Profit,* Archway, 1979.

Sam and Beryl Epstein, *Hold Everything,* Holiday House, 1973.

Sam and Beryl Epstein, *Look in the Mirror,* Holiday House, 1973.

Kathryn F. Ernst, *Danny and His Thumb,* Prentice-Hall, 1973.

Valerie Pitt, *Let's Find Out about Communications,* Watts, 1973.

Charles Keller and Richard Baker, compilers, *The Star-Spangled Banana and Other Revolutionary Riddles,* Prentice-Hall, 1974.

Alice Low, *David's Window,* Putnam, 1974.

Mary Calhoun, *Old Man Whickutt's Donkey,* Parents' Magazine Press, 1975.

Norma Farber, *This Is the Ambulance Leaving the Zoo,* Dutton, 1975.

Lee Bennett Hopkins, compiler, *Good Morning to You, Valentine* (poems), Harcourt, 1975, reissued by Boyds Mills Press.

Martha and Charles Shapp, *Let's Find Out about Houses,* Watts, 1975.

Eleanor Coerr, *The Mixed-Up Mystery Smell,* Putnam, 1976.

John Graham, *I Love You, Mouse,* Harcourt, 1976.

Bernice Kohn Hunt, *The Whatchamacallit Book,* Putnam, 1976.

Steven Kroll, *The Tyrannosaurus Game,* Holiday House, 1976.

Martha and Charles Shapp, *Let's Find Out about Summer,* Watts, 1976.

Barbara Williams, *If He's My Brother,* Harvey House, 1976.

Lee Bennett Hopkins, compiler, *Beat the Drum: Independence Day Has Come* (poems), Harcourt, 1977, reissued by Boyds Mills Press.

Daniel O'Connor, *Images of Jesus,* Winston, 1977.

Belong, Winston, 1977.

Journey, Winston, 1977.

(With others) Norma Farber, *Six Impossible Things before Breakfast,* Addison-Wesley, 1977.

Jean Fritz, *Can't You Make Them Behave, King George?,* Coward, 1977.

Patricia Lee Gauch, *Once upon a Dinkelsbuehl,* Putnam, 1977.

Tony Johnston, *Odd Jobs,* Putnam, 1977, published as *The Dog Wash,* Scholastic, 1977.

Steven Kroll, *Santa's Crash-Bang Christmas,* Holiday House, 1977.

Stephen Mooser, *The Ghost with the Halloween Hiccups,* Watts, 1977.

Annabelle Prager, *The Surprise Party,* Pantheon, 1977.

Malcolm E. Weiss, *Solomon Grundy, Born on Oneday: A Finite Arithmetic Puzzle,* Crowell, 1977.

Nancy Willard, *Simple Pictures Are Best,* Harcourt, 1977.

Jane Yolen, *The Giants' Farm,* Seabury, 1977.

Sue Alexander, *Marc, the Magnificent,* Pantheon, 1978.

William Cole, compiler, *Oh, Such Foolishness!* (poems), Lippincott, 1978.

Tony Johnston, *Four Scary Stories,* Putnam, 1978.

Steven Kroll, *Fat Magic,* Holiday House, 1978.

Naomi Panush Salus, *My Daddy's Moustache,* Doubleday, 1978.

Jan Wahl, *Jamie's Tiger,* Harcourt, 1978.

The Cat on the Dovrefell: A Christmas Tale, translated from the Norse by George Webbe Dasent, Putnam, 1979.

Lee Bennett Hopkins, compiler, *Easter Buds Are Springing: Poems for Easter* (poems), Harcourt, 1979.

Anne Rose, *The Triumphs of Fuzzy Fogtop,* Dial, 1979.

Daisy Wallace, compiler, *Ghost Poems,* Holiday House, 1979.

Jane Yolen, *The Giants Go Camping,* Seabury, 1979.

Patricia Lee Gauch, adapter, *The Little Friar Who Flew,* Putnam, 1980.

Patricia MacLachlan, *Moon, Stars, Frogs, and Friends,* Pantheon, 1980.

Clement Clarke Moore, *The Night before Christmas,* Holiday House, 1980.

Daniel M. Pinkwater, *The Wuggie Norple Story,* Four Winds, 1980.

Pauline Watson, *The Walking Coat,* Walker, 1980.

Malcolm Hall, *Edward, Benjamin, and Butter,* Coward, 1981.

Michael Jennings, *Robin Goodfellow and the Giant Dwarf,* McGraw, 1981.

Stephen Mooser, *Funnyman's First Case,* Watts, 1981.

Annabelle Prager, *The Spooky Halloween Party,* Pantheon, 1981.

Jean Fritz, adapter, *The Good Giants and the Bad Pukwudgies,* Putnam, 1982.

Tony Johnston, *Odd Jobs and Friends,* Putnam, 1982.

Ann McGovern, *Nicholas Bentley Stoningpot III,* Holiday House, 1982, reissued by Boyds Mills Press.

David A. Adler, *The Carsick Zebra and Other Animal Riddles,* Holiday House, 1983.

Tony Johnston, *The Vanishing Pumpkin,* Putnam, 1983.

Shirley Rousseau Murphy, *Tattie's River Journey,* Dial, 1983.

Valentine Davies, *Miracle on 34th Street,* Harcourt, 1984.

Sarah Josepha Hale, *Mary Had a Little Lamb,* Holiday House, 1984.

Stephen Mooser, *Funnyman and the Penny Dodo,* Watts, 1984.

Tony Johnston, *The Quilt Story,* Putnam, 1985.

(With others) Hans Christian Andersen *The Flying Trunk and Other Stories by Andersen,* new English version by Naomi Lewis, Andersen Press (England), 1986.

Jill Bennett, adapter, *Teeny Tiny,* Putnam, 1986.

Thomas Yeomans, *For Every Child a Star: A Christmas Story,* Holiday House, 1986.

Sanna Anderson Baker, *Who's a Friend of the Water-Spurting Whale?,* Cook, 1987.

Carolyn Craven, *What the Mailman Brought,* Putnam, 1987.

Jean Fritz, *Shh! We're Writing the Constitution,* Putnam, 1987.

Nancy Willard, *The Mountains of Quilt,* Harcourt, 1987.

Elizabeth Winthrop, *Maggie and the Monster,* Holiday House, 1987.

Caryll Houselander, *Petook: An Easter Story,* Holiday House, 1988.

Tony Johnston, *Pages of Music,* Putnam, 1988.

Cindy Ward, *Cookie's Week,* Putnam, 1988.

Tony Johnston, adapter, *The Badger and the Magic Fan: A Japanese Folktale,* Putnam, 1990.

Jane Yolen, *Hark! A Christmas Sampler,* Putnam, 1991.

(With others) *For Our Children* (song lyrics by various artists), Disney Press, 1991.

Jean Fritz, *The Great Adventure of Christopher Columbus: A Pop-up Book,* Putnam and Grosset, 1992.

Tony Johnston, *The Tale of Rabbit and Coyote,* Putnam, 1994.

Karen Pandell, *I Love You, Sun; I Love You, Moon,* Putnam, 1994.

Tony Johnston, *Alice Nizzy Nazzy: The Witch of Santa Fe,* Putnam, 1995.

Mary Ann Esposito, *Celebrations Italian Style,* Hearst, 1995.

Antonio H. Madrigal, adapter, *The Eagle and the Rainbow: Timeless Tales from Mexico,* Putnam, 1997.

Jane O'Connor, *Benny's Big Bubble,* Grosset & Dunlap, 1997.

Arnold L. Shapiro, *Mice Squeak, We Speak* (poem), Putnam, 1997.

Antonio H. Madrigal, *Erandi's Braids,* Putnam, 1999.

OTHER; UNDER NAME TOMIE dePAOLA

Conceived, designed, and directed the puppet ballet *A Rainbow Christmas* at Botolph in Cambridge, Massachusetts, 1971. Provided the foreword for *Raising Readers: Helping Your Child to Literacy* by Steve Bialostok, Penguin, 1992. DePaola's books have been published in many countries, including Denmark, France, Germany, Italy, Japan, the Netherlands, Norway, South Africa, and Sweden. DePaola's papers are housed in permanent collections at the Kerlan Collection, University of Minnesota, and the Osborne Collection, Toronto, Canada.

Adaptations

The Wind and the Sun was released as a sound filmstrip by Xerox Films/Lumin Films, 1973; *Andy* was released as a sound filmstrip by Random House, 1977; *Charlie Needs a Cloak* was released as a filmstrip with cassette, 1977, and as an audiocassette, 1990, both by Weston Woods. *Strega Nona* was released as a filmstrip with cassette by Weston Woods, 1978, was released on videocassette by OC Studios, 1985, and was adapted into a musical by Dennis Rosa (based on *Strega Nona, Big Anthony and the Magic Ring,* and *Strega Nona's Magic Lessons*) and was first produced in Minneapolis, MN, by the Children's Theatre Company, 1987. *Oliver Button Is a Sissy* was released as a filmstrip by Imperial Education Resources, 1980. *The Clown of God* was adapted into a play by Thomas Olson and first produced in Minneapolis by the Children's Theatre Company, 1981; it was also made into a motion picture, directed by Gary McGivney, by Weston Woods, 1982, and released as a 16mm film and videocassette by Weston Woods, 1984. *Pancakes for Breakfast* was made into a filmstrip by Weston Woods, 1982. *Strega Nona's Magic Lessons and Other Stories* was released on record and cassette by Caedmon, 1984, read by Tammy Grimes, it includes

Strega Nona; Strega Nona's Magic Lessons; Big Anthony and the Magic Ring; Helga's Dowry; Oliver Button Is a Sissy; Now One Foot, Now the Other; and *Nana Upstairs and Nana Downstairs.* The radio play *Big Anthony and Helga's Dowry* was performed by the Children's Radio Theatre, 1984. *The Night before Christmas* was released on cassette by Live Oak Media, 1984. *The Vanishing Pumpkin* was released as a filmstrip with cassette by Random House, 1984. *The Legend of the Bluebonnet: An Old Tale of Texas* was released as a filmstrip, directed by Forest Ann Miner, by the Listening Library, 1984, and as a filmstrip with cassette by Random House, 1985. *Now One Foot, Then the Other* was released as a motion picture and videorecording, directed by Don MacDonald, by Film-Fair Communications, 1985. *Sing, Pierrot, Sing* was released as a filmstrip by Random House, 1985; *The Mysterious Giant of Barletta* was released on cassette by Random House, 1985; *Mary Had a Little Lamb* was released as a filmstrip with cassette by Weston Woods, 1985; *The Legend of the Indian Paintbrush* was released as a filmstrip with cassette by Listening Library, 1988; *Tomie dePaola's Christmas Carols* was released on cassette by Listening Library, 1988. *Merry Christmas, Strega Nona* was released on cassette by Listening Library, 1988; it was also adapted as a play by T. Olson and first produced in Minneapolis by the Children's Theatre Company, 1988. *Mary Had a Little Lamb* was released on audio cassette by Live Oak Media, 1989. *Tomie dePaola's Mother Goose* was adapted into a play by Constance Congdon and first produced in Minneapolis by the Children's Theatre Company, 1990. *Return to the Magic Library: A Giant Tale* was released as a videorecording by TVOntario, 1990; *Big Anthony's Mixed-Up Magic* was released as a computer file by Putnam New Media, 1993; *Strega Nona* was released on audio cassette by Weston Woods, 1993.

Charlie Needs a Cloak has been adapted into braille and *Strega Nona* has been produced as a talking book. *The Art Lesson* was released on audio cassette, read by Tomie dePaola, by Listening Library, Inc. Filmstrips and videocassettes of *Let's Find Out about Houses, Let's Find Out about Summer, The Surprise Party, The Unicorn and the Sun, Shh! We're Writing the Constitution,* and *Tattie's River Journey* have been produced. DePaola is the subject of the videorecording *Tomie dePaola,* directed by R. Davies, J.S. Weiss, 1984, and the videocassette *A Visit with Tomie dePaola,* 1997. Spin-off products based on dePaola's books, such as the Strega Nona doll released by Simon & Schuster in 1995, have also been issued.

Work in Progress

Antonio, the Bread Boy, for Putnam; a new edition of *Now One Foot, Then the Other* with full-color illustrations, for Putnam.

Sidelights

Described as "one of the great masters of the picture book" by Marcus Crouch in *Junior Bookshelf* and as "one of the century's leading picture-book artists" by Anne Sherrill in *Dictionary of Literary Biography (DLB),* dePaola is perhaps the most prolific and popular contemporary creator of books for children in the early and middle grades. The author and/or illustrator of more than two hundred books as well as a professional artist, designer, and art teacher, he is recognized as an imaginative, versatile artist and writer whose works reflect his personal background and interests as well as his affection for and understanding of his audience. DePaola writes and illustrates autobiographical and semiautobiographical picture books and stories; informational and concept books; original stories, including several folktale and fairy tale variants; and retellings that often draw on his Italian and Irish heritage and his background as both a Roman Catholic and a resident of New England and the American West. Often acknowledged for the success of his autobiographical fiction, retellings, and informational books, he is also credited with compiling thoughtfully edited collections of poetry, song lyrics, riddles, folklore, and stories. His works center on subjects that have both personal relevance and child appeal—holidays; food; animals; clowns; clouds; family relationships; Bible stories and characters; saints; Mother Goose rhymes; folk and fairy tales; and legends, among others. In addition to traditional picture books, dePaola is the creator of well-received wordless picture books, pop-up books, and board books.

As a writer, dePaola uses a straightforward, direct prose style that includes clever wordplay and smatterings of foreign phrases. Although many of his books are humorous and whimsical, dePaola often addresses serious themes. His books often feature intergenerational bonds and stress the importance of individuality and equality as well as courage, personal sacrifice, the healing power of art, the deep joy of spirituality, and respect for the environment; he has also treated subjects such as old age, disability, and death. As an artist, dePaola has developed a signature style that reflects such influences as pre-Renaissance Italian art, folk motifs, and techniques from film and the theater. DePaola uses a variety of techniques to create his works, such as dark line with color applied within, layering acrylic paint to achieve an opaque look, and a combination of the two with colored pencil. He has also used mediums such as charcoal pencil and etchings for his art. DePaola's stylized illustrations are considered easily recognizable—cats, birds, hearts, flowers, and tousle-haired, round-cheeked children are often present, as are decorative borders composed of doorways, windows, and other frames. Praised for the luminous quality of his pictures, dePaola is considered a gifted artist whose works range from stately and elegant to wild and exuberant. Although his books have been criticized as erratic and facile and his texts are sometimes considered less effective than his art, dePaola is generally considered a writer and artist of uncommon talent and sensitivity, an author who is, in the words of a critic in *Publishers Weekly,* "as original as he is prolific."

DePaola was born in Meriden, Connecticut, to a father of Italian descent and a mother of Irish descent.

Speaking of his father, Joseph, who worked as a barber before becoming a salesman and union official, dePaola once told *SATA*, "[P]eople have an image of Italians being robust and loud. My father was just the opposite. He was a quiet and thoughtful man who was loads of fun and loved to cook. I grew up not knowing that men didn't cook." His mother Florence read aloud to Tomie and his older brother every night; dePaola informed *SATA* that this ritual "had a lot to do with my decision to become an artist. She would read the old fairy tales and legends, especially during the war, when my father was working the graveyard shift at a war plant job. I would come down, not able to sleep, and see my mother curled up in a chair with graham crackers and peanut butter, reading." The author once commented that his exposure to the children's radio program "Let's Pretend" and "the fact that my mother was in love with books and spent many long hours reading aloud to my brother and me … were the prime factors that caused me to announce to my first grade teachers that when I grew up I was going to make books with pictures." From the age of four, dePaola knew that he wanted to become an artist. He wrote in the *Fifth Book of Junior Authors and Illustrators,* "When I was very young, before I had even started to go to school, I promised myself a lot of things. One was that when I grew up, I would never tell children like myself things that weren't all true. Another was that when I grew up, I would be an artist and draw pictures, especially for books. I promised myself that I would write stories, too! That was a long time ago … and I can smile and say truthfully that I kept those promises to myself."

Recalling in *Fifth Book of Junior Authors* how he began preparing for his career, dePaola wrote, "I sat down and drew pictures—all over the place. By second grade, I was considered the 'best artist' by my teachers and classmates," a designation he held throughout his school years. DePaola later used an incident from his second grade year in which he refused to copy a Thanksgiving scene because "real artists don't copy" in his autobiographical picture book *The Art Lesson*. In 1940, dePaola started tap dancing lessons at Miss Leah Grossman's Dancing School. "I loved them," the author wrote in an autobiography for the Tomie dePaola celebration sponsored by the Meriden Public Library in his hometown; he added, "I would continue to take tap from Miss Leah and others until I went to Art School—years later." In 1979, dePaola included his boyhood tap dancing as an important feature of his autobiographical picture book *Oliver Button Is a Sissy*. In the same year that he started dancing lessons, dePaola was presented with a baby sister, Maureen. In the autobiography he wrote for the Meriden Public Library, the author stated, "[A]s far as I was concerned, she was mine. There are so many events surrounding her birth, some of which involved my Italian grandmother, that I could fill a book with them." In 1996, he did just that with his picture book *The Baby Sister*.

DePaola has written and illustrated several books with a Christmas theme; he recalled in *SATA* that the Christmas he was nine was one of his most memorable: "All my presents were art supplies: paints, brushes, colored pencils, all sorts of instruction books, watercolors, and even an easel." At around the same time, dePaola sent a drawing to Walt Disney and received a supportive letter back accompanied by an original drawing of Mickey Mouse. In sixth grade, dePaola began writing poetry. By the time he was a sophomore in high school, dePaola knew that he wanted to attend Pratt Institute in New York City and wrote to them to find out what classes to take in preparation. In 1952, he entered Pratt Institute on a scholarship.

In his autobiography for the Meriden Library, dePaola wrote that his experience at Pratt "was wonderful and trained me well." He added, "I learned to keep my mind open and not make any judgments about things until I knew more about them. I was like a vacuum cleaner, devouring everything." At Pratt, dePaola studied drawing, design, and painting in the illustration program and discovered such artists as Matisse and Picasso; he also developed a strong appreciation for religious artists Fra Angelico, Giotto, and Botticelli as well as for folk art. When he wasn't in class, dePaola explored New York City, went to art galleries, and fell in love with Greenwich Village: "That's where *my* people were," he told *SATA*. While at Pratt, dePaola began to define his style as an artist. He wrote in *Children's Books and Their Creators* that his style "hasn't really changed in over thirty-five years. The roots are there in my early drawings and paintings—things done way before I began illustrating books. There are white birds, pink tiled roofs, arched doors and windows. My early love of line and strong design and stylization has grown and been refined over the years, but the seeds are all there in the early work." In 1955, dePaola won a scholarship to the Skowhegan School of Painting and Illustration in Maine. He studied with artist Ben Shahn, who, he told *SATA,* "probably had the most impact on me of any of the teachers I had. He told me that being an artist was more than the kind of things you do. 'It's the way you live your life,' he said. I've never forgotten that."

After graduating from Pratt in 1956, dePaola spent six months in a small Benedictine monastery in Vermont, where he became, as he told *SATA*, "sort of the resident artist." DePaola commented that joining the Benedictines, an order involved in the arts, was "a very valid thing for me to do at that age. I think it solidified, not religious, but some deep spiritual values that I have. I have a very strong spiritual life and meditate very easily. I'm not a fundamentalist by any means, but I really believe in the strong power of prayer." His experience in the monastery, dePaola noted, "gave me a way to view life and realize that culture was an important thing as well. If you can add to the culture of the race of man, you're doing a really hot number. It certainly gave me time to delve even more into the study of art." After returning to secular life, dePaola maintained a relationship with the monastery by designing fabric for their weaving studio and starting them in a Christmas card business; he also began his career as a professional artist and designer and worked in summer theater. During this period, dePaola got married, a union that lasted for a

Inspired by the classic "porridge pot" tales of other cultures, dePaola created Strega Nona, the benevolent witch of a small village in Renaissance Calabria whose magic pasta pot creates big trouble for her inept assistant, Big Anthony. (From Strega Nona, *written and illustrated by dePaola.)*

year and a half; he told *SATA*, "A friend said it was my brief period. I was briefly in the monastery and briefly married." In 1962, dePaola began teaching art and theater at the university and junior college levels, a career that he combined with his painting and illustration for the next seventeen years.

In 1964, dePaola illustrated his first book, *Sound*, an informational picture book by Lisa Miller, the pseudonym of Bernice Kohn Hunt. Since that time, he has provided the pictures for fiction and nonfiction by such authors as Jean Fritz, Clement Clarke Moore, Norma Farber, Lee Bennett Hopkins, Tony Johnston, Nancy Willard, Jan Wahl, Jane Yolen, William Cole, Patricia MacLachlan, Steven Kroll, Patricia Lee Gauch, Robert Bly, Mary Calhoun, Daniel M. Pinkwater, Sara Josepha Hale, and Sam and Beryl Epstein as well as for collections. In 1966, dePaola wrote and illustrated his first book, *The Wonderful Dragon of Timlin*, a picture book about a young princess, a page, and a pink dragon with a talent for breathing fire. Writing in *School Library Journal*, Ann Currah predicted, "Little girls who adore dragons and princesses will probably enjoy this," while Kenneth Marantz of *Chicago Tribune Books Today* called the story "a tale a bit above ordinary." For the next six years, dePaola continued to create picture books featuring child and animal characters, illustrate the books of other authors, and teach. He spent four years in California, earning his master's degree from the California College of Arts and Crafts and a doctoral equivalency from Lone Mountain College. In 1971, dePaola returned to the east coast, settling in a small town in New Hampshire. However, before leaving California, dePaola had a breakthrough. In an interview with Phyllis Boyson in the *New Era*, he stated: "I didn't pay attention to my childhood memories and experiences

until 1971. I was feeling very ineffective.... I felt that I had a block in my work, and I went to group therapy with Margaret Fringe Keyes, who uses a lot of art as a means of therapy. I realized that I had locked up the child so effectively that it wasn't getting any say.... Through therapy, I realized that I had shoved the child in me into a closet. I had a feeling of loss—but no, I hadn't lost it. I finally opened the door and let it out of the closet. I remet my child and let it live again, and then I wrote *Nana Upstairs and Nana Downstairs*. With *Nana*, instead of making up a story, I took the risk of telling the truth."

Considered one of dePaola's best books as well as the author's favorite among his own works, *Nana Upstairs and Nana Downstairs* is credited with providing a new depth to dePaola's stories. The story, which was inspired by dePaola's relatives on his father's side, features four-year-old Tommy, his great-grandmother, and his grandmother, who all live in the same house—great-grandmother upstairs and grandmother downstairs. Nana Upstairs is bedridden and, when she sits, must be tied into a chair to avoid falling. When Tommy comes to visit, they talk and eat candy together, with Tommy tied into his chair as well. When Nana Upstairs dies, Tommy sees a shooting star; his parents tell him that the star may be Nana Upstairs sending him a kiss and, though she is no longer here, he can always call her back through his memory. Later, when Nana Downstairs dies, Tommy thinks of them both as Nana Upstairs. Writing in *DLB*, Anne Sherrill noted, "Though the book deals with the death of loved ones, the focus is on affection and lost memories." Melinda Schroeder of *School Library Journal* commented that although "the book gets a little soupy" after Nana Upstairs dies, "[c]hildren will want to hear this again and again...." Writing in *Bulletin of the*

THE LEGEND OF THE BLUEBONNET

AN OLD TALE OF TEXAS
RETOLD AND ILLUSTRATED BY
TOMIE dePAOLA

In his self-illustrated book, dePaola relates the Comanche Indian legend of the profusion of the bluebonnet, the state flower of Texas. (Cover illustration by dePaola.)

Center for Children's Books, Zena Sutherland stated, "This is one of the best … stories for very young children that shows the love between a child and a grandparent and pictures the child's adjustment to death." DePaola again features his grandmother as a character in *Watch Out for the Chicken Feet in Your Soup,* a picture book published in 1974. In this work, small Joey takes his friend Eugene to visit his old-fashioned grandmother, who puts chicken feet in her soup and uses the boys's coats to warm her bread dough. Joey is thoroughly embarrassed, but Eugene enjoys the soup, dons an apron, and helps Nana make bread dolls. At the end of the story, Joey reconciles with his grandmother, who gives him a hug and a special bread doll. The book also includes a sprinkling of Italian words as well as the recipe for bread dolls used by dePaola's grandmother. Anne Sherrill of *DLB* called the Italian grandmother "memorable and authentic," while a critic in *Kirkus Reviews* noted that both the "cozy pictures and his simple text … glow with a genuine warmth that other visitors of whatever background can't help sharing." A reviewer in *Publishers Weekly,* calling the book "[a] sure winner," concluded that Joey's grandmother is "the heart and soul of the maternal symbol…."

In 1979, dePaola published *Oliver Button Is a Sissy,* a picture book that he has described as mostly autobiographical. Young Oliver, who enjoys drawing, reading, and walking in the woods rather than playing sports, is teased and criticized. However, after he shows talent as a tap dancer, his schoolmates change the graffiti that read "Oliver Button Is a Sissy" to "Oliver Button Is a Star." Writing in *School Library Journal,* Marilyn R. Singer called *Oliver Button* "an attractive little book that might offer reassurance to those readers who will identify with Oliver, as well as good counsel for their parents and teachers." With *Now One Foot, Now the Other,* a book that is based loosely on his family's background, dePaola depicts how young Bobby helps his grandfather to walk after a stroke. "Like *Nana Upstairs and Nana Downstairs,*" wrote Zena Sutherland in *Bulletin of the Center for Children's Books,* "this is a loving testament to the special bond that can exist between a child and a grandparent." Writing in the *New York Times Book Review,* Natalie Babbitt noted that like *Nana Upstairs,* "this is a big and difficult story compressed into a small and simple story. Mr. dePaola is able somehow to leave nothing out—not even the horror of Bob's first efforts to speak after his stroke—and yet present a warm and positive picture of the power of love."

DePaola again portrayed himself as a character in *The Art Lesson,* a picture book published in 1989 in which first-grader Tommy, an aspiring artist, balks when his teacher asks the class to copy the Pilgrim that she's drawn on the board. Tommy, who has been told not to copy by his grown-up cousins in art school, strikes a bargain with his teacher: if he will draw the Pilgrim, she will let him draw another picture of his own. Writing in *Bulletin of the Center for Children's Books,* Roger Sutton commented, "While the illustrations hold few surprises, the story has the kind of specificity that characterizes the best of dePaola's texts…." Patricia Dooley of *School Library Journal* stated, "[I]t's gratifying to see the small non-conformist accommodated." Calling dePaola's own style "eminently copyable," the critic concluded that young artists should not be discouraged from copying dePaola before imitating Reubens. With *Tom,* a picture book published in 1993, dePaola recreates his close relationship with the paternal grandfather for whom he is named. Tom and Tommy are playful partners in crime; their boisterous laughter often causes Nana to banish them outside or to the cellar. Tom, a butcher, teaches Tommy to manipulate newly severed chicken feet; when Tommy takes them to school, he scares the other students and is sent to the principal's office. Undaunted, Tom winks at his grandson and vows to find more adventures for them to share. Writing in *Booklist,* Deborah Abbott predicted, "Youngsters will bask in the delicious conspiracy between grandfather and grandson…. For story hours, intergenerational units, and humor studies, this book is a treasure." Hanna B. Zeiger of *Horn Book* added, "With gentle humor and his usual mastery of line and composition, dePaola conveys the strong bond of affection between Tom and Tommy…."

With *The Baby Sister,* a picture book published in 1996, dePaola describes the events surrounding the birth of his younger sister, Maureen. In this story, Tommy prays nightly for a baby sister with a red ribbon in her hair. He expects his beloved Aunt Nell to babysit when his mother goes to the hospital; when stern Nana arrives in her place, Tommy is dismayed. However, he bonds with Nana during their time together, and when the baby comes home it is Nana who suggests that Tommy hold her. A reviewer in *Publishers Weekly* noted: "Reaching deep into the treasured memories of his own childhood, dePaola pulls out a plum.... [U]nder dePaola's sure, sensitive direction, a richly textured tale unfolds." A critic in *Kirkus Reviews* called *The Baby Sister* a "loving look back," adding that the story "is told with graceful economy" and that the illustrations impart "a glowing sense of the security and love that surrounds this large family."

In 1999, dePaola published his first chapter book, *26 Fairmount Avenue,* the first in a projected series of books titled after the address of the first home in which the dePaola family lived. Sally Lodge, interviewing the author for *Publishers Weekly,* commented that using words rather than pictures was a radical change for the illustrator. He himself said, "In picture books, the pictures move the story and the characters along, but with *26 Fairmount Avenue,* I had to find all those adjectives I learned to leave out over the years. Where before I had to reduce, reduce, reduce, now with this series I have to add, add, add. It's a very interesting process for me." A reviewer for *Bulletin of the Center for Children's Books* observed that the writing had "an understated, unassuming rhythm" and brought people and events "to easy life."

DePaola is well known for the series of picture books he has written about Strega Nona—Italian for "Grandmother Witch"—and her hapless helper Big Anthony. In researching fairy tales to illustrate, dePaola discovered a paucity of stories with Italian settings. Inspired by the classic "porridge pot" tales of other cultures, he changed porridge to pasta and created Strega Nona as the benevolent witch of a small village in Renaissance Calabria. The first book of the series, *Strega Nona: An Old Tale,* revolves around a magic cooking pot owned by the title character; the pot keeps on producing pasta until three kisses are blown to turn it off. When Nona's curious houseboy, Big Anthony, begins pasta production without knowing how to stop the pot, he fills the village with pasta until Strega Nona comes in to save the day. For his punishment, Big Anthony has to eat all of the pasta in the town. Writing in *Horn Book,* Anita Silvey claimed that dePaola "has given new vitality to the magic cooking pot theme" before concluding that he has created "an appealing, successful picture book." Zena Sutherland of *Bulletin of the Center for Children's Books* noted that "the familiar theme of a self-filling magical object is used to great effect" and predicted that "children will probably enjoy [the ending] tremendously." In *Big Anthony and the Magic Ring,* the teenage farm boy steals Strega Nona's magic ring, which turns him into the village ladies's man; however, when the local women become overly amorous, Anthony must be rescued by Strega Nona. Though Harold C. K. Rice, writing in the *New York Times Book Review,* is disconcerted about a "misogynistic undertone" to this tale, he concludes that the humor and "always profes-

sional, cartoon-Renaissance dePaola" makes this one of the best current picture books. Marjorie Lewis of *School Library Journal* added, "Kids old enough to know what Night Life is ... will find Big Anthony's predicament hilarious. Sexist, yes. But lots of fun anyway." In *Strega Nona's Magic Lessons,* Big Anthony—who wants to join Bambolona, the baker's daughter, in receiving *strega* lessons—disguises himself as a girl in order to become Strega Nona's apprentice. Dismayed when he thinks one of his spells turns Strega Nona into a frog, Big Anthony promises to swear off magic before Strega Nona, who was simply in hiding, reappears. Barbara Elleman of *Booklist* concluded, "Played for laughs—successfully," while Craighton Hippenhammer of *School Library Journal* stated, "DePaola's irrepressible illustrations add vibrancy and humor." In *Merry Christmas, Strega Nona,* Big Anthony loses the shopping list for the Christmas feast that Strega Nona is planning; since Christmas is the only time that Nona does not use her spells and potions, there is no way for her to prepare a last-minute feast. However, through the efforts of Big Anthony, the townspeople bring a feast of their own. A critic in *Publishers Weekly* noted: "The joyful ending and sparkling illustrations make this one of the most warmhearted selections of the season," while Ilene Cooper of *Booklist* claimed, "It's especially satisfying to see a bona fide story centered on Christmas that is funny, accessible, and contains a gentle message tucked neatly inside." Judith Gloyer of *School Library Journal* added, "Anthony is still a gangling, oafish, but good-natured helper. It's nice to see him do something right for a change. *Buon Natale!*"

In *Strega Nona Meets her Match,* dePaola introduces Strega Amelia, a witch friend of Nona's from the other side of the mountain whom Hanna B. Zeiger of *Horn Book* described as "bejeweled and bedecked like a fugitive from Bloomingdale's." Strega Amelia goes into competition with Strega Nona and, due to fancy equipment and free giveaways, surpasses her friend in business. When Amelia hires Big Anthony to help her, he gets everything backward, causing the townspeople to come back to Strega Nona to be cured. At the end of the story, the mayor tells Amelia that one *strega* is good enough for their town. Writing in *Booklist,* Carolyn Phelan noted: "DePaola's watercolor illustrations seem bolder, brighter, and more comical than in the original story.... A pleasure to read aloud, this features the broad humor that young children relish." Carol Fox of *Bulletin of the Center for Children's Books* concluded, "Here is a civil and generous account of business competition with the unshaken belief that goodness and business can coincide; both Sesame Street and Wall Street could benefit." *Strega Nona: Her Story* is a prequel to the first book about the wise witch. The story takes young readers from Nona's birth through her education as a village *strega* by her Grandma Concetta, including instruction on the secret ingredient—lots of love. When Concetta retires, she gives her practice, including her magic pasta pot, to her granddaughter; the story ends with the arrival of Big Anthony on Strega Nona's doorstep. Writing in *School Library Journal,* Karen MacDonald predicted: "Children will find many

After their naps, Nana Downstairs would comb out Nana Upstairs' beautiful silver-white hair.

Then Nana Downstairs would comb and brush her own hair.

Four-year-old Tommy experiences the deaths of his beloved grandmother and great-grandmother in dePaola's professed favorite work. (From Nana Upstairs and Nana Downstairs, *written and illustrated by dePaola.)*

of the paintings hilarious. Though this book is a mere teaser on its own, it serves as the perfect final installment in any Strega Nona story fest, leaving children wanting still more of that 'ingrediente segreto.'" With *Big Anthony: His Story,* dePaola wrote and illustrated a companion piece to *Strega Nona: Her Story* with a prequel that proves that Big Anthony, according to Sue Sherif of *School Library Journal,* "has bumbled from birth." DePaola depicts the accident-prone but well-meaning Anthony from infancy—when he spills holy water all over himself and everyone else at his christening—to his arrival at Strega Nona's door. Sherif concluded, "Big Anthony and Strega Nona certainly qualify as celebrities in the realm of picture books, and this latest installment will bring smiles to the faces of their young fans."

In addition to his "Strega Nona" series, dePaola has written and illustrated a popular series of picture books about Bill, a crocodile, and his friend-cum-toothbrush Pete as well as several board books about the Kitten Kids, young anthropomorphic felines whose experiences appeal to small children. DePaola has also received much acclaim for the individual titles for which he is both author and illustrator. His first informational book, *Charlie Needs a Cloak,* is considered one of the best

examples of dePaola's ability to make education fun. In this work, which tells the story of how shepherd Charlie makes himself a new red cloak, dePaola provides information on shearing, carding, spinning, weaving, and sewing while adding humor through the exploits of a mouse and a sheep. Writing in *Bulletin of the Center for Children's Books,* Zena Sutherland claimed, "for the child who would like to know how to make a new red cloak ... starting with the sheep, *Charlie Needs a Cloak* ... will be indispensable." With *The Clown of God: An Old Tale,* a retelling of the legend of a juggler who offers his talent as a gift to the Christ Child and is rewarded with a miracle, dePaola was praised for the sincerity of his message and the beauty and authenticity of his illustrations, which echo Fra Angelico and other Renaissance artists. Writing in the *New York Times Book Review,* Harold C. K. Rice said that "unlike so many picture books these days, this allusive art is not a self-indulgence but a spur to the artist's invention." DePaola has also been especially recognized for creating two other books with a religious theme. *Francis: The Poor Man of Assisi* is a picture book written to celebrate the eight-hundredth anniversary of the birth of the saint. Considered an outstanding presentation of the life of St. Francis, the work has, according to Natalie Babbitt of *Book World—The Washington Post,* "a glow that can only come from the deepest concern for the subject." *Christopher: The Holy Giant* tells the story of the deposed saint Christopher, who in legend carried the Christ Child on his back across a raging river. In her review of the book in *Horn Book,* Mary M. Burns said that dePaola's tales of the saints "are remarkable for innate spirituality without overt sentimentality. They are childlike—clear, precise, concrete—but never childish."

DePaola has also received acclaim for the works he has done in nontraditional formats such as the pop-up book and wordless picture book. For example, his pop-up book *Giorgio's Village,* which portrays a medieval Italian village in three-dimensional detail, is considered one of the most successful examples of its genre. A reviewer in *Publishers Weekly* called it "spectacular, amusing as well as educational ...." Barbara Elleman of *Booklist* stated that the "look and feel of another country comes magically alive." DePaola has also been credited for his compilations; for example, *Tomie dePaola's Mother Goose,* a collection of more than two hundred rhymes and songs, is now considered a standard source. Writing in *Horn Book* at the time of its publication, Ann A. Flowers said that *Tomie dePaola's Mother Goose* is "[d]estined to become a classic," while M. Hobbs of *Junior Bookshelf* concluded: "There is no doubt that this is not only, arguably, the American illustrator's best work to date, but that it will become a classic of nursery illustration."

In an interview with Phyllis Boyson of the *New Era,* dePaola commented, "I write a lot for children between three and seven years old, and young children can tell right away when you're not being honest. If a message rings true, they will sit and listen. My guess is that children respond to my work because it's simple and honest." Asked by Dennis Anderson of *Instructor* if he would ever give up his writing for children, dePaola replied, "Never. It's my calling. There's a marvelous southwestern Indian image—Pueblo, I think. It's a clay figure sitting with its mouth open surrounded by little figures—and it's called the storyteller. The storyteller has always been an extremely important figure in our culture. A good children's author/illustrator is the storyteller of a new era. Of today. And that's what I want more than anything else in the world." Writing in *Books for Your Children,* dePaola added, "It's a dream of mine that one of my books, any book, any picture, will touch the heart of some individual child and change that child's life for the better. I don't even have to know about it. I hope it's not a far-fetched dream. Meanwhile, I'll keep working, doing the best I'm capable of."

Works Cited

Abbott, Deborah, review of *Tom, Booklist,* January 15, 1993, p. 898.

Andersen, Dennis, "Tomie dePaola: Tough and Tender Storyteller," *Instructor,* March, 1980, pp. 32-38.

Babbitt, Natalie, review of *Francis: The Poor Man of Assisi, Book World—The Washington Post,* May 9, 1982, pp. 16-17.

Babbitt, review of *Now One Foot, Now the Other, New York Times Book Review,* September 20, 1981, p. 30.

Review of *The Baby Sister, Kirkus Reviews,* February 15, 1996, p. 294.

Review of *The Baby Sister, Publishers Weekly,* February 19, 1996, p. 214.

Burns, Mary M., review of *Christopher: The Holy Giant, Horn Book,* May-June, 1994, pp. 333-34.

Cooper, Ilene, review of *Merry Christmas, Strega Nona, Booklist,* November 1, 1986, pp. 407-08.

Crouch, Marcus, review of *The Legend of the Bluebonnet, Junior Bookshelf,* October, 1983, p. 197.

Currah, Ann, review of *The Wonderful Dragon of Timlin, School Library Journal,* May, 1966, p. 178.

dePaola, Tomie, "Involved with Dreams," *Books for Your Children,* summer, 1980, pp. 2-3.

dePaola, commentary in *Children's Books and Their Creators,* edited by Anita Silvey, Houghton Mifflin, 1995, p. 196.

dePaola, commentary in *Fifth Book of Junior Authors and Illustrators,* edited by Sally Holmes Holtze, Wilson, 1983, pp. 99-100.

dePaola, interview with Phyllis Boyson, *New Era,* May-June, 1981, pp. 76-80.

Dooley, Patricia, review of *The Art Lesson, School Library Journal,* April, 1989, p. 80.

Elleman, Barbara, review of *Giorgio's Village, Booklist,* October 1, 1982, pp. 243-44.

Elleman, review of *Strega Nona's Magic Lessons, Booklist,* December 15, 1982, p. 563.

Review of *Flix, Publishers Weekly,* November 19, 1979, p. 78.

Flowers, Ann A., review of *Tomie dePaola's Mother Goose, Horn Book,* January-February, 1986, p. 66.

Fox, Carol, review of *Strega Nona Meets Her Match, Bulletin of the Center for Children's Books,* December, 1993, p. 119.

Review of *Giorgio's Village, Publishers Weekly,* June 18, 1982, p. 74.

Gloyer, Judith, review of *Merry Christmas, Strega Nona, School Library Journal,* October, 1986, pp. 109-13.

Hippenhammer, Craighton, review of *Strega Nona's Magic Lessons, School Library Journal,* January, 1983, p. 58.

Hobbs, M., review of *Mother Goose, Junior Bookshelf,* February, 1986, p. 14.

Lewis, Marjorie, review of *Big Anthony and the Magic Ring, School Library Journal,* May, 1979, p. 50.

Lodge, Sally, "Tomie dePaola Mines His Childhood Memories," *Publishers Weekly,* March 15, 1999.

MacDonald, Karen, review of *Strega Nona: Her Story, School Library Journal,* October, 1996, p. 91.

Marantz, Kenneth, review of *The Wonderful Dragon of Timlin, Chicago Tribune Books Today,* May 8, 1966, p. 9A.

Review of *Merry Christmas, Strega Nona, Publishers Weekly,* September 26, 1986, p. 74.

Phelan, Carolyn, review of *Strega Nona Meets Her Match, Booklist,* November 1, 1993, p. 528.

Rice, Harold C. K., review of *The Clown of God: An Old Tale, New York Times Book Review,* December 10, 1978, pp. 72-3, 93.

Rice, review of *Big Anthony and the Magic Ring, New York Times Book Review,* April 29, 1979, p. 47.

Schroeder, Melinda, review of *Nana Upstairs and Nana Downstairs, School Library Journal,* September, 1973, p. 56.

Sherif, Sue, review of *Big Anthony: His Story, School Library Journal,* November 1, 1998, p. 83.

Sherrill, Anne, entry in *Dictionary of Literary Biography,* Volume 61, *American Writers for Children since 1960: Poets, Illustrators, and Nonfiction Authors,* Gale, 1987, pp. 15-26.

Silvey, Anita, review of *Strega Nona: An Old Tale, Horn Book Magazine,* October, 1975, pp. 458-59.

Singer, Marilyn R., review of *Oliver Button Is a Sissy, School Library Journal,* October, 1979, p. 138.

Sutherland, Zena, review of *Charlie Needs a Cloak, Bulletin of the Center for Children's Books,* June, 1974, p. 156.

Sutherland, Zena, review of *Nana Upstairs and Nana Downstairs, Bulletin of the Center for Children's Books,* October, 1973, pp. 24-25.

Sutherland, Zena, review of *Now One Foot, Now the Other, Bulletin of the Center for Children's Books,* May, 1981, pp. 168-69.

Sutherland, Zena, review of *Strega Nona: An Old Tale, Bulletin of the Center for Children's Books,* November, 1975, p. 42.

Sutton, Roger, review of *The Art Lesson, Bulletin of the Center for Children's Books,* March, 1989, pp. 168-69.

Review of *26 Fairmount Avenue, Bulletin of the Center for Children's Books,* June, 1999, p. 349.

Review of *Watch Out for the Chicken Feet in Your Soup, Kirkus Reviews,* October 1, 1974, p. 1057.

Review of *Watch Out for the Chicken Feet in Your Soup, Publishers Weekly,* October 7, 1974, p. 64.

Zeiger, Hanna B., review of *Strega Nona Meets Her Match, Horn Book,* November-December, 1993, p. 730.

Zeiger, review of *Tom, Horn Book,* July, 1993, p. 441.

For More Information See

BOOKS

Berg, Julie, *Tomie dePaola*, Abdo & Daughters, 1993.
Children's Literature Review, Gale, Volume 4, 1982, pp. 50-66, Volume 24, 1991, pp. 84-104.
Elleman, Barbara, *Tomie dePaola: His Art and His Stories*, Putnam, 1999.
Elleman, entry in *St. James Guide to Children's Writers*, 5th edition, St. James Press, pp. 317-20.
Roginski, Jim, compiler, *Newbery and Caldecott Medalists and Honor Book Winners*, Libraries Unlimited, 1982.
Stoddard, Jewell, entry in *Children's Books and Their Creators*, edited by Anita Silvey, Houghton Mifflin, 1995, pp. 195, 197.

PERIODICALS

Booklist, February 15, 1992, p. 1108; March 15, 1992, p. 1382; September 15, 1996, p. 246.
Bulletin of the Center for Children's Books, March, 1991, pp. 163-64.
Horn Book, November-December, 1994, pp. 710-11; November-December, 1996, pp. 722-23.
Kirkus Reviews, February 1, 1994, p. 140; September 1, 1995, p. 1279; February 15, 1996, p. 294; December 16, 1996, p. 59.
New York Times Book Review, November 15, 1998, p. 43.
Publishers Weekly, January 25, 1993, p. 86; April 20, 1998, p. 65.
School Library Journal, March, 1994, p. 214; May, 1996, p. 91; June, 1999, p. 113.

—*Sketch by Gerard J. Senick*

*   *   *

dePAOLA, Tomie
See dePAOLA, Thomas Anthony

*   *   *

DEWAN, Ted 1961-

Personal

Born 1961, in Boston, MA; married Helen Cooper (an author/illustrator); children: Pandora. *Education:* Attended Brown University (engineering and electronic music); also studied art with author/illustrator David Macaulay.

Addresses

Home—North London, England.

Career

Milton Academy, Boston, MA, physics instructor; illustrator and cartoonist, 1988—. *Member:* Society of Authors (chairman, Children's Writers and Illustrators Group); Royal Institution.

Awards, Honors

Mother Goose Award, shortlisted for *Times Educational Supplement* Information Award (for foreign editions), both 1992, both for *Inside the Whale and Other Animals;* shortlisted for Kurt Maschler Award, 1997, for *The Sorcerer's Apprentice.*

Writings

AUTHOR AND ILLUSTRATOR; FOR CHILDREN

(Reteller)
3 Billy Goats Gruff, Andre Deutsch (London), 1994.
Top Secret, Andre Deutsch, 1996, Doubleday, 1997.
(Reteller) *The Sorcerer's Apprentice* (based on *Der Zauberhling* by Wolfgang von Goethe; with Dewan's arrangement of story narration and accompanying music, including an original composition), Doubleday, 1997.
The Weatherbirds, Puffin, 1999.

ILLUSTRATOR; FOR CHILDREN

Steve Parker, *Inside the Whale and Other Animals*, Dorling Kindersley, 1992.
Steve Parker, *Inside Dinosaurs and Other Prehistoric Creatures*, Dorling Kindersley, 1993, Delacorte, 1994.
Kit Wright, *Rumpelstiltskin*, Hippo, 1998.

ILLUSTRATOR; FOR ADULTS

Grace L. Mitchell and Harriet Chmela, *I Am, I Can: A Preschool Curriculum*, Telshare, 1977.
Robert Ornstein, *The Evolution of Consciousness*, Prentice-Hall, 1991.
Robert Ornstein, *The Roots of the Self: Unraveling the Mystery of Who We Are*, HarperCollins, 1993.
James Burke and Robert Ornstein, *The Axemaker's Gift*, Putnam, 1995.

Dewan's illustrations have appeared in nearly every British newspaper and are featured regularly in the *Times* and the *Guardian*.

Sidelights

Ted Dewan is gaining renown as an illustrator with a quirky, engaging style all his own. Using his artistic skills, timely marketing, and creative concepts, Dewan encourages readers to find new appreciation for familiar material. *Books for Keeps* contributor Pam Harwood admired the author's "'cool' language" and "bright, lively pictures," which bring the time-honored story *Three Billy Goats Gruff* back to life. Dewan's new adaptation of *The Sorcerer's Apprentice* was released to coincide with the two-hundredth anniversary of the tale's original publication in Germany. Bringing the story's appeal to audiophiles as well as readers, Dewan complemented his version with a tape of narration, appropriate musical accompaniment, and his own original musical composition.

After studying engineering at Rhode Island's Brown University and teaching physics at Milton Academy in Boston, Dewan decided to make a career change. He

In Ted Dewan's self-illustrated retelling of the classic tale **The Sorcerer's Apprentice,** *an inventor creates a robot to clean his workshop, but the robot has ideas of its own.*

began illustrating books for children, starting with several volumes by science writer Steve Parker. *Inside the Whale* showcases Dewan's pen-and-ink and water-color drawings in a book that examines the morphology of the world's largest mammals. Similar in format, *Inside Dinosaurs and Other Prehistoric Creatures* investigates the processes used by scientists to recreate detailed models of dinosaurs. *School Library Journal* contributor Cathryn A. Camper praised both books for using "humor and imagination, instead of knives, to dissect ... literally and figuratively get[ting] to the guts of the matter."

With the success of his illustrations for Parker, Dewan moved on to create his own stories for children. Published in 1996, *Top Secret: Don't Breathe a Word* reveals, in a comic-book format, the complex technology and heroic bravery responsible for the legend of the tooth fairy. In it, the "new kid," one of seven turtle-like creatures, describes the dangerous mission with which his crew has been charged. Their goal: undetected tooth extraction from beneath the pillow of a sleeping girl and replacement of said tooth with a shiny coin. *School Library Journal* contributor Karen James noted Dewan's humorous peppering of technical jargon, such as "zip cable" and "Slumber Zone," to augment the text. Citing the combination of "catchy lingo of the narration and the Lego-like machines," a *Kirkus Reviews* critic called *Top Secret* "adventurous fun, especially for the mechanically inclined." *Booklist*'s Carolyn Phelan announced: "Chil-

dren will enjoy the visual wit and pizzazz that character-izes this original picture book."

Despite its Disney-popularized story line, *The Sorcerer's Apprentice,* Dewan's next endeavor, is no less original. True, it is based on a ballad by eighteenth-century German writer Johann Wolfgang von Goethe. It is doubtful, however, that Goethe could have imagined a robot cast in the title role. In a workshop that *School Librarian* contributor Anne Rowe described as "a cross between a metal workshop and Dr. Frankenstein's laboratory," Dewan's modern-day "sorcerer" puts to-gether gears, wires, bulbs, transistors, and other mechan-ical things to create new inventions. Because his workshop is becoming too cluttered with bits of left-over stuff, he wires together a savvy robot apprentice to clean up after him. The first robot, who quickly becomes addicted to technology himself in the form of television, accumulates enough stuff to build a successor to perform all the hard work; the new robot does the same. So it goes, until the robots revolt against the sorcerer, forcing the inventor to flip the "off" switch on the entire mechanical crew—all except his original apprentice. A *Publishers Weekly* contributor called *The Sorcerer's Apprentice* a "post-modern melodrama [that] cautions against cloning, environmental depletion and television," while a *Kirkus Reviews* critic appreciated the work as a "rollicking remake of the classic tale." Incorporating his interest in electronic music, Dewan created a tape of musical accompaniment to compliment this visual story.

The music, arranged by Dewan, is by Paul-Abraham Dukas and Camille Saint-Saens, with the exception of Dewan's original composition, "The March of the Robots." The entire package provides "a memorable take," wrote a critic in *Kirkus Reviews,* "capped by a rousing robot cheer: '1, 2, 4, 8, We were made to duplicate.'"

Works Cited

Camper, Cathryn A., review of *Inside Dinosaurs and Other Prehistoric Creatures, School Library Journal,* April, 1994, p. 144.

Harwood, Pam, review of *Three Billy Goats Gruff, Books for Keeps,* September, 1995, p. 10.

James, Karen, review of *Top Secret, School Library Journal,* March, 1997, p. 150.

Phelan, Carolyn, review of *Top Secret, Booklist,* April 1, 1997, p. 1337.

Rowe, Anne, review of *The Sorcerer's Apprentice, School Librarian,* November, 1997, p. 185.

Review of *The Sorcerer's Apprentice, Kirkus Reviews,* December 1, 1997, p. 1774.

Review of *The Sorcerer's Apprentice, Publishers Weekly,* January 12, 1998, p. 59.

Review of *Top Secret, Kirkus Reviews,* January 15, 1997, p. 140.

For More Information See

PERIODICALS

Booklist, July, 1992, p. 1935; March 15, 1994, p. 1345.

Books for Keeps, May, 1996, p. 24.

New York Times Book Review, June 28, 1992, p. 26.

Publishers Weekly, February 7, 1994, p. 88.

School Library Journal, July, 1992, p. 81.

Times Educational Supplement, September 29, 1995, p. 10; October 25, 1996, p. 12; October 3, 1997, p. 9; November 7, 1997, p. 11.

F

FATHER GOOSE
See GHIGNA, Charles

*　　*　　*

FITCH, Sheree 1956-

Personal

Born December 3, 1956, in Ottawa, Ontario, Canada; daughter of Kenneth Douglas and Dolores Shirley (Comeau) Fitch; divorced; children: two sons. *Education:* St. Thomas University, graduated (with honors), 1987; has attended writer's workshops.

Addresses

Home—Halifax, Nova Scotia, Canada. *Office*—c/o Writer's Federation of Nova Scotia, 1809 Barrington St., Ste. 901, Halifax, Nova Scotia B3J 3K8, Canada. *Agent*—c/o Doubleday, 1540 Broadway, New York, NY 10036.

Career

Children's author and performance poet. Worked as a government clerk; founder and president of Campus, a group for older, part-time students at St. Thomas University and the University of New Brunswick, while an undergraduate; founder and member of Enterprise Theatre, an alternative theatre troupe, while an undergraduate; performer and actress on stage, radio, film, and television. *Member:* Writer's Federation of Nova Scotia.

Awards, Honors

Queen's Fellowship, 1987; Atlantic Booksellers' Choice Award, 1990, for *Sleeping Dragons All Around;* Mr. Christie's Book Award, 1993, for *There Were Monkeys in My Kitchen!;* Ann Connor-Brimer Award, 1995, for *Mabel Murple.*

Sheree Fitch

Writings

POETRY FOR CHILDREN

Toes in My Nose, and Other Poems, illustrated by Molly Bobak, Doubleday Canada (Toronto), 1987, Boyds Mill Press, 1993.

Sleeping Dragons All Around (prose), illustrated by Michele Nidenoff, Doubleday Canada, 1989.

Merry-Go-Day, illustrated by Molly Bobak, Doubleday Canada, 1991.

With this collection of childhood poems, Fitch elicited comparisons to beloved children's poet Shel Silverstein.

There Were Monkeys in My Kitchen!, illustrated by Marc Mongeau, Doubleday Canada, 1992.

I Am Small, illustrated by Kim LaFave, Doubleday Canada, 1994.

Mabel Murple, illustrated by Maryann Kovalski, Doubleday Canada, 1995.

If You Could Wear My Sneakers!, illustrated by Darcia Labrosse, Doubleday Canada, 1997.

There's a Mouse in My House, illustrated by Leslie Watts, Doubleday Canada, 1998.

The Hullabaloo Bugaboo Day, illustrated by Jill Quinn, Pottersfield Press (Lawrencetown Beach, Nova Scotia), 1998.

The Other Author, Arthur, illustrated by Jill Quinn, Pottersfield Press, 1999.

If I Were the Moon, illustrated by Leslie Watts, Doubleday Canada, 1999.

Sun-Day, Moon-Day, Some Day Dreams, Pembroke Publications, forthcoming.

PLAYS

Light a Little Candle, produced at Eastern Front Theatre, 1996.

Rummabubba, Lid-Maker of the Snufflewogs, produced at Mermaid Theatre, 1997.

The Monkeys are Back and We're Out of Bananas, produced at Montreal Youth Theatre, 1998.

The Hullabaloo Bugaboo Day (adapted from book by same name), produced by Young Company Tour, at Theatre New Brunswick, 1998.

POETRY FOR ADULTS

In This House Are Many Women, Goose Lane (Fredericton, New Brunswick, Canada), 1996.

Contributor of poetry to periodicals, including *Fiddlehead* and *Alpha.* Author, with Graham Pilsworth, of weekly column/cartoon. Also author of *The Sweet Chorus of the Ha, Ha, He! Polyphony in Utterance: A Collection of Writings on Children's Poetry,* National Library of Canada, 1994.

Sidelights

Canadian poet-performer Sheree Fitch is the author of numerous children's books which are part of a body of work the author calls "utterachure," writings that are especially suited to oral presentation. Fitch performs her poetry in personal appearances as well as on television and radio. When presenting her work on the printed page, she has enlisted the help of several different illustrators. Fitch has also addressed an adult audience with her poetry, both in print and on CBC radio.

In 1987, when Fitch published *Toes in My Nose,* critic Joanne Stanbridge wrote in *Canadian Children's Literature* that the book "promises to generate some unforgettable author visits" and that "although the poems don't dance and sing on the page," they might do so when performed by Fitch. The poet elicited comparisons to Dennis Lee and Shel Silverstein from *Quill & Quire* writer Adele Ashby, who called the collection of thirty-six poems "zany" and suggested that "this is read-aloud poetry ... to reinforce the enjoyment of the subject."

Based on her five-year-old daughter's reaction, *Books in Canada's* Carole Corbeil recommended Fitch's *Sleeping Dragons All Around* as a fantastic book to read to children, because "the writing ... trips off the tongue." The rhyming story of a girl who has to brave a group of dragons on her way to get a late night snack was also praised by Jacqueline Reid-Walsh, a reviewer for *Canadian Children's Literature.* Reid-Walsh noted that the poem "is written in vivid free verse with strong rhythm, repetition and aural effects." In *Quill & Quire,* Anne Gilmore complimented the book for its "delightful sense of music and amusement."

A visit to the annual Canadian National Exhibition is the subject of Fitch's *Merry-Go-Day,* called "delightfully playful" by Phil Hall in *Books in Canada.* While reiterating the recommendation that Fitch's work should be read aloud, *Canadian Materials* reviewer Ray Doiron felt that the author "brought to life all the sights, sounds, smells and tastes" of the fair; he concluded that "one reading is not enough."

There Were Monkeys in My Kitchen! is a story poem reminiscent of *Sleeping Dragons All Around.* In this work, Willa Wellowby finds that an uninhibited group of monkeys has made a mess of her kitchen, but she cannot convince the Mounties that come to her rescue that the animals were there. Writing for *Quill & Quire,* Kit Pearson found that while "Fitch has a good ear for aural effects and uses long and nonsense words effectively," she should have "pared her text to avoid intimidating the young child." Bert Almon, a *Canadian Children's Literature* critic, called the book "a very funny narrative" and noted that "the language of the poetry fits the uproar of the action."

Mabel Murple takes a character from Fitch's *Toes in My Nose* and places her in a book-length story. The poet explores an imaginary world where Mabel lives, where there is much that is familiar to a young child but where absolutely everything is purple. In a review for *Quill & Quire,* Gwyneth Evans praised Fitch's "insouciant four-line stanzas" and felt that the book's ending—where the setting switches from a purple world to a green one— "provides an almost irresistible temptation to create our own verses about coloured worlds."

A collection of Fitch's prose poems called *I Am Small* expresses the thoughts of Small, a girl of about kindergarten age. *Canadian Materials* reviewer Mary-leah Otto called the book "a quiet, thoughtful collection," maintaining that Fitch's "expressions are pure childhood and pure delight to read." Another of Fitch's works, *If You Could Wear My Sneakers!,* part of a special project for UNICEF, was designed to illustrate several articles from the United Nations Convention on the Rights of the Child. *Quill & Quire* contributor Loris Lesynski found the poems "delicious," adding: "The goofiness of the poems and lightness of the art will put young readers at ease and inspire discussion."

Fitch's first book of poetry for adults, *In This House Are Many Women,* is a collection which includes three poems about the lives of people in a women's shelter. Reviewer Lesley D. Clement commented in *Canadian Literature* that Fitch's background as a children's writer was "everywhere evident in the collection's fantasies: from nightmarish through to whimsical." The subjects explored in the volume include women as mother figures, male-female attraction, and a housewife-turned-circus performer. Overall, Clement described the poems as "sensuous" and found interesting links between the several groupings of poems in the volume.

Secrets

Some things are for telling
Some things are for yelling
Some things are for whispering
To flowers or the sky
Other secrets wing their way
To light by and by

As a special project for UNICEF, Fitch and illustrator Darcia Labrosse produced a collection of poems interpreting fifteen of the articles of the United Nations Convention on the Rights of the Child. (From If You Could Wear My Sneakers! *)*

Works Cited

Almon, Bert, review of *There Were Monkeys in My Kitchen!, Canadian Children's Literature,* no. 81, 1996, pp. 43-44.

Ashby, Adele, review of *Toes in My Nose, Quill & Quire,* June, 1987, p. 10.

Clement, Lesley D., "The Compulsion to Sing," *Canadian Literature,* spring, 1996, pp. 136-38.

Corbeil, Carole, review of *Sleeping Dragons All Around, Books in Canada,* June-July, 1990, pp. 13-16.

Doiron, Ray, review of *Merry-Go-Day, Canadian Materials,* May, 1992, p. 162.

Evans, Gwyneth, review of *Mabel Murple, Quill & Quire,* June, 1995, p. 56.

Gilmore, Anne, review of *Sleeping Dragons All Around, Quill & Quire,* December, 1989, p. 22.

Hall, Phil, "In Praise of Playable," *Books in Canada,* October, 1991, pp. 52-53.

Lesynski, Loris, review of *If You Could Wear My Sneakers!, Quill & Quire,* April, 1997, p. 37.

Otto, Maryleah, review of *I Am Small, Canadian Materials,* October, 1994, p. 187.

Pearson, Kit, review of *There Were Monkeys in My Kitchen!, Quill & Quire,* October, 1992, p. 34.

Reid-Walsh, Jacqueline, review of *Sleeping Dragons All Around, Canadian Children's Literature,* no. 61, 1991, pp. 80-81.

Robertson, Barbara, review of *Merry-Go-Day, Quill & Quire,* July, 1991, p. 52.

Stanbridge, Joanne, review of *Toes in My Nose, Canadian Children's Literature,* no. 50, 1988, p. 76.

For More Information See

PERIODICALS

Books in Canada, December, 1992, p. 32; September, 1997, p. 33.

Canadian Book Review Annual, 1994, p. 450; 1995, p. 468.

Canadian Children's Literature, no. 78, 1995, p. 73.

Canadian Materials, March, 1990, p. 63.

Children's Book News, spring, 1990, p. 14; summer, 1995, p. 13; spring, 1997, p. 29.

School Library Journal, March, 1999, pp. 192-93.

FRENCH, Jackie 1950-

Personal

Born November 30, 1950, in Sydney, Australia; daughter of Barrie (a management consultant) and Valerie (a social reformer; maiden name, Edwards) French; married David Dumaresq (divorced); married Bryan Sullivan, January 20, 1988; children: (first marriage) Edward. *Education:* University of Queensland, B.A. *Politics:* "Fluctuating." *Religion:* "Nonspecific."

Addresses

Home—P.O. Box 113, Braidwood, New South Wales, Australia 2622.

Career

Public servant, 1973-75; farmer, 1975-85; writer, 1985—. *Member:* Australian Society of Authors, Braidwood Historical Society.

Awards, Honors

New South Wales Premier's Award, 1991; Shortlist, Children's Book Council of Australia (CBCA) Award, 1992, for *Rainstones;* Wilderness Society Award, 1993; Royal Blind Society Talking Book of the Year, 1994; Human Rights Award, 1994; Several West Australian Premier's Awards; Christian Education Award; two Commonwealth literary grants; Honor Book, CBCA, 1995, for *Somewhere around the Corner.*

Writings

FOR YOUNG PEOPLE

(And illustrator) *Smudge*, Childerset (Australia), 1988.

Rainstones (short stories), Angus & Robertson (Pymble, New South Wales), 1991.

The Roo that Won the Melbourne Cup, illustrated by Carol McLean-Carr, HarperCollins, 1991.

Walking the Boundaries, illustrated by Bronwyn Bancroft, Angus & Robertson, 1993.

Hairy Charlie and the Pumpkin, illustrated by Dee Huxley, Moondrake (Carlton, Victoria), 1994.

The Secret Beach, Angus & Robertson, 1995.

Annie's Pouch, illustrated by Bettina Guthridge, Angus & Robertson, 1995.

Somewhere around the Corner, Henry Holt, 1995.

Mermaids, photographs by Bernard Rosa, Angus & Robertson, 1995.

Mind's Eye, Angus & Robertson, 1996.

Summerland, Angus & Robertson, 1996.

A Wombat Named Bosco, illustrated by Bettina Guthridge, Angus & Robertson, 1996.

Beyond the Boundaries, Angus & Robertson, 1996.

The Warrior: The Story of a Wombat, illustrated by Bettina Guthridge, Angus & Robertson, 1996.

The Book of Unicorns, HarperCollins, 1997.

Dancing with Ben Hall and Other Yarns, illustrated by Gwen Harrison, Angus & Robertson, 1997.

Soldier on the Hill, HarperCollins, 1997.

There's an Echidna at the Bottom of My Garden, illustrated by David Stanley, Koala Books (Redfern, New South Wales), 1997.

The Boy with the Silver Eyes, illustrated by David Miller, Lothian (Port Melbourne, Australia), 1997.

There's a Wallaby at the Bottom of My Garden, illustrated by Bettina Gutheridge, Koala Books, 1997.

Daughter of the Regiment, Angus & Robertson, 1998.

The Little Book of Big Questions, illustrated by Terry Denton, Allen & Unwin (Sydney, Australia), 1998.

Felix Smith Has Every Right to Be a Crocodile, illustrated by David Stanley, Koala Books, 1998.

How the Aliens from Alpha Centauri Invaded My Math Class and Turned Me into a Writer ... and How You Can Be One Too, HarperCollins, 1998.

Stories to Eat with a Banana, HarperCollins, 1998.

Tajore Arkle, HarperCollins, 1999.

Hitler's Daughter, HarperCollins, 1999.

Captain Purrfect, Koala Books, 1999.

Charlie's Gold, HarperCollins, 1999.

"THE CHILDREN OF THE VALLEY" SERIES; ALL ILLUSTRATED BY VICTORIA CLUTTERBUCK

City in the Sand, Aird, 1992.

The Music from the Sea, Aird, 1992.

House of a Hundred Animals, Aird, 1993.

The Metal Men, Aird, 1994.

The Tribe that Sang to Trees, Aird, 1996.

FOR ADULTS

Organic Gardening in Australia, Reed (Australia), 1987.

Natural Rose Growing: An Organic Approach to Gardening, Angus & Robertson, 1988.

The Wilderness Garden: A Radical New View of Australian Growing Methods, Aird, 1993.

Backyard Self Sufficiency, Aird, 1993.

Organic Control of Household Pests, Aird, 1993.

Organic Control of Common Weeds, Aird, 1993.

A to Z of Useful Plants, Aird, 1993.

Book of Lavender, HarperCollins, 1993.

Book of Mint, HarperCollins, 1993.

Book of Rosemary, HarperCollins, 1993.

Book of Thyme, HarperCollins, 1993.

Book of Chili, HarperCollins, 1994.

Book of Garlic, HarperCollins, 1994.

Household Self Sufficiency, Aird, 1994.

The Organic Garden Problem Solver, HarperCollins, 1994.

Yates Guide to Herbs, HarperCollins, 1994.

Yates Guide to Edible Gardening, HarperCollins, 1994.

New Plants from Old, Aird, 1994.

Plants that Never Say Die, Lothian (Port Melbourne, Australia), 1995.

Soil Food: 1372 Ways to Add Fertility to Your Soil, Aird, 1995.

Jackie French's Top 10 Vegetables, Aird 1995.

The Pumpkin Book, Aird, 1997.

Growing Flowers Naturally, Aird, 1997.

Making Money from Your Garden, Earth Garden Books (Trentham, Victoria), 1997.

Jackie French's Household Herb Book, Earth Garden Books, 1998.

Seasons of Content, illustrated by Gwen Harrison, Angus &
    Robertson, 1998.
How to Guzzle Your Garden, HarperCollins, 1999.
*Wham Whomp Stamp Stomp and Other Interesting Ways to
    Kill Pests,* HarperCollins, 1999.

OTHER

Regular contributor to *Australian Women's Weekly,
Sydney Morning Herald, Burke's Backyard* and *Earth-
garden.* "Walking the Boundaries," a popular environmental children's outdoor program, is based on French's
book of the same name. French's children's books have
been translated into French and German.

Work in Progress

Missing You Love Sarah, and *A Memoir for Bunyips and
Mermaids,* both for HarperCollins.

Sidelights

Jackie French told *SATA:* "I wrote my first children's
book, *Rainstones,* living in a shed with a wallaby called
Fred, a black snake called Gladys, and a wombat called
Smudge. The editor at HarperCollins described it as the
messiest, worst spelt manuscript they'd ever received.
Now, tens of thousands of readers deeply love these
same short stories.

"The messiness was mostly due to Smudge, the wombat,
who had a particular hatred for my typewriter (an old
one I found at the dump) and so he left nightly droppings
on the keyboard. But the incorrect spellings were from
my dyslexia—I can't focus on single words to see if
they're spelt properly or not. (I profoundly hope
someone has checked this spelling before you read it.)

"I sent my first book off because I was broke, had a baby
to support, and could think of no other way to do it alone
in the bush. But I've always told stories. I'm a storyteller
by passion and by conviction. In any age, in any place,
I'd be a storyteller. But I also write because I believe
that giving children fiction is one of the most valuable
things you can give them.

"When you tell a child a story, you are telling them life
holds other possibilities. Encouraging fantasies of mermaids, and unicorns just around the corner, may well
foster creative imaginations that one day lead to social
reform, or new theories of the universe, or simply, a
knowing that life can be better.

"As well as my books for children, I'm one of the
Australian gurus of organic growing methods, with
books ranging from detailed accounts of my research
into alternative methods of weed or pest control, to more
popular gardening books. I'm also a regular on a popular
television gardening show and on many radio programs
around Australia. My husband, Bryan, and I also run an
experimental farm.

"My other work includes adult fiction (horrible way to
express it—it always sounds like I write pornography,

but how else do you differentiate children's books from
books for adults?), and various other books that are hard
to stuff into categories. (Literary diversity isn't fashionable in the 1990s. ... I do sometimes feel like
apologizing for a form of intellectual attention deficit
syndrome ... but the apology wouldn't be sincere.)

"I've also studied wombat ecology for twenty years, and
will tell wombat stories at a drop of the hat—or with
even less encouragement.

"I live with my husband, Bryan, and son, Edward, in a
deep valley on the Southern Tablelands of New South
Wales, Australia. We live in a house we built ourselves
with stone from the creek, with a homemade waterwheel
to power the computer when its too shady for the solar
panels, a rambling garden over-endowed with fruit and
roses, six wombats, a frequently drunk goanna, and a
mob of lyrebirds who dig up the asparagus."

French's stories reverberate with an intense interest in
environmental issues and a sensitive and fine description
of setting and character. The Australian landscape and

*In Jackie French's story for young readers, a drought
in Australia may necessitate a move which will separate
Annie from the animals she has befriended.(Cover
illustration by Bettina Guthridge.)*

its many life forms become the backdrop for the highly acclaimed *Rainstones,* a collection of five stories in which the author zealously brings the Australian bush to glorious life. As Kevin Steinberger, a reviewer for *Magpies,* maintained, French "explores [the Australian bush] with a keen multi-sensory perception that indicates a genuine affinity with the land and a passion for its life." In her review for *Horn Book,* Karen Jameyson also praised the author's poignant descriptions, explaining how readers "imbibe not just plot and character but a very distinct group of country settings as well. Casuarina trees sway in the breeze; mopokes call their distinctive cry; wombats grind grass in the moonlight." The last story in the book, "Dusty and the Dragon," which takes a stand against logging, becomes the forerunner for a continuing and fearless focus on environmental concerns in French's stories.

Somewhere around the Corner, another work distinguished by French's sensitive description of character and setting, transports Barbara, an Australian foster child, from a violent labor dispute in 1994 Sydney, back to Sydney, 1932, and the Great Depression. Here she meets Jim, a young boy her own age, who brings her home to his family. In this setting of hard times and misfortune, Barbara comes to know the loving warmth and support of a family for the first time. Writing for *School Library Journal,* Susan L. Rogers claimed: "Thorough character development and a captivating story save the novel from preaching." In her review for *Booklist,* Sally Estes declared, "French does a wonderful job of portraying the precariousness of life during the 1930s Depression as well as the courage and warmth of people who not only survived but managed, in many ways, to thrive despite adversity." "The author has an eye for setting and characterization," concluded *Voice of Youth Advocates* contributor Joyce A. Litton.

Works Cited

Estes, Sally, review of *Somewhere around the Corner, Booklist,* May 15, 1995, p. 1645.

Jameyson, Karen, review of *Rainstones, Horn Book,* July-August, 1992, pp. 498-99.

Litton, Joyce A., review of *Somewhere around the Corner, Voice of Youth Advocates,* October, 1995, p. 218.

Rogers, Susan L., review of *Somewhere around the Corner, School Library Journal,* July, 1995, p. 78.

Steinberger, Kevin, "Jackie French and the Green Crusade," July, 1994, p. 15.

For More Information See

PERIODICALS

Australian Book Review, February, 1993, p. 56; June, 1993, p. 59.

Bulletin of the Center for Children's Books, June, 1995, p. 343.

Magpies, March, 1992, p. 30; July, 1993, p. 26; November, 1993, p. 34; July, 1994, pp. 15-16; March, 1995, p. 21; March, 1996, p. 33; May, 1997, p. 34; September, 1997, p. 31; November, 1997, p. 33.*

G

Alan Garner

1934-

Old Men's Trousers & the Making Strange of Things

My name is Alan Garner, and I was born, with the cord wrapped twice round my throat, in the front bedroom of 47, Crescent Road, Congleton, Cheshire, at Latitude 53 degrees, 09' 40' N, Longitude 02 degrees, 13' 7' W, at 21.30 on Wednesday, 17 October 1934. My mother was a tailor, and my father a painter and decorator.

My mother's family were talented cranks, on every side; lateral thinking was a part of their equipment, and those that got away with it were respectable as well. Even the names are odd. There was a great-aunt Sophia Pitchfork; and a great-great-grand-uncle, J. Sparkes Hall, an inventor, of 308 & 310, Regent Street, London, Bootmaker to Her Majesty The Queen and Their Royal Highnesses The Prince and Princess of Wales. He designed the elastic sided boot, and demonstrated his English Cottage or Test House (which became the traditional Nineteenth Century worker's kitchen fire-cum-oven-cum-boiler) at the Paris Exhibition of 1867. His brother, Edward, designed and built church organs.

Perhaps a more typical gene was represented by the third brother, who was Professor of Systematic Memory, or Polymnemonics, on which he lectured, 'copiously illustrated by Novel, Curious, Extraordinary and Interesting Experiments (Schools at halfprices)'.

In the Eighteenth Century, the Halls cover their traces, but documentary fragments are indicative: early photographs suggest that a pawnbroker Hall, of Plymouth, had fashionable tastes; and so my great-great-great-great-grandmother may have been West African.

My father's family is quite different. They have been craftsmen for centuries. They have married locally, under strict cultural tabus, and have lived in the same house without a break of tenancy. My cousin lives there now. The house stands on the slopes of Alderley Edge, in a small area called The Hough, a wooded sandstone hill above the Cheshire Plain. The Edge is a Beauty Spot in summer and at weekends, but its long history and prehistory make it unsafe at all times. It is physically and emotionally dangerous. No one born to the Edge questions that, and we show it a proper respect.

So there are three main elements in me from the start. Families on the one side gifted, unstable, and, on the other, skilled, steady. And a hill that Garners have inhabited, and worked, for as long as anybody knows.

Born in Congleton, raised in Alderley, I have lived, since 1957, seven miles from both, near the Jodrell Bank radio telescope, in a mediaeval timber-framed house on a site that has been occupied by the living for eight thousand years, since the Mesolithic period at the end of the last Ice Age, and also by the dead. The mound that the house stands on is one of a group of tumuli. If I have any real occupation, it is to be here.

Therefore, I have spent the whole of my life, so far, on the Pennine shelf of East Cheshire. It is an area that encompasses most of the landscapes to be found in Britain. Within twelve miles, I can move through fen, dairy and arable farms, to sheep runs and bleak mountain tors. And, in this particular place, I find a universality that enables me to write.

Everywhere is special, in some way. It was not imperative that I should be born in Cheshire; but it was imperative that I should know my place. That can be achieved only by inheriting one's childhood landscape, and by growing in it to maturity. It is a subtle matter of owning and of being owned.

The landscape of childhood is itself unremarkable, for the child. Lack of any concept of things being other than they are found to be brings to childhood an innocence that hindsight can abuse. When we comment on the resilience of children, we should remember that what may now appear to have been brave or terrible was possibly unquestioned at the time. It was certainly unquestioned by me as an individual and by the generation of village children to which I belonged.

"God bless Mummy, God bless Daddy, make me a good boy and don't let the war end. Amen."

I gabbled that prayer every night from the age of six until God let me down in 1945, when I was nearly eleven. We were not a religious family. The first three pious requests were taught by my mother, who was enlisting the Holy Trinity as a child-minder, and the last bit was my own, because I had worked out that peace would axe my favourite wireless programmes.

The knowing innocence of childhood makes something peculiar of war. Lack of experience turns it into a bright game. There is no responsibility, no foresight, no sense of deprivation. The child is free to take what he wants from the mess; and the child is a callous animal, with little built-in morality.

The past was something called Pre-war. It seemed to have been an age of plenty. Adults would thumb through old mail order catalogues and talk of the good days. If the past was Pre-war, the future had no name. We were living in a geological time span called the Duration. We did not think beyond that.

The nearest I came to thinking was that I was between two periods, of which adults were aware, but I could not be: the Eldorado of Pre-war, of which I remembered only the vivid yellow and the taste and shape of a banana, and a return to an Elysium after the Duration: a 'once and future peace'. But I felt no sense of loss.

We lived a rural life on the edge of suburbia, far enough from Manchester for us to take their evacuees, but among the anti-aircraft batteries, and where the bombers would jettison for the dash home. I lay in bed, listening. Heinkel? Dornier? It was the wah-wah of German engines as the planes dragged their weight to Manchester. Then the guns. Out of bed and into the road to pick up hot shrapnel: metal with a texture like no other: steel sand.

Next morning we would swap our shrapnel and barter for sticky incendiary bombs that were more like bicycle pumps than fireworks. For some reason, shrapnel that had been 'hot-found' was worth more than 'cold-found', though there was nothing by which to tell the difference now. It was a matter of unquestioned honour: the only instance that was never challenged, in my experience of childhood.

The Polish pilot would have been our greatest prize, but we lost him. His fighter was in trouble, and he crash landed. He was dead when we arrived. We could not get the cockpit fully open before the fire reached the ammunition, and we had to leave his goggles and make do with a yellow handkerchief that had been around his neck. But the blood was real.

Our war was with the evacuees. We had them from Liverpool, Manchester, London and the Channel Islands. The worst were the Islanders. They were silent, foreign, could speak a secret language, and would not go home. Manchester, Liverpool and London fought dirty, but were scared both of woods and of open spaces. For us, a field was certain refuge from pursuit, even if it were empty. The possibility of a hidden cow lurking in the cropped grass was something that no townie would risk.

The adult plans for what they called the Home Front, (there appeared to be no Home Back; or, if there was, it did not concern them), were varied and improvised. My mother concocted the following stratagem against invasion while my father was guarding us from the Hun in North Wales.

I kept a bag of pepper by the door, next to Mum's poker. They were for the German paratrooper. When he knocked on the door, I was going to throw the pepper into his face, Mum would hit him with the poker, and then we would run upstairs and commit suicide by hurling ourselves head first from the bedroom window. That the window was only some nine feet above the ground, with stone mullions that would have made 'hurling' a problem did not make either of us question the efficacy of the scheme.

Peace, I thought, came when a sailor gave me a banana. But it was green. He told me that it was not ripe. I put it on the mantlepiece and watched it every day. When it was the yellow I remembered, and the smell was as I remembered, I peeled and ate it in a Proustian orgy. At that instant of biting into the fruit, I knew that the Duration was over. By colour, taste, smell and geometry, a banana, for me, bracketed World War II.

Then everything changed. The Belsen films were shown at our cinema. Although children were forbidden entry, we had always known the free way in. I saw the films four times. The not-dead corpse in the black skull cap, picking over his shirt and grinning at the camera that had come too late; the bulldozer ploughing the graceful, hideous ballet into the mass grave. It was right for us to see this, to remind us that what we children were playing was being played better by adults, because they were bigger and had more toys.

Can anything be summarised of our generation, bred in poverty and branded in war? Well, for me, I am not afraid of the dark, and the blackout gave me a childhood of stars. But I do wish that air raid sirens were not still used to call out the fire brigade. Also, to grow up in an improvised world, where others are trying to kill you, does develop an ability to distinguish between necessity and luxury, to arrive quickly at priorities, and to survive.

And what is the difference between me and my children? Materially, they are secure in a way that we never were. They are in a saner world, though it is not sane yet. And there is a factor to consider.

The blitz, the bag of pepper, the dead pilot meant little. But Belsen made sense. At the age of ten, I realised what all the fuss had been about. It was about the ovens and the people inside. Before seeing them, I knew a lot of facts, but could not give them a context. Then, within minutes, the facts came together in an image and I was violently wise.

My children and their generation have not had that shock; yet they are better informed than I was, and they are better informed because they have watched television.

I am not defending rubbish, or the trite, but pointing out that there is an argument for the medium of television's being the main cultural development of the century. It removes more barriers than it creates, and exposes liars more clearly than any previous news machine. As long as politicians and generals continue to fear the lens, and there are men and women willing to be killed serving it, future cameras may arrive in time for the not-dead corpse in the black skull cap.

I find this hard to explain to many people, who say that the world is getting worse because what they see on the news is so terrible. I try to explain that what they see has always gone on, but they have not been able to see it as it is happening, edited, focused. If a camera had been around to record how Athens dealt with an Aegean island that objected to paying taxes, the Parthenon and our model of Western thought would have been put into a different perspective indeed. This century has moved the portrayal of war from static engravings, with no corpses, of events long gone and in another country, to a young girl running naked in napalm into your house, in high quality colour, and now.

Television removes barriers. My attitudes in childhood were partly the innate callousness of an infant, and the war ended on the threshold of adolescence, when I was ready to become more aware of other people. I maintain that children now are more aware, more humane, because they have learned more through television than we did by living in an isolation that happened to be punctuated by random, and occasional, violence close at hand.

Rubbish there was, is and ever shall be. What has to be educated is choice. That is the difference. My children are richer in mind and spirit than I was, and from that richness grows compassion.

Let me stress that I see no miracle, no sudden generation of angels. But, where I tried to snatch the pilot's goggles, the next children may not let him put them on.

So, while Leningrad starved for nine hundred days and Belsen conducted its roaring trade, my childhood was happy, along with the other village children; and, in addition, unaware that all children did not commonly live as I lived, I spent ten years in two worlds.

The daily landscape for me was a bedroom ceiling in a brick cottage, with a porch. It was out of that porch my father stepped one January in the pre-dawn blackness and disappeared to join the army, while my mother and I cried, certain we should not see him again.

The bedroom was whitewashed, irregular plaster, steeply pitched, with rafters and purlins and ridge exposed. And I lay on my back beneath it through three long illnesses: diphtheria, meningitis and pneumonia.

I had no brothers or sisters. The Second World War came and went. The family survived. There were no tragedies. But the isolation caused by physical weakness and paralysis must have been increased by the more general isolation of a house threatened, bombed, blacked out. When I was bedfast, the rhythms of day and night were not imposed on me. Rather than sleep, I catnapped, or was in coma. Reality was the room.

The view from my window was, for five years, glued over with cheesecloth against bomb blast; but, even unrestricted, it was no more than a length of road where little happened, and which was closed by the spire and weathercock of a Victorian church, on which my great-great-grandfather had worked to build. Sideways rolling of my head made the spire wobble, the houses insecure, and people on the road change shape. I knew that the uneven window pane was the cause, but it still gave the room the greater reality. The ceiling did not wobble when I rolled my head.

There was a forest in the ceiling, with hills and clouds, and a road to the horizon. The way into the ceiling for me was harder at some times than at others. To enter the ceiling, I had to stare at the road and remove detail from the sides of vision by unfocusing my eyes. I had to block sound. I had to switch myself off. "Switching off" is not a good description, because there was a profound engagement in the activity of making the bed-bound "me" let go of me. The changes in sound and vision were felt by the "me" on the bed. I had to remove myself from that. I would concentrate on the concentration of the "me" concentrating. I thought of the thought of myself thinking. I observed the observer observing; until the observer was not the observed.

Whatever actually took place, the sensation was that of sliding out of phase with the boy in the bed. And the automatic result was to find that I had crossed the neutralised zone from the bed into the ceiling. I did not sleep. There was no relaxing of consciousness. It was the opposite. I had to think harder, relatively, than at any previous time of my life. The thoughts may have been unusual, but the thinking was not.

I could tell the difference between waking and sleeping because of something else that developed. It was the ability to programme myself for dreaming before I slept, rather like choosing from a menu. Generally, the dreams would come in their programmed order, though nightmares were frequent and unsought.

If I found myself in a nightmare, I would first check that I was dreaming, then watch for the approach of the nightmare's particular horror, and jump head-first into it to wake myself up. I always knew when I was dreaming, because I could control the dream. The ceiling, however, I could not predict. Once I was on the road in the ceiling, there was no effort needed to keep me there. I entered, and did not look back. I did not see the boy on the bed. I felt that I was awake.

The world of the ceiling was three-dimensional, objects were solid, visual perspectives true. I never ate or drank in the ceiling (as I later found was the rule for the Other World). There was no wind, no climate, no heat, no cold, no time. The light came from no source and was shadowless, as neon; but before I knew neon. And everywhere, everybody, everything was white.

Another peculiarity was that I could see in the dark. If I lay in bed, in the black room, the ceiling became fluorescent, or a negative film. And, when I went into the ceiling, the ceiling-world was lit by the same reversed light, and so were the people and so was I. Otherwise, the ceiling was, for me, 'natural'. I met people I knew, including my parents, and some who were only of the ceiling. None of the 'ceiling people' has turned up in later life, yet, and they had no names. The people I knew in both states of waking had no knowledge of the ceiling when I asked them. I soon stopped asking.

I 'lived' in the ceiling. But there was a difference between the ceiling and the bed that made the bed, with all its pain and debility, the permanent choice. Although the way to the ceiling was along the same road in the ceiling, the land beyond the road, from visit to visit, was inconsistent; and this inconsistency made the ceiling not more interesting but less. Each venture was separate rather than a learning, and such variety leads nowhere; it builds nothing; it has nothing to teach. And I wanted to learn. That was the difference. I would enter the ceiling by an act of will, but I left it through tedium. Sooner or later, I would stop whatever I was doing in the ceiling, turn around, and always be facing the same road-forest-cloud-hill picture that I saw from my bed. Then I would pull back, as a camera does, to the bed, and lie looking at the lime-washed plaster.

There was one terror in the ceiling: one motionless dread.

Sometimes I would look up, and see no road, no forest, clouds or hills, but a plump little old woman with a circular face, hair parted down the middle and drawn to a tight bun, lips pursed, and small, pebbled eyes. She sat wrapped in a shawl in a cane wheelchair and watched me. She was a waning moon: her head turned to the side, as if she had broken her neck. When I saw her, I knew that I could die. She must not enter the room, and I must not enter the ceiling. If I let her eyes blink, I should die. There was no night, day, dawn, dusk. The little old woman and I were locked.

The little old woman came only when my life really was threatened. She was a part of the plaster in the ceiling, not of my room but of my parents', and I was taken there when I was too ill to be left alone. She was my death, and I knew it.

A hundred and fifty yards from bed, and behind the house, was my other world. Later knowledge told me that it was an eroded fault-scarp, six hundred feet high, of the Keuper and Bunter Triassic sandstones. To me, it was the Edge, that cliff covered with trees, mined for copper and quarried for stone through centuries and then abandoned. When I was not confined to the house, I would spend my days and my nights on the Edge.

Woodland on a crag of coloured stone was just the beginning of that world for me. In the best sense, as a family, we have always known our place. We handled it as miners and stonecutters. We culled its timber for houses and fuel, grew food on its soil. At a deeper level, we accepted that there was a Hero King asleep in the ground, behind a rock named the Iron Gates. Our water supply derived from the Holy Well, which granted wishes to tourists at weekends, and an income for the child of our family who, on a Monday morning, cleaned out the small change.

Yet for no money would that child have climbed the yew that stood beside the well. "If I ever so much as see you touch that," my grandfather said, "I'll have the hide off you." And there was a memory that could hardly be restored to words: of how the well was not for wishing, but for the curing of barren women; and the offerings were of bent pins, not of pence. And grandad spoke of rags tied to trees there; but that had been a long time ago, he said.

So it is for a child born to the Edge. We knew our place, and knowledge passed beyond the material, such as where a band of white clay was under the fallen leaves which could be used as soap to clean up with before going home. It passed to the spiritual, too. I was brought up to respect both. They were there. Even the ghosts were those of relatives. Yet my relationship with that hill was different from that of the rest of my family. As a result of gained knowledge, for me the Edge both stopped, and melted, time.

I knew enough geology to become amazed. I could trace the tidal vortex in the strata: the print of water swirling for a second under the pull of wind and moon and held for two hundred and forty-three million years. I felt the white pebbles in the rock and wondered from what mountains they had come, by what river, to what sea.

And, in the fleeting, I found the vision. In knowing the moment of the vortex, and of the pebble, which, if I could have watched for long enough, was not rock but liquid, I lost all sense of 'me' upon the hill. As with the ceiling, a barrier was down. But, perhaps because I was not weakened, fevered, paralysed, the result was different. I felt not that I entered a world, but that a world entered me. There were no exploits such as the ceiling gave; no journeys; no people. Of the two landscapes, the ceiling was the more mundane. But the ceiling had showed me that time was not simply a clock; and so I was open to the hill and to the metaphors of time that the hill gave.

The years of bed had developed another freedom.

For most children, I know now, time drags. That is because inertia is uncommon, and days are filled with events. But where a child has only inertia, time must not rule. And I played with time as if it were chewing-gum, making a minute last an hour, and a day compress to a minute. I had to. If I had not kept time pliant, it would have set me as the pebble in the rock.

So I brought to the coloured cliff and my strength the craft of the white ceiling and my weakness. I switched myself off. And the universe opened. I was shown a totality of space and time. A kaleidoscope of images expanded so quickly that they fragmented. There were too many, too fast for individual detail or recall. They dropped below the subliminal boundary, but I felt the rip-tide of their surge, and the rip-tide has remained.

Yet, despite the hurry-burly beyond words, when I partook of the hill and the hill partook of me, there is a calm, which childhood could not give. For, if the child had been left with only a vision, if the "me" had not been replaced by a truer sense of self, I do not know what would have happened. I do not know that I could have grown. With only a blind vision, I do not know that I could have survived.

I said at the beginning that, as children, we accept 'normality' to be whatever is around us; and I have tried to describe two experiences to demonstrate what I mean. Man, though, at every age, is also an animal with instincts that need no teaching; and the strongest instinct is for life. Yet, in childhood, at three separate times, I died.

It was not medical death in the way that it can now be defined. It was the opinion of doctors, humane men, around the bed of an organism under the rough ceiling of a cottage below Alderley Edge.

The child was technically alive, but all systems were collapsing, and there was nothing more to be done for him. In one instance, meningitis, I heard my mother being helped to accept the imminent death by being told that for me to recover would be a cruelty, because the damage to brain and spine would be massive, and I should be a bedridden thing for the rest of my life: not a person, not a son.

What those humane men did not take into account, was that I was not yet dead. I could not signal, I was unable to communicate with the outside world, but I was not yet dead. I could hear. And I heard. I heard myself dismissed, written off. It was, to the animal in me, an attempt to kill my life.

I screamed, using no words, making no sound. The body was nearly dead. But fury then was greater than death, and, though nothing showed on the surface of the creature under the sheet, inside was war. I raged against the cosmos. Inside me was a zoo gone mad. Outside was calm, immobile, good-as-dead. And, I think, that is why I lived. I was too angry to die.

I lived. For what?

The point is that mine was a glorious childhood. I would not wish it on anyone, nor on me again. But it happened. And my good fortune was that I was able, as a child, to know my death, to face the ultimate, before experience scrambled my brains.

I am not arguing for life-at-all-cost. I hope I am not so arrogant that I would begin to tell other people in other circumstances what to do. Indeed, I am at a disadvantage. I have known my death and known its ways, but I have never felt so desperate that I have wanted to die. I have felt so desperate that I have wanted to live. I have pursued life through the Edge and the ceiling, and am simply relating a number of connected events that, though personal to me, may, by their simplicity, be of interest to others.

I speak as a survivor, and have described some techniques of survival, the pursuit of life, through the Edge and the ceiling, through inner and outer space and time, which I used as a child. They were the instincts of an animal, but they went on to teach me something more. They taught me that we transcend technique and that all experience can be made positive and turned to good. But we can never afford to stop.

If I had stopped, having survived, the technique of the Edge and the ceiling might have dwindled into a sloppy mysticism; but instead, I endured the rigours of an education that matched vision with thought, each to feed the other, so that dream and logic both had their place, both made sense, and legend and history could both be true.

In such a way, one mere survival was transcended, and is to this day. Each connection seen brings greater awe. My privileged childhood integrated me by forcing me to choose whether to live or to die; and, from that integration, I saw that inner and outer worlds did not collide, but communicated, through my very being, their harmonies of poetry and prose. I saw a unity at work outside myself.

I have often been asked by people who know this history whether that childhood made me a writer. I cannot answer. Certainly, I drew on the experience, but it is a chicken-and-egg question.

If I had not had the encounter with my death and the Damascan road provided by the Edge, would I have been granted the vision needed in order to write? If I had not been born with the stamina of will and the bloody-mindedness required of all writing, would I have meekly accepted the doctors' diagnosis, and conveniently complied? I do not know. All I can say is that many writers, significantly or not, have been only children, and have suffered long and life-threatening illness in isolation from human company. It is not for me to guess.

However, my wife has voiced a theory that may well be of literary import in the context of my experience at that given time. She is a teacher and critic, so I may put forward these thoughts without much fear of misrepresentation; and you may be sure that she will have checked them before they are spoken, since she says that, if a fiction can improve on the fact, I shall always choose the fiction.

My wife claims to find, in recent children's literature, little that qualifies as literature. She asked herself why this should be, after a Golden Age that ran from the late fifties to the late sixties in Britain. And she found that, generally, the writers of this Golden Age were children during the Second World War: a war waged deliberately against civilians.

The atmosphere that these children and young people grew up in was one of a whole community and a whole nation united against pure evil, made manifest in the person of Hitler. Parents were seen to be afraid. Death was a constant possibility. There was no expectation of security. The talk was of an idyllic time in the past, and the propaganda promised a better future.

Therefore, daily life was lived on a mythic plane: of absolute Good against absolute Evil; of the need to endure, to survive whatever had to be overcome, to be tempered in whatever furnace was required. These are spiritual, moral and philosophical issues, and, therefore, bound to have had an effect on the psyche of childhood at that time.

Those children who were born writers, and who would be adolescent when the full horrors became known, would not be able to avoid concerning themselves with the issues; and so their books, however clad, were written on profound themes, and were literature. The generation that has followed is not so fuelled, and its writing is, by comparison, effete and trivial.

Susan Cooper, an exact contemporary of mine at Oxford, has said: "I know that the shape of my imagination, and all its unconscious preoccupations, were moulded by having been a child in the war."

At a deeper level, and more enigmatically, Kurt Hahn said in 1947: "Education has no nobler task than to provide the moral equivalent of war."

So for my wife. I can testify to the weight of at least one part of her observations. She is right in saying that we were living on a mythic plane. I remember the frequency with which the Sleeping Hero under the hill behind the village was referred to by adults. They said of him, half (yet only half) in joke, that, since he was waiting to ride out when England should be 'in direst peril,' and, 'in a battle thrice lost, thrice won, drive the enemy into the sea,' it was about time for him to be doing. It showed me, at an early age, the enduring and genuine power of myth. In 1940, it was something the village turned to seriously. And I would add, on my own account, that, when I see the materialistic brats who have never had to ask twice to be appeased, muling and puling now as adults, I agree with Othello that 'the tyrant custom . . . hath made the flinty and steel couch of war my thrice- driven bed of down.' And, when I was on that bed, I felt, with Richard Crawshaw, 'all wonders in one sight. Eternity shut in a span.'

Educationalist and critic may dispute the matter; psychologist and philosopher, biologist and theologian, too. But, for me, there is no conflict. I am a writer. For me it is enough that, as a child, I saw, and came to know, my place.

In making the possibly hubristic claim to be a writer, I should say something about that process, which occupies my life day and night, awake and asleep, especially since my own understanding of the activity was resolved for me in the most recent novel, *Strandloper* by my being permitted to engage with the thought structures of a wise people who can neither read nor write. It would be apt if I could draw this essay together by trying to show how these events came about, and to give weight to the recent statement by another writer (whose words I now steal whenever approached for "hints" or "advice") that: "There is no use whatever trying to write a book unless you know that you must write that book or go mad, or perhaps die." It is as clear as that.

Having risked hubris, I can go further, but this is fact.

In writing I have never considered a reader. I have merely written as well and as passionately as possible from the resources of experience and ability within me; and those resources, if healthy, will have matured and changed through time. So the question of my "writing for children," has never concerned me, and I can understand that the resources of a twenty-year-old would superficially be of more interest to a reader half that age than to one twice that age. But when it comes to degrees of literary passion, a child of five and an adult of ninety are the same animal.

Over the years, I have come to feel that I had to create not only the books themselves but the atmosphere into which they could be published. Confirmation came quite recently when I discovered that the publisher's readers' reports for all my novels, until *The Stone Book*, had recommended rejection. Only the belief of the three strong editors I have worked with has got me into print.

The objections have tended to be the same. One has been universal: "It's not like his last novel." But it should not be like his last novel, since that novel has been written and there is no literary gain to be had from repetition.

In the particular: the reports on *The Weirdstone of Brisingamen* and *The Moon of Gornrath* objected to the perceived complexities of the Proper Nouns. Readers of the published books write to express the particular richness of the words and to ask where I get such magical names from. *Elidor* was thought to be emotionally unhealthy and intellectually too complex. The letters single out the reader's apprehensions of the numinous and of an understanding of Space Time and multi-dimensional theory. *The Owl Service* and *Red Shift* were found to be too difficult and demanding in their poetic structures and beyond the comprehension of the public. The letters, some of them metaphorically sobbing, ask how I know what it means to feel what is in the books. The comment is: "I thought it had happened only to me."

It would appear, and this is happy coincidence because I am not prolific but do move on, that the first readers of *The Weirdstone of Brisingamen* have been at the right stage of their development as each book was published. Such an experience can, of course, happen only once.

There are two quotations from my lips that may seem to be in conflict with what I am arguing and that the less sensitive critics often dog me with. The quotations are accurate, but have suffered in the uses to which they have been put by their having been taken baldly out of a subtle context, and not put back in, so that the younger and more idle are not aware of the whole nor do they conceive that the quotations may now be out of date. The words that I am using here should, if healthy, contain some ephemeral thought, because whatever may be written in the future, if worth the writing, will change both me and the reader. But what is worth having here will stay.

Strandloper, through its demands, has given me what I hope to be the strength to write the next novel on which I closed, but did not destroy, the file in 1977 after three years' research because I sensed the immaturity of my powers to deal with the matter then. Now, after *Strandloper* and another three years' research, we shall see.

***

I put the full stop at the end of *Strandloper*, looked at my watch, and wrote: '14.30. Tuesday. 25 April. 1995.' Then I went back to the full stop, and thought: Why didn't I do just that at the start? What I had undergone had all been in order to reach a full stop. The point was the point.

I had set off for it by deciding to do something useful on a hot day. I had opened a box I keep for newspaper cuttings, in case any of them should provoke an idea in the future, and started to cull the redundant. I chid myself for having amassed so much dross. Then I stopped, and read and re-read an item from *The Congleton Chronicle*, our local newspaper, of November 1977. I must have read the article before, otherwise it would not have been in the box, yet I had no memory of it, while now it burnt my brain.

It was a brief article, recording the anecdote of a twenty-year-old bricklayer, William Buckley, from the neighbouring hamlet of Marton, who had been transported for life to New Holland in 1803, had escaped into the bush, survived, and had lived for thirty-two years as an Aborigine. It was headed: "The Wild Man of Marton." I looked at my watch, and noted: '14.30. Tuesday. 21 June. 1983. William Buckley'.

So it had begun. Now it was finished. Why had something, presented as amusing and trivial, taken up precisely four thousand, three hundred and twenty-six days of my life and produced a novel at an average rate of 14.1 words a day, or approximately 0.5875 words an hour? There are two answers. The first is that it had been the most rewarding and demanding period of my life so far. The second is that I had no choice. I did not even have to defend myself by hiding behind Hazlitt's statement that: 'If a man leaves behind him any work which is a model of its kind, we have no right to ask whether he could do anything else, or how he did it, or how long he was about it.'

I'm going to try to communicate something of this experience, despite Hazlitt.

The first problem that has to be tackled may be phrased as: Why subject oneself to the ordeal of constructing a work of fiction? The answer is that the world is messy, and the truth hard to find in its tangled thickets. Truth is best found by the writer's taking the facts, pruning them, and then arranging what's left into the simplest possible pattern. This necessitates a degree of fabrication, which presents us with the paradox that the writer has to manipulate the facts in order to make what is essential clear and true. At its most extreme, reality can be expressed in art most accurately as myth. And, as I progressed into *Strandloper*, I became aware that the historical William Buckley's life matched the elements of the mythic Quest.

Next must be asked: What makes some people, regardless of cost to themselves and others, write at all? Freud would have it that the creative mind is a morbidity. Plato set poets, of which he was one, at the top of his hit list, against the day when he could establish his ideal state. And Professor Kay Redfield Jamison has made the grotesque discovery, in her surveys of writers, and of creativity, that some fifty percent of the significant innovators suffer from a lethal psychosis, lethal because of its fifty percent suicide risk, which is largely ignored by society since its occurrence in the general public is not more than one percent.

Clearly, then, we are not dealing with a dilettante hobby, or an occupation for gentlefolk. Writers are driven.

Yet the last impression I want to make is one of angst or gloom. The brain is too clever for that. The main drive is what C. S. Lewis cunningly calls "joy", and it is in finding that "joy" that the brain is at its most clever. And I am happiest when engaged in establishing and pursuing research.

In order to make sense, it's time for me to say a little of how I write: not How to Write: just how I write. I count as my main asset the combination of an academic's and a magpie's mind that sees, finds or makes connections and patterns where others don't. Also essential to creativity is the ability to doodle mentally and to play.

I read a newspaper cutting about a curious fellow from Marton. I know that I am pregnant with his story. I look at the story, and make a list of primary subjects that I shall have to learn in great detail before I can begin; and they will each consist of fibres, as in a rope, which will unwind, and have to be followed, in their turn, as I progress. And the fibres will have fibres. Here is the academic at work. I grow a bibliography. I read and read, and take notes: books of notes. The joy leads me on. I am learning what I did not know, and, unlike purely academic work, the subjects appear not to be linked. The magpie is gratified by the collecting; and the writer is awed as the unconnected themes begin to converge, apparently of their own accord (although I am aware of the more mundane theory of selective perception), and, for me, it is the point of convergence, where all makes an elegant and natural simplicity of resolution: that something that, subjectively, has always been waiting: the numinous as a book. But that point can't be reached by the academic element, which is a simple drudge. There comes a moment when all has been read. The intellect, then, has to be suppressed, because I can't 'think' something into being. That is the job of the unconscious. It shows, and tells, so that I 'see', 'dream', 'hear' and 'find'. Then the intellect is freed to edit what the unconscious wrote.

Before I say more of William, I should put the culling of the files into perspective.

It was the Summer Solstice of 1983. The last piece of original work that I had written, *The Stone Book Quartet*, was finished in the summer of 1977. Therefore, six years had gone by in silence. There was nothing to add. 'When may we expect the next novel?' said my publisher of the day. 'When it's ready,' I said, and got on with not writing.

Fortunately for my nervous system, I had never given much credence, if any, to the phenomenon of so-called "writer's block". I was more inclined to think of it as "writer's impatience", and to follow Arthur Koestler's

dictum: 'Soak; and wait.' For me, with *The Stone Book Quartet,* I had emptied my well, and nothing could be done until the water table was restored. And that's where I was at the Summer Solstice of 1983, until 2.30.p.m., when the well became a gusher.

My first problem was to find William. He was said to have been born in 1780, and brought up by his grandfather. I searched the parish registers. There was no record of him anywhere. Then a voice, which many writers learn to heed, said, internally: 'Bishop's Transcripts'. At the period I was concerned for, and for centuries before that, the priest of a parish was obliged not only to keep his registers but, each year, to make a copy and to send it to the Bishop's Palace. By the end of the Eighteenth Century, the concept of making a Bishop's Transcript had become something of a joke. One nearby incumbent of Marton kept the registers themselves in a bag by his chair, the easier to light his pipe with the spills that he made from them. So I was not optimistic as I sat in the County Record Office in Chester, contemplating the pile of uncatalogued sheets that the archivist had brought from the vaults.

The baptisms of the Bishop's Transcript were there for 1782. They were identical to those of the register, except for an additional entry: 'William, son of Eliza Buckley, March 31st.,' and, in the margin, in another hand, 'Illigitim.' The County Record Office went into spasm, as I yelled: 'Oh, William!'

The next part was easy, now that the clew was in my hand. Eliza was the teenage daughter of Jonathan Buckley.

The following day I was in the John Rylands Library of Manchester University, which holds the archive of the Marton estate. Within minutes, I had identified Jonathan Buckley's farm, such as it was (one acre, three roods and thirty perches of bits of land), from the rent books and maps, and the subsequent change of the house to a school, the year after the church register's recording of his death.

I had to see inside that house, to feel where William had grown up, to stand in the room from which he had gone out to spend thirty-two years as an Aborigine. I stooped under the beams. William had been six feet and five and seven-eighths inches tall. The headroom in the transport ship in which he had spent six months chained in darkness, with no sight of the sun, was five feet seven inches. By the end of many such moments, I felt that I knew William Buckley very well, simply by inference from what I found he had experienced. But I still had to meet him. Because of the research, I could identify his closest living relative, Arthur Buckley. I was warned that he was old, ill, reclusive, depressed and bad tempered. Nevertheless, I went to his house at Fiddler's Elbow, where he had been born and lived all his life. I knocked on the door. Silence. I was about to knock again when I heard a slow and distant shuffling. My adrenaline surged. I was going to be as near as it was possible to be to William Buckley. I was going to look into the gene pool.

There was a drawing of bolts, and the door opened enough for me to make out a blue eye behind thick lenses, and a spike of uncombed silver hair.

Then I did a stupid thing. I entered on a preamble. 'Mr. Buckley?'

Grunt.

'I'm sorry to bother you, but could you could spare me a few minutes? I'd like to talk to you.'

'I don't think so,' said a toneless voice, and the door moved to shut. Desperate, I said: 'My name's Alan Garner.' I was going to say: 'I'm a writer, and I'm working on a book about your family,' or something like that. But the door was pulled wide open, and Arthur Buckley said: 'You're Colin's lad!'

'Yes.'

'Come in! Come in! I know more about Garners than you do!'

And I had come in order to know more about Buckleys than he did.

He beckoned me into the kitchen with his head. He walked with difficulty and never let go of his trousers.

'Sit thi down. Tek thi bacca.' He welcomed me formally, and eased himself into the only arm chair. I fetched a stool from the table. He was agitated with pleasure as he told me how in the 1920s and '30s, he had, with his family and mine, made up the local brass band. Along the whole length of the mantle piece were curled and time-discoloured photographs of the band in uniform, with their instruments, fat Big Bill Garner in the middle, holding his baton.

Arthur Buckley talked obsessively, reliving the great days; but I noticed that, even sitting, he kept one hand on his trousers. I asked him what was wrong.

'My braces snapped last week.'

'Have you another pair?'

'No.'

'A belt? Any rope?'

'No. There's a strap for cases somewhere in the back bedroom, but I can't get up the stairs.'

I found the strap. Arthur Buckley leaned against the mantlepiece, while I stood behind, grappling him to me as I slotted the strap twice round him. The thought went through my head that, if the would-be Doctors of Philosophy, who write to me asking for opinions on my work and its relationship to structualism, deconstructualism, phenomenology, semiotics, the objective correlative, the hermeneutic circle, and, not least, my debt to Shklovsky's theory of *ostranenie* in Russian Formalism; if only they could see that writing lay more in trying to keep an old man's trousers up, and that from such moments came a *Strandloper*.

Arthur Buckley was tired. It was time to go. I said that I'd enjoyed our talk very much.

'Ay,' said Arthur Buckley. 'We've had a grand crack.'

I asked him whether I could come and talk again.

'If I'm here,' he said. 'Then I'll tell you the truth about Maurice Garner.'; We parted in good cheer. When I went back a few days later, Arthur Buckley was dead. I still do not know the truth about Maurice Garner, but I had gained much of the truth about William Buckley. I knew him now.

The rest of the English section of the book, and the transport to Australia, presented no intangible or irresolvable problems. I had only to follow the lines of the pattern. But then came alarm. The lines were there and flowing; yet they were starting to approach and to interact with other lines, a pattern I had dealt with: *The Stone Book Quartet*. The relationships were unavoidable. *The Stone Book Quartet* had been written as a sequel to *Strandloper*, beginning nine years before *Strandloper* was conceived.

That inner voice, which instructs but will not discuss, told me not to hesitate.

So I put my disconcertion aside, and obeyed. I continued to pursue the Lewisian "joy". And what can be said to have been among the particular qualities of *Strandloper*, to compensate for the difficulties, is that it has been a joyous work in its making. Everybody I have approached has been friendly, and eager to help. But beware. I should tell you that, whenever you are in the presence of a writer, anything you say will be taken down, and it will be used. The difference with *Strandloper* is that the victims have, without exception, not merely acquiesced. They have shared in the joy.

What happens is that the writer, either having written a paragraph, or about to start one, feels that something extra is needed: something slight: a seasoning more than an ingredient. These seasonings are beyond the skill of invention. And they make all the difference to what is written that changes a text from adequate to inspired.

A new butcher moved to our nearby village, which has an enclave of upwardly mobile, insecure executives, who expect servility, not only civility, from shopkeepers. To help him at weekends, he employs Raymond, a retired butcher, who was the apprentice of my father's best friend. I had not seen Raymond for nearly fifty years; but, the first time I went into the shop, we spontaneously broke into a loud exchange of improvised verbal abuse and scatology, and, lowering the executive tone further, all in broad dialect. I saw the young butcher's eyes flicker in alarm. 'Give over,' said Raymond. 'I've known our Alan since his bum were as big as me shirt button.' That was what had been missing. Within half an hour, it was in the book, making a tragic scene the more tense and human.

Nicknames cannot be invented, either. All the nicknames of *Strandloper* are of local men, provided mostly by the stone mason, Ken. His one misgiving is that Eggy Mo, an innocent in the book, a near-psychopath in reality, may not be the illiterate he is said to be.

Taxi driver, John, used to be a coalman, after his father, and so, inevitably in Cheshire, is known as Cobby. I asked him whether he would mind if I 'borrowed' him. He was so amused that he told me a rhyme long known in his family.

'Owd Cob and Young Cob and Young Cob's son.
Young Cob's Owd Cob when Owd Cob's done.'

He was giving me more than he knew. In Cheshire dialect, 'Cobby' is a coalman. But 'Cob' is 'chief man', 'governor of a gang', 'leader'. This was so important that the rhyme not only went into the dialogue, but changed the structure of the book, gave the name to one of its sections, and expressed the inexpressible, on many levels, when I was trying to say the unsayable at a cathartic resolution of an Aboriginal acceptance of the pain of what had to be, in order to achieve the purpose of a life. All from asking an ex-coalman if I could use his name, which I did, as well as the rhyme.

As a last example: I needed an opening for the first chapter of the transport to Australia: something memorable, poetic, yet indicative of a destroyed mind. It is: 'I chases 'em; I flaps my apron at 'em. But they sees me coming.

They sees my apron. But I'll get 'em. One day.' It is all the character ever says, but he says it for six months.

The fragmentation, and the rhythm, enabled me to create whole scenes in the smallest space, by using single phrases, or sentences, impressionistically, to show the duration of the voyage, even to its being used by the chaplain for the committal of the man's corpse to the sea.

In our son's first term at New College, Oxford, he was sitting by the lake with three friends, watching the ducks, when out of the bushes ran a scout, a college servant, towards the ducks, shouting: 'I chases 'em; I flaps my apron at 'em. But they sees me coming. They sees my apron. But I'll get 'em. One day.'

Nobody is safe. I was lucky. All whom the thieving magpie robbed, delight in the private joke. *Strandloper* is as much a novel made by a community as by an individual.

The reason for my turning out my files at the Summer Solstice was that I was too exhausted to do anything else. I had spent six weeks travelling in Canada, the United States and Australia.

The Australian visit had been arranged by my closest friend, who has given me the sobriquet of 'manky academic' instead of 'academic manqué'. He is Professor (now Emeritus) Ralph Elliott, a direct descendant of Martin Luther, nephew of Nobel Laureate Max Born, and cousin to Ben Elton and to Olivia Newton John. At the time of my visit, he was Master of University House at the Australian National University in Canberra. His speciality is runic inscriptions, in which he is the acknowledged ultimate authority, and an internationally respected scholar of Old and Middle English, especially of Chaucer and the Gawain poet, and of the works of Thomas Hardy. We met because he wrote to me to tell me that I must be the first writer since the Fourteenth Century to use the same dialect and landscape in my writing as the Gawain poet had used in *Sir Gawain and the Green Knight*. And we had, from different backgrounds and disciplines, arrived at the same answer in identifying the location of the Green Chapel.

We are also concerned in the nature of The Matter of Britain and the need for it to be kept alive by its working and reworking. For me, *Strandloper* is *Sir Gawain and the Green Knight*. The elements of The Matter of Britain are in both.

It was vital that I had seen Australia, seen its light and hues, smelt its smells, heard its sounds. Without them, it would have been an insult to dare the quest. The other ingredient, without which it would not have started, was the tireless generosity of Ralph Elliott and his position that gave him access to the libraries and archives of Australia. He had the means to dig out and photocopy rare books, unique books, diaries, notes, sketches, letters—all the paraphernalia of the land that was to become William Buckley's.

Ralph himself is a William Buckley. He left Germany as a teenager, one step ahead of the SS, to come to Britain, knowing three words of English. His mother told him that it was necessary to know only two in order to get by in that benighted land: 'Corned beef' and 'Darling'. His cousin said that, with one more word, he would be entirely at ease among the British. All he had to say, yet frequently, was 'Bugger'. Thus armed, Ralph set out from the chapel at midnight, pricking o'er the plain, to develop a career devoted to the enlightenment of the English language around the world.

So, for Australian documentary research, I had my mole; and I was kept secure and happy in the research. I had all the external facts I needed. The historical William Buckley was shipped out both as a convict and as a bricklayer, a mechanic, to build a new penal colony in what was arrogantly decreed by the British Government to be 'terra nullius': no one's land. One piece of William's workmanship survives: as fragments of a concrete armoury he built, which are now the crazy paving of a garden path in Ramsey Street. But William had brooded on other ideas. He had long decided to walk back home. The possibility of this was a common belief among the convicts: head north along the coast, reach China, turn left, and there you were. They even drew compasses on scraps of paper, to keep them from going off course.

The land was so hostile, and fear of the Indians so great, that little attempt was made to recapture an escapee. Either he would come back, begging to be let in, or he was never seen again. Once William Buckley was out of range of the sentries, he was presumed dead. The penal colony failed, after three months, for lack of water, departed, and founded Hobart. The land was left to itself.

Meanwhile, William followed the coast to China.

Unfortunately, he was inside the narrow mouth of Port Phillip, the caldera of an extinct volcano. He did not know how to get food or water, and his progress was slow, his physical condition not good and growing worse. After an unknown time, and some ninety-five miles of walking in terrible conditions, he completed the circuit of Port Phillip and found himself looking across the entrance, straight at the ship and into the camp.

Among the photocopies that Ralph sent me was a critical edition of the ghosted first-person account of William's life in the bush, which was recorded by a hack journalist from Hobart after William's return to the whites. From this, I was able to relate the Aboriginal names of physical features to their modern equivalents, and could plot William's long journey.

Instead of giving up when he saw the penal colony he had staggered ninety-five miles to escape, he turned away and continued to head north-east for China. But he was travelling south-west. This he continued to do for about two hundred miles. Then the text showed that he stopped, turned around, and set off, moving away from the sea, but in the right direction. Why had he been a hundred and eighty degrees out, and how had he come to discover his error? It is in the apparent anomalies that the most significant and exciting aspects of research are to be found. When I saw it, I felt time and space dissolve. I was with William Buckley, I was William Buckley, as I watched him work out his error. He had not realised that, in the Southern Hemisphere, in that mad land that seemed to have been designed to kill, where even the rivers were salt, the sun, at noon, was not in the south but in the north.

He made for China.

It had always been impossible. At last, his body, after another two hundred miles, and what must have been a total of more than a year of solitary stumbling, dehydrated and starved, gave out. But his mind did not. He could not walk, so he crawled. He crawled until he came to a low hillock, and, with fading vision, he saw a stick planted at the top of the hillock. A stick to help him to walk to China. He crawled for the stick, took hold of it, and, with that last effort, collapsed, and should have died.

He was found by a group of Aborigines. They had no knowledge of white men, but it was an Aboriginal belief that the dead became white. And here was this white giant, lying, not on a hillock, but on the grave mound of a hero, warrior, wise man, healer and law-giver, Murrangurk; and he was holding not a stick but Murrangurk's spear. Murrangurk had come back to his People. It was as if Arthur had returned from Avalon.

For thirty-two years William Buckley was Murrangurk.

Now, it would be understandable that, having made the journey from Tharangalkbek, the sky land, 'the gum tree country', Murrangurk would be in shock and have forgotten his language and his customs, but he would remember, given time: a few weeks or months. William had to have more going for him to be able to remain Murrangurk for thirty-two years. Also, I could infer something about Murrangurk.

Among Australian Aborigines, there is an unbreakable rule that, when someone dies, the name must never be spoken again. There is one exception. If the individual has been of the highest spiritual rank, that of shaman, the name may be spoken. So Murrangurk had been a shaman. Tough luck on William. Yet, thirty-two years later, the opportunistic British, who, within a few years, exterminated the irritating riggers, often for sport, were saved from death by the authority of a Murrangurk who was very much respected, and wholly in control. What had started out as a twenty-year-old bricklayer was now a leader of thinkers and of warriors.

That for me, the novelist, was the crux, the conscious reason for writing the book. How was a priest-philosopher-healer-leader of great intelligence to communicate his wisdom in a language that no European spoke? How could his only point of contact, the Cheshire dialect and the convict Cant of an immature man, be used to tell what he now knew?

Apart from his usefulness as an interpreter's being abused, and his laying of the first brick in what was to become Melbourne, William Buckley was discarded as a fellow of low intellect and brutish nature, who had fallen instantly to the level of the heathen, to the extent that he had not even tried to introduce to them the Word of God. That perhaps William had had no need; that perhaps he had been, initially, the acolyte, would never have been countenanced. And here I nearly foundered.

Ralph was in Europe on one of his too-rare visits, and we were talking. I said that I had reached a point beyond which I could not go. For the first time, despite six years' work, I should have to abort a book.

The impregnable barrier was the Aboriginal mind. I had no wish to invade their philosophy, which is largely sacred/secret, and is their last privacy and dignity, but, unless I knew something of it, my Aboriginal characters, and the change from William Buckley to Murrangurk, could not be shown as they naturally would have behaved. There was no way in. Any flim-flam I might concoct from

what I could deduce, however plausible, would produce a false story.

'No worries, mate,' said Ralph. 'I'm going home tomorrow.' Shortly after, I had a letter from one of Australia's anthropologists: the leading one, for my purpose; because not only is she anthropologist, but is a full member of an Aboriginal kinship group, is a female Elder, and of such high rank that she has the authority to adjudicate over both Men and Women's Matters. In her letter, she said that Ralph had told her that I was stuck, and she wanted to know whether she could help. She had a long-standing invitation to lecture in Lisbon, and the fee would pay her air fare to Manchester.

And so I engaged with the Aboriginal mind among the throng and coloured neon of Manchester airport. We recognised each other on sight, spontaneously broke into laughter, and, before we were clear of the carpark ramps, she had begun.

I continue to say 'she', because of her wish to remain anonymous. Her work involves negotiating, finagling and manoeuvering for the pure Aborigines, and she prefers to keep a low profile. To me, she is lovingly known as 'The Southern Sybil.'

Education in Aboriginal teaching is inferential, not, as with us, instructional. A pupil is shown something, or told a story, or given a statement in metaphorical images rather than through grammatical and syntactical logic; and, dependent on the reaction, is either moved forward or automatically returns to the start. It is akin to a fail-safe flow chart system of religious and philosophical wisdom. It is also a protection for the individual. We do not let people drive Formula I cars on the day they collect their driving licence.

As a result, Southern Sybil presents herself in such a way that the impatient, intolerant, inflexible (and therefore unsuitable) mind is irritated by what appears to be a deliberately elliptical and batty old woman. That is a serious, and frequently terminal, mistake. But stay with this Delphic nuisance, and things start to happen within oneself. A new grammar and syntax form. And thought takes a new shape: an Aboriginal shape. Once this is established, The Sybil uses both Hellenistic and Aboriginal models, both intellectually highly demanding, to express what has to be conveyed in the most efficient way.

I knew, fairly soon, that I had unwittingly passed a crucial test, from an Aboriginal point of view, and I asked The Sybil why she had crossed the world on Ralph's say-so. 'It was necessary,' she said. 'The only moment of doubt I had was when we were about to touch down at Manchester, and I thought: Dear God! What if Alan's not up to it? But when we both laughed before we spoke, I knew that we should dance well.'

That was 1989. We have danced well. And the dance goes on, and will, for it has led me to see what has always given spring to my step, why the books are eternally different, eternally the same. The Aborigine would call it my Dreaming, my song and my dance. The books are a vehicle for, and then detritus of, the journey. It is why, once my duty towards them has been discharged, I have no further interest in them per se; which is not to claim that I disparage them. They are swept up, and still exist, in the cumulative intricacy and simplicity of the dance. Already *Strandloper* is taking its place, giving way to the new song that it has made possible by my writing of that portion of spiritual autobiography, with the help of so many people, foremost among whom are: Ralph Elliott, Southern Sybil, William Buckley, and particularly my wife and our children, who have had to live the soaking and the waiting.

The magpie must also be given his due. It is not by chance that he occurs as a principal in Aboriginal Creation myths. Without him, the book would not be as it is, nor would I be as spiritually enlarged as I feel myself to be.

I woke one morning with that imperative voice in my head. I had learnt that the voice is also known to the Aboriginal mind, and held as the source of inspiration. It is called The Voice that Thunders. It said: 'Go to Marton church. Go now.'

Marton church is the oldest timber framed church in Europe, dating in its present form from 1393 and the focal point of *Strandloper*. I went. And, as I entered the church I had known all my life, I saw it through Aboriginal eyes for the first time, and was, as a human being, dumbfounded; and, as a writer, aware that all the cards had been finally dealt. An Aboriginal Elder, knowing nothing of architecture or of Christianity, would recognise Marton as sacred. For the magpie had discovered entoptic lines.

Entoptic lines were first published by two South African anthropologists, J. D. Lewis-Williams and T. A. Dowson, in 1988. They had noticed that the same abstract patterns tended to appear in all pre-literate art and iconography, in all places and at all times, from the upper palaeolithic cave paintings of France and Spain to the modern religious art of the Kalahari bushmen. There are about six patterns, and they are invariable: zig-zag, cross-hatching, honeycomb, dot, circle and spiral. Lewis-Williams and Dowson consulted neurologists, who reported the same patterns, which are found in only three conditions of the human brain. They appear to be projected as external images by people entering grand mal epileptic seizures; by many migraineurs; and as the result of shamans entering trance, or ecstatic, states. The ritual body painting of Aboriginal adepts, and the abstractions of the stained glass windows of mediaeval Marton, are the same. Both William Buckley and Murrangurk would have known them. What I had been expecting, a Green Man, or foliate head, disguised, our daughter found a few minutes later. No composer of *Strandloper* could have wished for more. The entoptic lines created the jacket of the book; and they made the climax of the story.

I can't end without admitting to having shortchanged you.

At the start, I dodged the question of why I have written by saying that I had no choice. But why no choice? Only with *Strandloper* have the last forty years become clear.

I am a member of a family of rural craftsmen, but I use my hands in a different way. Unconsciously, I have spent those forty years in trying to celebrate the land and tongue of a culture that has been marginalised by a metropolitan intellectualism, that churns out canonical prose through writers who seem unable to allow new concepts or to integrate the diversity of our language; who draw on the library, ignorant of the land; on the head, bereft of the heart; making of fair speech mere rustic conversation; so that I am led to ask: Have we become so lazy that we have lost the will to read our own language, except at its most anodyne, and, from that reading, too lazy to create? For true reading is creativity: the willingness to look into the open hand of the writer and to see what may, or may not, be there. A writer's job is to offer, not to direct.

Therefore, yes, I owe an apology to the academics, at whom you may well think I sneered. I am, in their jargon, a phenomenologist. I do have an affinity with Shklovsky's *ostranenie*, or 'the making strange of things'. But it is a philosophy arrived at by serendipity, by an empirical pragmatism, not by a conscious, or slavish, following of a school of literature. It is a happy accident, discovered later, that a writer has to be able to cope with Russian Formalism equally as with an old man's trousers. In that integration lie the victory over, and the achievement of, the self. And, from such victory and achievement, a greater good is served.

'There is only the fight to recover what has been lost,' T. S. Eliot says in *East Coker*. 'The rest is not our business.'

There were two spurs to my endeavour. The first was the realisation that a well meaning teacher had washed my mouth out with carbolic soap when I was five years old for what she called 'talking broad', which she did not know was the language of one of the treasures of English poetry. The second was that I have the earliest surviving example, which may have been the sum of his literacy, of writing by a Garner: the signature of another William: a slashed, fierce cross, made with the anger of a pen held in the fist as a dagger.

So it was gratifying when a Professor of Humanities at Saint Louis University wrote: 'There is, in [*Strandloper*], a kind of thesis about how a precious mythology was allowed to slip by a controlling politico-literary agenda.... But most of all, there is a refusal to grieve.... The people are dead, but the words lie like stones, indestructible as the land, and as invincible.'

To have been able to use my personal indoctrination into academe as a means to free a suppressed, concrete voice, to give a slashed cross a flowing hand, opened to offer our starved and arid prose if only one way out of the library, back to its enriching soil, has been a privilege and an apprenticeship. That apprenticeship—the quest from gash and slash of a cross, by way of carbolic soap, to the Voice that Thunders—is over. Now, I can begin. Indeed, I already have.

Writings

FICTION

The Weirdstone of Brisingamen: A Tale of Alderley, Collins, 1960, published as *The Weirdstone: A Tale of Alderley*, F. Watts, 1961, revised edition, Penguin, 1963, Walck, 1969.

The Moon of Gomrath (sequel to *The Weirdstone of Brisingamen*,) Collins, 1963, Walck, 1967.

Elidor, Collins, 1965, Walck, 1967.

The Old Man of Mow, Collins, 1966, Doubleday, 1970.

The Owl Service, Collins, 1967, Walck, 1968.

Red Shift, Collins, 1973, Macmillan, 1973.

The Breadhorse, Collins, 1975.

Alan Garner's Fairy Tales of Gold, four volumes, Collins, 1979, one-volume edition, Philomel Books, 1980.

The Alan Garner Omnibus (contains *Elidor, The Weirdstone of Brisingamen,* and *The Moon of Gomrath*), Lions, 1994.

Strandloper, Harvill Press, 1996.

Grey Wolf, Prince Jack, and the Firebird, Scholastic Children's Books, 1998.

The Well of the Wind, D.K. Publishers, 1998.

"THE STONE BOOK QUARTET" SERIES

The Stone Book, Collins, 1976, Collins & World, 1978.

Tom Fobble's Day, Collins, 1977, Collins & World, 1979.

Granny Reardun, Collins, 1977, Collins & World, 1978.

The Aimer Gate, Collins, 1978, Collins & World, 1979.

The Stone Book Quartet (contains *The Stone Book, Tom Fobble's Day, Granny Reardun,* and *The Aimer Gate*), Collins, 1983, Dell, 1988.

PLAYS

Holly from the Bongs: A Nativity Play, Collins, 1966.

The Green Mist, 1970.

Lamaload, 1978.

Lurga Lom, 1980.

To Kill a King, 1980.

Sally Water, 1982.

The Keeper, 1983.

Lord Flame, Harvill Press, 1996.

Pentecost, Harvill Press, 1997.

SCREENPLAYS

Places and Things (documentary), 1978.

Images (documentary), 1981.

Strandloper (feature film adapted from his novel), 1992.

LIBRETTI

The Bellybag, music by Richard Morris, 1971.

Potter Thompson, music by Gordon Crosse, 1972, Oxford University Press, 1985.

OTHER

(Editor) *A Cavalcade of Goblins,* Walck, 1969, published in England as *The Hamish Hamilton Book of Goblins: An Anthology of Folklore,* Hamish Hamilton, 1969.

(Compiler) *The Guizer: A Book of Fools,* Hamish Hamilton, 1975, Greenwillow Books, 1976.

The Lad of the Gad (folktales), Collins, 1980, Philomel Books, 1981.

(Reteller) *Alan Garner's Book of British Fairy Tales,* Collins, 1984, Delacorte, 1985.

(Reteller) *Jack and the Beanstalk,* Collins, 1985, Doubleday, 1992.

A Bag of Moonshine (folktales), Delacorte, 1986.

(Reteller) *Once upon a Time, Though It Wasn't in Your Time and It Wasn't in My Time, and It Wasn't in Anybody Else's Time . . .* (folktales), Dorling Kindersley, 1993.

(Reteller) *Little Red Hen,* D.K. Publishers, 1996.

The Voice that Thunders: Essays and Lectures, Harvill Press, 1997.

Also author of film adaptation of *Red Shift,* 1978. Member of International Editorial Board, Detskaya Literatura Publishers, Moscow. Manuscript collection is held at Brigham Young University, Provo, UT.

GHIGNA, Charles 1946-
(Father Goose, a pseudonym)

Personal

Surname is pronounced *Geen*-ya; born August 25, 1946, in New York, NY; son of Charles Vincent and Patricia (Pelletier) Ghigna; married Nancy Minnicks, June 24, 1967 (divorced June 5, 1973); married Debra Holmes (a writer), August 2, 1975; children: (first marriage) Julie Ann; (second marriage) Chip. *Education:* Florida Atlantic University, B.A., 1968, M.Ed., 1969; also attended Edison Community College, 1964-66, University of South Florida, 1968-69, and Florida State University, 1973. *Hobbies and other interests:* Baseball.

Addresses

Home—204 West Linwood Dr., Homewood, AL 35209.

Career

High school English teacher in Fort Myers, FL, 1967-73; Edison Community College, Fort Myers, instructor in creative writing, 1973; National Council of Teachers of English, Urbana, IL, poetry editor of *English Journal,* 1974; Alabama School of Fine Arts, Birmingham, poet-in-residence, 1974-93; Samford University, instructor in creative writing, 1979. Creator, director, performer on *Cabbages and Kings* (children's television series), Alabama Education Television, 1976. Correspondent for *Writer's Digest* magazine, 1989—. Author of nationally syndicated light verse feature "Snickers" for Tribune Media Services, 1993-98. Has given hundreds of readings at colleges and secondary schools.

Awards, Honors

Fellowship grants from the National Endowment for the Arts, the Library of Congress, the Mary Roberts

Charles Ghigna

Rinehart Foundation, and the Rockefeller Brothers Fund; First Place, *Writer's Digest* National Poetry Writing Competition, 1977, for "Divers"; nomination, Pulitzer Prize, 1990, for *Returning to Earth;* Helen Keller Literary Award, 1993; First Place, International Sakura Haiku Writing Competition, 1993, for "October"; Pick of the Lists, American Booksellers Association, 1994, for *Tickle Day: Poems from Father Goose,* and 1995, for *Riddle Rhymes;* Main Selection (month of August), Book-of-the-Month Club, 1999, for *See the Yak Yak.* Ghigna performed his poetry at the Library of Congress in 1978 and at the Kennedy Center for the Performing Arts in 1984; his poetry was featured on ABC-TV's *Good Morning America* in 1991.

Writings

FOR CHILDREN

Good Dogs, Bad Dogs, illustrated by David Catrow, Hyperion, 1992.

Good Cats, Bad Cats, illustrated by David Catrow, Hyperion, 1992.

The Day I Spent the Night in the Shelby County Jail, Best of Times, 1994.

Tickle Day: Poems from Father Goose, illustrated by Cyd Moore, Hyperion, 1994.

Riddle Rhymes, illustrated by Julia Gorton, Hyperion, 1995.

Animal Trunk: Silly Poems to Read Aloud, illustrated by Gabriel, Abrams, 1999.

Mice Are Nice, illustrated by Jon Goodell, Random House, 1999.

See the Yak Yak, illustrated by Brian Lies, Random House, 1999.

Christmas Is Coming, illustrated by Mary O'Keefe Young, Charlesbridge, in press.

Halloween Poems, illustrated by Clare MacKie, Running Press, in press.

FOR ADULTS; POETRY, EXCEPT AS NOTED

Plastic Tears, Dorrance (Philadelphia, PA), 1973.

Stables: The Story of Christmas (chapbook), Creekwood Press (Birmingham, AL), 1976.

Cockroach (one-act play), Contemporary Drama Service, 1977.

Divers and Other Poems, Creekwood, 1978.

Circus Poems, Creekwood, 1979.

Father Songs, Creekwood, 1989.

Returning to Earth, Livingston University Press (Livingston, AL), 1989.

Wings of Fire, illustrated by Patricia See Hooten, Druid (Birmingham, AL), 1992.

The Best of Snickers, Best of Times, 1994.

Speaking in Tongues: New and Selected Poems, 1974-1994, Livingston University Press, 1994.

Plastic Soup: Dream Poems, Black Belt (Montgomery, AL), 1999.

Love Poems, Crane Hill, 1999.

Works represented in anthologies, including *Southern Poetry: The Seventies,* North Carolina State University, 1977; *Italian-American Poets,* Fordham University, 1985; *American Sports Poems,* Orchard, 1988; *Creative Writer's Handbook* (1st, 2nd, and 3d editions), Prentice Hall, 1990, 1994, 1999; *Enjoy! Invitations to Literacy* and *My Buddy,* both for Houghton Mifflin, 1996; *Knock at a Star: A Child's Introduction to Poetry,* Little Brown, 1999; and *The 20th Century Children's Poetry Treasury,* Alfred A. Knopf, 1999. Contributor of hundreds of adult and children's poems to magazines and newspapers, including *Harper's, McCall's, Good Housekeeping, Ladies Home Journal, Kansas Quarterly, Texas Quarterly, Christian Science Monitor, Highlights for Children, Cricket, Ranger Rick, Jack and Jill, Children's Digest, Hopscotch,* and *Child Life.* Some of Ghigna's poems have been translated into Italian, German, French, and Russian.

Sidelights

Charles Ghigna is a poet who makes his living performing his poetry in schools, libraries, and elsewhere, as well as through the publication of his poems in book form. His *Riddle Rhymes* combines two popular genres of children's literature to "appealing" effect, according to Julie Corsaro in *Booklist.* By joining the fun of riddles to the playfulness of rhymes, Ghigna has produced "a lighthearted guessing game about everyday objects in a young child's life," noted Pamela K. Bomboy in *School Library Journal.* The topics covered by Ghigna's riddles include shadows, mirrors, leaves, rainbows, and kites.

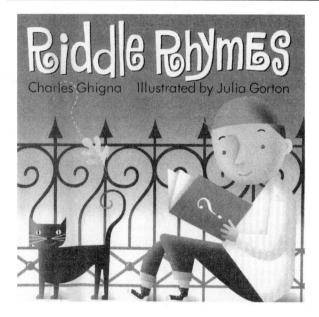

Ghigna's collection of rhyming riddles combines two popular forms of juvenile writing. (Cover illustration by Julia Gorton.)

"And because they are in verse, the riddles are especially fun to read out loud," remarked Campbell Geeslin in the *New York Times Book Review*.

In an interview with Tracy Hoffman, Ghigna commented: "My ideas [for poems] come from everywhere! They pop into my head when I least expect them. Many poem and story ideas come to me while I am driving or mowing or taking a shower! I also do 30-40 school visits each year. Sometimes ideas come to me while I'm around children, especially while I'm playing with my son and his friends. Ideas also come to me while looking out the window of my upstairs office. My son and I often spend time after school jumping on his trampoline. Sometimes after jumping we collapse on the trampoline and lie still looking up at the clouds and watching Mother Nature's movie screen. We always find something new to think about while looking toward the sky. Other ideas for poems and stories also come from memories of my childhood—which still hasn't ended!"

Among Ghigna's numerous publications for children are two associated books that exemplify in their design the basic concept of the book. In both *Good Cats, Bad Cats* and *Good Dogs, Bad Dogs,* Ghigna offers two humorous verses, one emphasizing the positive aspects of the animal, the other the negative. Each verse fills the space of half of the book, which must then be flipped over in order for the other, opposing, story to be read. Ghigna's rhymes work in concert with illustrations by David Catrow that literalize the humorous absurdity of such commonplace notions as the ideas that dogs defend those they love and cats always land on their feet. "By turns slapstick and sophisticated, the humor here will snare adults as well as children," remarked a reviewer for *Publishers Weekly*.

"I hope my poems offer children the opportunity to explore and celebrate the joys of childhood and nature, and to see some of the wondrous ironies all around them," Ghigna once commented. "I also hope my humorous poems tickle the funny bone of their imaginations. I usually do not sit down to write a poem with a preconceived 'goal.' I like to enter each poem with a sense of wonderment and discovery. My favorite poems are those that contain little surprises that I did not know were there until I wrote them."

Works Cited

Bomboy, Pamela K., review of *Riddle Rhymes, School Library Journal,* November, 1995, p. 89.

Corsaro, Julie, review of *Riddle Rhymes, Booklist,* November 15, 1995, p. 562.

Geeslin, Campbell, review of *Riddle Rhymes, New York Times Book Review,* April 7, 1996, p. 21.

Ghigna, Charles, interview on *www.inkspot.com.*

Review of *Good Cats, Bad Cats* and *Good Dogs, Bad Dogs, Publishers Weekly,* August 24, 1992, p. 78.

Hoffman, Tracy, "An Exclusive Interview with Father Goose, Charles Ghigna," on www.wordmuseum.com.

For More Information See

PERIODICALS

School Library Journal, April, 1993, p. 96.
Writer's Digest (interview), August, 1999, p. 6.

*   *   *

GOLDSMITH, Howard 1945-
(Ward Smith, Dayle Courtney)

Personal

Born August 24, 1945, in New York, NY; son of Philip (a motion picture engineer) and Sophie (Feldman) Goldsmith; *Education:* City University of New York, B.A.(with honors), 1965; University of Michigan, M.A.(with honors), 1966. *Politics:* Independent.

Addresses

Home—41-07 Bowne St., No. 6-B, Flushing, NY 11355-5629.

Career

Psychologist. Mental Hygiene Clinic, Detroit, MI, psychologist, 1966-70; writer and editorial consultant, 1970—. Audiovisual writer for educational publishers, including Encyclopaedia Britannica Educational Corp., 1970— and Harcourt Brace Educational Measurement, 1998—. *Member:* Society of Children's Book Writers and Illustrators, Poets and Writers, Science Fiction Writers of America, Phi Beta Kappa, Phi Kappa Phi, Psi Chi, Sigma Xi.

Awards, Honors

United States Public Health Service Fellowship, 1965; Arthur Rackham Fellowship, 1966, Phi Sigma Science Award, 1966, both from the University of Michigan.

Writings

PICTURE BOOKS

Turvy, the Horse that Ran Backwards, Xerox Education Publications, 1973.

What Makes a Grumble Smile?, illustrated by Tom Eaton, Garrard (Champaign, IL), 1977.

Toto the Timid Turtle, illustrated by Shirley Chan, Human Sciences, 1980.

The Tooth Chicken, Thomas Nelson, 1982.

Ninon, Miss Vison, Harlequin, 1982.

Mireille l'Abeille, Harlequin, 1982.

Toufou le Hibou, Harlequin, 1982.

Fortou le Kangourou, Harlequin, 1982.

Plaf le Paresseux, Harlequin, 1982.

Treasure Hunt, illustrated by Ulises Wensell, Santillana (Northvale, NJ), 1983.

Little Lost Dog, illustrated by Wensell, Santillana, 1983.

The Circle, Santillana, 1983.

The Square, Santillana, 1983.

Stormy Day Together, illustrated by Wensell, Santillana, 1983.

Welcome, Makoto!, illustrated by Wensell, Santillana, 1983.

The Contest, illustrated by Wensell, Santillana, 1983.

Maggie the Mink, illustrated by Russ Flint, T. Nelson/Ideals, 1984.

Sammy the Sloth, T. Nelson, 1984.

Helpful Julio, Santillana, 1984.

The Secret of Success, Santillana, 1984.

A Day of Fun, Santillana, 1984.

Pedro's Puzzling Birthday, Santillana, 1984.

Rosa's Prank, Santillana, 1984.

The Rectangle, Santillana, 1984.

The Twiddle Twins' Haunted House, illustrated by Jack Kent, HarperCollins/Caedmon, 1985.

Ollie the Owl, T. Nelson, 1985.

Kelly the Kangaroo, T. Nelson, 1985.

The Pig and the Witch, illustrated by Jeffrey Severn, Golden, 1990.

(Under pseudonym Ward Smith) *Little Quack and Baby Duckling,* Golden, 1991.

The Day My Dad and I Got Mugged, illustrated by Dorathye W. Shuster, University Classics, 1993.

The Christmas Star, illustrated by Byron Appleget, Reading Video, 1994.

Sleepy Little Owl, illustrations by Denny Bond, McGraw-Hill, 1997.

The Twiddle Twins' Music Box Mystery, illustrated by Charles Jordan, Mondo, 1997.

The Gooey Chewy Contest, illustrated by Charles Jordan, Mondo, 1997.

The Twiddle Twins' Amusement Park Mystery, illustrated by Charles Jordan, Mondo, 1998.

The Twiddle Twins' Single Footprint Mystery, illustrated by Charles Jordan, Mondo, 1998.

Hungry Little Hare, illustrated by Denny Bond, McGraw-Hill, 1998.

Shy Little Turtle, illustrated by Denny Bond, McGraw-Hill, 1998.

Late Little Robin, illustrated by Denny Bond, McGraw-Hill, 1999.

JUNIOR NOVELS

The Whispering Sea, Bobbs-Merrill (Indianapolis, IN), 1976.

(With Wallace Eyre) *Sooner Round the Corner* (novel), Hodder & Stoughton (London, England), 1979.

Invasion: 2200 A.D., Doubleday, 1979.

JUNIOR NOVELS; UNDER PSEUDONYM DAYLE COURTNEY; ILLUSTRATED BY JOHN HAM

Omen of the Flying Light, Standard (Cincinnati, OH), 1981.

The Knife with Eyes, Standard, 1981.

The Ivy Plot, Standard, 1981.

Flight to Terror, Standard, 1981.

Operation Doomsday, Standard, 1981.

Escape from Eden, Standard, 1981.

Tower of Flames, Standard, 1982.

Mysterious Strangers, Standard, 1982.

The Hidden Cave, Standard, 1982.

Jaws of Terror, Standard, 1982.

The Foxworth Hunt, Standard, 1982.

Three-Ring Inferno, Standard, 1982.

The Sinister Circle, Standard, 1983.

Shadow of Fear, Standard, 1983.

The House that Ate People, Standard, 1983.

The Trail of Bigfoot, Standard, 1983.

Secret of Pirates' Cave, Standard, 1984.

The Great UFO Chase, Standard, 1984.

The Olympic Plot, Standard, 1984.

SHORT STORIES

The Shadow and Other Strange Tales, Weekly Reader Books, 1977.

Terror by Night and Other Strange Tales, Weekly Reader Books, 1977.

(Editor, with Roger Elwood) *Spine-Chillers: Unforgettable Tales of Terror,* Doubleday, 1978.

(Editor) *Junior Classics,* Grosset & Dunlap, 1989.

PLAYS

The President's Train, Kane, 1994.

Thomas Edison Had a Bright Idea, Kane, 1994.

CONTRIBUTOR

More Science Fiction Tales, Rand McNally, 1974.

Adrift in Space and Other Stories, Lerner, 1974.

Crisis, edited by Roger Elwood, T. Nelson, 1974.

Horror Tales, Rand McNally, 1974.

Starstream: Adventures in Science Fiction, Western, 1976.

Future Corruption, edited by Roger Elwood, Warner Paperback, 1976.

Encore Readers, Scott Foresman, 1980.

Distant Worlds, Collins, 1980.

Incubo, Mondadori Editore (Italy), 1980.

The Year's Best Horror Stories, edited by Karl Wagner, DAW, 1982.

Top Horror, Heyne Verlag (Munich, Germany), 1984.

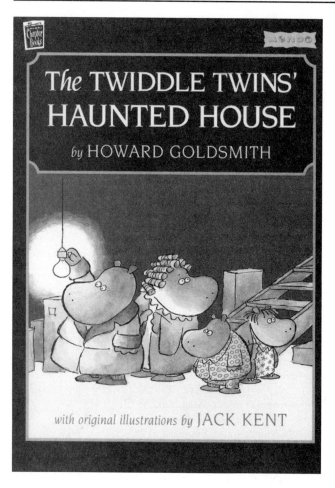

In Goldsmith's comical chapter book for beginning readers, hippos Timothy and Tabitha Twiddle are awakened by a strange sound in their new home, and they become convinced that it is a ghost.

Young Ghosts, edited by Isaac Asimov, HarperCollins, 1985.

Hitler Victorious, edited by Gregory Benford, Berkeley, 1987.

The Further Adventures of Batman, Bantam, 1989.

Visions of Fantasy, edited by Isaac Asimov, Doubleday, 1989.

Spooky Stories, T. Nelson, 1990.

Evil Tales of Evil Things, Checkerboard, 1993.

Tales of the Batman, DC Comics, 1995.

Dream Weavers, Penguin, 1996.

Contributor to adult and children's magazines (sometimes under pseudonym Ward Smith), including *Child Life, Young World, Scholastic Storyworks, Short Story International, London Mystery, Weekly Reader, Highlights for Children, Outlook, School, Opinion, Galaxy, Ideals, Comet* (West Germany), *Void* (Australia), *Crux* (Australia), *Wings,* and others.

OTHER

The Plastic Age, Educational Progress, 1979.

The Bend of Time, Educational Progress, 1979.

Work in Progress

An adult action/adventure novel titled *Danger Zone,* to be published by Books in Motion in 1999.

Sidelights

Howard Goldsmith is the author of plays, poetry, videos, and more than four dozen books, most of them for a children's audience ranging in age from preschool to young adult. In addition to his many picture books and beginning readers featuring animal characters—from owls and robins to hippos and kangaroos—Goldsmith has also written novels for middle-grade and young adult readers, among them *The Whispering Sea* and *Invasion: 2200 A.D.* Goldsmith's short fiction has appeared in such children's magazines as *Highlights for Children, Scholastic Storyworks, Child Life, Weekly Reader,* and *Disney Adventures.* "I have a horror of boring the reader...," Goldsmith once commented. "My plots emphasize suspense and mystery that, I hope, compel attention and intrigue the imagination. The challenge is greatest in writing for young people, especially the growing numbers of printed-starved, picture-oriented nonreaders and reluctant readers."

Goldsmith's first novel, *The Whispering Sea,* written in 1976, intrigues its readers with ghosts, astral projection, and other supernatural phenomena. The mystery begins as Bob and Lucy Carter and their parents rent a home for their summer vacation—an old mansion on the coast of Maine. According to local lore, the Carter's rental house is haunted, and strange events are constantly supporting the theory. The attic is strictly off-limits to the Carters; a reputed sea witch haunts the water; and murders, psychics, and possession become part of the story's tapestry. Investigating the mystery surrounding the weather-beaten house, Lucy becomes invaded by the spirit of Lucinda, the girl who occupied the house a century ago, before she drowned. It takes an exorcism to work Lucy free of the spirit.

Robert Bloch, author of *Psycho,* wrote: "*The Whispering Sea* works its magic—conjuring up evil spirits and eerie events without resorting to cheap shock-for-shock's-sake—but including enough chills and excitement to send shivers down the spines of young readers everywhere." While Andrew K. Stevenson found the novel to be "unconvincing" in his *School Library Journal* review, *Best Sellers* contributor Tony Siaulys argued that *The Whispering Sea* "has the elements of a good scare, without gore." Siaulys also praised the book as "interesting and very readable," expressing enthusiasm for reading Goldsmith's future works.

Invasion: 2200 A.D. is a science-fiction novel for preteens and teens. An alien scientist named Rog is on a mission to warn Earth's inhabitants of impending invasion by a race of mind-bending aliens, called Tuks. When he meets a farmer's son, Rog ends up getting entangled in a civil war between farmers and city-dwellers. *Invasion: 2200 A.D.* "has action, adventure, and science fantasy in abundance," according to *Children's Book Review Service* contributor Jennifer Brown.

In addition to writing novels, Goldsmith gives in to his "bent for whimsy for the sheer pleasure of it" by creating lighter books for the younger set. Many of his picture books feature young animal characters that illustrate a variety of emotions in ways that young children can identify with. For example, in *Sleepy Little Owl,* a small screech owl decides that sleeping all day makes him miss too much; he tries to stay awake past sunrise to search for adventure, but finds trouble instead. Little Owl realizes, after he is rescued by his parents, that he needs sleep just like everyone else. In addition to illustrating the problems that can occur when natural laws are ignored, the book also teaches listeners about the habits of nocturnal and diurnal animals. According to a *Children's Book Review Service* contributor, "each time children read [*Sleepy Little Owl*] they will learn something new." *School Library Journal* reviewer Patricia Manning enjoyed the story as "a pleasant little interlude."

Goldsmith's early chapter book series featuring the Twiddle Twins is full of the kind of silliness that is sure to capture the interest of beginning readers. In *The Twiddle Twins' Haunted House,* hippos Timothy and Tabitha are awakened by a strange sound, which they become convinced is caused by a ghost. A *Publishers Weekly* critic appreciated the way Goldsmith "exuberantly told" the mystifying story that puzzled the hippo family. The *Twiddle Twins' Music Box Mystery,* another book featuring the portly hippo pair, sets the twins to the task of figuring out who stole their prize music box—and trashed their house to boot. Calling the story "a lively satisfying whodunit played out in five short chapters," *School Library Journal* contributor Mary Ann Bursk complimented Goldsmith's writing. "He mixes both simple and complex sentences," wrote Bursk, "to create a varied text." Bursk believed that the story would likely spark classroom discussion and asserted that youngsters "will enjoy the fast pace and chuckle at the pictures." Approving of these "engaging beginning chapter books," *Booklist* critic April Judge wrote: "Independent readers ... will enjoy these well-paced refreshing mysteries."

Goldsmith himself recognizes the speedy pacing of his stories, commenting: "We can all recall plodding through acres of murky narrative and sunless prose. My dread of tedium has, to a large extent, shaped my style and guided my choice of subject matter...."

About his primary choice of audience, Goldsmith commented: "Nowhere is storytelling in its purest form more evident than in literature for young people—often underrated, deprecated, or ignored. Yet it is a craft, a discipline, and an art form in every way as sophisticated and demanding as adult fiction. And there is an intimacy of relationship between reader and writer that is seldom equalled."

Works Cited

Brown, Jennifer, review of *Invasion: 2200 A.D., Children's Book Review Service,* December, 1979, p. 37.

Bursk, Mary Ann, review of *The Twiddle Twins' Music Box Mystery, School Library Journal,* December, 1997, p. 90.

Judge, April, review of *The Twiddle Twins' Music Box Mystery, Booklist,* February 1, 1998, p. 918.

Manning, Patricia, review of *Sleepy Little Owl, School Library Journal,* February, 1998, p. 85.

Siaulys, Tony, review of *The Whispering Sea, Best Sellers,* May, 1977, p. 44.

Siaulys, Tony, review of *Sleepy Little Owl,* Review Service, February, 1998, p. 75.

Stevenson, Andrew K., review of *The Whispering Sea, School Library Journal,* October, 1977, p. 123.

Review of *The Twiddle Twins' Haunted House, Publishers Weekly,* November 22, 1985, p. 52.

For More Information See

PERIODICALS

Bulletin of the Center for Children's Books, May, 1977, p. 142.

School Library Journal, November, 1979, p. 77; April, 1986, p. 72.

*   *   *

GRIECO-TISO, Pina 1954-

Personal

Born March 27, 1954, in Melbourne, Australia; daughter of Bert (a railway employee) and Ida (Santosuosso) Grieco; married Alfredo Tiso (a joiner), January 17, 1981; children: Ben, Jason, Tristan. *Education:* Monash University, B.A. and diploma in education, 1976; University of Melbourne, B.A. (Italian language, culture, and literature), 1979. *Hobbies and other interests:* Graffiti, reading, movies, music, tae kwon do, roller-blading, leadlight art, travel, Egyptology, working with youth groups, astrology, the occult, the brain.

Addresses

Home—18 Daley St., Bentleigh, Victoria 3204, Australia. *Office*—Parkdale Secondary College, Warren Rd., Mordialloc, Victoria 3195, Australia. *E-mail*—grieco@eisa.net.au.

Career

Writer. Teacher of English and other languages at secondary schools and foreign language schools throughout Australia; Parkdale Secondary College, Mordialloc, Australia, teacher of English and French. *Member:* Australian Society of Authors, Fellowship of Australian Writers, Australian Literary Translators' Association, National Book Council of Australia.

Pina Grieco-Tiso

Awards, Honors

Regional prizes from Fellowship of Australian Writers, 1987, 1988, and 1990, for short stories, and 1989, for poetry; Coolum Prizes, 1989 and 1990; Rockhampton Poetry Award, 1989.

Writings

FOR YOUNG ADULTS; NOVELS

Blitz: A Bomber's Nightmare, Random House (Milsons Point, Australia), 1991.
Time Out, Random House, 1993.
Sticks and Stones, Random House, 1998.

OTHER

Author of a multilingual textbook for travelers and a bilingual (English and Italian) version of the "yellow pages." Work represented in anthologies, including *Anthology of Australian Poetry,* 1987. Contributor to periodicals, including *Viewpoint, Writer's News, Australian Woman's Weekly, Summer,* and *New Decade.*

Work in Progress

A young adult novel, *Marco;* a young adult novel about the rehabilitation of a young murderer; translating into English *The Honoured Society,* an adult novel, for Black Pepper.

Sidelights

Pina Grieco-Tiso told *SATA:* "Writing has been an enjoyable activity for me since primary school, where the well-meaning but strict, black-habited nuns scared me to death! My first stories were full of big, black aliens from outer space who came to kidnap earth children. For this brilliant and imaginative initiation into the world of writing, I remain deeply indebted to those nuns, some of whom I still see from time to time at reunions. In the following years my tastes in literature didn't progress too much from there—anything in the gothic horror genre was fine for me, and still is. I particularly enjoy it when the human psyche is explored, as in Anne Rice's vampire series.

"In my own writing, I too explore the psyche. Why do people do what they do? There has to be a reason, whether it is an innocent child playing hurtful, disturbing games in the playground or an older person suffering personality disorders that prohibit him from leading a 'normal' life. After all, what is normal, and who decides?

"Because of this, most of my writing is in the first person. I like to get into one person's head so that I can study how he, based on his knowledge of life, perceives the world around him, and perhaps I can understand human behavior better.

"This sort of writing also helps you understand yourself, and for this reason young people should be encouraged from an early age to write creatively and explore their own feelings. In this way they can develop their unique styles of writing. Argumentative writing can be learned; so can critical writing and even the narrative style. They all work to a formula. But creative writing can only be an original expression of one's feelings, and no rules apply. This makes it all the more exciting and adventurous—a sure winner for young people!"

For More Information See

PERIODICALS

Australian Book Review, March, 1991, p. 22; June, 1991, p. 45; February, 1993, p. 41.
Education Australia, No. 13, 1991, pp. 33-34.
Magpies, May, 1991, p. 34.
ViewPoint, winter, 1993, p. 41; spring, 1994, p. 5; spring, 1998, p. 44.

H

Barbara Hambly

HAMBLY, Barbara 1951-

Personal

Born August 28, 1951, in San Diego, CA. *Education:* University of California at Riverside, M.A. (medieval history); also studied at University of Bordeaux, France.

Addresses

Agent—c/o Del Rey Books, 201 East 50th St., New York, NY 10022.

Career

Writer. Has worked as a research assistant, high school teacher, and karate instructor. *Member:* Science Fiction Writers of America (president).

Writings

"DARWATH" SERIES

The Time of the Dark, Del Rey, 1982.
The Walls of Air, Del Rey, 1983.
The Armies of Daylight, Del Rey, 1983.
Mother of Winter, Del Rey, 1996.
Icefalcon's Quest, Del Rey, 1998.

"SUN WOLF" SERIES

The Ladies of Mandrigyn, Del Rey, 1984.
The Witches of Wenshar, Del Rey, 1987.
The Unschooled Wizard, (includes *The Ladies of the Mandrigyn* and *The Witches of Wenshar*), Doubleday, 1987.
The Dark Hand of Magic, Del Rey, 1990.

"SUN-CROSS" SERIES

The Rainbow Abyss, Del Rey, 1991.
Magicians of the Night, Del Rey, 1992.
Sun-Cross (includes *The Rainbow Abyss* and *Magicians of the Night*), Guild America, 1992.

"THE WINDROSE CHRONICLES"

The Silent Tower, Del Rey, 1986.
The Silicon Mage, Del Rey, 1988.
Darkmage (includes *The Silent Tower* and *The Silicon Mage*) Doubleday, 1988.
Dog Wizard, Del Rey, 1993.

"STAR TREK" BOOKS

Ishmael: A Star Trek Novel, Pocket, 1985.
Ghost Walker, Pocket, 1991.
Crossroad, Pocket, 1994.

NOVELS

The Quirinal Hill Affair, St. Martin's Press, 1983, published as *Search the Seven Hills,* Ballantine, 1987.

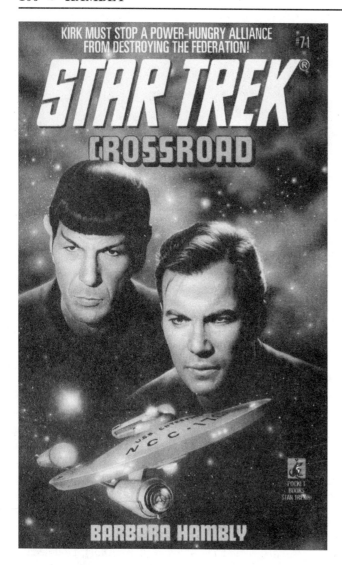

Based on the popular television show, Hambly's novel places Captain Kirk in a dangerous battle with a group of renegades trying to control his starship.

Dragonsbane, Del Rey, 1986.

Search the Seven Hills, Del Rey, 1987.

Those Who Hunt the Night, Del Rey, 1988, published in England as *Immortal Blood,* Unwin, 1988.

Beauty and the Beast (novelization of television script), Avon, 1989.

Song of Orpheus (novelization of television script), Avon, 1990.

Stranger at the Wedding, Del Rey, 1994, published in England as *Sorcerer's Ward,* HarperCollins, 1994.

Bride of the Rat God, Del Rey, 1994.

Traveling with the Dead, Del Rey, 1995.

Star Wars: Children of the Jedi, Del Rey, 1995.

A Free Man of Color, Bantam, 1997.

Star Wars: Planet of Twilight, Del Rey, 1997.

Fever Season, Bantam, 1998.

Dragonshadow, Del Rey, 1999.

OTHER

(Editor) *Women of the Night,* Warner Aspect, 1994.

(Editor) *Sisters of the Night,* 1995.

Contributor of short fiction to anthologies and other publications, including *Xanadu 2,* edited by Jane Yolen and Martin H. Greenberg, 1994; *South from Midnight,* Southern Fried Press, 1994; *Sandman: Book of Dreams,* 1996; and *War of Worlds: Global Dispatches,* 1996. Also author of scripts for animated cartoons.

Sidelights

Barbara Hambly's life experiences are as varied as her fiction. The ex-model, clerk, high school teacher, black belt karate instructor, and technical writer enjoys dancing, painting, studying historical and fantasy costuming, and carpentry—and she occasionally uses these varied activities as fodder for her writing. While Hambly's novels are primarily sword-and-sorcery fantasies, she also writes in a variety of other genres—everything from vampire stories to science fiction; recently she has enjoyed success with historical mysteries such as the popular *Free Man of Color* and *Fever Season,* and she has created novelizations based on the characters in television shows like *Beauty and the Beast* and *Star Trek.*

Hambly, who has served as president of the Science Fiction Writers of America, maintains that the urge to write is a big part of an author's makeup. "I think a person is a writer if they HAVE to write," she said during a July, 1997, online chat session with Barnes and Noble. "This is not an easy way to make a living. I think I would be doing this even if I were not making money at it. I think people who are true writers write because they have to. They can't NOT do it. They have stories in them to tell, and they have to tell them."

Considered a gifted storyteller, Hambly has garnered a wide readership, and critics have praised her work. "Hambly's writing is witty and fast-paced," wrote Elizabeth Hand of the *Washington Post Book World.* David Langford, in the *St. James Guide to Fantasy Writers,* remarked that Hambly "has a special talent for reclaiming and reworking familiar themes of fantasy, making them over into a seamless gestalt which is very much her own."

Hambly was born in the Naval Hospital of San Diego, California, on August 28, 1951. She grew up in southern California, attended the University of California, Riverside, and studied for a time at the University of Bordeaux in southern France. As a girl she was an avid reader. She fell in love with fantasy fiction after reading L. Frank Baum's classic turn-of-the-century children's tale *The Wizard of Oz,* and decided to become a writer. Hambly took a step in this direction when she earned a master's degree in medieval history. This gave her both the research skills and the knowledge base to craft historical novels.

Hambly took her first step toward a career in the writing of fiction when she penned a fantasy novel for her own enjoyment in 1978. She sold the book to a publisher on its first submission despite the fact she did not yet have an agent. "I always wanted to be a writer but everyone

Leia, Luke, Han Solo, and Chewbacca journey to the frozen world of Belsavis to search for the missing children of the Jedi warriors in Hambly's novel based on the Star Wars *films.*

kept telling me it was impossible to break into the field or make money," Hambly said in an interview with Elisabeth Sherwin in the *Davis Enterprise*. "I've proven them wrong on both counts."

In 1982, Hambly's writing career took off with publication of *The Time of the Dark,* the first book in the "Darwath Trilogy." The story centers on a race of creatures known as the "Dark Ones" who are eyeless, can fly, and have a taste for human flesh, as they attack a parallel Earth. Two citizens of Los Angeles, graduate student Gil Patterson and auto mechanic Rudy Solis, are drawn into the alternate world to do battle with the Dark Ones. Reviewer Michael W. McClintock of *Science Fiction and Fantasy Book Review* wrote that Hambly "draws Gil and Rudy effectively, and the plot shows at least the possibility of interesting development." Susan L. Nickerson in *Library Journal* described *The Time of the Dark* as "heart stopping," and noted that Hambly had written an "unusually effective" fantasy work.

The second book, *The Walls of Air,* published a year later, continues the adventure of Gil and Rudy, who have been taken to the Dark Ones' parallel world. There, Rudy becomes a wizard and Gil is transformed into an elite guard. Reviews for this novel were mixed. Nickerson however, praised Hambly's plot for its "brisk action" and a feeling of impending menace which "keeps the reader deeply involved." The third book in the saga, *The Armies of Daylight,* gave devotees an answer to the riddle of the Dark. Roland Green of *Booklist* wrote that Hambly's work features "intelligent characterization, sound storytelling, and creative use of magic." Thirteen years after *The Armies of Daylight,* Hambly resurrected Rudy and Gil in 1996 for the novel *Mother of Winter.* Here the characters must save Earth from a glacial freeze. "The story is involving, and the narrative intelligent," according to a *Publishers Weekly* reviewer.

Aside from the "Darwath" novels, the prolific Hambly has written more than two dozen other books. Among them is *Ishmael: A Star Trek Novel,* published in 1985. In Hambly's tale, one of a popular series of books based on the characters created by the late Gene Roddenberry, Spock travels back in time to visit Earth circa 1867 in an effort to thwart a Klingon plan to change human history. Roland Green of *Booklist* praised Hambly's effort, recommending it "not only for Star Trek collections but as a good novel in its own right." *Ishmael* grabs the reader's attention throughout "with humor, action and personal interplay," according to Roberta Rogow of *Voice of Youth Advocates.* Hambly added two other books to the "Star Trek" series: *Ghost Walker* in 1991 and *Crossroad* in 1994.

Hambly delved into the adventures of Princess Leia and Luke Skywalker in *Children of the Jedi* and *Planet of Twilight,* part of a series of books based on George Lucas's popular *Star Wars* films. "In [Hambly's] hands, the heroes of the New Republic take on a maturity and credibility that enhance their already engaging personalities," *Library Journal* contributor Jackie Cassada wrote of *Children of the Jedi.* Hambly's contribution rated "among the best in the series," a *Booklist* reviewer declared. The story takes Leia, Luke, Han Solo and Chewbacca on a journey to find the missing children of the Jedi. In *Planet of Twilight,* published in 1997, two factions battle for power on a planet called Nam Chorios. "Hambly is superior to most of the other SW authors at vivid word building [and] humor," wrote Roland Green of *Booklist.*

Perhaps Hambly's most successful original creation is the "Sun Wolf" series, which chronicles the adventures of what Langford described as "the unbrutal mercenary Sun Wolf and his hard-bitten lady, second-in-command Starhawk." *The Ladies of Mandrigyn,* the first book in the series, is a gory adventure about Sun Wolf's battle with the wizard Altiokis. It also deals with Sun Wolf's acceptance of the aging process, the emergence of his own innate wizard potential, and the realization that he loves Starhawk, his longtime loyal follower. The work should "please most fantasy readers," *Library Journal*

Set in nineteenth-century New Orleans, **A Free Man of Color** *centers on Benjamin January, a free Creole who returns to Louisiana after living in Europe and is promptly accused of murder.(Cover illustration by Jason Seder.)*

contributor Janet Cameron predicted. Subsequent books in the "Sun Wolf" series are *The Witches of Wenshar* and *The Dark Hand of Magic.* Hambly gave further proof of her versatility when she wrote *Dragonsbane,* a dragon fantasy novel. The book relates the adventures of a character named Prince Gareth as he deals with a demonic parent, love, rioting subjects, and a black dragon. "High school readers of both sexes will applaud with equal fervor," wrote Frank Perry in *Voice of Youth Advocates.*

In 1988, Hambly crafted a vampire story with an inventive twist: the vampires are the victims. *Those Who Hunt the Night* presents a mystery being who slashes open the coffins of vampires in London and lets in lethal sunlight that allows the stalker to kill the victims as it drinks their blood. A frightened vampire enlists the help of an ex-spy to find the culprit. Susan M. Schuller, writing in *Voice of Youth Advocates,* stated that Hambly

"delves into vampire lore with gusto, detailing the lust for blood and the killing urge among the undead."

While Hambly enjoyed writing her vampire book, she was so busy with other projects that a decade passed before she returned to the genre. *Traveling with the Dead* follows the adventures of James Asher, a former British espionage agent, and his wife, Lydia, who battle to prevent an alliance between human governments and the living dead. A *Library Journal* contributor believed that *Traveling with the Dead* "captures both the subtle ambiance of turn-of-the-century political intrigue and the even more baroque pathways of the human and the inhuman heart." A reviewer in *Publishers Weekly* remarked that Hambly's "vivid portraits" of the vampires "allow them to emerge as memorable personalities distinct from the viewpoints they represent."

Hambly has also ventured into the field of mystery writing. Her first novel in that genre was *A Free Man of Color,* published in 1997. Set in nineteenth-century New Orleans, the book follows the exploits of Benjamin January, a free Creole with dark brown skin. January, a trained surgeon, returns to Louisiana after living in Paris and promptly becomes a murder suspect. Hambly explained in her Barnes and Noble online interview that she did extensive research at the Historic New Orleans Collection in preparation for writing the book. "I did not think so much about writing in the voice of a black man, as writing in the voice of a historical character from another time and place," she said in an online chat. Hambly's attention to detail paid off handsomely. Marilyn Stasio, writing in the *New York Times Book Review,* praised *A Free Man of Color* as a "stunning first mystery"; Dick Adler of the Chicago *Tribune Books* described the novel as "magically rich and poignant." Assessing the author's work, a *Kirkus Reviews* contributor observed that Hambly has a talent for "goldstained description."

In *Fever Season,* the sequel to *A Free Man of Color,* January works at New Orlean's Charity Hospital while the city is in the grip of a cholera epidemic. January also realizes that free men of color are disappearing, and his investigations into the matter lead to a horrifying conclusion. According to a *Publishers Weekly* critic, *Fever Season* is "complex in plotting, rich in atmosphere, and written in powerful, lucid prose." A *Booklist* reviewer called the work "rich, intense, and eye-opening."

In 1999, Hambly returned to the Winterlands, the setting for *Dragonsbane,* with the sequel *Dragonshadow.* Mage Jenny Waynest and her husband, Lord John Aversin, must defend the land from a siege of demons from another plane of existence who prey on the magic and souls of dragons and wizards, and who capture Waynest and Aversin's young son. A reviewer in *Publishers Weekly* called *Dragonshadow* a "first-rate high fantasy" as well as "elegant, intelligent and entertaining." "Heartbreaking, wryly comic, and breathtaking, this is fantasy at its finest," enthused *Booklist* critic Roberta Johnson.

Although she juggles a hectic schedule, Hambly prides herself on the professionalism and thoroughness with which she practices her art. Her books go through first, second, and third drafts. Hambly begins her stories by working with a computer, printing out a hard copy and then going over it with a pen and rewriting, sometimes large portions, by hand. The technique has served her well. Hambly explained that if ever she suffers from writer's block, she retraces what she has written. She believes that hold-ups in her writing are likely her subconscious telling her that something is not right.

Continuing her prolific pace, Hambly is in the process of writing *Graveyard Dust,* the third book in the Benjamin January mystery series, and she has a new fantasy novel called *Fading of the Light* in the works. Hambly, who divides her time between Los Angeles and New Orleans, shares her two homes with her author husband, George Alec Effinger, and with the couple's two Pekinese cats. Hambly has said that her greatest writing gift is always having a story to tell. As she explained in her Barnes and Noble online interview, "If everyone has one superpower, mine is—thank God and knock on wood—that so far, I seem to have a cast-iron Muse; I seem to be able to work under just about any condition."

Works Cited

Adler, Dick, review of *A Free Man of Color, Tribune Books* (Chicago), July 6, 1997, p. 2.

Cameron, Janet, review of *The Ladies of Mandrigyn, Library Journal,* March 15, 1985, p. 599.

Cassada, Jackie, review of *Children of the Jedi, Library Journal,* March 15, 1995, p. 101.

Review of *Children of the Jedi, Booklist,* April 1, 1995, p. 1355.

Review of *Dragonshadow, Publishers Weekly,* February 8, 1999, p. 199.

Review of *Fever Season, Booklist,* May 15, 1998.

Review of *Fever Season, Publishers Weekly,* April 27, 1998, p. 48.

Review of *A Free Man of Color, Kirkus Reviews,* May 15, 1997, p. 741.

Green, Roland, review of *The Armies of Daylight, Booklist,* September 1, 1983, p. 31.

Green, Roland, review of *Ishmael: A Star Trek Novel, Booklist,* July, 1985, p. 1519.

Green, Roland, review of *Planet of Twilight, Booklist,* February 1, 1997, p. 907.

Hambly, Barbara, *Barnes and Noble Online Chat,* http://www.barnesandnoble.com, January 27, 1999.

Hand, Elizabeth, comments on Hambly in *Washington Post Book World,* January 29, 1989, p. 6.

Johnson, Roberta, review of *Dragonshadow, Booklist,* February 15, 1999, p. 1048.

Langford, David, essay on Hambly in *St. James Guide to Fantasy Writers,* St. James Press, 1995.

McClintock, Michael W., review of *The Time of the Dark, Science Fiction and Fantasy Book Review,* September, 1982, pp. 30-31.

Review of *Mother of Winter, Publishers Weekly,* September 16, 1996, p. 74.

Nickerson, Susan L., review of *The Time of the Dark, Library Journal,* May 15, 1982, p. 1014.

Nickerson, Susan L., review of *The Walls of Air, Library Journal,* March 15, 1983, p. 603.

Perry, Frank, review of *Dragonsbane, Voice of Youth Advocates,* August-October, 1986, p. 162.

Rogow, Roberta, review of *Ishmael: A Star Trek Novel, Voice of Youth Advocates,* February, 1986, pp. 393-94.

Schuller, Susan M., review of *Those Who Hunt the Night, Voice of Youth Advocates,* April, 1989, p. 42.

Sherwin, Elisabeth, interview with Hambly in *Davis Enterprise,* October 29, 1995.

Stasio, Marilyn, review of *A Free Man of Color, New York Times Book Review,* August 2, 1998, p. 24.

Review of *Traveling with the Dead, Library Journal,* August, 1995, p. 122.

Review of *Traveling with the Dead, Publishers Weekly,* March 13, 1995, p. 63.

For More Information See

PERIODICALS

Kirkus Reviews, August 1, 1996, p. 1107; November 15, 1997, p. 1678.

Library Journal, September 15, 1996, p. 101; June 1, 1997, p. 148.

Publishers Weekly, May 5, 1997, p. 197.

Voice of Youth Advocates, October, 1995, p. 232; August, 1998, p. 210.*

*   *   *

HASHMI, Kerri 1955-

Personal

Surname pronounced "Hash-mee"; Born March 4, 1955, in Melbourne, Australia; daughter of Harold (a dairy farmer) and Betty (a telegraphist) Normandale; married, 1982; children: Omar, Natasha. *Education:* Adelaide University, B.A. (with first class honors), 1976; Flinders University of South Australia, diploma in education, 1977. *Hobbies and other interests:* Reading, travel, cooking, languages.

Addresses

Home—Canberra, Australia.

Career

Birdwood High School, South Australia, teacher, 1978-79. Australian Department of Foreign Affairs, diplomat, 1980-86. *Member:* Childrens' Book Council of Australia.

Writings

You and Me, Murrawee, illustrated by Felicity Marshall, Viking, 1998.

Kerri Hashmi

Work in Progress

My Six Grandparents and *Philippine Diary, 1972.*

Sidelights

Kerri Hashmi told *SATA:* "I have always wanted to write since earliest childhood. I would love to be able to convey to children the magic of life on this planet, the diversity of its people and cultures, and the environment we all share. I enjoy traveling and reading so that I can learn about different places and people. I always have my ear tuned to pick up a new story."

For More Information See

PERIODICALS

Reading Time, November, 1998, p. 17.

*   *   *

HENKES, Kevin 1960-

Personal

Born November, 1960, in Racine, WI; married. *Education:* Attended University of Wisconsin—Madison.

Addresses

Home—Madison, WI.

Career

Writer and illustrator.

Awards, Honors

Children's Choice Book selection, Children's Book Council/International Reading Association, 1986, both for *A Weekend with Wendell;* notable book citation, American Library Association (ALA), 1988, and Keystone to Reading Award, Keystone State Reading Association, 1990, both for *Chester's Way;* Elizabeth Burr Award, Wisconsin Library Association, 1993, for *Words of Stone; Boston Globe-Horn Book* Award honor book, and Caldecott Honor Book, both 1994, both for *Owen; Booklist* "Top of the List" Picture Book Award, 1996, and American Booksellers Book of the Year (ABBY) Award, American Booksellers Association, 1997, for *Lilly's Purple Plastic Purse;* best books of the year citation, *School Library Journal,* 1997, Best Books, *School Library Journal,* 1998, and notable book citation, ALA, 1998, all for *Sun and Spoon.*

Writings

SELF-ILLUSTRATED

All Alone, Greenwillow, 1981.
Clean Enough, Greenwillow, 1982.
Margaret and Taylor, Greenwillow, 1983.
Bailey Goes Camping, Greenwillow, 1985.
Grandpa and Bo, Greenwillow, 1986.
Sheila Rae, the Brave, Greenwillow, 1987.
A Weekend with Wendell, Greenwillow, 1987.
Chester's Way, Greenwillow, 1988.
Jessica, Greenwillow, 1989.
Shhhh, Greenwillow, 1989.
Julius, the Baby of the World, Greenwillow, 1990.
Chrysanthemum, Greenwillow, 1991.
Owen, Greenwillow, 1993.
Lilly's Purple Plastic Purse, Greenwillow, 1996.

NOVELS

(Self-illustrated) *Return to Sender,* Greenwillow, 1984.
(Self-illustrated) *Two under Par,* Greenwillow, 1987.
The Zebra Wall, Greenwillow, 1988.
Words of Stone, Greenwillow, 1992.
Protecting Marie, Greenwillow, 1995.
Sun and Spoon, Greenwillow, 1997.
The Birthday Room, Greenwillow, 1999.

OTHER

Once around the Block, illustrated by Victoria Chess, Greenwillow, 1987.
Good-bye, Curtis, illustrated by Marisabina Russo, Greenwillow, 1995.
The Biggest Boy, illustrated by Nancy Tafuri, Greenwillow, 1995.
Circle Dogs, illustrated by Dan Yaccarino, Greenwillow, 1998.

Kevin Henkes

Oh!, illustrated by Laura Dronzek, Greenwillow, 1999.

Adaptations

A Weekend with Wendell was made into a filmstrip and a read-along audio cassette, both by Weston Woods, both 1988; Recorded Books made audiocassettes of *Words of Stone,* 1993, *Two under Par,* 1997, and *The Zebra Wall,* 1997; Listening Library made an audiocassette of *Sun and Spoon,* 1998. Weston Woods has made videocassette adaptations of *A Weekend with Wendell, Owen,* and *Chrysanthemum,* while Broderbund Software has created a "Living Books" CD-Rom game of *Sheila Rae, the Brave.*

Work in Progress

Dog and *Twice as Far,* both for Greenwillow.

Sidelights

The books of Kevin Henkes have been consistently praised for the funny and, above all, realistic way they portray children and the relationships they have with their parents and peers. Henkes is most famous for his picture books, many of which feature unforgettable mouse characters such as Lilly and Owen, but he has written several acclaimed novels as well. *Bulletin of the*

Center for Children's Books reviewer Betsy Hearne observed that Henkes's writing "sounds as if the author has been eavesdropping on children at play," while *Tribune Books* critic Mary Harris Veeder wrote: "Henkes's children are full of the imperfections and emotions which mark real life." As Martha Vaughan Parravano similarly noted in *Children's Books and Their Creators:* "Henkes is the creator of true picture books— in which text and illustrations work together to make a seamless whole—that exhibit an innate understanding of children and always contain a strong element of security and comfort."

Books played an important part of Henkes's childhood in Wisconsin. His family regularly visited the local public library, and checking out his own books and carrying them home was an important part of the ritual for Henkes. Illustrations often determined which books he would select, and the works of Crockett Johnson and Garth Williams were particular favorites. "I think I always knew [I would be an artist]," the illustrator told Ilene Cooper of *Booklist.* "My parents and my sisters encouraged me in that. There was an art museum near my house, and we used to make excursions there." As a high schooler, Henkes was encouraged by a teacher to develop his writing skills as well, and this gave him the idea for his future career. "I knew I liked to write, draw and paint," he said in a *Publishers Weekly* interview with Nathalie Op de Beeck, "and I wanted to find an art form to combine those things—that's when I rediscovered picture books."

Henkes attended the University of Wisconsin, where he majored in art. Between his first two years of college, he decided to travel to New York City to find a publisher who might be interested in his work. While breaking into publishing is usually very difficult, the idealistic student was undaunted. "I picked the week I would go to New York, made a list of my ten favorite publishers, and set up appointments," he told Op de Beeck. "I went thinking, 'I'll come back with a book contract.'" Henkes had done his homework and had included among his interviews one with Susan Hirschman, an editor at Greenwillow whom he had heard lecture on tape. He made a good connection with her, and when he returned to school, the nineteen year old had a contract for his first book in hand. In 1981, Henkes published his first picture book, *All Alone,* which he first drafted while he was still in high school.

Both *All Alone* and its follow-up, *Clean Enough,* are gentle stories relating ordinary, everyday activities of children. While critics did not find the text exceptionally distinguished, they did have praise for Henkes's artwork. Of *All Alone,* in which a little boy uses his imagination while outside alone, a *Publishers Weekly* reviewer stated that "muted colors [and] delicate lines reflect the sensitivity in the text." A *Kirkus Reviews* writer likewise observed that "Henkes paints with a delicate palette ... and the illustrations have a degree of feeling." Bathtime is the focus of *Clean Enough,* as a little boy considers how to get the water just the right temperature and remembers previous adventures in the tub. *School*

Library Journal contributor Joan W. Blos found this work "highly successful" and praised the text's "nuances of humor" as well as Henkes's "affectionate drawings."

After publishing *Margaret and Taylor,* which relates the travails of a boy who tries to overcome the nasty tricks of his older sister, and *Return to Sender,* in which a postal worker responds to a boy's letter to a superhero, Henkes tried his hand at his first animal characters. In *Bailey Goes Camping,* young rabbit Bailey is disappointed at being left behind while his older siblings go on a Bunny Scouts camping trip. His understanding mother, however, finds ways for him to enjoy camping activities while at home. The story "*truly* captures the world of the small child," Anne Devereaux Jordan Crouse remarked in *Children's Book Review Service,* adding praise for the book's "wit and warmth." With its gentle pastels and simple text, *Bailey Goes Camping* is "a cozy, comfortable book that will leave youngsters smiling," Denise M. Wilms wrote in *Booklist.* A loving spirit also infuses *Grandpa and Bo,* about a shared summer between a boy and his grandfather. The book "is a welcome addition to [Henkes's] growing list of accomplishments," a *Kirkus Reviews* critic stated, explaining that the artist's "soft pencil drawings accurately convey the story's mood of quiet simplicity."

Many of Henkes's most popular books feature a group of young mice whose adventures and concerns mirror those of children worldwide. "I found I could get much more humor out of animals, and besides it freed me from having to sketch from a human model," the artist revealed to Cooper. "I tried rabbits for a while, but I found mice to be the most fun. Now, I've really grown attached to some of my mouse characters, so I'd like to explore their lives a little bit more." The first of these mouse works is the Children's Choice Book *A Weekend with Wendell.* Wendell's parents have gone out of town, leaving Wendell to stay with Sophie's family for the weekend. Wendell, however, is a difficult houseguest, in spite of Sophie's attempts to be a good host. When the two play house, for example, Wendell is the father, mother, and children, leaving Sophie to be the dog; when they play hospital, Wendell makes himself the doctor, the patient, and the nurse, making Sophie be the desk clerk; and while playing bakery, Wendell is the baker—Sophie is a sweet roll. In the end she can bear it no longer; Wendell gets his comeuppance, and the two mice ultimately become close friends. The story is "divertingly recounted by Henkes with good humor and charm," a *Publishers Weekly* critic stated, adding that "the postures of his mice children speak volumes."

In 1987, Henkes brought out two more stories about his little rodent characters. In *Sheila Rae, the Brave,* boastful elder sister Sheila Rae impresses her meek younger sister Louise with her ability to combat dogs, bullies, and monsters in the closet. When Sheila Rae's imagination gets the best of her while taking a new route home from school, however, it is Louise who comes to the rescue. "Everything that happens here is completely credible," a *Publishers Weekly* writer commented, "hence appealing to kids' intuitions." *School Library*

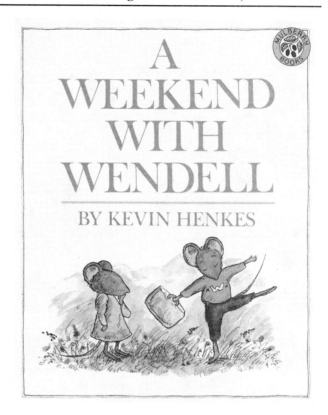

Sophie learns she must stand up for herself in Henkes's self-illustrated picture book. (Cover illustration by Henkes.)

Journal contributor David Gale likewise asserted that children would enjoy the book's humor and realism, and also praised Henkes's "bouncy watercolors" and "highly expressive faces." *Chester's Way* introduces one of the author's most popular characters, the imaginative and impish Lilly. When Lilly moves into the neighborhood, best friends Chester and Wilson both have some adjusting to do before the trio become good friends. "Henkes's vision of friendship captures the essence of the childlike," a *Publishers Weekly* critic noted, adding that "every sentence is either downright funny or dense with playful, deadpan humor." In this "amusing, believable story" with its "delightful little mice," Ann A. Flowers noted in *Horn Book,* the author-illustrator once again demonstrates "his strong empathy with the feelings of children."

The mid-1980s also saw the author introduce the first of what has since become a growing body of novels that address issues that confront children everywhere. *Two under Par* is the story of a boy, Wedge, as he tries to adapt to his new stepfather and stepbrother. When his mother becomes pregnant, Wedge feels more isolated than ever. One *Publishers Weekly* reviewer applauded *Two under Par,* in particular the "complicated process of learning acceptance and being accepted ... [which] Henkes explores with confidence and care." "Henkes's handling of Wedge's problems is masterful and shows a keen understanding of childhood," Robert Unsworth similarly remarked in *School Library Journal.* A new baby is also arriving in *The Zebra Wall,* prompting a

"Fuzzy's dirty," said Owen's mother.

"Fuzzy's torn and ratty," said Owen's father.

"No," said Owen. "Fuzzy is perfect."

And Fuzzy was.

Owen's parents insist that he give up his favorite blanket when school starts. (From Owen, *written and illustrated by Henkes.)*

visit by the eccentric and slightly annoying Aunt Irene. Adine, the young girl who must share her room with Aunt Irene during her stay, is none too pleased—about either new arrival. "This is not [just] another new baby story," claims a reviewer for *Publishers Weekly.* "Henkes knows that every worry in a child's life has many layers." Elizabeth S. Watson likewise concluded in *Horn Book* that *The Zebra Wall* "embodies genuine understanding of a ten-year-old's fears," making for a "beguiling story peopled with true characters."

Although he was earning critical and popular acclaim for his picture books featuring mice, Henkes was not content to merely repeat a formula in his work. The 1989 picture book *Jessica* is the story of Ruthie and the imaginary playmate who "becomes real" when Ruthie meets a similarly-named new student at school. "Not one extraneous element in text or pictures mars the lyrical, joyous tone," Mary M. Burns declared in *Horn Book,* while *Bulletin of the Center for Children's Books* writer Roger Sutton hailed the excellent design of the book, "with a witty use of white space and an imaginative variety of type and line placement." In his first venture outside of watercolors, Henkes used broad-stroked acrylic paintings in *Shhhh,* a gentle portrayal of a child awake in the quiet early morning. Henkes's artwork is perfect in conveying "the hushed world of a child's first waking moments," according to one *Publishers Weekly* critic. "How rewarding to watch an artist stretch, and achieve another perfect fit."

To the delight of his fans, Henkes has continued to explore the world of his young mouse characters in several critically acclaimed picture books. *Julius, the Baby of the World* features the return of spunky young Lilly, who is about to become a sister—much to her displeasure. Before the baby is born, Lilly is sure she will be a wonderful big sister as she watches her parents buy toys for the new arrival and talk to it through her mother's swollen belly. When little Julius is born, however, Lilly is disgusted by the attention he commands—attention that was, until recently, reserved for Lilly alone. She wishes Julius away. She pinches his tender flesh. She recites to him a mixed-up alphabet, to undo the lessons of her parents. However, when a visiting cousin voices *her* disapproval, big sister comes to Julius's defense. "There is much to admire, giggle over and learn from *Julius, the Baby of the World,*" Ann Pleshette Murphy wrote in the *New York Times Book Review.* "No matter how vitriolic a big sister may become, she really does love her little brother after all." Veeder concurred with this positive assessment in Chicago *Tribune Books,* admitting: "I've read this one over and over just for fun."

Other everyday concerns are explored in books such as *Chrysanthemum,* in which a girl discovers that being different can mean being special, and *Owen,* which earned Henkes a Caldecott Honor Book citation. Owen is about to start school, and so his nosy neighbor Mrs. Tweezers suggests to his parents that he needs to give up his cherished blanket, Fuzzy. The resourceful Owen thwarts every trick his parents use to make him give up Fuzzy, until his mother finds the perfect solution: turn Fuzzy into a series of handkerchiefs small enough to fit in his pocket. "Owen is a great addition to Kevin Henkes's many endearing characters," Hanna B. Zeiger wrote in *Horn Book;* as Hazel Rochman explained in *Booklist,* like previous Henkes heroes "Owen the mouse is a sturdy and vulnerable individual, and he is every-child." Rochman also had praise for how the artist can convey emotion "with a few simple lines," while a *Publishers Weekly* writer hailed the "characteristically understated humor" of Henkes's "spry text and brightly hued watercolor-and-ink pictures."

While *Owen* earned its creator his first major award citations, his next picture book has proven to be one of his most popular. *Lilly's Purple Plastic Purse* features the return of the spunky little girl mouse, now in school. Lilly loves everything about school, especially her teacher, Mr. Slinger. When her excitement over sharing her musical purse with him leads to a reprimand, however, Lilly's ardent devotion turns into anger. In portraying Lilly's journey from remorse to reconciliation, Henkes "once again demonstrates his direct line to the roller-coaster emotions of small children," a *Kirkus Reviews* writer stated. Reviewers highlighted the artist's use of humor as well as his ability to express feelings in his drawings; *School Library Journal* contributor Marianne Saccardi observed that "with a few deft strokes, Henkes changes Lilly's facial expressions and body language to reveal a full range of emotions." Ilene Cooper of *Booklist* likewise hailed Henkes's ability to

Lilly ran and skipped and hopped and flew all the way home, she was so happy.

And she really *did* want to be a teacher when she grew up—

Henkes's spunky heroine Lilly is angry when her excitement over showing her musical purse to her classmates leads to a reprimand from her beloved teacher.(From Lilly's Purple Plastic Purse, *written and illustrated by Henkes.)*

portray Lilly's mixed emotions, and commented: "That Henkes is able to bring this perplexity—and its some-times sweet solutions—to a child's level is his gift." The result of this gift, wrote M. P. Dunleavey in the *New York Times Book Review,* is "a book so delightful, so exuberant, honest and evocative of the passionate life that children live as we look on, that one considers nailing a proclamation to the door of the local bookseller or wearing a copy around one's neck to advertise it."

Throughout the 1990s, Henkes has continued developing his skills in the novel genre as well. In *Protecting Marie,* he portrays the world of twelve-year-old Fanny, who longs for the dog she feels is her destiny. Once she had a puppy, but her sixty-year-old father, a painter, gave it away after it proved too disruptive to his work. When her father unexpectedly brings home a well-trained adult dog, it helps build a bridge between the two. While the slow-moving story may require patience from its read-ers, a *Kirkus Reviews* critic suggested, "the reward is a cast of good-hearted, strongly individual characters moving through a simply told but multilayered story, rich in imagery and feeling." *Booklist* reviewer Hazel Rochman found that Henkes's novel portrayed the same feeling of "the child's powerlessness in a world run by unpredictable grownups" as his picture books do. "This is a rich a intensely developed story," Joanne Schott observed in the *Quill & Quire,* concluding that "adoles-cent Fanny is complex, true, and delightful to know."

The 1997 novel *Sun and Spoon* "offers another meticu-lously crafted, quietly engaging epiphany," according to a *Kirkus Reviews* writer. Ten-year-old Spoon is having difficulty adjusting to his first summer without his beloved grandmother, especially since his grandfather finds it too painful to play the card games they once shared with her. Fearing that he will lose his precious memories of his grandmother, Spoon takes her favorite deck of cards as a memento, triggering a family crisis. The resolution provides Spoon with new insights about himself and his family, and the book as a whole "glitters with small, memorable moments that seem true to life, yet fresh and unexpected," Elizabeth Spires remarked in the *New York Times Book Review. School Library Journal* contributor Marilyn Payne Phillips praised how the author "captures young angst with respect and honesty," while a *Publishers Weekly* reviewer hailed the use of "both sensitively planted metaphors and realistic experiences to explore different phases of the healing process." Although this novel is quieter and more complex than Henkes's picture books, the *Kirkus Reviews* critic observed, "it is infused with the same good humor, wisdom, and respect for children's hearts and minds that characterize all his works."

At no loss for story ideas, Henkes has authored several picture books illustrated by other artists. In the first such collaboration, *Once around the Block,* Henkes and illustrator Victoria Chess portray how a little girl turns the boredom of waiting for her father into a fun journey around the neighborhood. The conclusion—in which the girl comes home to find her bored father waiting for her return—is "a masterstroke of child appeal on the part of the author," Betsy Hearne observed in the *Bulletin of the Center for Children's Books.* "As in his other books," a *Kirkus Reviews* writer remarked, "Henkes creates a comfortable story with understated, believable charac-ters and events." *The Biggest Boy,* illustrated by Nancy Tafuri, similarly shows the author's sensitivity towards children's concerns by showing how a little boy imagines himself to be big and powerful. *New York Times Book Review* contributor Meg Wolitzer praised how in Henkes's text, "the parents encourage the child's fantasies of power and separation and take great pleasure in his responses," thus "liberating" the fears of child.

Similarly, the text of *Good-bye, Curtis* "sets a tone that's just right for preschoolers: straightforward and affection-ate without a hint of sentimentality," according to Carolyn Phelan in *Booklist.* Accompanied by the paint-ings of Marisabina Russo, *Good-bye, Curtis* relates the last day in the career of a mail carrier as the people on his neighborhood route show their appreciation. *Circle Dogs* is another "day-in-the-life" tale, this time of the everyday activities of a pair of dachshunds. The lively dogs sleep, eat, play, and meet people, revealed in a simple, sound-filled text that is accompanied by Dan Yaccarino's illustrations. "The diversity of words and sentence structures," observed a *Publishers Weekly* reviewer, "ensure a book that runs circles around the usual primer." The result is a "delightful book for the very young," as a *Kirkus Reviews* critic described it.

In his autobiographical sketch for *Sixth Book of Junior Authors and Illustrators,* Henkes explains his feelings on being an author of children's books: "I'm a very lucky person. I've known for a very long time that I wanted to be an artist and a writer—and that's exactly what I do for a living. Making books is my job, but more importantly, it is what I love doing more than anything else." By extending his range into novels, Henkes prevents the "job" from becoming routine: "I like trying new ways to fill the pages between two covers. Experimenting with words and paint and ink keeps my job interesting." Sharing this enjoyment of art and writing with his readers is one of his most important goals, as he wrote in *Children's Books and Their Creators:* "I hope that there is something about my books that connects with children, and something that connects with the adult readers. Even if something traumatic happens to one of my characters, I like to have my stories end on a hopeful note. That's my gift to the reader."

Works Cited

Review of *All Alone, Kirkus Reviews,* December 15, 1981, p. 1517.

Review of *All Alone, Publishers Weekly,* December 18, 1981, p. 70.

Blos, Joan W., review of *Clean Enough, School Library Journal,* October, 1982, p. 141.

Burns, Mary M., review of *Jessica, Horn Book,* May-June, 1989, p. 357.

Review of *Chester's Way, Publishers Weekly,* July 8, 1988, p. 53.

Review of *Circle Dogs, Kirkus Reviews,* July 15, 1998, p. 1035.

Review of *Circle Dogs, Publishers Weekly,* July 6, 1998, p. 59.

Cooper, Ilene, review of *Lilly's Purple Plastic Purse, Booklist,* August, 1996, p. 1904.

Cooper, Ilene, interview with Henkes, *Booklist,* January 1, 1997, p. 868.

Crouse, Anne Devereaux Jordan, review of *Bailey Goes Camping, Children's Book Review Service,* November, 1985, p. 25.

Dunleavey, M. P., "The Mouse that Boogied," *New York Times Book Review,* November 10, 1996, p. 41.

Flowers, Ann A., review of *Chester's Way, Horn Book,* September-October, 1988, p. 616.

Gale, David, review of *Sheila Rae, the Brave, School Library Journal,* September, 1987, p. 164.

Review of *Grandpa and Bo, Kirkus Reviews,* February 15, 1986, p. 303.

Hearne, Betsy, review of *A Weekend with Wendell, Bulletin of the Center for Children's Books,* October, 1986, pp. 27-28.

Hearne, Betsy, review of *Once around the Block, Bulletin of the Center for Children's Books,* March, 1987, p. 126.

Henkes, Kevin, autobiographical sketch, *Sixth Book of Junior Authors and Illustrators,* H. W. Wilson, 1989, pp. 123-24.

Henkes, Kevin, remarks in *Children's Books and Their Creators,* edited by Anita Silvey, Houghton, 1995, p. 303.

Review of *Lilly's Purple Plastic Purse, Kirkus Reviews,* June 15, 1996, p. 899.

Murphy, Ann Pleshette, review of *Julius, the Baby of the World, New York Times Book Review,* April 28, 1991, p. 22.

Review of *Once around the Block, Kirkus Reviews,* April 15, 1987, p. 638.

Op de Beeck, Nathalie, interview with Henkes, *Publishers Weekly,* August 12, 1996, p. 26.

Review of *Owen, Publishers Weekly,* September 20, 1993, p. 71.

Parravano, Martha Vaughan, "Kevin Henkes," *Children's Books and Their Creators,* edited by Anita Silvey, Houghton, 1995, pp. 303-04.

Phelan, Carolyn, review of *Good-bye, Curtis, Booklist,* October 15, 1995, p. 411.

Phillips, Marilyn Payne, review of *Sun and Spoon, School Library Journal,* July, 1997, p. 94.

Review of *Protecting Marie, Kirkus Reviews,* April 1, 1995, p. 469.

Rochman, Hazel, review of *Owen, Booklist,* August, 1993, p. 2060.

Rochman, Hazel, review of *Protecting Marie, Booklist,* March 15, 1995, p. 1330.

Saccardi, Marianne, review of *Lilly's Purple Plastic Purse, School Library Journal,* August, 1996, p. 122.

Schott, Joanne, review of *Protecting Marie, Quill & Quire,* June, 1995, p. 60.

Review of *Sheila Rae, the Brave, Publishers Weekly,* June 26, 1987, p. 71.

Review of *Shhhh, Publishers Weekly,* June 9, 1989, p. 65.

Spires, Elizabeth, "The Last Flip," *New York Times Book Review,* November 16, 1997, p. 47.

Review of *Sun and Spoon, Kirkus Reviews,* June 1, 1997, p. 873.

Review of *Sun and Spoon, Publishers Weekly,* June 16, 1997, p. 60.

Sutton, Roger, review of *Jessica, Bulletin of the Center for Children's Books,* February, 1989, p. 148.

Review of *Two under Par, Publishers Weekly,* March 13, 1987, pp. 84-85.

Unsworth, Robert, review of *Two under Par, School Library Journal,* June, 1987, pp. 96.

Veeder, Mary Harris, review of *Jessica, Tribune Books* (Chicago), May 14, 1989, p. 5.

Veeder, Mary Harris, review of *Julius, the Baby of the World, Tribune Books* (Chicago), August 12, 1990, p. 5.

Watson, Elizabeth S., review of *The Zebra Wall, Horn Book,* May-June, 1988, p. 352.

Review of *A Weekend with Wendell, Publishers Weekly,* July 25, 1986, p. 187.

Wilms, Denise M., review of *Bailey Goes Camping, Booklist,* September 15, 1985, p. 134.

Wolitzer, Meg, review of *The Biggest Boy, New York Times Book Review,* September 24, 1995, p. 29.

Review of *The Zebra Wall, Publishers Weekly,* March 11, 1988, pp. 104-05.

Zeiger, Hanna B., review of *Owen, Horn Book,* November-December, 1993, pp. 733-34.

For More Information See

BOOKS

Children's Literature Review, Volume 23, Gale, 1991, pp. 124-31.

PERIODICALS

Booklist, August, 1997, p. 1900.
Bulletin of the Center for Children's Books, March, 1995, p. 237; October, 1996, p. 62.
Horn Book, May-June, 1995, p. 325; November-December, 1995, p. 733.
Kirkus Reviews, July 15, 1995, p. 1024.
New York Times, December 3, 1990.
Publishers Weekly, July 27, 1990, p. 233; March 6, 1995, p. 69.
School Library Journal, January, 1990, p. 83; November, 1993, p. 82; October, 1995, p. 104; September, 1998, p. 173.

—*Sketch by Diane Telgen*

*   *   *

HOPKINSON, Deborah 1952-

Personal

Born February 4, 1952, in Lowell, MA; daughter of Russell W. (a machinist) and Gloria D. Hopkinson; married Andrew D. Thomas (an artist); children: Rebekah, Dimitri. *Education:* University of Massachusetts—Amherst, B.A., 1973; University of Hawaii, M.A., 1978. *Hobbies and other interests:* Reading, hiking, gardening, history.

Addresses

Home—P.O. Box 1052, Walla Walla, WA 99362. *Office*—Whitman College, 345 Boyer Ave., Walla Walla, WA 99362. *Electronic* mail—hopkinda@ whitman.edu.

Career

Manoa Valley Theater, Honolulu, HI, marketing director, 1981-84; University of Hawaii Foundation, Honolulu, development director, 1985-89; East-West Center, Honolulu, development director, 1989-94; Whitman College, Director of Development Administrative Services, 1994—; Whitman College, instructor (children's literature), 1998, 1999. Creative Fund Raising Associates, Honolulu, consultant, 1991—. Board member of the National Society of Fund Raising Executives, Aloha Chapter, 1985-91. *Member:* Society of Children's Book Writers and Illustrators.

Awards, Honors

Magazine Merit Award (Fiction Honor), Society of Children's Book Writers and Illustrators, 1991, for a story appearing in *Cricket;* work-in-progress grant recipient, Society of Children's Book Writers and

Deborah Hopkinson

Illustrators, 1993; Children's Book Award, International Reading Association, 1994, for *Sweet Clara and the Freedom Quilt;* Silver Honor, Parents' Choice Foundation, 1997, and Blue Ribbons, *Bulletin of the Center for Children's Books,* 1997, for *Birdie's Lighthouse.*

Writings

Pearl Harbor, Dillon, 1991.
Sweet Clara and the Freedom Quilt, illustrated by James Ransome, Knopf, 1993.
Birdie's Lighthouse, illustrated by Kimberly Bulcken Root, Atheneum, 1997.
A Band of Angels: A Story Inspired by the Jubilee Singers, illustrated by Raul Colon, Atheneum, 1999.
Maria's Comet, illustrated by Deborah Lanino, Atheneum, 1999.
Under the Quilt of Night, illustrated by James Ransome, Atheneum, 2000.

Work in Progress

Fannie in the Kitchen, illustrated by Nancy Carpenter, for Atheneum, 2001; *Bluebird Summer,* illustrated by Bethanne Andersen, for Greenwillow, 2001; *Girl Wonder,* illustrated by Terry Widener, for Antheneum, 2003.

We were cold and shivering by the time we reached Turtle Island. From the boat, it really did look like a giant black turtle hunched in the sea.

What wild, rough waters! Jagged boulders loomed over us, casting cold, eerie shadows. I remembered a story the fishermen told of a night when the lighthouse went dark, and a grand schooner slammed into these rocks and was lost.

I held my breath, terrified our little boat would be dashed to pieces, too. But Papa steered us through the maze of sharp rocks, and at last we landed safely.

Ten-year-old Birdie Holland must tend her father's lighthouse during a ferocious storm in Hopkinson's novel set in Maine during the 1850s. (From Birdie's Lighthouse, *illustrated by Kimberly Bulcken Root.)*

Sidelights

"As a girl, I always wanted to be a writer," Deborah Hopkinson once told *SATA*. "But I never knew what I wanted to write. Then, when my daughter Rebekah was about three, we were reading a lot of children's books. Having a full-time career and a child, I was very busy. But I thought, 'Maybe I'll try writing for children. At least the books are short!' I have since found out that simply because a story is short, that doesn't mean that it is easy to write!"

Hopkinson has since made a career as the author of several works of history or fictionalized history for young people. Her first book, *Pearl Harbor,* was published in 1991 as part of Dillon Press's "Places in American History" series. Aimed at older children, the book tells the story of the bombing of Pearl Harbor during World War II and includes photographs showing Pearl Harbor both during the war and today. Hopkinson's focus is on the memorial erected on the site of the bombing, but she also provides a history of the Hawaiian islands before, during, and since World War II. "There's

Hopkinson's picture book offers a fictional account of the choral group whose performances of traditional spirituals helped to fund Fisk University at the end of the Civil War. (Cover illustration by Raul Colon.)

plenty of information for students writing reports and prospective visitors without overwhelming recreational readers," noted Luann Toth in *School Library Journal.*

For her second book, Hopkinson decided to try her hand at historical fiction. *Sweet Clara and the Freedom Quilt* is about a slave girl who is separated from her mother and sent to work in the fields. She lives with an elderly woman named Aunt Rachel, who teaches her to sew. Clara becomes a seamstress, but she is always preoccupied with thoughts of her mother and freedom. Clara overhears other slaves discussing the Underground Railroad, and decides to use her sewing skills to help herself and other slaves escape. In her spare time she sews a quilt, but instead of patchwork, Clara's quilt is a map detailing an escape route. When she finally does escape the plantation, she leaves the quilt for other slaves to use in their own escape plans. A *Publishers Weekly* contributor called the book "a triumph of the heart." The story's basis in an actual event "brings power and substance to this noteworthy picture book," wrote the reviewer. Many critics were impressed with Hopkinson's strong protagonist. Calling *Sweet Clara and the Freedom Quilt* an "exciting addition to the study of African-American history," *Five Owls* critic Lyn Lacy praised the protagonist's depiction as a "resourceful and courageous freedom-seeker." *Booklist*'s Janice Del Negro also lauded the strength the author imbued in her main character: "Clara is a sympathetic and determined character not easily forgotten." Concluding her

positive review of the story, Lacy wrote, "*Sweet Clara*'s author Deborah Hopkinson breathes new life into her heroine and other characters with their use of ... 'old speech' [dialect] as a rich and valuable early-American oral tradition."

Hopkinson told *SATA:* "The idea for *Sweet Clara and the Freedom Quilt* came to me while listening to a National Public Radio story about African-American quilt history. I consider this story a wonderful gift, and feel very happy that I was able to tell it."

In addition to her books, Hopkinson also writes short stories, especially for *Cricket* magazine. While her main interest "is stories that also tell about history," she adds, "I also like to write about girls, because when I was a girl, there weren't many stories about the exciting things that girls can do!"

Like *Sweet Clara and the Freedom Quilt,* Hopkinson's picture book *Birdie's Lighthouse* is an example of the author's interest in telling historical stories with active female protagonists. Set in the 1850s, *Birdie's Lighthouse* takes the form of a diary kept by Bertha Holland, known as Birdie, a ten-year-old girl who tells of the year her father became the lighthouse keeper on Turtle Island off the coast of Maine. Birdie's brother is a sailor, just as her father once was, and on the night of a great storm, when her father is too ill to maintain the lighthouse, Birdie must use all she has learned at her father's side to make sure the beacon shines brightly enough to guide her brother home safely. "Period details and a spirited heroine with a clear voice make this book a genuine delight," stated a *Kirkus Reviews* critic. Other reviewers similarly emphasized Hopkinson's authentic setting in time and place and her reliance on actual historical figures in the creation of Birdie. Anne Parker, a reviewer for *School Library Journal,* dubbed *Birdie's Lighthouse* "a shining bit of historical fiction for elementary audiences."

Hopkinson returned to the topic of African-American history in the picture book *A Band of Angels: A Story Inspired by the Jubilee Singers.* This fictionalized account of how a group of singers managed to save the Fisk School (now Fisk University) in Nashville, Tennessee, a school established for freed slaves after the Civil War, is "both touching and inspirational," asserted Beth Tegart in *School Library Journal.* The story's narrator is a young girl—the great-great-granddaughter of Ella Sheppard, one of the original singers. The young narrator asks her Aunt Beth to tell yet again her favorite family story. Ella, who was born a slave, had attended Fisk for only a short time when she was asked to join a chorus that toured the northern states, raising money to help support the school. The chorus found little success performing the popular tunes of the day, but one night, in order to inspire a bored audience, Ella began singing the traditional spiritual song "Many Thousand Gone." Thereafter the group, named the Jubilee Singers for the spirituals or jubilees they sang, found enormous success touring throughout the world. "Hopkinson's ... lilting text interweaves subtle details about racial tensions after the Civil War while emphasizing the importance of education and of being true to oneself," commented a reviewer for *Publishers Weekly.* Janice M. Del Negro noted, in *Bulletin of the Center for Children's Books,* her appreciation of the author's note, which "clearly separates fact from fiction at the conclusion of the text." In *School Library Journal,* Tegart proclaimed the book "a fine read-aloud with a good story, uplifting pictures, and fascinating information."

Works Cited

Review of *A Band of Angels: A Story Inspired by the Jubilee Singers, Publishers Weekly,* January 4, 1999, p. 90.

Review of *Birdie's Lighthouse, Kirkus Reviews,* May 1, 1997, p. 722.

Del Negro, Janice M., review of *A Band of Angels: A Story Inspired by the Jubilee Singers, Bulletin of the Center for Children's Books,* February, 1999, pp. 204-05.

Del Negro, Janice M., review of *Sweet Clara and the Freedom Quilt, Booklist,* April 15, 1993, p. 1514.

Lacy, Lyn, review of *Sweet Clara and the Freedom Quilt, Five Owls,* March-April, 1993, p. 89.

Parker, Anne, review of *Birdie's Lighthouse, School Library Journal,* June, 1997, pp. 91-92.

Review of *Sweet Clara and the Freedom Quilt, Publishers Weekly,* February 8, 1993, p. 87.

Tegart, Beth, review of *A Band of Angels: A Story Inspired by the Jubilee Singers, School Library Journal,* February, 1999, p. 84.

Toth, Luann, review of *Pearl Harbor, School Library Journal,* April, 1992, p. 134.

For More Information See

PERIODICALS

Booklist, February 15, 1992, p. 1103; June 1 and 15, 1997, pp. 1718-19.

Horn Book, March-April, 1999, pp., 190-91.

Publishers Weekly, April 14, 1997, p. 74.

School Library Journal, June, 1993, p. 76.

*　　　*　　　*

HORENSTEIN, Henry 1947-

Personal

Born in 1947 in New Bedford, MA. *Education:* Attended University of Chicago; Rhode Island School of Design, M.F.A., 1973.

Career

Has worked as a free-lance photographer, magazine editor, book producer, industry consultant, and teacher. Has taught photography at Harvard University, University of Massachusetts, and, since 1981, at Rhode Island School of Design.

Writings

FOR YOUNG PEOPLE

Dog's Life, Macmillan, 1986.

Go, Team, Go!, Macmillan, 1988.

Spring Training, Macmillan, 1988.

(With Walt Hriniak and Mark Starr) *A Hitting Clinic: The Walt Hriniak Way,* introduction by Wade Boggs, Perennial Library, 1988.

Sam Goes Trucking, Houghton Mifflin, 1989.

Horse Farm, Knopf, 1989.

A Cat's Life, Sterling, 1990.

How Is a Bicycle Made?, Simon & Schuster, 1993.

How Is a Sneaker Made?, Simon & Schuster, 1993.

My Mom's a Vet, Candlewick (Cambridge, MA), 1994.

Farm Babies, Candlewick, 1996.

Zoo Babies, Candlewick, 1996.

Good Morning, Babies!, Shaw's Candlewick Press, 1996.

Good Night, Babies!, Shaw's Candlewick Press, 1996.

Baseball in the Barrios, Gulliver, 1997.

The Day I Met Splashy, Harcourt, 1998.

A Is for —-?: A Photographer's Alphabet of Animals, Harcourt Brace, 1999.

Arf! Beg! Catch!: Dogs from A to Z, Scholastic, 1999.

Baseball in the Barrios has been translated into Spanish.

ILLUSTRATOR

Brendan Boyd, *Racing Days,* Viking, 1987.

Brendan Boyd and Robert Garrett, *Hoops: Behind the Scenes with the Boston Celtics,* Little, Brown, 1989.

Carol Flake, *Thoroughbred Kingdoms: Breeding Farms of the American Racehorse,* foreword by Paul Mellon, Bulfinch Press, 1990.

Ned Dowd, *That's a Wrap: How Movies Are Made,* foreword by David Mamet, Simon & Schuster, 1991.

Bill Littlefield, *Baseball Days: From the Sandlots to "The Show,"* Little, Brown and Co., 1993.

OTHER

Black and White Photography: A Basic Manual, with drawings by Claire Nivola, Little, Brown, 1974.

Beyond Basic Photography: A Technical Manual, with drawings by Henry Isaacs, Little, Brown, 1977.

(With Eliot Tarlin) *ComputerWise: An Introduction to Understanding, Using and Buying a Personal Computer,* Vintage, 1983.

Black and White Photography: A Basic Manual, drawings by Carol Keller, Little, Brown, 1983.

(Editor) Robert Baker and Barbara London, *Instant Projects: A Handbook of Demonstrations and Assignments for Photography Classes,* Polaroid Corp., 1986.

(With Russell Hart and others) *The Photographer's Source: A Complete Catalogue,* Simon & Schuster, 1989.

(With Russell Hart) *Color Photography: A Working Manual,* with drawings by Tom Briggs, Little, Brown, 1995.

Branson, MO: Las Vegas of the Ozarks, foreword by the Lennon Sisters, Artisan, 1998.

Photography Imaging, Prentice Hall, in press.

Sidelights

Henry Horenstein is a photographer who has written and photographically illustrated a number of books for children. While the emphasis in these photo-essays for youngsters is often on the information to be imparted to the reader, Horenstein's bright, clear photos have garnered praise for adding to the informative text. For example, in *Sam Goes Trucking,* a six-year-old spends the day with his father, a short-haul trucker working in New England. Together, they check his rig, pick up a load of fish, and deliver it to its destination by the end of the day. Reviewers noted that Horenstein's photographs establish the warm relationship enjoyed by Sam and his father, and augment the informative text. *School Library Journal* contributor Susan Hepler remarked that "the well-designed and spacious layout allows readers to talk about what's going on or what is pictured." A reviewer for *Kirkus Reviews* asserted: "Bright, clear color photo-

Narrated by Hubaldo, a fifth-grader who lives in Caracas, Baseball in the Barrios *introduces enthusiasts in the United States to the passion with which Venezuelan youngsters pursue the sport. (Written and illustrated by Horenstein.)*

graphs give this look at a typical trucker's day plenty of visual appeal."

In *My Mom's a Vet,* Horenstein again centers on the relationship between a child and a parent on the job. Here, twelve-year-old Darcie agrees to spend a week assisting her mother in her work as a country veterinarian, and in exchange her mother will send her to gymnastics camp for a week. Critics noted that Horenstein does not shy away from depicting how hard a large-animal veterinarian works. Also elucidated are the emotional and physical strain suffered by veterinarians, who see cases of preventable injury, such as a horse who loses an eye because of owner neglect. "The variety of tasks [depicted] is fascinating as well as instructive," proclaimed a *Kirkus Reviews* commentator. "The pictures are crisp and well composed," added Elizabeth S. Watson in *Horn Book. School Library Journal* contributor Pamela K. Bomboy called *My Mom's a Vet* "a balanced presentation" of what a large animal veterinarian does, adding that "this is a worthy addition to career collections."

Horenstein wrote and illustrated two related books, *How Are Sneakers Made?* and *How Is a Bicycle Made?,* both of which earned positive reviews. The format for both books allowed Horenstein to clearly and creatively present detailed information about objects popular with young people. Deborah Stevenson, who reviewed both books for *Bulletin of the Center for Children's Books,* wrote: "Visually the books are a treat, with vivid color and textural contrasts in the photos of rainbows of sneakers and a panoply of exciting machines." Other reviewers similarly emphasized the success of Horenstein's photos. Janet M. Bair, writing for *School Library Journal,* described the text as "detailed and readable but not overwhelming."

Horenstein has written and illustrated or collaborated on several works for children and young adults with a sports theme. In *Go, Team, Go!,* Horenstein centers on a high school football team, covering try-outs; practices; games won and lost; the injury of a teammate; visits from college scouts; and the contributions made by the team band, waterboys, and cheerleaders. Reviewers emphasized the dominance of the author's photos over the minimal text, and praised the choice to focus on a high school over a professional team. *Booklist* reviewer Carolyn Phelan noted that for those football fans who don't live in a town big enough to support a pro team, high-school level football is "the only game in town." Those readers "will particularly enjoy this opportunity to look behind the scenes," Phelan predicted.

Along these same lines is *Baseball in the Barrios,* Horenstein's tribute to the love of baseball in Venezuela. Narrated by Hubaldo, a fifth-grader who lives in Caracas, the capital of this South American country, *Baseball in the Barrios* introduces enthusiasts in the United States to the passion with which Venezuelan youngsters pursue the sport, incorporating Spanish and English terms into the text. Like his other works for children, Horenstein's photos in *Baseball in the Barrios*

MY MOM'S A VET

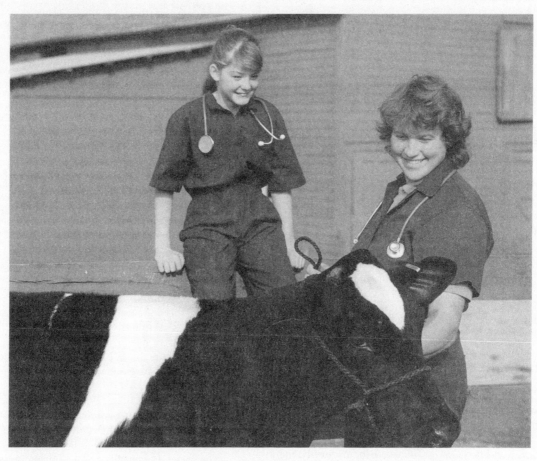

HENRY HORENSTEIN

Twelve-year-old Darcie spends a week assisting her mother in her work as a country veterinarian in Henry Horenstein's informative nonfiction book, illustrated with his photographs. (Cover photograph by Horenstein.)

garnered much of the critical attention. "The wonderful pictures perfectly capture Hubaldo and his friends' exuberant love of the game," noted Todd Morning in *School Library Journal.* Annie Ayers concluded her review in *Booklist* with the prediction that *Baseball in the Barrios* "will be fun for sports fans and effective for social studies units." A nostalgic homage to baseball, *Baseball Days: From the Sandlots to "The Show,"* by Bill Littlefield, also features Horenstein's pictures, deemed "rich and vivid" by *Quill & Quire* reviewer Tim Falconer.

Works Cited

Ayers, Annie, review of *Baseball in the Barrios, Booklist,* April 15, 1997, p. 1432.

Bair, Janet M., review of *How Are Sneakers Made?* and *How Is a Bicycle Made?, School Library Journal,* February, 1994, p. 94.

Bomboy, Pamela K., review of *My Mom's a Vet, School Library Journal,* June, 1994, p. 138.

Falconer, Tim, "Searching for Soul in among the Stats," *Quill & Quire,* March, 1994, pp. 77-78.

Hepler, Susan, review of *Sam Goes Trucking, School Library Journal,* July, 1989, p. 66.

Morning, Todd, review of *Baseball in the Barrios, School Library Journal,* June, 1997, p. 138.

Review of *My Mom's a Vet, Kirkus Reviews,* May 15, 1994, p. 699.

Phelan, Carolyn, review of *Go, Team, Go!, Booklist,* March 15, 1989, p. 1298.

Review of *Sam Goes Trucking, Kirkus Reviews,* February 15, 1989, p. 293.

Stevenson, Deborah, review of *How Are Sneakers Made?* and *How Is a Bicycle Made?, Bulletin of the Center for Children's Books,* October, 1993, pp. 47-48.

Watson, Elizabeth S., review of *My Mom's a Vet, Horn Book,* May-June, 1994, p. 334.

For More Information See

PERIODICALS

Booklist, April 1, 1989, p. 1384; September 15, 1993, p. 154.
Horn Book, July-August, 1997, p. 475.
School Library Journal, April, 1989, p. 96.

*　　*　　*

HUGHES, Carol 1955-

Personal

Born 1955, in Yorkshire, England; married John (an animation artist). *Education:* Attended Brighton College of Art, England.

Addresses

Home—San Francisco, CA.

Career

Worked as an animation artist for companies including Animation City (a production company); writer, 1995—.

Writings

Toots and the Upside Down House, with illustrations by Garrett Sheldrew, John Stevenson and Anthony Stacchi, Bloomsbury (London), 1996, Random House (New York), 1996.
Jack Black and the Ship of Thieves, Bloomsbury (London), 1997.
Toots Upside Down Again, Bloomsbury (London), 1998.

Adaptations

A live action/animated version of *Toots and the Upside Down House* is currently in the works.

Sidelights

Although Carol Hughes began her career as an artist, she now makes her living as an author of innovative books for young readers. Her works have won praise for their humorous approach to resolving interpersonal conflicts in families. Hughes grew up in Lancashire, England, where her parents were proprietors of a small inn. As a young girl, she hoped to become a ballerina, but her height proved to be a detriment, and in her teens Hughes began to devote more time to artistic pursuits. She studied at the Brighton College of Art and began working as an animation artist in the pre-computer era, when it was necessary to painstakingly draw and color every frame by hand. Marrying a former colleague, Hughes moved with her husband John from England to the United States, where John accepted a job in San Francisco, California, and Carol, unable to secure a work permit, began writing to pass the time.

Five years later, Hughes's first book, *Toots and the Upside Down House,* was published. Toots is a lonely little girl, an only child whose mother died years before; Toots does not even remember her. Her father, immersed in his stamp collection, pays little attention to her. Mired in boredom one day, Toots decides to try standing on her head, and is surprised at how different the living room looks from this perspective. She is also astonished by the sight of a little fairy running across the ceiling and vanishing through a miniature door.

Soon Toots herself, shrunk by the little fairies, escapes into this miniature upside down world, where she encounters fantastical talking plants and a host of other perverse-reverse phenomena, including frost that burns. She also discovers the evil house sprites, who are battling the good fairies for control of her house. By freezing the house's pipes, the evil ones hope to cause irreparable water damage to Toots's father's prized stamp collection. The scheming sprites try to win Toots to their side by promising to cast a spell that will win her father's attention. Ultimately, Toots sides with the good pixies, whose job is to protect the house. She saves the stamp collection, and returns renewed to the real world. Hughes's "elaborate hierarchy of tiny, mythical creatures," noted a *Publishers Weekly* reviewer, offer "much to spark the imagination." Writing for *Booklist,* Helen Rosenberg praised *Toots and the Upside Down House* for its "Alice in Wonderland feel," and deemed it "a well-crafted, fast-paced fantasy."

Hughes decided that Toots was worthy of a sequel, and *Toots Upside Down Again* was released in 1998. In this story, a flip on her garden swing places Toots once again in a magical upside down world, where she is reunited with Cadet Fairy Olive. The fairies enlist Toots to help combat a poisonous, ruinous weed, dispatched by the evil Waspgnat to blight the Fairy Squadron's Upside-Down Garden. *Books for Keeps* reviewer Andrew Kidd appreciated an especially "amusing confrontation with two haughty maggots (who pronounce their name 'Maggo')." Comparing *Toots Upside Down Again* to the work of J. R. R. Tolkien, Kidd recommended Hughes's "exciting fantasy" to "fluent upper junior readers or lower junior listeners."

Jack Black and the Ship of Thieves is another of Hughes's imaginative creations. *Carousel* critic Chris Stephenson cited the story's title alone as "a further display of the author's rich inventiveness, strong narrative drive, and sharp sense of fun." In this fast-paced fantasy story, title character Jack Black is experiencing a strained relationship with his honorable father, Captain Black. In contrast, he has nothing but admiration for his hero, a flying ace named Gadfly. When the captain allows Jack to go on the maiden voyage of *Bellerophon,* the world's largest airship, along with Gadfly, Jack is ecstatic. On board, Jack inadvertently discovers that his hero, Gadfly, is at the center of a plot to sabotage the craft. Before he can help, Jack falls out of the airship and into a mythical world full of sea monsters and pirates. Jack's father and his crew become stranded in the ice of the Polar Sea, but Jack, with the help of several new friends, comes to the rescue. "The novel teems with memorable characters," wrote Stephenson, "and is a nonstop, breathless adventure story, with hair's-breadth escapes and more twists and turns than a bowl of spaghetti." *School Librarian* contributor Cherrie Warwick found *Jack Black and the Ship of Thieves* "a superb book and impossible to put down."

Works Cited

Kidd, Andrew, review of *Toots Upside Down Again, Books for Keeps,* May, 1998, p. 25.

Rosenberg, Helen, review of *Toots and the Upside Down House, Booklist,* September 1, 1997, p. 125.

Stephenson, Chris, "Carol Hughes," *Carousel,* Spring, 1998, p. 29.

Review of *Toots and the Upside Down House, Publishers Weekly,* May 19, 1997, p. 76.

Warwick, Cherrie, review of *Jack Black and the Ship of Thieves, School Librarian,* November, 1997, p. 191.

For More Information See

PERIODICALS

Books, September/October, 1996, p. 24; Spring, 1998, p. 22.

Magpies, March, 1998, p. 39.

Times Educational Supplement, December 12, 1997, p. 40.

*   *   *

HUSAIN, Shahrukh 1950-

Personal

Born April 28, 1950, in Karachi, Pakistan; daughter of Prince Ahmed (a dog show judge) and Sabeeha (Ahmed) Husain; married Christopher Shackle (a professor), January 12, 1988; children: Adah Ahmed, Samira Lucy. *Education:* London School of Oriental and African Studies, London, B.A. (with honors), 1979. *Politics:* "Humanitarian." *Religion:* "Family credo, Muslim, pagan now." *Hobbies and other interests:* Magic, music, movies, storytelling, "things supernatural."

Addresses

Home—29 Winchester Ave., London NW6 7TT, England. *Agent*—Blake Friedmann Literary, Film, and Television Agency.

Career

Writer. *Member:* Society of Authors, Producers and Writers Guild of North America (Hollywood branch).

Writings

FOR CHILDREN

Focus on India, Hamilton (London, England), 1986.

Demons, Gods, & Holy Men from Indian Myths & Legends, illustrated by Durga Prasad Das, Peter Lowe (London), 1987, Schocken Books, 1987.

What Do We Know about Islam?, illustrated by Celia Hart, Peter Bedrick Books, 1995.

OTHER

(With D. J. Matthews and C. Shackle) *Urdu Literature,* Third World Foundation for Social and Economic Studies (London), 1985.

(Editor) *The Virago Book of Witches,* illustrated by Liane Payne, Virago (London), 1993.

Mecca, Evans Brothers (London), 1993.

Women Who Wear the Breeches: Delicious and Dangerous Tales, Virago, 1995, published in the United States as *Handsome Heroines: Women as Men in Folklore,* Anchor Books, 1996.

The Goddess, Little, Brown (Boston, MA), 1997.

The Virago Book of Temptresses, Virago, 1998.

Work in Progress

Erotic Myths; Book of Choices, a children's book; research on spiritual elements in psychotherapy, with a novel expected to result.

Sidelights

Shahrukh Husain comments: "My work is influenced by fairy tales, myths, and patterns in people's minds. I see events in stories. If they lend themselves to a natural structure, I want to write them. Oral storytelling also has a great influence on my work. I hear the voices who first told the stories to me."

For More Information See

PERIODICALS

School Library Journal, December, 1987, p. 107; May, 1997, p. 146.

J

JACKSON, Alison 1953-

Personal

Born August 22, 1953, in Alhambra, CA; daughter of Samuel (a physician) and Lorayne (a musician; maiden name, Swarthout) Coombs; married Stephen Jackson (a computer analyst), September 10, 1983; children: Kyle, Quinn. *Education:* University of California, Irvine, B.A., 1975; San Jose State University, M.L.S., 1977. *Politics:* Democrat. *Religion:* Protestant. *Hobbies and other interests:* Travel, snow skiing, waterskiing.

Alison Jackson

Addresses

Home—6213 Wynfield Ct., Orlando, FL 32819. *Office*—Seminole County Public Library, 245 Hunt Club Blvd., North Longwood, FL 32779.

Career

Long Beach Public Library, Long Beach, CA, children's librarian, 1977-80; Newport Beach Public Library, Newport Beach, CA, children's librarian, 1980-87; Fullerton Public Library, Fullerton, CA, children's librarian, 1987-97; Seminole County Public Library, Longwood, FL, children's librarian, 1997—; writer. *Member:* American Library Association, Society of Children's Book Writers and Illustrators, California Library Association, Southern California Council on Literature for Children and Young People, Florida Library Association.

Writings

My Brother the Star, illustrated by Diane Dawson Hearn, Dutton, 1990.
Crane's Rebound, illustrated by Diane Dawson Hearn, Dutton, 1991.
Blowing Bubbles with the Enemy, Dutton, 1993.
I Know an Old Lady Who Swallowed a Pie, illustrated by Judith Byron Schachner, Dutton, 1997.

Work in Progress

Thea's Tree (tentative title); *The Ballad of Valentine* (tentative title).

Sidelights

Alison Jackson told *SATA:* "I grew up in South Pasadena, California. I was always interested in writing as a child, and I served on the staff of both my school newspaper and yearbook while attending South Pasadena High School.

In Jackson's humorous rendition of a traditional folk song, a voracious woman invited to share a family's Thanksgiving feast proceeds to devour the entire dinner, down to the roasting pan.

"I only began writing seriously after entering college in 1971. I enrolled in the creative writing program at the University of California, Irvine, where I took a number of writing courses and learned many of the basic techniques necessary in writing fiction. At that time I had written a few short stories, but I had never attempted a novel-length work. And I certainly wouldn't have dared to send anything in for publication. I didn't think I had enough talent!

"In fact, it was not until 1988 (seventeen years later) that I summoned up enough courage to submit a manuscript to a major publisher. At that time I had been working as a professional children's librarian for over ten years and was married with a tiny baby of my own at home. I decided that I had read enough good children's books in the past ten years to try writing one myself. And by that time there was no doubt in my mind that I wanted to write for children—not adults.

"The problem was ... I needed something to write about. As luck would have it, a workshop was being conducted in our library. The class was titled 'How to Get Your Child into Television Commercials,' and I thought this would be a wonderful subject to write about. Why not?, I decided. I'll write about a kid on TV.

"So I did. I invented the character of Cameron Crane, a six-year-old terror who stars in television commercials. Then I came up with the idea of an older brother, Leslie,

who feels overshadowed by his brother and ignored by his parents—until he himself is given a chance to star on a county-wide basketball team. The result was *My Brother the Star,* which was published by Dutton Children's Books."

School Library Journal contributor Trish Ebbatson called *My Brother the Star* a "nicely written first novel.... Leslie is a likable and believable central character." Also voicing approval of Jackson's first novel, a *Kirkus Reviews* critic contended that "the author writes with unforced fluidity." "This is light fare," asserted Denise Wilms in *Booklist,* "but it moves easily." Wilms went on to recommend *My Brother the Star* as "one for the popular reading shelf."

Telling *SATA* about her next endeavor, Jackson continued: "I enjoyed writing about these two characters [Leslie and Cameron] so much that I created a sequel, *Crane's Rebound,* which came out the following year. Crane's Rebound recounts Leslie's adventures at a summer sports camp. Unfortunately, competition on the basketball court is not all Les is forced to contend with. He also has an obnoxious roommate, who happens to be a bully—and the best player on the team. In *Crane's Rebound,* I also feature a character who was introduced in my first novel. Her name is Bobby Lorimer. She is a feisty basketball-playing tomboy who develops a huge crush on Leslie while continuing to be one of his main adversaries on the court." *Booklist* critic Kay Weisman called Jackson's portrayal of Leslie's insecurities "right on target." She also noted Jackson's "comic touch that will appeal to sports fans and problem-novel enthusiasts alike."

Jackson told *SATA:* "The feisty character, Bobby Lorimer, proved to be so popular that I decided to write a third novel, just about her. Entitled *Blowing Bubbles with the Enemy,* this third book in the series deals with Bobby's instant unpopularity when she chooses to try out for the boys' basketball team at her junior high school. Not only does her tryout anger the boys at her school, but when Bobby is unjustly denied a spot on the team, the girls take up a crusade in her honor, nearly creating a civil war at Jefferson Junior High." A *Kirkus Reviews* critic contended that female readers will "enjoy Bobby's breezy voice, admire her gumption, and share her confusion over the awkwardness of boy-girl relationships." *School Library Journal* contributor Renee Steinberg also appreciated the "likeable, well-drawn heroine" of *Blowing Bubbles with the Enemy.* "Jackson's smooth prose style and believable characters make this an enjoyable read," wrote Steinberg.

Reflecting on her goals as an author, Jackson told *SATA:* "I have always enjoyed writing books for children. I especially feel that there is a need for good, funny stories that can be enjoyed by boys in the middle (third through fifth) grades. In the future, I intend to write more books about Leslie, Cameron, and Bobby. But I would also like to branch out and create new characters with other interests."

Jackson certainly branched out with the title character of her picture book, *I Know an Old Lady Who Swallowed a Pie*. The elderly lady seems to have one interest—eating everything. In this humorous take off on the traditional folk song, "I Know an Old Lady Who Swallowed a Fly," a woman, who has been invited to share a family's Thanksgiving feast, proceeds to devour not only a pie, but an entire feast, down to the roasting pan. The result is "an amusingly successful variation" on the original, remarked Gahan Wilson in the *New York Times Book Review*. Several reviewers complimented Jackson on her inventive, holiday-appropriate conclusion, in which the family finally trusses up the old lady with ropes and throws her out the door, where she floats away among the other enormous balloons in the Thanksgiving Day parade. Told in whimsical rhymes that mimic the original, the story prompted *Bulletin of the Center for Children's Books* critic Elizabeth Bush to predict: "Sing it once, and kids'll beg for seconds."

Responding to those cries for more from her youngest fans, Jackson told *SATA:* "After seeing the immense popularity of *I Know an Old Lady Who Swallowed a Pie*, I plan to continue writing picture books in addition to chapter books. Take-offs on familiar songs and stories are of particular interest to me.

"A number of sources have influenced my writing. One University of California, Irvine professor in particular, by the name of Oakley Hall, gave me much encouragement and advice. He taught me some of the finer points of plotting and characterization, and he continually emphasized the use of realistic detail.

"My children continue to be a source of humorous material for me. They have a logic and sense of perspective that is always fresh and entirely unique. In fact, as they grow older, I can already see a number of potential books in the works.

"I also pay close attention to the students who come into the library every day, either to do homework or just to chat with each other. I find that children will talk about almost anything, if I simply stay in the background. And I have already used quite a few of their inspirational conversations in my books.

"I think this is the real reason why I want to continue writing for children. They are so uninhibited and funny that I find them irresistible, not only as subjects in my work, but as members of my potential audience. So I feel safe in saying that as long as kids keep on reading ... I will continue writing books for them."

Works Cited

Review of *Blowing Bubbles with the Enemy*, *Kirkus Reviews*, November 1, 1993, p. 1392.

Bush, Elizabeth, review of *I Know an Old Lady Who Swallowed a Pie*, *Bulletin of the Center for Children's Books*, November, 1997, p. 87.

Ebbatson, Trish, review of *My Brother the Star*, *School Library Journal*, January, 1990, p. 104.

Review of *My Brother the Star, Kirkus Reviews*, September 1, 1989, p. 1328.

Steinberg, Renee, review of *Blowing Bubbles with the Enemy*, *School Library Journal*, January, 1994, p. 114.

Weisman, Kay, review of *Crane's Rebound*, *Booklist*, September 15, 1991, pp. 151-52.

Wilms, Denise, review of *My Brother the Star*, *Booklist*, January 1, 1990, p. 917.

Wilson, Gahan, "Perhaps She'll Die," *New York Times Book Review*, November 16, 1997, p. 56.

For More Information See

PERIODICALS

Booklist, November 1, 1993, pp. 521-23; September 1, 1997, p. 139.

School Library Journal, November, 1997, p. 84.

* * *

JIMENEZ, Francisco 1943-

Personal

Born June 29, 1943, in San Pedro, Tlaquepaque, Mexico; immigrated to United States, 1947, naturalized citizen, 1965; son of Francisco (a farm laborer) and

Francisco Jimenez

Maria (a cannery worker; maiden name, Hernandez) Gonzalez Jimenez; married Laura Catherine Facchini (a teacher), 1968; children: Francisco Andres, Miguel Antonio, Tomas Roberto. *Education:* Santa Clara University, B.A., 1966; Columbia University, M.A., 1969, Ph.D., 1972; attended Harvard University, 1989. *Politics:* Democrat. *Religion:* Roman Catholic.

Career

Educator, college administrator, author. Columbia University, New York, NY, instructor, 1971-72, assistant professor of Spanish, 1973; Santa Clara University, Santa Clara, CA, assistant professor, 1973-77, associate professor, 1977-81, professor of modern languages and literature, 1981—, Phil and Bobbie Sanfilippo Professor, 1986—, director of Division of Arts and Humanities, 1981—, director of Mexico Summer Study Program at Universidad Nacional Autonoma de Mexico, 1984—, member of board of trustees, 1981-87. Visiting professor at Universidad Nacional Autonoma de Mexico, summer, 1987; lecturer at California State University, Bakersfield, San Diego State University, California State College (now University), Dominguez Hills, Stanford University, University of Texas at Austin, Harvard University, University of Notre Dame, Graduate Theological Union, and Wellesley College. Director of Institute of Poverty and Conscience, 1985; member of board of directors of Far West Laboratory for Educational Research and Development, 1988-94. California State Commission for Teacher Preparation and Licensing, vice-chairman, 1976-77, chairman, 1977-79; vice-chair of California State Humanities Council, 1987-91; member of Western Association Accrediting Commission for Senior Colleges and Universities, 1989-92; member of bilingual advisory board of California Student Aid Commission. Member of board of directors of Circulo Artistico y Literario, 1980-. Consultant to WNET-TV. *Member:* Modern Language Association of America (member of Delegate Assembly, 1989-92), American Association of Teachers of Spanish and Portuguese, Hispanic Institute of the United States, National Chicano Council on Higher Education, National Association on Chicano Studies, Institute of Latin American Studies, American Association for Higher Education, Asociacion Latino Americana de Bellas Artes (member of board of directors, 1979—), Pacific Coast Council of Latin American Studies (member of board of governors, 1977-79), Association of California Teachers of Foreign Languages, Raza Administrators and Counselors in Higher Education.

Awards, Honors

Woodrow Wilson fellow, 1966; National Defense Foreign Language fellow, 1968-69, 1969-70, and 1970-71; Ford Foundation Summer Study Grant, 1969; 22nd *Arizona Quarterly* Annual Award for Best Short Story, 1973, for "The Circuit"; President's Special Recognition Award for Faculty from Santa Clara University (SCU), 1978; Outstanding Young Man of America Award, 1978, 1980; Distinguished Leadership in Education Award from California Teachers Association, 1979;

Jimenez's award-winning compilation features eleven autobiographical stories related to his childhood experiences in a migrant family. (Cover illustration by Susan Marquez.)

Woodrow Wilson Faculty Development Grant (honorary), Woodrow Wilson National Fellowship Foundation, 1983; Teaching Grant, SCU, 1983; Presidential Research Grant, SCU, 1985; award for "dedicated and continuous service in education" from Association of Mexican American Educators, 1986; Resolution of Commendation from California State Legislature and California State Commission on Teacher Credentialing, both 1986; Phil and Bobbie Sanfilippo Endowed University Academic Chair, 1986-98; Principal Director, "Japanese Language Staff Expansion," Grant for $100,000, The Japan Foundation, 1989-92; Principal Director, "Excellence through Diversity," Grant for $1,000,000, James Ervine Foundation, 1990-94; Americas Award for Children's and Young Adult Literature, 1997, Jane Addams Children's Award Honor Book, The Women's International League for Peace and Freedom Educational Fund, 1998, John and Patricia Beatty Award, California Library Association, 1998, and *Boston Globe-Horn Book* Award for Fiction, 1998, all for *The Circuit: Stories from the Life of a Migrant Child;* Smithsonian's Notable Books for Children, 1998, for *La Mariposa;* College of Arts and Sciences Dave Logathetti Award for

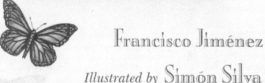

When Francisco begins first grade, his inability to speak English brings constant frustration until he daydreams about the class caterpillar and its ability to change and fly away. (Cover illustration by Simon Silva.)

Excellence in Teaching, 1998; Dia del Maestro: Teacher of the Year Award (University Category), Santa Clara County, 1998; Fay Boyle Endowed University Academic Chair, SCU, 1998; California State Assembly Certificate of Recognition, 1998; Professor Cedric Busette Memorial Award for outstanding contributions to Ethnic Studies, 1998; SCU Faculty Senate Professor, 1998-99.

Writings

FOR YOUNG PEOPLE

The Circuit: Stories from the Life of a Migrant Child, University of New Mexico Press (Albuquerque), 1997, hardcover edition, Houghton Mifflin, 1999.

La Mariposa, illustrated by Simon Silva, Houghton Mifflin, 1998.

OTHER

Episodios nacionales de Victoriano Salado Alvarez (title means "National Episodes of Victoriano Salado Alvarez"), translated from the original English by Nicolas Pizarro Suarez, Editorial Diana (Mexico City), 1974.

(With Gary D. Keller) *Viva la lengua! A Contemporary Reader* (Title means "Long Live Language"), Harcourt Brace Jovanovich, 1975, 2nd edition (with Keller and Rose Marie Sune Beebe), 1987.

(With Keller and Nancy A. Sebastiani) *Spanish Here and Now,* Harcourt Brace Jovanovich, 1978.

(Editor) *The Identification and Analysis of Chicano Literature,* Bilingual Press, 1979.

(Editor with Keller) *Hispanics in the United States: An Anthology of Creative Literature,* Bilingual Press, Volume 1, 1980, Volume 2, 1982.

(Editor) *Mosaico de la vida: Prosa chicana, cubana y puertorriquena* (title means "Mosaic of Life: Chicano, Cuban, and Puerto Rican Prose"), Harcourt Brace Jovanovich, 1981.

(Editor) *Poverty and Social Justice, Critical Perspectives: A Pilgrimage toward Our Own Humanity,* Bilingual Press, 1987.

Cajas de Carton, Houghton Mifflin, 1999.

Work represented in anthologies, including *Perspectivas: Temas de hoy y de siempre,* edited by Mary Ellen Kiddle and Brenda Wegmann, Holt, 1974, 2nd edition, 1978; *Purpose in Literature,* edited by Edmund J. Farrell, Ruth S. Cohen, and others, Scott, Foresman, 1979; *Fronteras,* edited by Nancy Levy-Konesky and others, Holt, 1989; and *Mexican American Literature,* edited by Charles Tatum, Harcourt, 1990. Contributor to *Dictionary of Mexican American History.* Contributor of articles, stories, and reviews to periodicals, including *American Hispanist, Arizona Quarterly, Bilingual Review, California History, Hispania, Los Angeles Times, Owl, Rivsersedge,* and *Tiempo.* Member of editorial advisory board of the series "Studies in the Language and Literature of United States Hispanos," Bilingual Press. Co-founder and West Coast editor of *Bilingual Review/La Revista Bilingue.*

WORK IN PROGRESS:

Christmas Gift, illustrated by Claire Cotts, for Houghton Mifflin; *Breaking the Circuit* (sequel to *The Circuit*), also for Houghton Mifflin.

Sidelights

Francisco Jimenez is an educator who has written textbooks on Spanish language and literature and has edited anthologies of literature written by other Latin Americans. "My primary goal in writing both scholarly and creative works is to fill the need for cultural and human understanding, between the United States and Mexico in particular," Jimenez comments. After numerous scholarly publications, Jimenez began publishing stories drawing on his experiences growing up in a family of migrant workers. These works, *The Circuit: Stories from the Life of a Migrant Child* and *La Mariposa,* have been praised for their moving depictions of obstacles commonly faced by children of migrant families, including language barriers, poverty, demanding physical labor, and sporadic school attendance. Critics noted that these are among the very few works available to young people on the plight of Chicano migrant workers.

The Circuit, which takes its title from Jimenez's oft-anthologized short story, ties together eleven autobiographical stories relating Jimenez's childhood experiences. His parents came to the United States from Mexico illegally and thus had no opportunities for legal employment. Forced to earn a meager living picking crops, the family spent years without a permanent home, moving every few months. Jimenez embodies his recollections in Panchito, the young protagonist of the stories. Panchito's desires are simple: to stay in one place and attend school without interruption. *Booklist* reviewer Hazel Rochman applauded Jimenez's decision not to idealize his characters. "Though the family is warm," wrote Rochman, "their bitter struggle creates anger and jealousy as well as love." In summary, Rochman stated: "Like Steinbeck's classic *Grapes of Wrath,* Jimenez's stories combine stark social realism and heartrending personal drama." Originally published by a university press, *The Circuit* was first intended for adult audiences. *Horn Book* editor Roger Sutton argued that the book's "distinction lies in the fact that it is *both* a children's and an adult book.... Jimenez's twelve stories ... have a transparency that speaks to the adult's desire for spare, clean writing and the young reader's need for immediacy." Commending Jimenez's child's-eye lens, "never filtered through adult hindsight or regret," Sutton noted that the adult reader is likely to feel "a healthy amount of anger at the conditions endured by farm workers. Children, though, will go from field to field with Francisco, hearing his stories as if from a friend. Both audiences," assured Sutton, "will be enriched."

Jimenez explains: "I write in both English and Spanish. The language I use is determined by what period in my life I write about. Since Spanish was the dominant language during my childhood, I generally write about those experiences in Spanish." It is lucky for the English-speaking members of his audience that Jimenez published *La Mariposa* in English. A picture book rendition of one particular episode in the young author's life, *La Mariposa* shows readers a rare view of some of life's most difficult challenges. Like his classmates, young Francisco is adapting to first grade. His is a task more complicated than that of his peers, however, because Francisco, a Mexican immigrant, speaks not a word of English. "Jimenez successfully captures the confusion and isolation of his protagonist in an unembellished, straightforward narration," asserted a *Kirkus Reviews* commentator. Young Francisco tries to pay attention in the classroom but the din of the foreign language around him gives him a headache. Daydreaming about the class caterpillar provides relief, and Francisco anticipates the caterpillar's transformation into a butterfly—*la mariposa* of the title. As Francisco draws a picture of the butterfly, he imagines changing into a butterfly himself and flying out of the classroom. Over several months, Francisco becomes increasingly isolated. In the winter, the well-meaning school principal gives him a winter coat from the lost-and-found, precipitating a fight with classmate Curtis, who recognizes the coat as his own and assumes Francisco has stolen it. By the end of the school year, some of these conflicts are resolved when Francisco wins an award for his butterfly drawing and offers it to Curtis. While *School Library Journal* reviewer Ann Welton felt the ending offered "no real resolution," a *Kirkus Reviews* critic contended that "the ending is impossibly happy." Welton captured opinions offered by both reviewers, emphasizing: "The strength of the book lies in its ability to capture the frustration and isolation experienced by children who do not speak the dominant language." Citing the book as especially suited for schools with an ESL population, Welton called *La Mariposa* "an excellent choice" for raising awareness of the challenges facing non-English-speaking students who attend English-speaking schools.

Works Cited

Review of *La Mariposa, Kirkus Reviews,* July 1, 1998, pp. 967-68.

Rochman, Hazel, review of *The Circuit, Booklist,* December 1, 1997, p. 619.

Sutton, Roger, "On *The Circuit,*" *Horn Book,* September-October, 1998, p. 532.

Welton, Ann, review of *La Mariposa, School Library Journal,* November, 1998, pp. 86-87.

For More Information See

BOOKS

Meier, Matt S., Conchita Franco Serri, and Richard A. Garcia, *Notable Latino Americans,* Greenwood (Westport, CT), 1997.

PERIODICALS

Publishers Weekly, October 5, 1998, p. 90.
Voice of Youth Advocates, February, 1999, pp. 410-13, 424.

* * *

JONES, Diana Wynne 1934-

Personal

Born August 16, 1934, in London, England; daughter of Richard Aneurin (an educator) and Marjorie (an educator; maiden name, Jackson) Jones; married John A. Burrow (a university professor), December 23, 1956; children: Richard, Michael, Colin. *Education:* St. Anne's College, Oxford, B.A., 1956.

Addresses

Home—9 The Polygon, Clifton, Bristol BS8 4PW, England. *Agent*—Laura Cecil, 17 Alwyne Villas, London N1 2HG, England.

Career

Writer, 1965—. *Member:* Society of Authors, British Science Fiction Association (BSFA).

Diana Wynne Jones

Awards, Honors

Carnegie commendation, 1975, for *Dogsbody;* Guardian commendation, 1977, for *Power of Three;* Carnegie commendation, 1977, and Guardian Award, 1978, both for *Charmed Life; Boston Globe-Horn Book* Honor Book award, for *Archer's Goon,* and *Horn Book* Honor List, for *Fire and Hemlock,* both 1984; *Horn Book* Fanfare List, 1987, for *Howl's Moving Castle;* Methuen Children's Award, and Carnegie commendation, both 1988, both for *The Lives of Christopher Chant;* Mythopoeic Fantasy Award in children's category, 1996, for *The Crown of Dalemark;* Best Books, *School Library Journal,* 1998, for *Dark Lord of Derkholm.*

Writings

FOR CHILDREN

Wilkins' Tooth, illustrated by Julia Rodber, Macmillan (London), 1973, published as *Witch's Business,* Dutton, 1974.
The Ogre Downstairs, Macmillan, 1974, Dutton, 1975.
Eight Days of Luke, Macmillan, 1974, Greenwillow, 1988.
Dogsbody, Macmillan, 1975, Greenwillow, 1977.
Power of Three, Macmillan, 1976, Greenwillow, 1977.

Who Got Rid of Angus Flint? (also see below), illustrated by John Sewell, Evans Brothers, 1978.
The Four Grannies (also see below), illustrated by Thelma Lambert, Hamish Hamilton, 1980.
The Homeward Bounders, Greenwillow, 1981.
The Time of the Ghost, Macmillan, 1981, Greenwillow, 1996.
Warlock at the Wheel and Other Stories, Greenwillow, 1984.
Archer's Goon, Greenwillow, 1984.
Fire and Hemlock, Greenwillow, 1985.
Howl's Moving Castle, Greenwillow, 1986.
A Tale of Time City, Greenwillow, 1987.
Chair Person (also see below), illustrated by Glenys Ambrus, Hamish Hamilton, 1989, Puffin, 1991.
Wild Robert, illustrated by Emma Chichester-Clark, Methuen, 1989.
Castle in the Air (sequel to *Howl's Moving Castle*), Greenwillow, 1991.
Aunt Maria, Greenwillow, 1991.
Black Maria, Methuen (London), 1991.
Yes, Dear (picture book), illustrated by Graham Philpot, Greenwillow, 1992.
Stopping for a Spell: Three Fantasies (includes *Chair Person, Who Got Rid of Angus Flint?,* and *The Four Grannies*), illustrated by Jos. A. Smith, Greenwillow, 1993.
Hexwood, Greenwillow, 1994.
Everard's Ride, NESFA (Framingham, MA), 1995.
The Tough Guide to Fantasyland, Vista (London), 1996.
Minor Arcana, Gollancz, 1996.
Deep Secret, Gollancz, 1997, Tor, 1999.
Dark Lord of Derkholm, Greenwillow, 1998.
Seeing Is Believing: Seven Stories, Greenwillow, 1999.

FOR CHILDREN; "DALEMARK" CYCLE

Cart and Cwidder, Macmillan, 1975, Atheneum, 1977.
Drowned Ammet, Macmillan, 1977, Atheneum, 1978.
The Spellcoats, Atheneum, 1979.
The Crown of Dalemark, Methuen, 1993, Greenwillow, 1995.

FOR CHILDREN; "CHRESTOMANCI" CYCLE

Charmed Life, Macmillan, 1977, Greenwillow, 1977.
The Magicians of Caprona, Greenwillow, 1980.
Witch Week, Greenwillow, 1982.
The Lives of Christopher Chant, Greenwillow, 1988.

FOR CHILDREN; PLAYS

The Batterpool Business, first produced at Arts Theatre, London, October, 1968.
The King's Things, first produced at Arts Theatre, February, 1970.
The Terrible Fisk Machine, first produced at Arts Theatre, January, 1971.

OTHER

Changeover (adult novel), Macmillan, 1970.
(Contributor) *The Cat-Flap and the Apple Pie,* W. H. Allen, 1979.
(Contributor) *Hecate's Cauldron,* DAW Books, 1981.
(Contributor) *Hundreds and Hundreds,* Puffin, 1984.

Christopher Chant discovers that he is destined to be the next great Chrestomanci and control the world's magic in Jones's fantasy novel. (Cover illustration by Greg Newbold.)

The Skiver's Guide, illustrated by Chris Winn, Knight Books, 1984.

(Contributor) *Dragons and Dreams,* Harper, 1986.

(Contributor) *Guardian Angels,* Viking Kestrel, 1987.

(Editor) *Hidden Turnings: A Collection of Stories through Time and Space,* Greenwillow, 1990.

A Sudden Wild Magic, Morrow, 1992.

(Editor) *Fantasy Stories,* illustrated by Robin Lawrie, Kingfisher, 1994.

Work in Progress

The Year of the Griffin, a sequel to *Dark Lord of Derkholm;* a collection of stories from the "Chrestomanci" cycle.

Sidelights

Diana Wynne Jones is a British author of prolific talents and wry humor who uses the fantasy genre—her particular interpretation of it, at any rate—to tell coming-of-age tales with a twist. "Her hallmarks," according to Kit Alderdice in a *Publishers Weekly* interview with the author, "include laugh-aloud humor, plenty of magic, and an imaginative array of alternate worlds." Alderdice went on to note that along with humor, there is also a "great sense of seriousness" present in all of Jones's novels, "a sense of urgency that links Jones's most outrageous plots to her readers' hopes and fears." But for Alderdice, "Jones's books are never grim, nor are they didactic."

This sentiment is echoed by Donna R. White writing in *Dictionary of Literary Biography.* White noted that Jones, while writing children's fantasy, stands the conventions of that genre on their heads. "Instinctively hostile to rules," White declared, "Jones employs her unbounded inventiveness to create fantasy worlds that break the conventions and show her readers the world from a new and imaginative angle. Jones specializes in surprising plot twists and slapstick humor, which she combines with scenes of serious drama."

Jones once told *SATA:* "When I write for children, my first aim is to make a story as amusing and exciting as possible, such as I wished I could have read as a child. My second aim is equally important. It is to give children—without presuming to instruct them—the benefit of my greater experience. I like to explore the private terrors and troubles which beset children." Mixing a potent brew of magic, myth, and fantasy, Jones typically tells the story of a youngster between the ages of ten and thirteen—often operating in a difficult relationship with the adult in their life—who undergoes some crisis as a result of the realization of magical powers. Working through this crisis, the protagonist often finds an "enhanced stature within the family, and feet set firmly on a career of using magic for good," according to Jessica Yates writing in *Twentieth-Century Young Adult Writers.* Yates went on to stress "how readable, funny, enjoyable, and 'unputdownable'" Jones's novels are.

Born in London on August 16, 1934, Jones had a childhood guaranteed to make a writer—or recluse—of a person. Much of her youth was informed by the horrors and vicissitudes of World War II. Evacuated at the age of five from London to the relative safety of Wales, Jones and her younger sister first stayed with their grandmother. Soon joined by their mother and a new baby sister, the reunion was anything but warm. Jones's mother, Marjorie, did not care for the Welsh-isms in the children's speech. In 1940 the family moved to Westmorland in northern England, where Jones and her siblings lived with other children evacuated from southern, urban areas. Here Jones had her first encounters with authors: both Arthur Ransome and Beatrix Potter lived nearby, and neither seemed to like children much. Relocation continued during the war years, landing the family next in a Yorkshire nunnery, and then back in a London suburb in 1942 after the worst of the Blitz was over.

It was at about this time that the young Jones determined she would be an author, a notion her parents scoffed at, despite the fact that her mother was Oxford educated and was herself searching for a suitable career. An opportunity seemed to present itself to Jones's parents when, in

Abdullah the carpet merchant longs to change his life, but his acquisition of a magic carpet brings more adventure and danger than he anticipated. (Cover illustration by Jos. A. Smith.)

1943, they took jobs running a cultural center for young adults in the rural Essex village of Thaxted. Jones's experience at Thaxted was anything but a country idyll, however. With the main house on the grounds used for the center, the three young girls were housed in a hastily prepared two-room shack with inadequate heating and no water. Left to their own devices by their busy and distant parents, the three girls bonded with each other for support and community. Irony and a strong sense of humor proved to be survival skills in such a situation.

Of all the privations of village life, the worst for Jones was the absence of reading material. By then a voracious reader, she soon made her way through the small local library, as well as the bookshelves of the school her parents ran. Such reading included the Greek myths, as well as *The Arabian Nights* and works by Homer. Each Christmas the girls' father would go to the cupboard where he kept a complete set of Ransome novels and pick one out for the three daughters as their communal present. To fill the literary void, Jones took to composing her own works, filling the pages of exercise books with two cliche-filled epics as a young teenager.

Jones attended Oxford's St. Anne's College, partly thanks to a near-photographic memory. There she studied under both C. S. Lewis and J. R. R. Tolkein, both of whom greatly influenced not only her writing style, but also her choice of genres. Graduating in 1956, Jones was married in that same year to a young man whom she had met at the Thaxted center several years before. For the next decade, Jones was busy with the difficult task of motherhood, raising three boys born in 1958, 1961, and 1963, respectively. Though she had always dreamed of being a writer, she had never thought of writing children's books, but her own tour of duty as a mother encouraged her in that direction. Determined that her children should never feel deprived of good books as she had during her childhood, Jones went in search of books to read to them. When she could not find good contemporary fantasy-literature, she decided to create some herself.

Though she did publish one adult novel in 1970, her first children's work, *Wilkins' Tooth,* did not appear until 1973. A story of two kids who set up in the revenge business and eventually tangle with the local witch, this first novel, published in the U.S. as *Witch's Business,* is important in that it "shows the unflagging inventiveness and sense of humor characteristic of Jones's style," according to Donna R. White in *Dictionary of Literary Biography.* Also, as Christopher Davis pointed out in the *New York Times Book Review,* no "authority but the child's own is ever recognized and adults are never appealed to." Thus, set in place with her first novel are Jones's twin pillars: a sense of humor and an adolescent protagonist largely bereft of parental supervision who must fend for him- or herself.

Jones's next novel, *The Ogre Downstairs,* relates the story of five stepchildren who deal with the trials of a blended family by creating magical spells with a chemistry set. Compared to the fantasy works of the Edwardian writer, E. Nesbit, Jones's second novel won favorable reviews and also introduced themes, such as displacement and alienation, that she would further develop in later novels. Much of Jones's later work hearkens back to the difficulties of her own childhood, when she was continually displaced during the war years and left to fend for herself emotionally.

Since these early novels, Jones has written several dozen books for young readers, all dealing in some way with magic and fantasy. Some of these, such as *The Homeward Bounders* and *A Tale of Time City,* with their alternate worlds, could be classified as science fiction. Her first book to win recognition, in the form of a Carnegie commendation, was the 1975 *Dogsbody,* in which the Dog Star, Sirius, is banished to earth in the form of a newborn puppy, there to become the object of the adoration of Kathleen, a neglected young girl whose father is in prison for terrorist activities. Indeed, 1975 was a watershed year for Jones, as she published two other novels; one of them, *Cart and Cwidder,* initiating the Dalemark quartet of books completed in 1993 with publication of *The Crown of Dalemark.*

When Ann Stavel notices strangers arriving at neighboring Hexwood Farm but never re-emerging, she investigates and discovers a machine that manipulates the boundaries of time and space. (Cover illustration by Jos. A. Smith.)

The Dalemark series, also including *Drowned Ammet* and *The Spellcoats,* was described by Donna R. White as "a more conventional kind of fantasy than Jones usually writes—almost High Fantasy." Jones creates a mythical medieval land, Dalemark, for these books, and tells the story of the North and South kingdoms and of characters young and old who go in search of the lost crown of Dalemark. Reviewing the last title in the series, *Booklist*'s Chris Sherman noted that "treachery, mystery, humor, and magic abound in this intriguing, well-crafted fantasy," and that Jones's "quirky characters" are so well drawn that "readers will feel they know them."

Jones has also written another fantasy series known as the "Chrestomanci" books, which include *Charmed Life, The Magicians of Caprona, Witch Week,* and *The Lives of Christopher Chant.* As Margaret Meek observed in *School Librarian,* the Chrestomanci Cycle takes place "in a universe where magic is normal and the unexpected commonplace." The books in this cycle are loosely linked together by the enchanter Chrestomanci, who appears in all four titles; the books are also united by

what White described in *Dictionary of Literary Biography* as "high-comedy, fast-paced adventure, and convoluted plots." Two of the books in this series, *Charmed Life* and *The Lives of Christopher Chant,* were award winners in Jones's native England.

Among Jones's non-series books are the award-winning *Howl's Moving Castle* and its sequel, *Castle in the Air,* and the 1981 novels *The Homeward Bounders* and *The Time of the Ghost,* the latter not published in the U.S. until 1996. Inspired by *The Arabian Nights* as well as fairy tales from Europe, the duo, *Howl's Moving Castle* and *Castle in the Air,* tell the story of Sophie Hatter, who must work as an apprentice hat-maker while her sisters go out into the world to seek their fortunes. Sophie is turned into an old crone and the Wizard Howl follows his moving castle around the countryside in the award-winning first novel, in which "wit and humor glint from the pages," according to *Horn Book*'s Ethel R. Twichell. The castle of the sequel is again Howl's, and this time he has become a genie in a bottle, while a young carpet-merchant purchases a magic carpet straight out of *The Arabian Nights.* Ann A. Flowers of *Horn Book* commented that this sequel "contains enough material for any number of books" and that it was "cleverly written, with flowing Middle-Eastern expressions and amusing, sardonic remarks."

Dubbed Jones's "most powerful novels" by White in *Dictionary of Literary Biography, The Homeward Bounders* and *The Time of the Ghost* both deal with the themes of alienation and displacement. In *The Homeward Bounders,* Jamie discovers that his world is simply a giant game board for the masters he calls "Them." Having discovered the secret, he is discarded from the game, destined to walk the borders between the worlds forever in a novel Judith Elkin, writing in *Times Literary Supplement,* described as "strangely compelling—rather like a monster jigsaw-puzzle in which the reader can become totally and intensely absorbed." Published in England the same year as *The Homeward Bounders, The Time of the Ghost* was not published in the U.S. until 15 years later, due to Briticisms that make for more difficult reading. Dealing in a fictional manner with Jones's years in Thaxted, the novel tells of four neglected sisters who live in a converted shack next to a boys' boarding school. In this tale, a ghost returns to the past and attempts to prevent her own death, to change history in effect. *Horn Book*'s Flowers concluded that the "Complex plot ... is absorbing, but equally interesting and frequently amusing are the family dynamics and the character sketches of the four fascinatingly eccentric sisters." *A Tale of Time City* also deals with Jones's childhood experiences during the war.

Three of Jones's early short novels for younger readers, *Chair Person, Who Got Rid of Angus Flint?,* and *The Four Grannies,* were also published later in the U.S., pulled together under one cover for the 1993 *Stopping for a Spell.* A critic for *Kirkus Reviews* commented that, "as usual, Jones's sly wit and irrepressible imagination are a delight—in fast-moving, easily read, laugh-aloud stories," while a *Publishers Weekly* reviewer concluded

DIANA WYNNE JONES

DARK LORD OF DERKHOLM

Teenage Blade and his magical siblings must set their land free from the tyranny of the evil bureaucrat, Mr. Chesney. (Cover illustration by Jos. A. Smith.)

that this collection was "an ideal introduction to the quirky humor and witchery that characterizes this author's work..."

Jones is an eclectic author who continues to push the bounds of the genre she has worked in for a quarter of a century. Not all of her works are served up with frothing bits of humor; the dark 1991 fantasy, *Aunt Maria,* is a horror story involving werewolves and zombies, while *Fire and Hemlock,* Jones's "most challenging book for adolescents," according to Donna R. White, is a book with a convoluted structure and shifting time perspectives which examines deep emotional states. 1994's *Hexwood* walks the bounds between science fiction and fantasy and deals in virtual reality. When young Ann, the teenage daughter of a British couple, notices strangers arriving at Hexwood Farm but never reemerging, she investigates, only to find that the boundaries of time and space are not what she thought. Sally Estes, writing in *Booklist,* called the novel "fast-paced" and the mystery "compelling." Estes also commented on the Jones trademark: "There's even a nice bit of humor." Joan Zahnleiter concluded in *Magpies* that "this challenging book is a satisfying read and one that is likely to

be re-read in order to extract full flavor from its many layers of meaning."

A commentator for *Publishers Weekly* noted of 1998's *Dark Lord of Derkholm* that "this expansive novel" was on a par with the author's best, managing to be at once "an affectionate send-up of the sword-and-sorcery genre and a thrilling fantasy adventure in its own right." Each year, package tours come looking for excitement in Derkholm, but this year, teenage Blade and his magical siblings must do something to set things right and set the land free from the tyranny of the evil bureaucrat, Mr. Chesney. "Thought-provoking and utterly engaging, this tour-de-force succeeds on numerous levels," the reviewer concluded. Flowers noted in *Horn Book* that one of the charms of the book "is the staggering magnitude of the invention," and concluded that the novel was "the author's best fantasy in some time."

Reviewers never seem to run out of superlatives for Jones's work. Her blending of Norse, Greek, and Celtic mythologies with fantastic elements of magic, ghosts, enchanted animals, and witches has led to an impressive body of work that is almost always characterized also by a large dollop of humor. As Elaine Moss noted in the *Times Literary Supplement,* "Diana Wynne Jones is a prolific novelist of enormous range who can raise hairs on the back of the neck one minute, belly laughs the next." As Jones herself put it in an autobiographical sketch for *Something about the Author Autobiography Series,* "I get unhappy if I don't write. Each book is an experiment, an attempt to write the ideal book, the book my children would like, the book I *didn't* have as a child myself."

Works Cited

Alderdice, Kit, "Diana Wynne Jones," *Publishers Weekly,* February 22, 1991, pp. 201-02.

Review of *Dark Lord of Derkholm, Publishers Weekly,* October 19, 1998, p. 82.

Davis, Christopher, review of *Witch's Business, New York Times Book Review,* May 5, 1974, pp. 22, 24, 26.

Elkin, Judith, "Walking the Bounds," *Times Literary Supplement,* March 27, 1981, p. 339.

Estes, Sally, review of *Hexwood, Booklist,* June 1, 1994, pp. 1803-04.

Flowers, Ann A., review of *Castle in the Air, Horn Book,* March-April, 1991, p. 206.

Flowers, review of *Dark Lord of Derkholm, Horn Book,* November, 1998, p. 732.

Flowers, review of *The Time of the Ghost, Horn Book,* November-December, 1996, pp. 736-37.

Jones, Diana Wynne, essay for *Something about the Author Autobiography Series,* Volume 7, Gale, 1989, pp. 155-70.

Meek, Margaret, review of *Charmed Life, School Librarian,* December, 1977, pp. 363-64.

Moss, Elaine, "Ghostly Forms," *Times Literary Supplement,* November 20, 1981, p. 1354.

Sherman, Chris, review of *The Crown of Dalemark, Booklist,* December 15, 1995, p. 698.

Review of *Stopping for a Spell, Kirkus Reviews,* May 15, 1993, p. 663.

Review of *Stopping for a Spell, Publishers Weekly,* May 24, 1993, p. 88.

Twichell, Ethel R., review of *Howl's Moving Castle, Horn Book,* May-June, 1986, pp. 331-32.

White, Donna R., essay on Jones in *Dictionary of Literary Biography,* Volume 161: *British Children's Writers Since 1960,* edited by Caroline C. Hart, Gale, 1996, pp. 225-32.

Yates, Jessica, essay on Jones in *Twentieth-Century Young Adult Writers,* St. James Press, 1994, pp. 332-34.

Zahnleiter, Joan, review of *Hexwood, Magpies,* July, 1994, p. 34.

For More Information See

BOOKS

Children's Literature Review, Volume 23, Gale, 1991, pp. 177-98.

Contemporary Literary Criticism, Volume 26, Gale, 1983.

Fifth Book of Junior Authors, edited by Sally Holmes Holtze, Wilson, 1983.

St. James Guide to Fantasy Writers, St. James Press, 1996.

PERIODICALS

Bulletin of the Center for Children's Books, July-August, 1975; July-August, 1993, p. 348; May, 1994, p. 290; October, 1996, p. 65.

Horn Book, May, 1994, p. 345; March, 1996, p. 209.

School Library Journal, October, 1992, p. 89; March, 1994, p. 236; October, 1998, p. 136.

Voice of Youth Advocates, February, 1994, p. 382; October 24, 1994, p. 223; August, 1995, p. 172; April, 1997, p. 42.

—Sketch by J. Sydney Jones

K

KEHRET, Peg 1936-

Personal

Surname is pronounced "carrot"; born November 11, 1936, in LaCrosse, WI; daughter of Arthur R. (an executive of Geo. A. Hormel Co.) and Elizabeth M. (a homemaker; maiden name, Showers) Schulze; married Carl E. Kehret (a player-piano restorer), July 2, 1955; children: Bob C., Anne M. *Education:* Attended University of Minnesota, 1954-55. *Hobbies and other interests:* Reading, gardening, antiques, watching baseball, animals, cooking.

Addresses

Home—P.O. Box 303, Wilkeson, WA 98396. *Agent*—Emilie Jacobson, Curtis Brown Ltd., 10 Astor Place, New York, NY 10003.

Career

Writer, 1973—. Volunteer for the Humane Society. *Member:* Authors Guild, Society of Children's Book Writers and Illustrators, Mystery Writers of America.

Awards, Honors

Forest Roberts Playwriting Award, Northern Michigan University, 1978, Best New Play of 1979, Pioneer Drama Service, and Best Plays for Senior Adults, American Theatre Association, 1981, all for *Spirit!*; Children's Choice Award, International Reading Association-Children's Book Council (IRA-CBC), 1988, and master list, Young Reader's Choice Awards in Nevada and Oklahoma, all for *Deadly Stranger;* Service Award, American Humane Association, 1989; Recommended Books for Reluctant Young Adult Readers, American Library Association (ALA), 1989, for *The Winner,* and 1992, for *Cages;* Books for the Teen Age, New York Public Library, 1992, for *Cages* and *Winning Monologs for Young Actors: 65 Honest-to-Life Characterizations to Delight Young Actors and Audiences of All Ages;* Young Hoosier Book Award, Association for Indiana Media Educators, 1992, Nebraska Golden Sower Award and Iowa Children's Choice Award, both 1993, Maud Hart Lovelace Award, 1995, and master list, Young Reader's Choice Awards in Vermont, Illinois, Oklahoma, Nebraska, Iowa, West Virginia, and Missouri, all for *Nightmare Mountain;* Young Adult's Choice Award, IRA, 1992, for *Sisters, Long Ago;* Texas Lone Star list, 1992, Recommended Books for Reluctant Young Adult Readers, ALA, Books for the Teen Age, New York

Peg Kehret

Public Library, Young Adult's Choice, IRA, Maud Hart Lovelace Award, and master list, children's book awards in Oklahoma, Illinois, South Carolina, Tennessee, Iowa, Indiana, Nebraska, Utah, and the Pacific Northwest, all for *Cages;* Pacific Northwest Writer's Conference Achievement Award, 1992; Young Adult's Choice, IRA, Pacific Northwest Young Reader's Choice Award, and Iowa Children's Choice Award, all for *Terror at the Zoo;* Sequoyah Award, Indiana Young Hoosier Book Award, and Honor Book, West Virginia Children's Book Award, all for *Horror at the Haunted House;* Quick Picks for Reluctant Young Adult Readers, ALA, and Children's Choices, IRA, both for *Danger at the Fair;* Children's Books of the Year, Child Study Children's Book Committee, 1995, for *The Richest Kids in Town;* Golden Kite Award, Society of Children's Book Writers and Illustrators, 1996, Notable Book, ALA, and PEN Center U.S.A. West Award for children's literature, both 1997, Dorothy Canfield Fisher Award, 1998, Mark Twain Award, 1999, and children's book awards in Oklahoma, Tennessee, Illinois, Texas, Kansas, Pennsylvania, Washington, New Hampshire, and Alabama, all for *Small Steps: The Year I Got Polio;* Maryland Black-Eyed Susan Award nominee, 1996-97, for *Danger at the Fair,* and 1998-99, for *Earthquake Terror;* Children's Crown Award, National Christian Schools Association, and West Virginia Children's Book Award, both 1998, Mark Twain Award list, 1998-99, and Utah Children's Choice Award, all for *Earthquake Terror.*

Writings

FOR CHILDREN

Winning Monologs for Young Actors: 65 Honest-to-Life Characterizations to Delight Young Actors and Audiences of All Ages, Meriwether (Colorado Springs, CO), 1986.
Deadly Stranger, Dodd, Mead, 1987, Troll, 1997.
Encore!: More Winning Monologs for Young Actors: 63 More Honest-to-Life Monologs for Teenage Boys and Girls, Meriwether, 1988.
The Winner, Turman (Seattle, WA), 1988.
Nightmare Mountain, Dutton, 1989.
Sisters, Long Ago, Cobblehill, 1990.
Cages, Cobblehill, 1991.
Acting Natural: Monologs, Dialogs, and Playlets for Teens, Meriwether, 1991.
Terror at the Zoo, Cobblehill, 1992.
Horror at the Haunted House, Cobblehill, 1992.
Night of Fear, Cobblehill, 1994.
The Richest Kids in Town, Cobblehill, 1994.
Danger at the Fair, Cobblehill, 1995.
Don't Go Near Mrs. Tallie, Pocket Books, 1995.
Desert Danger, Pocket Books, 1995.
Cat Burglar on the Prowl, Pocket Books, 1995.
Bone Breath and the Vandals, Pocket Books, 1995.
Backstage Fright, Pocket Books, 1996.
Earthquake Terror, Cobblehill, 1996.
Screaming Eagles, Pocket Books, 1996.
Race to Disaster, Pocket Books, 1996.
Small Steps: The Year I Got Polio, Albert Whitman, 1996.

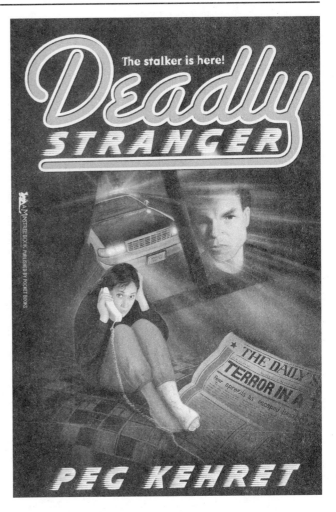

Katie Osborne is the target of a stalker who kidnapped her new friend in Kehret's suspenseful novel for middle graders. (Cover illustration by Mark Garro.)

The Ghost Followed Us Home, Minstrel, 1996.
Searching for Candlestick Park, Cobblehill, 1997.
The Volcano Disaster, Pocket Books, 1998.
The Blizzard Disaster, Pocket Books, 1998.
I'm Not Who You Think I Am, Dutton, 1999.
Shelter Dogs: Amazing Stories of Adopted Strays, Albert Whitman, 1999.
The Flood Disaster, Pocket Books, 1999.

PLAYS

Cemeteries Are a Grave Matter, Dramatic Publishing, 1975.
Let Him Sleep 'till It's Time for His Funeral, Contemporary Drama Service, 1977.
Spirit!, Pioneer Drama Service, 1979.
Dracula, Darling, Contemporary Drama Service, 1979.
Charming Billy, Contemporary Drama Service, 1983.
Bicycles Built for Two (musical), Contemporary Drama Service, 1985.

FOR ADULTS

Wedding Vows: How to Express Your Love in Your Own Words, Meriwether Publishing, 1979, second edition, 1989.

Kit felt trapped...
until she found
a way to set
herself free.

Peg Kehret

Author of *Nightmare Mountain* and *Sisters, Long Ago*

When young Kit, upset by troubles at home, shoplifts a bracelet, she is sentenced to community service at the Humane Society and learns a lesson about love and personal responsibility. (Cover illustration by Doron Ben-Ami.)

Refinishing and Restoring Your Piano, Tab Books (Blue Ridge Summmit, PA), 1985.

Also contributor to periodicals.

Work in Progress

Don't Tell Anyone, for Dutton, *The Secret Journey* and *My Brother Made Me Do It,* for Pocket Books.

Sidelights

Peg Kehret is the author of over two dozen children's novels; most of them, such as award-winners *Deadly Stranger, Nightmare Mountain,* and *Earthquake Terror,* serving up heavy doses of suspense and danger. Kehret has also written nonfiction for adults as well as for children. Her *Winning Monologs for Young Actors* and *Acting Natural* both reflect her own commitment to theater; the multi-talented Kehret has also penned six plays. The winner of the 1998 Dorothy Canfield Fisher Award, Kehret's *Small Steps* documents her own fight

with a childhood case of polio that left her temporarily paralyzed. In a *Booklist* review of Kehret's *Earthquake Terror,* Stephanie Zvirin neatly summed up the author's career to date: "Prolific author Kehret has a well-deserved reputation for writing good, solid thrillers for middle-graders."

Born in LaCrosse, Wisconsin in 1936, Kehret formed an early passion for words and writing. Paid three cents a story by her grandfather, she wrote, published, and sold her own newspaper about the dogs in her neighborhood. From this experience she gained valuable knowledge about pleasing an audience: her youthful broadsheet soon went out of business because she continually featured her own dog on the front page.

Kehret's idyllic childhood was shattered when she contracted polio in the seventh grade. As a result, she was paralyzed from the neck down and told that she would never walk again. "Much to everyone's surprise," Kehret once told *SATA,* "I made almost a complete recovery. I vividly remember the time when I got sick and my months in the hospital and my eventual return to school. Maybe that's why I enjoy writing books for young people; I recall exactly how it felt to be that age. I remember my friends and the books I liked and even what programs I listened to on the radio. When I write, it is easy for me to slip back in my imagination and become twelve years old again."

As a teen, Kehret dreamed of being either a veterinarian or writer, finally opting for the wordsmith business. "I'm glad I chose writing," Kehret told *SATA,* "but two of the main characters in my books want to be veterinarians. Dogs, llamas, and elephants have played important parts in my books." With high school came a new direction for Kehret's interest in words: theater. Cast as a hillbilly in a one-act play as a freshman, Kehret was seriously bit by the theater bug, working backstage or in acting roles in every production she could. Kehret briefly attended the University of Minnesota before marrying in 1955. Children soon followed and she lived the busy life of mother and homemaker, also volunteering for the Humane Society.

Kehret began writing in the early 1970s, spurred on by further work in community theater as well as her interest in research of various sorts. She began selling magazine stories, eventually logging over 300 of them before turning her hand to lengthier works. There followed one-act and full-length plays, including the award-winning *Spirit!,* as well as two adult nonfiction titles, before she began writing books for young people. Her initial juvenile title, *Winning Monologs for Young Actors,* appeared in 1986 and was followed by her first novel for young people, *Deadly Stranger.* The story of a kidnaping, this novel was dubbed a "cliffhanger" by a *Kirkus Reviews* contributor. "As soon as I tried writing from a youthful point of view," Kehret told *SATA,* "I knew I had found my place in the writing world."

Another popular early title from Kehret is *Nightmare Mountain,* a thriller involving young Molly and her visit to her aunt's ranch at the foot of Mt. Baker. The fun visit turns into a nightmare when her Aunt Karen falls into a coma and three valuable llamas are stolen. *Booklist*'s Denise Wilms observed that Kehret delivered "a fast-paced mystery-adventure tale with a heroine who, when forced to deal with disaster, shows courage and resourcefulness." Jeanette Larson concluded in *School Library Journal* that the book was a "satisfying novel that will keep readers guessing until the end." Reincarnation informs Kehret's next book, *Sisters, Long Ago.* When Willow comes close to drowning, she sees herself in another life in ancient Egypt. The girl who saves her seems to be her sister from Egyptian days, while her own sister, Sarah, is fighting a losing battle with leukemia. Bruce Anne Shook, writing in *School Library Journal,* noted that "suspense is maintained up to the very end, making this a page-turner . . . ."

One of Kehret's personal favorites, *Cages,* allowed her to write about a passion of hers, the Humane Society. When young Kit—who has an alcoholic stepfather and a mother in denial—gives in to a momentary urge and shoplifts a bracelet, she sets off a train of events that has lasting repercussions in her life. Caught, she is sentenced to community service at the Humane Society. There she falls in love with the homeless dogs and learns lessons about personal responsibility and facing her problems. As Andrea Davidson noted in *Voice of Youth Advocates,* the book "will appeal to young teen readers interested in getting out of the 'cages' represented by their problems." *School Library Journal* reviewer Sylvia V. Meisner concluded that Kit's determination to set herself free from "the cages of alcohol enablement, jealousy, and, ultimately, the secret of her crime make her an appealing protagonist."

Kehret's best-selling paperback book to date is the 1992 *Terror at the Zoo,* the story of an overnight camp-out at the zoo which goes very wrong. Another 1992 title is *Horror at the Haunted House,* which continues the adventures of Ellen and Corey from *Terror at the Zoo.* This time around, they help with a Halloween haunted-house project at the local historical museum, only to discover that the house really is haunted. Overcoming her fear of ghosts, Ellen helps find out who is stealing from the museum's collection. Donna Houser noted in *Voice of Youth Advocates* that this "fun, fast-paced novel can be read in an evening," while *Booklist*'s Chris Sherman concluded that readers "will be waiting in line for this action-packed novel, which combines a good mystery with an exciting ghost story, a little danger, and a satisfying ending that ties everything up neatly." Ellen and Corey appear again in *Danger at the Fair,* "this time sharing a thrill-a-minute adventure set at a county fair," according to *Booklist*'s Zvirin. Atop the Ferris wheel, Corey spies a pickpocket at work, but when Corey subsequently trails the thief, he is trapped inside the "River of Fear" ride. Zvirin concluded that the mystery-suspense components of the story, plus "a pair of enthusiastic, heroic, quite likable" protagonists all added up to a book "that won't stay on the shelf for long."

Kehret's comic novel traces young Peter's doomed money-making ventures and his budding friendship with his eager business partner, Wishbone Wyoming. (Cover illustration by Toby Gowing.)

Two other personal favorites of Kehret are *The Richest Kids in Town* and *Searching for Candlestick Park.* The former title is a departure for Kehret; a comic novel about Peter's money-making ventures that all go wrong. New in town, Peter desperately wants to save up enough money for a plane ticket to go back and visit his best friend. Peter enlists the help of some other kids, including Wishbone Wyoming, in some of his crazy money-making schemes. Their plans range from an alternative health club to a rubber-duck race, and all fail miserably and rather humorously. Finally Peter comes to see that he no longer needs to make money for a ticket; he has a new best friend in Wishbone. A critic for *Kirkus Reviews* concluded that there were "clever antics in this fun book," while *Horn Book* dubbed it a "read-aloud comedy." In *Searching for Candlestick Park,* 12-year-old Spencer is trying to find the father who left him and his mom three years before. Sure that his dad works for the San Francisco Giants, Spencer sets off on his bicycle from Seattle, accompanied by his cat, Foxey. Lauren Peterson noted in *Booklist* that Spencer's "honesty and integrity are repeatedly tested" in this "fast-paced, exciting adventure." A *Kirkus Reviews* contributor

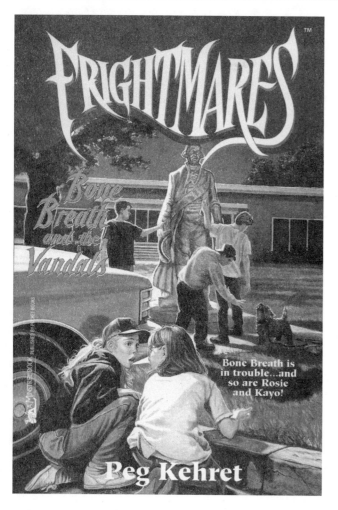

Rosie and her friend Kayo are pursued by vandals bent on defacing the school statue in Kehret's compelling book for young readers. (Cover illustration by Dan Burr.)

commented that "Spencer's impulsive escapade may give readers infatuated with the notion of running way some second thoughts."

With *Earthquake Terror,* Kehret returned to her more usual thriller format. When an earthquake destroys the only bridge to the mainland from the tiny island where Jonathan and his disabled sister Abby are staying, the young boy is pitted against nature. With no food or supplies, and unable to contact help, Jonathan must single-handedly save Abby, his dog, and himself. With displaced waters from the quake beginning to flood the island, the clock is ticking on Jonathan's efforts. "It will be a rare thriller fan who won't want to see what happens," Zvirin commented in her *Booklist* review. Roger Sutton, writing in the *Bulletin of the Center for Children's Books,* noted that Kehret's "focus on the action is tight and involving," while Elaine E. Knight concluded in *School Library Journal* that "Jonathan is a sympathetic and realistic character," and that this "exciting tale is a fine choice for most collections."

Kehret has also authored several titles in the "Frightmare" series, a competitor to the popular "Goosebumps" books. Kehret's books feature friends Rosie and Kayo who get involved in all manner of adventures and mysteries, from solving a kidnapping in Arizona in *Desert Danger* to solving a possible poisoning in *Don't Go Near Mrs. Tallie* to discovering vandals in the school with the help of a pet in *Bone Breath and the Vandals.* Using youthful protagonists Warren and Betsy, Kehret has also employed time travel to set up thrilling stories, as in *The Volcano Disaster,* in which Warren must survive the eruption of Mount St. Helens. *Booklist*'s Peterson, reviewing *Bone Breath and the Vandals,* noted that "Kehret delivers some likable characters and a thrilling plot that won't disappoint suspense fans."

Nonfiction for children has also received the Kehret touch. Of her several books of monologues for young actors, one of the most popular is *Acting Natural: Monologs, Dialogs, and Playlets for Teens.* "A wide range of topics is addressed in this sourcebook of 60 original scenes and monologues," noted Dianne G. Mahony in *School Library Journal.* Donna Houser commented in *Voice of Youth Advocates* that "all sections have their own merit because they deal with problems that are relevant to today's youth."

Kehret details her own battle with the paralyzing after-effects of polio in her award-winning *Small Steps: The Year I Got Polio.* "This heartfelt memoir takes readers back to 1949 when the author, at age 12, contracted polio," noted Zvirin in *Booklist.* Kehret describes the progress of the illness, the paralysis, and her slow recovery. Christine A. Moesch concluded in *School Library Journal* that Kehret's memoir was an "honest and well-done book." Yet another nonfiction title is Kehret's *Shelter Dogs,* stories of dogs that found a second life after being taken from Humane Society shelters. A *Kirkus Reviews* critic called the book "an amiable collection of short anecdotes," concluding that there was "a ready audience to cry over and gasp at the tale behind every dog."

Kehret has amassed a large body of work and a legion of loyal fans—both girls and boys—for her middle-grade thrillers. Blending exciting action, likable characters, and hi-lo language, Kehret writes books that lead her readers on to more difficult fiction and nonfiction. As she reported in an online source, "I do what I love and get paid for it. It's fun to use my creativity and I like being my own boss. Writing is hard work, but when one of my books wins an award, it's worth it."

Works Cited

Davidson, Andrea, review of *Cages, Voice of Youth Advocates,* June, 1991, pp. 97-98.

Review of *Deadly Stranger, Kirkus Reviews,* March 1, 1987, p. 373.

Houser, Donna, review of *Acting Natural: Monologs, Dialogs, and Playlets for Teens, Voice of Youth Advocates,* June, 1992, pp. 126-27.

Houser, review of *Horror at the Haunted House, Voice of Youth Advocates,* October, 1992, p. 224.

Kehret, Peg, "Frequently Asked Questions to Peg Kehret," http://users.owt.com/kehretbp/FAQ.html (April 15, 1999).

Knight, Elaine E., review of *Earthquake Terror, School Library Journal,* February, 1996, p. 100.

Larson, Jeanette, review of *Nightmare Mountain, School Library Journal,* October, 1989, p. 120.

Mahony, Dianne G., review of *Acting Natural: Monologs, Dialogs, and Playlets for Teens, School Library Journal,* August, 1992, p. 182.

Meisner, Sylvia V., review of *Cages, School Library Journal,* June, 1991, p. 126.

Moesch, Christine A., review of *Small Steps: The Year I Got Polio, School Library Journal,* November, 1996, p. 114.

Peterson, Lauren, review of *Bone Breath and the Vandals, Booklist,* May 1, 1995, p. 1573.

Peterson, review of *Searching for Candlestick Park, Booklist,* August, 1997, p. 1901.

Review of *The Richest Kids in Town, Horn Book,* spring, 1995, p. 78.

Review of *The Richest Kids in Town, Kirkus Reviews,* August 15, 1994, p. 1131.

Review of *Searching for Candlestick Park, Kirkus Reviews,* June 1, 1997, p. 874.

Review of *Shelter Dogs: Amazing Stories of Adopted Strays, Kirkus Reviews,* April 1, 1999, p. 535.

Sherman, Chris, review of *Horror at the Haunted House, Booklist,* September 1, 1992, pp. 56, 60.

Shook, Bruce Anne, review of *Sisters, Long Ago, School Library Journal,* March, 1990, pp. 218-19.

Sutton, Roger, review of *Earthquake Terror, Bulletin of the Center for Children's Books,* March, 1996, p. 231.

Wilms, Denise, review of *Nightmare Mountain, Booklist,* September 15, 1989, p. 184.

Zvirin, Stephanie, review of *Danger at the Fair, Booklist,* December 1, 1994, p. 664.

Zvirin, review of *Earthquake Terror, Booklist,* January 1, 1996, p. 834.

Zvirin, review of *Small Steps: The Year I Got Polio, Booklist,* November 1, 1996, pp. 492-93.

For More Information See

BOOKS

Science Fiction and Fantasy Literature, 1975-1991, Gale, 1992.

PERIODICALS

Booklist, February 15, 1990, p. 1166; May 15, 1992, p. 1672; September 1, 1994, p. 41; October 1, 1995, p. 314; August, 1998, p. 2005.

Bulletin of the Center for Children's Books, February, 1995, pp. 202-203; November, 1996, pp. 100-101; November, 1997, pp. 88-89.

Kliatt, July, 1993, p. 10; March, 1997, p. 40.

School Library Journal, September, 1994, p. 218; May, 1995, p. 108; December, 1995, p. 104; July, 1998, p. 96.

Voice of Youth Advocates, February, 1996, p. 373.

Small Steps:
THE YEAR I GOT POLIO

Peg Kehret

In her award-winning juvenile autobiography, Kehret documents her fight with a childhood case of polio that left her temporarily paralyzed.

—Sketch by J. Sydney Jones

*　　*　　*

KELLER, Holly 1942-

Personal

Born February 11, 1942, in New York, NY; married Barry Keller (a pediatrician), June, 1963; children: Corey (daughter), Jesse (son). *Education:* Sarah Lawrence College, A.B., 1963; Columbia University, M.A., 1964; studied printmaking at Manhattanville College; studied illustration at Parsons School of Design. *Hobbies and other interests:* Tennis, travel.

Addresses

Home—West Redding, CT.

Career

Writer. Redding Board of Education, member and vice chair, 1975-85.

Holly Keller

Awards, Honors

Children's Book of the Year, Library of Congress, 1983, for *Ten Sleepy Sheep;* best book of the year, *School Library Journal,* 1984, for *Geraldine's Blanket;* Children's Choice and Child Study Association Children's Book of the Year, both 1987, both for *Goodbye, Max;* Notable Children's Trade Book in the Field of Social Studies, National Council for the Social Studies-Children's Book Council (NCSS-CBC), 1989, for *The Best Present;* Fanfare Honor Book, *Horn Book,* and Reading Rainbow Review Book, both 1991, both for *Horace;* Pick of the Lists, American Booksellers Association, 1991, for *The New Boy,* 1992, for *Island Baby,* and 1994, for *Geraldine's Baby Brother;* Notable Children's Trade Book in the Field of Social Studies, NCSS-CBC, 1994, for *Grandfather's Dream.*

Writings

FOR CHILDREN; AUTHOR AND ILLUSTRATOR

Cromwell's Glasses, Greenwillow, 1982.
Ten Sleepy Sheep, Greenwillow, 1983.
Too Big, Greenwillow, 1983.
Geraldine's Blanket, Greenwillow, 1984, Nelson Canada, 1991.
Will It Rain?, Greenwillow, 1984.
Henry's Fourth of July, Greenwillow, 1985.
When Francie Was Sick, Greenwillow, 1985.
A Bear for Christmas, Greenwillow, 1986.
Lizzie's Invitation, Greenwillow, 1987.
Goodbye, Max, Greenwillow, 1987.
Geraldine's Big Snow, Greenwillow, 1988.

Maxine in the Middle, Greenwillow, 1989.
The Best Present, Greenwillow, 1989.
Henry's Happy Birthday, Greenwillow, 1990.
What Alvin Wanted, Greenwillow, 1990.
Horace, Greenwillow, 1991.
The New Boy, Greenwillow, 1991.
Furry, Greenwillow, 1992.
Island Baby, Greenwillow, 1992.
Harry and Tuck, Greenwillow, 1993.
Grandfather's Dream, Greenwillow, 1994.
Geraldine's Baby Brother, Greenwillow, 1994.
Rosata, Greenwillow, 1995.
Geraldine First, Greenwillow, 1996.
I Am Angela, Greenwillow, 1997.
Merry Christmas, Geraldine, Greenwillow, 1997.
Angela's Top-Secret Computer Club, Greenwillow, 1998.
Brave Horace, Greenwillow, 1998.
Jacob's Tree, Greenwillow, 1999.
What I See, Harcourt Brace, 1999.
A Bed Full of Cats, Harcourt Brace, 1999.
That's Mine, Horace, Greenwillow, 2000.

FOR CHILDREN; ILLUSTRATOR

Jane Thayer, *Clever Raccoon,* Morrow, 1981.
Melvin Berger, *Why I Cough, Sneeze, Shiver, Hiccup, & Yawn,* Crowell, 1983.
Roma Gans, *Rock Collecting,* Crowell, 1984.
Franklyn Mansfield Branley, *Snow Is Falling,* Crowell, 1986.
Branley, *Air Is All around You,* Harper & Row, 1986, revised edition, Crowell, 1986.
Patricia Lauber, *Snakes Are Hunters,* Crowell, 1988.
Franklyn Mansfield Branley, *Shooting Stars,* Crowell, 1989.
Patricia Lauber, *An Octopus Is Amazing,* Crowell, 1990.
Paul Showers, *Ears Are for Hearing,* Crowell, 1990.
Barbara Juster Ebensen, *Sponges Are Skeletons,* HarperCollins, 1993.
Patricia Lauber, *Be a Friend to Trees,* HarperCollins, 1994.
Wendy Pfeffer, *From Tadpole to Frog,* HarperCollins, 1994.
Patricia Lauber, *Who Eats What?: Food Chains and Food Webs,* HarperCollins, 1995.
Lauber, *You're Aboard Spaceship Earth,* HarperCollins, 1996.
Wendy Pfeffer, *What's It Like to Be a Fish?,* HarperCollins, 1996.
Stuart J. Murphy, *The Best Bug Parade,* HarperCollins, 1996.
Roma Gans, *Let's Go Rock Collecting,* HarperCollins, 1997.
Nola Buck, *Morning in the Meadow,* HarperCollins, 1997.
Wendy Pfeffer, *Sounds All Around,* HarperCollins, 1999.

Work in Progress

Illustrations for *Hear Your Heart,* by Paul Showers, and *What Will I Be,* by Anne Rockwell.

Sidelights

Holly Keller is an American author and illustrator whose picture books often feature animal protagonists drawn in

and ten came blowing bubbles.

When a little boy can't sleep and decides to count sheep, the animals materialize and throw a party in his room. (From Ten Sleepy Sheep, *written and illustrated by Keller.)*

a minimalist, flat, cartoon style. Keller's works are entertaining to read, but also have a message. Her picture books deal with issues ranging from adoption to fitting in, from sibling relationships to saying farewell to a beloved pet. She has created endearing characters, many of whom reappear in companion volumes. Her "Geraldine" books, featuring a plucky piglet, include *Geraldine's Blanket, Geraldine's Big Snow, Geraldine's Baby Brother, Geraldine First,* and *Merry Christmas, Geraldine.* Horace, another beloved character and a personal favorite of Keller's, is a whimsical young leopard adopted into a family of tigers. Horace makes appearances in the initial book, *Horace,* as well as in *Brave Horace* and *That's Mine, Horace.* A rambunctious possum named Henry is featured in *Too Big, Henry's Fourth of July,* and *Henry's Happy Birthday.* Other popular and award-winning picture-book titles from Keller include *Ten Sleepy Sheep, Goodbye, Max, The Best Present, Furry, The New Boy,* and *Island Baby.* Keller has also ventured into the realms of juvenile chapter-books with her "Angela" books, *I Am Angela* and *Angela's Top-Secret Computer Club.*

Keller was born on February 11, 1942, in New York City. An avid reader as a child, she spent much of her time by herself. Drawing also became an early form of self-entertainment; she made a project of copying all the bird illustrations from a book by the famous American naturalist illustrator, John James Audubon. Another school project, translating *Little Red Riding Hood* into Latin and illustrating it, served as a preview of things to come for Keller.

But illustrating children's books was still far in the future. Attending Sarah Lawrence College, where she planned to study art, Keller ultimately earned a degree in

history. At Columbia University, she earned a master's degree in history, yet all the time holding onto her love of drawing and painting. Married in 1963, Keller soon became the mother of two children and found herself living in rural Connecticut. She began taking classes in printmaking and suddenly her love of text and illustration began to coalesce when her instructor advised her to try children's illustration. A further course in illustration at the Parsons School of Design convinced her to put together a portfolio of her works which she showed to an editor at Greenwillow in 1981. Given an assignment to turn one set of drawings into a story within a week, Keller sat down and wrote her first picture book, *Cromwell's Glasses,* the tale of a young rabbit's anxiety at receiving his first pair of spectacles.

Carolyn Noah, reviewing the title in *School Library Journal,* noted that "this brief tale thoughtfully treats the difficulties that glasses present to a young child," and also supplies "a positive resolution." Noah concluded that the book would make "a serviceable addition to storytime collections." Already in place with this first book was Keller's characteristic cartoon-style black ink drawings filled in with watercolor, as well as her positive treatment of a difficult childhood issue.

Her next title, *Ten Sleepy Sheep,* features a human protagonist, a little boy who cannot fall asleep. Counting sheep does not help, for soon the animals are throwing a party in his room. A critic for *Kirkus Reviews* called the

When the blanket got dirty, Geraldine helped wash it.

Piglet Geraldine turns her favorite blanket into a more socially acceptable product, clothing for her dolls. (From Geraldine's Blanket, *written and illustrated by Keller.)*

From **Grandfather's Dream**, *Keller's self-illustrated tale about a grandfather's wisdom in recreating wetland feeding grounds for the cranes who departed when Mekong Delta canals drained the land during the Vietnam War.*

book "neatly done—and nice," with pictures in "perky (not pretty-pretty) pink and blue" and an overall effect that was "lightly whimsical." Margery Fisher noted in *Growing Point* that a "simple, irresistible joke is beautifully sustained in this elegantly produced picture-book." *Ten Sleepy Sheep* was voted a Library of Congress Children's Book of the Year and set Keller on course in her new career.

Too Big introduces Henry the possum, who has definite new-brother problems when baby Jake comes home from the hospital. Each time he tries to join in with activities—from sucking on a bottle to putting on a diaper—Henry is met by the statement, "You're too big." Finally even Henry gets the idea that he is too big for babyish things, and a new bike christens his role as older brother in a book that is "both touching and funny," according to Sarah Wintle in the *Times Literary Supplement*. Henry makes curtain calls in *Henry's Fourth of July* and *Henry's Happy Birthday*. In the former title, Henry has a great time at a Fourth of July picnic, running a sack race and watching the fireworks. *Booklist*'s Ilene Cooper concluded that this book was a "happy introduction" for young readers to the national holiday. In the latter title, Henry fears that his fifth

birthday is going to be a disaster, especially when his mother insists he wear a shirt and tie to his own party. But eventually, once he munches his cake and gets the present he's been waiting for, he decides things aren't so bad, after all. *Horn Book*'s Elizabeth S. Watson noted that the book was an "appealing and refreshingly honest approach to the traditional birthday party story."

Keller once told *SATA* that she wrote the "Henry" books because "he's just fun. He doesn't have any special meaning, except that he is always somewhat beleaguered somehow, which in a funny way was how my son Jesse was when he was very little. He always had this feeling that things weren't working out for him and that somehow he had been singled out for that misfortune."

With *Geraldine's Blanket,* which features a piglet who turns her favorite blanket into a more socially acceptable product—clothing for her dolls—Keller hit on a character that has become one of her hallmarks. Geraldine has been featured in four further titles to date. A *Kirkus Reviews* contributor, in a critique of the first book, called Geraldine "a piglet with aplomb," and especially noted the "deft, spare, pink-and-gold cartoons." *Booklist*'s Cooper concluded that the book was a "novel look at a familiar problem, and one that may provide a solution for some families." In *Geraldine's Big Snow,* the piglet is full of anticipation, waiting for the first snow of the season. "Geraldine may be a pig," commented Janet Hickman in *Language Arts,* "but her experience with waiting out a weather forecast will be familiar to young children wherever snow falls." Writing in *School Library Journal,* Trev Jones dubbed the title "fresh, appealing, and perfectly delightful." Geraldine returned in 1994 with a new baby brother in tow in *Geraldine's Baby Brother,* a further exploration of sibling rivalry. Harriett Fargnoli observed in *School Library Journal* that this "expressive pig's appeal remains timeless." A critic for *Kirkus Reviews* noted that the "whimsical line drawings add to the overall charm" of this "wise, funny, accepting little book." Geraldine's little brother, Willie, also makes an appearance in *Geraldine First,* in which he is copying everything Geraldine says and does. *School Library Journal* contributor Virginia Opocensky commented that, again, Keller managed to capture a normal sibling problem with "understated humor and a satisfying denouement," and that her "marvelously minimalist pen-and-watercolor drawings [extend] the story beyond the words." An over-large Christmas tree picked by Geraldine forms the plot crux of the 1997 *Merry Christmas, Geraldine.* Carolyn Phelan of *Booklist* called Keller's illustrations "beguiling" and declared: "fans of the series will enjoy watching this assertive heroine plow through every obstacle."

A personal experience of meeting a child troubled by the knowledge that she was adopted inspired Keller to create her popular and award-winning *Horace.* A little spotted leopard, the adopted Horace feels out of place with his family of striped tigers, especially at his birthday party when all his stripe-bearing cousins appear. Cooper noted in *Booklist* that adopted children would surely identify with Keller's "gentle story," but it would also appeal to those not adopted, "who simply feel like the odd one out." Anna Biagioni Hart, writing in *School Library Journal,* felt that "Keller's use of appealing animal characters in a fictional tale is a welcome approach" to the difficult issue of adoption. Horace makes a return in 1998's *Brave Horace,* in which he comes unglued in anticipation of going to his friend's monster-movie party. He promises himself he won't be scared, and relief is all he feels when the scary movie gets canceled. "This sensitive and entertaining picture book is just right for young children," noted *Booklist's* Carolyn Phelan, "who often need courage to overcome their own imaginations." *School Library Journal* contributor Jody McCoy called the book a "boon for timid youngsters."

"I think *Horace* and *Geraldine's Blanket* are my two favorites," Keller once told *SATA.* "I like *Geraldine* because she's really me, and *Horace* because it's a gentle and nice story, one of the better ones I've done." Individual titles that have earned Keller high marks with critics and readers include *Goodbye, Max,* the story of the death of a pet; *The Best Present,* a tale of a hospitalized grandmother; *The New Boy,* about being unwelcome at a new school; *Furry,* detailing the disappointment felt with a pet allergy; *Island Baby,* set

In Keller's easy-reader chapter book, Angela and her computer-whiz friends solve a mystery when someone breaks into the school's computer system.

in a tropical bird hospital; *Harry and Tuck,* a twin story; and *Grandfather's Dream,* a Vietnamese tale about a grandfather's wisdom.

Keller once said that she had no desire to write longer works for children, but like some character out of one of her own picture books, curiosity got the better of her. *I Am Angela,* an easy-reader chapter book, appeared in 1997, followed the next year by *Angela's Top-Secret Computer Club.* The first book details five episodes in the life of feisty Angela—including playing softball at camp, visiting the zoo with her Scout troop, creating a class exhibit, and becoming a dog walker. *Booklist's* Stephanie Zvirin noted that "there's always some goofy complication in the goings-on to ensure laughs." In the sequel, *Angela's Top-Secret Computer Club,* someone has broken into the school's computer system and chaos ensues, including adulterated report cards. Angela and her computer-whiz friends are called on to solve the mystery. *Booklist's* Kay Weisman concluded that Keller's "intrepid heroine hits just the right note in this upbeat mystery." Weisman also felt that the short chapters and line drawings would add "appeal for first-chapter-book readers."

Keller has also illustrated the work of others and continues to turn out picture books along with her popular chapter books. "Creating children's stories is the

"What could be wrong with Horace?" Mama asked
Mrs. Pepper when she picked him up after school.
Mrs. Pepper shook her head.

Keller's popular protagonist Horace, a little spotted leopard who is adopted by a family of tigers, comes unglued in anxious anticipation of his friend's monster-movie party. (From Brave Horace, *written and illustrated by Keller.)*

most wonderful job in the world," Keller told *SATA*. "I never think of it as being work."

Works Cited

Cooper, Ilene, review of *Geraldine's Blanket*, *Booklist*, June 15, 1984, p. 1484.

Cooper, review of *Henry's Fourth of July*, *Booklist*, April 1, 1985, p. 1120.

Cooper, review of *Horace*, *Booklist*, February 11, 1991, p. 1130.

Fargnoli, Harriett, review of *Geraldine's Baby Brother*, *School Library Journal*, August, 1994, p. 133.

Fisher, Margery, review of *Ten Sleepy Sheep*, *Growing Point*, March, 1984, p. 4220.

Review of *Geraldine's Baby Brother*, *Kirkus Reviews*, August 15, 1994, p. 1131.

Review of *Geraldine's Blanket*, *Kirkus Reviews*, March 1, 1984, pp. J5-6.

Hart, Anna Biagioni, review of *Horace*, *School Library Journal*, April, 1991, p. 97.

Hickman, Janet, review of *Geraldine's Big Snow*, *Language Arts*, January, 1989, pp. 65-66.

Jones, Trev, review of *Geraldine's Big Snow*, *School Library Journal*, February, 1989, p. 72.

McCoy, Jody, review of *Brave Horace*, *School Library Journal*, April, 1998, p. 102.

Noah, Carolyn, review of *Cromwell's Glasses*, *School Library Journal*, March, 1982, p. 136.

Opocensky, Virginia, review of *Geraldine First*, *School Library Journal*, May, 1996, p. 93.

Phelan, Carolyn, review of *Brave Horace*, *Booklist*, March 1, 1998, p. 1140.

Phelan, review of *Merry Christmas, Geraldine*, *Booklist*, September 1, 1997, p. 139.

Review of *Ten Sleepy Sheep*, *Kirkus Reviews*, September 1, 1983, p. J150.

Watson, Elizabeth S., review of *Henry's Happy Birthday*, *Horn Book*, November-December, 1990, p. 729.

Weisman, Kay, review of *Angela's Top-Secret Computer Club, Booklist,* August 19, 1998, p. 1140.

Wintle, Sarah, review of *Too Big, Times Literary Supplement,* September 30, 1983, p. 1050.

Zvirin, Stephanie, review of *I Am Angela, Booklist,* May 15, 1997, p. 1575.

For More Information See

BOOKS

Authors of Books for Young People, 3rd edition, Scarecrow Press, 1990.

Children's Books and Their Creators, Houghton Mifflin, 1995, pp. 363-64.

Children's Literature Review, Volume 45, Gale, 1997, pp. 43-61.

PERIODICALS

Booklist, March 15, 1992, p. 1388.

Bulletin of the Center for Children's Books, July, 1990, p. 269; March, 1998, p. 247.

Horn Book, May-June, 1990, p. 326; November-December, 1994, p. 720; November-December, 1995, p. 734; May-June, 1996, p. 325; July-August, 1998, p. 475; March-April, 1999, p. 193.

Kirkus Reviews, April 15, 1993, p. 531; July 15, 1995, p. 1025; February 15, 1998, p. 269; March 15, 1999, p. 452.

Publishers Weekly, April 5, 1991, p. 145; April 26, 1993, p. 77; March 23, 1998, p. 98.

School Library Journal, August, 1990, pp. 143-144; November, 1991, p. 100; November, 1992, p. 72; June, 1998, pp. 111-12.

Tribune Books (Chicago), September 13, 1992, p. 7.

—*Sketch by J. Sydney Jones*

*　　*　　*

KELLY, Fiona
See COLEMAN, Michael

*　　*　　*

KRAKAUER, Jon 1954-

Personal

Born in Brookline, MA, in 1954; son of Lewis Krakauer (a physician) and an art teacher; married Linda Moore, 1980. *Education:* Attended Hampshire College, MA, in the early 1970s. *Hobbies and other interests:* Mountain climbing.

Addresses

Home—Seattle, WA.

Career

Freelance journalist. Contributing editor to *Outside* magazine. Worked previously as a carpenter and a commercial fisherman.

Awards, Honors

National Magazine Award nominee, for an article that formed the basis of *Into the Wild;* Best Books for Young Adults, American Library Association, 1998, for *Into Thin Air: A Personal Account of the Mount Everest Disaster.*

Writings

Eiger Dreams: Ventures among Men and Mountains (essay collection), Lyons and Burford, 1990.

(Photographer) David Roberts, *Iceland: Land of the Sagas* (travelogue), Abrams, 1990.

Into the Wild (nonfiction), Villard, 1996.

Into Thin Air: A Personal Account of the Mount Everest Disaster (nonfiction), Villard, 1997.

Adaptations

Into Thin Air was adapted for television by TriStar Television and broadcast on ABC-TV, 1997, and into an audiocassette read by Krakauer, BDD, 1997.

Sidelights

"Straddling the top of the world, one foot in Tibet and the other in Nepal, I cleared the ice from my oxygen mask, hunched a shoulder against the wind, and stared absently at the vast sweep of earth below. I understood on some dim, detached level that it was a spectacular sight. I'd been fantasizing about this moment, and the release of emotion that would accompany it, for many months. But now that I was finally here, standing on the summit of Mount Everest, I just couldn't summon the energy to care," writes Jon Krakauer in his "Into Thin Air" account for *Outside* magazine. Later he speculated: "Reaching the top of Everest is supposed to trigger a surge of intense elation; against long odds, after all, I had just attained a goal I'd coveted since childhood. But the summit was really only the halfway point. Any impulse I might have felt toward self-congratulation was immediately extinguished by apprehension about the long, dangerous descent that lay ahead."

Krakauer was right to feel apprehension; as he began his descent down Everest, a winter storm invaded the mountaintop, stranding several of the climbers who had reached the summit after him. Lucky to make it back to camp in the diminished visibility caused by the storm and the darkness of descending dusk, Krakauer stumbled into his tent, thinking the others would be back soon. Several hours later he learned of the life-and-death struggle taking place further up the mountain, a struggle that ended with the deaths of eight climbers. Haunted by this tragedy and his connection to it, Krakauer first wrote the *Outside* article for which he was sent on the

JON KRAKAUER

Author of *Into the Wild* and *Into Thin Air*

EIGER
DREAMS

VENTURES AMONG
MEN AND MOUNTAINS

"Krakauer has taken the literature of mountains
onto a higher ledge." *–The New York Times Book Review*

In his collection of short pieces originally published as magazine articles, Krakauer relates his experiences and motivations as a mountain climber. (Cover photo by Ned Gillette.)

commercially-guided Everest expedition. When this format wasn't enough to do the tragic story justice or to bring its author the peace he sought, Krakauer expanded it into the best-selling book *Into Thin Air: A Personal Account of the Mount Everest Disaster.*

"I guess I don't try to justify climbing, or defend it, because I can't," related Krakauer in a discussion of *Into Thin Air* with Mark Bryant for *Outside.* "There's no way to defend it," he continued, "even to yourself, once you've been involved in something like this disaster. And yet I've continued to climb. I don't know what that says about me or the sport other than the potential power it has. What makes climbing great for me, strangely enough, is this life and death aspect. It sounds trite to say, I know, but climbing isn't just another game. It isn't just another sport. It's life itself."

Climbing and other risk-taking activities became a part of Krakauer's life at a young age. Born in Brookline, Massachusetts, in 1954, Krakauer was only two when he moved with his family to Corvallis, Oregon, experiencing his first climb a few years later at the age of eight.

Krakauer's father, who led his son up Oregon's 10,000-foot South Sister, was acquainted with Willi Unsoeld, a member of the first American expedition to Everest in 1963. Thus Krakauer's heroes became Unsoeld and his fellow climber, Tom Hornbein, and his dream became the Everest Summit. "I'd had this secret desire to climb Everest that never left me from the time I was nine and Tom Hornbein and Willi Unsoeld, a friend of my father's, made it in '63," Krakauer admitted to Bryant. "They were my childhood heroes, and Everest was always a big deal to me, though I buried the desire until *Outside* called."

Between his early dreams of Everest and his actual ascent of the mountain, Krakauer made several other climbs that eventually led to a writing career. It was while attending Hampshire College in Massachusetts during the early 1970s that Krakauer was introduced to Alaska by climbing writer David Roberts. "I became this climbing bum," recalled Krakauer in a *People* Magazine interview with William Plummer. "I worked as a carpenter in Boulder, Colorado, five months of the year, climbed the rest." Toward the end of the 1970s he met Linda Moore, a student at the University of Colorado at Denver, and married her three years later. Also a climber at one point in her life, Linda believed Krakauer would quit the risky sport, but he found himself unable to do so. As Krakauer explained in an *Outside Online* interview with Jane Bromet, " . . . when we got married I promised I'd quit climbing, and a few years later when I started climbing again I came within a millimeter of wrecking our marriage. So, then we went through a bunch of years where climbing was a big issue. Now it is less of an issue. It is how I make my living, to no small degree . . . . It's a huge part of who I am, and I wouldn't be a writer if it wasn't for climbing, and Linda understands that and she accepts it."

Writing and climbing first mixed for Krakauer back in 1974 when he climbed the Alaskan Arrigetch Peaks in the Brooks Range, making three ascents of previously unexplored peaks. These accomplishments prompted the American Alpine Club to request a piece for its journal; it was the first article Krakauer ever wrote. Three years later his first income-generating article, on climbing the Devil's Thumb, was published in the British magazine *Mountain.* With the encouragement and advice of Moore and Roberts (his climbing partner and writing mentor), Krakauer learned the craft of writing query letters and began pursuing the career of a freelance writer; in 1983 he quit his carpentry job and wrote full time.

"I have never received any formal training as a writer," Krakauer admitted in an *Outside Online* question-and-answer session. "I have always been a voracious reader, however, and whenever I read something that moves me, I re-read it many times to try and figure out how its author has worked his or her magic . . . . Like any craft, the harder and longer you work at your writing, the more likely you are to get better at it." While trying to hone his new craft, Krakauer wrote several different kinds of articles that drew on his past experiences; since he had been a carpenter, he wrote about architecture for

Architectural Digest, and having been a commercial fisherman, he made *Smithsonian* an offer to do an article on a commercial fishery in Alaska, which they accepted. "I was setting quotas that I would write ten query letters a week, and I definitely worked hard, but I got lucky," he observed in an online *Bold Type* interview. "Because I wanted to pay the rent, I didn't have any grandiose ambitions of being an artiste; I wanted to pay the ... bills, so I worked really hard."

As his new career progressed, however, Krakauer found himself focusing on outdoor subjects more than any others. "The problem is that none of [the other subjects] have captured my interest as much as the outdoor pieces," he observed in his *Bold Type* interview. "The pieces I've written for *Outside* magazine are definitely my best work, and they're virtually all about the outdoors." And so Krakauer's first book, *Eiger Dreams: Ventures among Men and Mountains,* published in 1990, is a collection of several magazine articles originally published in *Outside* and *Smithsonian.* While describing his experiences climbing Mt. McKinley, the North Face of the Eiger in Switzerland, and many others, Krakauer attempts to answer the question of why anyone would want to risk their life climbing a mountain. "The reader who knows little about climbing will learn much from *Eiger Dreams,* but Mr. Krakauer has taken the literature of mountains onto a higher ledge," maintained Tim Cahill in the *New York Times Book Review.* "His snow-capped peaks set against limitless blue skies present problems that inspire irrefutable human experiences: fear and triumph, damnation and salvation. There is beauty in his mountains beyond that expressed in conventional sermons. His reverence is earned, and it's entirely genuine."

The exploration of the impulse that drives risk-taking is the major thread that ties all of Krakauer's books together. In 1992 *Outside* magazine asked him to write about the life and death of twenty-four-year-old Christopher McCandless, an honors graduate whose admiration of the writer Leo Tolstoy prompted him to shed all of his worldly possessions and return to nature in search of transcendental experiences. Giving away his savings, McCandless adopted the name Alex Supertramp and wandered through the American West, eventually making his way to Alaska. There he hiked into the wild Alaskan bush near Denali National Park to live off the land; four months later he was found starved to death.

While researching McCandless's life, Krakauer found similarities in his own youthful adventures, similarities that helped him identify with this young man's life and death. "In 1977, when I was 23—a year younger than McCandless at the time of his death—I hitched a ride to Alaska on a fishing boat and set off alone into the back country to attempt an ascent of a malevolent stone digit called the Devils Thumb, a towering prong of vertical rock and avalanching ice, ignoring pleas from friends, family, and utter strangers to come to my senses," wrote Krakauer in his *Outside* article "Death of an Innocent." He continued: "The fact that I survived my Alaskan adventure and McCandless did not survive his was largely a matter of chance; had I died on the Stikine Icecap in 1977, people would have been quick to say of me, as they now say of him, that I had a death wish .... I was stirred by the mystery of death; I couldn't resist stealing up to the edge of doom and peering over the brink. The view into that swirling black vortex terrified me, but I caught sight of something elemental in that shadowy glimpse, some forbidden, fascinating riddle."

Krakauer's fascination with McCandless continued long after the publication of this original article. "I was haunted by the particulars of the boy's starvation and by vague, unsettling parallels between events in his life and those in my own," explained Krakauer in his introduction to *Into the Wild.* And so Krakauer spent the next year tracing the complex and twisting path that led to McCandless's death, the result of which became the author's first full-length book, *Into the Wild,* published in 1996. "In trying to understand McCandless," continued Krakauer in his introduction, "I inevitably came to reflect on other, larger subjects as well: the grip wilderness has on the American imagination, the allure high-risk activities hold for young men of a certain mind, the complicated, highly charged bond that exists between fathers and sons."

Reconstructing the last two years of McCandless's life, Krakauer drew from journals and postcards, as well as interviews with anyone who knew him during this time period. Thomas McNamee, writing in the *New York Times Book Review,* asserted that as Krakauer "picks through the adventures and sorrows of Chris McCandless's brief life, the story becomes painfully moving. Mr. Krakauer's elegantly constructed narrative takes us from the ghoulish moment of the hunters' discovery back through McCandless's childhood, the gregarious effusions and icy withdrawals that characterized his coming of age, and, in meticulous detail, the two years of restless roaming that led him to Alaska. The more we learn about him, the more mysterious McCandless becomes, and the more intriguing."

"I won't claim to be an impartial biographer," Krakauer stated in his introduction to *Into the Wild.* "McCandless's strange tale struck a personal note that made a dispassionate rendering of the tragedy impossible. Through most of the book, I have tried—and largely succeeded, I think—to minimize my authorial presence. But let the reader be warned: I interrupt McCandless's story with fragments of a narrative drawn from my own youth. I do so in hope that my experiences will throw some oblique light on the enigma of Chris McCandless." McNamee maintained that Krakauer does just what he set out to do: "Christopher McCandless's life and his death may have been meaningless, absurd, even reprehensible, but by the end of *Into the Wild,* you care for him deeply."

Like *Into the Wild,* Krakauer's next book began as an article requested by *Outside* magazine—an article on the commercialization of Mt. Everest climbing expeditions. In order to tell the story, Krakauer became a member of a team guided by Rob Hall, a respected and experienced

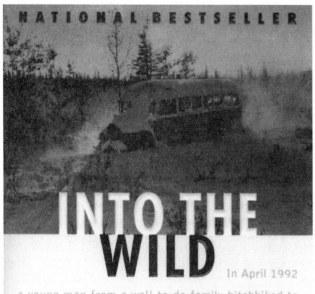

NATIONAL BESTSELLER

INTO THE WILD

In April 1992 a young man from a well-to-do family hitchhiked to Alaska and walked alone into the wilderness north of Mt. McKinley. His name was Christopher Johnson McCandless. He had given $25,000 in savings to charity, abandoned his car and most of his possessions, burned all the cash in his wallet, and invented a new life for himself. Four months later, his decomposed body was found by a moose hunter...

JON KRAKAUER

In his sympathetic biography, Krakauer traces the complex and twisting path that led to the death of twenty-four-year-old Christopher McCandless, who died of starvation in the Alaskan wilderness.

climber who had been on Everest seven times before. And so one of Krakauer's childhood dreams became a reality. "Secretly, I dreamed of climbing Everest myself one day; for more than a decade it remained a burning ambition," Krakauer confessed in his article "Into Thin Air," adding: "It wasn't until my mid-twenties that I abandoned the dream as a preposterous boyhood fantasy. Soon thereafter I began to look down my nose at the world's tallest mountain.... Despite the disdain I'd expressed for Everest over the years, when the call came to join Hall's expedition, I said yes without even hesitating to catch my breath. Boyhood dreams die hard, I discovered, and good sense be damned."

As he became acclimated to the altitude (higher than 17,600 feet) and culture of base camp, Krakauer met several of the other teams and climbers, commenting on them in his *Outside Online* interview with Bromet: "It's really appalling. There's a lot of inexperienced people here—and many people would say I'm one of them—and that's sort of scary. There's a lot of people here who shouldn't be here. And maybe I shouldn't be here. But the guides and the Sherpas make that possible, which is

kind of neat in a lot of ways. People who wouldn't have the time and the experience—but they have the money—can do this, so it's neat. But it's a challenge. I don't care how much you paid or what kind of guides or Sherpas you have, it's not going to be easy, I can tell that already. It demands determination and physical reserves. If you can get to the top of Everest, I say more power to you."

By the time summit-day was upon him, Krakauer and his teammates had already made three trips (over the course of six weeks) above base camp, going approximately 2,000 feet higher each time. This was Hall's way of acclimating his team to the altitude, a method which he assured them would enable them to climb safely to the 29,028-foot summit. From the beginning, Hall planned May 10 as his team's summit-day, mainly because the most favorable weather of the year was likely to fall on or around this date. This, of course, meant that other teams had their sights set on the same day, which could result in a dangerous gridlock on the summit ridge; so Hall and the other leaders held a meeting and assigned summit dates to the various groups. In the end, it was decided that Krakauer's team would share the May 10 date with Scott Fischer's team, and all other groups (except the South-African team, whose leader declared they would go to the top whenever they pleased) agreed to steer clear of the top of the mountain on this date.

Climbing with oxygen for the first time, Krakauer reached the South Col, the final camp from which his team would make its summit bid, at one o'clock on the afternoon of May 9, several hours before the last stragglers on Fischer's team. By 11:35 p.m., conditions were excellent and the teams left their tents on the South Col and headed toward the summit. The most important thing Hall had ingrained in his team was the predetermined turnaround time of one o'clock in the afternoon on May 10; no matter how close you were to the summit at this time, you were to turn around and head back down. During the ascent, various members of both teams suffered from numerous problems, including hypoxia, blindness, and several bottlenecks along the climbing route. Despite these obstacles, on May 10 Krakauer arrived at the summit with two other climbers and began his descent at approximately 1:17 p.m., reaching the South Summit around three. As he continued down from this point, the first clouds began to move in and it began to snow; these weather conditions in combination with the diminishing light made it difficult to determine where the mountain ended and the sky began. The lower Krakauer went, the worse the weather became, but by 5:30 p.m. he was within 200 vertical feet of camp, making it down the final steep bulge of rock-hard ice without a rope and stumbling into his tent about a half-hour later. At this point he was unaware that one teammate was already dead and that twenty-three others were in a life-and-death struggle to make it back to camp. The events that unfolded from there made heroes out of some, and are the reason that Krakauer has been unable to overcome his guilt for not having been able to do anything for the other climbers. In the end, a total of eight climbers died, including Krakauer's team leader Hall, and several others were severely injured.

Krakauer wrote in "Into Thin Air:" "Days later ... people would ask why, if the weather had begun to deteriorate, had climbers on the upper mountain not heeded the signs? Why did veteran Himalayan guides keep moving upward, leading a gaggle of amateurs ... into an apparent death trap?

"Nobody can speak for the leaders of the two guided groups involved, for both men are now dead. But I can attest that nothing I saw early on the afternoon of May 10 suggested that a murderous storm was about to bear down on us."

"Climbing mountains will never be a safe, predictable, rule-bound enterprise," mused Krakauer in "Into Thin Air." "It is an activity that idealizes risk-taking; its most celebrated figures have always been those who stuck their necks out the farthest and managed to get away with it. Climbers, as a species, are simply not distinguished by any excess of common sense. And that holds especially true for Everest climbers: When presented with a chance to reach the planet's highest summit, people are surprisingly quick to abandon prudence altogether." As proof of this, one need look no further than May 24th, just a couple weeks following the disaster Krakauer experienced; on this date the South-African team launched its summit bid. One of the climbers, Bruce Herrod, fell far behind, yet continued alone past the frozen body of Fischer to reach the summit at 5:00 p.m., where he found himself alone, tired, and out of oxygen. At 7:00 p.m. Herrod radioed camp a final time and was never heard from again; he is presumed to be dead, the desperate radio calls and deaths of the previous weeks having had no effect on him during his quest for the summit.

The book resulting from Krakauer's experiences on Everest generated much criticism from the friends and families of the victims as well as other climbers who survived the expedition. They accused Krakauer of being too judgmental of the actions of others and of earning money off the tragedy of others. "In writing the book I tried very hard to recount the events truthfully, in an even-handed, sympathetic manner that did not sensationalize the tragedy or cause undue pain to friends and families of the victims," contended Krakauer in another *Outside Online* discussion. He also answered some of the other criticisms during his interview with Bryant: "Plenty of people have said to me, 'Who are you to assess someone else's role or lack of experience or skill?' But I'm a working journalist, and I was there, and I was there to do a job—to tell what happened as best I could. I certainly feel bad that some people are hurt by my assessments, but somebody needed to step up and tell what went on up there."

Despite criticism from those involved in the tragedy, *Into Thin Air* was well-received by both critics and readers, who kept the book on the best-seller list for weeks. "Every once in a while a work of nonfiction comes along that's as good as anything a novelist could make up," maintained James M. Clash in *Forbes*. "Krakauer's new book, *Into Thin Air*, fits the bill." Alastair Scott, writing for the *New York Times Book Review*, pointed out that with *Into Thin Air* Krakauer "has produced a narrative that is both meticulously researched and deftly constructed. Unlike the expedition, his story rushes irresistibly forward. But perhaps Mr. Krakauer's greatest achievement is his evocation of the deadly storm, his ability to re-create its effects with a lucid and terrifying intimacy." *Sports Illustrated* contributor Ron Fimrite similarly praised Krakauer's account: "In this movingly written book, Krakauer describes an experience of such bone-chilling horror as to persuade even the most fanatical alpinists to seek sanctuary at sea level. Not that they're likely to do so."

In this way, Krakauer gets across the all-consuming need for climbers to climb, a need he himself cannot shake even after this tragedy—he continues to climb mountains. "There's something about it that is important to me—for some of us it's an important antidote to modern life," Krakauer stated in his interview with Bryant. "But climbing, for me, does have this transcendental quality, this ability to transport you, to enforce humility, to cause you to lose yourself and simply live in the moment. What other people may get from attending midnight mass, I still get from climbing. These are bad cliches, I know, but they're cliches that nevertheless ring true for me." And so through his climbing and writing Krakauer continues to work toward overcoming the tragedy of Everest. "Writing's a way to hang on to your sanity," he concluded in an *Entertainment Weekly* interview with David Hochman. "It's still very painful to me, but I think I've had an incredibly good life and have been lucky in climbing and writing. Now it's just a matter of getting the rest of my life under control again."

Works Cited

Bromet, Jane, "Summit Journal 1996: Jon Krakauer Turns His Eye—and Lungs—toward Everest," *Outside Online,* April 15, 1996.

Bryant, Mark, "Everest a Year Later: False Summit," *Outside,* May, 1997.

Cahill, Tim, "Travel," *New York Times Book Review,* June 10, 1990, p. 48.

Clash, James M., review of *Into Thin Air, Forbes,* May 19, 1997, p. 291.

Fimrite, Ron, review of *Into Thin Air, Sports Illustrated,* May 12, 1997, p. 18.

Hochman, David, "Cliff Notes," *Entertainment Weekly,* April 25, 1997, pp. 40-43.

Krakauer, Jon, *Bold Type* interview at http://www.bookwire.com/boldtype/krakauer/read.article$1258.

Krakauer, "Death of an Innocent: How Christopher McCandless Lost His Way in the Wilds," *Outside,* January, 1993.

Krakauer, introduction to *Into the Wild,* Villard, 1996.

Krakauer, "Into Thin Air," *Outside,* September, 1996.

Krakauer, responses to reader's questions, *Outside Online: The Lodge,* 1997.

Krakauer, "Summit Journal 1996: Jon Krakauer on Everest," *Outside Online,* May 23, 1997.

McNamee, Thomas, "Adventures of Alexander Supertramp," *New York Times Book Review,* March 3, 1996, p. 29.

Plummer, William, "Everest's Shadow," *People,* June 2, 1997, pp. 53-57.

Scott, Alastair, review of *Into Thin Air, New York Times Book Review,* May 18, 1997, Section 7, p. 11.

For More Information See

PERIODICALS

Economist, September 6, 1997, pp. 17-18.

Library Journal, November 15, 1995, p. 96.

Newsweek, April 21, 1997, p. 76.

New York Times, May 6, 1997.

New York Times Book Review, December 7, 1997, p. 12.

Outside, February, 1996; May, 1997.

Outside Online, February, 1996; May 20, 1997.

People, February 12, 1996, p. 35.

Publishers Weekly, February 20, 1990, p. 73; November 6, 1995, p. 76; May 5, 1997, p. 20; July 14, 1997, p. 18; September 22, 1997, p. 28.

School Library Journal, August, 1990, p. 178.*

L

LAIRD, Christa 1944-

Personal

Born December, 1944, in London, England; married Nigel Laird (an educator), 1968; children: Julian, Adam. *Education:* University of Bristol, degree in modern languages, 1966; University of Exeter, qualification in social work, 1968; University of Oxford, B.Litt, 1978.

Addresses

Home—82 Lonsdale Rd., Oxford OX2 7ER, England.

Career

Social worker, trainer, manager, largely with Oxford-shire Social Services. Author.

Awards, Honors

Janusz Korczak Literary Award, 1992, for *Shadow of the Wall.*

Writings

Shadow of the Wall, Julia Macrae (London), 1989, Greenwillow (New York), 1990.
The Forgotten Son, Julia Macrae, 1990.
But Can the Phoenix Sing?, Julia Macrae, 1993, Greenwillow, 1995.

Shadow of the Wall has been translated into several languages.

Sidelights

An English author of historical fiction for young people, Laird has been consistently praised for writing moving, thought-provoking works that successfully blend real facts, people, and events with invented characters and situations. Although she has written only three books, Laird is considered one of the most promising creators of young adult literature. The author has set two of her

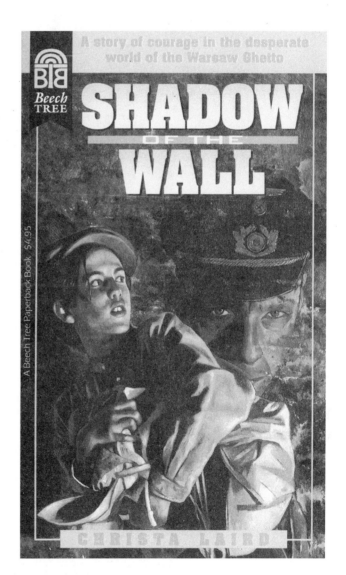

Christa Laird's novel, set in World War II Poland, features fourteen-year-old Misha Edelman who takes great personal risks to bring food and medicine to his widowed mother, who is stricken with tuberculosis. (Cover illustration by Daniel Mark Duffy.)

In her sequel to **Shadow of the Wall,** *Laird takes Misha through his experiences as a partisan in the forests of eastern Poland, a courier for the underground resistance in Warsaw, and a prisoner of war in Germany. (Cover illustration by Daniel Mark Duffy.)*

works, *Shadow of the Wall* and its sequel *But Can the Phoenix Sing?*, (also called *Beyond the Wall*) in the periods during and immediately following the Holocaust, while her third book, *The Forgotten Son,* takes place in twelfth-century France. All of Laird's stories feature young men who are searching for their identities in the face of social or personal difficulties, and her works explore sophisticated moral concepts such as the individual's capacity for good and evil and the emergence of courage from oppression. Recognized for her thorough research, Laird is noted for including an abundance of accurate information about the periods she depicts as well as prefaces and postscripts that provide further resources. Although her books contain war, death, cruelty, abandonment, and other difficult issues, Laird is also acknowledged for underscoring the humanity and universality of the situations she describes, and her books are often viewed as testimonies to the indomitability of the human spirit. In a 1998 autobio-

graphical essay for *Something about the Author Autobiography Series (SAAS),* Laird wrote that her "inclination to write was a maternal legacy; the subject matter, on the other hand, rather persistently paternal." She continued, "They say that all works of fiction are essentially autobiographical, and my sons tease me that my three books are all about searching for a lost father, which I suppose, in a way, they are."

Born in London, Laird arrived in the world less than three months after the 1944 death of her father at the Battle of Arnhem, the first attempt by the Allies to free Holland from Nazi occupation. "Perhaps the most poignant aspect of my father's death," Laird said, "is the fact that it was, in a very particular sense, unnecessary." Laird's father was born in Cologne, Germany, to a successful Jewish architect and his gentile wife. Shortly after Hitler's rise to power, the couple left Germany, making their way to Holland. Laird's father obtained a law degree from Oxford University, then volunteered for the armed forces, which as an alien he was not required to do. Later, he joined a parachute regiment. That led to his involvement in the Battle of Arnhem, where he was killed at age twenty-four.

Laird wrote in *SAAS,* "Overshadowed though it was by my father's death, my childhood, like most, contained both joys and miseries, and in my case there were definitely more of the former." Devoted to her mother, a writer who published magazine articles and short stories (several of which were broadcast on BBC radio), five-year-old Christa was upset and resentful when her mother remarried. "At that time, and for several years afterwards," Laird noted, "the secret that I hated my stepfather was one I chose to share, like a sacrificial offering, with only the most special or coveted of friends." She added, "Not that my stepfather was cruel or abusive in any way; distant, certainly, and unsure how to relate to children, with other more pressing things on his mind than how to win over a resentful and probably rather self-opinionated little girl." As an adult, Laird's attitude toward her stepfather mellowed; when he died, she remembered, "I was genuinely sad."

Many of Laird's happiest childhood memories are associated with her maternal grandparents: her grandfather, as Laird described him in *SAAS,* "was a dear and endlessly patient man," while her grandmother "was a more irascible, indeed fiery, character." Laird's grandfather took her to the London Zoo and played cards and board games with her, while her grandmother kept a jar of sweets in a secret place in the corner of her cupboard for Christa and her younger brother, Paul. When she was eight, Laird's grandparents booked expensive seats outside the Savoy Hotel for Coronation Day—the celebration of Queen Elizabeth II's ascension to the throne. Christa boasted to her mother afterwards that she "had been close enough to see the Queen's blue eyes as she passed in her golden coach!" Her grandparents also owned a cottage in North Devon on England's southwestern coast. As Laird noted in her *SAAS* essay, until her early teens she spent all of her holidays here, "when the days were always long and sunny and the hydrangea bushes in the cottage garden always in full bloom." On several occasions, Laird's mother took her and her brother to nearby Lundy Island. Laird has special memories of that lonely, windswept place. She recalled in her *SAAS* essay a particular adventure that occurred when the family stayed on Lundy for two nights: "The best moment then was when we stood watching the steamer depart with its cargo of day trippers, and we could begin to pretend that we had been shipwrecked and marooned, with only seabirds and wild deer and the ghosts in the ruined castle for company."

When Laird was about twelve, she was sent to the same boarding school her mother had attended; Laird wrote that they even shared the same math teacher, "who," the author noted, "could never decide which one of us was the less numerate." After a few days of homesickness, Laird adjusted well to her new school. She recalled, "I enjoyed both sports and academic work, so on the whole school was a positive experience; and several of the friends I made then are still my friends today." At fifteen, she made what she described as "probably the first major mistake in my life." Although she was considered an apt pupil with a particular talent for languages, Laird decided that she did not want to go to college, "I had had enough of school and discipline," she remembered. Her mother and stepfather sent Laird to a school in Switzerland where she could study French and German seriously; her experience in Switzerland, which she described in *SAAS* as "not much more than an enjoyable and fattening diversion," led her to change her mind about university. Returning to England, Laird crammed two years of study into one year at a London tutorial college. She wrote that "no less than three of my teachers in that year succumbed to nervous breakdowns or other health-related problems—coincidence rather than consequence, I hope." After passing her "A-level" exams, Laird was accepted by the University of Bristol. "I was to spend three of the happiest years of my life [there]," she wrote. Before starting college, Laird went to the United States for five months to get to know her father's twin sisters who had emigrated there in 1947. One of her aunts had married William Castle, the producer of *Rosemary's Baby* and other thrillers; staying in Beverly Hills with the Castles was, Laird acknowledged, "a dizzying experience" and "enough to spoil an impressionable eighteen-year-old for life!" Since her first visit, Laird has traveled elsewhere in America, including the Grand Canyon. "Few other places have made such a deep and lasting impression on me," she wrote.

In 1963, Laird began her course work at the University of Bristol. On her first day of classes, she met Nigel Laird, whom she would eventually marry. "Not that it was love at first sight, exactly," the author recalled in *SAAS*. "Love works in mysterious ways, and it took a good many shared classes, enough cups of coffee to float a battleship, and several months of sitting around in various bars for me to subtly persuade Nigel to persuade me that he was the man who should share my life." During her three years at university, Laird "lived in a constant state of exhilaration," she wrote in *SAAS*. She

enjoyed her classes, had a rich social life, traveled extensively in France and Germany, and became one of the early members of Amnesty International. After graduation, Nigel Laird went to teach in Austria as preparation for a career as a specialist in modern languages, while Christa went to the University of Exeter in Devon—the county in which she had spent her blissful summer holidays—to earn her degree in social work. Laird wrote that she "never seriously considered any career other than social work.... I *do* regret not having better career advice at that point."

After completing her degree, Laird became a child care officer, a social worker who worked with families and children. For her first post, she returned to Bristol, where Nigel was earning his post-graduate teaching qualification. In 1968, they married and settled in Coventry, a city that Laird described in *SAAS* as "famous for its wholesale destruction in World War Two and for the remarkable new cathedral built, in the spirit of reconciliation, alongside the shattered ruins of the old." While living in Coventry, the Lairds had two sons, Julian and Adam. After Julian's birth, Laird found that she adored her son but, as she noted in her *SAAS* essay, "he was not quite articulate enough at age one and a half to satisfy even my admittedly modest intellectual requirements." She continued, "So it was to fill a certain void that while he was taking his morning nap, I started to write my first novel." Directed to adults, the story describes a female terrorist, hospitalized after an injury, who develops a relationship with a social worker who has been assigned to protect her. "I expect," Laird offered, "the social worker was far too transparently 'me'"; the novel, she noted, "malingers to this day at the bottom of a drawer somewhere because last time I had a clear out I couldn't bring myself to throw it in the bin! I am mildly intrigued by this because I *have* succeeded in jettisoning manuscripts which have taken just as much time and effort to produce; perhaps it is because the idea of the 'good' terrorist is one which continues to fascinate me, both from an ethical and an aesthetic point of view. It makes one consider the gulf between public and private virtue, which has always struck me as one of *the* most interesting moral issues of our day."

In 1972, Nigel Laird was accepted as an schoolmaster at an independent school for boys in Oxford. Five years later, with her sons in nursery school, Christa was, as she wrote in *SAAS,* "ready to meet a fresh challenge." That, she decided, should be writing. "In a vague and visionless way ... I had always wanted to write," she explained. Despite her training in the social sciences, Laird admitted that her heart "belongs much more to languages and literature." She decided to return to her degree subject, German, to do literary research. In addition, as she noted in her essay, Laird was "fascinated by the subject of oppression and responses to it; the obvious solution seemed to be to combine these strands of interest and to write a thesis on a specific aspect of the German literary response to Nazism." Laird completed a thesis on fascist mentality in the works of German novelists Gunter Grass and Siegfried Lenz and received her B.Litt (now changed to M.Litt) from Oxford. She did some general literature teaching part-time and also returned to social work. However, while she was working on her research degree, Laird had come across a reference to Janusz Korczak, a heroic Polish Jew who was a pediatrician, writer, educator, broadcaster, and social worker. When the Nazis sealed off the Warsaw Ghetto in 1940, Korczak took two hundred children into its confines from an orphanage that he managed, and he tried to guarantee them safety as well as some quality of life. When the Nazis deported the children to the death camp of Treblinka, Korczak was offered the chance of a reprieve, but he is said to have replied, "Desertion is not in my vocabulary." Instead, he went with the children to his death. Laird realized that she needed to tell Korczak's story; in researching it, she discovered that "the sacrificial manner of Korczak's death was but an extension of his entire way of life."

Written while she worked full-time as a locum training officer, Laird's first book, *Shadow of the Wall,* was published in 1989. The novel is set in wartime Poland and tells the story of a fourteen-year-old Jewish boy, Misha Edelman, who lives with his two sisters in one of Janusz Korczak's orphanages in the Warsaw Ghetto. Misha, whose father is dead and whose mother is dying of tuberculosis, at great personal risk, tries to bring food and medicine to his mother from the other side of the wall. In the streets, he sees shootings and beatings as well as the effects of disease and starvation. In the orphanage, he sees Korczak struggle to provide the children with a haven of love and support. As life at the orphanage becomes ever more difficult and prospects for survival weaken, Misha and Korczak smuggle the boy's infant sister to the home of a gentile family. Mrs. Edelman dies soon after, and Misha, who then joins a resistance group, watches as Korczak marches at the head of the line of children bound for Treblinka. Among this group is the boy's other sister. After the train departs, Misha escapes from the ghetto through a sewer. *Shadow of the Wall* was praised as a gripping, heart-rending book that reflects Laird's smooth, skillful interweaving of true story and fictional narrative. Writing in *Horn Book,* Hanna B. Zeiger claimed that the interwoven stories are "a testament to the courage of those who survived as well as those who died," while Adrian Jackson of *Books for Keeps* declared, "The scene where the Doctor leads the children onto the train for Treblinka is etched in my mind." Writing in *Growing Point,* Margery Fisher commented, "A book like this can be an effective sermon against war and, more valuably, a proclamation of the strength of the human spirit." Betsy Hearne of *Bulletin of the Center for Children's Books* concluded that *Shadow of the Wall* "serves as bearable context for any young person exploring the important question of how the Holocaust could have happened." In 1992, Laird received the Janus Korczak Literary Award for *Shadow of the Wall.*

Laird followed the success of *Shadow of the Wall* with a second novel, *The Forgotten Son.* Published in 1990 and set in the twelfth century, this work features Peter Astrolabe, the fourteen-year-old son of the famous French scholars Abelard and Heloise. The couple married secretly after the birth of their son. When their union came to light, Abelard was emasculated and became a monk, while Heloise complied with Abelard's wishes and became a nun; their famous exchange of letters on love and suffering led to a popularization of their story as a romantic tragedy. Handed over to Abelard's sister at four months, Peter searches to discover the facts about his birth. His quest leads him to a new awareness, both about his identity and about the social forces that destroyed his parents. Calling the book "warm-hearted and moving," Margery Fisher of *Growing Point* noted that the forgotten boy of eight hundred years ago "can be understood by young readers in the 'teens today because his problem is not unlike that of any youth caught in the complexities of a broken family." *School Librarian* contributor Frank Warren agreed, noting that *The Forgotten Son* will "perhaps have added cogency for any readers who feel parental neglect or who are experiencing some sort of crisis in relation to personal identity." L. Atterton of *Books for Your Children* asserted: "The heart breaks for Heloise, for the honesty, passion, and unselfishness of her love [in this] exquisitely detailed and moving emotional awakening . . . ." Writing in *SAAS,* Laird noted, "The challenge for me was to find a fresh perspective on an ancient story, which has been retold by many writers and artists over the centuries, so the discovery that the lovers did actually have a son, about whom very little is known, was a gift." Laird enthused, "I loved writing *The Forgotten Son;* it is my favorite of the three books so far and, my family and I believe, the best, although it has done much less well in terms of sales than the others. Perhaps that is because the subject matter is less accessible or dramatic than the Holocaust—or perhaps our judgement is simply wrong."

After completing *The Forgotten Son,* Laird began writing a novel for adults about Misha, the protagonist of her first book, *Shadow of the Wall.* This sequel featured the character as a grown-up, and it contained little reference to its predecessor, except, the author wrote in *SAAS,* "through a few flashbacks, to his experiences after escaping from the ghetto." However, her publishers demanded a rewrite, so Laird focused on Misha's life after he left the Warsaw Ghetto. The result was *But Can the Phoenix Sing?,* a story for young people published in 1993. Laird takes Misha through experiences as a partisan in the forests of eastern Poland through his return to Warsaw, where he works as a courier for the underground resistance, to his capture by the Wehrmacht after the Warsaw Uprising of 1944. The novel also describes Misha's experience as a POW in Germany—always hiding his identity as a Jew—as well as his liberation and relocation to England. *But Can the Phoenix Sing?* includes tragedy: Misha's lover, Eva, a girl who leads him to the partisan group in the Parczew forest, is killed, and so are her twin brother and the doctor who is their friend. Laird frames the story through Misha's relationship with his teenage stepson, Richard. Now a teacher, Misha writes his story in a letter to Richard, who by now is estranged from his stepfather and has been involved in an anti-Semitic prank. Richard comments on the main narrative in letters to his girlfriend. Through Misha's letter, Richard gains both an understanding of his stepfather and realizations about himself. Writing in the *School Librarian,* Audrey Baker called *Phoenix* "much more than an adventure or war story," while Peter D. Sieruta of *Horn Book* predicted that "it is the intense, horrifying scenes of wartime struggle that will continue to burn in the reader's mind." Betsy Hearne of *Bulletin of the Center for Children's Books* also noted the intensity of the book, describing it as "undiluted by either the stepson's occasional outbursts in letters to a girlfriend ... or by the kind of historical explanation that occasionally marked the previous book." Hearne concluded that it is "a tribute to Laird's research that she has so completely absorbed factual information into the depth of a story." Writing in *Booklist,* Hazel Rochman commented, "What's splendid about this story is the account of the partisans.... Teens will be held by Misha's haunting discovery that cruelty and tenderness can co-exist 'not just in one culture or country ... but in one person even.'"

Writing in *SAAS,* Laird noted that both *Shadow of the Wall* and *But Can the Phoenix Sing?* are "about courageous responses to oppression, about human resilience and different sorts of courage, all themes which have fascinated me since my teens, perhaps because of my own pre-history." The author's two aunts were active in the Dutch Resistance in Amsterdam, and her grandparents concealed Allied airmen and weapons in their home, despite the fact that, as Laird commented, "my grandfather, archetypally Jewish to look at, lived in virtual seclusion at the top of the house and could ill-afford to run extra risks." She continued, "I remain fascinated by the quality of courage in its thousand manifestations, and haunted by the question of whether I could ever rise to the challenge, as my family did, of putting my own life at risk for the sake of others. At the end of *Shadow of the Wall,* I have written a brief outline of Korczak's life and have gone on to say: 'If these stories of love and horror have one message for those of us who live in happier circumstances, it is surely one of humility; for none of us knows the limits—good or evil, moral or physical—of which we are capable, until put to the test.'" Laird mused that good and evil can be found "in lots of different packages, and sometimes the packaging obscures their true character, so that they are not always immediately recognizable.... [I]t is worth remembering that one person's terrorist is often another person's freedom fighter. If there are such things as moral absolutes, they are elusive creatures, and typically easier to identify on someone else's territory than on one's own. These are some of the questions that have preoccupied me over the years, and, having no answers which are remotely satisfactory, I have tried instead to work them in some way into my books."

Works Cited

Atterton, J., review of *The Forgotten Son, Books for Your Children,* summer, 1991, p. 24.

Baker, Audrey, review of *But Can the Phoenix Sing?, School Librarian,* February, 1994, p. 31.

Fisher, Margery, review of *The Forgotten Son, Growing Point,* March, 1991, pp. 5484-85.

Fisher, Margery, review of *Shadow of the Wall, Growing Point,* September, 1989, p. 5213.

Hearne, Betsy, review of *But Can the Phoenix Sing?, Bulletin of the Center for Children's Books,* November, 1995, pp. 96-97.

Hearne, Betsy, review of *Shadow of the Wall, Bulletin of the Center for Children's Books,* May, 1990, p. 217.

Jackson, Adrian, review of *Shadow of the Wall, Books for Keeps,* March, 1991, p. 9.

Laird, Christa, essay in *Something about the Author Autobiography Series,* Volume 26, Gale, 1998, pp. 117-32.

Rochman, Hazel, review of *But Can the Phoenix Sing?, Booklist,* November 15, 1995, p. 548.

Sieruta, Peter D., review of *But Can the Phoenix Sing?, Horn Book,* March-April, 1996, p. 210.

Warren, Frank, review of *The Forgotten Son, School Librarian,* May, 1991, p. 72.

Zeiger, Hanna B., review of *Shadow of the Wall, Horn Book,* September-October, 1990, p. 604.

—Sketch by Gerard J. Senick

*   *   *

LENT, John 1948-

Personal

Born July 8, 1948, in Antigonish, Nova Scotia; son of Harry and Adrienne (Brown) Lent; married Jude Clarke, 1981. *Education:* University of Alberta, B.A. (with honors), 1969, M.A., 1971; doctoral coursework at York University, 1971-75.

Addresses

Home—2401 26th St., Vernon, British Columbia V1T 4T3, Canada. *Office*—Okanagan University College, 7000 College Way, Vernon, British Columbia V1B 2N5, Canada. *Agent*—c/o Thistledown Press, 633 Main St., Saskatoon, Saskatchewan S7H 018, Canada. *Electronic mail*—jlent@junction.net.

Career

Okanagan University College, Kelowna, British Columbia, Canada, professor of literature and creative writing, 1979—. Writer of poetry, fiction, non-fiction, and scholarly essays. *Member:* Writers Union of Canada, Associated Writing Programs-U.S.A.

Awards, Honors

Canada Council Doctoral Fellowship, 1971-73; Banff Centre Writing Fellowship, 1993; extended study leaves for writing, in Strasbourg, France, 1988, and in Edinburgh, Scotland, 1994.

John Lent

Writings

A Rock Solid, Dreadnaught Press (Toronto), 1978.
Wood Lake Music, Harbour Publishing (Vancouver), 1982.
Frieze, Thistledown Press (Saskatoon, Saskatchewan, Canada), 1984.
The Face in the Garden, Thistledown Press, 1990.
Monet's Garden, Thistledown Press, 1996.

Work in Progress

So It Won't Go Away, short fiction, and *Who Needs You,* a novel.

Sidelights

Canadian writer and teacher John Lent is the author of several volumes of poetry and prose, including *A Rock Solid, Wood Lake Music,* and *Frieze.*

Lent's *The Face in the Garden* is a novel of sorts, with two parts written in prose and the final part in verse. The plot revolves around a young man's efforts to comprehend his family history and current situation. He desires to understand his father and his own role as a man and to express his true self. In a collective review in *Canadian Literature,* John LeBlanc noted similar themes in the work *Wishbone* by Reg Silvester and *Working without a Laugh Track* by Fred Stenson. "Writing, in varying degrees, about the problems of their gender, these writers illustrate how much these problems are a matter of how our major forms of aesthetic practice, although male-dominated, are still inefficacious in expressing male feeling."

Because the protagonist's efforts to become a writer are also a focus in *The Face in the Garden,* the novel is "thinly disguised autobiography," noted LeBlanc. The style of the novel is impressionist in that it tries to present the chaotic nature of reality without being obliterated by that chaos. Thus a more straightforward narrative degenerates into poetry by the novel's end. "The work, bravely attempting to break out into the world, ends up being more withdrawn," concluded LeBlanc. "This is not an easy book," declared Elinor Kelly in a review for *Canadian Materials.*

Nineteen-ninety-six's *Monet's Garden* is a collection of linked stories that feature an unnamed narrator. In an online review at a *John Lent* website, Craig McLuckie stated that "Lent's postmodern structure dramatizes an ongoing disintegration and recuperation of self." McLuckie concluded that "*Monet's Garden* has an appeal to artists, writers, musicians and especially to the general reading public because of its stress on the joys and freshness to be found in day-to-day existence." According to Katheryn Broughton in *Canadian Materials,* the book "explore[s] family dynamics in the marriage of Charles and Colette, as well as in the lives of their three eldest children." Broughton believed that "readers ... who hope to sharpen their perceptions and discover a new way of looking at life through fiction, will emerge moved and eminently satisfied."

Lent once commented: "I have been living and writing in the Okanagan Valley of British Columbia now for twenty years and, in that sense, partly because of my commitment to this place, and partly because of certain aesthetics concerning place that I have naturally inherited from writers like Lowry and Joyce, my work has a strong, and, I hope, rich regional texture to it. That work is regional in another way, too, considering that my published work, both poetry and fiction, has surfaced through the dynamics and limitations of small rather than large publishing houses. I feel, however, that it is the vision in these works—especially my exploration of subjectivity and place—that grants it qualities that are not simply regional, but contemporary and international in every sense of those words. I am fascinated by how we attempt to see the world through our landscape/place and through our consciousness, and my hope is that I will unearth increasingly refined but accessible forms in fiction that will carry that vision."

Works Cited

Broughton, Katheryn, review of *Monet's Garden, Canadian Materials,* November 1, 1996.
Kelly, Elinor, review of *The Face in the Garden, Canadian Materials,* March 1, 1991, p. 128.
LeBlanc, John, "Male Expression," *Canadian Literature,* summer, 1992, pp. 179-81.
McLuckie, Craig, review of *Monet's Garden,* March, 1997, unpublished manuscript, available online: lentm cluckie2.html.

M–N

MANDEL, Brett H. 1969-

Personal

Born May 10, 1969, in Philadelphia, PA; son of Stephan (a manufacturer's representative) and Sharyn (a secretary; maiden name, Weissman; present surname, Dershovitz) Mandel; married Laura Weinbaum. *Education:* Hamilton College, B.A., 1991; University of Pennsylvania, M.G.A., 1993. *Politics:* Democrat. *Religion:* Jewish. *Hobbies and other interests:* Sports, politics.

Addresses

Home—2210 St. James St., Philadelphia, PA 19103. *Office*—City Controllers Office, 12th Floor MSB, 1401 Arch St., Philadelphia, PA 19102. *E-mail*—brett@libertynet.org.

Career

Philadelphia Independent Charter Commission, Philadelphia, PA, assistant policy director, 1992-94; Pennsylvania Economy League, Philadelphia, associate, 1994-96; City of Philadelphia, assistant city controller, 1996—. *Member:* Big Brothers/Big Sisters. Phi Beta Kappa.

Writings

Minor Players, Major Dreams, University of Nebraska Press (Lincoln, NE), 1997.
Philadelphia: A New Direction, Saint Joseph's University (Philadelphia, PA), 1999.

Sidelights

Brett H. Mandel once commented: "The idea that launched whatever writing career I have came to me as an inspiration to mix my love of baseball and desire to do more than play in a Sunday league with my need to find a job since my then-current job was ending. I came up with the idea to convince a minor league team to sign me to a player's contract for a season, so I could write a book on the minor league experience and tell the inside story of the young men who were chasing their dreams in the minor leagues. After ten months of phone calls and hard work, I was able to convince the Ogden Raptors of the Pioneer Rookie League to accept the idea and let me on board for their inaugural season. I really enjoyed the freedom to express my thoughts in a book format and hope I was able to convey everything I experienced to readers.

"My experience writing my first book and writing about minor league baseball probably does not describe the usual writing process. I typed away on a laptop computer while enduring fifteen-hour road trips on the team bus. One happy side effect was that the other players allowed me to spread across two seats so I could have enough elbow room. When not typing on the bus, I typed away in front of a television tuned into *Headline News.* I found that it was just enough distraction to give me a break whenever I wanted to look up, but enough repetition that I could tune it out when I needed to work. I was pretty much manic about the need to put something on paper (or on disk, I guess) and religiously typed for at least two hours each day for the seventy-seven days of the season. At the end of the season, I had over four-hundred pages of single-spaced text that I spent three months crafting into a story—again, with *Headline News* as background. Try it. Not only does it provide neutral background noise, but you'll never be more up on current events."

In a review of *Minor Players, Major Dreams, Booklist* critic Wes Lukowsky called the title "a fine baseball book," commenting on the unromanticized picture of minor league baseball that Mandel presents: "The money is poor, and the odds are stacked against the young players, most of whom, he notes incredulously, are unaware of the unique opportunity they've been given." A *Publishers Weekly* reviewer had equal praise for Mandel's book, stating, "when he's describing the games, or the ballparks, or the surprise of seeing Red Sox great Luis Tiant take the field as an opposing pitching coach.... Mandel makes an appropriate and likeable spy."

Works Cited

Lukowsky, Wes, review of *Minor Players, Major Dreams,* *Booklist,* February 15, 1997, p. 993.

Review of *Minor Players, Major Dreams, Publishers Weekly,* December 9, 1996, p. 53.

For More Information See

PERIODICALS

Library Journal, February 1, 1997, p. 82.

* * *

MARGOLIS, Jeffrey A. 1948-

Personal

Born July 13, 1948, in Philadelphia, PA; son of Alex H. and Sara B. (Schwartz) Margolis; married Ida R. Moskowitz, June 14, 1970; children: Jamibeth. *Education:* Temple University, B.S. Ed., 1970; Rowan University, M.A., 1975. *Politics:* Independent. *Hobbies and other interests:* Travel, "scripopholy," fishing.

Addresses

Home—304 North Lafayette Ave., Ventnor, NJ 08406. *Office*—687 Route 9, Cape May, NJ 08204. *E-mail*—Jamcounsel@aol.com

Career

Lower Cape May Regional School District, Cape May, NJ, guidance counselor, 1987—. Richard Stockton College of New Jersey, adjunct faculty member, 1986-95. Bethel Investment Club, vice-president. *Military service:* U.S. Army, 1970-76. *Member:* National Education Association, New Jersey Counseling Association, Phi Delta Kappa (past president).

Writings

On Your Own, privately printed, 1991.
Teen Crime Wave: A Growing Problem, Enslow, 1997.
Violence in Sports: Victory at What Price?, Enslow, 1999.

Sidelights

Jeff A. Margolis comments: "The focus of my writing has been to provide information and resources for young people. Having been a professional educator in both public schools and colleges, I believe that I have a pulse on material that is of high interest, yet of a readability level that most junior and senior high school students can understand.

"An informed and educated public is better able to understand the problems that plague our society today, like juvenile crime. With that understanding comes the hope that readers will begin to give critical thought to these problems and find ways to deal with them."

Teen Crime Wave, Margolis's contribution to Enslow's "Issues in Focus" series, explores the startling rise in juvenile crime in America during the 1980s and 1990s. The book provides young adult readers with "information helpful for reports and projects," according to reviewer Anne O'Malley in *Booklist.* "Margolis studies the teen crime phenomenon," O'Malley noted, "offering a solidly researched array of causes underlying the crisis, as well as a clearly detailed trip through the juvenile justice system...." A *Kirkus Reviews* critic called *Teen Crime Wave* a "thought-provoking book," citing a shocking statistic presented in Margolis's study: between 1983 and 1992, the number of juveniles arrested for homicide increased 128 percent, compared with a 9 percent increase in adults arrested for the same crime during that same period.

"My writings to date have been research-based," acknowledges Margolis, "with the frequent use of stories that are relevant to the material being presented. In the future I hope to continue with this style of writing and to make public appearances to interested civic and school

Jeffrey A. Margolis's informational book explores the startling rise in juvenile crime in America. (Cover photo by Eric R. Berndt.)

groups. I want to help facilitate a community-wide dialogue in an effort to find solutions to contemporary problems."

Works Cited

O'Malley, Anne, review of *Teen Crime Wave, Booklist,* August, 1997, p. 1889.

Review of *Teen Crime Wave, Kirkus Reviews,* June 1, 1997, p. 878.

For More Information See

PERIODICALS

School Library Journal, September, 1997, p. 228.

*   *   *

MASSIE, Elizabeth

Personal

Hobbies and other interests: Camping and cattle rustling.

Addresses

Agent—c/o Pocket Books, 1230 Avenue of the Americas, New York, NY 10020.

Career

Writer.

Awards, Honors

Bram Stoker Award for best novelette, Horror Writers Association, 1991, for "Stephen," and for best first novel, 1993, for *Sineater.*

Writings

FOR CHILDREN

1870: Not With Our Blood (Young Founders, No. 1), Demco Media, 1998.

(With Barbara Spilman Lawson) *Jambo, Watoto!* (picture book), illustrated by Marsha Heatwole, Creative Arts Press, 1998.

Dreams of the Dark, Harper, in press.

"DAUGHTERS OF LIBERTY" SERIES

Patsy's Discovery, Pocket Books/Minstrel (New York City), 1997.

Patsy and the Declaration, Pocket Books/Minstrel, 1997.

Barbara's Escape, Pocket Books/Minstrel, 1997.

FOR YOUNG ADULTS

Maryland: Ghost Harbor, Z-Fave, 1995.

FOR ADULTS; HORROR

Sineater (novel), Carroll & Graf (New York City), 1994.

In this installation in Elizabeth Massie's "Daughters of Liberty" trilogy, two girls living in Philadelphia during the American Revolution form the Daughters of Liberty to help the colonies gain their freedom. (Cover illustration by Ernie Norcia.)

Southern Discomfort: The Selected Works (short stories), introduction by Yvonne Navarro, photographs by H. E. Fassl, Dark Regions Press, 1994.

Shadow Dreams (short stories), introduction by Gary A. Braunbeck, Silver Salamander Press (Seattle, WA), 1997.

Work represented in anthologies, including *Dead End: City Limits,* edited by Paul F. Olson and David B. Silva, St. Martin's Press (New York City), 1991; *Revelations,* edited by Douglas E. Winter, Harper Prism (New York City), 1997; and *Darkside: Horror for the Next Millennium,* edited by John Pelan, Darkside Press, 1996.

Sidelights

Elizabeth Massie is a writer of both horror fiction and children's books. Among her most significant works is *Sineater,* a horror tale that received the Horror Writers Association's Bram Stoker Award for best first novel in 1993. *Sineater* concerns Joel Barker, a Southern youth whose father has been chosen by a religious sect to live alone and bear upon himself the sins of the sect's dead members. As a consequence of his father's peculiar predicament, Joel finds himself alienated from others in the community. After a series of gruesome murders occur in town, deranged sect leader Missy Campbell accuses Joel's father of the crimes. But Joel and his only friend, Missy's son Burke, determine to find the true murderer. Their efforts, however, lead them to particularly alarming realizations. A *Publishers Weekly* reviewer stated that "Massie's sharp observations and eye for detail bring her characters to life and lend credence to the unfamiliar setting and bizarre plot."

Massie has also had collections of her horror stories published. *Southern Discomfort,* her first collection, includes such tales as "Hooked on Buzzer," which features a youth with an intense affinity for electricity; "Abed," in which a widow is pressured by her mother-in-law into having a child; and "The Sick'un," wherein a schoolteacher makes a startling discovery when she investigates student absences. *Locus* reviewer Edward Bryant called *Southern Discomfort* "effective" and "attractive" and described Massie's work as "sensual, frequently erotic, and hard-edged."

Shadow Dreams, Massie's second horror collection, features more memorably disturbing tales, including "Snow Day," which concerns a young girl with an unappealing mother; "I Am Not My Smell," which chronicles an impoverished woman's final hours; and "Sanctuary of the Shrinking Soul," which relates a mother's loss of her child. Hank Wagner, in an online review at *HorrorNet,* concluded that "*Shadow Dreams* is not perfect, but it does gather a number of superlative stories from an excellent writer."

Among Massie's writings for children is the "Daughters of Liberty" trilogy comprised of *Patsy's Discovery, Patsy and the Declaration,* and *Barbara's Escape.* These books, set in Philadelphia during the American Revolution, recount the exploits of two girls, Patsy Black and Barbara Layman. In the first book in the series, the two twelve-year-olds form the Daughters of Liberty to help the colonies gain their freedom, and the girls' first task is to deliver a secret note they find to the Continental Congress. Reviewing *Patsy's Discovery* in *School Library Journal,* Mary M. Hopf noted that "the strength of this book lies in Massie's vivid descriptions of clothing, buildings, and items used in the late 1700s." In a review that echoed Hopf's sentiments, Kay Weisman asserted in *Booklist* that "Massie's strengths are believable characters and careful attention to setting details."

The second and third volumes of the series continue the adventures of Patsy and Barbara. In *Patsy and the Declaration* the girls set out to solve the mystery of the fire at the blacksmith's shop, and in *Barbara's Escape* two British soldiers steal the wagon Barbara is hiding in and she has to escape before they reach the British camp.

Jambo, Watoto! is Massie's first picture book, written with Barbara Spilman Lawson and illustrated with watercolor paintings by Marsha Heatwole. In this story, four cheetah cubs are instructed by their mother to remain hidden in the grass while she hunts, but are tempted out by a series of interesting animals. According to Anne Stanton, editor of *ForeWord* magazine: "Children between the ages of four and eight will identify with the cheetahs' struggle between freedom and obedience and delight in the whimsical drawings and lively text infused with African words."

Works Cited

Bryant, Edward, review of *Southern Discomfort, Locus,* January, 1994, p. 49.

Hopf, Mary M., review of *Patsy's Discovery, School Library Journal,* August, 1997, p. 138.

Review of *Sineater, Publishers Weekly,* May 23, 1994, p. 79.

Stanton, Anne, review of *Jambo, Watoto!, ForeWord,* August, 1998.

Wagner, Hank, review of *Shadow Dreams, HorrorNet,* http://www.horrornet.com (1998).

Weisman, Kay, review of *Patsy's Discovery, Booklist,* December 1, 1997, p. 637.

For More Information See

PERIODICALS

Publishers Weekly, August 30, 1991, p. 67; June 2, 1997, p. 72.*

*   *   *

McGRATH, Barbara B(arbieri) 1953-

Personal

Born September 29, 1953, in Natick, MA; daughter of Albert and Dorothy Barbieri; married William M. McGrath, April 16, 1978; children: Emily M., William Louis. *Education:* Lasell College, A.A. *Politics:* "Unenrolled." *Religion:* Roman Catholic.

Addresses

Home and office—7 Jennings Pond Rd., Natick, MA 01760. *E-mail*—bbmcgrath@aol.com. *Agent*—Barbara Bruce Williams, Concord, MA.

Career

Writer. Also worked as preschool teacher. Currently lectures at elementary schools throughout the United States, speaking on the writing process and literacy. *Member:* Society of Children's Book Writers and Illustrators.

Awards, Honors

Teachers' Choice Award, 1994, for *The M&M's Brand Chocolate Candies Counting Book.*

Barbara B. McGrath

Writings

The M&M's Brand Chocolate Candies Counting Book, Charlesbridge Publishing (Watertown, MA), 1994.
More M&M Math, Scholastic, 1998.
The Cheerios Counting Book, illustrated by Rob Bolster and Frank Mazzola, Jr., Scholastic, 1998.
The Goldfish Counting Book, illustrated by Rob Bolster and Frank Mazzola, Dancing Star Books, 1998.
The Baseball Counting Book, Scholastic, 1999.
The Goldfish Fun Book, HarperCollins, 1999.

Contributor to local newspapers.

Sidelights

Barbara B. McGrath once commented: "I taught preschool for sixteen years while writing public-interest articles for local newspapers. Then I focused on making learning fun—using a 'fun' subject to make the lesson memorable. I use brand-name products to teach hands-on lessons."

For More Information See

PERIODICALS

Publishers Weekly, June 6, 1994, p. 64.
School Library Journal, September, 1998, p. 194.

MEYERS, Susan 1942-

Personal

Born November 5, 1942, in Brooklyn, NY; daughter of Palmer (a writer) and Helvia (Ostman) Thompson; married Stephen A. Meyers; children: Jessica Lauren. *Education:* University of California, Berkeley, A.B., 1965.

Addresses

Home—107 Cornelia Ave., Mill Valley, CA 94941.

Career

Writer. *Member:* Writers Guild, Society of Children's Book Writers and Illustrators (member, board of directors).

Awards, Honors

Winner in mystery category, *Calling All Girls* Prize Competition, Dodd, Mead, 1966, for *Melissa Finds a Mystery;* Gavel Awards certificate of merit, American Bar Association, 1973, for article "Legal Supermarkets"; Outstanding Science Book for Children, National Science Teachers Association-Children's Book Council (NSTA-CBC), 1980, for *The Truth about Gorillas,* and 1981, for *Pearson, a Harbor Seal Pup.*

Writings

FICTION

Melissa Finds a Mystery, Dodd, Mead, 1966.
The Cabin on the Fjord, illustrated by Trina Schart Hyman, Doubleday, 1968.
The Mysterious Bender Bones, illustrated by Ib Ohlsson, Doubleday, 1970.
Meg and the Secret Scrapbook, Troll, 1995.
Cricket Goes to the Dogs, Troll, 1995.

FICTION; "P. J. CLOVER, PRIVATE EYE" SERIES

The Case of the Stolen Laundry, Simon & Schuster, 1981.
. . . *Missing Mouse,* illustrated by Gioia Fiammenghi, Dutton, 1985.
. . . *Borrowed Baby,* illustrated by Fiammenghi, Dutton, 1988.
. . . *Halloween Hoot,* illustrated by Fiammenghi, Lodestar, 1990.

NONFICTION

The Truth about Gorillas, illustrated by John Hamberger, Dutton, 1980.
Pearson, a Harbor Seal Pup, photographs by Ilka Hartmann, Dutton, 1980.
Insect Zoo, Dutton, 1991.

OTHER

(With Joan Lakin) *Who Will Take the Children?: A New Custody Option for Divorcing Mothers and Fathers,* Bobbs-Merrill (Indianapolis, IN), 1983.

TROLL 0-8167-3578-6 / $2.95 US / $3.95 CAN little rainbow

Meg and the Secret Scrapbook
Susan Meyers

When Meg Kelly discovers an old scrapbook in the attic of her new home, she also finds the close friendships she has desired in Susan Meyers's book for middle-graders. (Cover illustration by Susan Tang.)

(With Denise Saavedra and Paula Radisich) *Vinculos,* Whittier College (Whittier, CA), 1986.

Contributor of book reviews and articles to magazines. West coast editor, *Enter* magazine.

Work in Progress

Everywhere Babies, illustrated by Marla Frazee, for Harcourt.

Sidelights

Unlike some children's-book authors, Susan Meyers absolutely, positively did *not* want to be a writer when she grew up. "My father wrote for a living and it looked to me like hard and frustrating work," she recalled to *SATA.* While she set her sights on becoming, in turn, a veterinarian, a zookeeper, an artist, and an actress, tradition won out and Meyers ended up following in her father's footsteps. With several books of both fiction and nonfiction to her credit, she weaves action and humor into both the picture books and novels she writes for

young readers. Describing Meyers's 1991 nonfiction book *Insect Zoo* in *Booklist,* reviewer Leone McDermott called the study of all manner of bugs and other creepy-crawlies "a fun way to learn about the insect world."

Born in 1942, Meyers spent much of her childhood outdoors. "I always had pets—dogs, cats, rabbits, hamsters, and even a goat," the author remembered. "But until I went to school and until my sister was born—both of which happened at about the same time—I didn't have many playmates. I had to learn to amuse myself and to spend time alone. I don't remember finding this especially difficult. In fact, to this day, I enjoy being by myself—at least part of the time." Some of Meyers's time alone was actually spent in the company of a good book—*Heidi, The Swiss Family Robinson, Black Beauty, David Copperfield, The Saturdays, Homer Price,* and *Nancy Drew* were some of her favorites. "Whenever I finished a book I enjoyed, I wanted to read another one exactly like it," she remembered.

Having a writer for a father proved to be a strong influence on Meyers. "Though I wasn't aware of it at the time," she said, "I know now that I learned a great deal about writing by listening to my father talk about the plots for the radio and television scripts he wrote." Her mother proved to be influential as well; a wonderful storyteller with a vivid imagination, Meyers's mother has been the inspiration behind her daughter's effort to weave that same magic into her own stories. "I want ... [readers] to find the characters I create so alive and so interesting that they wish they were inside the book living the story with them. Of course, I don't always succeed," Meyers admitted, "... but I never stop trying."

Meyers has discovered that, as is common with many authors, her books reflect aspects of her own life, even if she doesn't always intend it. "When I visited relatives in Norway," she recalled, "the country and the people seemed so interesting that I had to write about them. That was how *The Cabin on the Fjord* began." Similarly, *The Mysterious Bender Bones* was inspired by "a true story I heard about an anthropologist who kept valuable fossil bones locked in a suitcase under his bed." Meyers's nonfiction works have also been inspired by her wide-ranging interests, particularly her love of nature. For instance, the photo essay titled *Pearson, a Harbor Seal Pup,* which Meyers created with the help of photographer Ilka Hartmann, compassionately documents the efforts of the California Marine Mammal Center to return a seven-month-old orphaned seal to its natural coastal habitat. Meyers's story both describes "the valuable work of the Center [and] sheds light on harbor seals in general," asserted Barbara Elleman in *Booklist.* A reviewer for *Bulletin of the Center for Children's Books* praised the combination of "crisp, straightforward text" and "good quality photographs."

The Truth about Gorillas was inspired by the movie *King Kong,* which upset Meyers due to its portrayal of gorillas as fearsome and dangerous to humans. She set about writing her book in "an attempt to set the record straight," because of her opinion that gorillas have been "so much maligned and misunderstood." Meyers's book portrays the creatures as gentle vegetarians, and documents in detail their physique, forager habits, and life cycle. Designed for young readers, the book explains such things as the gorilla's "fearsome" look—caused by a protruding browbone—and the fact that some gorillas have even exhibited the ability to learn sign language. *The Truth about Gorillas* was characterized as "an informative, easy-to-read book" by *Horn Book* contributor Nancy D. Lyhne, while a *Kirkus Reviews* contributor found the work "a personable introduction" to the species.

While her nonfiction titles are guided by Meyers's interests, her fiction has been limited only by her imagination. Of particular interest to young readers have been her "P. J. Clover, Private Eye" books, which feature two fifth-grade girls who team up to solve mysteries. In *The Case of the Halloween Hoot,* a costly Russian urn goes missing from school, and P. J. and her friend set about clearing the name of the janitor accused of taking the antique. Praising Meyers's "spunky duo," *Booklist* reviewer Kay Weisman noted that the author "keeps her pace brisk and drops plenty of hints" for readers willing to pay attention. A critic for *Kirkus Reviews* added that with its concentration on "brainwork" rather than violence, the book serves as an "entertaining entry in one of the better mystery series for middle-grade readers."

"Working with words gives me great pleasure," Meyers explained, describing her work as a professional writer. "I enjoy making sentences, deciding which should be long and which should be short, and where the commas should go. I like searching for words and phrases that say exactly what I mean. What is more, I've discovered that when you are a writer, life is rarely boring. Characters and stories are everywhere. There is always some new and fascinating subject to explore. The boundaries of your world expand and life seems full of possibilities."

Works Cited

Elleman, Barbara, review of *Pearson, a Harbor Seal Pup, Booklist,* April 1, 1981, p. 1156.

Lyhne, Nancy D., review of *The Truth about Gorillas, Horn Book,* August, 1980, p. 429.

McDermott, Leone, review of *Insect Zoo, Booklist,* September 15, 1991, p. 144.

Review of *Pearson, a Harbor Seal Pup, Bulletin of the Center for Children's Books,* May, 1981, pp. 176-77.

Review of *P. J. Clover, Private Eye: The Case of the Halloween Hoot, Kirkus Reviews,* January 1, 1990, p. 48.

Review of *The Truth about Gorillas,* Kirkus Reviews, July 1, 1980, p. 835.

Weisman, Kay, review of *P. J. Clover, Private Eye: The Case of the Halloween Hoot, Booklist,* February 15, 1990, p. 1170.

For More Information See

PERIODICALS

Booklist, June 15, 1980, p. 1540.

Kirkus Reviews, July 1, 1980, p. 835; March 1, 1981, p. 286.

School Library Journal, September, 1980, p. 61; August, 1981, p. 69; July, 1990, p. 77.

*　　*　　*

MORRISON, Lillian 1917-

Personal

Born October 27, 1917, in Jersey City, NJ; daughter of William and Rebecca (Nehamkin) Morrison. *Education:* Douglass College, B.S., 1938; Columbia University, B.S. (library science), 1942. *Hobbies and other interests:* Folk rhymes, outdoor sports, jazz, dance, films, and the arts in general.

Addresses

Office—116 Pinehurst Ave., New York, NY 10033.

Lillian Morrison

Career

New York Public Library, New York City, young-adult librarian, 1942-47, in charge of work with vocational high-schools, 1947-52, assistant coordinator of young-adult services, 1952-68, coordinator of young-adult services, 1968-82. Rutgers, The State University of New Jersey, summer library-school instructor, 1961; Columbia University, New York City, lecturer on library-school faculty, 1962, 1963. *Member:* Authors League, Phi Beta Kappa, R.E.N. American Center.

Awards, Honors

100 Best Children's Books, New York Public Library, for *I Scream, You Scream: A Feast of Food Rhymes.*

Writings

POETRY

The Ghosts of Jersey City, Crowell, 1967.
(With Jean Boudin) *Miranda's Music,* illustrated by Helen Webber, Crowell, 1968.
The Sidewalk Racer, and Other Poems of Sports and Motion, Lothrop, 1977.
Who Would Marry a Mineral?: Riddles, Runes, and Love Tunes, illustrated by Rita Floden Leydon, Lothrop, 1978.
Overheard in a Bubble Chamber and Other Sciencepoems, illustrated by Eyre de Lanux, Lothrop, 1981.
The Break Dance Kids: Poems of Sport, Motion, and Locomotion, Lothrop, 1985.
Whistling the Morning In: New Poems, illustrated by Joel Cook, Wordsong (Honesdale, PA), 1992.

POETRY; COMPILER

Yours till Niagara Falls, Crowell, 1950.
Black within and Red Without: A Book of Riddles, illustrated by Jo Spier, Crowell, 1953.
A Diller, a Dollar: Rhymes and Sayings for the Ten O'clock Scholar, Crowell, 1955.
Touch Blue: Signs and Spells, Love Charms and Chants, Auguries and Old Beliefs, in Rhyme (folklore), illustrated by Doris Lee, Crowell, 1958.
Remember Me When This You See: A New Collection of Autograph Verses, illustrated by Marjorie Bauernschmidt, Crowell, 1961.
Sprints and Distances: Sports in Poetry and the Poetry in Sport, illustrated by Clare and John Rose, Crowell, 1965.
Best Wishes, Amen: A New Collection of Autograph Verses, illustrated by Loretta Lustig, Crowell, 1974.
Rhythm Road: Poems to Move To, Lothrop, 1988.
At the Crack of the Bat: Baseball Poems, illustrated by Steve Cieslawski, Hyperion, 1992.
Slam Dunk: Basketball Poems, illustrated by Bill James, Hyperion, 1995.
I Scream, You Scream: A Feast of Food Rhymes, illustrated by Nancy Dunaway, August House (Little Rock, AR), 1997.

General editor, Crowell "Poets" and "Poems of the World" series, 1964-74. Contributor of poems to *Prairie Schooner, Sports Illustrated, Atlantic Monthly, Poetry Northwest.*

Work in Progress

Way to Go: New and Selected Poems of Sports and Motion, original poetry.

Sidelights

Inspired by her interest in popular verse as a form of folklore and her exposure to the works of numerous poets during her years as a librarian for the New York Public Library, Lillian Morrison has compiled several anthologies of subject-related poetry and folk verse geared for younger readers. Her books range from collections of short poems suitable for memorizing and inscribing in friends' autograph albums—*Remember Me When This You See*—to volumes of poems about sports. In addition to her compilations, Morrison has written several complete books of original verse, each volume focusing on a specific area of interest. In her more recent anthologies, such as *At the Crack of the Bat: Baseball Poems,* the former librarian intersperses such classics as

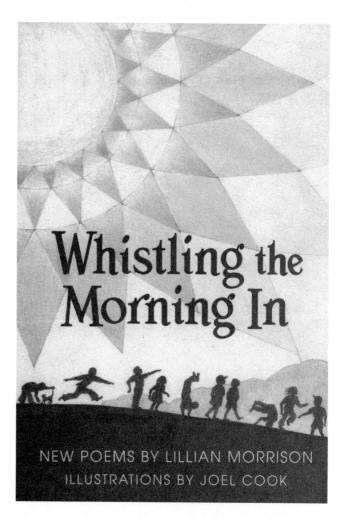

Morrison's collection of original poems focuses on nature and outdoor activities. (Cover illustration by Joel Cook.)

"Casey at the Bat" and "Take Me out to the Ball Game" with poems of her own invention. Zena Sutherland of *Bulletin of the Center for Children's Books* praised the book's "variety of style, form, mood, and subject," and its "unanimity of theme and high quality." *School Library Journal* contributor Renee Steinburg declared: "even those who don't look forward to opening day will be caught up in the excitement of the national pastime as chronicled in this varied volume."

Born in New Jersey in 1917, Morrison's childhood was full of the rhythms of the city: from the ebb and flow of traffic to the sing-song schoolyard chants sung to a game of jump rope. After graduating from high school and earning degrees from Douglass College and Columbia University, Morrison joined the staff of the New York Public Library in 1942. Once there, she quickly realized that she wanted to make books her life's work. Several decades after beginning her job, Morrison was appointed coordinator of young-adult services. Working with children on a daily basis put her in touch with the changing tastes and interests of young readers, and she began to look around for books that would serve as a bridge between poetry and readers who were rarely exposed to verse and whose tastes didn't often include a rhymed couplet. Morrison decided that the best way to introduce young people to poetry was to find poems on topics of interest to them. In 1965, after almost a decade of work, she published *Sprints and Distances: Sports in Poetry and the Poetry in Sport.* The volume is a collection of verse from both ancient and modern writers that reflects emotions young athletes—particularly young men, who tended to be least enamored of poetry to begin with—could identify with. "*Sprints and Distances* grew out of my feelings for sports and poetry both," Morrison once explained to *SATA*.

Morrison's collections of original poems include 1985's *The Break Dance Kids.* Supplementing her verse with illustrations, Morrison "capture[s] the immediacy of the body, and sometimes the mind, propelled into action and spurred on by the will to achieve," declared *Voice of Youth Advocates* critic Tony Manna in a review of the book. In her anthology *Slam Dunk: Basketball Poems,* as she had several years earlier with *At the Crack of the Bat,* Morrison intersperses poems of her own with the works of such authors as Jack Prelutsky, Walter Dean Myers, and May Swenson in a collection that received praise from *Booklist* contributor Carolyn Phelan as "a choice collection for those who find poetry in basketball, but don't expect to find basketball in poetry." The appearance in a poetry book of sports figures like Michael Jordan, Magic Johnson, and Shaquille O'Neal was bound to be a welcome surprise to reluctant readers attempting to tackle poetry for the first time, in the opinion of *School Library Journal* contributor Melissa Hudak.

From the world of sports, Morrison has broadened her focus to include science-fiction themes—*Overhead in a Bubble Chamber and Other Sciencepoems*—dance—*Rhythm Road: Poems to Move To*—and even food—*I Scream You Scream: A Feast of Food Rhymes.* In *I*

Morrison serves up a stew chock full of rhymes, chants, riddles, limericks, and rhyming jokes that all focus on something edible. (Cover illustration by Nancy Dunaway.)

Scream You Scream, Morrison serves up a stew chock-full of rhymes, chants, riddles, limericks, and rhyming jokes that all focus on something to do with edibles. True to its title, *Rhythm Road* contains over eighty poems guaranteed to have listeners moving to the beat of poets ranging from James Laughlin to Edgar Allan Poe. Another book featuring verses that almost dance off the page is *The Break Dance Kids: Poems of Sport, Motion, and Locomotion,* which *Voice of Youth Advocates* contributor Tony Manna maintained "cover[s] an impressive range of poetic types, forms, and content appropriate for readers of all ages who, once out of their armchairs and away from their desks, can make the poems come alive" through movement.

Behind each of Morrison's poetry collections is the desire to share her love of language with younger readers, and prove that poetry can speak to people on any number of levels, from basketball to boogie to blancmange. In Morrison's own poetry, she maintained, there is "always a strong kinetic feeling for me. Body movement seems to be involved. I am drawn to athletes, dancers, drummers, jazz musicians, who transcend misery and frustration and symbolize for us something joyous, ordered, and possible in life."

Works Cited

Hudak, Melissa, review of *Slam Dunk: Basketball Poems, School Library Journal,* November, 1995, p. 92.

Manna, Tony, review of *The Break Dance Kids: Poems of Sport, Motion, and Locomotion, Voice of Youth Advocates,* October, 1985, p. 278.

Manna, review of *Rhythm Road: Poems to Move To, Voice of Youth Advocates,* June, 1988, pp. 103-04.

Phelan, Carolyn, review of *Slam Dunk: Basketball Poems, Booklist,* October 1, 1995, p. 311.

Steinburg, Renee, review of *At the Crack of the Bat: Baseball Poems, School Library Journal,* June, 1992, p. 134.

Sutherland, Zena, review of *At the Crack of the Bat: Baseball Poems, Bulletin of the Center for Children's Books,* May, 1992, p. 243.

For More Information See

BOOKS

Hopkins, Lee Bennett, *Books Are by People,* Citation Press, 1969.

Sixth Book of Junior Authors and Illustrators, Wilson, 1989, pp. 199-200.

PERIODICALS

Booklist, September 1, 1985, p. 67; June 1, 1988, p. 1677; August, 1992, p. 2005; January 15, 1993, p. 901; November 15, 1997, p. 556.

Bulletin of the Center for Children's Books, April, 1988, p. 163.

Horn Book, May-June, 1993, pp. 303-06.

Kirkus Reviews, May 15, 1985, p. 48; March 1, 1988, p. 366.

New York Times Book Review, July 12, 1992, p. 23.

Quill & Quire, May, 1992, p. 36.

School Library Journal, August, 1985, p. 79; November, 1997, p. 95.

*   *   *

Thylias Moss

MOSS, Thylias (Rebecca) 1954-

Personal

Born February 27, 1954, in Cleveland, OH; daughter of a recapper for the Cardinal Tire Company and a maid; married John Lewis Moss (a business manager), July 6, 1973; children: Dennis, Ansted. *Education:* Attended Syracuse University, 1971-73; Oberlin College, B.A., 1981; University of New Hampshire, M.A., 1983.

Addresses

Office—P.O. Box 2686, Ann Arbor, MI 48106. *Agent*—Faith Hamlin, Sanford J. Greenburger Associates, 55 Fifth Ave., New York, NY 10003. *E-mail*—thyliasm@umich.edu.

Career

Poet and educator. The May Company, Cleveland, OH, order checker, 1973-74, data entry supervisor, 1974-75; junior executive auditor, 1975-79, Phillips Academy, Andover, MA, instructor, 1984-92; University of Michigan, Ann Arbor, assistant professor, 1993-94, associate professor, 1994-98, professor, 1998—. University of New Hampshire, Durham, visiting professor, 1991-92; Brandeis University, Waltham, MA, Fannie Hurst Poet, 1992. *Member:* Academy of American Poets.

Awards, Honors

Award from Cleveland Public Library Poetry Contest, 1978, for "Coming of Age in Sandusky"; four grants, Kenan Charitable Trust, 1984-87; artist's fellowship, Artist's Foundation of Massachusetts, 1987; grant, National Endowment for the Arts, 1989; Pushcart Prize, 1990; Dewar's Profiles Performance Artist Award in Poetry, 1991; Witter Bynner Prize, American Academy and Institute of Arts and Letters, 1991; Whiting Writer's award, 1991; Guggenheim fellowship, 1995; MacArthur fellowship, 1996; Best Book, *Village Voice,* 1998, and nomination, National Book Critics Circle Award, both for *Last Chance for the Tarzan Holler: Poems.*

Writings

POETRY

Hosiery Seams on a Bowlegged Woman, Cleveland State University Press (Cleveland, OH), 1983.

Pyramid of Bone, University of Virginia Press (Charlottesville, VA), 1989.

At Redbones, Cleveland State University Press, 1990.

Rainbow Remnants in Rock Bottom Ghetto Sky, Persea (New York City), 1991.

Small Congregations: New and Selected Poems, Ecco Press (Hopewell, NJ), 1993.

Last Chance for the Tarzan Holler: Poems, Persea, 1998.

OTHER

The Dolls in the Basement (play), produced by New England Theatre Conference, 1984.
Talking to Myself (play), produced in Durham, NH, 1984.
I Want to Be (for children), illustrated by Jerry Pinkney, Dial, 1993.
Tale of a Sky-Blue Dress (memoir), Avon, 1998.

ADAPTATIONS:

A selection of Moss's poems, read by the author, were recorded on an audiocassette titled *Larry Levis and Thylias Moss Reading Their Poems,* 1991.

Sidelights

Thylias Moss grew up the only child of doting parents in Cleveland, Ohio, met her future husband at age sixteen and has remained married to him ever since, and—though she grew up in working-class surroundings—has spent most of her adult life in the world of college English departments. Her later poetry collections have displayed a more relaxed state of mind, but Moss's early work is characterized by almost unremitting portraits of bitterness, anger, and despair.

Moss first won a poetry prize in 1978 for "Coming of Age in Sandusky." Her poems were collected for publication in 1983 as *Hosiery Seams on a Bowlegged Woman,* which was commissioned by Alberta Turner and Leonard Trawick of the Cleveland State University Poetry Center. Six years later came *Pyramid of Bone,* a volume written at the request of the University of Virginia's Charles Rowell. The book was a first runner-up in the National Book Critics Circle Award for 1989, and earned Moss praise from a reviewer in *Publishers Weekly* for her "rage and unyielding honesty." Reflecting on the difference between the author's life and her work, a critic in *Virginia Quarterly Review* observed: "If Thylias Moss's resume is sedate ... her poetry is anything but." The poems in *Pyramid* are full of disturbing images ("the vinegar she's become cannot sterilize the needle") and agonized statements ("The miracle was not birth but that I lived despite my crimes"), the critic noted.

Moss's third book, *At Redbones,* has a marginally less negative tone, and is also more faithful in its premise to the poet's upbringing. That premise is a mythical place called Redbones; part church and part bar, it serves as a refuge of sorts. Describing her own early influences, Moss cited the "explosions on Sundays" in church, when the preacher "made [the congregation] shout, made them experience glory that perhaps was not actually there .... I wanted to make what the preacher called 'text.'" Her other strong influence, she said, was akin to a bar, though she describes it as more of a schoolroom: the family kitchen on Saturday nights, where her father would sip whiskey and speak "mostly on the dialectics of the soul, asking the forbidden questions, giving words power over any taboo."

With the place called Redbones holding together the poems in her third book, Moss unites two salient influences from her childhood, but the effect is not necessarily—or even usually—comforting. Her images are of racism and brutality, a world in which the Ku Klux Klan is as ever-present as the laundry, and Christian faith offers no refuge: "Bottled Jesus is the / Clorox that whitens old sheets, makes the Klan / a brotherhood of saints." It is the world of sit-ins of the 1960s, when African Americans were denied service at the "whites-only" counters of Southern U.S. eating establishments, and sometimes beaten if they refused to give up their seats: "When knocked from the stool," she writes in "Lunchcounter Freedom," "my body takes its shape from what it falls into." This is a world rife with the old-fashioned racist imagery of Mammy in *Gone with the Wind,* of Buckwheat from *The Little Rascals* movies, of the Aunt Jemima logo on syrup bottles, her smiling face holding "Teeth white as the shock of lynching, thirty-two / tombstones," Moss writes.

Turning from race to religion, Moss describes a physical revulsion at the sacrament of Communion. In "Weighing the Sins of the World," receiving wine—Christ's symbolic blood—at the Eucharist, becomes a blood transfusion, and it turns out to be the wrong blood type, which is fatal. In "Fullness" she takes on, with similarly strong imagery, the literal substance (Christ's body) for which the bread of Communion is a symbol: "One day / the father will place shavings of his own blessed fingers / on your tongue and you will get back in line for / more. You will not find yourself out of line again. / The bread will rise inside you. A loaf of tongue."

The pun on "out of line" in the preceding quote illustrates Moss's facility with language, one of the elements of her poetry that earned her critical praise for *At Redbones.* Sue Standing of *Boston Review,* for instance, wrote enthusiastically that "if *At Redbones* were a light bulb, it would be 300 watt; if it were whiskey, it would be 200 proof; if it were a mule, it would have an awfully big kick." Gloria T. Hull in *Belles Lettres,* also reviewing *At Redbones* along with several other works by female African-American poets (including Maya Angelou), commented that "Thylias Moss is the youngest of this group ... and the one with whom I was most intrigued. She possesses absolutely stunning poetic skill.... [which] she unites with one of the bleakest, most sardonic visions I have ever encountered by an African-American woman writer." Marilyn Nelson Waniek in *Kenyon Review* was slightly more limited in her praise, but still found "a fine rage ... at play in these pages."

With *Rainbow Remnants in Rock Bottom Ghetto Sky,* Moss continues to explore race images, and also looks at menstruation, grandmothers, and history. With this volume, however, critics were less effusive in their praise. *Choice* reviewer H. Jaskoski said that the poems offer "predictable sentiments in unexceptional free verse," and that Moss "brings up the topics young black female poets seem expected to interpret." Mark Jarman in *Hudson Review* referred to poet Charles Simic's

I want to be all the people I know, then I want to know more
people so I can be them too. Then they can all be me.
I want to be a new kind of earthquake, rocking the world as if
it's a baby in a cradle.

As a little girl contemplates her future, she dreams of intriguing possibilities in Moss's lyrical picture book.
(From I Want to Be, *illustrated by Jerry Pinkney.*)

praise of Moss as a "visionary storyteller" but added, "but she tells no stories." Jarman also assailed Moss's use of strained metaphor: though he confessed to admire the "ambition" of her poems, he wrote that she showed "a kind of complacence in assuming that putting one thing on one side of an equals sign and one on another is imagination." In some cases, critics have seemed unwilling to allow Moss sufficient freedom as a poet, as when Jarman criticized her use of a colloquialism: "This is the first poet I have encountered who ... actually has used the word *hopefully* as it is currently employed, which is to say incorrectly."

Though *Rainbow Remnants in Rock Bottom Ghetto Sky* was met with some negative reviews, many other critics found much in the collection to praise. "Using intricately woven, well-crafted sentences, [Moss] writes accessible, sensual, feminist poems about pregnancy, bonding between women, and racial and ethnic identity," wrote Judy Clarence in *Library Journal.* Clarence added that "there's a sense of hopefulness, of the poet's and our individual ability to survive, even to rejoice, in a very imperfect world." A *Publishers Weekly* reviewer also praised the collection, declaring: "Moss refuses to accept things as they are.... [her] writing expertly simulates the processes of her fecund mind, with thoughts

overlapping and veering off on tangents that bring us back, with fuller knowledge, to a poem's central concern."

Prairie Schooner reviewer Tim Martin, who also praised *Rainbow Remnants in Rock Bottom Ghetto Sky,* commented that "readers who delight in originality of image, language, and the striking metaphor might be urged to read Moss. Several poems are tours de force of sheer description." Martin continued that the poet transforms everyday objects and chores into "startling new ways of seeing reality.... one gladly accepts as a good trade the occasional excess or lapse in exchange for the times she hits the mark and wakes us up with her use of language."

Small Congregations is a compilation drawn from the three preceding volumes and arranged into three sections. The collection's themes, according to Elizabeth Frost in *Women's Review of Books,* can be identified respectively as religious symbolism, the mythology of African-American life, and racist images. The familiar viewpoints on race and religion are combined in "The Adversary," wherein Moss expresses metaphorical sympathy for the devil as a sort of cosmic black man: "Poor Satan. His authority denied him / by a nose, a longer, pointier Caucasian nose. / Where's the gratitude for Satan who is there / for God no matter what; Satan / who is the original Uncle Tom." In her "Interpretation of a Poem by Frost," Moss both pays tribute to and parodies the poet Robert Frost's famous "Stopping by Woods on a Snowy Evening," which in her treatment becomes another instance of white racism: "A young black girl stopped by the woods, / so young she knew only one man: Jim Crow." But when Moss turns her vision away from God and whites, and inward toward the African-American home and hearth, the vision often becomes tender, as in "Remembering Kitchens": "... and I remove Mama's sweet potato pie, one made / —as are her best—in her sleep when she can't / interfere, when she's dreaming at the countertop / that turns silk beside her elegant leaning, I slice it / and put the whipped cream on quick, while the pie / is so hot the peaks of cream will froth; these / are the Sundays my family suckles grace."

With *I Want to Be,* a book for children illustrated by Jerry Pinkney, Moss took a new and refreshing direction. As a little African-American girl walks home, thinking about the question often asked by adults— "What do you want to be when you grow up?"—she finds in herself some intriguing answers: "I want to be quiet but not so quiet that nobody can hear me. I also want to be sound, a whole orchestra with two bassoons and an army of cellos. Sometimes I want to be just the triangle, a tinkle that sounds like an itch." Though reviewers worried that these metaphors might be a bit challenging for young readers, for adults they are much more comprehensible than those found in Moss's earlier work. The book, which suggests a different and fascinating side of Moss, found praise with critics. "The untrammeled exuberance of a free-spirited youngster, eager to explore everything, sings through a poetic story," wrote a critic for *Kirkus Reviews,* later calling the work "exhilarating, verbally and visually: the very essence of youthful energy and summertime freedom."

Moss continued her success as a poet with *Last Chance for the Tarzan Holler,* which reviewer Fred Muratori, in *Library Journal,* called "a massive, acid-edged tribute to mortality in all of its contradictions and wrenching ironies." In this collection, which was nominated for the National Book Critics Circle Award and named a "Best Book of 1998" by the *Village Voice,* Moss seeks to "finish knowing herself / in time to begin to know something else," touching such topics as sexuality, religion, and motherhood. In his *Library Journal* review, Muratori called the work "loquacious and impassioned, precise and ragged, willing to risk even boredom in its drive to get at the heart of humanity's conflicted, necessary obsessions." A *Publishers Weekly* reviewer commented, "Moss meditates, starkly and unsentimentally, on death and motherhood, on God, and, beneath them all, on sex and power." Calling the collection's poems "unflinching" and "brilliant," reviewer Donna Seaman, in a piece for *Booklist,* called it "a book of extraordinary range."

Moss's second book to appear in 1998, *Tale of a Sky-Blue Dress,* marked a departure from her previous works. This book, a memoir of the author's childhood, recounts the physical, emotional, and sexual abuse Moss endured as a child at the hands of her babysitter, a teenage girl living in the same apartment building. The book opens with descriptions of a comfortable childhood, adoring parents, and domestic and familial rituals. The warmth of such scenes diminishes, however, when Moss's new babysitter introduces the child to humanity's dark side. The sitter, Lytta Dorsey, frequently wears a blue dress that is several sizes too small and displays an emotionally disturbed mind to her small charge. Moss, seeking to protect her loving parents from distress, endured the abuse for four years, and never told them of the tortures she was forced to submit to. She also relates in the book that she was "fascinated with the pull of darkness," according to a reviewer for *Booklist.* Moss writes that Lytta gave her "the gift of darkness" in her life, a life in which her parents had kept her wrapped in a blanket of wonder, protection, and comfort. According to *Detroit Free Press* writer Barbara Holliday, "she thinks perhaps the novelty of cruelty made it exciting." "Is it true," writes Moss in *Tale of a Sky-Blue Dress,* "that I would not be a writer, if not for Lytta?" adding however, "I am not ready to admit to her necessity in my life."

Eventually raped by her tormentor's brother with his sister's encouragement, Moss entered adolescence troubled by the abuses she had suffered. She was drawn into relationships with men that mimicked her abusive relationship with Lytta and undermined her self-esteem. Finally, at the age of sixteen, Moss met a young air force sergeant whose patient understanding and love helped her move beyond the pain of her childhood.

Tale of a Sky-Blue Dress received positive recognition from reviewers. A *Kirkus Reviews* critic called the book "an elegant, forthright exploration of the effects of evil on a fragile life" and "a stylish, well-wrought memoir that forgoes self-pity for redemption." "This is a story that reads like poetry, even when the memories are the bleakest," declared *Tribune Books* writer Sharman Stein. *New York Times Book Review* critic Paula Friedman commented that "her analysis of her own surrender is impressive in its depth and unwillingness to settle for the simple role of victim."

Works Cited

Clarence, Judy, review of *Rainbow Remnants in Rock Bottom Ghetto Sky, Library Journal,* May 15, 1991, p. 86.

Friedman, Paula, review of *Tale of a Sky-Blue Dress, New York Times Book Review,* September 13, 1998, p. 26.

Frost, Elizabeth, review of *Small Congregations: New and Selected Poems, Women's Review of Books,* March, 1994, pp. 11-12.

Holliday, Barbara, "From Childhood Horror, a Writer Emerges," *Detroit Free Press,* 1998.

Hull, Gloria T., review of *At Redbones, Belles Lettres,* spring, 1991, p. 2.

Review of *I Want to Be, Kirkus Reviews,* August 1, 1993, p. 1006.

Jarman, Mark, review of *Rainbow Remnants in Rock Bottom Ghetto Sky, Hudson Review,* spring, 1992, pp. 163-64.

Jaskoski, H., review of *Rainbow Remnants in Rock Bottom Ghetto Sky, Choice,* February, 1992, p. 896.

Review of *Last Chance for the Tarzan Holler: Poems, Publishers Weekly,* February 23, 1998, p. 69.

Martin, Tim, review of *Rainbow Remnants in Rock Bottom Ghetto Sky, Prairie Schooner,* summer, 1994, p. 156.

Moss, Thylias, *I Want to Be,* Dial, 1993.

Muratori, Fred, review of *Last Chance for the Tarzan Holler: Poems, Library Journal,* February 15, 1998, p. 146.

Review of *Pyramid of Bone, Publishers Weekly,* January 20, 1989, p. 143.

Review of *Pyramid of Bone, Virginia Quarterly Review,* summer, 1989, p. 100.

Review of *Rainbow Remnants in Rock Bottom Ghetto Sky, Publishers Weekly,* April 15, 1991, p. 141.

Seaman, Donna, review of *Last Chance for the Tarzan Holler: Poems, Booklist,* February 15, 1998, p. 970.

Standing, Sue, review of *At Redbones, Boston Review,* February, 1991, p. 28.

Stein, Sharman, "For One Memorist, Self-pity, For Another, Self-Respect," *Tribune Books,* August 2, 1998, section 14, p. 11.

Review of *Tale of a Sky-Blue Dress, Booklist,* June 1, 1998, p. 1708.

Review of *Tale of a Sky-Blue Dress, Kirkus Reviews,* June 1, 1998, p. 799.

Waniek, Marilyn Nelson, review of *At Redbones, Kenyon Review,* fall, 1991, pp. 214-26.

For More Information See

BOOKS

Bloom, Harold, *The American Religion,* Simon & Schuster (New York City), 1992.
Contemporary Women Poets, St. James Press, 1998.
Dictionary of Literary Biography, Volume 120: *American Poets since World War II,* Gale, 1992, p. 220-22.

PERIODICALS

Booklist, October 1, 1993, pp. 353-54.
Georgia Review, winter, 1998, pp. 755-72.
Kirkus Reviews, March 15, 1998, p. 368.
Kliatt, July, 1995, p. 19.
Publishers Weekly, July 5, 1993, p. 7.
School Library Journal, September 1993, p. 216.

*   *   *

MURRAY, Kirsty 1960-

Personal

Born November 21, 1960; daughter of Guy Martin (a sculptor) and Phyllis (Nairn) Boyd; married John Murray, December 17, 1982 (divorced, March 5, 1994); married Ken Harper (a teacher), February 14, 1998; children: (first marriage) Ruby, William, Elwyn; step-children: (second marriage) Isobel, Romanie, Theodore. *Education:* Attended Royal Melbourne Institute of Technology (Melbourne, Australia).

Career

Author. Worked variously as a forest ranger, secretary, caterer, life model, waitress, graphic artist, administrator, art teacher, craftsperson, laborer, barmaid, editor, and researcher. Served on various school councils in the United Kingdom and Australia. *Member:* Australian Society of Authors, Amnesty International.

Writings

Maneaters and Blood Suckers, Allen & Unwin, 1998.
Howard Florey: Miracle Maker, Allen & Unwin, 1998.
Tough Stuff, Allen & Unwin, 1999.

Kirsty Murray

Circus of Secrets, Allen & Unwin, 1999.

Work in Progress

Market Blues, a novel for middle graders.

*   *   *

NELSON, Jim A.
See STOTTER, Mike

P

PARKS, Gordon (Alexander Buchanan) 1912-

Personal

Born November 30, 1912, in Fort Scott, KS; son of Andrew Jackson (a dirt farmer) and Sarah (Ross) Parks; married Sally Alvis, 1933 (divorced, 1961); married Elizabeth Campbell, 1962 (divorced, 1973); married Genevieve Young (a book editor), August 26, 1973;

Gordon Parks

children: (first marriage) Gordon, Jr. (deceased), Toni Brouillaud, David; (second marriage) Leslie. *Education:* Attended public high schools in Minneapolis, MN, three-and one-half years. *Politics:* Democrat. *Religion:* Methodist.

Addresses

Home—860 United Nations Plaza, New York, NY 10017. *Agent*—(Film) Ben Benjamin, Creative Management Associates, 9255 Sunset Blvd., Los Angeles, CA 90069.

Career

Photographer, writer, film director, songwriter, and composer. Held various jobs before 1937, when he focused on photography; photographer with Farm Security Administration, 1942-43, Office of War Information, 1944, and Standard Oil Co. of New Jersey, 1945-48; *Life* magazine, New York City, photojournalist, 1948-72; *Essence* magazine, New York City, editorial director, 1970-73; film director, 1968—, has directed productions for Warner Brothers-Seven Arts, Metro-Goldwyn Mayer, and Paramount Pictures. President, Winger Enterprises, Inc. Composer of concertos and sonatas performed by symphony orchestras in the United States and Europe. *Member:* Directors Guild of America (member of national board, 1973-76), Authors Guild (member of board, 1973-74), Authors League of America, Newspaper Guild, Black Academy of Arts and Letters (fellow), American Federation of Television and Radio Artists, American Society of Magazine Photographers (past member of board), American Society of Composers, Authors, and Publishers, American Federation of Television and Radio Artists, National Association for the Advancement of Colored People, Directors Guild of New York (member of council), Urban League, The Players (New York City), Kappa Alpha Mu.

Awards, Honors

Rosenwald Foundation fellow, 1942; Frederic W. Brehm award, 1952; two Mass Media Awards, National Conference of Christians and Jews, 1964, for outstanding contributions to better human relations; Carr Van Anda Journalism Award, University of Miami, 1964, Ohio University, 1970; named photographer-writer who had done the most to promote understanding among nations of the world in an international vote conducted by makers of Nikon cameras, 1967; honorary A.F.D., Maryland Institute of Fine Arts, 1968; honorary Litt. D., Kansas State University, 1970; Carr Van Anda Journalism Award, Ohio University, 1970; Spingarn Medal, National Association for the Advancement of Colored People (awarded annually to one black American for distinguished achievement), 1972; Georgia Children's Book award, 1972, for *J. T.;* honorary H.H.D., St. Olaf College, 1973, Rutgers University, 1980, Pratt Institute, 1981; Christopher Award, 1980, for *Flavio;* President's Fellow award, Rhode Island School of Design, 1984; World Press Photo award, 1988; Artist of Merit, Josef Sudek Medal, 1989. Additional awards include Photographer of the Year, Association of Magazine Photographers; awards from Syracuse University School of Journalism, 1963, Philadelphia Museum of Art, 1964, Art Directors Club, 1964, and University of Miami, Coral Gables, 1964; honorary degrees from Fairfield University and Boston University, both 1969, Macalaster College and Colby College, both 1974, Lincoln University, 1975, Columbia College, 1977, Suffolk University, 1982, Kansas City Art Institute, 1984, Art Center and College of Design, 1986, Hamline University, 1987, American International College and Savannah College of Art and Design, both 1988, University of Bradford (England) and Rochester Institute of Technology, both 1989, Parsons School of Design, 1991, Manhattanville College and College of New Rochele, both 1992, Skidmore College, 1993, Montclair State University, 1994. Stockton School, East Orange, NJ, renamed Gordon Parks Academy in honor of Parks, 1998.

Writings

Flash Photography, [New York City], 1947.
Camera Portraits: The Techniques and Principles of Documentary Portraiture, F. Watts, 1948.
(And director) *Flavio* (also see below), Electra Studios, 1961.
The Learning Tree (autobiographical novel; also see below), Harper, 1963.
A Choice of Weapons (autobiography), Harper, 1966.
(And photographer) *A Poet and His Camera* (poems), Viking, 1968, published in England as *Gordon Parks: A Poet and His Camera,* Deutsch, 1969.
(Director, producer, and composer of score) *The Learning Tree* (screen adaptation of the novel), Warner Brothers-Seven Arts, 1968.
(Photographer) Jane Wagner, *J. T.,* Van Nostrand Reinhold, 1969.
(And photographer) *Born Black* (essays), Lippincott, 1971.
(And photographer) *Gordon Parks: Whispers of Intimate Things* (poems), Viking, 1971.

(And photographer) *In Love* (poems), Lippincott, 1971.
(And director) *Shaft* (screenplay), MGM, 1971.
(And director) *Shaft's Big Score,* MGM, 1972.
(And director) *The Super Cops,* MGM, 1974.
(And photographer) *Moments without Proper Names* (retrospective exhibition of photographs with verse), Viking, 1975, Secker & Warburg (London), 1975.
Leadbelly, MGM, 1976.
Flavio, Norton, 1978.
To Smile in Autumn: A Memoir, Norton, 1979.
Shannon (novel), Little, Brown, 1981.
Voices in the Mirror: An Autobiography, Doubleday, 1990.
Arias in Silence, Little, Brown, 1994.
Glimpses toward Infinity, Little, Brown, 1996.
(Photographer) Philip Brookman, *Half Past Autumn: A Retrospective,* Bulfinch Press, 1997.

Author of television documentaries produced by National Educational Television, including *Mean Streets.* Author of *Martin* (ballet), 1990. Contributor to *Show, Vogue, Venture,* and other magazines.

Adaptations

Selections from *The Learning Tree* and *A Choice of Weapons,* read by the author, were recorded on audiocassette, both by Scholastic Records, both 1970.

Sidelights

A published poet, filmmaker, novelist, composer, and photojournalist, Gordon Parks is well known as the first African American to ever be signed as a director to a major Hollywood film studio. His directorial debut, *The Learning Tree,* filmed in 1968, was based on his own childhood in Fort Scott, Kansas, where Parks, the youngest of fifteen children, was raised in abject poverty. Not only did the multi-talented Parks write the autobiographical novel upon which the film was based, he also wrote the screenplay adaptation, composed the soundtrack, directed, and produced the film. Parks has recounted the events of his life in several autobiographical works in addition to *The Learning Tree,* and his photographs for major magazines like *Life* and *Vogue* chronicle the mid-twentieth-century development of the African-American consciousness. "As passionate as he is peace-seeking despite all the hurt he has endured, Parks, in his words as well as in his actions, has become a pioneer as both an artist and a defender of the human spirit," stated John Brosnahan in *Booklist.*

Forced to leave high school in the midst of the Great Depression in order to support himself after his mother died, Parks turned to photography, and eventually worked his way up to a job freelancing for the prestigious *Life* magazine. Parks would spend more than two decades on staff at the magazine, while also turning his attention to several other vocations—among them film director and composer. "I am often asked why I do so many different things," Parks commented to *SATA.* "I used to wonder about this myself, and for a long time I passed it off as a sort of professional restlessness. But, in retrospect, I know that it was a desperate search for security within a society that held me inferior simply because I was black. It was a constant inner rebellion against failure. I was a poor black boy who wanted to be somebody.... Basketball, football, and photography—simple pleasures for other boys of my age, had to make money for me. In my fright, I set up all sorts of hypothetical tragedies for myself, then I would contemplate an alternative to offset whatever tragedy I felt might strike. For instance, I would imagine I had lost my legs in an accident. Then, just as quickly I would daydream myself into a situation whereby I would play music or perhaps compose for a living. Or if I lost my sight or hearing I could learn Braille and somehow survive by writing.... with all the tragic possibilities considered, and all the alternatives accounted for, I could push on with a little less fear."

Despite his love of photography, Parks also felt the need to channel his self-expression into other forms, namely writing. His first novel, *The Learning Tree,* parallels his own childhood in Kansas. In the novel, teen protagonist Newt Winger grows to manhood despite being beset by economic and personal tragedies similar to those endured by Parks. Parks also composed several volumes of poetry illustrated with his photographs, and has illuminated the human condition in photo essays such as *Flavio,* based on a 1961 *Life* piece about a young Brazilian boy's rescue from a Rio de Janeiro slum. Taken to the United States and treated for malnutrition, the boy ultimately made the choice to return to his native country and resume a life of hardship in a volume that a *Publishers Weekly* contributor characterized as "both poignant and depressing."

Since publication of *The Learning Tree,* Parks has continued in an autobiographical vein with several other books, among them *A Choice of Weapons,* which discusses his years from age sixteen through his efforts to become a successful photographer. *To Smile in Autumn* covers the years 1943 through 1979, the period during which Parks rose to success in the film industry, writing and directing the box-office smash *Shaft* in 1971. *To Smile in Autumn* covers the author's experiences photographing everything from dead Harlem gang leaders to heiress-and-designer-jeans-purveyor Gloria Vanderbilt and addresses Parks's personal quandary—how to be a successful African American working as a representative of the white business elite. The book contains forty photographs by Parks, many that depict such civil-rights leaders as Malcolm X and Stokeley Carmichael. *School Library Journal* contributor Alice M. Fellows called the book a "thoughtful eye-witness account ... of the Civil Rights movement," and a critic for *Kirkus Reviews* praised the book as a reflection of its author's "genuine accomplishments and truly wrenching conflicts."

Voices in the Mirror, published in 1990, takes another step backward in Parks's life, returning to the Kansas city where he spent his mid-teens and endured racism, poverty, and, ultimately, the death of his mother. Following Parks during his efforts to make a living on his own and establish himself in his chosen vocation, the book also serves as a tribute to Parks's family and to the African Americans who fought for racial equality during the 1950s and '60s. *Voices in the Mirror* "underscores a belief in dignity and the difference one man can create," according to *School Library Journal* contributor Mike Printz. A *Publishers Weekly* reviewer declared that Parks's "exhilarating, inspirational autobiography provides a searing view of what it's like to be black in America." Parks's fascinating life is further documented in *Half Past Autumn: A Retrospective,* a volume designed to accompany a 1997 traveling exhibit of almost three hundred examples of his photographic work.

Remarking on the many outlets his creativity has found over the years, Parks once commented: "I go on attempting to reveal my experiences, each time in a different way, through a different medium, hoping that, in some small way, they might make a dent—some mark—on our times. If only I could feel that a photograph, a piece of music or a film of mine could help put an end to hatred, poverty, bigotry, or war, the pain of those early years would have been worth while."

Works Cited

Brosnahan, John, review of *Voices in the Mirror: An Autobiography,. Booklist,* November 1, 1990, p. 494.

Fellows, Alice M., review of *To Smile in Autumn: A Memoir, School Library Journal,* March, 1980, p. 149.

Review of *Flavio, Publishers Weekly,* January 2, 1978, pp. 56-57.

Printz, Mike, review of *Voices in the Mirror: An Autobiography, School Library Journal,* February, 1991, p. 107.

Review of *To Smile in Autumn: A Memoir, Kirkus Reviews,* October 1, 1979, pp. 1193-94.

Review of *Voices in the Mirror: An Autobiography, Publishers Weekly,* October 12, 1990, p. 52.

For More Information See

BOOKS

Berry, S. L., *Gordon Parks,* Chelsea House, 1991.

Bush, Martin H., *The Photographs of Gordon Parks,* Edwin A. Ulrich Museum of Art (Wichita, KS), 1983.

Donloe, Darlene, *Gordon Parks,* Melrose Square (Los Angeles, CA), 1993.

Harnan, Terry, *Gordon Parks: Black Photographer and Film Maker,* illustrated by Russell Hoover, Garrard, 1972.

Roslansky, John D., editor, *Creativity,* North-Holland Publishing, 1970.

Turk, Midge, *Gordon Parks,* illustrated by Herbert Danska, Crowell, 1971.

PERIODICALS

American Visions, February-March, 1993, pp. 14-19.

Booklist, August 19, 1997, p. 1845; February 15, 1999, p. 1025.

Library Journal, January, 1992; June 15, 1997, p. 64; February 1, 1998, p. 83.

Life, October, 1994, pp. 26-29; September, 1997, pp. 94-99.

New York Times Book Review, December 9, 1990, p. 19;
    March 10, 1996, p. 16; December 7, 1997, p. 38.
Publishers Weekly, October 12, 1990 p. 52.
School Library Journal, February, 1991, p. 107.

Smithsonian, April, 1989, pp. 66-75.
Washington Post Book World, November 18, 1990, p. 4.*

*   *   *

Autobiography Feature

Robert Newton Peck

1928-

Soup's Best Pal

It began with a woman. Everything worthwhile does. Her name was Miss Kelly, and she taught first, second, third, fourth, fifth, and sixth in a tumble-down, one-room, dirt-road school in rural Vermont.

She believed in scholarship, manners, and soap.

But more, she believed in *me*. In all of us, telling us that in America you don't have to be what you're born. Haven Peck, my father, killed hogs for a living. Hard work, but he was a harder man. Like all hard men, he was kind, quiet, and gentle. I wanted to be like Papa, yet I wasn't sure I'd grow up only to kill hogs.

"Robert," said Miss Kelly, "perhaps you'll surprise us all, and amount to something."

It was years later when somebody pointed to a large building and said, "That's a library." I didn't believe it, because in Miss Kelly's little one-room school, we all knew what a library was. Not a building. It was a *board*. A three-foot-long shelf in the corner, a plank, upon which sat our few precious wornout books. According to custom, we washed our hands before touching them.

So there we sat in her school, soldier straight, learning about people like Mark Twain and Calvin Coolidge, and Ty Cobb and Charles Lindbergh and Booker T. Washington.

We were the sons and daughters of illiterate farmers, millworkers, and lumberjacks. Some of the folks, in town, called us uproaders. And we called *them* downhillers. But I knew they could do what I had me an itch to do.

They could *read*.

Sometimes, at home, a learned scholar would stop by, and he was always asked, following supper, to read to our family. There was only one book in our mountain home. It was black and large, yet we never referred to it as our Bible. It was known only as The Book

Then, after I'd fetched it, the clerk of the local feed store in town (if he happened to be our guest) would read to us. Mama's usual favorite was Isaiah, especially the part about swords into plowshares and spears into pruning hooks.

We listened.

The grown-up people nodded their heads, as if absorbing and agreeing with whatever verses were being read. As an interesting aside here, you might be surprised to learn that a neighbor of ours named his two sons Chapter and Verse.

At school, our teacher Miss Kelly read to us by the hour. She gave us *Tom Sawyer* and *The Wind in the Willows* and *Ivanhoe*, in an effort to lead us from the bondage of ignorance and poverty.

She earned her thirteen dollars a week.

I was the youngest of seven children, yet the first to attend any school. Papa and Mama had opposed my going. Yet when I finally introduced Papa to Miss Kelly, initially he said nothing. But he took off his hat.

"Thank you," Miss Kelly told my father, "for giving me Robert. I shall try to be deserving of your trust."

"We hope he's got manners," Papa told her with a straight face. "And whatever he breaks, we'll pay for."

Miss Kelly smiled.

At school, I met Soup.

He was a year and four months older than I was, and became my best pal. When a boy has a best friend, he's the richest kid on Earth. His real and righteous name was Luther Wesley Vinson, and he grew up too, to become a minister.

It's only honest to admit here, as an aside, that when I was in college I seriously considered becoming a minister . . . in order to become the first Protestant Pope. However, upon viewing my character (or lack of it) I decided I was unworthy. Were I a preacher, my worry would be that my flock might harken to some of my eccentricities and be like me. But today, were I a minister, I would fight pro-left organizations such as the National Council (and World Council) of Churches.

During much of my so-called mature life, I've protected my soul and my wallet by avoiding doctors, lawyers, and the clergy. Yet three of my closest and dearest cronies all became ministers . . . Hank Gooch, Fred Rogers, and Soup Vinson.

Robert Newton Peck

The Vinsons lived uproad from the Pecks. And most times, Soup and I were nothing but trouble, to everyone in our path.

He started it, and I usually caught the blame, and often Miss Kelly's ruler. She didn't have to fill out a form, or assemble witnesses, in order to whack a kid. Those were the sensible days in education. One ruler was worth a dozen rules.

Somehow, both Soup and I came to realize, as our behinds were smarting, that Miss Kelly was our ticket out of a sewer, or a manure pile. She was a small and resolute candle, flickering in darkness, proud to be a teacher, prouder still of all we learned.

"Teachers and farmers," Miss Kelly once informed us, "are alike. But I'm luckier, because a farmer has to go to his garden. My garden comes to me."

We were the young, the green, the growing. Buds of life, opening to her warmth, her sunshine, and her strength. She called us "her flowerbed of pansy faces." We were hers, we knew, and she was ours. In her shoddy clothes, she stood ramrod straight, instilling in us all the sterling, character-building Vermont virtues and values.

She liked *me* the best.

Every kid thought the same. Now you know why Miss Kelly deserved to bear that most noble of titles: Teacher.

As a first grader, I viewed our Miss Kelly as being very tall. As years flew by, she magically grew shorter. When, at age nineteen, I came home from Europe and World War II, she was almost tiny. She rushed up to me, hugged me with her thin little arms, and said, "Praise God."

Everyone in the county called her Miss Kelly.

Lots of people bowed to her as she passed, holding her head up high, a patrician among peasants, a beacon in their

darkened world. One of the toughest brawlers in town, a man named Buck Dillard, a lumberjack, always brought her a dressed capon for Christmas.

He had never attended school. Yet local rumor held that Miss Kelly had, one evening, taught Buck Dillard to write his name. He sported a big, mean wood-hook scar across his face and had a slightly crippled hand which had been crushed beneath a log. Some folks claimed there was little good in him. Others claimed none.

Buck weighed close to three hundred pounds, and for some strange reason, nobody kidded him much. Not even when he silently sobbed at Miss Kelly's funeral.

She died at age ninety-seven. For me, this was difficult to believe, because when we were her pupils, Soup and I both suspected that Miss Kelly was at least 144. I am most thankful that she lived to share in my success as a writer. I've dedicated more than one book to her, and she became almost as proud of me as I will ever be of her.

Dedications, in the front of a book, offer readers an insight into what an author believes and holds dear. *Clunie,* my short novel about a retarded child, bears a dedication which reads as follows:

"This book is dedicated to kids who will never read it, hoping that the kids who can will care."

Writing is not showing off with big words. Nor is teaching. The dearest rabbi who ever lived, a Nazarene carpenter, preached of little things in common terms ... loaves and fishes, a camel passing through the eye of a needle, a mustard seed.

Tangibles. Stuff, not abstracts.

My latest novel, *Jo Silver,* is dedicated to a remarkable woman, elderly only in years and winters, whom I met on a Montana mountain, a lady this author shall ever remember. Her name is Sally Old Coyote.

Dedications are gestures of thanks.

Soup is dedicated "to the Reverend Luther Wesley Vinson, a shepherd of his flock, from his first sheep."

Other pals warrant a salute.

Banjo pays tribute to a college buddy, who was my best man when I married Dorrie, my favorite librarian. "I dedicate this book to a great guy who will always be my pal ... and I'll always be his ... Fred Rogers." Yes, you're right, TV's famous Mister Rogers.

Fred and I don't see eye-to-eye on anything. You name it, we differ on it. Yet we've always been able to disagree without becoming disagreeable. Pals forever.

That is America.

We are God's garden of variety, in color, race, and creed. How dismal life must be to live in a country where there's only one political party, one origin, or one faith.

In the summer of 1984, in Los Angeles, we Americans all held a party for the entire world, the Olympic Games. (Russia didn't come. No matter, as Communists never enjoy anything and seldom grin.) What I liked best was watching two athletes hug each other, one white and one black, or one from Japan and one from Brazil, and a Frenchman hugged a German!

It was a blend of music, fun, excellence. People smiled and praised one another, a party of human brotherhood and sisterhood.

With Soup, named for the author's boyhood friend.

In my opinion, now that we've seen what works and what doesn't, we ought to dissolve the United Nations, and instead, hold the Olympic Games every year or two. We'd replace talk with action, mediocrity with excellence; and best of all, replace hatred with friendship. Sure, I was rooting for our USA kids. But when that courageous Belgian boy rolled over the finish line in his wheelchair, the *world* cheered.

Oh, I love our USA. I'm the corniest flag-waving patriot ever to skip along the pike. If you can't find scores of things, and folks, to admire in these United States, then perhaps loving is beyond your reach and grasp.

For example, take Early Pardee.

His real name was Earl. He was illiterate, as so many wise and poetic mountain people are.

Early Pardee and I were hunting, one cold day in Vermont, resting, our backs against spruce trees and sitting in snow. Two red foxes were dragging a dead snowshoe hare across a white meadow. It was too doggone beautiful to raise a gun and cut down.

Early spat out a brown stream of Red Man, and spoke. "Ya know, Rob . . . them snowshoes be the bread of winter."

It was true, what Early Pardee said, because all of life is predatory. Roots of a tree clutch at earth the way the talons of a hawk stretch for an unwary rabbit. Even a carrot is a predator, one orange talon, stabbing into the earth to seek that which is not yet its own.

Unfortunately, we now smother in a world of law, much of which (civil law and canon law) is enacted by senile males, in churches, courts, and legislatures. Divine Law is all that really counts, law ordained by God and practiced by Nature.

Today, trouble is, we're all up to our vulnerable wallets in *lawyers*. We citizens want less law, and more referenda. Lawyers dominate Congress, lobbies, government bureaus, state legislatures, city and town councils, and our courts. I hold even less respect for judges. In short, lawyers should practice the law, but should not be allowed to determine which laws are enacted, many of which benefit themselves.

No lawyer should run for office. We ought to board-up all law schools for at least twenty years. Laboratory experiments should use lawyers instead of white mice, as lawyers multiply more rapidly, and are less loveable.

We citizens are always warned: "You can't take the law into your own hands." Poppycock! This is exactly where law belongs, in *our* hands, not in the hands of lawyers and judges.

Now then, on to more pleasing matters.

Earth, our beautiful planet today has only one problem. *Excess human population.*

This dreaded disease, human pregnancy, is the mother lode which spawns disease, poverty, litter, crime, animal annihilation, and war. Not to mention traffic, or din.

Because of this mire of people, which I dub *peoplution,* our animals are dying. Whale, panther, moose, bluebird, even our American eagle is endangered.

Human life is no more sacred than *all* of life. Morality, therefore, is acreage per head, for all of Earth's bio life.

As I write these words, there is mass starvation in Africa, and today's newspapers abound with heart-wrenching photographs of emaciated children.

Nature's corrections are always massive, occurring without pity. Horrible, yet because of this starvation, many other forms of life will survive in Africa, and future generations may hopefully prosper. Perhaps it is part of some unknown Divine Order which a mortal mind cannot, or will not, comprehend.

Religion and sociology save no life. Only our Earth's *biology* has that honor.

God's will cannot be fairly translated into human words. To humanize God is demeaning. Prayer should not offer God direction, only gratitude, for a brutal beautiful natural balance created to work so well. "In the beginning, God created." *We* did not. Ergo, we best not criticize Divine Order, its drought, or its rain.

I wish not to improve the world. Instead, to give thanks I'm allowed to be part of it, a very insignificant part.

Even though I work as a writer, and speaker, it's a pity that *language,* was invented. It's fouled religion. God's purpose should not be etched into words, and Moses erred in herding us, like sheep, down that dreadful wordy path.

My own Bible is often read.

I thankfully accept God's rain and rainbow, God's leaf and tree. But if you tell me God spoke in words, I'm changing my pew. Blue Goose, a red Huron warrior, once said that he had never seen God; yet whenever he looked at a sundown sky, he knew that God sees Blue Goose.

God and sunsets are best absorbed by silent unspoken feelings of gratefulness, not described by the paltry and petty words of prophets or authors or priests or preachers, or nuns, or nitwits like me.

The future of our planet Earth depends on women, not warriors. The soil we walk upon is not neuter. Earth is female. Pour seed into her and she bears fruit. The atmosphere which surrounds Earth, however, is male. The wind carries pollen, seed, and spore. Sometimes by a bee or a bird.

Advice to Women: For a sweetheart, choose a physically strong man. He will be secure in his manhood to be tender, gentle, delicate. Only the unproven sissy will bully you. Manhood, like trees, is rooted in soil. If you are a woman, beware of a man who does not yet own *land.*

You know who taught me a few things?

Ed Nocker.

I met Ed away out in the middle of nowhere, in our Florida Everglades. He was dumping a mixture of acorns and corn mash onto the ground. I asked him why. Answer, to capture some wild hogs. "All I do," Ed said, "is git 'em lazy enough to depend on me. Soon as that happens, they're my slaves."

What he told me, I thought, applies to citizens and government. So I told Ed I'd someday write about him. Thus I have, but I won't send him this article. Ed can't read.

But he sure can cook possum.

Peck with Thunderbolt.

When I met Ed, his mule, Esme, had just died. Only mule he'd ever owned who would lift up a hoof to shake hands. He showed me the harness he'd made for her, then a mound of fresh amber sand he'd dug for her, under which she lay buried.

That, my friends, is the core of research for a writer, or for anyone curious to learn.

Research is a dirt road!

It is *getting* off *pavement* to find the Ed Nockers of America, rural sachems of distant domains, unwashed, unread, yet rarely unwise. Don't go to talk. Go to listen. Meet enough Eds, and you'll be EDucated.

Speaking of the Florida outback, land, and hardy folk (human or mule), I just finished a novel about a Florida cattle ranch, and a determined and scrawny little widow trying to raise calves and children. Ed Nocker would respect Violet Beecher and maybe so will you. *Spanish Hoof* is a book I'm proud to author.

There's music in it too.

Not surprising, as so many of my books feature a simple song or two which I've composed. I play self-taught ragtime piano, by ear, sometimes by fingers. To get raised as an uproader country boy means you've been treated to a spate of toe-tapping tunes.

We had us a near and dear neighbor, Miss Haddie, who'd sit barefoot on a half-broke, front-stoop rocking chair, and plunk a banjo which she'd fashioned by her own two hands. Miss Haddie (can't recall her final name) could almost make her banjo go out and bring in the mail. Or so it sounded to Soup and me, her fan club.

Music enters a child's *soul,* not his mind. It enters through an ear, not an eye. Even today, a sheet of music looks to me about as easy to savvy as a page in the Tokyo phonebook.

Some of the most spiritual and rewarding moments of my fun-packed life occurred when I sang *lead* in three barbershop quartets. A lead singer has to snarl out the most authoritative part, and he's also usually the best looking. *Names* of barbershop quartets are always fun. We were the Humbugs, the Deep Throats, and the Broadjumpers.

We were beer, cigars, outrageous macho jokes, and best of all, *buddies.* Dave, Pete, Don ... I miss y'all more than remembering can abide, or a heart can hold.

Rob Peck is a sentimental slob.

Soon, I intend to attempt a book about many of the people who have so enriched my life. Not celebrities, just common folk. Peasants, like me. Lumberjacks, farmers, hermits, ladies like Miss Haddie and Sally Old Coyote, men like Buck Dillard and Ed Nocker and Early Pardee. Their wit and wisdom ought to get *shared* as well as remembered.

A man keeps only what he gives away.

Whoa!

Hold it right there. My book won't be free. I'll sweat to write it and you'll sweat to buy it. America's fount is human sweat. Government cannot create wealth. Our fortunes are created by selling goods and services to each other. The brighter a person is, the more he wants to stand independent, and shun federal aid.

Pick any nonprofit governmental institution and you've got a pigsty mess. God sure did a nifty thing creating *greed.*

Too abrasive a word? Okay, then aspiration.

That's when the son of a pig butcher worked toward becoming an author. And if Miss Kelly said it was okay, it's okay. America, in the long run, must reward brains, guts, and ambition or stupidity.

Complainers and gripers rarely amount to squat. They're usually too occupied with wailing about people who are busily handling the chores.

Speaking of chores, *work is* a solid thing to believe in. Vermonters usually do. Granite folk on granite land. Much like their statues in village squares, they are the granite sentries of liberty, standing free.

Sure, I remember the guys I played on teams with, and drank beer with, and sang with ... but I don't guess I remember them any more fondly than the men I worked alongside. Farmers, lumberjacks, old woodhooks at a paper mill, men I helped slaughter hogs, and fellow soldiers when I was a seventeen-year-old private overseas in the U. S. Army.

These special people, so many of them unschooled, sit upon an honored throne in my heart.

In later years, I worked as an advertising executive in New York City, with people whose hands were always clean. Yet sometimes, their mouths, deeds, and souls were filthy. They frittered away their money on an analyst's couch. Why? Because they somehow suspected that what they did for a living served no rightful purpose. Their work built nothing. Fed no one.

Ask yourself this. Who got chosen by the carpenter of Nazareth to be His closest friends? Were they the richly-robed Pharisees and Sadducees? Not hardly. His friends were Galilean fishermen, men who sweated, and no doubt smelled of fish heads and salt from the sea.

Work!

That dirty four-letter word. Yet where would any of us be without it? Begging our government for support, I dare suppose. My happiest mornings are when I jump out of bed at six o'clock, knowing I have a lot to do. And I'm so grateful God has given me the back to start it (that's the tough part) and the will and fortitude to get it completed. Never quit when you're tired. Only when you're done.

Advice to kids: As you're growing up, find a type of *work* you enjoy. Any wimp can enjoy play, or TV.

Also, here's an extra bonus thought, one I discovered by personal experience: People who do hard *physical* work talk more sense to me than people who rarely soil their hands.

This is why, in this author's opinion, education better get up off its duff and move outdoors. Kids are being raised today who couldn't even kill a chicken, pluck it, gut it, or cook it. From their limited scope of living, they probably conclude that survival is ordering up a coke and fries at Burger World.

If you eat meat, you ought to be able to butcher it yourself, instead of tripping blissfully through life thinking that a hamburger is made by Du Pont out of soybeans.

Perhaps what is really being butchered is education. How long has it been since *you* have actually touched a cow? Go touch her. She's as warm and sweet as her milk.

People in America today are possibly becoming teachers at too young an age, too often fresh-hatched out of a college egg. From one cloister to another. Now then, I'm not quite sure how this would work, but perhaps the noble title of *teacher* should only be bestowed upon a citizen who has ventured off a campus and into the real outside world, and has actually accomplished something. Maybe a teacher should be no younger than thirty, or forty.

Little saddens me more than my suspecting that educational institutions judge teachers on the criterion of what *degree* they hold.

For kids, education should perhaps consider balancing all of its conceptual thought with tangible training, so that a youngster doesn't graduate from college able to manipulate a telephone, a pencil, a keyboard ... and little else.

Some teachers, the lesser ones, gripe about some self-concocted disorder known as Burn Out. These teachers should be allowed to work in the chipper room in a paper mill, where the noise is literally deafening, for an eight-hour shift. I did. Then, when your relief man reports drunk, you work another eight hours. This might convince a teacher or two that a classroom ain't so doggone awful.

What I'm saying is not that I dislike teachers. No way. I'd just like to remind a few complainers that all jobs have a negative and a positive side. The goose that'll lay a golden egg will also drop a lot of other stuff.

Laugh Department: I speak to groups of teachers rather often. Generally, they're a super bunch and love to laugh. The biggest round of applause I ever received was after I'd

With Great Island Karl, Peck's 2,600-pound Charolais bull.

confessed that I had attended only one PTA meeting at a school, where my kids went, and *one* was quite enough. The ovation came when I said, "I'm convinced that teachers and parents should never meet."

A most jovial, bright, and friendly fellow was this junior-high principal I met near Chicago. After speaking at his school, the two of us escaped to a local pub for refreshment. He had recently returned from a national convention in Austin, a meeting of principals and superintendents. The most popular session had been called *Career Change.*

I asked him why so many upper-echelon educators wanted *out.* His answer startled me. "Politics," he said. "In my opinion, public education is becoming swamped with too many political causes, and not enough learning or fun."

His daughter, age of ten, was in elementary school. She came home with a list of new words. One of them was *feminist.* She spelled it for him. But then the young principal asked his daughter what it meant. Her reply? "Lesbian." This was not, he said, a definition supplied by her teacher, but rather a consensus of student conclusion.

Thus, we all might conclude that more of today's education could embrace a few studies which are tangible as opposed to conceptual and abstract.

Today's child is eager, almost salivating, to *drive* the family car. But have we adults ever manifested the courage, or foresight, to insist that the child understands even the most rudimentary concepts of an engine? Worse yet, do any of us so-called adults know?

Can we put a worm on a hook? Or remove a hooked catfish and prepare it as a meal? In other words, we should be fully-vested as people, not helpless, incomplete, *over-texted* weaklings, wondering when Mom (or Swift & Company) is going to spoon-feed us.

Are we men? Or do we merely wear trousers?

I hope you long-suffering folks who are reading this gig won't mind if I continue to ramble a mite, sort of like an old Vermont cowpath, going nowhere. But, come to think of it, cowpaths *do* go to worthy places; to a barn for the welcome hands of milking, to the shade of a meadow elm, or to a cool brook. So I'll ramble, talking to you over the back fence, as if you're Rob Peck's next-door neighbor.

Here goes:

1. Two people recently robbed me. One, a mugger, stuck a gun in my ribs and took my money. The other robber, a college prof I never met, applied for a federal grant, and took *your* money as well as mine. Of the two, I respect the mugger more. At least he tackled his own dirty work.

2. Cost-of-living adjustments do accomplish one thing. They continually increase everyone's cost of living.

3. The amount you earn has little to do with your eventually becoming wealthy. Study the difference between income and capital. It's pig simple. Capital is how much you *save.* Always save half, and you'll be rich beyond measure. The man who told me so was Mr. Carliotta, born in Greece, who came to America as a penniless boy, spoke no English, and prospered in full measure. He drove a big black Cadillac and respected America more than a few of us who were hatched here. People who have to *have* so many things, early in life, often wind up with *having nothing.* They feel that they have to buy a stereo, flashy clothes, jewelry, fancy cars, and eat in expensive restaurants. Some complain that their salaries are too meager, yet if their salaries doubled or tripled, they would continue to squander instead of save. Regardless of their income level, nothing would be left. All spent. Poor people load their supermarket carts with junk food and carbonated beverages. Most of it is outrageously expensive. What I would do, were I poor, is go to the meat department and buy a large left-over bone. Sometimes they'll give it to you for free, because they're discarded as scraps. Then buy big sacks of potatoes, carrots, onions, rice, turnips, and barley … and prepare a nutritious stew, in one pot. It sure would beat Fritos.

4. Never buy anything, including religion, from someone who telephones you. Whenever one of these pesky people call, politely ask him, or her, to hang on because there's someone knocking at your door. Five minutes later, hang up the phone.

5. In my hands I hold two objects: an acorn, and my Bible. Were I *forced* to choose only one, to cherish forever, I would keep the acorn, as it is entirely of God's making.

6. Men are smarter than women. Because no man

would consider buying a shirt that buttons up the back.

7. If you wish to have friends, *be a friend* to someone. Learn where his soft spot is. (We all have them, areas in our mind where we can be easily hurt.) So don't stomp on somebody else's. Tiptoe graciously around it, and never let him know that you are aware he has a vulnerable underbelly which is undefended against a barbed tongue.

8. Justly so, people who try so hard to get *something for nothing* end up with far less than the rest of us who pay a merchant for its worth and value.

9. Education is not a social service. In truth, it is a commodity, like pork jowls. Health is also a personal concern. It is not a governmental problem that legions of us prefer our forks to exercise, smoke to fresh air, and booze over orange juice.

10. We need new prisons. They should be enclosed, colorful factories (not gray dungeons) where criminals learn a craft, produce products other than license plates, and earn a wage. A modern prison could, on cheap labor, support itself without a penny of public funds.

11. One tiny birth-control pill, properly used, accomplishes more to preserve our beautiful planet than ten social workers or twenty environmentalists.

12. Socialism is merely shared poverty. The disease of socialism could have been cured, like a ham, had only the unfortunate victim (the socialist) been raised on a farm.

13. Authors, old buildings, and retired hookers have one thing in common. If they manage to stand up long enough, they become quaint.

14. Taxation is theft. We all realize, however, that our city, state, and national governments can't operate without it. I'm willing to pay reasonable taxes, yet I believe we could dispense with the Internal Revenue Service. Instead of taxing income, which is largely impossible, *tax sales*. Every product or service purchased should be federally and locally taxed, at very low rates. Best of all, this sales tax arrangement would not only eliminate the expense of running the IRS, it would do away with the horrors of filling out those idiotic tax forms every April. We also need a Constitutional Amendment that requires our federal government to *balance the budget!*

15. Most of my wisdom (what little I have) was given to me by a mother, a father, an aunt and a grandmother ... none of whom could read or write. Yet I am so grateful to all of my teachers who taught me their crafts and artistry.

16. I like movies in which cop cars crash.

17. A child's first musical instrument should be a ukulele, because it so simply embraces the prime blending of melody, harmony, and rhythm.

18. Judges should not be former lawyers. A judge should be a citizen; like you, me, and the jury. If the systems in your body became as fouled-up as our judicial system, think how sick you'd be.

19. I respect teachers, so much so that I intensely distrust their unions who prey upon teachers and rob them of their money. Worse yet, when a teachers union hops into bed with a political party, education gets a slap in the face

20. The teachers who are characters in my books are always strict, sensitive, and caring.

21. The dumber people are, the louder they play a radio. This explains the origin of dumb's double meaning.

22. Every school needs a hero. But first, learn how a hero *acts*. He makes other kids feel big. The bigger they all feel, the higher they hold him, and the louder they cheer.

23. I'm sick of seeing blue jeans. Denim bores me almost as much as a Meryl Streep movie. Why, in any one school, are some teachers dressed so neatly and others dressed as slobs?

24. For some reason, even though I'm a jingo patriot, I just can't abide "The Star Spangled Banner." "Rockets red glare and bombs bursting in air" isn't what our Republic is all about. Besides, at ball games, hardly anyone sings it, and worse, we all stand there thoroughly bored, until it's over. Musically speaking, its range isn't within the capabilities of our limited voices, unless we're operatic sopranos. I vote for "America the Beautiful."

25. The high point of my life would be for me to visit a high school and meet a principal who is not a former football coach.

26. There is only one ironclad rule in today's public school. All other rules may be broken. One cannot. Never alter the lunch schedule!

27. If you're a blacksmith who is working on a stallion, always heft up a front hoof first, for safety. When you meet a stranger, shake his hand, before you're tempted to stomp on his toes.

28. Most automobile damage could have been avoided had the drivers employed a modicum of courtesy. After a two-car crash, it is usually the driver yelling the louder who is at fault. Brakes are poor

Soup and his friend, Rob Peck.

Mending a saddle.

substitutes for brains.

29. Farmers are the hardest-working people I know. Also the healthiest and happiest. Maybe there's a connection.

30. Ethnic jokes will always be told. It is natural and normal to snicker at the other fellow, especially if he's different, or hails from somewhere else. Up in Montana, every joke I heard began as follows: "Seems like there's these two guys from Idaho." And faces were already smiling.

31. Cowards always kick a dead lion. Politically speaking, Richard Nixon is a dead lion, but the cowards are still kicking. I pity them, and I'd guess old Mr. Nixon pities them too.

32. Winners always smile, whether they win or lose. Losers grumble, make up excuses, frown, cuss. They throw golf putters, tennis racquets, and tantrums. But your opponent won't remember the score. He will remember whether or not you were a lady or a gentleman.

33. Not long ago, upon hearing of his death, I wept. And then sat at my piano and played all of the 'S Wonderful songs he had written … "Lady Be Good" and "Embraceable You" and "My Love Is Here to Stay." Wherever you are, Ira Gershwin, I pray there's a piano and angels to sing you the kind of delightful music you gave to us.

34. As I write these words, a cat is sleeping with her head resting on the toe of my boot. I wish my foot were bare, to appreciate her comfort.

35. Many of today's schools are too big. Middle schools and high schools should be smaller, just for one neighborhood, so that the ridiculous cost of busing could go toward improving the salaries and quality of teachers and the manners of students.

36. Teachers, please *hug* your kids. Some of them have never been lovingly touched. Only slapped.

Miss Kelly hugged Soup and me. So hug even the pupil who is defiant. Why? It is the rule-breaker who will someday explore the stars.

37. She hugged *me* the most.

38. Never let humility encumber you. Arrogance is a lot more fun. *Humble* is useful, however, as it's the name of my oil company.

39. Women, please learn that men are interested only in one thing. But, after you feed us, our interests may be augmented into other areas.

40. Compared to the work of so many talented authors, my novels aren't really so doggone great. Yet secretly, I truly believe that I am the best teacher of creative writing in the entire galaxy. If you don't believe it, read *Secrets of Successful Fiction* and also *Fiction Is Folks*. But please, when talking to students, do *not* refer to them as *text* books, a term which makes my book about as appealing as eating a mattress. They are *fun* books, filled with the meat and potatoes of my craft, not written by a prof, but by a pro. Humor is my chief teaching tool. I've learned far more wisdom from clowns than I have from funeral directors.

41. Every hunting dog should own a man.

42. I own a dog who owns me. He's getting old, lame, and blind. Soon I must take him, a shovel and my gun, into the woods for our last trip together. He will not die indoors with a vet or a needle. I promise you he will feel no pain. I will feel it all. It will be our final outing, as friends.

43. Manhood is doing what has to be done.

44. One of the biggest thrills of my life happened in Missouri, in 1982, when I won the Mark Twain Award. The little bronze bust of Mark Twain that they gave me is here, in my den, and stands only seven inches high. Rob Peck stood seven feet that evening and he's been growing ever since.

45. If you possess courage and will, it will amaze you how much you'll accomplish on a day when you feel absolutely rotten.

46. Ain't it just peachy that the fools of the world hold their own annual festival. It's called New Year's Eve. And if you climb into your car on 31 December, and venture out on a highway, you'll be the biggest fool of all, especially in some flimsy Japanese car.

47. If your aim is to bore people, tell them about everything and everyone you hate. To charm your friends, tell them what you like.

48. My idea of a crashing bore is a guy who was born in Texas, served in the Marines, and then went to Notre Dame.

49. My favorite conversational ploy at a stand-up cocktail party is to corner a liberal and torture it.

50. I smoke cigarettes. Too many. But all of you nonsmokers will be amused to know that I once bought a suit with three pairs of pants, and burned a hole in the jacket. Have you ever tried to wear out three pairs of green pants?

Where is America going? West, and South. Places like Boston, New York, and Philadelphia (and their Ivy League colleges) represent our rich heritage of yesterday.

Peck with Conan.

But today, what I call Cowboy America is now holding the reins of command. The Northeastern Establishment doesn't know Roy Acuff from Roy Clark ... but folks who do, control elections.

Folks who do, cheer the United States and *not* the United Nations. They holler "U-S-A!" and *not* "U-N."

Cowboy America is positive, prosperous, and pleasant. More than a difference of geography, I see it as a difference of attitude. I live in Florida. Driving a car, one time, I entered a northeastern state, and noticed an official roadside sign which "welcomed" me to its border. It read "Conviction Means Loss of License." In contrast, as a motorist enters a particular southern state, the sign reads "Drive Friendly."

In short, Harvard's nasal wail of doom (so many Ivy League men talk slightly pained, as though their Fruit-of-the-Looms are a size too tight) is becoming unheard in most of our country.

It's rather a pity that the headquarters for all three broadcasting networks (ABC, CBS, NBC) are all in New York City, and continually pumping out NYC philosophies across the plains where most of us people live. That, however, will also change. Say what you will about the rural electronic evangelists, at least they're offering a balance for the see-saw.

No, I'm not, in any way whatsoever, a member of The Moral Majority.

Yet I must observe that much of what is broadcast, music-recorded, and filmed these days could use a bath. As obscenity comes, also comes censorship. I'd prefer a powder-blue-suited electronic evangelist for a neighbor rather than a foul-mouthed, hip-grinding, pot-smoking, herpes-carrying, gender-questionable electronic guitarist.

To conclude this tirade, I guess my personal preferences for America can be best typified by hearing old Gene Autry singing "Back in the Saddle Again." And that is Cowboy America.

Well, that's it. It's all I have to prattle and here's hoping it's enough. I can hear you screaming. "Too much!"

Whatever you do, don't let innocent children read any of this glop. We can't allow them to grow up into another warped and twisted Robert Newton Peck. Heaven forbid! Yet I must confess to you that Rob Peck has led one heck of a great life. It's been a ball. And a brawl. The rich and famous are often attacked.

Mediocrity resents talent. And believe me, I resent all those talented people.

My first hurdle, whenever I lecture (do a gig) at a college or university, is to open up minds. Not the minds of students, because theirs are already open. I try, and often fail, to open the minds of the faculty. They resent me, because I represent success in the off-campus world. Colleges persist in evaluating someone by what degree he holds, or what title. At lunch, bank presidents never ask me. On a campus, there are so many doctors I feel like I'm watching television's *General Hospital.*

Life is fun. It's a hoot and a holler. If you can't revel in America and enjoy all the wonderful Americans you meet, you wouldn't be happy in Heaven or even in Florida.

I doubt I'll go to Heaven, that is, if I have a choice. So many of my closest buddies will probably go somewhere further south, where there's a red piano, a red poker table, and a red pool table with corner pockets that are eight inches wide. And I'll be there, filling inside straights with bourbon, and making old Hades a Heaven for the ladies.

Looking back, I sure ain't missed much, so I probably won't be missed.

Don't panic.

I'm not going just yet, because I have more books to write, more horses to tame, and a lot more songs to sing. Every day ought to represent the whole of a person's life. A full day.

My three morning rules are these: Up at 6:00, breakfast at 6:15, and at 6:30 ... back to bed. But come to think about it, my life has been mostly work. I was a mite too busy for hopes, prayers, or dreams. So here's my personal motto.

"Wish not for apples. Grow strong trees."

An Update Spring 1999

How old am I?

Come Y2K, I'll turn 72.

Maturity, it's so delightful to discover, is not the crimson blush of ripening youth. It ain't peachy. Instead, becoming a senior citizen is more of a silver-haired shine, as opposed to being one of those stuttering relics on Golden Pond.

Looking ahead, we'll be holding a major election in the year 2000. Already I'm receiving loads of letters that beg me to run for president. Should I take them seriously? Most of the letters were written in Crayola.

No, I won't run. No time. Too busy playing tennis everyday. Singles as well as doubles. Recently, I was in a club singles match with an excellent player who was only 39. As golfing friends rolled by, riding in shade and seated in a golf cart, one taunted me with a needling: "Hey, Rob ... why don't you play somebody your own age?"

Quickly I quipped: "Because they're all dead."

Yes, there's fun.

And a few frets as well.

A few years ago (1991) my local doctor, here in Florida, sent me to Nashville, Tennessee, to the Vanderbilt Voice Center. I was under a doctor's observation every month for over two years.

The inevitable finally happened.

In December of 1993 several physicians pried open my mouth to a circle the size of a Hula Hoop, or so it felt. The doctors, plus two or three children and a small dog, crawled into my mouth, down my throat and slashed at "my condition."

Doctors refuse to say the word "cancer." That is understandable, because the term is so abrasive that it can spook folks into a panic.

Nor did they use the term "surgery."

What they did was nibble a part of me, removing some of my throat (I can't pronounce the Latin version). It resulted in being a permanent prevention of my continuing to harmonize in SPEBSQSA ... a Society for the Preservation and Encouragement of Barber Shop Quartet Singing in America. I was in their 60-man chorus, plus a fourth of a socially unpardonable quartet:

The Broad Jumpers.

A loss to the world of music? Hardly. Fellow members often describe the quality of my singing voice as "a snore calling to its mate."

No more barbershopping.

However, my new white Yamaha grand piano oft reverberates with my untalented yet enthusiastic ragtime. And jazz. Undaunted, what's left of my voice still bleats out the creatively clever lyrics of a few original ditties. All by ear, but sometimes I also use my fingers.

"Never had a lesson," I brag to my captive audience, guests that I earlier hogtied to their chairs.

They respond: "We believe it."

Alas, the Nashville operation, as my Tennessee surgeon ruefully informed me, "didn't quite get it all." So, he insisted that "we" ought to undergo another "procedure." And this jolly caper is cheerfully called "radiation."

They zapped me 64 times: 32 on one side of my neck, 32 on the other.

Believe me, it doesn't hurt. But by the time they've blasted the last gamma ray (or whatever the Star Trek crew likes to call it) I feel sort of like saying: "Uncle! Stick a fork in me. Yank me out of the oven as I'm ready to be carved."

Nifty news: I licked cancer!

During all of this entire ordeal, I just couldn't as much as write a comma. Started novels that filled up stacks of paper, yet went nowhere. Spirit was gone. So, by the way, was my wife of 35 years who divorced me to marry a guy who's 31 years younger than I. Believe it or not, I soon met him and immediately liked him. We sometimes play tennis.

Then I met my adorable Sam, and as soon as she came home to Florida from Venezuela, we got hitched. Dorrie, my first wife, brings her new husband, Keith, to visit us once in a while. We are all good friends.

I'm so grateful we four are so mature.

Also thankful that my writing career was gradually reborn, thanks to a large and ferocious Everglades critter.

Here's how it happened.

The author with the horse he named for Ronald Reagan.

Four or five years ago, when Sam was down yonder in Latin America, a series of horrendous events took place in South Florida. Not too long a drive from my Orlando (Longwood, actually) home. It was a situation that required two experienced hunters, so they claimed, to hurry. And bring weaponry. The problem? A gigantic wild boarhog was on a tear, a rampage, terrorizing a small swamp community of poor folks who reside in stilt shacks. On stilts so that the cottonmouths don't crawl into one's bed at night.

A hunting buddy called me. We both volunteered and raced to their rescue, taking along a brace of tracking dogs; a blue tick and redbone. Plus our guns.

Wet weather. Stupidly lost my compass.

Sadly, after we finally located this big boar, we soon lost one of our beloved dogs. The boar ripped him to bloody bits. Creeping in close enough to squeeze off a shot required a passel of patience. Yet this was slowly accomplished.

A monster of a "hawg." Huge tusks curved above his snout; and down below, a pair of white rippers like railroad spikes and stiletto sharp.

Had to break my rule: *If you kill it, you ought to eat it.* However, eating this old codger would be similar to chewing up a truck tire. Where I live in Florida, we eat a plenty of wild hog, but each one weighs about a hundred pounds.

This old rascal had to be destroyed.

He had already attacked and slaughtered two small children, a teenage boy, a 300-pound swamper who was one of the toughest men I ever met up with, and a half-

Peck on his five-hundred-acre ranch in Florida.

growed bull. In rage, this beast had also torn something else apart ... a Jeep.

We nailed him.

My gun is over a century old. It is a single-shot Montgomery & Ward original Texas Ranger 12-gauge shotgun. The shell was what's called a ball, one lead slug, and it hit that devil just behind the shoulder. Over he fell, kicked for a spell, and died. No more little children would die screaming.

The boar weighed 480 pounds.

For a short while, I kept his handsome head in my garage. It was infested with ticks and stunk worse than a wet farm dog in heat. Can't figure out why Sam (my wonder wife) didn't seem to be keen on having the head of that big tusker indoors.

Women sure do take understanding.

Right after he fell dead, my friend and I posed for photographs with him, one of which I shipped off to my editor at Random House, in New York City.

"Quick," she gasped, "write the book!"

Y'all know the happy ending.

Nine Man Tree.

Sam, whom I call Sugar because she calls me Sweet Pea, seemed to be far more pleased with the novel than the stench in our garage. Near the kitchen. Oh, in case you

happen to ponder how come I refer to Sam as *my wonder wife:* chalk it all up to the fact that she is so brilliant and so beautiful, and whenever we make an entrance, arm in arm, people are going to naturally conclude ... "I *wonder* what she sees in Rob."

As you know, presuming of course that you are well read, a high percentage of my 60-odd books takes place in my native state of Vermont, where Soup and I grew up together.

Long ago. A fond memory.

Following an interesting and successful New York City advertising career on Madison Avenue, then moving over to the client side of a giant corporation, I retired in 1974, and we moved to Florida, where, years ago, I attended, and graduated from, college. The South is going to be home for the rest of my life.

Here, in Dixie, is where I aim to establish Robert Newton Peck as a Southern author. Several of my novels have taken place in Florida. Many more shall soon follow.

Cowboy Ghost is one of my best.

What is it about? A primitive cattle drive across the wilderness toe of the Florida peninsula, back in the rugged era of 1924.

History informs us that the American cowboy originated here in Florida. He truly did. Centuries before there ever was a place called Texas, or Montana, cowhands pushed horses, cattle, mules, oxen, and wagons across the burning Florida flats, battling Seminoles, heat, or hurricanes.

Before the year 1600.

Having hailed from generations of Vermont farmers, and educationally smothered in the academic traditions of New England, naturally, as a young school boy, I was spoonfed myths and misbeliefs about American history. For example, we naive students were automatically taught an outright *lie* ... that the Confederate flag was the official highflying symbol of a slave ship.

Wrong!

To begin with, the first slaves in America were not black. They were *red*. My people, American Indians (and please resist that insipid term recently coined for us: Native Americans) who were captured by the saintly Pilgrims and Puritans of Massachusetts. You remember them, the holier-than-thou, white-collared hypocrites who came to the New World to seek freedom.

Trouble is, the Pilgrims and Puritans weren't so supportive on extending freedom to their Indian neighbors, the people who earlier had shared their corn with them, and even taught them how to plant it.

It gets worse.

Slave ships were built in New England, manned by New England seamen, commanded by New England sea captains, and owned by New England mercantile companies. The profits gleaned from this insidious slave trade were seized by greedy Yankee hands and then deposited into the Yankee banks of Boston.

Those self-righteous Bible walloping New England preachers somehow managed to look the other way on slave market day.

As for the burgeoning practice of slavery itself, Massachusetts was first to enact it legal. Ironically, far to the south, Virginia was the first state to declare slavery illegal.

A surprising percentage of my fan mail has begun, in recent years, to support my position on the above. We see fact, not fancy.

Oh, and while we're briefly touching on the subject of mail, please understand that I can't answer every fan letter. Sometimes I write close to 100 letters a week, to kids all over America and the world. However, if there's a *correct school address*, plus a brief and cordial missive from a teacher or librarian (even a sentence or two), I will willingly respond. Group letters, please, are most easily handled if mailed flat (unfolded) and in one package to:

Robert Newton Peck, 500 Sweetwater Club Circle
Longwood, Florida 32779

And, a bonus, for adults only, please. My home telephone number is (407) 788-3456.

Moving right along, and into a far more rewarding subject, I am now a grandfather. My little blond cherub of a grandchild, a boy, is named Stephen. He is four. And, because I am 71, the pair of us share our secret childhood that no one else can savvy.

A private club.

My children, Christopher Haven Peck and Anne Houston Peck (Stephen's mom), grew up knowing my best friend, who, you may remember, also served in my first wedding as my Best Man. His name is Fred Rogers. You know him. No doubt you have visited his Neighborhood on PBS - TV.

Recently I snapped a photo of Fred and his talented concert-pianist wife, Sara Joanne, reading *Hamilton* to Stephen.

Hamilton is my only picture book. Needless to say, it's about a pig. Seems like I can't get away from writing about pigs, wild or domesticated. Ultimately I'll be remembered as . . .

Robert Newton Pork

By the time Stephen is coming up nine or ten, I can introduce him to another very early boyhood sidekick, Luther Wesley Vinson. He was a real person and later also became my literary lunatic in the "Soup" series.

A new adventure is in progress: *Soup Up.*

As of late, Sam and I are being invited to dozens of state conventions that we relish attending: groups of reading teachers (IRA) and also state gatherings of *librarians*. Frequently at these, I'm asked for an opinion on today's public and private education, and on what is lacking in the average curriculum.

My comment is a simple one.

Human physiology.

For my dough, one of the necessities of providing a comprehensive basic education for a youngster is to *start with the student* himself. Teach him about his body (or hers) and how it functions: the respiratory system, the nervous system including a brain, the digestive complex.

Most important: the reproductive gear!

Far too many of our young girls are getting pregnant with unplanned and unwanted babies, and the cause isn't some mysterious ingredient in the drinking water. The core is pig-simple easy:

"Life is fun. It's a hoot and a holler."

Teach 'em the mechanics of how to prevent a sperm from uniting with an ovum.

For their sake. For the sake of Planet Earth.

We all share one universal trait, in common. Each and every one of us resides on our Big Blue Marble, originally a delightful sphere. That is, until humanity stupidly began to multiply in an out-of-control way, and alarmingly converting our earthly Heaven into an over-populated Hell.

There is only one mother-lode problem on our planet. Motherhood. And it is the source of most of the thorns in all of our sides.

The problem is not intercourse.

It is pregnancy!

As world population rises, and it is doing just that at a frightening rate, ask yourself these pivotal questions:

Is *air* cleaner?

Fresh water more pure?

Oceans more free of contaminates?

Land displaying less litter?

Fewer *traffic jams?*

Less *road rage?*

Will there be fewer *crimes?*

Will we hear less *noise* pollution?

More habitat *room for animals?*

Will there be *fewer wars?*

A cowboy American.

The common solution is merely common sense. As we *reduce the number of human beings,* all of the above problems (plus numerous others, such as our future's twenty-digit telephone dialing) will gradually abate.

Panthers, whales, and manatees might get a chance to thrive, raise young, and live as Mother Nature intended.

Earth, our home, is critically ill.

Our planet's future wellness, as well as prosperity, rests in the capability of young human *females.*

Boys (even *men,* based on all I have personally and reluctantly observed) cannot be trained to care about much more than their own sexual gratification. Certainly not the weighty responsibility of pregnancy prevention. Most males are too stupid, too apathetic; and worse . . . in many societies, they'll actually brag about how many women they knock up.

If you really want to be totally nauseated by herding males, eavesdrop on the primal dialogue you'll hear in any Sports Bar.

Ironic. How devoid of *sportsmanship* appear.

Ergo, a woman must learn to defend herself against her worst natural enemy. Sperm.

Young people in love are not necessarily evil. No, they are merely uninformed. Bear in mind, please, that today's generation of passionate teens are constantly being bombarded by sexual hype. Movies, rock music, rap, TV, radio,

romance novels . . . all exalting the joyful jubilation of "getting it on." Alas, so few messages further precaution.

We adults must lead, not just nag or criticize. A pity there's so little moral leadership in Washington, D. C., as Slick has led us down a sorry road.

Even though reality forces my acceptance of being merely a plain ol' country boy who somehow struck it lucky, at least my books try to uplift. Not degrade. Not to titillate in the gutter, but to direct minds upward, to stars. I write about my own kind, plain people, and mostly poor, who labor in mud. Yet are raptured by a rainbow.

Sometimes it discourages an author when the novel he's attempting to write isn't quite ripening for harvest. But it almost always eventually does.

However, if I puff up too uppity, I just fumble into a desk drawer to retrieve a rumpled letter, written on a shabby sheet of blue-lined notebook paper. The three tiny holes are no longer round but ripped. It was mailed to me a few years ago, from a boy named Charlie.

Hi, Rob, I like your books better than literature.

The author today in Longwood, Florida.

Writings

FOR CHILDREN; FICTION :

A Day No Pigs Would Die, Knopf, 1972.

Millie's Boy, Knopf, 1973.

Soup, illustrated by Charles Gehm, Knopf, 1974.

Bee Tree and Other Stuff, illustrated by Laura Lydecker, Walker, 1975.

Faun, Little, Brown, 1975.

Soup and Me, illustrated by Charles Lilly, Knopf, 1975.

Wild Cat, illustrated by Hal Frenck, Holiday House, 1975.

Hamilton, illustrated by L. Lydecker, Little, Brown, 1976.

Hang for Treason, Doubleday, 1976.

King of Kazoo, words and lyrics by Robert Newton Peck, illustrated by William Bryan Park, Knopf, 1976.

Rabbits and Redcoats, illustrated by L. Lydecker, Walker, 1976.

The King's Iron, Little, Brown, 1977.

Last Sunday, illustrated by Ben Stahl, Doubleday, 1977.

Patooie, illustrated by Ted Lewin, Knopf, 1977.

Trig, illustrated by Pamela Johnson, Little, Brown, 1977.

Eagle Fur, Knopf, 1978.

Soup for President, illustrated by T. Lewin, Knopf, 1978.

Trig Sees Red, illustrated by Pamela Johnson, Little, Brown, 1978.

Basket Case, Doubleday, 1979.

Clunie, Knopf, 1979.

Hub, illustrated by Ted Lewin, Knopf, 1979.

Mr. Little, illustrated by Ben Stahl, Doubleday, 1979.

Soup's Drum, illustrated by Charles Robinson, Knopf, 1980.

Trig Goes Ape, illustrated by Pamela Johnson, Little, Brown, 1980.

Kirk's Law, Doubleday, 1981.

Justice Lion, Little, Brown, 1981.

Soup on Wheels, illustrated by Charles Robinson, Knopf, 1981.

Banjo, illustrated by Andrew Glass, Knopf, 1982.

Trig or Treat, illustrated by Pamela Johnson, Little, Brown, 1982.

Dukes, Pineapple Press, 1983.

Seminole Seed, Pineapple Press, 1983.

Soup in the Saddle, illustrated by Charles Robinson, Knopf, 1983.

Soup's Goat, illustrated by Charles Robinson, Knopf, 1984.

Spanish Hoof, Knopf, 1985.

Jo Silver, Pineapple Press, 1985.

Soup on Ice, Knopf, 1985.

Soup on Fire, illustrated by Robinson, Delacorte, 1987.

Soup's Uncle, illustrated by Robinson, Delacorte, 1988.

Hallapoosa, Walker & Co., 1988.

The Horse Hunters, Random House, 1988.

Arly, Walker & Co., 1989.

Soup's Hoop, illustrated by Robinson, Delacorte, 1990.

Higbee's Halloween, Walker & Co., 1990.

Little Soup's Hayride, Dell, 1991.

Little Soup's Birthday, Dell, 1991.
Arly's Run, Walker & Co., 1991.
Soup's in Love, Delacorte, 1992.
Little Soup's Turkey, Dell, 1992.
Little Soup's Bunny, Dell, 1992.
Soup Ahoy, Knopf, 1994.
A Part of the Sky (sequel to *A Day No Pigs Would Die*), Knopf, 1994.
Soup 1776, Knopf, 1995.
Nine Man Tree, Random House, 1998.
Cowboy Ghost, HarperCollins, 1999.

ADULT FICTION

The Happy Sadist, Doubleday, 1962.

NONFICTION:

Path of Hunters: Animal Struggle in a Meadow, illustrated by Betty Fraser, Knopf, 1973.
Secrets of Successful Fiction, Writer's Digest Books, 1980.
Fiction Is Folks: How to Create Unforgettable Characters, Writer's Digest Books, 1983.
My Vermont, Peck Press, 1985.
My Vermont II, Peck Press, 1988.

OTHER

Also author of songs, television commercials, and jingles. Adapter of novels *Soup and Me, Soup for President,* and *Mr. Little* for television's *Afterschool Specials,* American Broadcasting Companies, Inc. (ABC-TV).

PETERSON, Jean Sunde 1941-

Personal

Born January 3, 1941, in Estherville, IA; daughter of Elvin (a farmer) and Sylvia Sunde; married Reuben Peterson (a university professor), June 3, 1963; children: Sonia, Nathan. *Education:* Augustana College, B.A., 1962, M.A.T., 1982; University of Iowa, M.A., 1991, Ph.D., 1995. *Religion:* Lutheran. *Hobbies and other interests:* Writing, music, gardening.

Addresses

Home—117 Brookfield Dr., Lafayette, IN 47905. *Office*—LAEB 1446, Room 5108, Department of Educational Studies, Purdue University, West Lafayette, IN 47907-1446.

Career

Teacher and counselor. High-school English teacher, 1962-66, 1975-85; instructor of teaching methods, 1972-88; teacher and counselor, gifted education, 1985-90; counselor and counselor educator, 1995—; licensed professional counselor, 1996—. *Member:* American Counseling Association, National Association for Gifted Children, American School Counseling Association, Association for Counselor Education and Supervision.

Awards, Honors

South Dakota Teacher of the Year Award; Award for Excellence in Research, American Mensa Education & Research Foundation; Distinguished Alumni Achievement Award, Augustana College; Spirit of Excellence Award, International Black Hills Seminars; Best Books for the Teen Age, New York Public Library, and Midwest Independent Publishers Association Award, both for *Talk With Teens about Self and Stress: 50 Guided Discussions for School and Counseling Groups.*

Writings

(Contributor) *Counseling the Gifted and Talented,* edited by L. Silverman, Love (Denver, CO), 1992.
Talk with Teens about Self and Stress: 50 Guided Discussions for School and Counseling Groups, Free Spirit (Minneapolis, MN), 1993.
Talk with Teens about Feelings, Family, Relationships, and the Future: 50 Guided Discussions for School and Counseling Groups, Free Spirit, 1995.
(Contributor) *Counseling Children and Adolescents,* second edition, edited by A. Vernon, Love, 1998.
(Contributor) *Underserved Gifted Populations,* edited by Joan F. Smutny, Hampton Press (Cresskill, NJ), in press.

Also co-editor with S. VanBockern of a special issue of *Reclaiming Children and Youth,* vol. 6, no. 4. Contributor to journals and magazines, including *Journal for the Education of the Gifted, Journal of Secondary Gifted Education, Journal of Counseling and Development, Journal of Adolescent Research, Gifted Child Quarterly, Roeper Review, Gifted Child Today, Gifted* (Australia), and *Reclaiming Children and Youth.* Also contributor to *Reconstructing Mental Health Education: Transformative Teaching Practices,* edited by G. McAuliffe, C. Lovell, and K. Eriksen, in press.

Work in Progress

Currently researching topics related to counselor education, counseling interventions, adolescent and young-adult development, and underachievement. Latest manuscript is *Hearing the Voices: Why Nonmainstream Children Aren't Selected,* an ethnographic look at

Jean Sunde Peterson

teacher-student interaction, with attention to cultural value-orientations.

Sidelights

With many years of teaching and counseling experience behind her, Jean Sunde Peterson has determined that one of the best methods for helping students to steer through the difficult and often confusing teenage years is to encourage them to talk and then to respond to them nonjudgmentally. Often, though, parents and educators have trouble getting children to open up. Recognizing this, Peterson wrote two books which are essentially manuals that teach adults how to create environments in which children feel comfortable enough to discuss any problems they may have, as well as their thoughts on life in general. Through her years of conducting discussion groups with students, Peterson has discovered methods to entice a variety of children into a group, and to get results once she has them there.

Her two books are the culmination of her experiences with groups. First, Peterson published *Talk with Teens about Self and Stress: 50 Guided Discussions for School and Counseling Groups*. The title is indicative of the book's content. The intention of the book is to provide a blueprint for adults who would like to become group leaders and lead discussion sessions with teenagers.

Peterson targeted teachers, youth leaders, counselors, and parents who want to have a better understanding of what makes individual children tick and to help them make it through tough transitions. "Through the groups, students gain self-awareness, and that in turn helps them to make better decisions, solve problems, and deal more effectively with their various environments," Peterson writes in the book, describing the goal of the sessions. In the introductory chapter, Peterson describes what the sessions are, how to get groups together, and how to attract "difficult" and reluctant children. She also presents guidelines for individuals who want to lead groups, and provides a special note for parents. The book is organized into three sections: "The Self," "The Self and Others," and "Stress." Peterson includes sample sessions dealing with each of these subjects. She also provides an array of discussion topics such as "Personal Strengths and Limitations," "Perfectionism," "When We Need Courage," "How Others See Us," "Tolerance and Compassion," "Substance Abuse," and "Responding to Authority." Each of these topics has a list of objectives and suggestions for discussions, as well as activity sheets, background information, and instructions on how to conclude a particular session. The book struck a chord with some critics, who appreciated it for its altruistic value. Reviewing *Talk with Teens about Self and Stress* for *Voice of Youth Advocates,* critic Evie Wilson-Lingbloom called it an "outstanding guidebook" for those adults grappling with creating supportive relationships with teens. The reviewer also believed it was a "welcome resource." Likewise, Bruce A. Maloof, writing for *Science Books & Films,* admired the project's objective. However, Maloof felt that its message may not reach its intended audience, that it may be too advanced for inexperienced group leaders, and that it does not provide much new material for experienced counselors.

Peterson's second book, *Talk with Teens about Feelings, Family, Relationships, and the Future: 50 Guided Discussions for School and Counseling Groups,* expands the scope of the first book, adding topics that focus on feelings, family, relationships, and the future. The guidelines presented could be used in community settings, in treatment centers, or in a classroom setting, particularly in health, home-economics, social-science or language-arts classes. In a thorough introduction, Peterson describes the intent of the guided sessions, what they are, how to organize them, how to adjust sessions for various types of children, and how to recruit children. She also explains how the reader can perform a self-assessment to determine their capability to lead sessions. Guidelines and tips for leaders on how to behave ethically and how to begin and end sessions are included. *Talk with Teens about Feelings, Family, Relationships, and the Future* was also appreciated by some critics. Noting that it is "rare" that a guidebook "is as strong on process as it is on content," *Voice of Youth Advocates* contributor Susan Rosenzweig lauded the book. "This is an excellent, highly recommended resource," Rosenzweig wrote.

Peterson's book provides a blueprint for adults who would like to become leaders of group discussion sessions with teenagers. (Cover photo by David Coates.)

Peterson once commented: "Almost all my research and writing has been practitioner-oriented, and my teaching background and current clinical work continue to provide many avenues to explore. Each successive part of my varied career evolved rather seamlessly from what came previously. My writing interests have matched my career development, with attention to English-teaching methodology first, then to the affective concerns of special school populations, then to sociological and anthropological perspectives on teacher-student interaction, and finally to issues in counselor education. I hope to continue to write well into retirement."

Works Cited

Maloof, Bruce A., review of *Talk with Teens about Self and Stress: 50 Guided Discussions for School and Counseling Groups, Science Books and Films,* April, 1994, p. 70.

Peterson, Jean Sunde, *Talk with Teens about Self and Stress: 50 Guided Discussions for School and Counseling Groups,* Free Spirit, 1993.

Rosenzweig, Susan, review of *Talk with Teens about Feelings, Family, Relationships, and the Future: 50 Guided Discussions for School and Counseling Groups, Voice of Youth Advocates,* April, 1996, pp. 65-66.

Wilson-Lingbloom, Evie, review of *Talk with Teens about Self and Stress: 50 Guided Discussions for School and Counseling Groups, Voice of Youth Advocates,* April, 1994, p. 58.

For More Information See

PERIODICALS

Children's Bookwatch, March, 1994, p. 8; October, 1995, p. 1.
Kliatt, March, 1996, p. 30.

*   *   *

PETTIT, Jayne 1932-

Personal

Born May 23, 1932; married Irving Pettit, Jr., September 10, 1955; *children:* Robin Pettit Guillard, Susan Pettit McCrindle, Bruce F. *Education:* Susquehana University, B.S. (music); Rowan College, M.A. Ed; University of Pennsylvania, graduate work in writing and art history. *Religion:* Episcopalian. *Hobbies and other interests:* Gardening, traveling, reading, cooking, music, and collecting books, old movies, shells, Santas, and angels.

Addresses

Home—76 Club Course Drive, Hilton Head, SC 29928.

Career

Educator in independent and public schools for seventeen years. Teaches English as a second language to Latino adults. Author of children's books.

Awards, Honors

"Newest and Greatest Read-alouds," Libraries Unlimited, 1994, and "Best Books for the Teen Age," New York Public Library, 1996, both for *My Name Is San Ho;* Children's Book of the Year selection, Child Study Children's Book Committee, 1996, for *Maya Angelou: Journey of the Heart;* Notable Children's Trade Book in the Field of Social Studies, National Council for Social Studies and Children's Book Council, 1997, for *A Time to Fight Back.*

Writings

Amazing Lizards, Scholastic, 1990.
My Name is San Ho, Scholastic, 1992.
A Place to Hide: True Stories of the Holocaust, Scholastic, 1993.
A Time to Fight Back: True Stories of Wartime Resistance, Houghton Mifflin, 1994.
Maya Angelou: Journey of the Heart, Lodestar, 1996.
Michelangelo: Genius of the Renaissance, Franklin Watts, 1998.
Jane Goodall: Pioneer Researcher, Franklin Watts, 1999.
A Man with a Dream: The Life of Martin Luther King, Jr., Franklin Watts, in press.

OTHER

The Chef's Palate Cookbook, J. Pettit, 1992.

Jayne Pettit

Work in Progress

A book on women of the Civil War.

Sidelights

Jayne Pettit's lifelong focus has been on educating young people; first by teaching in the classroom, and then by writing books. Since 1990 she has written books directed to children and young adults, most of which are historical biographies about courageous people who have overcome tremendous odds to survive or accomplish a personal goal. An excerpt from one title, *My Name is San Ho,* was used as educational content for an enrichment program sponsored by Heath Publishing Company. Only two early works have explored other subjects—her first book, *Amazing Lizards,* and *The Chef's Palate Cookbook.* Many of her works, including *Amazing Lizards,* have been published internationally.

Following the publication of *Amazing Lizards,* Pettit began writing about the impact major events, historical and personal, can have on people's lives. Her first book in this genre, *My Name is San Ho,* tells the story of a young Vietnamese boy who witnesses the ravages of war, is separated from his mother and sent to Saigon for safety, and, years later, is reunited with her in the United States. The story is written as a first person narrative from San Ho's perspective as an adult. The first chapter establishes a historical backdrop for San Ho's story. Born in a small South Vietnamese village to a mother already widowed by the Vietnam War, his childhood memories begin with gunfire, Viet Cong raids, and napalm attacks. Danger and fear are omnipresent.

When the war escalates, creating even greater insecurity, San Ho's mother sends him to Saigon to live with friends and attend Catholic school. There, separated from family, he experiences loneliness amid great uncertainty about his future. Three years later, his mother and her American GI husband, now living near Philadelphia, send for him to join them. As a teenager in the United States, San Ho struggles to acclimate himself to a new culture and language, while striving to be accepted by his schoolmates. Carolyn Phelan in *Booklist* described the story as "sufficiently involving to make readers care what happens next," and a *Publishers Weekly* reviewer maintained that *My Name is San Ho* "powerfully depicts the effects of war on its innocent victims." The book also garnered praise from *School Library Journal* contributor Diane S. Marton, who called it a useful tool "in communities having not only new residents from Vietnam but also immigrants from other countries in conflict."

Pettit continues the theme of personal courage in the face of adversity as she recounts the stories of six men and women who saved Jewish people during the holocaust. *A Place to Hide* includes well-known rescuers such as Oskar Schindler and Miep Santrouschitz as well as unsung heroes who risked their own lives to save people they didn't know. Pettit's honest, eye-opening accounts of a Catholic priest in Assisi who hides refugees in monasteries, and another about how the Danish people manage to evacuate eight thousand Jews, offer a glimpse into the lives of ordinary citizens during World War II. Sarah Mears, in a review for *School Librarian,* applauded the author's matter-of-fact approach as making the stories "all the more moving."

A Time to Fight Back: True Stories of Wartime Resistance is a compilation of stories about courageous acts of young people from different countries during World War II. As in *My Name is San Ho,* the author uses the introduction to explain events preceding the war so that readers can understand the historical context. In a review for *Voice of Youth Advocates,* Jennifer Lynn Joynt stated that "Pettit relays each of the stories with elegant prose which entices the reader to read on."

The stories cover a wide range of experiences in different countries, including those of two children in the "Resistance"—one who delivers contraband newspapers in Belgium and another who rescues a downed British airman in France. The most common theme, however, is survival. In addition to Elie Wiesel's recollection of life in the death camps, readers learn about a Polish girl trying to hide from the Nazis, a British child's evacuation from London to the United States during the Blitz, and a Japanese-American girl and her family's internment in Manzanar, a California detention camp. Hazel Rochman of *Booklist* commented: "The facts about ordinary kids in wartime are so compelling that this can serve as an introductory work." Betsy Hearne, writing in *Bulletin of the Center for Children's Books,* called *A*

Time to Fight Back "a well-intentioned book that shows signs of diligent research on an important subject."

The author's next endeavors explore the lives of two remarkable people: Maya Angelou and Michelangelo. The biography of Angelou, entitled *Maya Angelou: Journey of the Heart,* is a straightforward, compassionate account of an unsettled childhood marked by sexual abuse and victimization. Angelou's ability to overcome these obstacles is revealed in the path her journey takes, as she goes on to become an author, a poet, performer, and civil rights activist. Marilyn Makowski, writing in *School Library Journal,* called *Maya Angelou: Journey of the Heart* an "interestingly told account." A similar format unfolds in *Michelangelo: Genius of the Renaissance* as readers learn what life experiences enabled Michelangelo to believe in himself and his talent enough to undertake great artistic challenges.

Works Cited

Hearne, Betsy, review of *A Time to Fight Back: True Stories of Wartime Resistance, Bulletin of the Center for Children's Books,* March, 1996, p. 238.

Joynt, Jennifer Lynn, review of *A Time to Fight Back: True Stories of Wartime Resistance, Voice of Youth Advocates,* June, 1996, pp. 123-24.

Makowski, Marilyn, review of *Maya Angelou: Journey of the Heart, School Library Journal,* April, 1996, pp. 148-49.

Marton, Diane, S., review of *My Name Is San Ho, School Library Journal,* March, 1992, p. 241.

Mears, Sarah, review of *A Place to Hide, School Librarian,* November, 1994, p. 170.

Review of *My Name Is San Ho, Publishers Weekly,* April 27, 1992, pp. 268-69.

Phelan, Carolyn, review of *My Name Is San Ho, Booklist,* March 1, 1992, p. 1280.

Rochman, Hazel, *A Time to Fight Back: True Stories of Wartime Resistance, Booklist,* April 1, 1996, p. 1360.

For More Information See

PERIODICALS

Books for Keeps, March, 1995, p. 28.
Bulletin of the Center for Children's Books, February, 1992, p. 167.
Kirkus Reviews, April 15, 1992, p. 542; January 15, 1996, p. 140; February 15, 1996, p. 298.

*   *   *

PORTER, Janice Lee 1953-

Personal

Born October 16, 1953, in Highland Park, IL; daughter of Harold Joseph (a secondary-school English teacher and administrator) and Jane Irving (a library aide and literary analyst) Perry; married Jeffrey M. Peters, 1978 (divorced, 1979); married Anthony Peyton (A. P.) Porter (a writer), February 2, 1991; children: Jai Imani Perry

Henry, Adecola Peyton Porter, Joseph Lee Porter. *Education:* Kansas City Art Institute, B.F.A., 1978. *Politics:* "No particular affiliation, but I hate capitalism." *Religion:* "No particular affiliation, but God created everyone." *Hobbies and other interests:* Walking and reading.

Addresses

Home and office—1001 Sheridan Ave. N., Minneapolis, MN 55411.

Career

Painter and illustrator, specializing in book arts. Graphic designer in Missouri Valley, IA and Minneapolis, MN, 1976—; painter, private commissions and shows, 1976—; illustrator, editorial and commercial, 1985—; illustrator, children's books, 1990—. *Member:* Society of Children's Book Writers and Illustrators, Book Illustrators Guild.

Awards, Honors

Best Book, Chicago Reading Roundtable, 1997, for *Colors of Mexico;* finalist, Minnesota Book Awards, 1999, for *M Is for Minnesota.*

Janice Lee Porter

Illustrator

A. P. Porter, *Kwanzaa,* Carolrhoda Books (Minneapolis, MN), 1991.

Marlene Targ Brill, *Allen Jay and the Underground Railroad,* Carolrhoda Books, 1993.

Linda Lowery, *Wilma Mankiller,* Carolrhoda Books, 1996.

Jim Haskins and Kathleen Benson, *Count Your Way through Greece,* Carolrhoda Books, 1996.

Lynn Ainsworth Olawsky, *Colors of Mexico,* Carolrhoda Books, 1997.

Lynn Ainsworth Olawsky, *Colors of Australia,* Carolrhoda Books, 1997.

Claire H. Blatchford, *Going with the Flow,* Carolrhoda Books, 1998.

Emily Abbink, *Colors of the Navajo,* Carolrhoda Books, 1998.

Isabell Monk, *Hope,* Carolrhoda Books, 1998.

Linda Lowery, *Pablo Picasso,* Carolrhoda Books, 1998.

Linda Lowery, *Aunt Clara Brown: Official Pioneer,* Carolrhoda Books, 1999.

Holly Littlefield, *Colors of India,* Carolrhoda Books, 1999.

OTHER

Dori Hillestad Butler, *M Is for Minnesota,* University of Minnesota Press, 1998.

Eric Hoffman, *No Fair to Tigers,* Redleaf (St. Paul, MN), 1999.

Work in Progress

The sequel to *Hope,* called *A Special Place,* written by Isabell Monk, for Carolrhoda Books; a book for babies and toddlers, called *Under a Mother's Heart,* also by Isabell Monk; *When Katie Was a Teacher,* for Redleaf Press; and *Jesse Owens,* written by Jane Sutcliffe, for Carolrhoda Books.

Sidelights

Janice Lee Porter told *SATA:* "I am first and foremost a painter. I've painted since childhood. When I was young, my parents supported my artwork. Dad bought me supplies; Mom hung the paintings on the wall. At the end of my first year at Kansas City Art Institute, I committed myself to painting as a life-long endeavor. I turned to illustration in about 1987; it was both a natural extension of the graphic arts field I was working in and a way to make money making pictures.

"My mother was a woman of many opinions, and one of her opinions during the early '80s was: 'You should illustrate children's books. You live in the same town as Lerner Books ... try them.' So eventually, I did. I must say, my artwork sat in some drawer at Lerner for several years. Finally I met an editor/author there who seemed to take a special interest in my artwork and assured me he could get me work, which he did. By the time the contract was drawn up, I was both engaged to be married to this editor/author, Anthony Porter, and readying to illustrate a book he had written, *Kwanzaa.*

"In the nine years since, I've lived the conflicted life of a book illustrator. Illustrating is very difficult work, in my opinion. A lot of research is required, which is fun and enlightening, but the stage of whittling the results of that research down into thirty-two great sketches that will become thirty-two great paintings—paintings with continuity—is not easy. I'm always trying to honor the story, its mood, my own sense of what makes a good picture, and my own mood—how I feel like painting for the two or three months I spend on the book. Besides being difficult, illustrating requires that I constantly respond to other people's ideas, and my own ideas for paintings lie dormant. When I come back to those ideas, I have to shake them off and spend months breathing life into them again.

"On the up side, the demands of illustrating have quickened me, strengthened my technical skills, and caused me to think about pictures serially. Now I am engaged in making one-of-a-kind books, which is satisfying both my need to create a piece of art from my soul and the habit I am in, as an illustrator, of turning pages to see what comes next.

"The job assignments for the books I have illustrated have come to me; I rarely choose what to work on. So it is interesting, and probably significant, that I illustrate books about either people from countries other than the United States, or Americans who live outside the dominant culture of white America. I myself live on the fringe of American life. I try to live around as many cultures as possible, and I am an artist living with a writer in a mixed-race family. I'm white, my husband is black, my kids are mixed. So illustrating *Hope* was especially fun for me. I pulled the look of the characters out of my life. The other great joy of that project was meeting and becoming friends with the author, Isabell Monk. Other than my husband, the authors of my other books reside out of state, and I never meet or even talk to them, which is a bit weird to me."

In *Hope,* which *School Library Journal* reviewer Eunice Weech called "a beautifully told and illustrated book," Porter's young title character learns about her biracial heritage from her great-aunt Poogee. Hope has overheard the term 'mixed' used in reference to herself. Aunt Poogee tells Hope that this means she is made of "generations of faith 'mixed' with lots of love." Weech appreciated Porter's "lively, expressive full-page [acrylic] paintings," which show the history of Hope's ancestors on both sides of her family. "A must-have title," concluded Weech enthusiastically.

Porter offered *SATA* perceptions of her experiences illustrating other books for children: "Stylistically, the most fun I've had with a book was with *Aunt Clara Brown.* Once I found the approach I wanted, which was simpler and used a more limited palette than the rest of my books; the pictures flowed. I intend to pull from this style in future work.

"*M Is for Minnesota* stood out a bit from the other books. That book I approached purely as a painting.

Many of the pages were not occupied by people, unusual for my books. The time I spent painting landscapes and buildings in Minnesota has inspired me to begin on-site outdoor paintings.

"As for other writers and illustrators who influence me, the list is endless. There is so much fine work out there, and I look at both illustrated books and fine art all of the time. What has most impact on me is probably local influence: the work and lives of the artists and writers who live in my town and whose work I can see 'in the flesh.'

"My advice to others: Get thoroughly involved in your art form, enjoy it, get better at it. I'm sure I've spent too much time doubting my own work and being a bit of a chameleon stylistically, trying to second-guess what was wanted. Forget all that. When I look at a really great book of art, I can tell that the illustrator is doing exactly what he or she feels like doing and has gotten good at it.

"What's up ahead: I am falling in love with book arts—from the marriage of serial images, or illustration, to one-of-a-kind art pieces or small editions of beautiful books. I'm working on books in the latter category right now, all for adults so far. Grownups need pictures, too. Included in these adult art books are a book of illustrated social commentary, written by my husband, A. P. Porter, an illustrated book of poetry, written by Jeannie Piekos, and a one-of-a-kind art piece book called 'Banana Cake,' also a collaboration with my husband, and based on our honeymoon experiences in Jamaica. In addition to the adult books, I am still illustrating children's books. Through the year 2000, I am determined to concentrate on my own artwork."

Vital to her work, Porter told *SATA,* is "a global orientation"—a recognition that "any group of people which attempts to demean or bury another's culture is deluded and dangerous." This philosophy of cultural respect has obviously influenced Porter's choice of titles to which she has contributed her brightly colored illustrations. Among the several nonfiction books for young children illustrated by Porter, is *Count Your Way through Greece,* written by Jim and Kathleen Benson. Porter's illustrations mimic a style native to Greece, while the text offers bits of information on Greek architecture, history, art, and culture. Each piece of information is associated with a Greek number from one to ten; that is where the counting comes in. "Porter's paintings capture the sunlit landscape perfectly," remarked Judith Constantinides in *School Library Journal.*

Porter's ability to evoke a region or culture in her paintings is pivotal in several of her other works, including *Colors of Australia, Colors of Mexico,* and *Colors of the Navajo,* books in the "Colors of the World" series published by Carolrhoda Press. Each work presents ten colors and associates each with a place, tradition, or object connected to the topic country or culture. In *Colors of the Navajo,* reviewed by Darcy Schild for *School Library Journal,* "each page of text is paired with a childlike painting done in vivid colors," depicting events in the history of the Navaho nation. In *Colors of Mexico,* "large, cheery oil paintings done in bright hues and with bold strokes reflect the countryside and various aspects of Mexican culture," wrote *School Library Journal* contributor Denise E. Agosto. Orange is the color of the monarch butterflies that spend each winter in the Sierra Madres, for example, and green is the color of Mayan jade. Porter's illustrations for *M Is for Minnesota,* an ABC book, also incorporate unique qualities of a specific region-in this case, the Gopher State. "Porter's atmospheric images perfectly capture the northern landscape and its inhabitants," contended reviewer Kathleen Squires in *Booklist.*

Works Cited

Agosto, Denise E., review of *Colors of Mexico, School Library Journal,* October, 1997, p. 121.

Constantinides, Judith, review of *Count Your Way through Greece, School Library Journal,* August, 1996, p. 138.

Schild, Darcy, review of *Colors of the Navajo, School Library Journal,* December, 1998, p. 98.

Squires, Kathleen, review of *M Is for Minnesota, Booklist,* January 1, 1999, p. 862.

Weech, Eunice, review of *Hope, School Library Journal,* June, 1999, p. 104.

For More Information See

PERIODICALS

Booklist, September 15, 1996, p. 243.
School Library Journal, June, 1998, pp. 96, 130.

R

REECE, Gabrielle 1970-

Personal

Born January 6, 1970, in California. *Education:* Attended Florida State University.

Addresses

Home—Marina del Rey, CA.

Career

Professional volleyball player, model, and corporate spokesperson for companies. Team Nike (volleyball team), team player.

Awards, Honors

Most Valuable Player, 4-Woman Pro Beach Volleyball Tour, 1992; Offensive Player of the Year, 4-Woman Pro Beach Volleyball Tour, 1994, 1995.

Writings

(With Karen Karbo) *Big Girl in the Middle,* Crown (New York City), 1997.

Contributing editor, *Elle* magazine, 1994-95. Contributor of feature articles to *Sports for Women.*

Sidelights

Reece is a volleyball player, model, and commercial spokesperson who is staking a claim in the publishing world. As a student at Florida State University, Reece majored in communications, and her education has come in handy. Reece wrote articles for *Elle* magazine in 1994 and 1995, and in 1997 she began a regular feature column in *Sports for Women,* a magazine for female athletes.

In 1997, Reece released her autobiography, *Big Girl in the Middle.* Co-authored with Karen Karbo, *Big Girl in the Middle* explores the personal and professional life of the multi-talented Reece. Describing a challenge that women athletes face, Reece observes in *Big Girl:* "Everything a woman does has an emotional component. Paying attention to my emotional side without surrendering is one of the toughest parts of playing professional sports." Reece also explains that her prowess as an athlete was hard earned, but she credits the hard work for giving her a strong character. "And it's the same for all girls who choose to play sports. The discomfort inflicted ... taps into her character, forces her to grow."

The breadth of Reece's talents is as imposing as her height (six feet, three inches tall). Although her literary voice is growing, the central focus of her career remains athletics, an activity from which she draws powerful benefits. "For girls," she writes in *Big Girl,* "it's especially good for them to be forced to work as a team with other girls ... it forces them to deal with unpleasant, ungracious emotions and get over it. It forces girls to rely on each other. It gives them confidence in other girls."

Works Cited

Reece, Gabrielle, and Karen Karbo, *Big Girl in the Middle,* Crown (New York City), 1997.

*　　*　　*

ROCK, Maxine 1940-

Personal

Born April 29, 1940, in Brooklyn, NY; daughter of Louis (an engineer) and Jean (a housewife; maiden name, Rubin) Hochman; married, August 3, 1963; children: Lauren, Michael. *Education:* New York University, B.S., 1960; University of Michigan, M.A., 1962, doctoral study, 1963.

Maxine Rock

Addresses

Home and office—370 Valley Green Dr., Atlanta, GA 30342. *Agent*—Agnes Birnbaum, Bleecker Street Associates, 532 LaGuardia Place, New York, NY 10012.

Career

Journalist, educator, author. National Parks Association, Washington, DC, associate editor of *National Parks,* 1962-66; University of Maryland at College Park, instructor in journalism, 1966-67; *Atlanta Journal,* Atlanta, GA, feature writer, 1967-71; Georgia Conservancy, Atlanta, director of information and founding editor of *Georgia Conservancy,* 1971-73; Georgia State University, Atlanta, instructor in journalism, 1975-82; writer, 1980—. North Buckhead Civic Association, Atlanta, founder and member of board of trustees, 1971, president, 1974; founder and member of Atlanta Coalition on the Transportation Crisis, 1972; founder and co-administrator of Atlanta's City-Wide League of Neighborhoods, 1973; chairman of urban environment section of Atlanta mayor's Committee on the Energy Crisis, 1975; member of media study group of Leadership Atlanta, 1975; Founder and vice-chair, PATH Foundation, 1991—. *Member:* National Parks and Conservation Association (member of board of trustees), American Society of Journalists and Authors, National Writers Union, National Association of Science Writers, Dixie Council of Journalists, Zoological Society of Atlanta (founder, 1972).

Awards, Honors

Atlanta Foundations Award from Leadership Atlanta, 1977-78; science writing award from *Grolier Science Yearbook,* 1978; second prize from *Reader's Digest* "drama in nonfiction" contest, 1981; first prize from *Writer's Digest* "drama in nonfiction writing" contest, 1982; award from Women in Journalism, 1982; Best Feature Writing, American Society of Journalists, 1993; Award of Excellence in Medical Journalism, 1998; William Harvey Award, 1999.

Writings

JUVENILE NONFICTION

Kishina: The True Story of Gorilla Survival, epilogues by Terry Maple and Gerald Lentz, Peachtree (Atlanta, GA), 1996.
Totally Fun Things to Do with Your Dog, illustrated by Ed Shems, Wiley, 1998.
Totally Fun Things to Do with Your Cat, illustrated by Ed Shems, Wiley, 1998.

OTHER

(With David M. Taylor) *Gut Reactions: How to Handle Stress and Your Stomach,* Saunders, 1980.
Fiction Writer's Help Book, Writer's Digest Books (Cincinnati, OH), 1982.
Report on Student Work Programs Leadership Conference at Berry College, October 4 and 5, 1982, The College (Mount Berry, GA), 1982.
The Marriage Map: Understanding and Surviving the Stages of Marriage, Peachtree, 1986.
The Automobile and the Environment, introduced by Russell E. Train, Chelsea House, 1992.

Also the contributor of more than one thousand articles to local, national, and international publications, including *Smithsonian, McCalls, Travel,* and *Atlanta.*

Sidelights

Maxine Rock has been a professional freelance writer and journalist for twenty-five years and served as a professor of journalism for ten years. During that decade, she remained an active journalist, because, as she once commented, "writing is an active, changing profession, and one cannot merely step back, observe, and teach. To be a writer, you must write as well as talk about writing."

Whether writing for child or adult audiences, Rock's goal is to "gather facts about a specific subject and weave them into dramatic, readable tales that give readers not only knowledge, but a *feel* for the material presented." Rock's background in journalism serves her young readers well, delivering to them the interesting and well-filtered results of her often extensive research. In *Kishina: A True Story of Gorilla Survival,* the author neatly outlines the study of the first gorilla born and

Rock offers young readers a wealth of activities to share with their pet dog. (Cover illustration by Randy Verstraete.)

successfully raised in captivity. "Ably distilling years of research," wrote a *Publishers Weekly* critic, "Rock describes the work of the many scientists and veterinarians who have vigilantly tracked Kishina's development." The resulting book introduces readers to gorilla physiology, psychology, and social behavior, as well as issues of ecology and extinction. Moreover, "the author beautifully illustrates the significant biological and behavioral kinship between gorillas and humans," noted Joseph A. Mannino in *Science Books & Films.* Readers follow Kishina's development from her abandonment as an infant and resulting care from humans, through her mature maternal role with her own offspring, and her successful incorporation into a new family of gorillas at a Florida animal preserve. Rock emphasizes the great advances in human understanding of the gorilla since Kishina's birth in 1972, noting the endangerment of these animals in the wild, and arguing for the continuance of support from zoos and animal preserves for this and other species threatened with extinction. "Portraying Kishina's intelligence and sophisticated emotional life,

the author pleads her case persuasively," concluded a *Publishers Weekly* reviewer.

Rock has also written two books for children with pets. In *Totally Fun Things to Do with Your Dog,* Rock presents information on how to play games with a dog, how to go jogging with a dog, and how to enter a dog in a show. *Totally Fun Things to Do with Your Cat* follows a similar format with cat-comparable activities. Reviewers of *Totally Fun Things to Do with Your Dog* emphasized that Rock presents information on dog ownership in a spirited, often humorous way that encourages building a bond with a pet through play rather than through training or caring for it. *School Library Journal* contributor Carol Kolb Phillips did, however, appreciate the "clear step-by-step instructions on training" in addition to the many other elements that contributed to "a lively read." "Children will devour this interesting, offbeat treat," predicted Kathleen Squires in *Booklist,* "not only because of the pleasing activities but also because of the accessible, well-organized form and Ed Shems' adorable illustrations."

Works Cited

Review of *Kishina, Publishers Weekly,* May 6, 1996, p. 82.

Mannino, Joseph A., review of *Kishina, Science Books & Films,* March, 1997, p. 52.

Phillips, Carol Kolb, review of *Totally Fun Things to Do with Your Dog, School Library Journal,* August, 1998, pp. 183-84.

Pollock, Jean, review of *Kishina, School Library Journal,* July, 1996, pp. 95-96.

Squires, Kathleen, review of *Totally Fun Things to Do with Your Dog, Booklist,* June 1, 1998, p. 1760.

*　　　*　　　*

ROWLAND, Florence Wightman 1900-1997

OBITUARY NOTICE—See index for *SATA* sketch: Born January 2, 1900, in Newark, NJ; died March 24, 1997, in Nice, CA. Children's writer. Rowland received her A.B. degree in 1923 from the University of Southern California, and her general secondary teaching certificate in 1938 from the University of California, Los Angeles. A writer for children, Rowland was an honorary member of the Southern California Women's Press Club. Her first book was *Austrian Colt* (1950), followed by *Jade Dragons* (1954), *Juddie* (1958), *Eo of the Caves* (1959), *Pasquala of Santa Ynez Mission* (1961), *The Singing Leaf* (1965), *Let's Go to a Hospital* (1968), *School for Julio* (1969), *Little Sponge Fisherman* (1969), *Amish Boy* (1970), *Amish Wedding* (1971), and *Robbie of the Kirkhaven Team* (1973). A prolific writer, Rowland also contributed more than three hundred short stories, poems, and articles to magazines, including *McCall's, Good Housekeeping,* and *Everywoman's,* as well as to major juvenile publications.

—Obituary by Robert Reginald and Mary A. Burgess

RYBAKOV, Anatoli (Naumovich) 1911-1998

OBITUARY NOTICE—See index for *SATA* sketch: Born January 14 (some sources say January 1), 1911, in Chernigov, Russia (now Ukraine); died December 24, 1998, in Manhattan, NY. Author. Russian novelist Anatoli Rybakov was well known for his work *Children of the Arbat* (1987), which for the first time in print, promoted the advent of detente and described the horrors of the Stalin regime. The story also did much to raise awareness of—and lend credibility to—the initiatives and reform advocated by Mikhail Gorbachev. Rybakov and his Jewish family lived during his early years in the Arbat district of Moscow. He was arrested in 1933 for alleged involvement in counter-revolutionary activity and sentenced to a three-year exile in Siberia. Rybakov began writing in 1948 and published the children's book *Kortik* (1948), which was later made into a movie. Stalin thought highly of the young author's work, including *Voditeli* ("The Drivers," 1950), which won a Stalin Prize. Rybakov also published *Heavy Sand,* a first among novels as it openly addressed German anti-Semitism during World War Two. *Children of the Arbat* described the Stalin regime in the 1930s and was unique not only for bringing the subject into the open, but for the fact that the author was no dissident but instead, a respected Soviet author with many published children's works. Later publications by Rybakov included *Fear* (1992) and *Dust and Ashes* (1996).

OBITUARIES AND OTHER SOURCES:

PERIODICALS

Chicago Tribune, December 24, 1998, p. 12.
London Times, January 22, 1999.
New York Times, December 24, 1998, p. A17.
Los Angeles Times, December 25, 1998, p. A48.
Washington Post, December 24, 1998, p. B6.

S

SALISBURY, Graham 1944-

Personal

Born April 11, 1944, in Philadelphia, PA; son of Henry Forester Graham (an officer in the U.S. Navy) and Barbara Twigg-Smith; married second wife, Robyn Kay Cowan, October 26, 1988; children: Sandi Weston, Miles, Ashley, Melanie, Alex, Keenan, Zachary, Annie Rose (adopted). *Education:* California State University at Northridge, B.A. (magna cum laude), 1974; Vermont College of Norwich University, M.F.A., 1990. *Politics:* "Middle of the road."

Graham Salisbury

Addresses

Office—520 SW Sixth Ave., Suite 830, Portland, OR 97204. *Agent*—Fran Lebowitz, Writers House, 21 West 26th St., New York, NY 10010.

Career

Writer. Worked variously as a deckhand, glass-bottom boat skipper, singer-songwriter, graphic artist, and teacher; manager of historic office-buildings in downtown Portland, OR. *Member:* Society of Children's Book Writers and Illustrators, American Library Association, Hawaiian Mission Children's Society, National Council of Teachers of English.

Awards, Honors

Parents Choice Award, Bank Street College Child Study Children's Book Award, Judy Lopez Memorial Award for Children's Literature, Women's National Book Association, Best Books for Young Adults, American Library Association (ALA), and Best Books, *School Library Journal,* all 1992, Notable Trade Book in the Language Arts, National Council of Teachers of English (NCTE), and Oregon Book Award, both 1993, all for *Blue Skin of the Sea;* Parents Choice Honor Award, Editors' Choice, *Booklist,* Scott O'Dell Award, Best Books for Young Adults, ALA, Notable Children's Books, ALA, and Books in the Middle, *Voice of Youth Advocates,* all 1994, Teacher's Choice, International Reading Association, Notable Children's Trade Book in the Field of Social Studies, National Council for the Social Studies and Children's Book Council (NCSS-CBC), Notable Children's Books, Library of Congress, Books for the Teen Age, New York Public Library, Hawaii Nene Award, California Young Reader Medal, and Oregon Book Award, all 1995, all for *Under the Blood-Red Sun;* Oregon Book Award, 1998, and Parents Choice Honor Award, both for *Shark Bait;* Best Books for Young Adults, ALA, and Junior Literary Guild pick, both 1999, both for *Jungle Dogs.* PEN/Norma Klein Award for an emerging voice among American writers of children's fiction, 1992, and John Unterecker Award

A series of eleven interlinking stories, Salisbury's novel centers on two boys growing up in Hawaii during the 1950s and '60s.

for Fiction, Chaminade University and Hawaii Literary Arts Council, for body of work.

Writings

Blue Skin of the Sea, Delacorte, 1992.
Under the Blood-Red Sun, Delacorte, 1994.
Shark Bait, Delacorte, 1997.
Jungle Dogs, Delacorte, 1998.

Contributor to anthologies, including *Ultimate Sports: Short Stories by Outstanding Writers for Young Adults,* edited by Donald R. Gallo, Delacorte, 1995; *Going Where I'm Coming From: Memoirs of American Youth,* edited by Anne Mazer, Persea, 1995; *No Easy Answers: Short Stories about Teenagers Making Tough Decisions,* edited by Donald R. Gallo, Delacorte, 1997; *Working Days: Short Stories about Teenagers at Work,* edited by Anne Mazer, Persea, 1997; *Dirty Laundry: Stories about Family Secrets,* edited by Lisa Rowe Fraustino, Viking, 1998; and *Time Capsule: Short Stories about Teenagers throughout the Twentieth Century,* edited by Donald R. Gallo, Delacorte, 1999.

Contributor to periodicals, including *Bamboo Ridge, Chaminade Literary Review, Hawaii Pacific Review, Journal of Youth Services in Libraries, Manoa: A Journal of Pacific and International Writing, Northwest, Booklist, ALAN Review, SIGNAL Journal,* and *Hawaii Library Association Journal.*

Sidelights

Characterizing himself as an author who writes for and about teenage boys, Graham Salisbury has published four well-received novels: *Blue Skin of the Sea, Under the Blood-Red Sun, Shark Bait,* and *Jungle Dogs,* all of which are set on the Hawaiian islands where Salisbury was raised. In addition to an exotic island setting, his fictional coming-of-age novels feature intricate interpersonal relationships that can make the task of growing up most difficult. "I've thought a lot about what my job is now, or should be, as an author of books for young readers," Salisbury noted in an article in the *ALAN Review.* "I don't write to teach, preach, lecture, or criticize, but to explore. I write to make good use of the amazing English language. And if my stories show boys choosing certain life options, and the possible consequences of having chosen those options, then maybe I will have finally done something worthwhile."

While Salisbury entered the world in the city of Philadelphia, Pennsylvania, during the second World War, generations of his family had lived far from the U.S. mainland, on the islands of Hawaii. Salisbury's ancestors were missionaries who went to Hawaii in the early nineteenth century. His father, a young ensign in the U.S. Navy, was at Pearl Harbor during the Japanese attack on December 7, 1941; although he survived that ordeal, he died a few years later when he was shot down in his fighter plane on April 11, 1945—his son's first birthday.

Given his family history, it is not surprising that Salisbury spent little time in Pennsylvania; he and his mother made their home in the Hawaiian islands. In turn, he has set his books on the islands as he remembers them from his childhood. "I can *feel,* even now, the rocking of my stepfather's deep-sea charter fishing boat, the hot sun on my shoulders, salt itching under my T-shirt after swimming," Salisbury once told *SATA.* "I can hear the constant rumble of waves and smell the sweet aroma of steaks cooking at the hotels in the village of Kailua-Kona. I can even make myself shudder when I remember the time I got caught in quicksand in Kanehoe, Oahu, and had to wait, sinking slowly, while my friend ran for help."

Unlike many writers, Salisbury was not interested in books as a child. Because of his father's untimely death, Salisbury was raised without a solid male role-model to provide guidance, and he was left with a lot of time on his hands in which to wander the islands with his friends. His mother, whom Salisbury has described as "wonderful but needy," was immersed in her own problems and was often absent from the home, both emotionally and physically. Salisbury was left to search

Fourteen-year-old Hawaiian Eric is torn between his loyalty to his police chief father and the animosity he and his friends feel toward Navy sailors from a destroyer docked nearby. (Cover illustration by Rick Lieder.)

for guidance and approval from other adults in his life: friends, relatives, and teachers.

Salisbury attended boarding school from grades seven through twelve, and this experience provided him with the structure and guidance that he had missed earlier in life. However, until Salisbury's college days at California State University at Northridge, where he graduated with a bachelor's degree in 1974, the idea of being a writer never occurred to him. "I didn't read until I was a little past thirty," Salisbury confided to *SATA*. "Sure, I escaped with Edgar Rice Burroughs and Louis L'Amour a couple of times, and I read the required *Iliad* and *Odyssey* in high school, but I didn't read of my own choice until my first son was born. Then I read Alex Haley's *Roots,* which changed my life forever." It was *Roots* that inspired Salisbury to become a voracious reader and then to write books of his own. He also went on to obtain his master's degree in fine arts degree at Vermont College of Norwich University in 1990.

Salisbury began by writing what he calls "memory pieces": autobiographical vignettes that eventually got stretched and shaped into fiction. The pieces retained the island setting and the themes of relationships that informed his memories—most markedly the relationship that Salisbury had always desired but never had as a boy: that between father and son. But it was the medium of fiction that would allow his imagination full reign. And writing fiction was what Salisbury enjoyed most.

The author's first novel, *Blue Skin of the Sea,* was published in 1992. Composed of a series of eleven interlinking short-stories, the book centers on two boys, Sonny Mendoza and his cousin Keo, who are growing up in Hawaii during the 1950s and 60s, at a time when the old island ways were getting lost due to the increasing influx of tourists and other newcomers. Keo is fearless, while Sonny, whose mother died when he was very young, is more thoughtful and introspective. But as friends the two cousins balance one another. Throughout the book, the boys learn to deal with the school bully, try to cope with their growing attraction to girls, figure out ways to earn spending money, and jump other hurdles of everyday teen life. Along the way they meet up with a Hollywood film crew, sent out to the Mendoza's corner of Kona to film actor Spencer Tracy in *The Old Man and the Sea.* The boys, thinking that the props make the action look unrealistic, decide to educate the veteran actor in how to deal with real, rather than fake sharks. A *New York Times Book Review* critic termed *Blue Skin of the Sea* an "impressive debut," while *Five Owls* contributor Gary D. Schmidt deemed the novel "entertaining, moving, and poignant," adding praise for the Salisbury's realistic depiction of island life, with all its "pressures and tensions and loves and fears." *Blue Skin of the Sea* won several awards, and was chosen one of the American Library Association's Best Books for Young Adults.

Salisbury took four years to write *Blue Skin of the Sea;* in fact, he claimed in an interview with Janet Benton in *ALAN Review* that he actually "taught" himself to write while working on the book: "I wrote all the stories ... as individual stand-alone stories, then wove them together with the 'dream memory' thread which, luckily, seems to have worked.... As far as I am concerned, [all the characters in the book] actually lived on this earth and I, for a while, knew them and learned from them. Writing fiction is like that for me. It's one of the great glories of reveling in this art form."

Reflecting upon his father's experiences during and after the bombing raid at Pearl Harbor, Salisbury began a new novel when he imagined what it would be like to be there, as a boy, during the bombing and its aftermath. *Under the Blood-Red Sun,* published in 1994, is the story of a Japanese-American eighth-grader named Tomikazu "Tomi" Nakaji, whose parents had left Japan to find a better life in the United States, settling on the island of Oahu. Set during World War II, the novel shows how Tomi's life is suddenly, radically altered after the Japanese attack on Pearl Harbor. Where baseball, school assignments, and a local bully once occupied his thoughts, young Tomi now must worry about battling the increased tensions between Japanese immigrants and native islanders. Of real difficulty is toning down his elderly grandfather's proud display of his Japanese heritage, a heritage which is now viewed with suspicion by the Nakajis' American neighbors. Praising Salisbury for "subtly reveal[ing] the natural suspicions of the Americans and the equally natural bewilderment of the Japanese immigrants," *Booklist* contributor Frances Bradburn stated: "It is a tribute to the writer's craft that, though there are no easy answers in the story, there is empathy for both cultures." *Voice of Youth Advocates* reviewer John R. Lord also praised the work, noting that "in a time when positive co-existence is being touted in our schools, this novel is an outstanding example of thought-provoking—and at the same time eerily entertaining—prose for the YA reader."

The world of boyhood is central to Salisbury's writing, and it contains elements that he well remembers, particularly what he calls the "Silent Code of Conduct." In his *ALAN Review* interview, he recalled a scene from his youth, when he and friends were surfing. While sitting on their surfboards, legs dangling knee-deep in the salt water, one of the boys pointed out to a nearby reef and stated, simply, "'Got one shark surfing with us,' as if it were a mullet, or one of those fat hotel-pond carps," Salisbury remembered. "The strength in my arms suddenly felt like jelly," he continued, and stories of the infrequent shark attacks around the island of Oahu reeled through his mind. "None of us moved. None of us started paddling in to shore. We just kept sitting there with our legs, from the knee down, dangling underwater," Salisbury recalled. "I sat there with the rest of them, keeping an eye on the shark ... trying not to look nervous, which I was." Salisbury attributes the young boys' desire to be accepted to "that unspoken 'code,' lurking in the corner of [our] mind."

In Salisbury's novel *Shark Bait,* that silent code of male conduct weighs heavily on fourteen-year-old protagonist Eric Chock, nicknamed "Mokes" or "tough guy." Mokes is unsure where his loyalties lie when he and his school friends hear through the grapevine that tensions between native kids and Navy sailors from a destroyer docked nearby are about to spark a showdown. Mokes's father, the police chief in their small Hawaiian town, working to uphold the law and keep the peace, imposes a six o'clock evening curfew, but Mokes's best friend, seventeen-year-old Booley, plans to go to the fight and vows to kill one of the white sailors if he has the chance during the brawl. Mokes wants to obey his father, but also feels he should stand by his friend in battle. Things take a sharp turn for the worse when it is discovered that one of the island kids is going to the fight with a loaded gun. Praising Salisbury's "surefooted" portrayal of "the teen milieu of fast cars, faster girls, rivalries, and swagger," Elizabeth Bush of the *Bulletin of the Center for Children's Books* commended the novel as "a lot more diverting than luaus and ukuleles." While somewhat concerned about Salisbury's casual treatment of alcohol and drug use among his teen protagonists, *School Library Journal* contributor Coop Renner

deemed *Shark Bait* "a consistently engaging, well-written problem novel in a well-realized setting."

In *Shark Bait,* Salisbury's characters speak Pidgin English, a dialect used by many people native to the islands, which required the novelist to make several editorial passes through the manuscript to tone down the dialect, so that readers could get the flavor of the language without having to struggle to understand each word. *Booklist* contributor Helen Rosenberg praised Salisbury's use of dialect for adding to his "colorful picture of island life, complete with love interests and local superstitions. Along with the local color, there's some riveting action and a [powerful] climax."

Salisbury followed *Shark Bait* with another well-received novel for young adults, *Jungle Dogs.* Again featuring a Hawaiian setting, the book centers on a twelve-year-old named Boy Regis growing up in a tough neighborhood in which he must learn to conquer his fears and stand up for his convictions. Boy's older brother, who belongs to a gang, believes he must fight all his younger sibling's battles for him, often making things more difficult for Boy. At the same time, Boy's family relies on income he earns from his paper route—a route requiring that he daily pass a pack of wild jungle dogs on one of the paths to his deliveries. A *Publishers Weekly* reviewer praised the novel as a "tightly drawn drama," noting that Salisbury's "somewhat exotic scenery and dialect are backdrop for sharp characterizations and inventive, subtle plot twists." Janice M. Del Negro of the *Bulletin of the Center for Children's Books* maintained: "The lush Hawaii setting adds a physical dimension that strongly colors the action as Boy faces both canine and human packs with tenacity and nerve that will hearten young readers confronting their own demons."

"There are so many things to learn about writing—about thought, about feelings and passions, about storytelling, about craft, about commitment, and about one's own personality and habits," Salisbury told *SATA*. "But in my mind, one element is most important. Without it a writer will struggle endlessly. That element is discipline. Someone once said that a published writer is an amateur who didn't give up. There's so much truth in that. Discipline, to me, means consistent—almost habitual—writerly thinking, writing, rewriting, revising, and submitting.

"The important thing for me to understand as a writer for young readers is that though the world has changed, the basic needs of young people haven't. There are many, many kids out there with holes in their lives that they desperately want to fill. I can write about those holes. I can do this because I am human and have suffered and soared myself. Strange as it sounds to say, I—as a writer—consider myself lucky, indeed, to have all the holes I have in my own life. Because when I write, I remember, I understand, I empathize, and I feel a need to explore those holes and maybe even fill a couple of them—for myself and for any reader with a similar need who happens to stumble onto my work."

Although he still has many relatives in Hawaii, Salisbury—who goes by the nickname "Sandy"—has returned to the mainland. He lives in Portland, Oregon, with his family. His hobbies include boating, fishing, biking, and running, and he also enjoys researching his family history in Hawaii, both the positive and negative aspects of his Anglo-Saxon missionary past and its role in the colonization of the native Hawaiian people. While identifying with native Hawaiians' concern that their traditional culture is being destroyed, Salisbury maintains that looking back and apportioning blame is not constructive. As he told Benton, "We are all new people. The people of the past are dust."

Works Cited

Benton, Janet, "'Writing My Way Home': An Interview with Graham Salisbury," *ALAN Review,* winter, 1997.

Review of *Blue Skin of the Sea, New York Times Book Review,* May 2, 1993, p. 24.

Bradburn, Frances, review of *Under the Blood-Red Sun, Booklist,* October 15, 1994, p. 425.

Bush, Elizabeth, review of *Shark Bait, Bulletin of the Center for Children's Books,* December, 1997, pp. 138-39.

Del Negro, Janice M., review of *Jungle Dogs, Bulletin of the Center for Children's Books,* February, 1999, p. 216.

Review of *Jungle Dogs, Publishers Weekly,* July 13, 1998, p. 78.

Lord, John R., review of *Under the Blood-Red Sun, Voice of Youth Advocates,* October, 1994, p. 216.

Renner, Coop, review of *Shark Bait, School Library Journal,* September, 1997, p. 225.

Rosenberg, Helen, review of *Shark Bait, Booklist,* September 1, 1997, p. 107.

Salisbury, Graham, "A Leaf on the Sea," *ALAN Review,* fall, 1994, pp. 11-14.

Schmidt, Gary D., review of *Blue Skin of the Sea, Five Owls,* May-June, 1992, p. 66.

For More Information See

PERIODICALS

ALAN Review, winter, 1996, pp. 35-45.

Bulletin of the Center for Children's Books, November, 1994, p. 102.

Horn Book, September-October, 1995, pp. 634-39.

Kirkus Reviews, October 15, 1994, p. 1415; July 1, 1997, p. 1035; July 15, 1998, p. 1041.

Publishers Weekly, June 15, 1992, p. 104; July 13, 1992, p. 22; October 31, 1994, p. 64.

School Library Journal, July, 1995, p. 50.

*　　　*　　　*

SAYLES, Elizabeth 1956-

Personal

Born January 6, 1956, in Brooklyn, NY; daughter of William (a commercial artist) and Shirley Leah (an

Elizabeth Sayles and daughter, Jessica Dow.

editor; maiden name, Weinstein) Sayles; married Matthew Justin Dow (a musician), September 5, 1993; children: Jessica Frances Dow. *Education:* Attended Philadelphia College of Art, 1974-77, and School of Visual Arts, New York. *Religion:* Jewish.

Addresses

Home—318 Fulle Drive, Valley Cottage, New York 10989. *Agent*—Cornell and McCarthy, LLC-2-D Cross Highway, Westport, CT 06880.

Career

Children's book illustrator. Graphic artist with own design studio in New York City; adjunct professor of illustration, School of Visual Arts, New York City. *Exhibitions:* Society of Illustrators, New York City; Columbus Museum of Art, Ohio; Edward Hopper Art Gallery, Nyack, NY; Every Picture Tells a Story Gallery, Los Angeles, CA; Chemers Gallery, Orange County, CA. *Member:* Graphic Artists Guild (National Board member, 1982-85).

Awards, Honors

Best Book, *Parents* magazine, 1995, for *Not in the House, Newton!;* Book of the Month, American Booksellers Association, 1995, for *The Sleeping Porch.*

Illustrator

Chuck Thurman, *A Time for Remembering,* Simon & Schuster, 1989.

Pegi Deitz Shea, *Bungalow Fungalow,* Clarion, 1991.

Janice May Udry, *What Mary Jo Shared,* Scholastic, 1991.

Louise Borden, *Albie the Lifeguard,* Scholastic, 1993.

Susan Tews, *Nettie's Gift,* Clarion, 1993.

Connie K. Heckert, *Dribbles,* Clarion, 1993.

Libba Moore Gray, *The Little Black Truck,* Simon & Schuster, 1994.

Mary Pope Osborne, *Molly and the Prince,* Knopf, 1994.

Karen Ackerman, *The Night Crossing,* Knopf, 1994.

Karen Ackerman, *The Sleeping Porch,* Morrow, 1995.

Judith Heide Gilliland, *Not in the House, Newton!,* Clarion, 1995.

Kathi Appelt, *The Thunderherd,* Morrow, 1996.

Tom Paxton, *The Marvelous Toy,* Morrow, 1996.

Pam Conrad, *This Mess,* Hyperion, 1998.

Mary McKenna Siddals, *Millions of Snowflakes,* Clarion, 1998.

Nancy Jewell, *Five Little Kittens,* Clarion, 1999.

Pat Mora, *The Rainbow Tulip,* Viking, 1999.

Sayles's illustrations have also appeared on dust jackets, in magazine and newspaper articles, and on the video-cassette packaging for the *Dinosaur!* series, from A & E cable network.

Work in Progress

Illustrating *Morning Song,* by Mary McKenna Siddals, for Henry Holt; *Ribbons for Mikele,* for Morrow.

Sidelights

Elizabeth Sayles left a successful career in graphic design—with clients including the Whitney Museum of American Art, UNICEF, and Arista Records—to turn her artistic hand to children's book illustration and jacket design, blending her artwork subtly with story text. Noted for her warm and somewhat soft-focus pastels, Sayles has illustrated over a dozen children's books, several of them award-winners.

Born in Brooklyn on January 6, 1956, Sayles grew up in Nyack, New York, raised in a family that encouraged her early artistic endeavors. "I come from a 'book' family," Sayles told *SATA*. "My father, a designer and illustrator; and my mother, a writer and editor, produced books together. My father also worked for a children's book publisher and brought lots of books home. He set up drawing tables for my brother and me right next to his in our attic. So, I always drew. My favorite illustrator then and now was Garth Williams."

Perspective was always an element Sayles enjoyed playing with, even as a child. Later in college, at the Philadelphia College of Art, she began learning about other artists. One of her favorites, Edward Hopper, was born in Nyack, New York, where Sayles grew up. Another early favorite for Sayles was Thomas Hart Benton, whose work later inspired her own, especially in

The Little Black Truck, a story set in the 1920s and '30s. In college Sayles was first introduced to pastels, and from that time on, she has continued to use them for her artwork. "After college," Sayles told *SATA,* "I did a few different jobs before establishing a *design* studio which I had for about ten years before mustering the courage to concentrate solely on illustration. For a short while I did both design and illustration, but happily the illustration jobs took over." At one point Sayles set up as a freelance illustrator in her hometown, moving into the very house where Edward Hopper had lived. "His use of light and shadow has always had a big influence on me," Sayles told *SATA.*

Sayles's picture book debut came in 1989 with the publication *A Time for Remembering,* written by Chuck Thurman. In this work, a terminally ill grandfather tries to prepare his grandson for the inevitable; helping him work through the grieving process with a flower which the boy will ritually throw away upon the old man's death. Patricia Pearl, writing in *School Library Journal,* noted that the "psychologically accurate theme is carried out through a brief, quiet, declarative text superimposed upon double-page spreads of soft, hazy, warmly colored illustrations of the grandfather and the boy at the hospital and during happier times."

More of Sayles's signature "soft" artwork is served up in *Bungalow Fungalow,* written by Pegi Deitz Shea. Fifteen poems celebrate the joy of a young boy during a vacation at his grandparents' seaside bungalow. Ellen Fader observed in *Horn Book* that "Elizabeth Sayles's art is full of the pale, sandy color of the beach; softly focused drawings shimmer with intense heat." Fader concluded that this book is a "fine choice in summer and in the middle of winter, when the book's images will warm readers with the relaxing glow of an unhurried family vacation." *School Library Journal* contributor Andrew W. Hunter noted that Sayles's illustrations "are realistic yet impressionistic in style, and capture the boy's enjoyment of the seashore and the time he spends with his family."

In 1993, three books illustrated by Sayles were published: *Albie the Lifeguard, Nettie's Gift,* and *Dribbles.* Described by *Booklist*'s Hazel Rochman as an "upbeat outsider story about a small boy who finds strength in himself to join his friends," *Albie the Lifeguard* provided Sayles with more opportunity to complement and expand on text. Albie decides not to join the swim team with the rest of his buddies, instead staying home and playing lifeguard in his backyard pool. "Sayles's warm pastels show Albie enjoying himself alone and with others, his solitary imaginative play as full of joyful movement and vitality as his social times with his smiling buddies," Rochman commented. A critic for *Publishers Weekly* noted that "Sayles's pastels have a dreamlike quality—as if viewed through stage scrim— softening the impact of Albie's perceived shortcom-ings." Reviewing the same title in *School Library Journal,* Liza Bliss concluded that "Sayles's pastels suggest the power and unity of the fantasy that prepares Albie to meet his challenge when he is ready."

Sayles's playful pastel drawings echo the fanciful mood of Judith Heide Gilliland's story of a young boy and his magical red crayon.

Nettie's Gift, written by Susan Tews, once again employs the intergenerational theme of grandparents and grandchildren. Grandma Nettie tells young Sarah, an only child, stories of her adventures at Sarah's age. These memories are turned into an imaginary friend for Sarah. Hanna B. Zeiger noted in *Horn Book* that the "rich, figurative language of the story and the warm illustrations, glowing with autumnal colors, blend to perfection in this tale of friendship imagined and real." Other reviewers also praised Sayles's autumnal palette. Writing in *Booklist,* Kay Weisman noted that "Sayles makes effective use of browns and oranges in the quiet autumnal story," and went on to comment that "her artwork—with its indistinct faces and fuzzy, faraway look—lends a tranquil atmosphere to this mood piece." A *Publishers Weekly* contributor concluded a review of the book by stating that "Sayles's autumn pastel illustrations lure readers into a wistful late-afternoon light where sharp edges are blurred and fading forms

catch bits of sun in luminous patches—creating an ideal mood for a girl to discover the wealth of her solitude."

Another story about death—this time told from the point of view of four cats—is *Dribbles.* An old cat, Dribbles, moves into a home populated by three others, and after they finally become friends, Dribbles dies. Virginia E. Jeschelnig observed in *School Library Journal* that "Sayles's rich pastel illustrations, with their subtle, painterly compositions, are the ideal accompaniment to the thoughtful text." A reviewer for *Publishers Weekly* concluded that "Sayles's full-page pastels, in soft ambers and creams, offer a gentle, cat's-eye view of friendship, love and loss; her illustrations of the three bereaved cats gazing out the window is particularly moving."

"I am very disciplined when I work," Sayles told *SATA.* "I am in my studio from about 10 a.m. to 5 p.m. Monday through Friday unless I have a meeting or have to go to

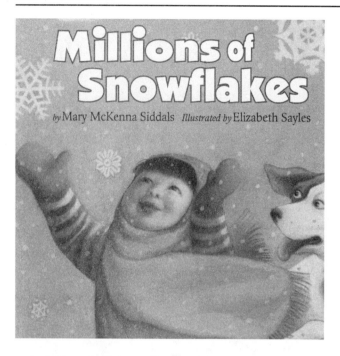

Sayles's charming illustrations enhance Mary McKenna Siddals's joyful counting verse about a young girl's delight in a snowfall.

the library for research or whatever. I work with pastel on paper, but before doing a final painting I do lots of sketches which must be approved by the editor and art director. A children's picture book—from the time I get the manuscript through thumbnail sketches, final sketches, and final art—can take a couple of years, but probably just three months of actual work."

The Little Black Truck by Libba Moore Gray reprises the idea of *The Little Engine That Could* and *Mike Mulligan's Steam Shovel,* but this time it is a little black truck that gets a second chance at life. The truck fetches produce against an ever-changing seasonal backdrop in the initial part of the truck's existence during a bygone era. Discovered rusting in the woods much later, the little truck is revived by the grandson of the man who may have earlier operated her. "The pictures," noted Mary Harris Veeder in *Booklist,* "in which landscapes almost always dominate, are soft-edged images that blanket rural life and the little black truck with an aura of affection." A *Publishers Weekly* critic concluded that "Sayles portrays the romantic mood of the story in handsome, larger-than-life pastels," with "warm greens, browns and blues" which "depict a shimmering heartland." Writing in *School Library Journal,* Cynthia K. Richey compared Sayles's "impressionistic, full-color illustrations" with their "soft, sculptural shapes and rounded use of line" to the work of *Jumanji* creator Chris Van Allsburg.

A *Parents* magazine Best Book, *Not in the House, Newton!* tells the story of a young boy and his magical red crayon. Everything Newton draws becomes real, and he ultimately flies off in an airplane he sketches. *Booklist*'s Susan Dove Lempke called Sayles's illustra-

tions for this book "cozy and intimate," while a *Kirkus Reviews* contributor commented that "Sayles's softened pastels create the right mood for the adventure." Another award-winning title, *The Sleeping Porch,* tells of a family's delight moving into their first home, until a leaky roof forces them to retreat to the sleeping porch to get a dry night's sleep. "Sayles's pastel illustrations," noted *Booklist*'s Kay Weisman, "rich in hues of purple and orange, convey the warmth and closeness the family shares." Jane Marino commented in *School Library Journal* that "Sayles's appealing pastel illustrations are dominated by various shades of purple that serve as warm backgrounds for the comforting glow of the porch's light."

Sayles has worked with a score of different authors, creating her subtle pictorial effects to work in tandem with text. However, as she told Melissa Myers in *The Journal News* of Rockland County, New York, "I think the pictures are the most important. The illustrator can definitely make or break the story." Sayles is picky when it comes to choosing manuscripts to illustrate. "I look for good stories," she told Myers. "When I read them I get pictures in my mind. Children's books do not have a lot of words, but every word is important." Having a child has also been a strong influence on Sayles's art. As she told Myers, "I have one daughter who critiques my work and inspires me now. I can see the work differently." Sayles continues to work primarily in pastels, and uses both friends and the children of friends as her models.

Sayles has depicted images from thunderstorms to snowflakes, and from mysterious toys to messy rooms. Her illustrations for Kathi Appelt's *The Thunderherd* were dubbed "dreamy pastel paintings" by *Booklist* reviewer Kay Weisman, while her artwork for Mary McKenna Siddals's *Millions of Snowflakes* was called "evocative" by Kathy Piehl in *School Library Journal.* Piehl went on to note that Sayles's illustrations "create winter surroundings made for playful exploration." Illustrating the popular folk song by Tom Paxton, *The Marvelous Toy,* Sayles "creates a satisfyingly unique 'marvelous toy' ... that fits the description in the song," according to Lisa Dennis in *School Library Journal.* Dennis also noted that the "combination of cozy charm and unpredictable whimsy" in Sayles's artwork "is a perfect match for the playful text." And reviewing Sayles's illustrations for Pam Conrad's *This Mess,* Stephanie Zvirin of *Booklist* praised the artist's work in a manner that could stand as a fitting tribute to her work as a whole. Zvirin wrote that "the artwork, in a rainbow of color, literally floats across the pages, reflecting both the comedy and the fantasy. Ordinary things here become extraordinary opportunities for fun."

Works Cited

Review of *Albie the Lifeguard, Publishers Weekly,* May 24, 1993, p. 87.

Bliss, Liza, review of *Albie the Lifeguard, School Library Journal,* June, 1993, p. 70.

Dennis, Lisa, review of *The Marvelous Toy, School Library Journal,* August, 1996, pp. 127-28.

Review of *Dribbles, Publishers Weekly,* August 9, 1993, p. 478.

Fader, Ellen, review of *Bungalow Fungalow, Horn Book,* July-August, 1991, p. 473.

Hunter, Andrew W., review of *Bungalow Fungalow, School Library Journal,* June, 1991, p. 98.

Jeschelnig, Virginia E., review of *Dribbles, School Library Journal,* November, 1993, p. 82.

Lempke, Susan Dove, review of *Not in the House, Newton!, Booklist,* December 15, 1995, p. 708.

Review of *The Little Black Truck, Publishers Weekly,* April 11, 1994, p. 64.

Marino, Jane, review of *The Sleeping Porch, School Library Journal,* May, 1995, p. 81.

Myers, Melissa, "Hopper House Book Fair Points Spotlight on Local Authors," *The Journal News,* November 29, 1998.

Review of *Nettie's Gift, Publishers Weekly,* March 15, 1993, p. 87.

Review of *Not in the House, Newton!, Kirkus Reviews,* October 15, 1995.

Pearl, Patricia, review of *A Time for Remembering, School Library Journal,* January, 1990, pp. 90-91.

Piehl, Kathy, review of *Millions of Snowflakes, School Library Journal,* September, 1998, p. 182.

Richey, Cynthia K., review of *The Little Black Truck, School Library Journal,* August, 1994, pp. 131-32.

Rochman, Hazel, review of *Albie the Lifeguard, Booklist,* February 15, 1993, p. 1066.

Veeder, Mary Harris, review of *The Little Black Truck, Booklist,* June 1, 1994, p. 1837.

Weisman, Kay, review of *Nettie's Gift, Booklist,* March 1, 1993, p. 1239.

Weisman, Kay, review of *The Sleeping Porch, Booklist,* March 1, 1995, p. 1246.

Weisman, Kay, review of *The Thunderherd, Booklist,* May 15, 1996, p. 1590.

Zeiger, Hanna B., review of *Nettie's Gift, Horn Book,* July-August, 1993, p. 431.

Zvirin, Stephanie, review of *The Mess, Booklist,* April 15, 1998, p. 1450.

For More Information See

PERIODICALS

Booklist, March 15, 1994, p. 1346.
Publishers Weekly, April 25, 1994, p. 79; August 15, 1994, p. 94; August 12, 1996, p. 83; April 20, 1998, p. 65.
School Library Journal, June, 1993, p. 90; July, 1994, p. 100; September, 1994, p. 190; January, 1996, pp. 83-84; August, 1996, p. 115; April, 1998, p. 97.

—*Sketch by J. Sydney Jones*

*   *   *

SMITH, Ward
See GOLDSMITH, Howard

STEVENS, Greg
See COOK, Glen (Charles)

*   *   *

STILES, Martha Bennett 1933-

Personal

Born in Manila, Philippine Islands; daughter of Forrest Hampton and Jane (Bennett) Wells; married Martin Stiles (a professor of chemistry), 1954; children: John Martin. *Education:* Studied at College of William and Mary; University of Michigan, B.S., 1954. *Religion:* Episcopalian.

Addresses

Home—861 Hume-Bedford Rd., Paris, KY 40361.

Career

Writer. *Member:* Authors Guild, South Carolina Poetry Society, University of Kentucky Library Associates, Phi Beta Kappa, Detroit Women Writers.

Martha Bennett Stiles

Awards, Honors

University of Michigan, Avery and Jule Hopwood Awards (both major and minor); Kentucky Arts Council, Al Smith Fellowship; University of Missouri, citation for distinguished contribution to children's literature; Society of Children's Book Writers and Illustrators (SCBWI), Judy Blume Novel-in-Progress Grant; Frankfort Arts Foundation, short fiction prizes, 1984 and 1986.

Writings

FOR CHILDREN

One among the Indians, Dial, 1962.
The Strange House at Newburyport, Dial, 1963.
Darkness over the Land, Dial, 1966.
Dougal Looks for Birds, illustrated by Iris Schweitzer, Four Winds, 1972.
(Reteller) *James, the Vine Puller: A Brazilian Folktale,* illustrated by Larry Thomas, Carolrhoda (Minneapolis, MN), 1974.
The Star in the Forest: A Mystery of the Dark Ages, Four Winds, 1979.
Tana and the Useless Monkey, Elsevier/Nelson, 1979.
Sarah, the Dragon Lady, Macmillan, 1986.
Kate of Still Waters, Macmillan, 1990.
Island Magic, illustrated by Daniel San Souci, Atheneum, 1999.

CHAPBOOKS

(With Bobbie Ann Mason) *Landscapes,* Frankfort Arts Foundation, 1984.
Kentucky *Bestiary,* Frankfort Arts Foundation, 1986.

OTHER

Lonesome Road (novel), Gnomon (Frankfort, KY), 1998.

Contributor of articles to periodicals, including *Thoroughbred Record, Maryland Horse, Michigan Quarterly Review, Esquire, New York Times,* and fiction to periodicals including *Ingenue, Seventeen, Virginia Quarterly Review, TriQuarterly, Georgia Review,* and the *Missouri Review.*

Sidelights

Author Martha Bennett Stiles is most well-known for her historical novels for young people, which have captured the favor of reviewers for their intricate plotting, realistic characters, fully realized settings, and poignant human dilemmas. "I have written historical fiction," Stiles once commented, "because I am fascinated by why we are as we are." In addition to her historical YA novels, Stiles has written a novel for adults, as well as several children's picture books, noted for their humorous and unusual scenarios.

In *Darkness over the Land,* set in Munich, Germany, during and after World War II, Stiles conveys the turmoil of the war through the consciousness of the preadolescent narrator, Mark Elend. Mark's parents, like many others of the time, neither support nor actively

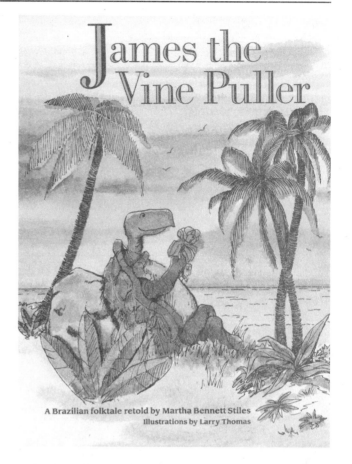

An ingenious turtle convinces a selfish whale and elephant to share their food in Stiles's version of a traditional Brazilian folktale.

oppose Nazi rule. Young Mark thus lives out the contradictions between what he is taught in his Nazi-run school and what he increasingly perceives to be the grim reality around him. Stiles depicts "the fears, hardships, and insecurity of life in Nazi Germany during the war years," remarked a reviewer for *Booklist.* Stiles also portrays the feelings of the Elend family when they are subject to the contempt of the occupying American forces after the war, who consider all Germans equally guilty of the crimes committed by some. "Never before have I read a story of the war so grimly real yet so lacking in morbidity," commented Ruth Hill Viguers in *Horn Book.*

With *The Star in the Forest: A Mystery of the Dark Ages,* Stiles created what *School Library Journal* contributor Ruth M. McConnell called a "suspenseful historic romance" for high school students. The novel features an extensive cast of both real and fictional characters, identified in a list at the back of the book. Set in sixth-century Gaul, the medieval mystery has been considered complex by several reviewers. The plot centers on the fate of Valrada, whose father, Lord Eurik of Poijou, intends to marry her to the cousin she is certain killed her beloved brother. Soon after Lord Eurik himself remarries upon the death of his wife, he is killed in battle, and his young pregnant wife becomes the center of a disputed inheritance claim between her unborn child and Valrada's evil cousin. McConnell praised Stiles for "good characterization (even of the animals)" and "a stunning climax."

Stiles's books for younger children include *Dougal Looks for Birds,* a gently humorous story of a boy's first birdwatching outing with his parents. Dougal not only spots the elusive great blue heron his father seeks but manages to capture a little girl's lost parakeet and becomes a hero. "The mixture of realism and whimsy in text and illustration ... is palatable, and the humor of the style is appealing," commented Zena Sutherland in the *Bulletin of the Center for Children's Books.*

Another of Stiles's humorous books for children, *Tana and the Useless Monkey,* is set in a poor Spanish-speaking country. The story tells how Tana's love for Pepito, her uncle's pet monkey, gives the monkey a chance to show he isn't as useless as Tana's father assumes. Only the farm's "useful" animals receive a blessing every year from the church, and a heartbroken Tana stays behind with Pepito on the special day. The two are thus home to intercept the dreaded government inspectors and warn the farmers to hide the livestock from the greedy government. The result, according to *Booklist* reviewer Denise M. Wilms, is a story that is "light and undemanding." A critic for *Kirkus Reviews* contended that Stiles's plot is "predictable," but the book is "none the worse for it—Pepito is an endearing, ingenious scamp, the other animals behave amusingly true to form, and even the adults act like reasonable, good-natured people."

Sarah, the Dragon Lady is a chapter book about a girl from New York City, who is stuck with her illustrator mother in rural Kentucky for a summer, while her parents make a trial separation. Sarah quickly befriends an adventurous local girl named Annette and eventually acquires some understanding of her working mother, and of her parents' marital problems. "Stiles' lively characters and realistic situations are sketched with true precision and humor," remarked a critic for *Kirkus Reviews.* "The story's large cast of interesting supporting characters is also a plus," concluded Ilene Cooper in *Booklist.*

For middle-grade readers is *Kate of Still Waters,* a moving coming-of-age story set in rural Kentucky, where Kate Chiddens and her family struggle to hold on to the family farm in the face of drought, the killing of their sheep by wild dogs, and other calamities. "The story's strength lies in its portrayal of farm life," wrote Denise Wilms in *Booklist.* "This isn't a simple book with a happy ending," Wilms continued, "it's a considered, very real picture of a complicated, demanding life." Kate had hoped to one day take over the family farm herself, but the tough times they face make her wonder if they won't lose the farm before she is old enough to run it. During the course of the year, Kate learns to stomach some of the less pleasant aspects of farming and begins to understand the changes she sees in her parents—her mother is forced to take a job in town,

and her father withdraws into himself. Writing in *Bulletin of the Center for Children's Books,* reviewer Kathryn Pierson praised Stiles's characterizations as "strong and believable." Pierson especially appreciated the empathetic teenage characters of Kate and her friends, asserting: "It is refreshing for fictional teenagers to be goal-oriented and sometimes serious, instead of superficially suburban." Other reviewers singled out Stiles's many scenes of animal husbandry for special praise, comparing the energy, grit, and poignancy of these scenes to those in the works of James Herriot. The result, concluded a *Kirkus Reviews* critic, is a "sensitive, honest picture of a threatened way of life."

Works Cited

Cooper, Ilene, review of *Sarah, the Dragon Lady, Booklist,* January 1, 1987, p. 712.

Review of *Darkness over the Land, Booklist,* May 1, 1967, p. 951.

Review of *Kate of Still Waters, Kirkus Reviews,* August 15, 1990, p. 1174.

McConnell, Ruth M., review of *The Star in the Forest, School Library Journal,* March, 1979, p. 151.

Pierson, Kathryn, review of *Kate of Still Waters, Bulletin of the Center for Children's Books,* December, 1990, p. 103.

Review of *Sarah, the Dragon Lady, Kirkus Reviews,* October 1, 1986, p. 1512.

Sutherland, Zena, review of *Dougal Looks for Birds, Bulletin of the Center for Children's Books,* September, 1972, p. 18.

Review of *Tana and the Useless Monkey, Kirkus Reviews,* August 15, 1979, p. 933.

Viguers, Ruth Hill, review of *Darkness over the Land, Horn Book,* February, 1967, p. 74.

Wilms, Denise M., review of *Kate of Still Waters, Booklist,* September 15, 1990, p. 157.

Wilms, Denise M., review of *Tana and the Useless Monkey, Booklist,* September 1, 1979, p. 47.

For More Information See

PERIODICALS

Booklist, November 1, 1972, p. 247; October 1, 1979, p. 232.

Bulletin of the Center for Children's Books, May, 1967, pp. 147-48; February, 1987, p. 120.

Kirkus Reviews, June 15, 1979, p. 691.

Publishers Weekly, November 23, 1998, p. 61.

School Library Journal, April, 1979, p. 64; November, 1990, pp. 140, 142.

*　　　*　　　*

STOTTER, Mike 1957- (Jim A. Nelson)

Personal

Born January 6, 1957, in London, England; son of James (a bank messenger) and Eleanor (a bank clerk; maiden

Mike Stotter

name, Osborne) Stotter; married Lorraine Desmond (a school assistant), January 5, 1980; children: Lee James, Paul Michael, Kieran Patrick. *Education:* Attended grammar school in London, England. *Politics:* Conservative. *Religion:* Church of England.

Addresses

Home—189 Snakes Lane E., Woodford Green, Essex IG8 7JH, England. *Electronic mail*—michael@mjstotter.demon.co.uk.

Career

BBC-TV, Middlesex, England, film clerk, 1974-78; London Transport, Essex, England, bus conductor, 1978-80; Centre-File Ltd., London, England, control clerk, 1980-82; Alpine Drinks, London, sales supervisor, 1982-84; bank messenger in London, 1986-87; Deutsche Bank, London, administrative assistant, 1987-99, central records administrator, 1999—; writer, 1990—. *Member:* Crime Writers Association.

Writings

McKinney's Revenge (novel), R. Hale (London, England), 1990.
Tombstone Showdown (novel), R. Hale, 1991.
McKinney's Law (novel), R. Hale, 1993.
Tucson Justice (novel), R. Hale, 1994.

(Under pseudonym Jim A. Nelson) *Death in the Canyon* (novel), R. Hale, 1997.
The Best-Ever Book of the Wild West (nonfiction), Larousse Kingfisher (New York City), 1997.
Step into the North American Indian World (nonfiction), Lorenz Books, 1999.

Work represented in anthologies, including *A Treasury of Cat Mysteries,* edited by Martin H. Greenberg, Carroll & Graf (New York City), 1998; *The Best of the American West,* edited by Greenberg and Ed Gorman, Berkley Publishing (New York City), 1998; *Speaking of Murder II,* edited by Greenberg and Gorman, Berkley Publishing, 1998; *Future Crimes,* edited by Greenberg and Gorman, DAW Books (New York City), 1999; and *Berkley Western Treasury II,* edited by Greenberg and Gorman, Berkley Publishing, 1999. Contributor to magazines, including *Mystery Scene, Mystery Review, Book and Magazine Collector, Million,* and *Old Dark House.* Editor, *Shots* (crime and mystery magazine); past editor, *Westerner.*

Work in Progress

Custer's Gold, a historical novel; research for a children's book, *Myths and Legends of the World.*

Sidelights

Mike Stotter told *SATA:* "I began writing back in 1990 when a friend mentioned that his publisher was looking for new writers and, since I liked westerns, why didn't I try writing one. I did, and that's how it all began. I had always loved the Old West era, even from childhood, having been reared on *Bonanza, Branded, Wagon Train,* and a whole lot more. If I stopped to analyze why, then you'd have a long wait for the answer.

"I was pleased that Kingfisher Larousse approached me to write *The Best-Ever Book of the Wild West.* It gave me the opportunity to redress some misconceptions created by Hollywood and pulp fiction novels at ground level. It was an enjoyable project, and I used my two younger sons as sounding boards for ideas, to gauge their reactions and to see whether or not the subject was of general interest to them. The fact that they still pull the book off the shelf at home and read it says volumes.

"In writing *The Best-Ever Book of the Wild West* I had to consider some important points. One of the paramount factors was never to be condescending to the readers. The fact that people die in the most unglamorous ways wasn't to be glossed over. Home life was harsh (no television or cable!). The image of a palisaded fort or a one-horse town had to be done away with; the meticulous research carried out on Fort Laramie and Tombstone bears this out. The American Indian wasn't always the savage that Hollywood made him out to be. In fact, in some circumstances, the lifestyle of the Indians was more desirable than that of the townsfolk. Not all cowboys were white men. As today, the Old West was multicultural with people flocking to the new land from all over the world to work in the military, industry, commerce, and entertainment. I think the illustrations and text bring this out.

"Working on *Step into the North American Indian World* was a natural extension to *The Best Ever Book of the Wild West.* Here I could explore the fascinating and often complex world of the North American Indian. Western literature is filled with writings on Indian tribes, though the truth is more colorful and exciting than any fictional story.

"The history of the North American Indian has been chronicled in many nonfiction books. In the *Step into* book I have tried to encompass details on most of the major tribes, their beliefs, customs, and traditions. Of course I have covered previously explored ground, but I still had to make it as fresh and exciting as possible for new readers.

"The goal in this work is to entertain and educate the reader, and perhaps make them stop and think once in a while. That was my challenge and one I hope I've met.

"I continue writing westerns, both full-length novels and short stories, and I still enjoy it. A current project is a children's book on myths and legends from around the world. Although it is not assigned to a publisher, it is a project that fascinates my children and me."

For More Information See

PERIODICALS

School Library Journal, January, 1998, p. 134.

*   *   *

STRUG, Kerri 1977-

Personal

Born November 19, 1977, in Tucson, AZ; daughter of Burt (a heart surgeon) and Melanie Strug. *Education:* Attended University of California, Los Angeles, 1996-98, Stanford University, 1998—.

Addresses

Office—P.O. Box 34B, Balboa Island, CA 92662 (fan club). *Agent*—Jill Peterson Management, 58 Parker Avenue, San Francisco, CA 94118.

Career

Gymnast. Participant in numerous gymnastics competitions and member of gymnastics teams, including Junior Pacific Alliance Team, Indianapolis, IN, 1989; Junior Pan Am Games Team, Tallahassee, FL, 1990; World Gymnastics Championship Team, Indianapolis, IN, 1991; U.S. Olympic Team, Barcelona, Spain, 1992; Hilton Challenge Team, Los Angeles, CA, 1993; Team World Championship Team, Dortmund, Germany, 1994; World Champion Team, Safae, Japan, 1995; U.S. Olympic Team, Atlanta, GA, 1996. Participant in

gymnastics exhibitions and tours. Has endorsed products and served as a spokesperson for corporations, including Becton Dickinson (Ace Bandage), Danskin, and Athlete Direct on America Online, and charities, including Special Olympics and Children's Make-a-Wish. Also worked as an intern for *Entertainment Tonight* and KNBC-TV, Los Angeles, CA.

Awards, Honors

First all around and second all around, both American Classic, both 1989; second place for uneven bars and balance beam, Dutch Open, 1990; first place for vault, U.S. Gymnastics Championships, 1991; first place for vault, United States vs. Romania, 1991; first place for vault and balance beam, U.S. Gymnastics Championships, 1992; second place all around and floor exercise, U.S. Gymnastics Championships, 1992; first place all around and for uneven bars, balance beam, and floor exercise, American Classic/World Championships Trials, 1993; first place for uneven bars and second place for uneven bars, Coca-Cola National Championships, 1993; first place for balance beam and second place all around, McDonald's American Cup, 1993; second place all around, Reebok International Mixed Pairs, 1993; first place all around, NationsBank World Team Trials, 1994; first place all around and for uneven bars, U.S. Olympic Festival, 1995; first place all around and for balance beam and floor exercise, and second place for vault and uneven bars, McDonald's American Cup, 1996; Silver Medal, World Championships, 1991; Olympic Bronze Medal, 1992; Silver Medal, Team World Championships, 1994; Bronze medal, World Championships,

Kerri Strug

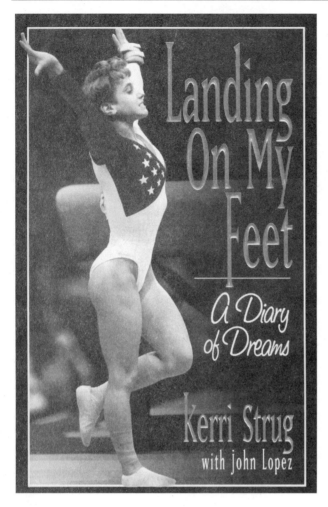

Strug's autobiography, co-written with John Lopez, is a chronicle of her life up until the 1996 Olympics that details her training regime. (Cover photo by Al Tielemans.)

1995; Olympic Gold Medal, 1996; Olympic Spirit Award, 1996.

Writings

(With Greg Brown) *Heart of Gold,* Taylor (Dallas, TX), 1996.

(With John Lopez) *Landing on My Feet: A Diary of Dreams,* Andrews & McMeel (Kansas City, MO), 1997.

Sidelights

Kerri Strug became an international figure at age eighteen during the 1996 Olympics in Atlanta when she made her medal-winning vault on an injured ankle. As she relates in her autobiography, *Landing on My Feet: A Diary of Dreams,* and in the children's book *Heart of Gold,* it was the culmination of years of work and competition that began with Strug's interest in gymnastics at age four as she imitated her older sister Lisa. At thirteen, she left home to train with Bela Karolyi in preparation for the 1992 Olympics. In Barcelona, Strug

was the youngest athlete to have ever competed in Olympic games but missed the all-around finals by .014 of a point, finishing fourth on the U.S. team. Karolyi retired after the 1992 games, leaving Strug with a succession of coaches and a series of injuries that included a torn stomach muscle and a back injury. When Karolyi came out of retirement in 1995, Strug returned to his gym and began preparing for the 1996 Olympic games.

In the final rounds of the women's team competition, the U.S. group was in first place, ahead of the skilled Russian and Romanian teams. In the final event, the vaulting routine, two of the U.S. competitors failed to earn high marks and pressure mounted for Kerri, who had not yet had her turn. Her first attempt on the vault fell short, and Strug felt her ankle give way on landing. "There was such momentum," she noted in *Heart of Gold.* "The bone was shoved forward and then back in place." The injury tore the medial and lateral ligaments, and Strug had to make the decision as to whether she would make the final vault. Karolyi has been criticized for encouraging her to make an attempt, but his protege's final effort was historic. Strug managed to complete a second vault and landed squarely on two feet before collapsing in pain. Her final vault secured a gold medal for the U.S. Women's Team, and though Strug was unable to continue in the individual competition, she earned worldwide recognition for her perseverance.

Strug commented in an interview with *Sports Illustrated* writer Jane Leavy that she feels there is a double standard for male and female athletes. "If it's a boy, it's fine, he's tough.... When it's a gymnast, we're being abused and ruining our bodies. It's the same thing—the athlete wants it, and the coach helps you get through it." After Strug held her landing, then collapsed on the mat after the final vault, she was carried to the podium by Karolyi and stood on one leg with her teammates to receive her medal to the "Star-Spangled Banner." Following the win, Karolyi advised Strug to stay with the rest of the team that included Jaycie Phelps, Dominique Moceanu, Amy Chow, Shannon Miller, Amanda Borden, and Dominique Dawes, but Strug chose to retain an agent. Instead of traveling with the team on sanctioned tours, she enrolled at the University of California, Los Angeles. "My parents said 'We love you and we're glad about everything, but you're still our kid. You need to go to college when it's appropriate,'" she told Leavy in the interview. Strug was able to tour on weekends with noted Olympians and other sports figures and perform routines that favored her damaged ankle. "She could teach a course in irony," said Jane Leavy in *Sports Illustrated.* "The little girl who never had time to go to birthday parties helped Bill Clinton celebrate his fiftieth. The great grandchild of Jewish immigrants who never had time for religion went to Israel to help light the torch at the 1997 Maccabiah Games."

Strug's book *Heart of Gold,* which she wrote with Greg Brown, was published as part of the "Positively for Kids" series. The book is meant to serve as a "road map" for children, providing insight into the struggles and goals of one young gymnast as she worked her way toward the 1996 Olympics. "My parents, Burt and Melanie, had the wisdom to let us try different things and then found the courage to allow us to follow our own interests," Strug wrote in her book. "Some kids are pushed into gymnastics by their parents. My parents never pushed me into the sport. I always pulled them, each step of the way."

In *Heart of Gold,* Strug writes about the hard decisions that had to be made in pursuing her dream. "I never went into gymnastics thinking of it as a career. I did it because I loved it. But slowly, as I improved, my family and I knew I would have to move away to reach my goals. At first, my parents discouraged me from moving away from home. Soon, however, they realized that I needed the chance to pursue my dreams, which could not be fulfilled if I stayed home. Thanks to Lisa's experiences in gymnastics, we knew what to expect."

Strug's second book, *Landing on My Feet,* which she wrote with John Lopez, is a chronicle of her life up to the 1996 Olympics, detailing her training regimen. Kathryn Ruffle commented in *Library Journal* that the book is "well written and interesting."

Works Cited

Leavy, Jane, "Happy Landing," *Sports Illustrated,* August 11, 1997, pp. 54-57.
Ruffle, Kathryn, review of *Landing on My Feet, Library Journal,* November 1, 1997, p. 81.
Strug, Kerri, and Greg Brown, *Heart of Gold,* Taylor (Dallas, TX), 1996.

For More Information See

PERIODICALS

Children's Digest, June, 1997, p. 12.
Life, January, 1997, pp. 68-74.
Newsweek, August 5, 1996, pp. 40-44; September 30, 1996, p. 67.
Sports Illustrated, August, 1996, pp. 40-45; August 12, 1996, p. 104; September 9, 1996, pp. 9-10; October 7, 1996, p. 26.
Time, August 28, 1995, p. 73; August 5, 1996, pp. 32-39, 42-44, 58; September 16, 1996, p. 93.

*   *   *

SWAN, Susan 1944-

Personal

Born September 13, 1944, in Coral Gables, FL; daughter of Arnold H. (a plastics designer) and Regis (deGlanville) Swan; married Terry Rasberry, 1995. *Education:* Florida State University, B.A., 1966, M.F.A., 1968.

Susan Swan

Addresses

Home and studio—1300 Ravenwood Dr., Arlington, TX 76013.

Career

Illustrator. *Member:* Graphic Artists Guild, Society of Children's Book Writers and Illustrators, Westport Artists, Inc. (secretary, 1974, president, 1975).

Awards, Honors

Citation for Merit from 15th Exhibition of Society of Illustrators; Book of the Year List, American Institute of Graphic Arts, 1973, for "Random House Math" Series, *Book 2;* Outstanding Science Book for Children, National Science Teachers Association-Children's Book Council Joint Committee, 1980, for *Dinosaur Mysteries;* numerous Bronze Awards at 3-Dimensional Art Directors and Illustrators Show, including 1996, for *Mummies;* awards from various bestowing bodies, including Graphic Design: USA, *Art Direction Magazine,* New York Book Show, The Educational Press Association of America; and the Art Director's Club of New Jersey.

Illustrator

Ruth B. Gross (reteller), *The Mouse's Wedding,* Scholastic, 1972.

Claire Merrill, *A Seed Is a Promise,* Scholastic, 1973.

Lee Vinson, *The Early American Song Book,* Ridge, 1974.

Eleanor B. Heady, *Plants on the Go: A Book about Reproduction and Seed Dispersal,* Parents' Magazine Press, 1975.

Jane Thayer, *I Don't Believe in Elves,* Morrow, 1975.

The Pop-up Book of Trains, Random House, 1976.

Mary Francis Shura, *Chester,* Dodd, Mead, 1980.

Carol Hellings White, *Holding Hands: The Complete Guide to Palmistry,* photographs by Jerry Sopko, Putnam, 1980.

Mary Elting and Ann Goodman, *Dinosaur Mysteries,* Platt & Munk, 1980.

Plays Children Love: A Treasury of Contemporary and Classic Plays for Children, edited by Coleman A. Jennings and Aurand Harris, foreword by Mary Martin, Doubleday, 1981.

The Twelve Days of Christmas, Troll (Mawah, NJ), 1981.

Francene Sabin, *Louis Pasteur, Young Scientist,* Troll, 1983.

Keith Brandt, *John Paul Jones, Hero of the Seas,* Troll, 1983.

Mary Francis Shura, *Eleanor,* Dodd, Mead, 1983.

Shura, *Jefferson,* Dodd, Mead, 1984.

Drew Stevenson, *The Case of the Horrible Swamp Monster,* Dodd, Mead, 1984.

Rita Schlachter, *Winter Fun,* Troll, 1986.

Michael J. Pellowski, *Who Can't Follow an Ant?,* Troll, 1986.

Drew Stevenson, *The Case of the Visiting Vampire,* Dodd, Mead, 1986.

Chris Arvetis and Carole Palmer, *What Is an Iceberg?,* Checkerboard, 1987.

Virginia Ferguson and Peter Durkin, *Autumn Leaves,* SRA School Group (Santa Rosa, CA), 1994.

Andrew Gutelle, *But Not Nate!,* Time-Life for Children (Alexandria, VA), 1994.

Joyce Milton, *Mummies,* Grosset & Dunlap, 1996.

John Archambault and David R. Plummer (adaptors), *I Love the Mountains: A Traditional Song,* Silver (Parsippany, NJ), 1999.

Deanna Wundrow, *Jungle Drum,* Millbrook (Brookfield, CT), 1999.

Jane B. Mason, *The Flying Horse: The Story of Pegasus,* Grosset & Dunlap, 1999.

Stephanie Spinner, *Snake Hair: The Story of Medusa,* Grosset & Dunlap, 1999.

Joyce Sidman, *Just Us Two: Poems about Animal Dads,* Millbrook, in press.

Sidelights

Susan Swan is a prolific illustrator whose preferred media include watercolor, dye, colored pencil, and paper sculpture. She is known for illustrating children's books with brightly colored paper collages, as in the concept book *But Not Nate!,* a humorous story that teaches the concept of opposites. *Jungle Drum,* a story that reveals a symphony of jungle sounds, tickles the sense of sight as well as sound, thanks to Swan's artistic contribution. *Booklist* reviewer Kathleen Squires noted, "Swan's textured, cut-paper animals stay cleverly in the background, peeking out of the lush vines and trees."

Likewise, Swan's cut-paper illustrations for Joyce Milton's early science-reader *Mummies* add significant enjoyment to the text. The clear, informative text covers the building of the pyramids, the Egyptians' beliefs about the afterlife, the process of mummification, and how the pharaohs were buried. Swan's illustrations of masks, mummies, and the ornate decorations of ancient, royal Egyptian tombs combine with Milton's text to create "one of the most attractive easy-to-reads around," wrote *Booklist*'s Ilene Cooper. *School Library Journal* contributor Gale W. Sherman, singled out Swan's "eye-catching" illustrations as an attractive enhancement to the straightforward text. "*Mummies* is sure to be popular with budding Egyptologists and beginning readers who want 'real stories,'" Sherman predicted.

Works Cited

Cooper, Ilene, review of *Mummies, Booklist,* November 15, 1996, p. 597.

Sherman, Gale W., review of *Mummies, School Library Journal,* June, 1997, p. 110.

Squires, Kathleen, review of *Jungle Drum, Booklist,* March 15, 1999, p. 1336.

For More Information See

PERIODICALS

School Library Journal, March, 1995, pp. 180-81.

*   *   *

SWEENEY, Joyce (Kay) 1955-

Personal

Born November 9, 1955, in Dayton, OH; daughter of Paul (an engineer) and Catharine (a bookkeeper; maiden name, Spoon) Hegenbarth; married Jay Sweeney (a marketing director), September 20, 1979. *Education:* Wright State University, B.A. (summa cum laude), 1977; graduate study in creative writing at Ohio University, 1977-78. *Politics:* Democrat. *Religion:* Unity. *Hobbies and other interests:* Native American religions, natural history, theater, poetry.

Addresses

Home—Coral Springs, FL. *Agent*—George Nicholson, Sterling Lord Literistic, Inc., 65 Bleecker St., New York, NY 10012.

Career

Philip Office Associates, Dayton, OH, advertising copywriter, 1978; Rike's Department Store, Dayton, advertising copywriter, 1979-81, legal secretary, 1980-81; freelance advertising copywriter in Dayton, 1981-82; full-time writer, 1982—. Leader of creative writing workshops in Ormond Beach and Ft. Lauderdale, FL. *Member:* Society of Children's Book Writers and Illustrators, Florida Council for Libraries, Mystery Writers of America.

Joyce Sweeney

Awards, Honors

Delacorte Press First Young Adult Novel Prize, and Best Books for Young Adults citation, American Library Association (ALA), both 1984, both for *Center Line;* Best Books for Reluctant Readers, ALA, 1988, for *The Dream Collector; The Dream Collector* and *Face the Dragon* were named Books for the Teen Age by the New York Public Library, 1991; Best Books for Young Adults, ALA, 1994, for *The Tiger Orchard;* Best Books for Young Adults, ALA, and Books for the Teen Age, New York Public Library, both 1995, Nevada Young Readers' Award, young adult category, and Evergreen Young Adult Book Award, Washington Library Association, both 1997, all for *Shadow;* Books for Reluctant Readers, ALA, Books for the Teen Age, New York Public Library, and Nevada Young Readers' Award List, all 1997, all for *Free Fall;* Best Books, ALA, 1999, for *The Spirit Window.*

Writings

YOUNG ADULT NOVELS

Center Line, Delacorte, 1984.
Right behind the Rain, Delacorte, 1985.
The Dream Collector, Delacorte, 1989.
Face the Dragon, Delacorte, 1990.
Piano Man, Delacorte, 1992.
The Tiger Orchard, Delacorte, 1993.
Shadow, Delacorte, 1994.
Free Fall, Delacorte, 1996.
The Spirit Window, Delacorte, 1998.

OTHER

Sweeney wrote a monthly column on local books and authors for the Fort Lauderdale *News/Sun-Sentinel* and contributed book reviews to periodicals. Contributor of

short stories and articles to periodicals, including *New Writers, Playgirl, CO-ED, Green's Magazine,* and *Writer.* Contributor of poetry to reviews, including *Blue Violin* and *Poetry Motel.* Sweeney's young adult titles have been translated in Danish, Dutch, Hebrew, and Italian. *Free Fall* was adapted for audio cassette by Recorded Books Inc., 1997.

Work in Progress

Young adult thrillers, including one about high school basketball.

Sidelights

Simply put, Joyce Sweeney is a "master at depicting the inner working of families," according to *Horn Book* reviewer Patty Campbell. Sweeney writes realistic fiction, much of it focused on male protagonists, which deals heavily with family issues and friendship. In her first novel, *Center Line,* Sweeney announced an intention of putting the family under the magnifying lens and probing its structure, its strengths, and its dysfunctions. The winner of Delacorte's Prize for Outstanding First Young Adult Novel, *Center Line* traces the adventures and misadventures of five young brothers on their own in the world, escaping an abusive father. Subsequent novels have dealt with teen suicide, divorce, homosexuality, fantasized love, the supernatural, and environmental concerns—all against the backdrop of family relations. "Perhaps it's because I didn't have one in the traditional sense that I am always writing about families," Sweeney told *Authors and Artists for Young Adults* in an interview.

"My father died when I was very young," Sweeney noted, "and I was an only child, so it was just me and Mom." Sweeney's first five years were spent in a rural town near Dayton, Ohio, where she developed a lifelong love for the outdoors and nature. It was a rude awakening for her to move to Dayton just before beginning school. "I may not have realized it at the time," Sweeney said, "but I missed the country and didn't really like the city. When I went to school I was doubly an outsider—a country kid and one who was already bookish. I just had no idea how to relate to the other kids."

Books were an important part of Sweeney's childhood: *Heidi, The Wizard of Oz, Peter Pan.* "Any book where you could fly away and create your own reality. I can say I was literally surrounded by books as a kid. By age eight, I was already talking about becoming a writer." By the fourth grade Sweeney had moved on to the novels of Steinbeck and was also attempting to sell her own work—mostly poetry—in magazines. During her elementary school years, Sweeney was withdrawn. "I kept my own counsel," she recalled. But with the advent of adolescence, this changed. High school presented a new beginning to her, and she took advantage of it, inspired in part by the writings of Norman Vincent Peale. As a freshman in high school she met the boy who would later become her husband. These were also

Haunted by strange nightmares, Zack receives therapy and thereby discovers his long-lost father.

years of intense experimentation with things religious. "I bounced everywhere from spiritualism to fundamentalism," Sweeney noted. "At heart I was an anthropologist; I just didn't have the word for it then." In high school she also continued writing, branching out to fiction, influenced by a teacher who had actually published short stories and who could show her the ropes of publishing.

For reasons of economy, Sweeney lived at home during college, studying English and creative writing at Wright State University. As a college freshman, she sold her first piece of fiction to *New Writers,* and in her junior year she sold another story, this time to *Playgirl.* "That second sale was an affirmation for me," Sweeney said. "It told me that I could actually build a career as a writer." After graduation, Sweeney took more creative writing courses in a master's program at Ohio University. Though she did not complete the degree, the experience was a positive one for her. "You're not taught how to write fiction in English classes. No one talks about how to stay in point of view, for example. For this you have to take creative writing courses. And I

had some great teachers like Daniel Keyes who taught me valuable lessons. Also just being around professional writers was an inspiration. Here is this person who writes books for a living, and he goes to the dentist. He does shopping. He's a human like me. This made it seem possible for me to become a writer, too."

Sweeney married in 1979, and there followed several years of working in advertising and as a legal secretary, which left her little time to work on her writing. Finally, however, Sweeney's husband, who had known her since she was fourteen, and knew of her dreams of becoming a writer, convinced her that the only way to become a writer was to do it full time. In 1980 she started the long process that led to her first publication. Not long thereafter, Sweeney and her husband moved from Ohio to Florida, where they still reside.

"Like most YA writers, I never really considered myself one," Sweeney commented. "I never realized I was writing YA novels with my first two books. When I was growing up I was deeply influenced by J. D. Salinger and John Knowles. They wrote novels that happened to have young protagonists. But these were novels first. At that time there was no such thing as a YA novel. When I finished my first novel, my agent told me I had a YA book and I almost felt insulted. I had no idea what sorts of books were being published as YA, but when I read some of the titles, I realized that they were good literature."

Sweeney's first publication, *Center Line,* written as an adult novel with youthful protagonists, does indeed have some mature scenes, but its premise—five brothers escaping an abusive father to learn about family responsibilities on their own—was a natural winner with young readers. A year in the writing, this first published novel was inspired by some reading Sweeney was doing at the time about the Beatles as very young men in Hamburg, Germany. "Here were these irresponsible, overgrown kids in Hamburg," Sweeney explained, "and they had to learn to look out for each other. Something similar was happening with me, too. In my marriage I was having to learn about responsibilities by caring for another human, my husband. I thought this would make a great centerpiece for a story about real coming of age." The writing was the easy part. Then came selling it. Sweeney's agent submitted the manuscript to almost thirty publishers before putting it in the pool of first-book contestants for the Delacorte YA prize. Winning that prize secured publication for *Center Line* as well as a healthy advertising budget for the book.

Center Line tells the story of the Cunnigan brothers: oldest brother Shawn, Steve, Chris, Rick, and Mark. Their mother has been dead for a number of years, and their alcoholic father regularly beats one or the other of the boys. To escape this intolerable situation, Shawn cashes out his college account. The brothers steal their father's car and hit the road, determined to live on their own until they grow up. What follows is a classic road adventure, as the quintet travel from one little town to the other.

Fourteen-year-old Deidre is intent upon winning the affections of the twenty-six-year-old musician living next door.

The skills of each brother come into play: Chris proves to be the Romeo of the group and scores so well in that domain that he even shares his surplus with his brothers. Young Mark earns money during difficult times as a "blind" guitarist in a shopping mall. Along the way, Steve drops out to marry an older woman, and the remaining four end up in Florida working on a fishing pier. Things are fine for a time until discontented Rick and Shawn get into a fight, and Rick blows the whistle on his brothers. An understanding judge, however, remands the others to Shawn's custody—their father has since disappeared—and all is neatly wrapped into a happy but cautionary ending.

Reviewers and readers alike reacted as positively as the Delacorte prize committee. Sue Estes, writing in *Booklist,* concluded that *Center Line* is a "powerful novel for mature teenagers," while a reviewer in *Bulletin of the Center for Children's Books* commented that "this is a strong first novel ... with fast-moving adventure, a gritty sense of place, and controlled scenes of comedy, drama, and pathos." In a lengthy *Wilson Library Bulletin* review, Patty Campbell compared Sweeney's first novel to *The Outsiders* by S. E. Hinton, noting however that

"*Center Line* has a plot twist that makes it a much more subtle and interesting work than *The Outsiders.*" That plot twist is the enemy within, Rick, who turns against his brothers. A critic in *Publishers Weekly* noted that "the author writes engagingly and her young readers are more than likely to put her book on the bestseller lists." Such was the case; *Center Line* was also optioned for a movie.

Sweeney followed this initial success by reworking a novella she had written before *Center Line.* Again, she was not consciously writing a YA novel but exploring a difficult time in her own life through a brother and sister in *Right behind the Rain.* Kevin is twenty-one, handsome, and a talented dancer with a part in an upcoming movie. He goes home to Ohio for the summer, where his younger sister, Carla, is dazzled by his success. But Carla soon sees that Kevin is deeply unhappy. His success has become a burden to him, perfection a prison. Others see only the golden boy; Carla is the only one to see possible danger ahead, and when Kevin buys a gun one day, it is left to her to talk him out of killing himself.

"The book was inspired by feelings I personally had during college," Sweeney explained. "I felt I had to be perfect: the four-point student. I also took care of our home when mom was working. And I had to be the perfect girlfriend as well as future great writer. I finally worked things out, but I definitely had suicidal feelings for a time. And it is amazing how many kids respond to this when I visit at schools. Invariably there is at least one student in the crowd who says 'How did you know I was feeling like this?' "

Reviewers again reacted positively. A *Publishers Weekly* commentator noted that the "simple, sensitive writing conveys all the emotions of a memorable summer," while a critic in *Kirkus Reviews* emphasized the "close, caring relationship between brother and sister" that "is easy to believe," and concluded that this relationship "[is] the novel's strongest asset and one readers will appreciate." Sweeney commented that "one of the obvious weird things about my life is that I was an only child and have devoted my whole career to writing about sibling relations."

Since her third novel, Sweeney has consciously been writing for the YA market. "It's where I feel at home," she maintained. "In fact now the only time I get inspired is when it's a book for kids. I used to think that I would somehow graduate to adult fiction from YA, but no longer. This is where I can make a difference; this is my audience. And the teen years are where the important decisions are made, ones that affect the rest of a lifetime." Sweeney's third book, *The Dream Collector,* is a reworking of important lessons she learned as a teenager entering high school. "If you make a wish, you can work it out," Sweeney said in her interview. "It's important kids understand that. It's not so much magic as willing something to happen. But then of course you have to watch out what you wish for. That's what makes the dramatic tension in *The Dream Collector.*"

Four boys shed their macho facades and share their darkest secrets when they are trapped in an underground cave. (Cover illustration by Danilo Ducak.)

Becky is fifteen and faced with a quandary—what to get the members of her family for Christmas with her limited funds and their sometimes extravagant lists. She opts to buy everyone a self-help book that describes how an individual can make his or her wishes become reality. Like a genie released from the bottle, the gift books unleash conflicts in the family as well as joyful surprises. Brother Tim gets the kitten he wanted; Scott manipulates family finances to get a fancy racing bike; their mother, who wanted lots of money, leaves their father for another man; the budding poet, Julia, finally gets published; and Becky herself goes on a date with the neighbor, only to discover she likes his friend Tom more. A reviewer in *Publishers Weekly* commented that "Sweeney ably delineates family relationships as she explores the nature of dreams and the pitfalls of ambition," adding that "her affecting and tender novel presents a perfect blend of humor and dramatic tension." Susan Rosenkoetter, writing in *Voice of Youth Advocates,* commented that while *The Dream Collector* "doesn't have the lingering emotional impact of *Center Line* ... [it] will have wider appeal."

Challenges to friendship, the agony of teen love, and dreams from the past inform the next three Sweeney titles, *Face the Dragon, Piano Man,* and *The Tiger Orchard.* In *Face the Dragon,* best friends Eric and Paul join four other teens in an accelerated class at high school. *Beowulf* becomes not just the subject matter for the class, but the theme of the book as well, as each of the characters in Sweeney's story has to confront his or her own personal dragon. Eric has always felt under the shadow cast by the more confident Paul, and determines not only to tackle the demon of public speaking, but also to battle Paul for the attentions of another student, Melanie. Though Eric has always considered him supremely confident, Paul is in fact racked by fears that he may be homosexual. When their teacher exposes these fears, Eric comes to Paul's defense, much like Beowulf's comrade, Wiglaf. Barbara Chatton noted in *School Library Journal* that the "frank language of adolescents is aptly depicted and flows naturally," and *Booklist*'s Stephanie Zvirin concluded her review by stating that "Sweeney says a lot about jealousy, pride, and embarrassment, and about what friendship really is."

Jeff, twenty-six, is the *Piano Man,* a talented young musician who lives next to fourteen-year-old Deidre, a budding chef. Falling in love with this older man, Deidre decides that the way to Jeff's heart is through his stomach, but in fact Jeff's heart belongs to another, gourmet cooking or no, and Deidre's love affair is destined for the garbage bin before it can get to the cooker. Subplots involve other wrong choices by women: Deidre's widowed mom is dating again, but not happily, and her cousin Suzie is going out with an abused teen who keeps her at arm's length. "This is far from a formula treatment of the not-smooth course of true love," observed Zena Sutherland in *Bulletin of the Center for Children's Books.* "The plots are smoothly integrated, the characters are well-defined and consistent, and the writing has, in both dialogue and exposition, a natural flow." Susan R. Farber commented in *Voice of Youth Advocates* that "Sweeney is expert at portraying the highs and lows, the dreams and expectations of young women in love (lust? like?)," while a *Kirkus Reviews* contributor applauded the "deft dialogue, willing players, and plausible events" that constitute this novel.

The Tiger Orchard, another well-regarded YA book by Sweeney, tells the story of Zack, who is haunted by strange nightmares. In therapy he tries to uncover the secrets these dreams might hold for him, and discovers that his father—who his mother always said was dead—is actually living. "The past is uncovered, secrets are revealed, and Zack finds his father as he finds the truth," noted Claire Rosser in *Kliatt.* Rosser added that "the real story here is the revelation of long-held, destructive secrets, and in the healing power of the revelation." A *Publishers Weekly* reviewer maintained that Sweeney displays "remarkable insights into family relationships and human nature."

For her next effort, Sweeney again turned to her own experiences for inspiration. "When my husband was a kid, his family had no pets," Sweeney noted. "And when I was growing up, we had lots of them. So his dream was to have pets galore. We adopted cats all over the place it seemed, and then feline leukemia struck. Over the course of several years we lost five cats. That loss touched me profoundly. I knew I wanted to use the material somehow in a book, but not a dead-pet story. Something more. Then I decided I wanted to write a supernatural story. I enjoy those tales myself and wanted to try my hand at one. It came to me that this might be the perfect way to use the grief I felt for the loss of those cats. Grief can alter your perceptions, so this would open up the whole question of whether the supernatural event in this case—the return of a cat—was indeed supernatural or if it was the result of emotions at work."

The eponymous cat in *Shadow* has been dead for a year, but thirteen-year-old Sarah still grieves its passing. Add this to the continual feuding between her older brothers, Brian and Patrick, a father who dotes on Brian and a mother who picks on him, and a girlfriend who nearly cuckolds one brother with the other, and a recipe for domestic disaster is in place. Soon Sarah begins seeing her dead cat, and after confiding this to the housekeeper, Cissy, who has a natural proclivity for things supernatural, she is informed that her cat is probably returning in the spirit to warn her of impending danger. Further complications ensue when Sarah realizes she is in love with her childhood friend, Julian. When she confides her experiences with Shadow to Julian, his skepticism nearly destroys their newfound relationship. The impending danger becomes all too real when Brian discovers his girlfriend about to make love with his brother Patrick. An enraged Brian nearly strangles Patrick; they are stopped only by what appears to be the ghost of Shadow.

"This page-turner is a psychic novel built around realistic feelings, emotions, hates, fears, and love," noted Bonnie Kunzel in *Voice of Youth Advocates.* Kunzel deemed the work "well-written and bound to be a teen pleaser with its mixture of sibling rivalry, romance, and psychic revelations." Bruce Anne Shook, writing in *School Library Journal,* observed that "characters are realistically drawn, and the plot is riveting," and noted that the conclusion, "as Shadow withdraws and Sarah finds a new kitten suspiciously like him, is nicely done." A *Publishers Weekly* reviewer felt that Sweeney "offers believably complex characters" and "challenges conventional views of reality."

Sweeney's books are equally as popular with young male readers as with young women. She writes about male protagonists with enough reality to elicit letters from these fans asking for more—more adventure, more sports. "I was definitely a tomboy, but I wasn't allowed to really act out the adventure and athletics that boys did at that time," Sweeny explained. "There was a sense of frustration at that double standard. That is one reason I seem to be able to write male characters well. I'm doing now what I couldn't do myself as a kid. Also, I seem to be more in touch with the male psyche than the female. It may be my upbringing, raised by a single mom, and

Thirteen-year-old Sarah sees the ghost of her dead cat, Shadow, and believes the spirit is warning her of impending danger.

taught to be tough, resilient, in control, not dependent on anyone else. It's easy for me to be macho."

Sweeney spread her tomboy wings with *Free Fall,* the story of four young boys—two antagonistic brothers and their friends—who get trapped in an underground cave. Neil and Randy are high school athletes and best friends. Together with Neil's younger brother David and his friend Terry, they explore a cave in Florida's Ocala National Forest. There is tension between the boys from the outset, but it reaches a climax when they realize they are lost. No spelunkers, these four have come ill-prepared. Neil tries to climb out but falls and breaks a leg. David ultimately comes to the rescue by finding an underwater passage out of the cave, but not before the quartet have shed their macho facades and share their darkest secrets. *Booklist's* Ann O'Malley commented that "Sweeney mixes excitement with finely crafted characters and credible psychological underpinnings to deliver a powerful punch." A reviewer in *Horn Book* called *Free Fall* a "taut survival story" and noted that "the book features gritty, realistic dialogue and insightful characterizations." Pam Carlson concluded in *Voice of Youth Advocates* that the novel is "a gripping,

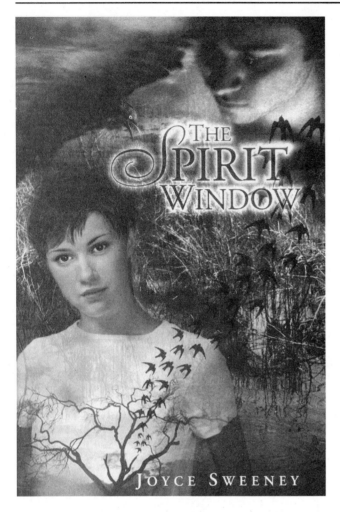

Miranda struggles against her father when he wants to develop the pristine Florida marshland their family owns. (Cover illustrations by Ericka Meltzer.)

sometimes scary tale of survival and brotherhood." A *Publishers Weekly* commentator felt *Free Fall* "goes beyond the action genre.... Lean and skillfully wrought, this novel hooks the reader and doesn't let go."

Environmental matters combine with another dysfunctional family in *The Spirit Window,* the story of Miranda and her summer visit to her dying grandmother on a Florida island. Miranda is accompanied by her psychiatrist father, Richard, and his new, young, and spoiled wife, Ariel. Grandmother Lila and her son do not see eye to eye on the property that she will leave behind at her death: he intends to develop it but she wants it preserved. To this end, she leaves it to her young, part-Cherokee assistant, Adam, who shares her beliefs in preservation and to whom Miranda is strongly attracted. Miranda soon finds herself torn between loyalty to family and her feelings for Adam in this "gentle story about two adolescents far wiser and more mature than the adults in their lives," according to Beth Anderson, writing in *Voice of Youth Advocates.* A reviewer in *Bulletin of the Center for Children's Books* noted that "Sweeney has a strong sense of place that contributes to an overall setting of mood that is very effective," while

School Library Journal contributor Angela J. Reynolds concluded that a "love story, a mystery, and a spiritual journey combine to make this a satisfying read."

A "satisfying read" is not necessarily what Sweeney sets out to do in her fiction, but if that is part of the result so much the better. "I try not to think of my audience a lot," Sweeney commented. "Mostly I try to work through some experiences in my own life, thoroughly disguising myself, by the way, usually in the guise of one of the male characters. I don't think of message. My unconscious knows what the message is, but I don't want to be thinking about that. Instead, I want to put issues out there, to open things up for discussion. I certainly want to be a force for good, but that has to come naturally through the story. It can't be forced and planned."

Sweeney, who in the future plans to write thrillers for YA readers as well as sports books, feels there is a real mission in writing for the teen audience. "I hope parents understand that people who write YAs care very deeply about kids and are trying to address issues that affect them and help them work through such issues. In the end, we believe that information is better than ignorance."

Works Cited

Anderson, Beth, review of *The Spirit Window, Voice of Youth Advocates,* April, 1998, pp. 50-51.

Campbell, Patty, "The Young Adult Complex," *Wilson Library Bulletin,* March, 1984, pp. 502-03.

Campbell, Patty, "The Sand in the Oyster," *Horn Book,* November-December, 1994, pp. 756-59.

Carlson, Pam, review of *Free Fall, Voice of Youth Advocates,* June, 1996, p. 102.

Review of *Center Line, Bulletin of the Center for Children's Books,* June, 1984, pp. 194-95.

Review of *Center Line, Publishers Weekly,* February 10, 1984, p. 194.

Chatton, Barbara, review of *Face the Dragon, School Library Journal,* October, 1990, p. 145.

Review of *The Dream Collector, Publishers Weekly,* November 24, 1989, p. 72.

Estes, Sue, review of *Center Line, Booklist,* April 1, 1984, p. 1110.

Farber, Susan R., review of *Piano Man, Voice of Youth Advocates,* April, 1992, p. 37.

Review of *Free Fall, Horn Book,* Spring, 1997, p. 84.

Review of *Free Fall, Publishers Weekly,* June 24, 1996, p. 62.

Kunzel, Bonnie, review of *Shadow, Voice of Youth Advocates,* October, 1994, pp. 218-19.

O'Malley, Ann, review of *Free Fall, Booklist,* July, 1996, p. 1819.

Review of *Piano Man, Kirkus Reviews,* May 15, 1992, p. 676.

Reynolds, Angela J., review of *The Spirit Window, School Library Journal,* March, 1998, p. 224.

Review of *Right behind the Rain, Kirkus Reviews,* May 1, 1987, p. 726.

Review of *Right behind the Rain, Publishers Weekly,* May 8, 1987, p. 72.

Rosenkoetter, Susan, review of *The Dream Collector, Voice of Youth Advocates,* February, 1990, p. 348.

Rosser, Claire, review of *The Tiger Orchard, Kliatt,* March, 1995, p. 12.

Review of *Shadow, Publishers Weekly,* May 27, 1996, p. 81.

Shook, Bruce Anne, review of *Shadow, School Library Journal,* September, 1994, pp. 242-43.

Review of *The Spirit Window, Bulletin of the Center for Children's Books,* May, 1998, p. 341.

Sutherland, Zena, review of *Piano Man, Bulletin of the Center for Children's Books,* June, 1992, p. 281.

Sweeney, Joyce, interview with J. Sydney Jones for *Authors and Artists for Young Adults,* Gale, conducted June 1, 1998.

Review of *The Tiger Orchard, Publishers Weekly,* January 30, 1995, p. 101.

Zvirin, Stephanie, review of *Face the Dragon, Booklist,* September 15, 1990, p. 157.

For More Information See

PERIODICALS

Booklist, December 15, 1989, p. 827; July, 1994, p. 1936; April 1, 1995, pp. 1404, 1416; April 1, 1997, p. 1310.

Kirkus Reviews, May 1, 1984, p. 153; November 15, 1989, p. 1678; October 1, 1990, p. 1398; May 1, 1996, p. 694.

School Library Journal, April, 1984, p. 127; June, 1987, p. 114; November, 1989, p. 129; April, 1992, p. 150; November, 1996, p. 126.

Times Literary Supplement, August 24, 1984, p. 954.

Wilson Library Bulletin, January, 1990, p. 7; September, 1994, p. 127.

—Sketch by J. Sydney Jones

T

TRELL, Max 1900-1996

OBITUARY NOTICE—See index for *SATA* sketch: Born September 6, 1900, in New York, NY; died February 3, 1996, in Englewood, NJ. Writer, journalist, and film producer and director. Trell received his B.A. degree in 1923 from Columbia University, and did graduate study at the Sorbonne, University of Paris, from 1929 to 1930. He served with the U.S. Navy during World War I, underwent officer's training, and served with the U.S. Army Signal Corps making training films from 1942 to 1946, eventually attaining the rank of captain. He began his writing career as a reporter for *Zits Theatrical Weekly* (1924) and the *New York Daily News* (1925-1927), as a story editor for Warner Brothers from 1927 to 1932, and as an associate editor for *Pictorial Review* (1934-1939), all in New York City. He produced and directed two films for Columbia Pictures: *Arrivederci Roma* (1960) and *The Making of Oliver Cromwell* (1970). Trell was a member of Screen Writers Guild West. He received an Academy Award for his story and narration of *Climbing the Matterhorn* (1947), and a Freedoms Foundation Award in 1948 for his story and continuity of *Dick's Adventures*, a syndicated cartoon feature based on American history. His first book, *Tom and Mot* (1930), was for children, and was followed by *Lawyer Man* (1934), *Shirley Temple: My Life and Times* (1938), *Now I Am Eight* (by Shirley Temple as told to Max Trell) (1938), *Just This Once* (1950), and *The Small Gods and Mr. Barnum* (1971). Trell was the author of a daily syndicated juvenile column for King Features from 1926 to 1956, a syndicated cartoon feature, *Dick's Adventures,* and he produced five volumes of text adaptations of the *Prince Valiant* comic strip, drawn by Hal Foster, from 1951 to 1954, and in two final volumes, *Prince Valiant in the Days of King Arthur* and *Prince Valiant on The Inland Sea* (1977). He also produced five screenplays, including *High Conquest* (1947), *Climbing the Matterhorn* (1947), *Sixteen Fathoms Deep* (1948), *New Mexico* (1950), and *Hell Below Zero* (1954).

OBITUARIES AND OTHER SOURCES:

PERIODICALS

The San Diego Union-Tribune, June 14, 1997, pp. B5-7.

—*Obituary by Robert Reginald and Mary A. Burgess*

*   *   *

TRIPP, Janet 1942-

Personal

Born November 26, 1942, in Lake City, MN; daughter of Sumner Richard (a machinist) and Arline (a teacher; maiden name, Leverstrom; present surname, Schmidt) Lombard; married Richard Tripp (a computer programmer), October 19, 1963; children: Jennie, Bill, Jonathan. *Education:* Macalester College, Northwestern Hospital School of Nursing, R.N., 1963; University of Minnesota—Twin Cities, B.A., 1992. *Religion:* Congregational, United Church of Christ.

Addresses

Home—5150 Logan Ave. S., Minneapolis, MN 55419.

Career

University of Minnesota-Twin Cities, Minneapolis, pediatric nurse at university hospital; Metropolitan Medical Center, Minneapolis, psychiatric nurse; Hennepin County Medical Center, Minneapolis, psychiatric nurse; writer. *Hurricane Alice: A Feminist Quarterly,* editor and staff writer, 1984-90; *Signs: Journal of Women in Culture and Society,* intern, 1991-92. Works as parish nurse for a local church and as a writing teacher. *Member:* National Organization for Women.

Awards, Honors

Valata Dakota Fletcher Award, from Women's Studies Department at University of Minnesota-Twin Cities,

1992, for outstanding feminist writing; resident at Norcroft, a writing retreat for women, 1994.

Writings

Lorraine Hansberry, Lucent Books (San Diego, CA), 1998.

Work represented in anthologies, including *The Book Group Book: A Thoughtful Guide to Forming and Enjoying a Stimulating Book Discussion Group,* Chicago Review Press (Chicago, IL), 1993, 2nd edition, 1995; and *Between the Heartbeats: Poetry and Prose by Nurses,* University of Iowa Press (Iowa City, IA), 1995. Contributor to periodicals, including *Utne Reader, Star Tribune* (Minneapolis, MN), *Melpomene,* and *Women's Studies Quarterly.*

Work in Progress

Sunday's Child, a biography of Anna Arline Leverstrom; research on women's spirituality and the "wheel of the year."

Sidelights

Janet Tripp told *SATA:* "Reading and writing have been fervent interests all my life—reading in the sunshine, my back against the house foundation, reading among the sprawling branches of the lilac bush, reading in the corner easy chair in my bedroom, sneaking minutes with a book while the babies napped, reading during long waits while 'carpooling' growing children, and now reading through supper breaks at the hospital where I work.

"Reading leads to writing. It began with 'Dear Diary' at age fifteen. Thirty-eight volumes later, I am now sharing the joys with others as a teacher of memoir and journal writing. I learn what I think as my pen talks to me on the white, listening page. In the journal I explore the blurry borders of what is barely conscious, pulling it into awareness.

"My work as a psychiatric nurse is fed by all my interests: journaling, biography, spirituality, and healing. My women's groups tie it all together. Reading, writing, and the spirit, all in one simmering stew I call my life."

For More Information See

PERIODICALS

School Library Journal, January, 1998, p. 135.

*   *   *

TRUESDELL, Sue
See TRUESDELL, Susan G.

TRUESDELL, Susan G. 1959-
(Sue Truesdell)

Personal

Education: Pratt Institute, BFA (communication design—illustration), 1981.

Addresses

Home—Tenafly, NJ.

Career

Illustrator.

Illustrator

Dennis Haseley, *The Pirate Who Tried to Capture the Moon,* HarperCollins Children's, 1983.
Alvin Schwartz, *Unriddling: All Sorts of Riddles to Puzzle Your Guessery,* HarperCollins Children's, 1983.

Tall Tim trims thin twin trees.

Illustrator Susan G. Truesdell collaborated with author Nola Buck on a collection of verbal-dexterity testers related to the holiday season in Santa's Short Suit Shrunk and Other Christmas Tongue Twisters.

Mitchell Sharmat, *The Seven Sloppy Days of Phineas Pig,* Harcourt Brace, 1983.

Anne Leo Ellis, *Dabble Duck,* HarperCollins Children's, 1984.

Betsy C. Byars, *The Golly Sisters Go West,* HarperCollins Children's, 1985.

Joan Robins, *Addie Meets Max,* HarperCollins Children's, 1985.

Phyllis Root, *Soup for Supper,* HarperCollins Children's, 1986.

Susan Shreve, *Lily and the Runaway Baby,* Random House Books for Young Readers, 1987.

Bill Grossman, *Donna O'Neeshuck Was Chased by Some Cows,* HarperCollins Children's, 1988.

Jocelyn Stevenson, *O'Diddy,* Random House Books for Young Readers, 1988.

Jean Little, *Hey World, Here I Am!,* HarperCollins Children's, 1989.

Amy Hest, *Travel Tips from Harry: A Guide to Family Vacations in the Sun,* William Morrow, 1989.

Joan Robins, *Addie Runs Away,* HarperCollins Children's, 1989.

Betsy C. Byars, *Hooray for the Golly Sisters!,* HarperCollins Children's, 1990.

Laura Geringer, *Look Out, Look Out, It's Coming!,* HarperCollins Children's, 1992.

Alvin Schwartz, *And the Green Grass Grew All Around,* HarperCollins Children's, 1992.

Barbara M. Joosse, *Wild Willie & King Kyle, Detectives,* Clarion, 1993.

Joan Robins, *Addie's Bad Day,* HarperCollins Children's, 1993.

Betsy C. Byars, *The Golly Sisters Ride Again,* HarperCollins Children's, 1994.

Barbara M. Joosse, *The Losers Fight Back: A Wild Willie Mystery,* Clarion, 1994.

Nola Buck, *Creepy Crawly Critters: And Other Halloween Tongue Twisters,* HarperCollins Children's, 1995.

Nola Buck, *Santa's Short Suit Shrunk: And Other Christmas Tongue Twisters,* HarperCollins Children's, 1997.

Barbara M. Joosse, *Nugget and Darling,* Clarion, 1997.

Barbara M. Joosse, *Ghost Trap: A Wild Willie Mystery,* Clarion, 1998.

Roberta Karim, *This Is a Hospital, Not a Zoo!,* Clarion, 1998.

Linda L. Strauss, *A Fairy Called Hilary,* Holiday House, 1999.

Jean Craighead-George, *How to Talk to Your Dog,* HarperCollins, 1999.

Also provided cover art for *Witcracks,* by Alvin Schwartz, with interior art by Glen Rounds, published by HarperCollins Children's Books, 1993.

Sidelights

Sue Truesdell, a graduate of the distinguished Pratt Institute in Brooklyn, New York, is the illustrator of over two dozen books for children. In one of her first titles, the whimsical 1983 Dennis Haseley book *The Pirate Who Tried to Capture the Moon,* Truesdell used black-and-white drawings with a centerpiece glowing golden moon whose hue intensified on every page. She

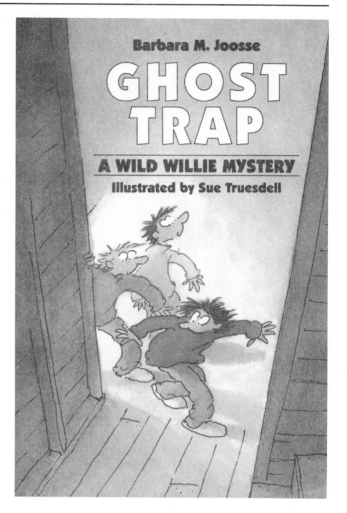

Friends Willie, Kyle, and Lucy try to determine whether Kyle's new house is haunted. (Cover illustration by Truesdell.)

has also illustrated several books by acclaimed authors Betsy C. Byars, Joan Robins, and Alvin Schwartz. Nonfiction writer Nola Buck has also paired with Truesdell for a number of titles, including 1995's *Creepy Crawly Critters: And Other Halloween Tongue Twisters.* For this preschool-age reader, Truesdell created watercolor illustrations of children's celebrations of the holiday twinned with an array of witches, goblins, bats, and other creatures cavorting on the pages. Pamela K. Bomboy, writing in *School Library Journal,* declared that Truesdell's drawings "add to the amusement" of *Creepy Crawly Critters.*

For their 1997 collaboration *Santa's Short Suit Shrunk: And Other Christmas Tongue Twisters,* Truesdell and Buck once again return to the delight of verbal-dexterity testers, and the pleasant nature of the season provides ample opportunity for Truesdell's pen. A tired little boy in a department store, for instance, queries, "Is Christmas shopping stopping soon?" Again, humor and recurring characters, including dogs and a boy named Sam, reappear throughout the pages. A *School Library Journal* assessment by Jane Marino found that "Truesdell's lively illustrations are well suited to the material," while *Horn Book*'s Roger Sutton found the art-filled pages possessed "a pleasing unity."

Truesdell has illustrated several titles by Barbara M. Joosse, including her 1997 reader for ages five to eight, *Nugget and Darling.* Nugget is Nell's beloved dog, but their relationship is dramatically altered when Nugget finds a kitten and Nell adopts it. A series of minor jealousy crises erupts, but in the end all find that there's more than enough love for everybody. Two reviews noted that Joosse's story had delved into rather coy, heart-tugging territory, but Truesdell's characterizations of the pets' faces "are a hoot, smoothly tempering the inherent sentimentality of the story," declared Stephanie Zvirin in *Booklist,* while a *Publishers Weekly* reviewer termed both text and art "full-bodied and pleasingly idiosyncratic."

Truesdell also illustrated Joosse's young detective-fiction series, beginning with 1993's *Wild Willie & King Kyle, Detectives,* which introduces the two neighborhood pals. Their story was continued in *The Losers Fight Back* in 1994, and the 1998 title *Ghost Trap: A Wild Willie Mystery* reunited the friends. In it, Kyle's family moves back into Willie's neighborhood but buys an older home in great need of repair. Willie's new friend Lucy finds herself resenting Kyle, but the decrepit state of the house—and its treasure-filled attic—gives all three ample opportunity for potential detective work. Lucy discovers that the previous owner died in Kyle's very bedroom, and tensions escalate; a clever parrot and Willie's graciousness help end the conflict. Susan Hepler, writing in *School Library Journal,* praised "Truesdell's big-nosed, large-eyed, loosely limned characters."

Whimsical drawings by the accomplished illustrator also help tell the story for Roberta Karim's *This Is a Hospital, Not a Zoo!* In this 1998 reader, Truesdell depicts a little boy who confounds the medical professionals when he metamorphoses into various animals according to his selection of which animal cracker to eat. Stephanie Zvirin, reviewing the story for *Booklist,* described it as the perfect accompaniment to "Truesdell's funny, irresistible artwork."

Works Cited

Bomboy, Pamela K., review of *Creepy Crawly Critters: And Other Halloween Tongue Twisters, School Library Journal,* November, 1995, p. 88.

Hepler, Susan, review of *Ghost Trap: A Wild Willie Mystery, School Library Journal,* June, 1998, p. 111.

Marino, Jane, review of *Santa's Short Suit Shrunk: And Other Christmas Tongue Twisters, School Library Journal,* October, 1997, pp. 45-46.

Review of *Nugget and Darling, Publishers Weekly,* February 24, 1997, p. 91.

Sutton, Roger, review of *Santa's Short Suit Shrunk: And Other Christmas Tongue Twisters, Horn Book,* November-December, 1997, p. 695.

Zvirin, Stephanie, review of *Nugget and Darling, Booklist,* March 1, 1997, p. 1172.

Zvirin, review of *This Is a Hospital, Not a Zoo!, Booklist,* March 1, 1998, p. 1140.

For More Information See

PERIODICALS

Booklist, September 15, 1995, p. 168; September 15, 1997, p. 237.

Horn Book, July-August, 1998, p. 491.

School Library Journal, August, 1998, p. 141.

V–W

VOJTECH, Anna 1946-

Personal

Surname is pronounced "*Voi*-tek"; born February 6, 1946, in Prague, Czechoslovakia; daughter of Leonard (a clerk) and Anna (Jenneova) Vojtech; married Roland Baumgaertel, March 27, 1970; children: Mathis, Lukas. *Education:* Attended University of Fine Arts, Prague, Czechoslovakia, 1965-70, University of Fine Arts, Antwerp, Belgium, 1968, and Academy of Fine Arts, Hamburg, Germany, 1969.

Addresses

Home—3 Bartlett St., Marblehead, MA 01945.

Career

Academia (publishing house), Prague, Czechoslovakia, assistant editor, 1964-65; Phillips & Deutsche Grammophon Gesellschaft, Hamburg, Germany, illustrator/designer, and Verclas & Boltz (advertising agency), Hamburg, worked in art department, 1969-70; National Film Board of Canada, Montreal, artist and animator, 1971-72; International Cinemedia, Montreal, artist, 1973-75. Created part of exhibition "Man and His Environment," Biosphere Pavilion, Montreal, 1973; creator of seven filmstrips for Museum of Natural History, Ottawa, Canada, 1973; set designer and creator of props for film *Cocology,* Aquilon Film, Montreal, 1977. *Exhibitions:* Gallery Laurent Tremblay, Montreal, Gallery de Vieu marche, Ottawa, and Gallery Passion, Boston, 1975-76; Gallery Laurent Tremblay, Montreal, Cowansville, and Botanical Garden, Montreal, 1981; Centre d'Art, Montreal, and Boston Athenaeum, 1982; and International Exhibition of Botanical Illustration, Pittsburgh, 1983.

Awards, Honors

Chris Bronze Plaque Award, Columbus International Film Festival, 1982, for filmstrip *My Food and Your*

In this Native-American pourquoi tale illustrated by Anna Vojtech, the sun god creates strawberries to reconcile a quarreling husband and wife. (From The First Strawberries: A Cherokee Story, *retold by Joseph Bruchac.)*

Food = Our Food; second prize in printmaking, Marblehead Arts Festival, 1983.

Illustrator

Louise Darios, *Tous les oiseaux du monde* (title means "All the Birds of the World"), Beachemim (Montreal), 1974.

Madeline Kronby, *A Secret in My Pocket,* McClelland & Stewart, 1976.

Jane Mobley, *The Star Husband,* Doubleday, 1979.

Ghillean T. Prance, *Wildflowers for All Seasons,* Crown, 1989.

Deborah Eaton, reteller, *The Elves and the Shoemaker: A Traditional Tale,* Barksbee (Morristown, NJ), 1992.

Joseph Bruchac, reteller, *The First Strawberries: A Cherokee Story,* Dial, 1993.

Betsy James, *Blow away Soon,* Putnam, 1995.

Philemon Sturges, *Ten Flashing Fireflies,* North-South Books, 1995.

Joseph Bruchac, *The Maple Thanksgiving,* Celebration Press (Glenview, IL), 1996.

(And reteller, with Philemon Sturges) *Marushka and the Month Brothers: A Folktale,* North-South Books, 1996.

Elizabeth Jane Coatsworth, *Song of the Camels: A Christmas Poem,* North-South Books, 1997.

Nancy Luenn, *Otter Play,* Atheneum, 1998.

Jean Craighead George, *Giraffe Trouble,* Disney Press, 1998.

George, *Elephant Walk,* Disney Press, 1998.

Holly Young Huth, reteller, *The Son of the Sun and the Daughter of the Moon: A Saami Folktale from Russia,* Atheneum, 1999.

Also illustrator of filmstrip *My Food and Your Food = Our Food.* Contributor of illustrations to a series of readers by Houghton. Contributor of illustrations to *Magook, Nous, Audubon,* and *Horticulture.*

Sidelights

Czech artist Anna Vojtech brings a striking sense of color and shape to her illustrations for stories by such well-known authors as Jean Craighead George, Elizabeth Jane Coatsworth, and Joseph Bruchac. Done in a wide variety of media, including acrylic, pencil, and watercolor, Vojtech's illustrations are especially well-suited to folk tales due to their stylization, the illustrator's focus on detail, and her liberal use of color. Commenting on the counting book *Ten Flashing Fireflies, School Library Journal* contributor Patricia Pearl Dole noted that Vojtech's intensely colored illustrations "reflect the universal mystery and excitement of playing outdoors on a summer night."

Vojtech was born in Prague in 1946. "My childhood with my two older brothers, Vojta and Vaclav, was rough but beautiful," she once recalled to *SATA,* "climbing trees, playing cowboys and Indians, and all kinds of adventures, but I still managed to play secretly with my dolls and all the little girlish things that my brothers considered as stupid." An imaginative child, Vojtech "painted and scratched my imaginings on paper, schoolbooks, sidewalks, walls, fences and all suitable and unsuitable surfaces," she remembered. "When I scratched a masterpiece with my hairpin on our fancy

A young girl is sent out by her wicked stepmother into a blizzard to accomplish a series of impossible tasks in **Marushka and the Month Brothers,** *a Slavic folktale retold by Vojtech and Philemon Sturges and illustrated by Vojtech.*

furniture, my talents weren't appreciated at all, to say the least."

Vojtech's family home was full of music, laughter, affection, and noise. "My mother was a bottomless well of creative ideas which she used in our everyday life," Vojtech told *SATA.* "Once she made a cake that looked like a piano. It was one piano lesson I mastered and fully enjoyed." Vojtech inherited her mother's creativity, but did not fully appreciate that gift until she had children of her own. "I really understand the wisdom of my mother's creativeness and playfulness," she recalled. "She managed to have an office job, household, three children and still give us and many other people joy, smiles, and love." Although Vojtech takes her job as an illustrator and artist seriously, she strives to also incorporate the playfulness of her mother's approach to life in her work.

Vojtech's contribution to *Marushka and the Month Brothers* is characteristic of her illustration work. The story of a young girl sent out by her wicked stepmother into a blizzard to accomplish a series of impossible tasks is based on a Slavic folktale. The girl is aided by twelve brothers who control the weather, enabling her to fulfill her stepmother's requests. Praising the illustrator's "well-lit faces" and "changing angles," *School Library Journal* contributor Carolyn Noah maintained that Vojtech's "interesting composition lifts this treatment above the ordinary." "The compositions are dramatic and the figures remarkably expressive," remarked Pam McCuen in *Bulletin of the Center for Children's Books.* McCuen also noted that "Vojtech's love for her native land ... is apparent in her illustrations." Ann A. Flowers added in her *Horn Book* review that "Vojtech's delicate watercolor illustrations ... give a distinctly European peasant flavor" to this Cinderella tale.

Vojtech moves with ease from Slavic tales to stories from other cultures, contributing illustrations to several books by Native-American author Joseph Bruchac. In *The First Strawberries: A Cherokee Story,* Bruchac recounts the ability of the sun god to reconcile the first husband and wife after an argument. The sun puts beautiful berries in the path of the angry wife, causing her to stop on the road away from her home long enough for her repentant husband to catch up with her and make amends. Vojtech's "attractive watercolor and colored-pencil illustrations show an idealized pastoral world," wrote *School Library Journal* contributor Lauralyn Persson. *Horn Book* reviewer Martha V. Parravano noted that "the watercolor illustrations focus on the strong faces" of the main characters, "and on the beauty of the small details of the landscape."

The natural world figures prominently in Vojtech's art, and many of her illustration projects feature animal protagonists. In *Otter Play,* a story by Nancy Luenn, "gently shaded forms, precisely drawn yet softened at the edges and suffused with sunlight," contribute to the appealing story of an otter family, according to *Booklist* contributor Carolyn Phelan. In *Blow away Soon,* the cycles of life in the desert are symbolized in what *School Library Journal* contributor Barbara Kiefer termed "textured paintings ... bright with desert golds, corals, and turquoise, colors that suggest the true wealth of the ... [region's] simple treasures." Vojtech's illustrations for Elizabeth Jane Coatsworth's *Song of the Camels: A Christmas Poem* make the desert vistas "more full of meaning" in a book that "honors both its subject matter and its audience," in the opinion of *Booklist* reviewer Carolyn Phelan. In a review for *School Library Journal,* Jane Marino declared that Vojtech's use of contrasting colors gives the work "its own, unspoken rhythm," calling *Song of the Camels* "a haunting and visually arresting book."

Vojtech numbers Czech gothic painters like Trebonsky among her major influences. Other artists who have inspired her include Brueghel, Bosch, Piero della Franscesca, Chagall, and Czech filmmaker/illustrator Jiri Trnka. Work creating animation and storyboards for films taught Vojtech to analyze stories in pictures rather than words. This ability, along with her love of detail, made her transition from artist to book illustrator a natural step, and Vojtech continues to produce illustrations—mostly in watercolor—in addition to branching out into wood carving and puppetry.

Works Cited

Dole, Patricia Pearl, review of *Ten Flashing Fireflies, School Library Journal,* August, 1995, pp. 129-30.

Flowers, Ann A., review of *Marushka and the Month Brothers: A Folktale, Horn Book,* March-April 1997, p. 207.

Kiefer, Barbara, review of *Blow away Soon, School Library Journal,* August, 1995, p. 124.

Marino, Jane, review of *Song of the Camels: A Christmas Poem, School Library Journal,* October, 1997, p. 45.

McCuen, Pam, review of *Marushka and the Month Brothers: A Folktale, Bulletin of the Center for Children's Books,* March, 1997, p. 260.

Noah, Carolyn, review of *Marushka and the Month Brothers: A Folktale, School Library Journal,* November, 1996, p. 102.

Parravano, Martha V., review of *The First Strawberries: A Cherokee Story, Horn Book,* March-April, 1994, p. 209.

Persson, Lauralyn, review of *The First Strawberries: A Cherokee Story, School Library Journal,* September, 1993, p. 222.

Phelan, Carolyn, review of *Otter Play, Booklist,* March 15, 1998, p. 1250.

Phelan, review of *Song of the Camels: A Christmas Poem, Booklist,* November 15, 1997, p. 564.

For More Information See

PERIODICALS

Booklist, July, 1993, p. 1969; June 1, 1995, pp. 1786, 1789; August, 1998, p. 2014.

Kirkus Reviews, September 15, 1996, p. 1408.

Publishers Weekly, June 28, 1993, p. 76; June 5, 1995, p. 61; February 9, 1998, p. 95.

School Library Journal, July, 1998, p. 79.

*   *   *

WARNER, Sunny (B.) 1931-

Personal

Born October 10, 1931, in New York, NY; daughter of David (a photographer) and Valedith (a stylist; maiden name, Bertrand) Popouciado; children: Geoffrey B. Cook, Michael Warner, Jennifer Warner. *Education:* Rhode Island School of Design, B.F.A., 1953; also attended American School in Paris, Atelier 17, Paris, and State University of New York at Stony Brook.

Addresses

Home and office—3001 East Lester St., Tucson, AZ 85716.

Career

Writer and illustrator. Freelance illustrator and graphic designer, including package designs and illustrations for toy manufacturers, 1951-90. Trinity Square Repertory Company, Providence, RI, art director, designer of

Sunny Warner

posters and promotional graphics, and costume designer, 1964-77. Rhode Island School of Design, teacher of illustration; graphic design teacher at a school for the gifted, in Providence.

Awards, Honors

Award for best Sunday magazine cover, Newspaper Guild of America, 1964, for a cover for *Providence Sunday Journal;* also earned award of excellence from an advertisers' show in Providence.

Writings

Tobias and His Big Red Satchel, self-illustrated, Knopf (New York City), 1961.
The Magic Sewing Machine, Houghton (Boston, MA), 1997.
Madison Finds a Line, self-illustrated, Houghton, 1999.

Illustrator of books by other authors.

Work in Progress

Tangerina and *The Day We Met Charlie,* for older children; a picture book, *The Moon Quilt.*

Sidelights

Sunny B. Warner told *SATA:* "My parents were portrait photographers with a studio a block from Washington Square. That's also where we lived. [Manhattan] was a different world then: it belonged to children as well as adults. I was free to navigate galleries, museums, and, best of all, the library. I adored Wanda Gag's *Millions of Cats, Mr. Popper's Penguins,* the "Mary Poppins" books, *Peter Pan, Alice in Wonderland, The Little Princess, The Secret Garden, Dr. Doolittle,* Dr. Seuss, the "Oz" books, the strange, dark *Princess and Curdie,* and *Curdie and the Goblins.* Even the smell of them was intoxicating. Maybe books were especially important because I was the only child in my family.

"In the thirties, Manhattan was alive with artists from the Works Progress Administration painting murals in banks, schools, libraries, everywhere you looked. The sight of these artists actually at work was tremendously exciting to me at age seven or eight. At school, I had a mural of my own going. It was painted on brown paper across the back wall of third grade at public school PS 41. It was a circus procession. I loved that school.

"Eventually I did get to do a mural. It was eighty feet long, for Nathan's Famous Restaurant at Atlantic City. I designed a picture history of its raffish rise from a 1907 hot-dog stand in Coney Island (hot dogs cost five cents each then) to a renowned restaurant in Atlantic City. Included were many famous hot-dog aficionados shown enjoying the product.

"I have been blessed with three wonderful children: Geoffrey, Michael, and Jennifer. I had illustrated several children's books, but it wasn't until the oldest, Geoffrey, was around three years old that I wrote one. It was inspired by Geoffrey's interest in tools and 'fixing' things, and also by a certain scene in a horrible ongoing story my husband's father used to tell his children at bedtime about a favorite character they had made up and named Little Picknose. Picknose cut the beard off an old man who had managed to get it stuck in a pot of glue. In my story, the hero's name was Tobias, and the name of the book was *Tobias and His Big Red Satchel.* It did very well and has been translated into German, Swedish, Danish, and Afrikaans.

"It wasn't until the arrival of my first grandchild, Madison Roze, that I was inspired to write another children's book. I wrote and illustrated *Madison Finds a Line* and then finished a manuscript called *The Magic Sewing Machine.* A new picture book, *The Moon Quilt,* is in the design stage, and two longer stories for older children are in the works as well.

"In 1994 I moved to Tucson, Arizona, and I've been celebrating the sunlight and mountains and clear air ever since. I've just built my lifelong dream studio, with skylights, drawing tables, and etching press. I am gearing it up for making monoprints and woodcuts, and look forward to launching some new, exploratory journeys into book illustration."

Warner's childhood love for good stories comes to fruition with her self-illustrated children's book, *The Magic Sewing Machine*. Left motherless, her young main characters, Olya and Sacha, are sent to live in a dark, gruesome orphanage under the harsh discipline of Miss Schnaap. Amid these grim circumstances comes relief from a magic sewing machine given to them by their dying mother. Warner snatches the children out of the grips of hard times and does so with surprising twists of story and illustrations that move characters and readers out of the darkness and into the light. Commenting on the author's artwork, a critic for *Kirkus Reviews* described the illustrations as "effectively composed to convey somber moods, humorous moments, and scenes of lasting harmony," and regarding story, the critic noted that "the dastardly adults and resourceful heroes combine for dramatic storytelling." Writing for *Booklist*, Susan Dove Lempke concluded that Warner's story and illustrations have "just enough evil to create pleasurable shivers and a highly satisfactory conclusion for all."

Works Cited

Lempke, Susan Dove, review of *The Magic Sewing Machine*, *Booklist*, September 15, 1997, p. 243.
Review of *The Magic Sewing Machine*, *Kirkus Reviews*, July 15, 1997, p. 1118.

For More Information See

PERIODICALS

Publishers Weekly, June 23, 1997, p. 91.
School Library Journal, September, 1997, p. 198.*

*   *   *

WILBUR, Richard (Purdy) 1921-

Personal

Born March 1, 1921, in New York, NY; son of Lawrence Lazear (a portrait artist) and Helen Ruth (Purdy) Wilbur; married Mary Charlotte Hayes Ward, June 20, 1942 ; children: Ellen, Christopher, Nathan, Aaron. *Education:* Amherst College, A.B., 1942; Harvard University, A.M., 1947. *Politics:* Independent. *Religion:* Episcopal.

Addresses

Home—87 Dodswells Road, Cummington, MA 01026. *Agent*—(theater only) Gilbert Parker, William Morris Agency, 1325 Avenue of the Americas, New York, NY 10019.

Richard Wilbur

Career

Harvard University, Cambridge, MA, Society of Fellows, junior fellow in Society of Fellows, 1947-50, assistant professor of English, 1950-54; Wellesley College, Wellesley, MA, associate professor of English, 1955-57; Wesleyan University, Middletown, CT, professor, 1957-77; Smith College, Northampton, MA, writer-in-residence, 1977-86. Lecturer at colleges, universities, and Library of Congress. Traveled to Russia, September, 1961, as U.S. specialist for the Department of State. *Military service:* U.S. Army, 1943-45, technician, third class. *Member:* American Academy of Arts and Sciences, Dramatists' Guild, American Academy of Arts and Letters (past president), Academy of American Poets (chancellor emeritus), Chi Psi, PEN.

Awards, Honors

Harriet Monroe Prize, *Poetry* magazine, 1948; Oscar Blumenthal Prize, 1950; Guggenheim grant, 1952, 1963; Prix de Rome, 1954; Edna St. Vincent Millay Memorial Award, 1957; elected to American Academy and Institute of Arts and Letters, 1957; Pulitzer Prize for poetry, and National Book Award, both 1957, both for *Things of This World;* Boston Festival Award, 1959; Ford fellow, 1960; honorary L.H.D., Lawrence College, 1960, and Washington University, 1964; Cane Award, 1962; Bollingen Prize for translation (co-recipient), 1963, for *Tartuffe;* honorary D.Litt., Amherst College, 1967, and Williams College, 1975; Children's Spring Book Festival Middle Honor award, *Washington Post Book World*, 1973, for *Opposites;* Pulitzer Prize, 1988, for *New and*

Collected Poems; Gold Medal, American Academy and Institute of Arts and Letters, 1991.

Writings

The Beautiful Changes, and Other Poems, Reynal & Hitchcock, 1947.

Ceremony, and Other Poems, Harcourt, 1950.

(Editor and contributor) *A Bestiary* (anthology), Pantheon, 1955.

(Translator) Jean Baptiste Poquelin de Moliere, *The Misanthrope,* Harcourt, 1955, published in England as *The Misanthrope: A Comedy in Five Acts,* Methuen, 1967.

Things of This World: Poems, Harcourt, 1956.

(Contributor) *The New Landscape in Art and Science,* edited by Gygory Kepes, Theobald, 1956.

Poems, 1943-1956, Faber, 1957.

(Author of lyrics with John Latouche and Dorothy Parker) *Candide* (comic opera based on the satire by Voltaire), based on the book by Lillian Hellman, music by Leonard Bernstein, Random House, 1957.

(Editor) Edgar Allan Poe, *Complete Poems of Poe,* Dell, 1959.

(With Robert Hillyer and Cleanth Brooks) *Anniversary Lectures,* U.S. Government Printing Office, 1959.

Advice to a Prophet, and Other Poems, Harcourt, 1961, Faber (London), 1962.

(Contributor) *Major Writers of America,* Harcourt, 1962.

(Contributor) *The Moment of Poetry,* edited by Don C. Allen, Johns Hopkins Press, 1962.

Loudmouse (for children), Collier, 1963, published with illustrations by Don Almquist, Collier, 1968.

(Translator) Jean Baptiste Poquelin de Moliere, *Tartuffe: Comedy in Five Acts,* Harcourt, 1963.

The Poems of Richard Wilbur, Harcourt, 1963.

(Author of introduction) *Poems of William Shakespeare,* Pelican, 1966.

Complaint, Phoenix Book Shop, 1968.

Walking to Sleep: New Poems and Translations, Harcourt, 1969.

Digging for China: A Poem, illustrated by William Pene Du Bois, Doubleday, 1970.

(Translator) Jean Baptiste Poquelin de Moliere, *The School for Wives: Comedy in Five Acts,* Harcourt, 1971.

(And illustrator) *Opposites* (for children), Harcourt, 1973.

(Author of introduction) Edgar Allan Poe, *The Narrative of Arthur Gordon Pym,* D. R. Godine, 1973.

(Editor with Alfred Harbage) *The Narrative Poems, and Poems of Doubtful Authenticity,* Penguin, 1974.

Seed Leaves: Homage to R. F., prints by Charles Wadsworth, D. R. Godine (Boston, MA), 1974.

The Mind-Reader: New Poems, Harcourt, 1976.

Responses: Prose Pieces, 1953-1976, Harcourt, 1976.

(Editor and author of introduction) Witter Bynner, *Selected Poems,* Farrar, Straus, 1978.

(Translator) Jean Baptiste Poquelin de Moliere, *The Learned Ladies: Comedy in Five Acts,* illustrated by Enrico Arno, Harcourt, 1978.

(Translator) Moliere, *Four Comedies,* Harcourt, 1978.

Pedestrian Flight: Twenty-one Clerihews for the Telephone, Palaemon Press (Winston Salem, NC), 1981.

Advise from the Muse, illustrated by Timothy Engelland, Deerfield Press (Old Deerfield, MA), The Gallery Press (Dublin, Ireland), 1981.

(Translator) Jean Racine, *Andromache: Tragedy in Five Acts,* illustrated by Igor Tulipanov, Harcourt, 1982.

The Whale, and Other Uncollected Translations, BOA Editions (Brockport, NY), 1982.

On My Own Work, Aquila (Portree, Scotland), 1983.

(Translator) Jean Racine, *Phaedra: Tragedy in Five Acts,* illustrated by Igor Tulipanov, Harcourt, 1986.

New and Collected Poems, Harcourt, 1988.

(And illustrator) *More Opposites,* Harcourt, 1991.

(Translator) Jean Baptiste Poquelin de Moliere, *The School for Husbands,* Dramatists Play Service (New York City), 1991.

(Translator) Moliere, *The Imaginary Cuckold; or, Sganarelle,* Dramatists Play Service, 1993.

A Game of Catch, (picture book) illustrated by Barry Moser, Harcourt, 1994.

(Translator) Jean Baptiste Poquelin de Moliere, *Amphitryon,* Dramatists Play Service, 1995.

Runaway Opposites, illustrated by Henrik Drescher, Harcourt, 1995.

The Catbird's Song: Prose Pieces, 1963-1995, Harcourt, 1997.

Responses II, Prose Pieces, Harcourt, 1997.

The Disappearing Alphabet, illustrated by David Diaz, Harcourt, 1998.

(Translator) Jean Baptiste Poquelin de Moliere, *Don Juan,* Dramatists Play Service, 1998.

General editor, "Laurel Poet" series published in original paperback editions by Dell. Contributor to anthologies. Author of critical papers.

Adaptations

Several sound recordings have been made of Wilbur reading selections of his poetry and translations.

Sidelights

A former poet laureate of the United States, Richard Wilbur is one of the most acclaimed English-language poets of the twentieth century. Awarded the 1957 Pulitzer Prize for poetry as well as the National Book Award for his poetry collection *The Things of This World,* Wilbur has received numerous other honors, including membership in the American Academy of Arts and Letters. Wilbur has supplemented his poetic work with essays, short stories, and several books for young people, including *Loudmouse, The Disappearing Alphabet,* and *Opposites.* He has also done a great deal of work as a translator, bringing works by French authors Moliere, Racine, and Voltaire into English-language versions.

Born in New York City in 1921, Wilbur attended Amherst College, graduated, got married, and served in the U.S. armed forces in Italy and Germany during World War II. Returning to the United States, he enrolled in Harvard's graduate school, and published his first book of poetry, *The Beautiful Changes, and Other*

Poems, the same year he received an M.A. in English. Many of the forty-two poems included in this first collection were influenced by young Wilbur's wartime experiences. Numerous other volumes of poetry followed, as well as essays and critical works, several discussing the philosophy of American writer Edgar Allan Poe.

The text of Wilbur's picture book *A Game of Catch* was originally published as a short story in *New Yorker* magazine in the early 1950s. The story focuses on two boys whose plans to spend the afternoon tossing the ball to each other in a vacant lot are disrupted when a third boy—without a baseball glove but with a desire to include himself in the other boys' activity—causes constant disruption. In its depiction of the escalating intrusiveness of the third boy despite the two players' efforts to ignore him, the book portrays "the pain and the power of the outsider," according to *Booklist* contributor Hazel Rochman.

Unlike *A Game of Catch,* Wilbur's other books for children often feature selections of his poetry. His 1973 work *Opposites* and its 1991 sequel, *More Opposites,* were selectively combined into *Runaway Opposites,* illustrated by Henrik Drescher. Containing fifteen short poems, *Runaway Opposites* deals with contrasts in many forms. Characterizing the work as "verbally and visually demanding," *Booklist* contributor Mary Harris Veeder noted approvingly that the book would appeal to "young artist-rebels" looking for new ways to juxtapose words and pictures. The poems range from illustrating simple relationships between objects to illuminating more complex associations. *Bulletin of the Center for Children's Books* contributor Deborah Stevenson commended the book's willingness to test "artistic boundaries," and noted the "energetic" effect and "appealing gaudy sinisterness" of the illustrations.

The Disappearing Alphabet, another droll book of rhyme, posits the gradual disappearance of letters of the alphabet amid fun wordplay. "If B were absent, say, from BAT and BALL,! There'd be no big or little leagues AT ALL," Wilbur writes in what a *Publishers Weekly* contributor referred to as "plenty of brain tickling words ... and a plethora of visual puns." A critic for *Kirkus Reviews* dubbed Wilbur's book "a sly and beautiful upending of the world of letters," and *Horn Book* reviewer Jennifer M. Brabander similarly remarked that *The Disappearing Alphabet* will have readers "laugh[ing] at the nonsensical wordplay while catching a glimpse of the formative—and transformative power of language."

Works Cited

Brabander, Jennifer M., review of *The Disappearing Alphabet, Horn Book,* September-October, 1998, p. 618.

Review of *The Disappearing Alphabet, Kirkus Reviews,* September 15, 1998, p. 1391.

Review of *The Disappearing Alphabet, Publishers Weekly,* August 17, 1998, p. 70.

How strange that the banana's slippery PEEL, Without its **P**, would be a slippery EEL! It makes you think! However, it is not Profound enough to think about *a lot.*

Prominent poet Wilbur posits the gradual vanishing of letters of the alphabet amid fun wordplay in his picture-book collection of twenty-six short verses. (From The Disappearing Alphabet, *illustrated by David Diaz.)*

Rochman, Hazel, review of *A Game of Catch, Booklist,* March 1, 1994, p. 1262-63.

Stevenson, Deborah, review of *Runaway Opposites, Bulletin of the Center for Children's Books,* April, 1995, p. 288.

Veeder, Mary Harris, review of *Runaway Opposites, Booklist,* April 15, 1995, p. 1497.

Wilbur, Richard, *The Disappearing Alphabet,* illustrated by David Diaz, Harcourt, 1998.

For More Information See

BOOKS

Bixler, Frances, *Richard Wilbur: A Reference Guide,* G. K. Hall (Boston, MA), 1991.

Conversations with Richard Wilbur, edited by William Butts, University Press of Mississippi (Jackson, MS), 1990.

Cummins, Paul F., *Richard Wilbur: A Critical Essay,* Eerdmans (Grand Rapids, MI), 1971.

Dictionary of Literary Biography, Volume 169: *American Poets since World War II,* Gale, 1996, pp. 297-311.

Edgecombe, Rodney Stenning, *A Reader's Guide to the Poetry of Richard Wilbur,* University of Alabama Press (Tuscaloosa, AL), 1995.

Field, John, *Richard Wilbur: A Biographical Checklist,* Kent State University Press, 1971.

Hill, Donald L., *Richard Wilbur,* Twayne, 1967.

Hougen, John B., *Ecstasy within Discipline: The Poetry of Richard Wilbur,* Scholars Press (Atlanta, GA), 1995.

Michelson, Bruce, *Wilbur's Poetry: Music in a Scattering Time,* University of Massachusetts Press, 1991.

Richard Wilbur's Creation, edited and with an introduction by Wendy Salinger, University of Michigan Press (Ann Arbor, MI), 1983.

Rosenthal, M. L., *The Modern Poets,* Oxford University Press, 1965.

PERIODICALS

Kirkus Reviews, February 15, 1994, p. 236.

New York Times Book Review, March 14, 1999, p. 30.

Publishers Weekly, March 28, 1994, p. 95.

School Library Journal, April, 1994, p. 132; May, 1995, p. 117.

*   *   *

WORTIS, Avi
See AVI

Y–Z

YOUNGER, Barbara 1954-

Personal

Born March 20, 1954, in Baltimore, MD; daughter of Ernest (a stockbroker) and Nancy (an artist and homemaker; maiden name, Wenger) Kiehne; married Clifford Younger (an electrical engineer), August 20, 1977; children: Katherine, Laura. *Education:* Duke University, A.B., 1976; University of North Carolina at Chapel Hill, M.L.S., 1977. *Religion:* Presbyterian.

Barbara Younger

Addresses

Home—404 North Churton St., Hillsborough, NC 27278. *Electronic mail*—Youngers@visionet.com.

Career

School librarian in Pittsburgh, PA, 1978-79; Dedham Public Library, Dedham, MA, children's librarian, 1979-82; writer. *Member:* Society of Children's Book Writers and Illustrators.

Writings

(With Lisa Flinn) *Food for Christian Thought,* Abingdon (Nashville, TN), 1991.

(With Flinn) *Tents, Clouds, and Angels,* CSS Publishing (Lima, OH), 1992.

(With Flinn) *Making Scripture Stick: 52 Unforgettable Bible Verse Adventures for Children,* Group Books (Loveland, CO), 1993.

(With Flinn) *Creative Ways to Offer Praise: 100 Ideas for Sunday Worship,* Abingdon, 1993.

(With Flinn) *Hooray for Children's Church,* Abingdon, 1995.

(With Flinn) *Boredom-Busting Ideas to Involve Children in Adult Worship,* Group Books, 1996.

A Moment with God for Children: Prayers for Little Ones, Dimensions for Living, 1997.

(With Flinn) *One Morning in Joseph's Garden,* Abingdon, 1998.

Purple Mountain Majesties: The Story of Katharine Lee Bates and "America the Beautiful" (juvenile), illustrated by Stacey Schuett, Dutton (New York City), 1998.

Work in Progress

Two picture-book biographies, one of Sarah Josepha Hale and one of Jane Taylor, author of the song "Twinkle, Twinkle, Little Star," both for Dutton; a chapter book.

Sidelights

Barbara Younger told *SATA:* "I grew up in Baltimore, where I spent many hours reading, making a good home for my dolls, climbing pine trees, and writing stories and poems. My parents were enthusiastic about my creative pursuits, and we had a house filled with stray cats and dogs and plenty of visiting family and friends to add to the fun. I never gave up the great book characters of my youth: Pooh, Babar, Ramona, Alice, Laura Ingalls, and Peter Rabbit. By the time I was in high school, I was fairly certain that I wanted to do something in the field of children's books when I grew up.

"At Duke University, I wrote countless term papers and learned the frustrations and joys of historical research. Several of my papers connected the history and development of children's literature with American and British social history. When I realized with some sadness that it was time to graduate, I knew that I needed to come up with an occupation. I asked myself, 'What do you like most in the world?' The answer came clearly, 'Children's books.' I decided in that instant to become a children's librarian.

"After getting my library degree at Chapel Hill and marrying a man I had met at Duke, we moved to Pittsburgh, where I worked as a school librarian. When we relocated to Massachusetts two years later, I found a job I loved as the children's librarian of the Dedham Public Library.

"We moved to North Carolina soon after my first daughter was born. I decided to stay at home with her and, of course, we read book after book every day. Before long, I had a second daughter who liked stories, too. Soon I decided the time had come to write children's books of my own. The daily mail took on a whole new meaning as I waited for word from publishers. In time, as my writing improved, the many rejection letters I received sometimes included encouraging notes from editors and invitations to send more of my work.

"Once my daughters started school, I volunteered to read to their classes and other classes in their elementary school. Around this time a good friend, Lisa Flinn, and I began writing books of creative program ideas for churches. We were delighted when Abingdon Press published our first book. Not too long after that, my first picture book, *Purple Mountain Majesties: The Story of Katharine Lee Bates and 'America the Beautiful,'* was accepted for publication. What a happy day that was!

"I live in a big, yellow, one-hundred-fifty-year-old house in the small town of Hillsborough with my husband, daughters, two cats, visiting mice and ants, and a collection of dolls, old toys, buttons, hat boxes, bookmarks, and, of course, books."

Younger described how she came to write her biography of Bates. "When I was a little girl, I liked to climb tall pine trees in my backyard. Once I reached the top I would survey the world around me and sing. One of the songs I remember singing is 'America the Beautiful.'

"Years later, I took my daughters to a story hour at our local library. Enjoying some restful solitude in the adult section, I began to browse among the shelves. I came upon a collection of American songs. Leafing through the book, I stopped at 'America the Beautiful.' When I read about Katharine Lee Bates and her rugged climb to the top of Pikes Peak in a prairie wagon, I knew immediately that the story would make a wonderful picture book.

"I began to research the writing of the song and was intrigued with the information I uncovered. When I visited the Wellesley College Archives, I was especially moved to be able to hold in my hands Katharine's girlhood diary, the diary she kept on her trip west, and the diary in which she made an entry the day before she died. Katharine's diary is a running theme throughout my book.

"I was glad to learn from her diary that Katharine had visited Niagara Falls and the World's Columbian Exposition on her trip west, and that she rode the first Ferris wheel at the Exposition on her way home. I knew these places would make intriguing illustrations, which they did, thanks to the splendid talent of the book's illustrator, Stacey Schuett.

"When I was a girl I took a train ride across America with my family. I have never forgotten the magnificence of the American landscape that I saw from the windows of the train. In 1893, almost one hundred years before my train ride west, Katharine Lee Bates made a similar trip that inspired the writing of one of my favorite songs!

"Since the publication of *Purple Mountain Majesties,* I have had a wonderful time talking to groups of children about the book and how I came to write it. I bring along a photograph of Katharine with her collie dog and a copy of the diary upon which the story is based. I also enjoy showing old and new postcards of Colorado Springs and Pikes Peak, a real ticket to the World's Columbian Exposition, and advertising cards from the fair. I often wear a vest a friend stitched for me, decorated with purple mountains and amber waves of grain. In some classrooms, when my talk is finished, the children sing the song to me, and it is always a wonderful moment.

"I have received letters and cards from children, decorated with purple mountains and waterfalls and Ferris wheels. Many of the children say that they would like to be writers when they grow up. I've received letters from adults, too. Perhaps my favorite is from William Bates, Jr. He wrote to tell me that he felt *Purple Mountain Majesties* captures the essence of Katharine Lee Bates better than anyone else who has written about her. He should know; he remembers visiting with his Great-Aunt Katharine in her Wellesley home when he was a little boy!"

Barbara Younger culls circumstances, setting, and thoughts from Katharine Lee Bates' diary and writings to create her children's book, *Purple Mountain Majesties: The Story of Katharine Lee Bates and "America the Beautiful."* Younger recreates the woman whose train ride across America inspires her to write about the natural splendors of the American Landscape. Bates, a young teacher from Wellesley, traveling to Colorado from Massachusetts, keeps an attentive eye on all she sees, records these sights in her diary, and later writes the memorable words to "America the Beautiful." John Peters, writing for *Booklist,* described how "Younger offers an energetic account of Bates' early life." A critic for *Kirkus Reviews* noted Younger's ability to "make a living character out of Bates, whose quirks and full-bodied charm gracefully flow from the letters and diary exerpts."

Works Cited

Peters, John, review of *Purple Mountain Majesties: The Story of Katharine Lee Bates and "America the Beautiful," Booklist,* July, 1998, p. 1881.
Review of *Purple Mountain Majesties: The Story of Katharine Lee Bates and "America the Beautiful," Kirkus Reviews,* June 1, 1998, p. 818.

For More Information See

PERIODICALS

Horn Book, July-August, 1998, p. 517.
Publishers Weekly, June 8, 1998, p. 60.
School Library Journal, August, 1998, p. 158.

*   *   *

ZARIN, Cynthia 1959-

Personal

Born July 9, 1959, in New York City; daughter of Michael (a lawyer) and Renee (an administrator; maiden name, Kroll) Zarin; married Michael Seccareccia, January 24, 1988 (divorced, 1996); married Joseph Goddu (an art dealer), December 6, 1997; children: Rose; stepchildren: Anna, Jack. *Education:* Radcliffe College, B.A., 1981; Columbia University, M.F.A., 1984.

Addresses

Office—c/o George Nicholson, Sterling Lord Literistic, 65 Bleecker Street, New York, NY 10014.

Career

New Yorker magazine, New York City, staff writer, 1984-94; Princeton University, Princeton, NJ, lecturer in creative writing, 1993-97; Cathedral of St. John the Divine, New York City, artist-in-residence, 1994—; Johns Hopkins Writing Seminars, Baltimore, MD, visiting poet, 1998. *Member:* PEN

Cynthia Zarin

Awards, Honors

Ingram Merrill Award, 1989, for *The Swordfish Tooth;* Lavan Award, Academy of American Poets, 1994; National Endowment for the Arts Award, 1997.

Writings

The Swordfish Tooth: Poems, Knopf, 1989.
Fire Lyric: Poems, Knopf, 1993.
Rose and Sebastian (picture book), illustrated by Sarah Durham, Houghton Mifflin (Boston, MA), 1997.
What Do You See When You Shut Your Eyes? (picture book), illustrated by Sarah Durham, Houghton Mifflin, 1998.
Wallace Hoskins, the Boy Who Grew Down (picture book), illustrated by Martin Matje, DK Ink, 1999.
Albert, the Dog Who Liked To Ride in Taxis (picture book), illustrated by Martin Matje, DK Ink, in press.

Sidelights

Cynthia Zarin is a poet whose books of poetry, *Fire Lyric* and *The Swordfish Tooth,* offer a purity of language and a slightly offbeat perspective on mundane, typically overlooked topics. Her picture books for children, including *Rose and Sebastian* and *What Do You See When You Shut Your Eyes?,* encourage her preschool audience to look at things from a fresh perspective.

In *Rose and Sebastian,* Rose is a young child who is used to the noisiness of New York, where she lives in an apartment with her mother. The noises made by Sebastian, the rowdy boy who lives upstairs, however, are a different story—they are scary. Summoning her courage, Rose goes upstairs to confront her fear and meet Sebastian. To her delight, Rose learns to appreciate the exuberance of a noisy new friendship. "Zarin offers not only a glimpse of apartment life, but establishes Rose as a captivating heroine who wants to overcome her fears, and does," remarked a critic in *Kirkus Reviews.* Susan Hepler, a reviewer for *School Library Journal,* likewise called *Rose and Sebastian* "a nice supplement to the preschool read-aloud shelf on overcoming fears."

What Do You See When You Shut Your Eyes? is less a storybook than a humorous game. Rhyming questions and answers encourage children to use their five senses and their imaginations to participate in the fun. Zarin's text "expresses a poet's sensibility," asserted a reviewer for *Publishers Weekly,* "an ability to observe, a sense of the absurd, an affection for the everyday, an eye for juxtaposition." Noting that the author ends with a question about dreams, *School Library Journal* contributor Olga R. Barnes called *What Do You See When You Shut Your Eyes?* an apt bedtime story as well as "a pleasant addition to a lesson on imagination or the senses."

Works Cited

Barnes, Olga R., review of *What Do You See When You Shut Your Eyes?, School Library Journal,* September, 1998, p. 186.

Hepler, Susan, review of *Rose and Sebastian, School Library Journal,* September, 1997, p. 198.

Review of *Rose and Sebastian, Kirkus Reviews,* August 15, 1997, p. 1316.

Review of *What Do You See When You Shut Your Eyes?, Publishers Weekly,* August 17, 1998, p. 71.

For More Information See

PERIODICALS

Booklist, January 15, 1989, p. 832.

Bulletin of the Center for Children's Books, October, 1997, p. 72.

Publishers Weekly, July 19, 1993, p. 239; June 30, 1997, p. 76.*